The Law of Agency

Seventh edition

G H L Fridman   QC, FRSC, MA, BCL, LLM

of the Ontario Bar and of the
Middle Temple, Barrister-at-law;
Emeritus Professor of Law, University of Western Ontario

Butterworths
London, Charlottesville, Dublin, Durban, Edinburgh, Kuala Lumpur,
Singapore, Sydney, Toronto, Wellington
1996

United Kingdom	Butterworths, a Division of Reed Elsevier (UK) Ltd, Halsbury House, 35 Chancery Lane, LONDON WC2A 1EL and 4 Hill Street, EDINBURGH EH2 3JZ
Australia	Butterworths, SYDNEY, MELBOURNE, BRISBANE, ADELAIDE, PERTH, CANBERRA and HOBART
Canada	Butterworths Canada Ltd, TORONTO and VANCOUVER
Ireland	Butterworth (Ireland) Ltd, DUBLIN
Malaysia	Malayan Law Journal Sdn Bhd, KUALA LUMPUR
New Zealand	Butterworths of New Zealand Ltd, WELLINGTON and AUCKLAND
Singapore	Reed Elsevier (Singapore) Pte Ltd, SINGAPORE
South Africa	Butterworths Publishers (Pty) Ltd, DURBAN
USA	Michie, CHARLOTTESVILLE, Virginia

A CIP Catalogue record for this book is available from the British Library.

ISBN 0 406 99718 7

Typeset by Phoenix Photosetting, Chatham, Kent
Printed and bound in Great Britain by
Redwood Books, Trowbridge, Wiltshire

TO JANET

Preface

The years since the appearance of the last edition of this work have seen a number of developments of which notice has been taken in the preparation of this edition. New legislation has come into force regarding the authority of agents of a company, viz, the amendments to the Companies Act 1985 enacted by the Companies Act 1989. The regulation and effects of the agency relationship in the conflict of laws have been changed by the Rome Convention, as enacted by legislation in 1990. Smaller, but no less important, amendments have been made by the Carriage of Goods by Sea Act 1992 and the Sale of Goods (Amendment) Act 1994. New Regulations have been made to deal with the class of commercial agents recognised by English law in consequence of EC Directives.

Some passages in the book have been rewritten to take into account changes of opinion by the author, occasionally the consequence of reviews that have made valid points. Other passages have required to be rewritten in consequence of more recent, or newly incorporated, decisions from England, Australia, Canada and New Zealand. Among the more important English cases that have been discussed in detail are *Yasuda Fire & Marine Insurance Co of Europe Ltd v Orion Marine Insurance Underwriting Agency Ltd; United Bank of Kuwait Ltd v Hammoud; Presentaciones Musicales SA v Secunda; The Choko Star; Kelly v Cooper; Marcan Shipping (London) Ltd v Polish SS Co; Boyter v Thomson; Clark Boyce v Mouat; Meridian Global Funds Management Asia Ltd v Securities Commission;* and *Siu Yin Kwan v Eastern Insurance Co Ltd.*

These changes indicate that the law of agency is still capable of evolution and alteration. It is very much alive and functioning.

I have endeavoured to state the law as at the end of March 1996.

London, Ontario   G H L Fridman
April Fools Day
1996

Contents

Table of statutes

References in this Table to *Statutes* are to Halsbury's Statutes of England (Fourth Edition) showing the volume and page at which the annotated text of an Act may be found.

List of cases

PART I

The nature of agency

SUMMARY

Introduction

The employment of another to perform certain tasks is a commonplace of life. From simple instances of the use of others, in domestic or agricultural activities, there have developed many complex situations, largely the result of the development of commercial life and the need for specialised activity in the fields of commerce, industry, and shipping (to mention only a few illustrations). In turn this has resulted in greater complexity of the law governing the relationships arising from the use of another as a substitute or, in some circumstances, as a representative. In modern English law, as in other legal systems, there are many different relationships of this kind. The law of agency, with which this book is concerned, deals with one particular one.

Others sometimes seem to resemble, but are distinct from, the relationship that exists in law between a principal and an agent. Like agency, however, they can involve questions of law concerning the liability of someone for the acts or omissions of another. For the most part, as will appear in due course, these questions of law concern liability, or immunity from liability, in tort.[1]

One such relationship is that between what used to be called master and servant. Another is the one arising when someone makes use of the services of an independent contractor. The distinction between these examples is the distinction between a contract of service and a contract for services. It has an important effect in the law concerning vicarious tort liability. There are situations in which someone who has contracted to supply services sub-contracts with another to perform all or part of those services.[2] By way of contrast there are circumstances when someone who is under a personal legal duty delegates its performance to another, although, in law, the duty is characterised as 'non-delegable' (which means that the party obliged by such duty will be liable for its non-feasance or misfeasance and cannot escape such liability by the process of delegation).[3] Finally there are situations in which a contractual obligation is vicariously fulfilled or performed by another on behalf of the party who has contracted to fulfil or perform it.[4] Where this occurs, not only may there arise questions about the proper performance of the contract, but also questions as to the ability of the

---

1 Below, chs 2, 13.
2 Cp, for example, the situation in cases of sub-bailment: below, pp 169–170.
3 Salmond and Heuston *Law of Torts* (20th edn 1992) pp 477–480; *Winfield and Jolowicz on Tort* (14th edn 1994) pp 616–618; Fleming *Law of Torts* (8th edn 1992) pp 389–392; Fridman *Law of Torts in Canada*, Vol 2 (1990) pp 340–343.
4 Which must be contrasted with the situation where a contract is assigned to someone not originally a party.

one actually performing the contract to rely on terms of the contract, such as a term that limits or excludes liability for non-performance or improper performance causing loss or damage to the other original contracting party (what has been called 'vicarious immunity').[5]

Although such relationships and the problems they create will have to be considered and discussed in conjunction with the law of agency in various parts of this book, it must be emphasised at the outset that the principles of law that regulate those relationships and resolve those problems are not part of the law of agency. There is a close connection between that law and the law concerned with master and servant, independent contractors, sub-contractors, non-delegable duties, and vicarious performance of a contract. But, for reasons that will emerge later, a sharp differentiation should be maintained between the law of agency on the one hand and the law relating to these other situations.

The law of agency deals with and governs only the relationship that arises when one party, called the principal, employs another, the agent, to perform certain tasks on behalf of, and in the name of the principal. The employment of someone in this way creates problems of many kinds in respect of the rights and duties of the various interested parties, resulting from the introduction of a third person between the one who wishes a particular undertaking to be performed and the one in respect of whom the undertaking is performed or is intended to be performed. Instead of there being two persons directly connected in law with each other by the unilateral act of one or the mutual acts of both, the employment of an agent introduces another person, whose conduct can affect in a variety of ways the legal position of the one on whose behalf the agent acts and the one with whom the agent deals. The complications resulting from this necessitate special rules of law to regulate and resolve them. These rules form the subject-matter of this book.

The origin and development of those rules must first be examined, in order to explain their nature and complexity.

Despite Bracton's use of Romanistic language, in saying that contracts can be made through agents,[6] it would seem that the English law of agency owes nothing to Roman law.[7] Maitland[8] traces the origin of agency in English law to the doctrine of 'uses'; and this doctrine Holmes[9] and Holdsworth[10] say derives

---

5 Below, pp 325–329.
6 Bracton f 200 (described by Maitland as 'a piece of inept Romanism': Pollock and Maitland *History of English Law* (cited hereafter as P & M) ii p 225 note 5; cf f 286 (cited by Holmes 'Agency' (1891) 5 HLR 1 at p 2 note 2).
7 Except possibly in respect of a shipmaster's liability for the torts of his crew, below, p 8. For a contrary view, which suggests a very Romanistic basis for the English law of agency, particularly with respect to authorisation of torts, see Tedéschi 'Authorization of Torts' (1969) 4 Israel LR 1, at pp 15–24. It should be noted that Roman law never advanced very far towards a general law of agency: cf Holmes 'Agency' (1890) 4 HLR 345 at p 351: cf Müller-Freienfels 'Legal Relations in the Law of Agency' (1964) 13 Am J Comp L 193–194. The different origins of the law may explain the differences between agency in common law and civil law systems, which has caused problems in regard to the international sale of goods, leading to a convention in 1983: Bonell 'The 1983 Geneva Convention on Agency in the International Sale of Goods' (1984) 32 Am J Comp L 717.
8 P & M ii at p 226.
9 'Early English Equity' (1884) 1 LQR 162.
10 *History of English Law* (cited hereafter as HEL) iv p 411.

from the Germanic *Salman*, or *Treuhand*, a person to whom the fulfilment of a particular task was entrusted, usually the transference of land in order that he might make a conveyance according to his grantor's directions.[11] Whether this be true or not, it is accepted that, in the early mediaeval period, instances of agency do occur, although the law is in its infancy.[12] Kings and prelates empower agents to borrow money in their name: attorneys are appointed for some purposes— though it is not until later that attorneys are appointed for the purpose of conducting litigation.[13] Elected knights and burgesses must bring 'full powers' to parliament for the representation of the shires and boroughs. 'But of any informal agency, of any implied agency, we read very little.'[14]

Maitland suggests that the start of the modern law is to be found in the position of the clergy. He cites a case in the reign of Edward I,[15] 'where an abbot was sued for the price of goods purchased by a monk and come to the use of the convent': and he comments that 'the legal deadness of the monks favours the growth of a law of agency'.[16] Hence, possibly, the alleged connection between agency and uses.[17] The influence of the Church and of canon law upon secular law is admitted by Professor Müller-Freienfels.[18] But he suggests two other origins. One is the Anglo-Saxon concept of the Mund, especially applied in the relation between master and servant (*ballivus*); the other is the Norman institution of the *attornatus*, which, as already noticed, was important in procedure and later penetrated into the substantive law. He concludes that, although the Church in several ways promoted the development of the law of agency, this influence was inadequate to bring the institution of agency to full fruition. The mediaeval community, he states, was satisfied with no more than a rudimentary concept of agency.

It is clear that even in mediaeval times there was liability in *debt* on the part of a principal in respect of goods bought or acquired by his agent, on the basis that the principal had thereby obtained the use and benefit of the goods.[19] Mercantile necessity, going even beyond this, imposed liability on a master for the acts of his apprentices and agents.[20] In addition to the liability which arose on the part

11 Holmes 'Early English Equity' (1884) 1 LQR 162 at p 163.
12 P & M ii p 225.
13 HEL ii pp 315–317. On the use of attorneys in conducting litigation, see Birks *Gentlemen of the Law* (1960) chs 1–3.
14 P & M ii p 225.
15 *YB* 33–5 Ed I, p 567. Other cases can be cited to the same effect: see *Randolph v Abbott of Hailes* (1313–14) Eyre of Kent, 6 & 7 Ed II (27 Selden S 32); *Parker v Prior of Blythburgh* (1315) YB 8 Ed II (37 Selden S 131); Simpson *History of the Law of Contract* (1975) p 540, notes 1, 2.
16 P & M ii p 226 note 1: cf HEL viii p 223. A similar tale can be told of the law relating to corporations.
17 Cf also, the alleged connection between uses (or trusts) and undisclosed principals: below, p 257.
18 (1964) 13 Am J Comp L at p 195.
19 Stoljar *Law of Agency* (1961) pp 14, 37–39. He also refers to the liability of a principal upon a deed and the liability of an agent to account: ibid pp 14–17. See also Geva 'Authority of Sale and Privity of Contract: The Proprietary Basis of the Right to the Proceeds of Sale at Common Law' (1979) 25 McGill LJ 32 at pp 38–45. On the difference between the situation where a contract was under seal and where it was an 'informal transaction', see Simpson, op cit at pp 552–554.
20 Red Book of Bristol i, 66. Cf also the London rules as to brokers: *Liber Albus* (RS) i, 269, 400–401 (on this and the previous note see HEL ii p 387). Brokers were known as early as 1391 at the very least: HEL viii p 102.

of ecclesiastical persons as principals, another illustration of a rudimentary agency relationship existing at this time is to be found in the law of husband and wife. At least by the time of Edward I it seems to have been possible for a husband to be made liable on a contract made by his wife (although such contract was void) if money or goods under it 'had come to the profit of the husband'.[1] Her contracts were his if he previously authorised or subsequently ratified them.[2]

The liability in *debt* of a principal for the price of goods bought or acquired by his agent was broadened into a contractual liability in assumpsit.[3] Gradually, agency as a general relationship giving rise to contractual liability emerged from agency which gave rise to liability in certain specific instances, in respect of which certain specific writs were applicable. By the end of the mediaeval period the common law had arrived at the position that a principal could be made liable on a contract made on his behalf by an agent,[4] if the principal ratified what the agent had done,[5] or had given him express authority to make the contract, or, apparently, if the agent acted 'within the scope of an authority to do acts of a particular kind'.[6]

Two important classes of persons, brokers and factors, were coming into prominence in mercantile practice, and were distinguished: the one being classed as agents, the other as servants.[7] At this time[8] the common law seemed to draw no distinction between principal and agent and master and servant: for, in respect of tortious liability as well as contractual, everything depended upon the command of the principal or master.[9] 'In both cases there must be a particular authority to do the acts complained of: and if the factor was to be protected from personal

---

1 HEL iii p 524: cf the case referred to by Maitland (note 15 above). See also Simpson, op cit pp 545–549. He criticises Holdsworth's theory that the liability of the husband was based on the wife's lack of property.

2 *YB* 21 Henry VII Mich pl 64: *YB* 27 Henry VIII Mich pl 3; HEL iii p 529. (For an earlier case, see *Anon v Musket* (1313) Eyre of Kent 6 & 7 Ed II 45.) This was finally accepted as the general rule of law in *Manby v Scott* (1663) 1 Lev 4: subject to the addition of the law relating to a deserted wife's agency of necessity: *James v Warren* (1706) Holt KB 104: this has now gone: below, p 134.

3 Stoljar *Law of Agency* pp 39–40; Simpson, op cit pp 554–556. See also Geva (1979) 25 McGill LJ 32 at pp 45–49.

4 *YB* II Hen IV Mich pl 53; HEL viii p 223, note 9.

5 For the way in which Coke CJ interpreted or reinterpreted Roman and mediaeval law to produce the basis for the modern common law of ratification, see Procaccia 'On the Theory and History of Ratification in the Law of Agency' (1979) 4 Tel Aviv U Studies in Law 9 at pp 21–24.

6 HEL viii pp 223–224, note 1, citing *YB* 8 Ed IV Mich pl 9. Note the argument by Geva (1979) 25 McGill LJ 32 that the 'property' approach did not and could not apply to the situation with respect to servants, factors and bailiffs because such parties could own property whereas monks and wives could not. Hence 'purchase by a servant or a bailiff, while potentially distinguishable from a purchase by a monk or a married woman, was not treated differently' Geva, above at p 41.

7 Note the argument by Geva (1979) 25 McGill LJ 32 at pp 49–53, about the property right of one who employed a factor in the proceeds of a sale by the factor of another's goods. For the development of the position of factors, see also Munday 'A Legal History of the Factor' (1977) 6 Anglo-American LR 221.

8 The situation may be described as different in modern law: cf below, pp 317–319.

9 HEL iii pp 382–387: vii pp 227–228.

liability he must be able to show that authority had been given to him in very wide terms.'[10]

It must be stated, however, that, although isolated instances of something like an agency relationship are to be found and are considered in the cases, there is no greatly developed legal institution which can be described as agency, and there is little law on the subject.[11] The designation 'agent' was not used in the common law before the seventeenth and eighteenth centuries; indeed the idea of 'representation' was merged with other 'service' functions of auxiliaries.[12] With the development of commercial life in many ways, such as the growth of trading companies,[13] from the seventeenth century onwards, the law of agency grew in importance and extent, and eventually agency emerged as a separate concept distinct from the relationship of master and servant.[14] Such development was clearly assisted and encouraged by the introduction of both equitable and civil law rules.

The Court of Chancery began to deal with the relation of principal and agent as if it were a relationship of cestui que trust and trustee;[15] and Holt CJ introduced ideas employed by the Court of Admiralty in respect of the relations of shipowners, masters, and merchants into the law dealing with the relations of principal and agent and master and servant. Indeed, Holdsworth went so far as to say[16] that Holt CJ's decisions upon this branch of the law of agency were largely instrumental in procuring it for the common law. If this had not been done, the whole, and not merely parts of the topic might have been developed by the Court of Chancery.

It is possible that the maritime law affected the contractual liability of principals.[17] This went further than the common law, and made shipowners liable for contracts made by the master where the owner had not authorised or ratified the making of the contract, as long as the master had acted in case of necessity, or within the scope of the powers conferred upon him by his contract of

10 HEL viii p 228: *Barton v Sadock* (1611) 1 Bulst 103; *Southern v How* (1618) Cro Jac 468. Simpson, op cit p 556, suggests that the underlying idea is that of a contrast between a *general* authority and a *special* authority: cf below, pp 38–40. It would also seem to indicate the beginnings of the ideas of 'implied authority' and 'apparent authority': below, pp 68–79, 122–132.

11 HEL viii pp 226–227.

12 Müller-Freienfels (1964) 13 Am J Comp L at p 197.

13 HEL viii pp 192–222.

14 Müller-Freienfels (1964) 13 Am J Comp L. Cf also Stoljar *Law of Agency* pp 49–51.

15 See *Burdett v Willett* (1708) 2 Vern 638; *Speerman v Degrave* (1709) 2 Vern 643: see also Dowrick, 17 MLR 24 at p 28, note 20. Note, however, the argument by Geva (1979) 25 McGill LJ 32 at pp 42–43, 44–45 against the view propounded by Ames (*Lectures on Legal History* p 116) that, as between factor and principal, title was always in the factor, who could be treated as a trustee for the principal. On the similarity between agents and trustees in modern law, see below, pp 23–36: see Waters *The Constructive Trust* (1964) ch IV. Cf Waters *Law of Trusts in Canada* (2nd edn 1984) pp 42–46. Note that the Court of Chancery also early recognised and gave effect to the position of undisclosed principals, HEL v p 298.

16 HEL viii p 299.

17 In this respect it is to be noted that English common law of agency is now part of Canadian maritime law, even to a contract made in Quebec: *QNS Paper Co v Chartwell Shipping Ltd* [1989] 2 SCR 683. And the law of salvage (cp below, p 139) has its origin in the general maritime law, denoting the close connection between agency and salvage: Tetley 'The General Maritime Law—The Lex Maritima' (1994) 20 Syracuse J of Int Law and Commerce 105 at p 132.

employment, or by the law of the sea.[18] But the effect of Holt CJ's decisions was felt largely in the law of liability for torts committed by an agent or servant. By maritime law the master of a ship was liable not only for his own torts but also for the torts of his crew. This was based in part on the Roman law relating to the quasi-delictual liability of ship-masters, etc for their employees,[19] and it was justified on the ground that the masters had the opportunity to choose good men.[20] The common law said that the owners of a ship were not liable for the torts of master and crew.[1] But the maritime law eventually held that owners were liable.[2] And in 1691, Holt CJ introduced this notion into the common law in the case of *Boson v Sandford*,[3] where he said that 'whoever employs another is answerable for him and undertakes for his care to all that make use of him'. Other cases occurred in which Holt CJ introduced the same principle outside the field of shipowner and master.[4] Various reasons were given for this: first, that the employer was better able to bear the loss and was really the one whose trust in the servant brought it about;[5] secondly, that the act of the servant was that of the master provided that the servant 'acts in execution of the authority' given him;[6] thirdly, the original mediaeval idea,[7] that the master was liable if he profited by the act or contract of his servant.[8]

It was Holt CJ's approach that eventually became the modern law. The modern rules of vicarious liability in tort sprang from his idea that the employer of another person should be liable for the wrongs the latter commits. But throughout the eighteenth century, and even later, there are echoes of the other views. Thus, as late as 1867, in *Barwick v English Joint Stock Bank*,[9] it was thought that the servant's or agent's act had to be for the master's or principal's benefit, if it was to involve him in tortious liability—a view which has now gone.[10] However the distinction between agents and servants, in so far as it may affect liability for torts committed by them on the part of their principal or master, is still a matter of debate producing much uncertainty.[11]

18 HEL viii p 249.
19 Dig 4, 9, 1.2.
20 It was apparently quite a strict liability: see HEL viii p 251 citing *Morse v Slue* (1672) 1 Mod Rep 85.
 1 *Waltham v Mulgar* (1605) Moore KB 776.
 2 HEL viii p 252.
 3 (1690) 2 Salk 440.
 4 *Turbervil v Stamp* (1697) Comb 459; *Jones v Hart* (1698) 2 Salk 441: cf *Lane v Cotton* (1701) 1 Salk 17.
 5 *Hern v Nichols* (1700) 1 Salk 289; *Wayland's Case* (1706) 3 Salk 234.
 6 *Middleton v Fowler* (1698) 1 Salk 282; *Ward v Evans* (1703) 2 Salk 442.
 7 Above, p 5.
 8 *Boulton v Arlsden* (1697) 3 Salk 234.
 9 (1867) LR 2 Exch 259.
10 Below, pp 317–319.
11 In this respect it should be noted that the originally distinct notions of principal and agent and master and servant were first combined, to produce a separate and distinct area of law, by Mr Justice Holmes, long before he became a judge, in lectures delivered at Harvard and later published: 'Agency' (1891) 4 HLR 345, 5 HLR 1. The approach taken by Holmes significantly influenced American writers and judges, and eventually became incorporated into American law in the *Restatement of Agency*, first published in 1933, and later revised in 1958. The American view, in contrast with that of English courts and writers, has been that the law of master and servant is an integral part of the law of agency. For reasons which will become clear later, such

So far as contract is concerned, the early part of the eighteenth century was still largely preoccupied with the notions of express authority and ratification. Any possible injustices that might have occurred could be cured by appeals to equity. It was in the latter part of the eighteenth century and the early part of the nineteenth century that the leading ideas of the modern law of agency emerged in more or less their present-day form.[12] The use of estoppel;[13] the law of undisclosed principals;[14] the wide authority of factors and other similar agents at common law and under the Factors Act 1889[15]—to name only a few examples— all appear at this time in more or less their present form. What happens in the nineteenth century is that these developments are refined, to meet the needs of the commercial community.[16]

These needs are at the basis of the history of this part of the law. The mediaeval community was not sufficiently open and mercantile in character to require more than a rudimentary notion of agency (just as it needed only an elementary law of contract). The growth in importance of commercial life (especially with the rise of trading companies, the ancestors of modern limited liability companies) showed that, both in contract and tort, agency was a vital relationship. To begin with, insufficient distinction was made between the relationship of principal and agent and that of master and servant—since liability in both instances rested on the notion of command or authorisation, there was little point in any subtle distinction: but the developments which resulted from the necessity for the introduction of maritime and mercantile law ideas into the common law after the end of the seventeenth century made such a distinction more important: and demanded a more subtle and complex notion of agency. This the common law courts proceeded to formulate—assisted, when the common law could not provide all the required features, by the Court of Chancery, which by the use of the analogy of the trust relationship helped to establish the modern shape of the agency relationship.

a view seriously conflicts with what is conceived of as being the essential nature of agency and the agency relationship. Although most American writers have accepted the Holmesian analysis (but see Conard 'What's Wrong with Agency' (1949) 1 J of Leg, Ed 540) there is some modern thought to the effect that this approach was misconceived and has resulted in incongruous legal decisions and the improper use of agency in inappropriate situations: see Estes 'Cinderella's Slipper: Agency' (1977) 10 John Marshall Journal of Practice and Procedure 225.

12 Cf Stoljar *Law of Agency* p 14: Müller-Freienfels (1964) 13 Am J Comp L, p 197.
13 *Pickering v Busk* (1812) 15 East 38; below, ch 6.
14 *Rabone v Williams* (1785) 7 Term Rep 360n; *Thomson v Davenport* (1829) 9 B & C 78: see Goodhard and Hamson 'Undisclosed principals in Contract' (1931) 4 CLJ 320 at p 321; Müller-Freienfels 'The Undisclosed Principal' (1953) 16 MLR 299 at p 302; Stoljar, *Law of Agency* pp 204–211. On the situation of such principals and their agents, see below, pp 253–272.
15 Below, pp 290–300.
16 Note the argument by Atiyah (*The Rise and Fall of Freedom of Contract* (1979) pp 496–501) that agency was originally dependent on the idea of 'reasonable reliance' not upon agreement: but that the importance of the will of the parties, agreement, and the notion of 'authority', was stressed by the House of Lord in *Cox v Hickman* (1860) 8 HL Cas 268. Atiyah's book is designed to establish that the true basis of contract is 'reliance', not the 'classical' notion of 'freedom of contract', with its emphasis on agreement which, he suggests, was contrary to eighteenth-century notions of contract and is now outmoded. Hence his argument with respect to agency, in so far as agency is an aspect of contract. It should be stated that the views of Atiyah are not generally accepted: nor are they necessarily acceptable.

Thus the sources of the modern law of agency are partly the common law and partly equity, maritime and mercantile law. This may help to explain the difficulties attached to the definition of agency, and the explanation of the nature and scope of agency in contrast with other relationships. The mingling of the various rules from their different sources has sometimes tended to confuse agency, as it is *now* understood, with other relationships that existed or emerged before, or at the same time as, the relationship of principal and agent. The clarification of this confusion is the subject of the first part of this book.

CHAPTER 1

The definition of agency

A tentative definition. Though it is true that agency does not allow of a brief description, and the whole law cannot be compressed into a sentence that is both short and significant,[1] this does not render either impossible or useless an attempt to summarise succinctly what is involved in the concept of agency. To a large extent, the nature and content of such a summary depends upon the outlook of the particular writer who is expounding the subject. None the less, such a summary can provide a guide to the student in the search for the features which distinguish agency from other legal relationships. The following is therefore suggested as a tentative, brief description of what agency involves:[2]

> Agency is the relationship that exists between two persons when one, called the *agent*, is considered in law to represent the other, called the *principal*, in such a way as to be able to affect the principal's legal position in respect of strangers to the relationship by the making of contracts or the disposition of property.

It seems virtually impossible to define agency except in terms of its consequences. A person is an agent only in so far as his acts can result in some alteration of the legal situation of the one for whom he acts or purports to act. Hence the indication in an Australian case[3] that the secretary of a Builders' Labourers' Federation was not its agent because the secretary was not authorised to create legal relations between the Federation and third parties. On this ground the accused was not guilty of corrupt acts as an agent (although his appeal failed on other grounds). In contrast, in a New Zealand case, *L C Fowler & Sons Ltd v St Stephens College Board of Governors*,[4] a travel agent in New Zealand, who had a history of acting as the agent for the school in arranging overseas tours, was held to be the agent of the school, not of the plaintiff company that had arranged the part of a sporting tour going to the United Kingdom and France. Hence the school was liable, as principal, for money owing under a contract made by the travel agent with the plaintiff company. The basis for this determination was the statement by Thomas J that agency was a word used 'to

---

1 Stoljar *Law of Agency* p 1. The discussion that follows (in the form in which it appeared in the fourth edition, 1976, pp 8–13) was invoked and applied by Hallett J in the Nova Scotia case of *Gerco Services Ltd v Astro* (1982) 48 NSR (2d) 541 at 557.
2 It was quoted and relied on by Valin J in *Labreche v Harasymiw* (1992) 89 DLR (4th) 95 at 107.
3 *R v Gallagher* [1986] VR 219.
4 [1991] 3 NZLR 304. Another issue in this case concerned the doctrine of election as between principal and agent: below, pp 242–243.

connote the relationship which exists where one person has the authority or capacity to create legal relations between another person and a third party'.[5] Whether such a relationship did exist in any given situation depended not on the terminology but on the true nature of the arrangement or the exact circumstances of the relationship.[6]

The suggestion has been made that overmuch emphasis has been placed upon the power of the agent to affect the principal's position, with consequent neglect of the realities of the situation so far as concerns the agent.[7] The commentator in question would prefer to see more interest taken by writers and courts in what the agent does and what he is supposed to be doing. By way of response, it is suggested that, while there may be indications in the cases that the historical concept of agency may be undergoing some revision, or at least some measure of reconsideration by the courts,[8] the traditional point of view, that agency as a relationship is dependent upon the extent to which, and ways in which one person can produce legal consequences for another, is still of the greatest importance, and remains the vital issue when it comes to determining whether someone is an agent. Having said this, several features of the definition suggested above require elaboration and comment.

First, it is meant to indicate that although there may be many situations in which one person represents or acts on behalf of another, it is only when such representation or action on another's behalf affects the latter's *legal* position, that is to say his rights against, and liabilities towards, other people, that the law of agency applies. The law of agency has no relevance to social or other non-legal obligations. Thus, the law of agency has no application to the kind of situation in which, for example, a man sends his wife to represent him at a wedding, and to congratulate on his behalf the bride and groom. For in such circumstances the representation is intended to serve a social purpose, not a legal one. However, the legal purpose intended to be achieved by the employment of an agent need not be a complex or sophisticated one. A mother who tells her son to buy milk from the milkman is making an agent of him, in the same way as a company makes agents of directors who enter into contractual obligations on behalf of the company. Clearly, the more important the transaction, the more necessary will it be to determine accurately the legal position of the interested parties. But, at least for the purposes of definition and comprehension, the only distinction that can validly be drawn is between the use of another person to fulfil some social or similar obligation or purpose, and the employment of another person to execute or discharge some legal obligation, or achieve some legal result.

---

5 [1991] 3 NZLR at p 306.

6 Ibid. Cp below, p 28. But in Canada an adjuster appointed to investigate an accident and a solicitor who was not negotiating a contract or handling litigation have been held to be 'agents' for evidentiary purposes: *Karl's Sporthaus Ltd v Allstate Insurance Co of Canada* (1983) 147 DLR (3d) 381; *Penderville Apartments Development Partnership v Cressey Development Corpn* (1990) 43 BCLR (2d) 57.

7 Reynolds 'Agency: Theory and Practice' (1978) 94 LQR 224. See, also, *Bowstead and Reynolds on Agency* (16th edn 1996) at pp 14–20.

8 Fridman 'The Abuse and Inconsistent Use of Agency' (1982) 20 U of Western Ontario LR 23, to which a response is suggested in Bowstead and Reynolds, op cit at p 20: a response with which the present author disagrees.

The second feature of the definition given above is that it stresses the importance of the way in which the *law* regards the relationship that has been created.[9] It is the effect in law of the way the parties have conducted themselves, and not the conduct of parties considered apart from the law, or the language used by the parties,[10] that must be investigated, in order to determine whether the agency relationship has come into existence.

This is not always an easy problem to solve and it can involve some intricate analysis of the facts and the nature of the relationship between the parties.[11] It must be solved, however, if the true legal relationship between the parties, and the incidents of such relationship, are to be classified, understood, and applied.[12]

9 The objection was raised by one reviewer of the fourth edition of this book (Bridge (1977) 14 JSPTL 150) that this definition did not accommodate estate agents who merely introduce prospective house purchasers to a vendor. It is certainly true that such agents do not normally create contractual relationships between their principals and third parties: and that they may not make their principals liable for deposits obtained by them from such third parties (see *Sorrell v Finch* [1977] AC 728, [1976] 2 All ER 371, discussed below, pp 49, 82). However, as the writer of the review pointed out, an estate agent may affect the legal position of the vendor, by making a misrepresentation: and may make the vendor liable to pay commission in certain circumstances (below, pp 189–201, 411–421). The precise legal quality of the relationship between an estate agent and a vendor who 'employs' him is far from certain, at least as regards some of its aspects: see Murdoch 'The Nature of Estate Agency' (1975) 91 LQR 357. Perhaps the most satisfactory approach to adopt is to say that the agency of estate agents is an anomalous type of agency, that has some practical utility, but does not conform to the normal commercial agency. It has been referred to as *incomplete agency*: below, p 30, note 17. Such agents have also been called 'canvassing agents': *Chitty on Contracts* (27th edn 1994), vol 2, para 31–002.

10 The terms 'agency' and 'agent' are often used wrongly in a commercial or business sense, not as meaning or involving the strict legal relationship of principal and agent which is the subject-matter of this book: cf Powell *Law of Agency* (2nd edn 1961) p 29. Thus dealers in goods may be described as agents, though in fact purchasers of goods from a manufacturer or wholesaler, and sellers of such goods to the public at large. What the term 'agency' really means in such a context is that the dealer in question is the approved dealer in goods of the kind in question: cf *Powell* pp 27–28. See, eg *Kennedy v De Trafford* [1897] AC 180 at 188 per Lord Herschell; *WT Lamb & Sons v Goring Brick Co Ltd* [1932] 1 KB 710; *International Harvester Co of Australia Pty Ltd v Carringan's Hazeldene Pastoral Co* (1958) 100 CLR 644.

Similarly someone who was an intermediary for an English company doing business in Israel was not an agent of the English company: *Vogel v R and A Kohnstamm Ltd* [1973] QB 133, [1971] 2 All ER 1428.

11 For examples, see *Moorgate Mercantile Co Ltd v Twitchings* [1977] AC 890, [1976] 2 All ER 641, when an organisation that supplied information about hire purchase to the dealers and finance companies was not the agent of such a dealer or finance company; *Garnac Grain Co Inc v HMF Faure and Fairclough Ltd* [1968] AC 1130n, [1967] 2 All ER 353 in which an intricate sales relationship was held not to involve any agency: *Bart v British West Indian Airways Ltd* [1967] 1 Lloyd's Rep 239, where the Court of Appeal of Guyana held that a 'middleman' who sent pools coupons to England was not the agent of the investor for the purpose of the contract of carriage with respect to the coupons: *Crampsey v Deveney* [1969] 2 DLR (3d) 161, where the Supreme Court of Canada held that a mother who was joint tenant of land with her children was not their agent when she contracted to sell it. Contrast *Royal Securities Corpn v Montreal Trust Co* (1967) 59 DLR (2d) 666; affd (1967) 63 DLR (2d) 15 where a broker was held to be the agent for *both* parties in a loan transaction, not merely an *interpreter* between them of the suggested terms. If there is no special requirement that money collected by someone acting on behalf of another should be kept in a separate fund, the relationship between the parties may simply be that of debtor and creditor, not one of agency: *R v Robertson* [1977] Crim LR 629.

12 Or if questions of tax liability are involved: *Customs and Excise Comrs v Paget* [1989] STC 773, [1990] CLY para 4584, where a photographer sold photos of students to a school, and the headmaster sold them at a higher price to parents. The headmaster was a principal not an agent of the photographer.

In this connection two factors merit consideration, in the light of their necessity for the understanding of the legal nature and function of the agency relationship. They are: *the consent of the parties* and *the authority of the agent*.

Consent. Several of the definitions proffered by leading writers introduce, and indeed revolve around, the idea that principal and agent have agreed, either in the form of a contract, or otherwise, that the agent should represent the principal. Thus Bowstead[13] says that agency is:

> '... the fiduciary[14] relationship which exists between two persons, one of whom expressly or impliedly consents that the other should act on his behalf so as to affect his relations with third parties and the other of whom similarly consents so to act or so acts.'

The *American Restatement of the Law of Agency*[15] defines agency as

> '... the relationship which results from the manifestation of consent, by one person to another, that the other shall act on his behalf and subject to his control, and consent by the other so to act.'

Similarly, Seavey[16] spoke of agency as 'a consensual relationship'; and Powell[17] included the notion of agreement on the part of the agent in his definition of agent. There is judicial support for this view. In *Garnac Grain Co Inc v HMF Faure and Fairclough Ltd*,[18] Lord Pearson said: 'The relationship of principal and agent can only be established by the consent of the principal and the agent.'

---

13 *Bowstead and Reynolds on Agency* (16th edn 1996) Article 1.
14 This word was added in the 15th edition. It is not disputed that agency creates fiduciary duties (below, pp 174–188): but this is a *consequence* of the relationship: it is not an essential feature of it.
15 *Restatement, Second, Agency* (1958) para (1): cf Conant 'The Objective Theory of Agency' (1968) 47 Nebraska LR 678, who argues that contractual agency and agency which involves estoppel (below, pp 111–114) are based on manifestations of consent by the principal. For another discussion of the theory of contract and agency, see Barnett, 'Squaring Undisclosed Agency Law with Contract Theory' (1987) 75 Calif LR 1969.
16 'The Rationale of Agency' (1920) 29 Yale LJ 859 at p 868: cf also ibid, pp 863–864.
17 *Law of Agency* p 5. By way of contrast, see the stimulating article by Dowrick 'The Relationship of Principal and Agent' (1954) 17 MLR 24, esp at pp 25–28. See also Müller-Freienfels 'Legal Relations in the Law of Agency' (1964) 13 Am J of Comp L 193 at p 203. Professor Müller-Freienfels, it is suggested, has unfortunately misinterpreted what is said below at p 59. He appears to read what is stated there as meaning that whenever the agent acts on behalf of another there is an implied contract: but in fact a distinction is drawn between a true implied contract and the agency relationship or aspects of it arising by estoppel when the agent cannot really be said to be impliedly consenting to act as an agent, though his conduct is treated by the law as making him an agent, for certain purposes at least.
18 [1967] 2 All ER 353 at 358. See also *Branwhite v Worcester Works Finance Ltd* [1969] 1 AC 552 at 573, [1968] 3 All ER 104 at 113 per Lord Morris to the effect that it was a question of fact whether there is an agency. Similarly in *Royal Securities Corpn v Montreal Trust Co* (1967) 59 DLR (2d) 666 at 686, Gale CJHC of Ontario stated that one of the essential requisites for, or ingredients of an agency relationship was the consent of both the principal and the agent (the others being authority given to the agent by the principal allowing the former to affect the latter's legal position, and the principal's control of the agent's activities).
Furthermore, in *Guerin v R* (1984) 13 DLR (4th) 321 at 322–323 Dickson J (later CJC) indicated that one reason the Crown was not the agent of an Indian band was that the Crown's authority to act on the band's behalf lacked a basis in contract.

However his lordship went on to say that they would be held to have consented 'if they have agreed to what in law amounts to such a relationship, even if they do not recognise it themselves and even if they have professed to disclaim it'. But consent was necessary, either expressly or by implication from their words or conduct.

This statement by Lord Pearson is open to criticism.[19] First of all it indicates that *consent* is the basis of agency, whereas, it is suggested, it is for the law to determine what is or is not agency, admittedly on the basis of the factual arrangements between the parties, but, in a sense, outside those arrangements in that it is a question of legal construction rather than of mechanical determination. A second criticism is that it seems to exclude from the scope of agency situations in which the parties have not truly consented to any such relationship, yet such a relationship arises. There are circumstances in which the relationship arises (at least for certain purposes) against the real wishes of one, if not both, of the parties. In situations of this kind the agency relationship, as far as certain of its effects are concerned, has no contractual, or even consensual, basis. Indeed the conduct which gives rise to the particular effects in question may have occurred without the cognizance, let along the approval of the person who is treated as the principal, and possibly without the agent's intending to act for the benefit of such principal. The contrast here is between agency arising by consent, and agency arising from estoppel. The dichotomy between consent and estoppel, or as he prefers to express it, between *contract* and estoppel, has been criticised by Professor Stoljar[20] on the ground that it is a dichotomy that is unreal, giving rise to a controversy that is beside the point. His view is that agency is really always contractual, involving two distinct contracts, one between the agent and the third party, the other between the principal and the third party. This gives rise, in his opinion, to a theory of 'transmissible contracts' or 'transmissible contract-interests'. This is not only difficult to grasp conceptually, it is also misleading as a guide to the rationale of the various types of agency relationship that can arise, and inaccurate as a description of what the law is doing when it recognises the existence and effects of an agency relationship.

The possibility that agency may exist, at least for certain purposes, even where no consent, and certainly no contract, can be found as between principal and agent, is evidenced by the decision of the House of Lords in *Boardman v Phipps*,[1] in which it was held that parties to whose acting as agents no consent had ever been given could be treated as 'self-appointed agents'. A comparison of these cases leads to the conclusion that it is not completely satisfactory to base agency upon consent, even though, in many instances, consent is a relevant, and possibly a determining, factor in the existence as well as the scope of an agency

---

19 Fridman 'Establishing Agency' (1968) 84 LQR 224 at pp 225–231.
20 *Law of Agency* pp 18–36. But see Dowrick [1963] CLJ 148; Conant 'The Objective Theory of Agency: Apparent Authority and the Estoppel of Apparent Ownership' (1968) 47 Nebraska LR 678 at p 683; Fishman, 'Inherent Agency Power—Should Enterprise Liability Apply to Agents' Unauthorized Contracts?' (1987) 19 Rutgers LJ 1. On 'agency by estoppel' see below, ch 6.
1 [1967] 2 AC 46, [1966] 3 All ER 721; discussed in Fridman, (1968) LQR 224 at pp 231–239, and by Hope JA in *Walden Properties Ltd v Beaver Properties Pty Ltd* [1973] 2 NSWLR 815 at 833. See further, below, pp 182–185.

relationship. But this is not the same as to say that the relationship and its effects always arise from and are determined by agreement.

This is borne out, it is suggested, by the fact that not all the incidents of the agency relationship, ie, the rights and duties which attach to the parties, arise as a result of any special agreement between them, although they may be limited or otherwise affected by such an agreement. Many such incidents are attached to the relationship by virtue of some rule of law. As Dowrick validly pointed out,[2] much of the law relating to agency is derived from equity, quasi-contract, or tort. For example, some of the obligations incumbent upon an agent are 'imposed by law, irrespective of agreement, and may properly be classed as quasi-contractual'.[3] An example is the duty of the agent to hand over to his principal money belonging to him, and received to the principal's use.[4] By virtue of the law of torts, an agent who acts gratuitously, in the absence of contract because there is no consideration, is still obliged to exercise care in the handling of his principal's affairs.[5]

In *Branwhite v Worcester Works Finance Ltd*,[6] Lord Wilberforce suggested that 'some wider conception of vicarious responsibility other than that of agency, as normally understood, may have to be recognised in order to accommodate some of the more elaborate cases which now arise when there are two persons who become mutually involved or associated in one side of a transaction.' The *Branwhite* case divided the House of Lords on the issue of agency. It involved a hire-purchase transaction made by the hirer with a dealer and financed by the respondent finance company. The latter failed in an action to recover arrears of instalments because of fraud on the part of the dealer's manager causing a mistake that rendered the hire-purchase agreement void. The hirer then sued the finance company for the return of the deposit paid by him. The House of Lords held in favour of the hirer, on a ground that is not relevant here. However, the majority also held that the dealer was not the agent of the finance company. The dealer was not held out by the finance company as its agent and possession by the dealer of the forms of the finance company was not enough to constitute agency.[7] Lords Wilberforce and Reid disagreed with this. As the language of Lord Wilberforce cited above indicates, the consent of the finance company to the situation as it existed between the company and the dealer was sufficient to permit a court to impose the consequences which result from agency.[8] In Lord Wilberforce's words: 'It is consensual not contractual.'

That agency may be consensual without being contractual is undeniable. But as Colman J put it in *Yasuda Fire and Marine Insurance Co of Europe Ltd v Orion Marine Insurance Underwriting Agency Ltd*,[9] if there is no contract it will

---

2 (1954) 17 MLR 24 at pp 28–34. Cf above, pp 7–9. On the fiduciary aspects of agency, see Waters *The Constructive Trust* (1964) ch IV: cf below, pp 174–188.
3 Dowrick (1954) 17 MLR 24 at p 32. Today one would refer to restitution rather than quasi-contract.
4 *Lyell v Kennedy* (1889) 14 App Cas 437; *Dixon v Hamond* (1819) 2 B & Ald 310.
5 Below, pp 160–164.
6 [1968] 3 All ER 104 at 122.
7 [1968] 3 All ER 104 at 113 per Lord Morris.
8 Ibid at 122.
9 [1995] QB 174 at 185 [1995] 3 All ER 211 at 219.

be sufficient 'if there is consent by the principal to the exercise by the agent of authority and consent by the agent to his exercising such authority on behalf of the principal'. In that case an agency relationship was held to exist between the parties because the plaintiff had entrusted to the defendant the making of transactions binding upon the plaintiff. Hence the plaintiff was entitled to inspect records kept by the defendant relating to the operations conducted by the defendant on behalf of the plaintiff. The fact that there was no contract of agency was irrelevant.

But the consent that is vital is not as Lord Wilberforce suggested, to 'a state of fact upon which the law imposes the consequences which result from agency', but to the exercise of authority by the agent. Hence, in several cases involving similar circumstances to those in the *Branwhite* case, it was sometimes held that the supplier of goods or dealer was not the agent of a finance company[10] and sometimes that such supplier or dealer was the finance company's agent.[11] As stated in an Australian case,[12] merely because the dealer or supplier possessed the forms of the credit provider, received a commission from the credit provider for introducing a debtor or filled in the charges on the forms, did not turn the supplier or dealer into the agent of the credit provider. In coming to this conclusion the court followed the majority in the *Branwhite* case, in the same way as the more recent English cases where the same problem was involved.

The idea that to be an agent it is necessary, or sufficient, to act with the authority of the alleged principal is further illustrated by another group of cases. These concern mortgages or guarantees signed by a wife at the instigation, urging or request of the husband. By virtue of such documents the wife made herself liable to a bank for the payment or repayment of sums of money. In these cases the wife argued that the transaction was invalidated by reason of mistake brought about by the conduct of the husband or undue influence on his part. A key question in each instance was whether the husband could be regarded as the agent of the bank. If so, then the bank would be affected by the misconduct of the husband and, consequently, would be unable to enforce the wife's prima facie liability. As pointed out by Lord Browne-Wilkinson in *Barclays Bank plc v O'Brien*,[13] at one time it was believed that this was on the ground of a special equity. In the *O'Brien* case, however, it was asserted that the fundamental decision, by the Privy Council in *Turnbull & Co v Duval*,[14] was really based on agency theory, ie that the husband was the agent of the bank for the purpose of obtaining the wife's agreement to a contract which made her liable to the bank in certain circumstances. Such domestic agency, as it may be called, was different from the agency relationship between husband and wife to be considered later.[15]

---

10 *Mynshul Asset Finance v Clarke (t/a Peacock Hotel)* [1992] CLY 487; *JD Williams & Co (t/a Williams Leasing) v McAuley, Parsons & Jones* [1994] CCLR 78. Despite the provisions of the Consumer Credit Act 1974, s 56, under which a finance company can be liable for oral or written representations, warranties or conditions made by a dealer in the course of antecedent negotiations with an eventual buyer.
11 *Woodchester Leasing Equipment Ltd v Clayton and Clayton (t/a Sudbury Sports)* [1994] CCLR 87.
12 *Custom Credit Corpn Ltd v Lynch* [1993] 2 VR 469 at 486.
13 [1993] 4 All ER 417 at 427–428.
14 [1902] AC 429.
15 Below, pp 144–149.

It was an agency that arose between bank and husband and stemmed from the grant by the bank of authority to the husband to bring about the desired contractual nexus between the wife and the bank. In some instances the argument based on such agency was not uniformly successful. The wife's failure to succeed was not always because of any failure to establish the necessary agency,[16] although sometimes that was the reason why the defence failed.[17] The rationale of these cases appears to be that the creditor entrusted the husband with the task of obtaining the wife's signature, and as a consequence, by the application of agency principles,[18] the creditor was affixed with notice of the husband's misconduct, if he was guilty of such vitiating behaviour.

Lord Wilberforce has not been the only critic of the idea that consent to the existence of an agency relationship, ie, to the exercise of authority on behalf of another, is essential. One form of such attack is based upon the problems arising from making a principal liable for the unauthorised acts of his agent, if consent to the exercise of power is stressed as the basis for the relationship.[19] It is argued that the common law utilises the concept of estoppel, in the form of 'apparent authority',[20] for the objective idea of holding someone to the expectations which his acts reasonably create,[1] in order to make up for the deficiencies, and to fill the gaps, resulting from the 'consent' or 'agreement' exposition of agency. Estoppel, or the objective approach, if accepted as bases for, or explanations of, agency, should lead to a rationalisation of agency in terms akin to the reasoning that appears in tort cases. This would produce an approach to agency that resembles more closely the American view of agency to which reference has been made earlier.[2] While 'consent' should not be over-emphasised as the explanation of agency, it may be added that it cannot altogether be ignored. In the modern law of agency, what has happened, it may be suggested, is not that 'consent' has ceased to be relevant and important: rather that modifications have been made to the pristine idea of agency, so as to make it more adaptable, and to cause it to conform much more to modern needs and requirements.

Attempts to base agency relationships upon a single theory of contract or to distinguish between only two bases for the emergence of an agency relationship are unprofitable, it is suggested, because neither a contractual explanation nor a simple division into two categories will provide an adequate framework within

---

16 *Kingsnorth Trust Ltd v Bell* [1986] 1 All ER 423, [1986] 1 WLR 119; *Midland Bank plc v Shephard* [1988] 3 All ER 17; *Bank of Credit and Commerce International SA v Aboody* [1990] 1 QB 923, [1992] 4 All ER 955 (overruled, on different grounds, by the House of Lords in *CIBC Mortgages plc v Pitt* [1994] 1 AC 200, [1993] 4 All ER 433).

17 Eg *Coldunell Ltd v Gallon* [1986] QB 1184, [1986] 1 All ER 429; *CIBC Mortgages plc v Pitt* [1994] 1 AC 200, [1993] 4 All ER 433. However, as stated in the *O'Brien* case, above at 428, in some of these cases, the earliest of which is *Avon Finance Co Ltd v Bridger* [1985] 2 All ER 281, even in the absence of agency, if the debtor has been guilty of undue influence or misrepresentation the creditor may not be able to enforce a surety contract if the creditor had actual or constructive notice of the debtor's conduct.

18 Below, pp 229–231.

19 Reynolds 'Agency: Theory and Practice' (1978) 94 LQR 224 at pp 226–227; *Bowstead and Reynolds on Agency* (16th edn 1996) pp 17–20.

20 Below, ch 6.

1 Cf *N & J Vlassopulos Ltd v Ney Shipping Ltd, The Santa Carina* [1977] 1 Lloyd's Rep 478, especially at 483 per Roskill LJ. See also Atiyah *The Rise and Fall of Freedom of Contract* pp 496–501.

2 Above, p 8 note 11.

which to discuss the law. There are instances of agency arising from consent. There are also situations in which the agency relationship and its effects come about by the operation of the doctrine of estoppel. In addition, however, there are examples of the agency relationship and its consequences which cannot be treated either as consensual or as based upon estoppel.[3]

An alternative division into agency arising by act of the parties and agency arising by operation of law is also misleading and narrow. Where an agency relationship comes into existence because of the consent of the parties, it may be said to arise by their acts. The conduct of the parties is accepted by the law as giving rise to a specific legal relationship with particular legal consequences. But the foundation of this relationship and its consequences is to be seen in the acts of the parties. Where an agency relationship comes about because of the operation of the doctrine of estoppel, it may be said that, here again, the law is interpreting the conduct of the parties as having a certain legal effect. In this respect agency by estoppel is similar to agency arising from consent, ie by act of the parties. At the same time, however, agency by estoppel is really agency by operation of law, in that it is only because the law regards the situation as one having the effect of an agency relationship in toto or for specific purposes that such relationship may be said to arise. In this respect, as in the absence of any true consent on the part of the principal, agency by estoppel resembles agency which arises entirely by operation of law, for example, agency of necessity. Where this is said to emerge it is sometimes the case that a relationship which may come about by consent, even contract, creates an agency even though the primary and original purpose of the relationship, or the consent which underlies it, was not the creation of an agency relationship. Hence, it is suggested, though the consent of the parties, ie their acts, may originate the ultimate agency relationship recognised and effectuated by the law, that relationship is not itself consensual or based upon the acts of the parties. It is an agency relationship which is the creation of the law, for reasons of policy.

Authority. The question of the authority of an agent is at the very core of agency.[4] It is complex and difficult, but it must be understood if the nature of agency is to be comprehended. Authority, at one time, was regarded as the cornerstone of the agency relationship.[5] It remains a vital feature; and the scope

---

3 Below, pp 111–132. Eg, agency of necessity, insofar as it may be regarded as involving agency at all: below, pp 134–144. So, too, there are situations in which one party appears to be treated as an agent to effect some policy of the law: eg, a receiver put in by creditors, who is the agent of the company not of debenture holders: *Standard Chartered Bank Ltd v Walker* [1982] 3 All ER 938, [1982] 1 WLR 1410; a mortgagee regarded as the agent of the mortgagor to effect insurance: *Re National Bank of Canada and Co-operative Fire and Casualty Co* (1989) 53 DLR (4th) 519; a salesman engaged by a broker: *McKee v Georgia Pacific Securities Corpn* (1988) 20 BCLR (2d) 12.

4 This sentence was quoted by the Nova Scotia Court of Appeal in *R v Arnold* (1994) 129 NSR (2d) 356 at 358. See also *R v Kelly* [1992] 14 Cr App Rep (5) 170 at 183 per Cory J.

5 See eg *Digest of English Law* para 132; Dowrick (1954) 17 MLR 24 at p 35, note 57; Powell *Law of Agency* p 7. Cf Gale CJ HC in *Royal Securities Corpn v Montreal Trust Co* (1967) 59 DLR (2d) 666 at 686. Hence the dispute over authority in several Canadian cases: *Calgary Hardwood and Veneer Ltd v Canadian National Rly Co* [1979] 4 WWR 198; *Rockland Industries Inc v Amerada Minerals Corpn of Canada Ltd* [1978] 2 WWR 44; revsd [1979] 2 WWR 209, [1980] 2 SCR 2; *Canadian Laboratory Supplies Ltd v Engelhard Industries Ltd* [1979] 2 SCR 787.

of an agent's 'authority' is frequently the key to an understanding of that relation-ship and its consequences.

The notion of authority is extremely artificial, in the sense that there are many instances in which an agent is regarded as having authority to act even where it is impossible to say that he has been invested with such authority by the principal. To describe the reason why the agent's acts produce a change in the principal's legal position by speaking of his 'authority' to act on behalf of the principal is hardly very explanatory.[6] For the purpose of explaining the *effects* of the agency relationship, the notion of authority is extremely useful. It enables a lawyer to state concisely and simply what the agent can and cannot do, and how he can affect his principal, beneficially or adversely. But as a means of describing the legal nature of the agency relationship, the notion of authority is unsatis-factory, because it does not go far enough. It describes the purposes of the agency relationship, in that it is a relationship by which one person 'permits' (or, in law is regarded as 'permitting') another person to act for him; but it does not say why this permission (or authorisation) is so vitally important to the agency relationship.

This missing explanation is provided by the analysis of the relationship in terms of the agent's power to affect his principal's legal position.[7] Modern writers have begun to accept this idea as the explanation of the agency relationship.[8] Thus Seavey[9] called agency:

> 'a consensual relationship in which one (the agent) holds in trust for and subject to the control of another (the principal) a power to affect certain legal relations of that other.'

Powell said that an agent was a person who (inter alia) 'has power to affect the legal relations of his principal with a third party'.[10] Dowrick[11] described the essential characteristics of an agent as being that '. . . he is invested with a legal power to alter his principal's legal relations with third persons'; and adds that 'the principal is under a correlative liability to have his legal relations altered'.

There are many instances of such a power-liability relation. Agency is only one of them.[12] By the agency relationship the agent is invested by the law with 'a facsimile of the principal's own power'.[13] For example, in respect of the making of a contract[14] the agent, in effect, acts in such a way that he produces the same

---

6 Cf Montrose 'The Basis of the Power of an Agent in Cases of Actual and Apparent Authority' (1938) 16 Can BR 757 at pp 761–763.
    This and the following sentences to the end of the paragraph were quoted in *R v Arnold*, above.
7 This sentence was quoted in *R v Arnold*, above.
8 See the citations in Dowrick (1954) 17 MLR 24 at p 36, note 63.
9 'The Rationale of Agency' (1920) 29 Yale LJ 859 p 868.
10 *Powell* p 7.
11 (1954) 17 MLR 24 at p 36: for the explanation of the terms 'power' and 'liability' see Hohfeld *Fundamental Legal Conceptions* pp 50–60. Salmond *Jurisprudence* (12th edn, 1966) pp 228–231; Dias *Jurisprudence* (5th edn 1985) pp 33–39.
12 Hence the similarity between agency and certain other relations. See pp 23–37.
13 Dowrick (1954) 17 MLR 24 at p 37. Hence an agent's authority is always limited to the *power* of the principal to act on his own behalf: see *Wilkinson v General Accident Fire and Life Assurance Corpn Ltd* [1967] 2 Lloyd's Rep 182.
14 Below, pp 216–222.

The definition of agency 21

results as if the principal had acted personally and the agent had never appeared on the scene at all.[15] This power is strictly controlled by the law. It may not be abused or misused, so as to benefit the agent to the detriment of the principal.[16] It may not be excessively exercised beyond the limits of its use as created by acts of the parties or operation of law. Its exercise results in liabilities on the part of principal and agent alike—though the liabilities differ.

The use of this terminology, it is suggested, underlines the argument put forward earlier, that the agency relationship is one that is created by the law, not by the conduct of the parties. The parties, by contract or otherwise, may bring these powers and liabilities into existence and operation: they may even restrict, or broaden their scope.[17] But, in the absence of any special agreement, the power arising from the creation of the agency relationship is derived from the law itself. Indeed the power in question may arise or vest in the absence of any agreement, as is shown by the whole idea of agency by estoppel.[18] Montrose[19] argued, for example, that the basis of agency is the endowment by the principal of the agent with the power to act, coupled with the exercise of that power by the agent. This endowment of the agent with the power to act results from *either* (i) agreement with the agent that the principal will be bound, which gives rise to actual authority of the agent, ie agency arising by act of the parties; *or* (ii) the principal's showing the third party an intention to be bound by the agent's acts, and his leading the third party reasonably to believe that he will be so bound, which gives rise to apparent authority on the part of the agent, ie agency by estoppel. The notion of authority may be used to describe the way in which the powers of the agent have been circumscribed by the agreement or conduct of the parties. But it does not adequately explain, in legal terms, the nature of the relationship between principal and agent.[20] This can best be done by talking of the powers and liabilities that emerge from the creation of the agency relationship.

Agency as a power-liability relationship. Once it is recognised that the essence of agency is this power to affect the principal's legal relations with the outside world, the law of agency can be more readily understood.[1] Much of it is concerned with the way in which the conduct of principal and agent (or two persons who are treated in law as being principal and agent) affects third parties. Even the relationship inter se of principal and agent is important not merely from the point of view of those parties themselves, but also from the point of view of

---

15 This is not completely true, since there are instances in which the agent does not drop out of the picture completely (below, pp 231–243). But this is in order to safeguard the third party, rather than to affect the principal's position.
16 Below, pp 174–188.
17 Subject to certain qualifications, such as illegality.
18 Below, pp 111–114. Contrast the view of Conant (1968) 47 Nebraska LR 678.
19 'The Basis of the Power of an Agent in Cases of Actual and Apparent Authority' (1938) 16 Can BR 757.
20 Cf Dowrick (1954) 17 MLR 24 at p 37, note 69: see also Seavey (1920) 29 Yale LJ 859 at pp 860–861, where he shows that 'power' and 'authority' must be distinguished.
 1 This sentence was quoted by the Nova Scotia Court of Appeal in *Scott v Trophy Foods Inc* (1995) 123 DLR (4th) 509 at 519.

the rights and liabilities of strangers to the relationship. These two aspects of the agency relationship have been differentiated as *external* and *internal*.[2] They may be considered and discussed separately, but it must not be forgotten that they interact. For example, the way the agent binds a third party to his principal can affect the agent's right to remuneration or indemnity. Whether the agent has properly performed or exercised his authority may be connected with the position of a third party as a result. The principal's right to determine the agent's authority, as between himself and the agent, can affect the third party's rights.

The law of agency is therefore concerned with the powers and liabilities of principal and agent, ie, the powers of the agent and the liabilities of the principal. The purpose of this book is to discuss how those powers and liabilities arise and may be determined, and what they involve. To do this, it is first necessary to differentiate agency from other relationships which similarly give rise to powers and liabilities. The purpose of such differentiation is to clarify and stress the fact that an agent affects the legal position of his principal by the making of contracts or the disposition of property. This power is the essence of the agency relationship. It distinguishes the position of an agent from that of others who have the power to affect the legal relations of another person. Such others do not possess the same kind of power as an agent, in that either they cannot affect the legal position of someone else by the making of a contract, or they cannot dispose of someone else's property effectively to alter the title of the original owner. Only an agent can do both. In this connection it is also relevant to differentiate various kinds of agents in terms of the content of their respective authorities, ie the nature and extent of their powers. Such a differentiation brings out the features of the agency relationship now being stressed, ie its effects upon the contractual and proprietary position of the principal, by showing how the most important kinds of agents evolved, and now exist, for precisely such purposes, namely to make contracts for another and to dispose of another person's property.[3]

---

2 Müller-Freienfels (1964) 13 Am J of Comp L 193 at p 198; cf Hay and Müller-Freienfels 'Agency in the Conflict of Laws and the 1978 Hague Convention' (1979) 27 Am J Comp L 1 at pp 8, 16, referring to national choice-of-law rules with respect to the 'internal' relationship (principal-agent) and the 'external' relationship (principal-third party). Cf Stoljar *Law of Agency* p 17.
3 This paragraph was quoted in *Scott v Trophy Foods Inc*, above.

CHAPTER 2

Agency and other legal relationships

Three features of agency emerge from what was said in the previous chapter. They are service; representation; power to affect the legal position of the principal. An agent performs a service for his principal; he represents him to the outside world; he can acquire rights for his principal and subject his principal to liabilities. There are other relationships recognised by the law which show some of these features.[1] In light of the origins of the modern concept of agency, this is not surprising. The modern relationship of principal and agent emerged alongside and out of other relationships.[2] For a long period, no great differentiation was made between them; indeed while the law of agency was elementary and rudimentary no differentiation may have been necessary or possible.

In the course of time the law hardened into more rigorously defined categories of relationships, each governed by special rules. Recent commercial developments may have assimilated some of these distinct relationships. That has been suggested in respect of developments in international trade.[3] 'Representatives' who are not strictly agents in the traditional sense, may share some of the characteristics of such agents, raising issues relating to their liability to the party they represent or the liability of such party to others.[4] At the present time, however, the changes that have been suggested should occur as a consequence of such characteristics have not been firmly or clearly incorporated into the law of agency.

A. Agency and trusts[5]

At first sight there appears to be a close similarity between the situation of a trustee and that of an agent. Trustees, like agents, can affect the legal position of

---

1 Cp above, p 3, referring to sub-contracting, delegation of non-delegable duties, and vicarious performance of contracts.
2 Above, pp 6–9.
3 Hill *Freight Forwarders* (1972) especially pp 38–49; Hill 'Confirming House Transactions in Commonwealth Countries' [1972] 3 J of Maritime Law and Commerce 307. See also his earlier article, 'Agents with special responsibility' [1964] JBL 306. On the subject of 'confirming houses' reference may be made to *Rusholme Bolton and Roberts Hadfield Ltd v SG Read & Co (London) Ltd* [1955] 1 All ER 180, [1955] 1 WLR 146; *Sobell Industries Ltd v Cory Bros & Co Ltd* [1955] 2 Lloyd's Rep 82; *Anglo-African Shipping Co of New York Inc v J Mortner Ltd* [1962] 1 Lloyd's Rep 610.
4 Cf Reynolds 'Agency: Theory and Practice' (1978) 94 LQR 224, at pp 230–237.
5 Street 'Trusteeship and Agency' (1892) 8 LQR 220: Waters *The Constructive Trust* ch IV: The Agent as a Constructive Trustee; Waters *Law of Trusts in Canada* (2nd edn 1984) pp 42–46.

the people with whose affairs (ie property) they are dealing. To some extent they seem to share and enjoy the same kind of powers. Maitland[6] suggested that the law of trusts and the law of agency have a common origin in the early doctrine of uses. Whether this be correct or not, it is certainly true that by the eighteenth and nineteenth centuries the Court of Chancery treated the agent as more or less in the position of a trustee, so far as the principal's confidence in the agent was concerned.[7] And the development of certain of the rules of law of agency bears out the first impression of a comparison and indicates a similarity and an analogy of some kind between the position of agents and that of trustees.[8]

First, just as a trustee can pass a valid legal title free of the beneficiary's interest to bona fide purchaser for value without notice of the existence of a trust, so agents can sometimes achieve the same result, thereby defeating their principal's claim to property which has been transferred to a third party.[9] At common law, there were instances in which by the operation of the doctrines of implied or apparent authority,[10] certain kinds of agents,[11] if entrusted in the ordinary course of business with goods for the purpose of dealing with them in various ways could validly sell to third persons so as to pass title, even without actual authority to do so.[12] But they could not achieve a similar result by pledging the goods.[13] The Factors Acts[14] made considerable changes in the law, by giving more scope to 'mercantile agents',[15] to defeat the principal's title by their own acts in relation to third parties. Furthermore, by the doctrine of 'apparent authority' an agent may be able to divest his principal of title.[16] To this extent, therefore, agents and trustees seem to be very alike. However, it is important to point out that, whereas the trustee is invested with legal *title*, the agent has no title to the property in question: all he has is the *power* to dispose of *his principal's* title, a power which may stem from his *authority*. And, whereas a trustee always has title, the agent's power to dispose of his principal's title depends upon the flexible ideas of implied and apparent authority.

Secondly, the duties of an agent towards his principal resemble very greatly at least some of those which a trustee owes towards his beneficiary.[17] This can

---

6 P & M ii p 226: see above, p 4.

7 See the cases referred to in Dowrick, 17 MLR 24 at p 28, note 30.

8 Cf Seavey 'The Rationale of Agency' (1920) 29 Yale LJ 859 at p 863. '[Agency] is rather the result of a grant of power by the principal and the assumption of a fiduciary obligation by the agent. It is analogous to a trust rather than to a contract.' But an agent may be, and usually is, subject to much greater control by his principal, than is a trustee by his cestui que trust: ibid at pp 867–868.

   A person can be an agent and a trustee at the same time, although one status or relationship may predominate: *Trident Holdings Ltd v Danand Investments Ltd* (1988) 49 DLR (4th) 1: cf *Allen v Richardson Greenshields of Canada Ltd* (1988) 48 DLR (4th) 98. Note also the fiduciary character of agency: below, pp 174–188: cf *Burns v Kelly Peters & Associates Ltd* (1988) 41 DLR (4th) 577.

9 Below, pp 279–300.

10 Below, pp 68, 122.

11 Below, pp 40–42, 79–80.

12 *Pickering v Busk* (1812) 15 East 38.

13 *Paterson v Tash* (1743) 2 Stra 1178.

14 The earliest was 1823: the one in force now is the consolidating Act of 1889.

15 As defined in the Acts: below, p 291.

16 Below, pp 128–132, 281–290.

17 Below, pp 174–188.

be summarised by saying that an agent, like a trustee, in respect of a beneficiary, must not let his duty to his principal conflict with his own interest.[18] The latter must give way before the former. But the similarity must not be taken too far, since trustees are bound by various duties imposed on them by the Trustee Act 1925, whereas the duties of an agent are not derived from statute.[19]

Thirdly, certain equitable remedies in respect of property in the hands of an agent may be pursued by the principal against an agent, in the same way that they are available to the beneficiary against the trustee. For example, an agent who makes a secret profit out of his agency must account for it in equity, in the same way as a trustee who makes a secret profit out of his trust.[20] Moreover, the principal's property, if mixed with the agent's, may be followed in the same way as a beneficiary's if mixed with the trustee's, ie the agent is treated as being trustee for the principal.[1] However, it is arguable whether the agent, like the trustee,[2] can be sued where the principal's money has been converted into some other form of property or mingled with some other fund of money. This was said by Powell[3] to be possible. But Hanbury[4] and Dowrick[5] argued that the following or tracing of property originally belonging to the principal, so as to enable him to recover it no matter into what form it has been converted, is not possible.

---

18 See eg *Parker v McKenna* (1874) 10 Ch App 96 at 118 per Lord Cairns LC. On damages for breach of fiduciary duty see *Canson Enterprises Ltd v Boughton & Co* (1991) 85 DLR (4th) 129, where the Supreme Court of Canada, in various different opinions, discussed the connection, and the difference between damages in tort, damages for breach of contract and damages in equity: Fridman *Restitution* (2nd edn 1992) at pp 381–384.

19 Except in special cases, such as bribery and corruption: below, p 188.

20 Below, pp 181–188.

 1 *Foley v Hill* (1848) 2 HL Cas 28 at 35–36 per Lord Cottenham LC; *Lupton v White* (1808) 15 Ves 432: *Re Hallett's Estate, Knatchbull v Hallett* (1880) 13 Ch D 696.

    This idea was employed in *Aluminium Industrie Vaassen BV v Romalpa Aluminium Ltd* [1976] 2 All ER 552, [1976] 1 WLR 676. There the separation of the proceeds of the sale of certain goods bought by the defendants from the plaintiffs and then resold to third parties entitled the plaintiffs to hold the defendants accountable for such proceeds, since the money in question was the product of goods ownership in which remained in the plaintiffs (the original sellers) until full payment of the purchase price.

    This case has been both distinguished and followed: *Borden (UK) Ltd v Scottish Timber Products Ltd* [1981] Ch 25, [1979] 3 All ER 961; *Re Bond Worth Ltd* [1980] Ch 228, [1979] 3 All ER 919; *Re Peachdart Ltd* [1984] Ch 131, [1983] 3 All ER 204; *Hendy Lennox (Industrial Engines) Ltd v Grahame Puttick Ltd* [1984] 2 All ER 152, [1984] 1 WLR 485; *Re Andrabell Ltd* [1984] 3 All ER 407; *Clough Mill Ltd v Martin* [1984] 3 All ER 982, [1985] 1 WLR 111; *Armour v Thyssen Edelstahlwerke AG* [1991] 2 AC 339, [1990] 3 All ER 481; *Len Vidgen Ski and Leisure Ltd v Timaru Marine Supplies (1982) Ltd* [1986] 1 NZLR 349; *Pongakawa Sawmill Ltd v New Zealand Forest Products Ltd* [1992] 3 NZLR 304; *Fosters Brewing Group Ltd v Monte Rosa Pty Ltd* (1991) 57 SASR 272; *Chattis Nominees Pty Ltd v Norman Ross Homeworks Pty Ltd* (1992) 28 NSWLR 338.

    See further, below, p 256.

 2 *Re Diplock, Diplock v Wintle* [1948] Ch 465; [1948] 2 All ER 318; sub nom *Ministry of Health v Simpson* [1951] AC 251, [1950] 2 All ER 1137.

 3 *Law of Agency* (2nd edn) pp 25, 208–211, 214–215. Cf Waters *The Constructive Trust* p 335 who clearly comes out in favour of the application of the doctrine of tracing.

 4 *Principles of Agency* (2nd edn 1960) pp 5–7.

 5 17 MLR 24 at p 29.

These last two writers relied on the case of *Lister & Co v Stubbs*,[6] where a principal was unable to claim investments purchased by the agent with a secret, corruptly obtained commission culled from third persons and accountable for to the principal. The court took the view that the relationship between principal and agent was that of debtor and creditor not trustee and cestui que trust. This case has been subjected to much criticism,[7] and the attitude therein adopted is probably not consistent with modern views as to the character of the relationship of principal and agent.[8] It was also criticised and doubted by the Privy Council in *A-G for Hong Kong v Reid*,[9] where it was said that the decision was not consistent inter alia with the principle that a fiduciary must not be allowed to benefit from his own breach of duty. Hence the position of a trustee and that of an agent, in this respect, may be closer than once thought.[10]

These resemblances should not be allowed to create the impression that agency and trusteeship are the same type of relationship. Sufficient differences abound to negate this.

Firstly, the relationship of principal and agent, while not necessarily always consensual in origin, more often than not arises by contract, or at least agreement between the parties,[11] and, even when it arises by operation of law, as opposed to agreement between the parties, involves the consent of *one* of the parties.[12] With certain exceptions, however, a trust may be created without the consent of the beneficiary or the trustee. Moreover, whereas the relationship of principal and agent in general can be created by agreement without any special form,[13] there are instances in which trusts must be in writing.[14]

Secondly, the agent represents his principal, and can create contractual relations between his principal and third persons, besides involving his principal in other forms of liability, such as those arising from the commission of some tort by the agent. But a trustee is not in any way the representative of his beneficiary: hence the trustee does not involve his beneficiary in personal responsibility for the trustee's acts, whether in contract or tort.

Thirdly, actions between principal and agent may be barred by the operation of the Limitation Act 1980. But no such limitation is operative to an action by a beneficiary against a trustee in respect of fraud, fraudulent breach of trust, or the recovery of trust property or its proceeds, in certain circumstances.[15] On the other

---

6 (1890) 45 Ch D 1. In *Canadian Pacific Airlines Ltd v CIBC* (1987) 42 DLR (4th) 375, the airline and travel agency were held to be principal and agent, not debtor and creditor: upheld on appeal (1990) 71 OR (2d) 63. Cp *Air Canada v M&C Travel Ltd* (1993) 108 DLR (4th) 592 where the relationship between a travel agency and the airline was one of trust, not one of debtor and creditor.

7 Waters *The Constructive Trust* pp 284, 339–340; Goff and Jones *The Law of Restitution* (4th edn 1993) pp 668–669.

8 As to which see *Boardman v Phipps* [1967] 2 AC 46, [1966] 3 All ER 721.

9 [1994] 1 All ER 1 at 9–11.

10 Note also the principal's common law right to trace in certain circumstances: *Taylor v Plumer* (1815) 3 M & S 562: below, p 277.

11 Above, pp 14–19.

12 Below, pp 133–150.

13 There are exceptions, such as power of attorney: below, p 57.

14 Law of Property Act 1925, s 53.

15 Where the trustee is party or privy to the fraud, or in possession of property, or the property or its proceeds was received by him and converted to his use: Limitation Act 1980, s 21.

hand, the equitable doctrine of laches (where it has not been affected by statute) may still operate to defeat the claims of a beneficiary. However, the differences between agents and trustees may not be so great in this respect: for there are cases in which agents have been treated as trustees, at least for the purposes of avoiding the statute of limitations.[16]

B. Agency and bailment

Bailment is the delivery or transfer of possession of a chattel (or other item of personal property) with a specific mandate which requires the identical res either to be returned to the bailor or to be dealt with in a particular way by the bailee.[17] It is obvious, therefore, that in a bailment the power of dealing with the thing bailed is transferred to the bailee by the bailor, who becomes liable to have his rights over the thing in question affected by what the bailee does. But a bailee may not be rendering any service to the bailor. In fact the situation may be quite the reverse, as where a chattel is loaned gratuitously for the benefit of the borrower.

It is possible that an agent may be the bailee of his principal's goods. Indeed this is very often an essential part of the agent's authority, eg in the case of auctioneers or factors.[18] But it is unusual for a bailee to be the agent of the bailor.[19] There are also two important distinguishing features between agency and bailment. First, the bailee does not represent the bailor. He merely exercises, with the leave of the bailor (under contract or otherwise), certain powers of the bailor in respect of his property.[20] Secondly, the bailee has no power to make contracts on the bailor's behalf; nor can he make the bailor liable, simply as bailor, for any acts he does. However, it must be added that, in exercising some of the powers of the bailor over the property, eg to have the property repaired or serviced, the bailee may incidentally involve the bailor in liability on a contract made for the purpose. Such situations greatly resemble those in which an agent makes the principal liable on a contract entered into by the agent in the course of his implied or apparent authority, or in situations of necessity.[1]

---

16 Eg *Betjemann v Betjemann* [1895] 2 Ch 474; *North American Land and Timber Co Ltd v Watkins* [1904] 1 Ch 242; affd [1904] 2 Ch 233.

17 Paton *Bailment in the Common Law* p 6; Palmer *Bailment* (2nd edn 1991) pp 1–3.

18 Below, pp 40, 45.

19 See however *Smith v General Motor Cab Co Ltd* [1911] AC 188; and compare the Nova Scotia case of *Scott Maritimes Pulp Ltd v B F Goodrich Canada Ltd* (1977) 24 APR 181. Note also *Aluminium Industrie Vaassen BV v Romalpa Aluminium Ltd* [1976] 2 All ER 552, [1976] 1 WLR 676, in which it was argued that the buyer became bailee of the goods on behalf of the seller, to whom they were accountable for the proceeds. The seller was succesful in attaining the proceeds, but on the basis of agency rather than bailments. See also the cases cited on p 25, note 1; and see below, p 173.

20 *Albermarle Supply Co Ltd v Hind & Co* [1928] 1 KB 307.

1 *Tappenden v Artus* [1964] 2 QB 185, [1963] 3 All ER 213: Fridman 'The Authority of Bailees' (1964) 114 LJ 265.

C. Agency and sale

At first sight there would appear to be a clear distinction between the relationship of principal and agent and that of vendor and purchaser of goods. That this distinction is not so clear is manifested in decisions in which the question has arisen whether the 'seller' of goods was a seller or an agent, acting for the 'buyer/principal', or, vice versa, whether the 'buyer' of goods was a buyer or an agent, acting for the 'seller/principal'.[2]

Confusion between sellers and agents may arise where the buyer asks the seller to obtain goods which the seller does not own or possess at the time of the contract. It becomes a question of fact whether the transaction between the parties involves the seller in procuring goods for the buyer as the latter's agent, or is a straightforward sale under the terms of which the seller undertakes to obtain the goods and resell them to the buyer. If the first is the true explanation of the situation, the duty of the 'seller' is not absolute, in the sense that he will be liable if he does not obtain the goods: his duty is to use his care and skill, as an agent, to endeavour to obtain what the buyer/principal wants.[3] If the correct interpretation of the arrangement between them is that it is a sale by a seller of goods which he does not own, then the seller will be absolutely liable (subject to any other terms of the contract) if he fails to obtain the required goods. Similarly, an agent will not be liable if the goods obtained are defective, unless, for example, he acted negligently in his purchase:[4] a seller will be liable in accordance with the express or statutorily implied terms of the contract.[5]

Confusion between buyers and agents may arise where the function of the 'agent' is really as a 'middleman', eg, a retail dealer or supplier of goods, who obtains goods from a wholesale supplier or a manufacturer for subsequent resale to retail customers or suppliers who, in turn, will be dealing with retail dealers or shopkeepers. Such 'middlemen' are sometimes referred to as 'agents', when in fact they are franchisees of the manufacturer, or of the supplier or distributor of the manufacturer's goods, perhaps with a 'sole agency' or special dealership in his goods. Such 'agents' are really buyers, acting as principals on their own behalf. Consequently, they are not liable to the manufacturer or supplier, in the way an agent might be for failure of duty: nor do their contracts with other parties, whether suppliers, retail dealers or individual customers, involve the party who sold to them in any form of liability, for example, for

---

2   See, for example, two Canadian cases illustrating both situations: *Re CA MacDonald & Co Ltd* (1959) 18 DLR (2d) 731; *B and M Readers' Service Ltd v Anglo Canadian Publishers Ltd* [1950] OR 159. In *Jackson Securities Ltd v Cheesman* [1986] 4 NSWLR 484 brokers speculating on the futures market for a client were agents, not sellers to their principal.

  A seller who agreed that title to goods would pass at the time of carriage of the goods to the buyer, and then contracted with a carrier for such carriage was the agent of the buyer in making the contract of carriage: from principal he became an agent: *Texas Instruments Ltd v Europe Cargo* [1990] CLY 440. Therefore when the carrier lost or damaged the goods the seller could sue the carrier as a party to the contract of carriage.

3   *Anglo-African Shipping Co of New York Inc v J Mortner Ltd* [1962] 1 Lloyd's Rep 610; cf below, pp 158–164 on the agent's duty of care.

4   Below, pp 158–160; *Ireland v Livingston* (1872) LR 5 HL 395.

5   Fridman *Sale of Goods in Canada* (4th edn 1995) chs 7, 8.

misrepresentations, or defective goods.[6] Any money received by such 'agents' from their customers will belong to the 'agent' not to the party who sold to him, and will be part of such 'agent's' property in the event of his bankruptcy or liquidation.[7] This will, or may be, the case even if the contract of sale is one of 'sale or return'.[8]

In all these situations, the problem must be resolved by a careful examination of the facts and, most importantly, the exact nature of the relationship arranged between the parties. In this respect courts pay considerable attention to the question whether one party, the alleged 'agent', is accountable for moneys received by him to the other party, the alleged 'principal'.[9]

This became of particular importance in *Aluminium Industrie Vaassen BV v Romalpa Aluminium Ltd*[10] (the *Romalpa* case) and subsequent decisions in which that case was sometimes followed and sometimes distinguished.[11] Goods were sold by the plaintiffs to the defendants on the terms that the goods remained in the ownership of the sellers until the buyers had met all that was owing to the sellers, no matter on what grounds. The goods had to be stored in such a way that they could be identified as the property of the seller. But the buyers could resell the goods or any part of them to other parties, the proceeds of such sales having to be kept in a separate account. When the buyers, who had sold some of the goods, became insolvent, the sellers claimed the money kept in that separate account. Their claim was successful at trial and in the Court of Appeal. That court held that, vis-à-vis the sellers the original buyers were principals, but vis-à-vis parties who bought from them the original buyers were the agents of the original sellers, the plaintiffs. Hence they were accountable to the plaintiffs for the proceeds of those sub-sales. The decision in this case was said to be based on the particular contract, and the particular terms, that governed the parties. The case has been criticised, but accepted in later English, Scottish, Australian and New Zealand decisions, even when the facts in a given case permitted the court to distinguish, and therefore not follow the result in the *Romalpa* case. Nonetheless, it follows from the decision that a party can be a principal and an agent at one and the same time. That is a situation that, previously, occurred only where an agent acted for an undisclosed principal in making a contract on the latter's behalf.[12]

---

6 See eg *Branwhite v Worcester Works Finance Ltd* [1969] 1 AC 552, [1969] 3 All ER 104, above, p 16. Note also the provisions of the Consumer Credit Act 1974, s 56.

7 *Re Nevill, ex p White* (1871) 6 Ch App 397 (upheld on appeal sub nom *John Towle & Co v White* (1873) 29 LT 78).

8 But see *Weiner v Harris* [1910] 1 KB 285, where a person buying on sale or return was held to be an agent (at least for the purposes of the Factors Act, on which see pp 290–300, below). See also *Garnac Grain Co Inc v HMF Faure and Fairclough Ltd* [1968] AC 1130n, [1967] 2 All ER 353.

9 Cf *R v Robertson* [1977] Crim LR 629: cf *B and M Readers' Service Ltd v Anglo Canadian Publishers Ltd* [1950] OR 159. See *Michelin Tyre Co Ltd v MacFarlane (Glasgow) Ltd* (1917) 55 SLR 35, which also deals with the situation where resale prices are fixed by a manufacturer. For a case where payment of commission did not involve the creation of an agency relationship between the parties, see *Limako BV v H Hentz & Co Inc* [1979] 2 Lloyd's Rep 23.

10 [1976] 2 All ER 552, [1976] 1 WLR 676.

11 For the cases in question see above, p 25, note 1.

12 Below, pp 256–257.

D. Agency and representation

Some commercial arrangements involve the participation of intermediaries between two parties who ultimately enter into some kind of contractual relationship in a manner which, by language or action, suggests that the intermediary is acting as an 'agent'. The true situation may be that the intermediary is an agent, at least for some purposes and as regards one party: or he may be acting as a principal (and in no way capable of being treated as an agent as respects either his relations with the party with whom he is dealing or the relations between that party and any other). Thus one who, in the common law is sometimes termed a 'commission agent', and sometimes called a 'commission merchant',[13] is an agent vis-à-vis the party who has appointed him as his representative to deal with third parties.[14] However, such an agent deals in his own name with the third party, and does not create contractual privity between his principal and such third party. In consequence it was held by the House of Lords in *Ireland v Livingston*[15] that the relationship between such an agent and his principal was compounded of the relationships involved in agency and sale of goods. In consequence in a later case, *Cassaboglou v Gibb*,[16] there was considerable difficulty experienced by the court in determining the damages payable by a commission agent who failed to supply his principal with goods of the right quality. In the event if was held that the right test was not that applicable as between buyer and seller, but that applicable between principal and agent.

Despite such a consequence, it may be questioned whether 'agents' of this class are truly agents in the sense in which that expression is traditionally understood, and is used in this book.[17] The argument has been raised that such representatives, whose 'commission' is the task with which they are entrusted (the term 'commission' not being used in this context to refer to the normal mode of payment of an agent[18]), should be regarded as agents in the true, and fullest sense.[19] This would result in some expansion of the traditional notion of agency. Hence there may be considerable opposition to any such assimilation. Were traditional views of agency to undergo revision, it would be more likely that commission merchants could be more properly described as 'commission agents'.[20]

---

13 Hill 'The Commission Merchant at Common Law' (1968) 31 MLR 623, for a comprehensive account.
14 Usually as a buyer of goods: *Ireland v Livingston* (1872) LR 5 HL 395 at 407–409; *Robinson v Mollett* (1875) LR 7 HL 802 at 809–810; *Cassaboglou v Gibb* (1883) 11 QBD 797 at 803–804; *Montgomerie v UK Mutual SS Association Ltd* [1891] 1 QB 370 at 372; but also sometimes as a seller; *Armstrong v Stokes* (1872) LR 7 QB 598; *Kirkham v Peel* (1881) 44 LT 195.
15 (1872) LR 5 HL 395.
16 (1883) 11 QBD 797.
17 This kind of agency, along with the 'agency' of a 'canvassing' or 'introducing' agent, such as the estate agent or real estate broker, is referred to as *incomplete agency* in *Bowstead and Reynolds on Agency* (16th edn 1996) pp 8–9.
18 Below, pp 189–201.
19 Hill 'Agents with Special Responsibility' [1964] JBL 120; cf Reynolds 'Agency: Theory and Practice' (1978) 94 LQR 224 at pp 233–235.
20 Note, also, 'commercial agents': below, pp 50–51. Though described as agents, and, now, in England, treated as such, they seem to be more like representatives than agents.

E. Agency, servants and independent contractors[1]

This is an extremely difficult topic, because fundamentally it is one of definition, of determining the scope of the application of the law of agency and the agency relationship. For historical reasons there has been considerable debate on the issue whether the master-servant relationship should be included within the scope of the relationship of principal and agent.[2] As a result, to one writer at least, the position is one of 'terminological disorder' which has been the 'source of . . . various quite sterile controversies as to how an "agent" should be distinguished or defined'.[3] For reasons which will emerge, however, it is suggested that in the context of this book and the attempt to clarify the scope of the law of agency, the distinction between agents, servants and independent contractors is not without theoretical importance. It is also of great practical importance.[4]

Some statutes refer, and apply only to agents, such as the Factors Act 1889, which speaks of 'mercantile agents'. This has been held to exclude servants,[5] but not necessarily independent contractors.[6] Some statutes acknowledge the distinction between agents and servants, and agents and independent contractors,[7] or define those within their scope in terms, such as 'a person employed under a contract of service', which exclude agents.[8] Furthermore, on the question of termination there may be a distinction, in that an agent, except in certain circumstances, can be dismissed at any time,[9] whereas at common law a servant must always be given notice, or must be dismissed for some lawful justification.[10] An agent can make his principal liable for torts committed by him only if they were expressly authorised, or ratified by the principal, or within the scope of the agent's authority. A servant makes his master liable for authorised torts or those committed in the course of the servant's employment. There may be an important difference here.[11] An agent may make his principal liable for his torts in circumstances in which an independent contractor may not make his employer

---

1 See also below, pp 303–315.
2 Cf the reference to the American development, p 8 note 11, above.
3 Stoljar *Law of Agency* p 10; cf *Bowstead and Reynolds on Agency* (16th edn 1996) p 24.
4 Cf Conant 'Liability of Principals for Torts of Agents: A Comparative View' (1968) 47 Nebraska LR 42 at pp 43–48, where a similar opinion is expressed and developed. See, also, Hamilton 'Vicarious responsibility for agents: Contract or tort?' (1993) 137 Sol J 512.
5 *Hayman v Flewker* (1863) 13 CBNS 519 at 527 per Willes J; *Lowther v Harris* [1927] 1 KB 393.
6 *Weiner v Harris* [1910] 1 KB 285.
7 Eg, Crown Proceedings Act 1947, s 38; see *Moukataff v British Overseas Airways Corpn* [1967] 1 Lloyd's Rep 396.
8 Long Service Leave Act 1967 (S Aus), considered by the Judicial Committee of the Privy Council in *Australian Mutual Provident Society v Allan* (1978) 18 ALR 385. See now the Long Service Leave Act 1987 (S Aus).
9 Below, pp 389–392.
10 This point is brought out very well in *Martin-Baker Aircraft Co Ltd v Canadian Flight Equipment Ltd* [1955] 2 QB 556 at 582, [1955] 2 All ER 722 at 735–736, where there was no agency, therefore notice was required: see also a Canadian case *Keshen v S Lipsky & Co* (1956) 3 DLR (2d) 438, where a person was held to be an *agent* and therefore not entitled to notice. This was referred to in *Lowe v Rutherford Thompson McRae Ltd* (1971) 14 DLR (3d) 772. On dismissal of an employee see the provisions of Part V of the Employment Protection (Consolidation) Act 1978, dealing with 'unfair dismissal'.
11 Below, pp 308–312.

liable.[12] A principal may be liable on a contract made by his agent where the employer of an independent contractor would not be bound by a contract made by his independent contractor, nor would a master be bound by a contract made by his servant.

It is useful to begin the discussion by an attempt to define what is meant by a servant and an independent contractor.

> A *servant* is one who, by agreement, whether gratuitously or for reward, gives his service to another.
> An *independent contractor* is one who by agreement, usually for reward, provides services for another.

Both terms describe people who (like agents) have power to act for others: and it is clear, from, eg the law of tort, that they can, and do affect the legal position of others. Another common feature between servants, independent contractors, and agents is the provision of service of one kind or another. To the extent to which a servant or independent contractor can make the person for whom he acts liable, it may be said that such categories evince the feature of representation which is an essential part of the concept of agency. Must they also, therefore, be included under the heading of agents? This raises the issue, whether, within the class of agents can be included those who cannot affect the contractual or proprietary position of the principal, but can affect his liability in another way, eg by the commission of torts.

In the first place, it is important to distinguish between servants and independent contractors.[13] The test is usually given as being one of *control*.[14] The servant is said to be someone who is completely subject to the control of his master as to what he does and how he does it: whereas an independent contractor is his own master, but must provide what he has contracted to provide in the way of work or services, though he can determine his own method of performance in so far as the terms of his contract permit. To quote *Salmond and Heuston*:[15]

> 'A servant . . . works under the supervision and direction of his employer, an independent contractor is one who is his own master. A servant is a person engaged to obey his employer's orders from time to time: an independent contractor is a person engaged to do certain work, but to exercise his own discretion as to the mode and time of doing it—he is bound by his contract, but not by his employer's orders.'

---

12 Below, pp 307–308.
13 *Salmond and Heuston on the Law of Torts* (20th edn 1992) pp 449–452; Atiyah, *Vicarious Liability in the Law of Torts* (1967) pp 31–69; cf *Restatement, Second, Agency*, para 220 (2). Cf *O'Kelly v Trusthouse Forte plc* [1984] QB 90, [1983] 3 All ER 456, CA.
14 Cf *Australian Mutual Provident Society v Allan* (1978) 18 ALR 385. Cf *Rodale Press Inc v Webster Industries Ltd* (1983) 47 NBR (2d) 328; *Thorne Riddell Inc v Rolfe* [1984] 6 WWR 240. But for a discussion of new ways to view 'employment' and 'employers' see Kidner 'Vicarious liability: for whom should the "employer" be liable?' (1995) 15 Legal St 47.
15 *Salmond and Heuston on the Law of Torts* p 449: citing *Honeywill and Stein Ltd v Larkin Bros (London's Commercial Photographers) Ltd* [1934] 1 KB 191 at 196 per Slesser LJ. See also a workmen's compensation case, *Lee Ting Sang v Chung Chi-Keung* [1990] 2 AC 374 at 382, [1990] 2 WLR 1173 at 1176, cited with approval in *Hall v Lorimer* [1994] 1 All ER 250, [1994] 1 WLR 209, a tax case.

However, this theoretical distinction is sometimes hard to apply, for there may be many servants (in the eyes of the law) who cannot really be regarded in practice as being subject to such overriding control.[16] But the distinction nevertheless exists in law.

Secondly, in the light of the above differentiation, the question arises whether *agents* can be distinguished in any way from servants and independent contractors; or can be regarded as being synonymous with either servants or independent contractors, or both. Various possibilities and tests have been suggested.

Agents are distinct from both servants and independent contractors.[17]—
Thus an agent is distinct from a servant, in that an agent is subject to less control than a servant, and has complete, or almost complete, discretion as to how to perform the undertaking. As Seavey said:[18] 'A servant ... is an agent under more complete control than is a non-servant.' The difference is 'in the degree of control rather than in the acts performed. The servant sells primarily his services measured by time: the agent his ability to produce results.'[19] This distinction can be criticised: for servants may have very wide discretion, and may not really be subject to control at all in practice, while agents may have their power to act circumscribed by detailed instructions.

Other alleged distinguishing features are equally unreliable. Thus, it is not always helpful to look at the mode of remuneration employed, because either servants or agents can be paid (a) by salary or wages; (b) by commission. Nor does the length of service conclude the matter since either servants or agents can be employed (a) for one occasion, or a few occasions; (b) regularly, or irregularly; (c) for fixed hours, or without fixed hours. Finally it cannot be said

---

16 Eg doctors and similar persons: *Salmond and Heuston* pp 451–452 and cases there cited; cf *Atiyah* pp 83–95. But a ship's pilot is an independent professional man *Esso Petroleum Ltd v Hall Russell & Co Ltd* [1989] AC 643, [1989] 1 All ER 37. The suggestion has been made that the distinction is whether or not the person employed is an integral part of a business: see *Stevenson, Jordan and Harrison Ltd v MacDonald and Evans* [1952] 1 TLR 101 at 111 per Denning LJ. For a case in which it was pointed out that the control test is unrealistic in the case of a professional man, or a man of some particular skill and experience, see *Morren v Swinton and Pendlebury Borough Council* [1965] 2 All ER 349, [1965] 1 WLR 576; cf *Beloff v Pressdram Ltd* [1973] 1 All ER 241 and two New Zealand cases, *Perry v Satterthwaite* [1967] NZLR 718: *Scott v Trustees, Executors and Agency Co Ltd* [1967] NZLR 725.

The problem has taken on importance in connection with liability for national insurance contributions and claims: see *Whittaker v Minister of Pensions and National Insurance* [1966] 1 QB 156, [1966] 3 All ER 631; *Ready Mixed Concrete (South East) Ltd v Minister of Pensions and National Insurance* [1968] 2 QB 497, [1968] 1 All ER 433; *Market Investigations Ltd v Minister of Social Security* [1969] 2 QB 173, [1968] 3 All ER 732; *Construction Industry Training Board v Labour Force Ltd* [1970] 3 All ER 220; *Global Plant Ltd v Secretary of State for Health and Social Security* [1972] 1 QB 139, [1971] 3 All ER 385; *Ferguson v John Dawson & Partners (Contractors) Ltd* [1976] 3 All ER 817, [1976] 1 WLR 1213. See also a tax case where the same issue arose: *Hall v Lorimer* [1994] 1 All ER 250, [1994] 1 WLR 209; and *Massey v Crown Life Insurance Co* [1978] 2 All ER 576, [1978] 1 WLR 676.

17 *Hewitt v Bonvin* [1940] 1 KB 188 at 194–196 per Du Parcq LJ; *Davie v New Merton Board Mills Ltd* [1958] 1 QB 210 at 219, [1958] 1 All ER 67 at 71, per Jenkins LJ; affd [1959] AC 604, [1959] 1 All ER 346.

18 29 Yale LJ 859 at p 866. Cf Conant (1968) 47 Nebraska LR 42 at p 46.

19 29 Yale LJ 859 at p 866.

that a person who works for only one employer is a servant, whereas one who works for several is an agent. Some servants may work for several people, thereby raising the question, who is the master for the purposes of liability:[20] while it would be possible for an agent to be bound to work for only one principal and still remain an agent.

These factors may be relevant to the question of *control*. But, as already seen, it is difficult to base any distinction between agents and servants on the issue of control.

On the other hand, can it be said that agents and independent contractors are distinguishable? An independent contractor is free from control on the part of his employer, and is only subject to the terms of his contract. But an agent may or may not be completely free from control. It all depends upon the terms of his employment, with the result that sometimes an agent looks more like an independent contractor and sometimes more like a servant, from the point of view of the control exercisable over him. An independent contractor may not be employed for the purpose of creating contractual relations between his employer and third persons, for example, a tailor or a butcher. Such people work for themselves. But an independent contractor may be employed for just such a purpose, ie to make contracts, for example in the case of an auctioneer or broker, who are clearly agents. Moreover, there are certain independent contractors who on some occasions may be acting for themselves, and at other times may be creating legal relations between their employers and third persons. For example, a solicitor may start by giving advice (independent contractor), and then as a consequence make a contract for his employer with another person (agent).

The conclusion may, therefore, be drawn that, using the suggested tests, it is difficult to produce a completely satisfactory threefold division between agents, servants and independent contractors, which will operate throughout the law, and enable all three expressions to be used generally in all branches of the law.[1]

Agents include servants and independent contractors. From what has been said above, it would seem that in some way or another the category of agents might be considered to include within its scope the two categories of servants and independent contractors. For the elements of control and liability, which are important in the definition of the two latter categories, are also relevant (and in the same way) to the conception, if not the definition of an agent. But the question is: how are these three categories connected? There are three possible ways.

---

20 See, eg *Mersey Docks and Harbour Board v Coggins and Griffiths (Liverpool) Ltd* [1947] AC 1, [1946] 2 All ER 345; *Garrard v Southey & Co* [1952] 2 QB 174, [1952] 1 All ER 597; *Gibb v United Steel Companies Ltd* [1957] 2 All ER 110, [1957] 1 WLR 668; *Bhoomidas v Port of Singapore Authority* [1978] 1 All ER 956. Note, however, the attitude of the Court of Appeal in *Savory v Holland, Hannen and Cubitts (Southern) Ltd* [1964] 3 All ER 18. Control may not be the only test: see *Ready Mixed Concrete (East Midlands) Ltd v Yorkshire Traffic Area Licensing Authority* [1970] 2 QB 397, [1970] 1 All ER 890.
 1 Cf also the kind of problem raised in *Heaton's Transport (St Helens) Ltd v Transport and General Workers' Union* [1973] AC 15, [1972] 3 All ER 101, and the solution therein, which may have had an important impact on the whole question of the definition and scope of agency: see further below, p 309.

First, the term agent can be used to cover both servants and independent contractors. In other words, all agents are *either* servants *or* independent contractors—the differences between the two being in respect of control. This is the view expressed in *Salmond and Heuston on Torts*,[2] at least for the purposes of the law of torts, though agency in contract is said to differ from agency in the law of torts. Diagrammatically this view can be presented thus:

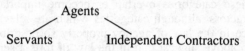

Agents

Servants   Independent Contractors

Another view[3] (A) is that agents and servants are types of a class called 'agents' (who are distinct from independent contractors from the point of view of control). The difference between agents (in this strict sense) and servants, here, is that agents make contracts with third parties on behalf of the principal, while servants do not. Alternatively, (B) agents and servants are types of a class called 'servants' the distinction being said to be based upon the nature of the employment: those whose employment is more or less continuous are servants (properly so called), those whose employment is intermittent, or confined to a particular occasion, agents, so that a servant is a continuous sort of agent.[4] The diagrams representing the above views are these:

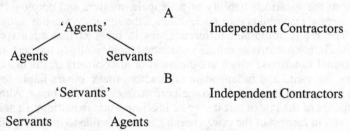

A

'Agents'   Independent Contractors

Agents   Servants

B

'Servants'   Independent Contractors

Servants   Agents

Powell originally adopted the view that some agents were servants, some independent contractors and some neither servants nor independent contractors but in a class by themselves.[5] In the second edition of his book[6] he appears to have abandoned this view in favour of there being no clear-cut distinction

---

2 (20th edn 1992) p 448. The *American Restatement, Second, Agency*, 2, 14N, also suggests the same sub-division, though it is stated that whereas a servant is always a kind of agent, an independent contractor may or may not be an agent. Treating the relationship of master and servant as part of the relationship of principal and agent involves the Restatement in considering a number of topics which, it is suggested, do not rightly fall within the realm of agency at all, eg, the common employment doctrine (which still subsists in the United States), and the duty of a master to take reasonable care for the safety of his employee: *Restatement, Second, Agency*, paras 473–528. These matters rightly belong to the law of *employment*, not *agency*: see Fridman *The Modern Law of Employment* (1963) pp 186–211.

3 Wright, 15 Can BR 285 ff.

4 Erle CJ in *Tobin v R* (1864) 16 CBNS 310 at 350. Cf also Seavey on the difference of control; 29 Yale LJ 859 at p 866. He concluded that servants are agents who have power to subject their principals to liability for torts not involving representation as well as such other powers as the principal may have given them.

5 *Law of Agency* (1952) p 25.

6 *Law of Agency* (2nd edn 1961) pp 10, 14.

between *agents* and independent contractors and a simple distinction between servants and independent contractors, into which categories he would subdivide agents.

A suggested solution. The present writer rejects the attempts to assimilate servants and independent contractors with agents. While there are areas of the law where these categories overlap or become important, servants and independent contractors, although categories which are relevant in the law of tort, have no place in the law of agency properly so described. Many of the writers referred to above suggest that in the law of torts a separate concept of agency is neither helpful nor relevant. Indeed they go so far as to say that agency is a relevant concept only in the law of contract. Herein, it is suggested, lies the vital point. Agency is really a relationship that has meaning and importance in the fields of contract and property. For the normal purpose of the agency relationship is for the agent to make a contract or dispose of property on the principal's behalf.[7]

For the purposes of vicarious tortious and criminal liability, it may well be relevant and necessary to consider these relationships of employer and independent contractor, and master and servant, compare them with the relationship of principal and agent, and show how they are important.[8] The rules relating to the vicarious liability of principals, masters and employers seem to bear a strong resemblance to each other, although they are not altogether the same. The really important difference lies in the fact that agents can make principals liable for torts or crimes committed incidentally to the performance of their normal functions, which are the making of contracts or the disposition of property. Servants and independent contractors make others liable for torts or crimes committed incidentally to the performance of *other* tasks. Although for the purposes of the law of tort it may be less important to distinguish agents from others, yet, in respect of the law generally, it is advisable to make this distinction because only agents, as a class, possess the power of affecting their principals by the making of contracts *and* the disposition of property. Incidentally to the performance of these tasks (which are the normal purposes of agency) the agent may involve his principal in tortious or other liability. But that is only incidental.

Thus it is suggested that, the term 'agent' can best be used to denote a relationship that is very different from that existing between a master and his servant, or an employer and his independent contractor. Although servants and independent contractors are parties to relationships in which one person acts for

---

7   Cf Wright, 15 Can BR 285 at pp 287–288; *Bowstead and Reynolds on Agency* (16th edn 1996) p 496. Cf also, with special reference to the doctrine of *ratification* (below pp 84–110); Tedeschi 'Authorization of Torts' (1969) 4 Israel LR 1 at pp 9–15: Conant (1968) 47 Nebraska LR 42 at pp 46–47. Seavey preferred to include under 'agents' servants who can involve their masters in tortious liability: 29 Yale LJ 859 at p 866. Contrast the following statement: '. . . this junction of the tort doctrine of respondeat superior with the contract institution of representations is apt to obscure important problems rather than elucidate them:' Rheinstein *Problems and Challenge of Contemporary Civil Law of Obligations* in *Essays on the Civil Law of Obligations* (ed J Dainow 1969) p 22; with which compare the comments of Estes 'Cinderella's Slipper: Agency' (1977) 10 John Marshall J of Practice and Procedure 225.

8   Below, pp 303–312.

another, and thereby possesses the capacity to involve that other in liability, yet the nature of the relationship and the kind of acts in question are sufficiently different to justify the exclusion of servants and independent contractors from the law relating to agency, unless at any given time a servant or independent contractor is being employed as an agent, when he should be called such.[9] In other words, the term 'agent' should be restricted to one who has the power of affecting the legal position of his principal by the making of contracts or the disposition of property: but who may, *incidentally*, affect the legal position of his principal in other ways.[10] That is the sense in which the term agent is used in this book.

9 Cf Conant (1968) 47 Nebraska LR 42 at p 48.
10 The passage from 'Although servants and independent contractors' to here was quoted in *Scott v Trophy Foods Inc* (1995) 123 DLR (4th) 509 at 520.

CHAPTER 3

Some different kinds of agents

As indicated in an earlier chapter, one of the most important features of the agency relationship, if not the most important, is the authority of the agent. This is concerned with the functions entrusted to the agent, as well as the mode of exercising those functions. In some degree, as will become evident, the agent's authority is derived from, or defined by the particular kind of agency he undertakes. A later chapter will illustrate in greater detail the nature of the authority possessed by some agents by virtue of their employment in a particular way arising from the kind of agency they usually undertake. It will be seen that, as a result of legal and commercial developments, certain kinds of agents, distinguished by name and function, have been invested, as a matter of law, with varying functions, stemming from the authority they possess as agents employed in a particular trade, business or profession, unless there has been some agreement to the contrary expressly made between the parties. So that such explanation and discussion may be better understood, these various kinds of agents will now be described.

General and special agents. One preliminary distinction, sometimes drawn, is that between general agents and special agents. It has been said[1] that, for the purpose of liability 'the general agent may be said to bear the same relation to the special agent that a servant bears to an independent contractor.' In view of the rejection of these terms, as being useless in the law of agency,[2] it is suggested that this is not a helpful statement.

Whatever difference there may be lies in the breadth of the agent's authority.

A general agent is one who has authority to do some act in the ordinary course of his trade, business or profession, as agent on behalf of his principal, or to act for his principal in all matters or in all matters of a particular trade or business or

---

1 Seavey 'The Rationale of Agency' (1920) 29 Yale LJ 859 at p 885. This statement is made at the end of a discussion of the reasons why a principal is made liable for acts of his agent in excess of the authority actually granted him. Seavey says this is because: (i) trust has been reposed in the agent; (ii) the principal controls the agent; (iii) business convenience demands it: (1920) 29 Yale LJ 859 at pp 884–885. This makes the contractual liability of a principal for his agent's acts like the tortious liability of a master for the acts of his servant. But this contractual liability will only apply where the agent is a general agent, whose apparent authority is considerable: (for 'apparent' authority see below, pp 122–132).
2 Above, pp 31–37.

of a particular nature.³ Thus the director of a limited liability company has been held to be the general agent of the company, so as to make valid a notice to quit given by such director to the company's tenant.⁴ In *Swiss Air Transport Co Ltd v Palmer*,⁵ the idea of general authority was utilised to make an importer and exporter of wigs liable for cargo sent by his agent, but not for the price of an air ticket obtained by the agent for his own personal transportation to a destination other than that of the goods. Swanwick J held that the agent had been held out as having 'general authority' to pledge the principal's credit for the cost of the freight of goods, including, but not restricted to wigs, but that such general authority would not apply to air tickets, as personal travel was not within the scope of the defendant's business or the agent's duties. A special agent is one whose authority is limited to doing some particular act, or to representing his principal in some particular transaction, not being in the ordinary course of his trade, profession, or business as an agent. The *American Restatement*⁶ says such an agent is one who has authority 'to conduct a single transaction or series of transactions not involving continuity of service', in contrast with the definition of a general agent in terms of authority 'to conduct a series of transactions involving continuity of service'.⁷

From this it would appear that two different tests are put forward. One is the nature of the employment, the other is continuity of employment. The latter test does appear to invoke one of the suggested tests for distinguishing between servants and agents.⁸ As already seen, it is not very satisfactory. Nor is it considered as necessarily determining the difference, for the *Restatement* goes on to say that the difference between general and special agents is one of degree, and the discretion involved in special agency may not be in any way distinctive from that involved in special agency.⁹ Hence this test is not very valuable: nor

---

3 Digest of Civil Law para 140: *Bowstead and Reynolds on Agency* (16th edn 1996) pp 33–34; *Chitty on Contracts* (27th edn 1996) Vol 2, p 7. See the discussion in the Canadian case of *McLaughlin v Gentles* (1920) 46 OLR 477, which was concerned with the liability of an undisclosed principal for the acts of an agent with limited authority: cf below, pp 72–76. Compare with this the institution of procura found in the Common German Commercial Code of 1861, by which an agent is empowered 'to carry on a commercial enterprise'. This has far-reaching effects: see Müller-Freienfels 'Legal Relations in the Law of Agency' (1964) 13 Am J of Comp L 193 at pp 208–209.

4 *Harmond Properties Ltd v Gajdzis* [1968] 3 All ER 263, [1968] 1 WLR 1858. See also *Excess Life Assurance Co Ltd v Firemen's Insurance Co Ltd* [1982] 2 Lloyd's Rep 599 on 'general agent' in relation to an insurance policy. In *Arsenal Football Club Ltd v Smith* [1979] AC 1, [1977] 2 All ER 267, the managing agent of a house was held to be a person who received the rents in receipt of the house under the General Rate Act 1967. On the idea of 'managerial agents', see Bowstead and Reynolds, op cit, Art 29.

5 [1976] 2 Lloyd's Rep 604.

6 *Restatement, Second, Agency*, para 3.

7 Ibid. Cf *Buller v Maples* 9 Wall 766 (1869) at 773–774: 'The purpose of [a special agency] is a single transaction, or a transaction with designated persons . . . Authority to buy for a principal a single article of merchandise by one contract, or to buy several articles from a person named is a special agency, but authority to make purchases from any persons with whom the agent may choose to deal, or to make an indefinite number of purchases, is a general agency': cited in Seavey (1920) 29 Yale LJ 859 at p 882.

8 Above, pp 33–34.

9 *Restatement, Second, Agency*, para 3, Comments a, c.

does it support the idea that the difference between general and special agents is the same as the difference between servants and agents, since that difference is also not easily based upon the test of continuity of service.[10] The other test, relating to the nature of the employment, may seem to differentiate between servants and independent contractors, as Seavey suggested.[11] In reality it deals not with the difference between two relationships (each an example of the agency relationship) but with the difference between two grants of authority and what they entail. As previously argued, for the purposes of the law of agency the contrast between servants and independent contractors is immaterial.[12] Both can be distinguished from agents, as that term is being used in this work.

Hence the distinction really concerns the nature of the authority given to an agent, and the extent to which a particular agent can affect the position of his principal.[13] However, the importance of distinguishing between two classes of agent, general and special, may not be very great.[14] The authority of a special agent will depend upon the express or implied terms of the agreement he has made with his principal: and that of a general agent must also be determined either by such express or implied terms or by what is *usual* having regard to the kind of work which the agent normally, in the ordinary course of his business, undertakes. Therefore, to discover the nature and extent of the authority conferred on an agent, it is insufficient to determine whether he is a general or special agent. The express, implied, or usual authority[15] of the agent in question must still be investigated. Hence the utility of the terms general and special agent is doubtful; and the distinction between these two kinds of agent, even if theoretically or colloquially justifiable, is of little practical value.[16]

Factors and mercantile agents in general. Before the first Factors Act was passed,[17] Abbott CJ in *Baring v Corrie*[18] defined the common law idea of a factor in the following terms:

> '. . . a person to whom goods are assigned for sale by a merchant residing abroad or at a distance away from the place of sale. . . . [He] normally sells in his own name without disclosing that of his principal.'

He went on to say that the result of this was that the principal

> 'with full knowledge of these circumstances trusts him with the actual possession of goods and gives him authority to sell in his own name.'

---

10 Above, pp 33–34.
11 Above, pp 32–34.
12 Above, pp 31–37.
13 Seavey (1920) 29 Yale LJ 859 at pp 882–883.
14 *Bowstead* pp 24, 109. Cf Powell *Law of Agency* p 31.
15 These terms are explained and discussed more fully below, pp 64–79.
16 See the discussion in Stoljar *Law of Agency* pp 42–43.
17 In 1823. The development of the common law and the contents of the various statutes are described and discussed in Munday 'A Legal History of the Factor' (1977) 6 Anglo-American LR 221.
18 (1818) 2 B & Ald 137 at 145: see also Holroyd J at 148. The expression 'factor' is now used very differently, eg, in the sense of credit factoring: *Bowstead and Reynolds* p 35. Cf below, p 43, referring to credit-brokers.

In a later case, *Stevens v Biller*,[19] decided not long before the most recent and consolidating Factors Act 1889, Cotton LJ defined a factor as

'an agent entrusted with the possession of goods for the purposes of sale.'

This definition repeats the idea that the factor has possession of goods and is given that possession in order to sell the goods, but it omits the idea that the factor sells in his own name. It was decided in that case that an agent is still a factor,[20] even if instructed by his principal to sell goods in the *principal's* and not in his own name. For

'there may be a factor who, as between himself and his principal is not justified in selling except in his principal's name.'[1]

In other words, the terms of the contract between the principal and agent will not have the effect of altering the kind of agency involved, even though it will effect an otherwise normal incident of such agency.

The common law was affected by the Factors Acts, which, when interpreted by the courts, widened the scope of the old law of factors and made it applicable to other people. The culmination was the Factors Act 1889 which contained a new definition for the purposes of the statute. It does not speak of a 'factor' or an 'agent', but of a 'mercantile agent', which is said to mean one:[2]

'. . . having in the customary course of his business as such agent authority to sell goods or to consign goods for the purpose of sale, or to buy goods, or to raise money on the security of goods.'

This definition really enshrines earlier decisions.[3] It is not confined to factors, but extends to various other kinds of mercantile agents. However, it does distinguish agents from servants, as Willes J said in *Hyman v Flewker*:[4]

'The term "agent" does not include a mere servant or caretaker or one who has possession of goods for carriage, safe custody, or otherwise as an independent contracting party: but only persons whose employment corresponds to that of some known kind of commercial agent like that class (factors) from which the Act has taken its name.'

In that case an agent for procuring business for insurance offices, with whom someone deposited pictures with instructions to sell them, was held to be an 'agent' within the Factors Act, although normally his business was not to sell goods. It is sufficient if goods are entrusted to someone as agent for sale, consignment for sale, or pledge even on only one occasion, and for only one

---

19 (1883) 25 Ch D 31 at 37. In the 17th century a factor was said to be a *servant: Southcote's Case* (1601) 4 Co Rep 83b: cf above, p 6.
20 Not a broker.
1 *Stevens v Biller* (1883) 25 ChD 31 at 35 per Chitty J.
2 Factors Act 1889, s 1(1).
3 'New, but . . . mainly declaratory.' Chalmers *Sale of Goods Act* (18th edn 1981) p 291. But this definition has no relevance to the common law definition of a factor: *Rolls Razor Ltd v Cox* [1967] 1 QB 552 at 568.
4 (1863) 13 CBNS 519 at 527. See also *Cole v North Western Bank* (1875) LR 10 CP 354 (clerk in charge of delivery orders was not an agent within the Acts).

principal, as in *Weiner v Harris*[5] and *Lowther v Harris*[6] as long as he is not merely a servant[7] or bailee.[8] Thus it would seem that despite the use of the words 'in the customary course of his business', to be a 'mercantile agent' it is not necessary to carry on business normally as a factor (in the common law sense seen above), nor as some known kind of commercial agent like a factor; what is necessary is that authority is given 'to sell goods or to consign goods for the purposes of sale, or to buy goods, or to raise money on the security of goods'.[9]

Although the effect of this development from the Factors Act has been to include within the scope of the legislation various different kinds of agents, it is still convenient to distinguish between them by name: for, although as regards the disposition of property their power may be the same, in some other respects they are to be distinguished.

Brokers. Brokers, like factors, are mercantile agents.[10] There is, however, a distinction between these classes of agents in that brokers are agents who are *not* given possession of goods or documents of title. A broker is:

> 'an agent employed to make bargains and contracts between persons in matters of trade commerce and navigation. Properly speaking, a broker is a mere negotiator between other parties . . . He himself . . . has no possession of the goods, no power actual or legal of determining the destination of the goods, no power or authority to determine whether the goods belong to buyer or seller or either.'[11]

He is not entrusted with the possession of the goods he sells.[12] Unlike a factor[13] he may not sell in his own name. 'The principal therefore who trusts a broker has a right to expect that he will not sell in his own name.'[14] Both brokers and factors

---

5 [1910] 1 KB 285 overruling *Hastings Ltd v Pearson* [1893] 1 QB 62. See the judgment of Aikins J in the Canadian case of *Thorsen v Capital Credit Corpn Ltd and Active Bailiff Service Ltd* (1962) 37 DLR (2d) 317.
6 [1927] 1 KB 393.
7 *Lowther v Harris* (above).
8 *Staffs Motor Guarantee Ltd v British Wagon Co Ltd* [1934] 2 KB 305, on which see the decision of the Privy Council in *Pacific Motor Auctions Pty Ltd v Motor Credits (Hire Finance) Ltd* [1965] AC 867, [1965] 2 All ER 105 (commented on and approved, in another connection, by the Court of Appeal in *Worcester Works Finance Ltd v Cooden Engineering Co* [1972] 1 QB 210, [1971] 3 All ER 708).
9 Cf *Powell* pp 218–220.
10 See *Story on Sale* paras 78–118. In consequence of this development, and the proliferation of different types of brokers the view has been expressed that the distinction between factors and brokers, once vital, is now no longer important: *Bowstead and Reynolds* pp 34–35.
11 *Fowler v Hollins* (1872) LR 7 QB 616 at 623 per Brett J. For a discussion of different types of brokers, see the judgment of Gale CJHC of Ontario in *Royal Securities Corpn v Montreal Trust Co* (1967) 59 DLR (2d) 666 at 686. A salesman employed by a broker is the agent of the broker, who will be liable for the salesman's negligence: *McKee v Georgia Pacific Securities Corpn* (1988) 20 BCLR (2d) 12. But an employee who was not a sales agent had no authority to bind an insurance broker in *O'Riordan v Central Agencies Camrose Ltd* (1987) 37 DLR (4th) 183.
12 *Baring v Corrie* (1818) 2 B & Ald 137 at 143 per Abbot CJ.
13 Above, pp 40–41.
14 *Baring v Corrie* (above). For a case illustrating the scope of a broker's authority, and the question whether the broker has acted negligently, see *Stafford v Conti Commodity Services Ltd* [1981] 1 All ER 691, [1981] 1 Lloyd's Rep 488, dealing with brokers in the commodities futures market.

negotiate sales. However, the difference between these two classes of agents in respect of the possession of goods may stem from the fact that brokers also negotiate other contracts, not involving the handling of goods by the broker himself. For example, stockbrokers deal with the sale of stock or shares (which are not goods within the meaning of the Sale of Goods Act 1979).[15] Insurance brokers arrange policies of insurance. Other brokers deal in the hiring of ships on charterparties. A more recent growth is that of the credit-broker, whose function is to arrange credit for those who wish to purchase goods. Some of these different types of brokers have given rise to special legal problems, or may be governed by particular legislation.

Thus stockbrokers have long been regulated by their own rules and customs, as well as by the general law of agency.[16] Insurance brokers, in respect of whom there have been many decisions dealing with liability for negligence or breach of the agent's duty of care,[17] are now regulated by a special statute,[18] which provides for their registration and training, the regulation of their conduct, and the maintenance of their discipline by special proceedings, akin to those applicable in relation to other professions. 'Credit-brokers' are defined[19] as those carrying on the business of effecting certain introductions. These are (i) of individuals desiring to obtain credit to persons carrying on certain specified business,[20] to individuals desiring to obtain credit to finance the purchase or provision of a dwelling for himself or a relative, or to persons carrying on a business in the course of which he lends money on the security of land; (ii) of individuals obtaining goods on hire to persons carrying on specified businesses;[1] (iii) of those wishing to obtain credit, or goods on hire, to other credit-brokers. Such credit-brokers are now regulated by the provisions of Part X of the Consumer Credit Act 1974.[2] It should also be noted that, under the Sale of Goods Act 1979,[3] the implied condition that goods sold will be reasonably fit for the particular purpose for which the goods are being bought, will be applicable where the purchase price or any part of it is payable by instalments and the goods were

15 Sale of Goods Act 1979, s 61(1); *Benjamin's Sale of Goods* (4th edn 1992) para 1–079; Fridman *Sale of Goods in Canada* (4th edn 1995) p 17.
16 For the law relating to brokers on the Stock Exchange, see Cooper & Cridlan *Law and Practice of the Stock Exchange* (1971) pp 118–179: see also Rider 'The Fiduciary and the Frying Pan' (1978) 42 Conv 114. For a Canadian case on the duty of stockbrokers to their clients, see *Volkers v Midland Doherty Ltd* (1985) 17 DLR (4th) 343.
17 On which see below, pp 158–164; for discussion of the situation with respect to insurance agents or brokers, which has caused difficulty in Canada, see Baer 'Annual Survey of Canadian Law: Insurance Law' (1980) 12 Ottawa LR 610 at pp 626–629; Irvine 'The Insurance Agent and his Duties: Some Recent Developments' (1979–1980) 10 Can Cas on the Law of Torts 108; Snow 'Liability of Insurance Agents for Failure to Obtain Effective Coverage' (1978–1979) 9 Manitoba LJ 165. A leading Canadian case is *Fine's Flowers Ltd v General Accident Assurance Co of Canada* (1977) 81 DLR (3d) 139, Ont CA. See also Merkin, 'Transferred Agency in the Law of Insurance' (1984) 13 Anglo-Amer LR No 3 at 33.
18 Insurance Brokers (Registration) Act 1977.
19 Consumer Credit Act 1974, s 145(2). See also ibid, s 189(1) and the Contracts (Applicable Law) Act 1990 s 5, Sch 4.
20 These are set out in the Consumer Credit Act 1974, s 145(2).
 1 These are set out in the Consumer Credit Act 1974, s 145(4).
 2 On which see Guest and Lomnicka *An Introduction to the Law of Credit and Security* (1978) pp 64–65; Goode *Consumer Credit Act 1974* (1974) ch 23.
 3 S 14(3)(b).

previously sold by a credit-broker to the seller, as long as the buyer has made known the purpose in question to the credit-broker (unless the buyer did not rely, or it was unreasonable for him to rely, on the skill or judgment of the credit-broker).[4]

Del credere agents.[5] These, again, are mercantile agents. Such agents, in return for an extra commission, called a del credere commission, promise that they will indemnify the principal, if the third party with whom they contract in respect of goods fails to pay what is due under the contract.

At one time it was thought that the liability of such agents was primary, ie, that the principal could call upon the del credere agent for payment before the third party had actually failed to pay. But this view, put forward by Lord Mansfield in *Grove v Dubois*,[6] was rejected in *Morris v Cleasby*,[7] where it was clearly stated that the agent was only secondarily liable, as a surety for the person with whom he dealt. Lord Ellenborough said[8] that:

'A commission del credere is the premium or price given by the principal to the factor for a guarantee, it presupposes a guarantee.'

It should be noted that a contract of del credere agency is not a contract of guarantee but a contract of indemnity. Hence it does not come within the requirement of the Statute of Frauds[9] that a promise to answer for the debt, default, or miscarrage of another person should be evidenced by a note or memorandum in writing.[10] This is because the agent is not totally unconnected with the transaction he is undertaking: he is deriving some benefit from it.[11] Therefore, since writing is not necessary for the proof of the existence of a del credere agency such an agency may be implied from the conduct of the parties.[12]

Since the decision in *Morris v Cleasby* shows that the del credere agent's liability is secondary, it is clear that such an agent can only be made liable for breach of contract if the person with whom he has contracted on his principal's behalf, and for whom he has gone surety, has failed to pay what is due under the contract. For no other breach of contract on the third party's part can the del credere agent be sued by the principal. Such an agent is merely a guarantor of the

---

4 For this purpose a credit-broker is a person acting in the course of a business of credit-brokerage carried on by him, that is a business of effecting introductions of individuals desiring to obtain credit (a) to persons carrying on any business so far as it relates to the provision of credit, or (b) to other persons engaged in credit-brokerage: Sale of Goods Act 1979, s 61(1). This definition is narrower therefore than the definition in the Consumer Credit Act 1974.
5 See Chorley, 45 LQR 221, 46 LQR 11, for the history of this form of agency.
6 (1786) 1 Term Rep 112.
7 (1816) 4 M & S 566.
8 Ibid, at 574.
9 Retained by the Law Reform (Enforcement of Contracts) Act 1954.
10 *Couturier v Hastie* (1852) 8 Exch 40; *Sutton & Co v Grey* [1894] 1 QB 285 (not really a case of del credere agency for the agreement was for the sharing of commission on stock exchange profits and losses).
11 *Sutton & Co v Grey* [1894] 1 QB 285 at 288 per Brett MR.
12 *Shaw v Woodcock* (1827) 7 B & C 73.

buyer's solvency.[13] Thus in *Thomas Gabriel & Sons v Churchill and Sim*[14] it was held that a seller was not entitled to litigate or dispute about the *performance* of the contract of sale with his del credere agent who had negotiated the contract. The agent's liability only extended to a liability to pay the price of the goods (if certain or ascertained) on default or insolvency of the buyer. This liability of the agent was carried to its logical conclusion in *Churchill and Sim v Goddard*:[15]

> The plaintiffs (del credere agents for X) were payees of a bill of exchange accepted by the defendants (buyers). It was held that the plaintiffs personally could sue for payment—although only agents—because they were personally liable for any failure by the defendants to pay the price.[16]

In view of this limitation of the liability of del credere agents, it is noteworthy that in more recent times more use has been made of *confirming* agents, who accept liability not merely for payment, but for the contract being completed vis-à-vis the confirmer.[17]

Auctioneers. Auctioneers are agents whose ordinary course of business is to sell by public auction, that is by open sale, goods or other property. They may or may not be given possession of the goods, but it is clear that, when given such possession, auctioneers are 'mercantile agents' within the Factors Act 1889.

A peculiarity of auctioneers is that they are agents for both parties to the sale which they negotiate.[18] Another is that an auctioneer, although an agent, may personally sue for the price of goods sold and delivered by himself as auctioneer,[19] even if his commission has been paid.[20] It is also the case that where an auctioneer sells goods by knocking them down with his hammer at an auction, after which he delivers the goods to the purchaser, then, even though the auctioneer is an agent, not a principal, if the vendor of the goods lacked title to them, the auctioneer, as well as the purchaser, will be liable in conversion to the true owner, despite the innocence of the auctioneer when he handled the goods (or the purchaser when he acquired them).[1] The Court of Appeal have now applied the same principle as is applicable to sales 'under the hammer', to a sale

---

13 *Rusholme Bolton and Roberts Hadfield Ltd v SG Read & Co (London) Ltd* [1955] 1 All ER 180 at 183, per Pearce J. In *Toycorp Ltd v Milton Bradley Australia Pty Ltd* [1992] 2 VR 572, the agents who purchased goods from the manufacturer for retailers, and described themselves as acting as del credere agents, were not liable for the unpaid price of goods. They were the agents of the retailers only in respect of the placing of orders and credit.
14 [1914] 3 KB 1272.
15 [1937] 1 KB 92 [1936] 1 All ER 675.
16 For the personal liability of agents and their right to sue, see below, pp 231–243, 249–253.
17 *Sobell Industries Ltd v Cory Bros & Co Ltd* [1955] 2 Lloyd's Rep 82. See also *Rusholme Bolton and Roberts Hadfield Ltd v SG Read & Co (London) Ltd* [1955] 1 All ER 180; *Anglo-African Shipping Co of New York Inc v J Mortner Ltd* [1962] 1 Lloyd's Rep 610.
18 *Hinde v Whitehouse* (1806) 7 East 558. See *Chaney v Maclow* [1929] 1 Ch 461, on signature for the purposes of the Law of Property Act 1925, s 40 (see now the Law of Property (Miscellaneous Provisions) Act 1989, s 2).
19 *Williams v Millington* (1788) 1 Hy Bl 81.
20 *Chelmsford Auctions Ltd v Poole* [1973] QB 542, [1973] 1 All ER 810.
1 *Barker v Furlong* [1891] 2 Ch 172; *Consolidated Co v Curtis & Son* [1892] 1 QB 495.

which followed a provisional bid.[2] Under this practice, the highest bid at the auction is treated as being 'provisional', until the highest bidder stipulated that he would stand on his bid. The test of the auctioneer's liability would seem to be whether or not he has sold the goods.[3] Once he does so, he makes himself liable for conversion if the auctioneer's principal, the vendor of the goods, lacked title.

Shipmasters. A shipmaster is the captain, or similar officer of a ship, who has been appointed by the owner or owners of the ship to conduct the voyage of the ship to a favourable termination. Such an agent has wide authority in his conduct of the affairs of the ship, ie, with respect to its navigation, control of the crew and passengers, handling of the cargo. In consequence of emergencies, his authority may be considerably widened, with regard to the disposition or salvage of the ship by reason of necessary implication, or of its cargo, under the doctrine of agency of necessity.[4]

Solicitors and counsel. Their employment is necessary in the conduct of legal business, particularly, but not exclusively, litigation. In exercising such capacities, they frequently involve their clients in legal responsibility for the agreements made on their behalf in and out of court. However it has been held that a solicitor has no implied authority to receive a notice (in the particular instance a notice under the Bankruptcy Act then in force) on behalf of his client.[5] On the other hand a client's solicitor and counsel did have implied authority, as between themselves and the client, to compromise a suit without reference to the client for instructions, as long as such compromise did not include matters that were collateral to the intended action: (they also were invested with ostensible, or apparent authority, as between themselves and the opposing litigant, to compromise such suit without proof of authority).[6]

There is also the issue of the liability of a firm of solicitors for the acts of a partner or employee. This, too, seems to turn on the actual, implied or ostensible or apparent authority of a solicitor, which was the subject of consideration in *United Bank of Kuwait v Hammoud*; *City Trust Ltd v Levy*.[7] There the Court of Appeal dealt with two cases where a solicitor gave undertakings, purportedly on behalf of his firm, but without the knowledge of his partners or his employers, that the firm in question had control of certain funds, with the result, in both instances, that the bank lent money that was not repaid. When the firms of

---

2 *RH Willis & Son v British Car Auctions Ltd* [1978] 2 All ER 392, [1978] 1 WLR 438: see ibid at 442 per Lord Denning MR declining to follow cases which suggested that there was a difference: *National Mercantile Bank Ltd v Rymill* (1881) 44 LT 767; *Turner v Hockey* (1887) 56 LJQB 301.

3 *RH Willis & Son*, above, at 443 per Lord Denning MR, 444–445 per Browne LJ.

4 *The Unique Mariner* [1978] 1 Lloyds Rep 438; *The Choko Star* [1989] 2 Lloyd's Rep 42; revsd [1990] 1 Lloyd's Rep 516; below, pp 136–139.

5 *Singer v Trustee of the Property of Munro* [1981] 3 All ER 215, [1981] 1 WLR 1358.

6 *Waugh v HB Clifford & Sons Ltd* [1982] Ch 374, [1982] 1 All ER 1095: for 'implied' and 'apparent' authority see below, pp 68, 122; cf *Scherer v Paletta* [1966] 2 OR 524; *Propp v Fleming* (1968) 64 WWR 13. See, generally, Vandervort, 'The Lawyer–Client Relationship in Ontario: Use and Abuse of the Authority to Act' (1984) 16 Ottawa LR 526; Fridman, 'Lawyers as Agents' (1987) UNBLJ 9; Siegal 'Abandoning the Agency Model of the Lawyer–Client Relationship: A New Approach for Deciding Authority Disputes' (1990) 69 Nebraska LR 473 especially at pp 516–527, discussing the competing interests at stake.

7 [1988] 3 All ER 418.

solicitors in question were sued by the banks the Court of Appeal held that the undertakings had been given by a solicitor who had actual authority to represent himself as a practising solicitor with an established firm, and, since the undertakings were given in the context of underlying transactions that were part of the usual business of a solicitor, the banks were entitled to conclude and had proved that the solicitor had ostensible or apparent authority to bind the firms which employed him as partner or assistant solicitor. Worthy of note are the comments by Staughton LJ[8] that old cases on the types of transaction that were or were not within the ordinary authority of a solicitor should be treated with caution. The work solicitors do can be expected to have changed since those cases. It has changed in recent times; and it is changing now. The learned judge preferred to have regard to expert evidence of today in deciding what is the ordinary authority of a solicitor. Much, therefore, may depend on the particular kind of activity or transaction in or on which the solicitor is engaged in respect of which it is sought to make him or his partners or employers liable.

One problem arising from the employment of solicitors and barristers as agents is that of liability for the negligent performance of their duties. A solicitor is liable in negligence if he acts without due care and skill in the conduct of his business as a solicitor, ie, advising a client, drawing up a will. Indeed a solicitor can be liable to a potential beneficiary who has been deprived of succession through the solicitor's negligence.[9] A solicitor may even owe a duty of care to his client's opponent in hostile litigation, where the solicitor accepts responsibility towards that opponent. Such was the case in *Al-Kandari v JR Brown & Co*[10] where the solicitors undertook to release their client's passport. This made them custodians of the document and involved them in a duty to the plaintiff, their client's wife who was engaged in litigation over custody of the children of the marriage.

Where the negligence alleged against the solicitor consists of some failure in advocacy, in a case in which a solicitor has acted as an advocate, solicitors and barristers have been assimilated.[11] It was held by the House of Lords, in *Rondel v Worsley*,[12] that a barrister could not be sued for negligence in respect of his conduct in court, as an advocate. However, in *Saif Ali v Sydney Mitchell & Co*[13] the House of Lords held that barristers were not immune from suit for negligence where the alleged neglect related to neither advocacy nor pre-trial work which

---

8 Ibid at 427.
9 See now *White v Jones* [1995] 2 AC 207, [1995] 1 All ER 691; cf *Whittingham v Crease & Co* [1978] 5 WWR 45. But not in all instances: the circumstances may reveal no duty of care owed to the prospective beneficiary: *Clarke v Bruce Lance & Co* [1988] 1 All ER 364, [1988] 1 WLR 881, CA. On the solicitor's liability in negligence, for breach of contract, see *Groom v Crocker* [1939] 1 KB 194, [1938] 2 All ER 394; *Clark v Kirby-Smith* [1964] Ch 506, [1964] 2 All ER 835; *Cook v S* [1967] 1 All ER 299, [1967] 1 WLR 457; *Heywood v Wellers* [1976] QB 446, [1976] 1 All ER 300: cf Brazier 'The Innocent Purchaser and his Professional Advisers' (1976) 40 Conv 179 at pp 191–194. For the agent's duty of care and skill see below, pp 158–164.
10 [1988] QB 665, [1988] 1 All ER 833, CA.
11 Courts and Legal Services Act 1990, s 62, which gives immunity from liability for negligence or breach of contract.
12 [1969] 1 AC 191, [1967] 3 All ER 993. This immunity should not be extended further than necessary in the interests of justice and public policy: *Somasundaram v M Julius Melchior & Co* [1989] 1 All ER 129 at 136.
13 [1980] AC 198, [1978] 3 All ER 1033: cf *Rees v Sinclair* [1974] 1 NZLR 180.

was so intimately connected with the conduct of a case that it could be said to involve preliminary decisions affecting the way the action was conducted when it came to a hearing. Dicta in the case[14] suggested that solicitors acting as counsel or advocates were entitled to the same immunity as a barrister on much the same grounds as first propounded in *Rondel v Worsley*, namely, that public policy required that advocates possess such immunity, since to make an advocate potentially liable for the way he conducted himself in court might impede the proper performance of his duties: and advocates were subjected to control by, and discipline at the hands of, the court before which they practised and in front of which they committed the alleged negligence or other wrongful conduct. These dicta were accepted, approved and adopted by the Court of Appeal, in a case involving the conduct of solicitors in relation to the way a criminal trial proceeded, *Somasundaram v M Julius Melchior & Co*.[15] The courts, therefore, distinguished between the functions of lawyers, whether barristers or solicitors, giving immunity to advocates but not to those performing other functions. This dichotomy and the immunity are now confirmed by statute.[16]

This may not be the position in Canada. In Ontario it was held[17] that an action is potentially available in respect of the failure by a lawyer (in a jurisdiction where all practitioners are both barristers and solicitors) to appear in a civil case, with the result that his neglect may have brought about the loss of the suit by his client. The judgment is by one judge sitting alone: and it arose out of a preliminary question of law, whether or not a statement of claim disclosed a cause of action. However, it would appear to be a very persuasive decision, at least in that, and similar, jurisdictions, in Canada, if not elsewhere in the common law world.

Estate agents. Estate agents seem to be in a very odd situation, so far as concerns the general law of principal and agent.[18] Unless given express authority in such respect, an estate agent has no authority to make a binding contract of sale between his client and a third party.[19] Thus an estate agent does not share the normal capacity of an agent, as defined earlier. However, such agents have been held liable to their clients for breach of fiduciary duties,[20] failure to exercise

---

14 [1978] 3 All ER 1033 at 1039, per Lord Wilberforce, 1046, per Lord Diplock, 1048, per Lord Salmon.
15 [1989] 1 All ER 129 at 136. But a solicitor would not have such immunity where a barrister had also been engaged to advise, as in the instant case.
16 See above, note 11.
17 *Demarco v Ungaro* (1979) 95 DLR (3d) 385, per Krever J.
18 Murdoch 'The Nature of Estate Agency' (1975) 91 LQR 357; cf Brazier (1976) 40 Conv 1979 at pp 179–182. Note the regulation of estate agents under the Estate Agents Act 1979, which applies to those performing 'estate agency work', as defined in s 1(1) of the Act. It does not apply to those doing things within s 1(2) (3) (4) of the Act. See also the Property Misdescriptions Act 1991; Estates Agents (Provision of Information) Regulations 1991, SI 1991 No 859; Estate Agents (Undesirable Practices) (No 2) Order 1991, SI 1991 No 1032. On the payment of commission to estate agents, see below, pp 411–421.
19 Murdoch, 91 LQR 357 referring to *Godwin v Brind* (1868) LR 5 CP 299n; *Chadburn v Moore* (1892) 61 LJ Ch 674; *Rosenbaum v Belson* [1900] 2 Ch 267; *Keen v Mear* [1920] 2 Ch 574.
20 *Andrews v Ramsay* [1903] 2 KB 635; *Regier v Campbell-Stuart* [1939] Ch 766, [1939] 2 All ER 235; cf *Yorkland Real Estate Ltd v Dale* (1987) 60 OR (2d) 460; *Ocean City Realty Ltd v A & M Holdings Ltd* (1987) 44 RPR 312 (but see *Knoch Estate v Jon Picken Ltd* (1991) 83 DLR (4th)

reasonable care and skill,[1] or the unauthorised appointment of a sub-agent.[2] They have also been held liable to third parties, as well as their principals, where the agent has been guilty of a negligent misrepresentation with respect to the property with which the estate agent was dealing on his client's behalf.[3]

After some difference of opinion as to whether the principal would be liable to a third party in the event that the estate agent misappropriated a deposit given by such third party to the agent in respect of property being handled by the agent on his client's behalf the House of Lords eventually held, in *Sorrell v Finch*,[4] that an estate agent possessed neither implied nor apparent authority to receive and accept such deposit, with the result that the principal, the owner of the property, was not liable to the prospective purchaser who had lost his deposit by reason of the impropriety of the estate agent.

Agents with special responsibility. The suggestion has been made[5] that, in the light of what has been happening in recent years, especially as regards the evolution of certain new types of agents, viz, forwarding, confirming and advertising agents, the old, Victorian concept of agency is becoming outdated. The writer in question put forward the idea that a new category of agents should be recognised, under the rubric of 'agency with dual responsibility'. Agents within this classification would be liable to their principals according to the normal rules of agency, and directly responsible to third parties, subject to a right of indemnity from their principals. This would obviate the problem of deciding whether a person has contracted as an agent (without personal liability) or as a principal (thus involving himself in responsibility to the other contracting party).[6] Such a breakdown of the traditional agency pattern, in situations in which the financial status of the agent is as important as, if not more important

447). See also *Kelly v Cooper* [1993] AC 205, where the Privy Council held that since some agents acted for several principals, some of whom might be competing and have conflicting interests, a term was to be implied into the contract with such an agent that he was entitled to act for other principals selling similar properties and to keep confidential information obtained from each principal. That contract determined the agent's fiduciary duty.

1 Murdoch (1975) 91 LQR 357 at p 358; as to standards of competence, see now the Estate Agents Act 1979, s 22.
2 *John McCann & Co v Pow* [1975] 1 All ER 129, [1974] 1 WLR 1643.
3 *Dodds v Millman* (1964) 45 DLR (2d) 472; *Academy Aluminium Products Ltd v McInerny Realty Ltd* (1980) 113 DLR (3d) 289; cf *Chand v Sabo Bros Realty Ltd* (1979) 96 DLR (3d) 445; *Komarniski v Marien* (1979) 100 DLR (3d) 81; *Roberts v Montex Development Corpn* (1979) 100 DLR (3d) 660; *Hauck v Dixon* (1975) 10 OR (2d) 605; *Olsen v Poirier* (1978) 21 OR (2d) 642; *Canada Trust Co v Sorkos* (1992) 90 DLR (4th) 265; *Finstad v Neilson* (1993) 10 Alta LR (3d) 310; *Longshaw v Houghton* (1993) 29 RPR (2d) 190; *MacDonald v Gerriston* (1994) 39 RPR (2d) 292. So, too, where fraud is alleged: *Harland v Fancali* (1994) 121 DLR (4th) 182.
4 [1977] AC 728, [1976] 2 All ER 371; for earlier discussion see below, pp 81–82. On the subject of pre-contract deposits, see now the Estate Agents Act 1979, s 19.
5 Hill 'Agent with Special Responsibility' [1964] JBL 306; Hill *Freight Forwarders* (1972), especially pp 38–39; Hill 'Confirming House Transactions in Commonwealth Countries' (1972) J of Maritime Law and Commerce 307. For other suggestions with respect to the need for change, see Reynolds 'Agency: Theory and Practice' (1978) 94 LGR 224 especially at pp 226–227. Contrast *Bowstead and Reynolds on Agency* (16th edn 1996) at pp 17–20.
6 Below, pp 237–242; see, for examples of the problems, *Henry Browne & Sons Ltd v Smith* [1964] 2 Lloyd's Rep 476; *Bridges and Salmon Ltd v The Swan (Owner)* [1968] 1 Lloyd's Rep 5.

than, that of the principal, is an interesting suggestion. But it does not seem to have been adopted by the courts.[7]

Commercial agents. This category of agents which is new to English law was recognised by the Commercial Agents (Council Directive) Regulations, made in 1993.[8] These came into effect on 1 January 1994. In respect of the particular class of agents defined therein they create or impose special requirements, designed to bring the law in England into conformity with continental law, where this class of agents originated.[9]

A commercial agent is defined as 'a self-employed intermediary who has continuing authority to negotiate the sale or purchase of goods on behalf of another person (the "principal"), or to negotiate and conclude the sale or purchase of goods on behalf of and in the name of that principal'. However the following are excluded from the operation of the regulations: officers of companies or associations: partners; insolvency practitioners as defined in the Insolvency Act 1986, s 388: gratuitous agents; agents operating on commodity exchanges or in commodity markets; Crown Agents; those whose activities as commercial agents are to be considered secondary.

Thus the regulations apply only to agents dealing with goods (a term that may cause difficulties). Those dealing with land or services are excluded, as are distributors who purchase for resale. Commercial agents within the regulations need not be authorised to make contracts, but may simply be authorised to introduce business. The definition indicates that such agents act 'in the name of the principal', which is a civil law, not common law concept: agents acting for undisclosed principals[10] are excluded, as may be agents acting for unnamed principals. Independent, ie self-employed, intermediaries are within the regulations: not employees of such persons. Moreover to be a commercial agent the person in question must have continuing authority.[11]

When the regulations apply they impose certain obligations on the parties[12] that, in certain respects, may differ from the rules of the common law that are considered in this book. Thus either party is entitled to a signed written document setting out the full terms of the agency contract between them. The parties must act in good faith towards each other (an idea that is not, thus far, part of English

---

7 For modern examples of the use of 'classical' or 'traditional' concepts as regards the possible liability of such agents in negligence to their principals, see *Club Speciality (Overseas) Inc v United Marine (1939) Ltd* [1971] 1 Lloyd's Rep 482; *Marston Excelsior Ltd v Arbuckle, Smith & Co Ltd* [1971] 2 Lloyd's Rep 306; *The Maheno* [1977] 1 Lloyd's Rep 81 at 86, per Beattie J (forwarding agent). Cf also, *J Evans & Son (Portsmouth) Ltd v Andrea Merzario Ltd* [1976] 2 All ER 930, [1976] 1 WLR 1078.

8 SI 1993 Nos 3053, 3173, made under the European Communities Act 1972, s 2(2), as a consequence of the EC Council Directive 86/653001. For elaboration and discussion see Reynolds [1994] JBL 260 at pp 265–270; Bell and O'Toole 'Legal protection for commercial agents' (1994) 138 Sol J 10; Davis 'The demise of commercial agents' (1994) 144 NLJ 388.

9 For a limited account of the law of various countries in Europe regarding such agents, see *Agency and Distribution Agreements: An International Survey*, edited by Agustin Jausas, International Bar Association, 1994, at pp 23, 29, 72, 89, 107, 120, 126, 162, 186.

10 Below, pp 253–272.

11 See also Sch 1 to the regulations for other limitations on the scope of the regulations: Reynolds [1994] JBL at p 266. Note also some conflict of laws issues discussed ibid at pp 267–268.

12 See regs 3, 5, 7, 10, 11, 14, 15, 17, 18, 19.

common law – though it is recognised in the United States and, to a certain extent, in Canada[13]). The agent must comply with reasonable instructions, make proper efforts to negotiate and conclude transactions, communicate all necessary information to the principal, act dutifully as well as in good faith. Such obligations are not excludable by agreement to the contrary. Also non-excludable, to the detriment of the agent, are certain provisions about payment of commission, including those concerning the time at which commission is payable. It is also not permitted to exclude the provision that the right to commission can only be extinguished when it is established that the contract between the third party and the principal will not be executed because of a reason for which the principal is not to blame (another concept not known to the common law). Special restrictions apply to the termination of an agency contract, although the principal can summarily terminate the agent's authority. Other provisions deal with termination by frustration of the contract.[14] Commission may also be payable on a transaction concluded after the agency contract has been terminated under certain circumstances.[15]

Close examination of the regulations suggests, as some commentators have already noted,[16] that there may be some difficult, even awkward questions to be resolved in the future with respect to their interpretation and application.

13 Fridman *Law of Contract in Canada* (3rd edn 1994) pp 78–79, 522–523.
14 On which see Treitel *Frustration and Force Majeure* (1994) paras 15–076–15–079.
15 Regs 8, 9.
16 See the references in note 8 above.

PART II

The varieties of agency

SUMMARY

CHAPTER 4

Agency created by contract

A. The creation of contractual agency

Basically agency is a relationship arising from consent usually expressed in the form of a contract.[1] In modern times it is correct to say that in most instances of an agency relationship there is a contract of agency between principal and agent. Even where such relationship arises from consent, however, it is not always necessary for a contract to exist between the parties. Although agency is a consensual relationship, resulting from agreement between the parties that one should act as agent for the other, it does not follow that all such agreements are strictly contractual, manifesting all the features of the common law contract. An agency may be gratuitous. If so it is not truly contractual. Admittedly the main difference between purely consensual and contractual agency lies in the absence or presence of consideration, in the form of remuneration of the agent for what he undertakes to do. The other obligations which arise as between principal and agent[2] arise by operation of law, irrespective of whether the agent is remunerated by the payment of commission. It may be argued that because a principal is always under a duty to indemnify his agent (unless there is an agreement to the contrary)[3] wherever there is an agreement to act as an agent there is always consideration moving from the principal, viz, the implied promise to indemnify the agent. If this is so then all instances of agency by agreement are cases of contractual agency. It is suggested, however, that the duty to indemnify is not truly to be regarded as providing consideration for the promise to act as an agent, but rather as an obligation imposed by the law wherever the relationship of principal and agent arises. In fact, where the agency is not strictly contractual, the principal does not promise to indemnify the agent; he is compelled by the law to do so, whether he wishes to or not (except where the law relieves him of such obligations for reasons which will be considered later).

1 Possibly this is what Lord Pearson meant in the *Garnac* case, quoted above, p 14. It is argued by Professor Müller-Freienfels 'Legal Relations in the Law of Agency' (1964) 13 Am J of Comp Law 193 at pp 203–207 that consent is unnecessary for the grant of the agency power, in that the principal can authorise an agent to act for him without communicating such intention to the agent, therefore without requiring the assent of the agent to act as an agent. It is suggested, however, that unless the agent acts for the principal, there is no true agency relationship in existence: and once the agent acts for the principal, following upon the principal's signification of authority, there is agreement, even if the agent has not previously heard of such authority, as long as the third party has received notice from the principal. Cf below, pp 59–61 on implied contracts of agency.
2 Below, chs 8, 9.
3 Below, pp 201–203.

Apart from the absence of the duty to pay the agent, gratuitous, purely consensual agency differs from contractual agency, ie agency for reward, only marginally. As will be seen the obligations of the agent may well differ slightly, where he is acting by agreement but not under contract. Such differences are comparatively minor, and will be discussed at an appropriate place.[4] Here it is only necessary to point out that, as far as creation of the agency relationship is concerned, purely consensual agency differs from contractual agency only in that no contract is required. Simple agreement, without the formalities of offer and acceptance, consideration, etc, necessary for the emergence of a contract at common law, is all that is needed. However, the emphasis is really upon agency arising from contract. Such a contract may be express or implied.[5] As Lord Romilly MR said in *Pole v Leask*:[6] 'The common division of the modes by which agency may be constituted is threefold. It is either by writing or it is by parol, or it is by mere employment'. This recognises the possibility of an express, written or contract of agency, or one that is implied from the conduct of the parties.

A. EXPRESS CONTRACT

Consent. As with other contracts, the parties must consent freely to the creation of the relationship between them. Their minds must be ad idem. There must be no fraud, duress, misrepresentation or mistake. It is unnecessary in the present context to consider these matters more fully, as they are governed by the rules applicable to contract.

Form. In general, no special form of contract is required. Even if the agent is appointed to make a contract (such as the purchase of land) which is now required to be in writing, signed by or on behalf of each party to the contract,[7] the appointment of the agent need not be in writing.[8] Under the older Statute of Frauds the agent was held to acquire the equitable estate in the land for his principal: and the courts did not allow the absence of a written contract of agency to operate in such a way as to perpetrate a fraud on the principal.[9] Presumably the same would apply under the new provision. But a statute[10] may require an interest in land to be created or disposed of by an agent 'lawfully authorised in writing', in which event the agent is incompetent to create or dispose of the interest on behalf of his principal unless he has been appointed by writing. Where

4 Below, pp 155–164.
5 Or created ex post facto, by ratification: below, ch 5.
6 (1860) 28 Beav 562 at 574.
7 Law of Property (Miscellaneous Provisions) Act 1989, s 2, repealing and replacing the Law of Property Act 1925, s 40: on the new provision see Pettit, 'Farewell Section 40' (1989) The Conveyancer 431; Annand (1989) 105 LQR 553 at 555–558. The Act is based on Law Comm No 164, published in 1987.
8 The same would be true of contracts of guarantee, the only other contracts which still come within the provision of the Statute of Frauds: see Law Reform (Enforcement of Contracts) Act 1954.
9 See *Mortlock v Buller* (1804) 10 Ves 292 at 311; *Heard v Pilley* (1869) 4 Ch App 548; *Rochefoucauld v Boustead* [1897] 1 Ch 196.
10 Eg Law of Property Act 1925, ss 53(1), 54.

an agent is appointed to execute a deed, his authority must itself be created by a deed,[11] except where the agent executes the deed in the presence, and with the authority of the principal.[12] The traditional name for a document containing the agent's authority, when the principal is giving the agent wide general powers to act on his behalf, is 'power of attorney'.[13] Such documents no longer have to be sealed, as long as the instrument is clear on its face that it is intended to be a deed and is validly executed as a deed. This means that it is signed by him in the presence of a witness attesting to his signature, or is signed at his direction in his presence and the presence of two witnesses who attest to his signature; and that the document is delivered by him or someone authorised to do so on his behalf.[14]

Under the Corporate Bodies' Contracts Act 1960 a corporation may contract in exactly the same way as a private person. That statute does not apply to companies formed and registered under the Companies Act 1985, nor to existing companies as defined in that Act.[15] In effect, however, a company may contract in a manner similar to that employed by a private person, depending on whether such a person would require a seal or writing, or could contract by parol.[16]

Capacity. The general rule is that both principal and agent must be capable of acting as principal or agent. Whether such capacity exists is a matter for the general law of contract.

Mentally incompetent persons, corporations, and minors either have no capacity, or only a limited capacity to appoint an agent. A mentally incompetent person can only appoint an agent during a lucid interval.[17] At common law, which

---

11 *Berkeley v Hardy* (1826) 5 B & C 355. For the law governing deeds and their execution, see new Law of Property (Miscellaneous Provisions) Act 1989, s 1: Annand, loc cit supra at 553–555.

12 *Ball v Dunsterville* (1791) 4 Term Rep 313. This is sometimes referred to as the Amanuensis Rule, since the agent is acting really as a clerical help: See Stoljar *Law of Agency* pp 284–285. This sentence was referred to, and relied on by Virtue J in *Royal Bank of Canada v Bauman* (1986) 46 Alta LR (2d) 68 at 79.

13 The giving of a power of attorney is a unilateral act. Its validity does not depend upon 'acceptance' by the attorney: *Abbott v UDC Finance Ltd* [1992] 1 NZLR 405 at 414.

14 Law of Property (Miscellaneous Provisions) Act 1989, s 1, Sch 1, amending the Powers of Attorney Act, 1971, ss 1, 7. To sign includes making one's mark: ibid, s 1(4). Delivery by certain persons, eg, solicitors or their agents, in the course of or in connection with a transaction involving the disposition or creation of an interest in land, results in a *conclusive* presumption of the requisite authority to deliver vis-à-vis a purchaser.

   Note that the change in the law abolishing the necessity for a seal does not apply to corporations sole: s 1(10). Nor, in view of the reference in the Act to 'an individual', does this change apply to corporations aggregate.

15 Corporate Bodies Contracts Act 1960, s 2, as amended by the Companies Consolidation (Consequential Provisions) Act 1985, s 30, Sch 2. For 'existing company' see the Companies Act 1985, s 735(1)(b) viz companies formed and registered under former Companies Acts (with certain exceptions): *Halsbury's Statutes* (4th edn Reissue 1991) Vol 8 at p 597.

16 Companies Act 1985, s 36, as substituted by the Companies Act 1989, s 130(1) (which applies to certain unregistered companies: ibid, s 718, Sch 22, SI 1985 No 680, as amended by SI 1990 No 1394): *Halsbury's Statutes* (4th edn Reissue 1991) Vol 8 at pp 154–155. See also the Powers of Attorney Act 1971, s 1(3).

17 *Drew v Nunn* (1879) 4 QBD 661. But there may be cases when a mentally incompetent person (or a drunkard) can be treated as a principal if the third party contracts in ignorance of his condition and without taking advantage of it: *Molton v Camroux* (1849) 4 Exch 17: *Imperial Loan Co v Stone* [1892] 1 QB 599; see also *Hart v O'Connor* [1985] AC 1000, [1985] 2 All ER 880, requiring equitable fraud before a contract will be unfair. Cf Havers J obiter in *Taylor v Walker* [1958] 1 Lloyd's Rep 490 at 514: contrast Hudson, 37 Can BR 497. But not for the purposes of a

is now affected by recent legislation, a corporation was required to have the power to appoint an agent by virtue of the instrument which created it, ie the appointment of an agent could not be ultra vires the corporation.[18] An infant can only appoint an agent in circumstances in which he himself has the power to act. This restricts an infant's capacity to appoint an agent to the kinds of valid contracts which he himself can make.[19] But an infant (other than a married woman) cannot give a valid power of attorney.

There are certain qualifications in respect of capacity which are peculiar to the law of agency, and must be noted. Although a person may be a principal and so act through an agent whenever he has capacity to act personally, there are instances when he must act personally and therefore cannot appoint an agent to act on his behalf. For example, under section 6 of the Statute of Frauds Amendment Act 1828 an action is not maintainable on any representation about the character, conduct, credit, ability, trade or dealings of any other person to enable that person to obtain credit, money or goods on the strength of such representation, unless it is in writing, signed by the representor. It has been held that a fraudulent representation made by an agent will not render the principal liable under this statute.[20] But there can be liability for a *negligent* misrepresentation made by an agent, even if not in writing, since the statute will not apply.[1] On the other hand, if the principal is obliged by his office or position to exercise personal skill, or discretion, or a power, or authority conferred on him, then, in general, he cannot delegate such task to an agent.[2] This is of special

power of attorney: *Daily Telegraph Newspaper Co Ltd v McLaughlin* [1904] AC 776. On the subject of contracts by such persons, see Fridman 'Mental Incompetency, Part I' (1963) 79 LQR 502 at pp 509–516. For an American view, see Meiklejohn, 'Incompetent Principals, Competent Third Parties and the Law of Agency' (1985–86) 61 Indiana LJ 95. As to the effect of a supervening insanity upon an existing agency relationship, see below, pp 398, 407.

18 On the doctrine of ultra vires, since the European Communities Act 1972, s 9, see below, pp 354–355. The result may be that the ultra vires appointment of an agent may have legal consequences for the corporation, if the agent thus appointed transacts with 'a person dealing with a company in good faith.'

19 But the Manitoban case of *Johannson v Gudmandson* (1909) 11 WLR 176, suggests that a minor can contract *to his advantage* through an agent.
Powell (*Law of Agency* pp 298–299) thought that the capacity of minors to appoint agents was uncertain, apart from the Law of Property Act 1925, s 129 (which has now been repealed by the Powers of Attorney Act 1971, s 8, on the ground that married women who are minors can execute powers of attorney and no longer need the protection of the earlier provision). In *Re Shephard, Shephard v Cartwright* [1953] Ch 728 at 735, [1953] 2 All ER 608 at 618; Denning LJ said: '. . . the appointment by an infant of an agent . . . has always been void.' This would not seem from the cases to be strictly accurate. Indeed Lord Denning MR retracted this statement in *G(A) v G(T)* [1970] 3 All ER 546 at 549, in which it was held that a minor could appoint an agent to pay maintenance for the support of his illegitimate child, since that was a lawful act for him to do, and one which he could be compelled to do. For the cases, and a discussion of the whole matter, see Webb 'The Capacity of the Infant to appoint an Agent' (1955) 18 MLR 861 arguing in favour of the capacity stated in the text.

20 *Williams v Mason* (1873) 28 LT 232; *Swift v Jewsbury* (1874) LR 9 QB 301; *Hirst v West Riding Union Banking Co* [1901] 2 KB 560. As to the effect of a representation made on behalf of a limited liability company by a duly authorised agent, viz, its assistant secretary, see *UBAF Ltd v European American Banking Corpn* [1984] QB 713, [1984] 2 All ER 226, CA.

1 *W B Anderson & Sons Ltd v Rhodes (Liverpool) Ltd* [1967] 2 All ER 850.

2 *Ingram v Ingram* (1740) 2 Atk 88; *Hawkins v Kemp* (1803) 3 East 410.

importance in relation to the position of an agent who wishes to delegate the exercise of his authority to a sub-agent.[3]

Secondly, capacity to act as an agent is not completely governed by the same rules as capacity to act as a principal. For example, a minor (provided of sound mind) even though incompetent to be a principal in respect of a particular contract, may none the less act as an agent in the making of such contract. It is irrelevant to his capacity to act as an agent that, because of his infancy, he may not be liable to the third party on the contract, where an adult agent would have been personally liable.[4] However, where a contract is required to be in writing signed by or on behalf of each party to the contract,[5] one party cannot be the agent of the other for the purposes of satisfying the statutory requirement.[6]

Validity. The purposes of the contract of agency must be lawful and possible. Therefore if the contract of agency is illegal by the law of the place where it is to be performed it cannot be treated as valid and enforceable in the country where it was entered into by the parties. In a Canadian case, *Gillespie Management Corpn v Terrace Properties*,[7] the plaintiff, a British Columbia company contracted with the defendant company to manage the latter's property in the State of Washington. The law of that State required the plaintiff to be licensed as a real estate broker in order to conduct such business within the State. The plaintiff was not so licensed. When the defendant company broke the contract, and the plaintiff sued in British Columbia, it was held that the contract, which was to be performed in Washington, involved an illegal performance. Therefore the plaintiff could not sue on the contract in British Columbia, just as the plaintiff could not sue in Washington State.

The effect of the doctrine of frustration, or impossibility of performance upon an existing contract of agency will be considered in a later chapter[8].

B. IMPLIED CONTRACT

As with other contracts the agency relationship may be impliedly created by the conduct of the parties, without anything having been expressly agreed as to terms of employment, remuneration, etc. The assent of the agent will be implied from

---

3 Below, pp 164–171.
4 *Smally v Smally* (1700) 1 Eq Cas Abr 6, 283. So, too, a company which could not legally carry on the business of real estate or insurance could act as the agent of an undisclosed principal in such business: *Commonwealth Trust Co v Dewitt* (1974) 40 DLR (3d) 113. For the personal liability of agents see below, pp 231–243.
5 Law of Property (Miscellaneous Provisions) Act 1989, s 2.
6 *Bird v Boulter* (1833) 4 B & Ad 443 at 447, per Littledale J. This was under the old provisions of the Statute of Frauds, later the Law of Property Act 1925, s 40, since repealed and replaced by the 1989 Act. But one party could authorise the other's *agent* to sign: *Bird v Boulter*, above: *Wilson & Sons v Pike* [1949] 1 KB 176, [1948] 2 All ER 267, CA. As for acting as agent for the principal and the third party, see below, p 179.
7 (1989) 62 DLR (4th) 221. See also *Gilbert v Gilbert* (1985) 86 NBR (2d) 260: power of attorney for an illegal purpose.
8 Below, pp 397, 399.

the fact that he has acted intentionally on another's behalf.[9] But in general it will be the assent of the principal which is more likely to be implied, for, except in certain cases, 'it is only by the will of the employer that any agency may be created.'[10] Such assent may be implied where the circumstances clearly indicate that he has given authority to another to act on his behalf.[11] This may be so even if the principal did not know the true state of affairs. Thus in *Biggar v Rock Life Assurance Co*:[12]

> An insurance agent employed by the defendants put false statements in the policy signed by X. He invented the answers on X's behalf and with the permission of X, even though X did not know he was inventing, and had not authorised him to invent, but had authorised him to fill in the form on his behalf. It was held that he was X's agent not the company's, despite the fact that he had exceeded whatever power had been given him.

Mere silence will be insufficient. There must be some course of conduct to indicate the acceptance of the agency relationship.[13] The effect of such an implication is to put the parties in the same position as if the agency had been expressly created.

9 It is suggested that Professor Müller-Freienfels ('Legal Relations in the Law of Agency' (1964) 13 Am J of Comp L 193 at p 203) has misinterpreted the meaning of this sentence, and takes it to refer to *all* relationships, when it is intended to relate only to *contractual* agency.
10 *Pole v Leask* (1861) 8 LT 645 at 648, per Lord Cranworth. It is to this manifestation of assent by the principal that Professor Müller-Freienfels is referring: (1964) 13 Am J of Comp L. 193.
11 As in *Townsends Carriers Ltd v Pfizer Ltd* (1977) 121 Sol Jo 375 where it was held the conduct of a landlord and a tenant indicated that each had allowed their associates to negotiate on their respective behalfs: therefore such associates were agents to give and receive a notice in writing to determine the lease. See also *R v Duffin* [1993] 4 WWR 201, where a dealer allowed someone who said he had sold a truck on behalf of the dealer to take possession of a truck even though the person claiming to have sold the truck did not return with the cheque as promised. The latter then sold the truck to a second dealer. It was held that the one who obtained possession of the truck was the agent of the first dealer. In *Advanced Mobile Welding Co v Quartz Ventures Ltd* (1991) 60 BCLR (2d) 235 a construction company was held to be the agent of a developer where documentary and discovery evidence was consistent with such conclusion. Contrast *Vogel v R and A Kohnstamm Ltd* [1973] QB 133, [1971] 2 All ER 1428 and an Australian case, *Bridle Estates Pty v Myer Realty Ltd* (1977) 15 ALR 415, an agent appointed only to negotiate, not to make an offer capable of acceptance. So, too, in a Canadian case, *Bank of British Columbia v Andrews and Struss* [1979] 6 WWR 574, the deposit by a co-owner with a bank of a certificate of title to certain land, revealing that the land was owned by two people as tenants in common, did not mean that the other co-owner had made the depositor of the certificate into his agent to deal with the land. See also *Bank of Montreal v Canadian Westgrowth Ltd* (1990) 72 Alta LR (2d) 319, parent corporation providing 100% wholly owned subsidiary with free management services and interest-free loans, also sharing same officers, directors, meetings, auditor and year end: no agency contract between the two companies.
12 [1902] 1 KB 516. Cf the following Canadian authorities: *Reid v Traders General Insurance Co* (1963) 41 DLR (2d) 148 at 152 per Ilsley CJ: *Baker v Judgment Recovery (Nova Scotia) Ltd* (1967) 64 DLR (2d) 442 at 448–449 per Fielding J: *Boutilier v Traders General Insurance Co* (1969) 7 DLR (3d) 220 at 233–237 per Coffin JA.
13 For illustrations of the way in which the courts approach the question, see: *Customs and Excise Comrs v Pools Finance (1937) Ltd* [1952] 1 All ER 775 (agency found); *Bottomley v Harrison* [1952] 1 All ER 368 (no agency found); *Sykes v Millington* [1953] 1 QB 770, [1953] 1 All ER 1098; *Alsey Steam Fishing Co Ltd v Hillman (Owners), The Kirknes* [1957] P 51 at 64–67, [1957] 1 All ER 97 at 106, per Willmer J (agency found); *Re Transplanters (Holding Co) Ltd* [1958] 2 All ER 711, [1958] 1 WLR 822 (auditors held not to be agents of a company); *Lawson v Hosemaster Machine Co Ltd* [1966] 2 All ER 944, [1966] 1 WLR 1300 (receiver of a company was company's agent, so as to permit ratification of his unauthorised act) see also *Standard*

A distinction should be mentioned here between an implied contract of agency and agency by estoppel. The former is an instance of agency created by agreement between the parties before the agent acts on behalf of the principal. The principal is willing that the agent should act on his behalf. The agent in fact has authority so to act. But the existence and scope of his authority are discoverable by reference only to the conduct of the parties, and not by the examination of any express agreement. On the other hand[14] agency by estoppel exists even where the principal did not want, or appoint, the agent to act on his behalf. There is no contract of agency implicitly in existence between the parties. None the less, the law considers the agency relationship to exist, and gives effect to such a relationship.

B. The authority of contractual agents

A. DEFINITIONS

Varieties of authority. Once it has been determined that an agency relationship has been created, it is necessary to establish the scope of such relationship. By this is meant the exact nature and extent of the power possessed by the agent. The power of an agent to affect the legal position of his principal is a concept already examined.[15] The nature and extent of such power are explicable in terms of 'the agent's authority', which is an artificial notion of law.[16] This is the central, most important feature of the whole relationship. Upon it depend not only the legal relations of the principal and his agent but also the relations which may emerge between the principal and the third party or the agent and the third party. At this juncture it is sufficient to state, without further elaboration, that the principal will only be bound to the third party by acts which are within the agent's authority. Anything that the agent does in excess of that authority will not affect the principal, unless the principal adopts what the agent has done in accordance with the doctrine of ratification.[17] Moreover, if the agent acts outside his authority, he may be liable to his principal for breach of the contract of agency, or otherwise,[18] or to the third party for breach of the implied warranty of authority.[19]

Chartered Bank Ltd v Walker [1982] 3 All ER 938, [1982] 1 WLR 1410, CA; *Bart v British West Indian Airways Ltd* [1967] 1 Lloyd's Rep 239 (no agency between pools investor and consignor of coupons to England); *Branwhite v Worcester Works Finance Ltd* [1969] 1 AC 552, [1968] 3 All ER 104 (above, p 16) (no agency between car dealer and finance company). Cf the Canadian case of *Crampsey v Deveney* (1969) 2 DLR (3d) 161: mother not the agent of her children with whom she was the joint tenant of land; *Weitzman v Hendin* (1986) 31 DLR (4th) 109; affd (1989) 61 DLR (4th) 525: solicitor acting for bank in connection with mortgage investment company not the agent of the bank when incorporating the company; *Smith v Lasko* [1987] 5 WWR 412: principal of car dealership not agent of the dealership when purchasing car and selling it to the plaintiff after having made limited use of, and using dealer plates on car.

As to the agency of shop stewards vis-à-vis a trade union, see *Heatons Transport (St Helens) Ltd v Transport and General Workers' Union* [1973] AC 15 [1972] 3 All ER 101.

14 Below, ch 6.
15 Above, pp 12 ff.
16 Above, p 19.
17 Below, ch 5.
18 Below, pp 155 ff.
19 Below, pp 243–249.

The elucidation of the agent's authority is complicated by the fact that in a sense, there is not one unique, integrated notion of authority but, instead, there are several varieties of authority. The particular one involved in any given agency relationship depends upon the type of agency that is under consideration. When the agency relationship has been created by contract (or consent), the relevant variety of authority is *actual*, or as it is sometimes termed, *real* authority.

Actual authority. Actual authority is the authority which in fact the agent has been given by the principal under the agreement or contract which has been made between them, or by virtue of subsequent ratification.[20] In *Freeman & Lockyer v Buckhurst Park Properties (Mangal) Ltd*,[1] Diplock LJ said:

> 'An "actual" authority is a legal relationship between principal and agent created by a consensual agreement to which they alone are parties. Its scope is to be ascertained by applying ordinary principles of construction of contracts, including any proper implications from the express words used, the usages of the trade, or the course of business between the parties.'

To this agreement, of course, a third party contracting with the agent was a stranger. Indeed he might be totally ignorant of the existence of any authority, ie that an agency relationship was in existence. This would occur where the principal was undisclosed, a situation which gives rise to certain important differences and anomalies.[2] Nevertheless, if the agent did enter into a contract pursuant to the 'actual' authority, it would create contractual rights and liabilities as between the principal and the third party. Such actual or real authority may be sub-divided into three categories, viz, express authority; implied authority; and usual, or customary authority.[3]

---

20 *Roy's Midway Ltd v Economical Mutual Insurance Co* (1986) 33 NBR (2d) 387. The authority may be contained in an implied term in the agency agreement: *Smith v Mosher Limestone Ltd* (1981) 121 DLR (3d) 290. Such authority may be limited in law or in fact: *Manitoba Securities Commission v Aronovitch* [1981] 4 WWR 344; *Kohn v Devon Mortgage Ltd* [1984] 1 WWR 544; revsd on appeal [1985] 4 WWR 543. In *Jawara v Gambian Airways* [1992] NPC 61 the Privy Council held that an agent was justified in believing that he had specific authorisation and approval from his principal to accept the offer of a contract. On the implication of a term into a contract of agency see also *Kelly v Cooper* [1993] AC 205 below, p 175.

1 [1964] 1 All ER 630 at 644. Thus actual authority to pay certain penalties required of a ship could be found in the relevant documents in *The Pindaros* [1983] 2 Lloyd's Rep 635. But the employee who engaged in discussions with a potential purchaser had no actual authority (nor any apparent authority) in *Discount Kitchens v Crawford* [1989] CLY 51. Nor did the pilot of an aircraft have actual authority to carry out unlawful air taxi work (or to carry passengers from Gatwick to earn money for the carriers, his employers) in *Gurtner v Beaton* [1993] 2 Lloyd's Rep 369. But he did have apparent or ostensible authority. Cp the similar conclusion, as regards the senior manager of the branch office of the bank communicating decisions on behalf of the bank although the plaintiff knew the manager's actual authority was limited, in *First Energy (UK) Ltd v Hungarian International Bank Ltd* [1993] 2 Lloyd's Rep 194. See further below, p 116.

    A collector of taxes did not have actual authority to make an agreement to accept taxes due by payment in arrears: *Re Selectmove* [1995] 2 All ER 531, [1995] 1 WLR 474.

2 Below, pp 253–272.

3 In the *Freeman* case, above, Diplock LJ and in *Hely-Hutchinson v Brayhead Ltd* [1967] 3 All ER 98 at 102, Lord Denning MR, divided actual authority into express or implied authority, and made no separate mention of usual or customary authority: but it is suggested, in the light of what is said later, that it may be useful to differentiate *implied* from *usual* authority, if only for explanatory purposes, even if, for practical purposes, there is no difference; cf *Bowstead and Reynolds on Agency* (16th edn 1996) p 104.

In the first place the agent's authority may be *express*: that is, it may be specifically created and limited by the terms of the agreement, or contract, which gives rise to the agency relationship.[4] 'It is *express* when it is given by express words, such as when a board of directors pass a resolution which authorises two of their number to sign cheques.'[5]

Secondly, it may be *implied* from the nature of the business which the agent is employed to transact. In the *Freeman* case,[6] Willmer LJ differentiated express actual authority from implied actual authority, an instance of the latter occurring if the agent in question had been appointed by the company of which he was a director to some office which carried with it authority to make such a contract of the kind involved on behalf of the company. This would occur if the board of directors appointed one of their number to be managing director.[7] This is a valid use of the term 'implied authority', for it shows that the contract of agency is to be interpreted in the light of what it is necessary to imply into it in order to make it effective. Moreover, where such implications can be made they are made on the basis that the principal has in fact consented to the agent's having authority to act in such a manner or as regards such a transaction. If there is evidence[8] that the principal has specifically not so consented, then these implications cannot be made. As will be seen below these considerations make it right and imperative to confine the term *implied authority* to the kind of authority now being discussed, and not to confuse it with apparent authority, though the term is sometimes used indiscriminately to refer to either kind of authority. The important feature is that the consent of the principal is a necessary part of implied authority: hence such authority is one aspect of an agent's actual, or real authority.[9]

Thirdly, the agent's actual authority may include what is often called his *usual*, or *customary* authority. This is the authority which an agent in the trade,

4 *Freeman and Lockyer v Buckhurst Park Properties (Mangal) Ltd* [1964] 2 QB 480 at 488, [1964] 1 All ER 630 at 635, per Willmer LJ. An authority to make representations relating to the manner in which a contract will be enforced is distinct from an authority to make, vary or terminate a contract: *State Rail Authority of New South Wales v Health Outdoor Pty Ltd* (1987) 7 NSWLR 170 at 194 per McHugh JA.

5 *Hely-Hutchinson v Brayhead Ltd* [1967] 3 All ER 98 at 102 per Lord Denning MR: italics in original.

6 [1964] 2 QB 480 at 488, [1964] 1 All ER 630 at 635.

7 *Hely-Hutchinson v Brayhead Ltd*, above, at 102 per Lord Denning MR. For an example of the implied authority of an agent to pay his principal's cheques into the *agent's* account, see *Souhrada v Bank of New South Wales* [1976] 2 Lloyd's Rep 444. So, too, in *Bell Group Ltd v Herald & Weekly Times Ltd* [1985] VR 613 a broker had implied authority to follow the rules and regulations of the Australian Stock Exchange. See also *Merrill Lynch Royal Securities Ltd v Newman Manning Ltd* (1984) 52 BCLR 103. But a branch manager did not have implied actual authority to make certain representations in *British Bank of the Middle East v Sun Life Assurance Co of Canada (UK) Ltd* [1983] 2 Lloyd's Rep 9. Nor did a pilot have implied actual authority to carry out unlawful air taxi work or to carry the injured passengers in *Gurtner v Beaton* [1993] 2 Lloyd's Rep 369.

8 See eg *First Energy (UK) Ltd v Hungarian International Bank Ltd* [1993] 2 Lloyd's Rep 194 (but the agent was held to have ostensible or apparent authority).

9 Cf Lord Denning MR in the *Hely-Hutchinson* case, above: 'Actual authority, express or implied, is binding as between the company and the agent, and also as between the company and others, whether they are within the company or outside it.' See *Rhodian River Shipping Co SA v Halla Maritime Corpn* [1984] 1 Lloyd's Rep 373 for an illustration of actual express and implied authority.

business, profession, or place in which the particular agent is being employed would usually, normally, or customarily possess, unless something was expressly said by the principal to contradict it. It is the authority which persons dealing with the agent, with the knowledge of the trade, etc, would expect him to have. Such authority is really a variety of implied authority, in the sense in which that expression has been explained above, and for the same reasons, and not an independent kind of authority.[10] As Lord Denning said in the *Hely-Hutchinson* case[11] in respect of the appointment by a board of directors of one of their number as managing director: 'They thereby impliedly authorise him to do all such things as fall within the usual scope of that office.' This form of authority may be contrasted with the more general notion of implied authority on the ground that it is based upon the more specific idea of settled and well-understood trade, business or professional usages and customs, evidence of which will have to be produced should a dispute arise. There are certain trades, businesses or professions, in which agents are employed, in respect of which a body of case-law has settled what an agent in such trade, business or profession may usually or customarily do for the purpose of effectuating the transaction in respect of which he is employed. In such circumstances the usage or custom may be said to have hardened into law so as to have become part of the implied authority of such agents.[12] In other instances, what may be implied into an agency relationship as far as usages or customs are concerned is still a matter for debate and decision.

B. EXPRESS AUTHORITY

Deeds. If the agent's authority is contained in a deed, when it is called a 'power of attorney',[13] the deed will be strictly construed according to the rules of construction which are usually applicable to deeds of all kinds.[14] Of special note are the following rules.

---

10 Cf *Bowstead and Reynolds on Agency* (16th edn) p 106. See *Bell Group Ltd v Herald & Weekly Times Ltd*, above. See also Stone 'Usual and Ostensible Authority – One Concept or Two?' [1993] JBL 325, arguing that usual and ostensible authority are distinct, criticising the approach of the Court of Appeal in *City Trust Ltd v Levy* [1988] 3 All ER 418, [1988] 1 WLR 1051.
11 [1967] 3 All ER 98 at 102.
12 Below, pp 79–83.
13 'The so-called power is not really a power but is merely a manifestation of the authority given by the principal to the agent.' Falconbridge, 17 Can BR 675, n 4. But a power of attorney confers authority to act on the agent: it is not a direction to act: the agent must pay regard to the subsequent orders of the principal after the power of attorney has been given: *Holt* (1983) 12 A Cr LR 1.
    A power of attorney gives the agent, the donee of the power, actual authority: *Ericksen Industries Ltd v Chevron Canada Resources Ltd* (1987) 53 Alta LR (2d) 35.
    The deed no longer has to be sealed: above p 57. For the situation under the previous law, see *Byblos Bank SAL v Al-Khudhairy* [1987] 1 FTLR 35 at 47–48 per Nicholls LJ.
14 See, eg, *Pich v Cleall* (1987) 49 Alta LR (2d) 401, agent not liable for failing to invest: did not receive money to do so. In this instance the construction is in favour of the principal, ie the grantor, not against him. For criticisms, see Stoljar *Law of Agency* pp 91 ff. Cf *Bowstead and Reynolds on Agency* (16th edn) pp 111–112.

The authority is limited to the purpose for which it was given.[15] In this respect it is important to note that under s 10 of the Powers of Attorney Act 1971, if a general power of attorney is in the statutory form or in a similar form expressed to be made under the Act, it confers on the donee or donees of the power authority to do on behalf of the donor, ie the principal, 'anything which he can lawfully do by an attorney'.[16] Thus, if the words are unqualified, viz, 'I appoint A to be my attorney in accordance with s 10 of the Act', the only restriction of the agent's authority will stem from the principal's incapacity to act through an agent, eg where he is entering into a contract of marriage. Subject to the situation in cases where the statutory or similar language is used, the use of general words in the deed will therefore not confer any power to act that exceeds the proper performance of the particular special duty or duties contained in the deed. This is of particular importance so far as the issue of bills of exchange and the borrowing of money are concerned. Thus, if the power of attorney allows the agent 'from time to time to negotiate, make sale, dispose of, assign and transfer' property this will not amount to an authority to borrow money, eg, by pledging the property.[17] Hence also where, by a power of attorney, the principal agreed in advance to ratify whatever the agent did or purported to do under the power, this could not be construed so as to extend the agent's authority beyond the purposes set out in the deed.[18]

Secondly, if general words are used, then they are limited by other, special words, which describe the particular acts which the agent is authorised to perform. Thus in a case which was concerned with the agent's authority to borrow money, *Jacobs v Morris*:[19]

A power of attorney gave the agent power to purchase goods in connection with a certain business and to make, draw, sign, accept or indorse for and on behalf of the principal, bills of exchange or promissory notes if they should be necessary for the purchase of goods or in the conduct of the business. The agent, purporting to act in pursuance of the power, borrowed money and gave bills of exchange drawn on the principal in respect of the loan. It was held that the agent had exceeded the authority given him in the power of attorney; therefore the principal was not liable on the bills.

Thirdly, where the operative part of the deed is ambiguous, the recitals will govern the construction of the power of attorney. Thus in *Danby v Coutts & Co*:[20]

---

15 Which must be legal: *Gilbert v Gilbert* (1985) 86 NBR (2d) 260. If the subject-matter of the power of attorney no longer exists the authority will be terminated by frustration (below, p 399): *Smith v Humchitt Estate* (1990) 48 BCLR (2d) 361.

16 See also the Powers of Attorney Act 1971, s 7 which deals only with procedure for acting: it does not enlarge the scope of things which may be done by the donee of the power: *Clauss v Pir* [1987] 2 All ER 752 at 756. The agent may not exercise the power for his own benefit unless expressly authorised to do so: *Elford v Elford* (1922) 64 SCR 125; *Tim v Lai* (1986) 5 BCLR (2d) 245; *Gilbert v Gilbert* (1985) 86 NBR (2d) 260; *Powell v Thompson* [1991] 1 NZLR 597.

17 *Jonmenjoy Coondoo v Watson* (1884) 9 App Cas 561: see also *Re Dowson and Jenkin's Contract* [1904] 2 Ch 219; *Green v Whitehead* [1930] 1 Ch 38.

18 *Midland Bank Ltd v Reckitt* [1933] AC 1: nor would it amount to ratification, since ratification can only be retrospective: below, p 104.

19 [1902] 1 Ch 816. See also *Hogg v Snaith* (1808) 1 Taunt 347. Cf *Hayes v Standard Bank of Canada* [1928] 2 DLR 898.

20 (1885) 29 Ch D 500.

The operative part of a power of attorney did not mention any term for which the power was to continue. But the recitals stated that the purpose of the deed was so that the principal should have an agent while he was abroad. It was therefore held that the agent's authority was limited to the period of the principal's absence from the country.

In short the authority conferred by a power of attorney is that which is 'within the four corners of the instrument either in express terms or by necessary implication.'[1] What is meant by 'necessary implication' may be illustrated by *Re Wallace, ex p Wallace*:[2]

The power of attorney authorised the agent 'to commence and carry on, or to defend, at law or in equity, all actions, suits, or other proceedings' which concerned the principal's personal estate. It was held that this authorised the agent to sign on the principal's behalf a bankruptcy petition against one of the principal's debtors.

What might be described as the converse situation is illustrated by a case involving not a power of attorney but a debenture deed. In *Newhart Developments Ltd v Co-operative Commercial Bank*,[3] a debenture deed provided that the defendants could appoint a receiver for the plaintiffs, under certain circumstances. Such receiver, when appointed, would be the agent of the plaintiffs and would have the powers to take proceedings in the plaintiffs' name for the purpose of collecting and getting in property charged by the debenture and to carry on or concur in carrying on the plaintiffs' business. A receiver was appointed, shortly after which the plaintiffs issued a writ against the defendants, claiming damages for breach of contract. The writ was issued without any attempt having been made to seek the consent or concurrence of the receiver. When the defendants applied to the court to have the writ set aside on the ground of irregularity, in that it was issued without the receiver's knowledge or consent, it was held that the construction of the debenture deed did not involve the inference that the normal powers of the directors with respect to bringing actions had been taken away from them. Consequently, the writ had been properly issued.

Written and parol authorisation. The approach of the law where the agent's authority is contained in a document not under seal or is given by parol is less stringent. If there is a document, the ordinary rules of construction of documents are to be employed in determining the scope of the agent's authority. There is a general rule, however, that if the document involved is not a deed, or the contract of agency is parol, the agent's authority is to be construed having regard to the

---

1 *Bryant, Powis and Bryant Ltd v La Banque Du Peuple* [1893] AC 170 at 177 per Lord MacNaghten. Hence someone who deals with an agent known to be acting under a power of attorney could not rely on the agent's having powers in excess of those granted in the power, ie could not rely on apparent authority or estoppel: *National Bank of Canada v Anemid* (1989) 39 BLR 108. Contrast *Ericksen Industries Ltd v Chevron Canada Resources Ltd* (1987) 53 Alta LR (2d) 35 where the agent under a power of attorney had actual *and* apparent authority. On apparent authority and estoppel, see below, pp 122–132.
2 (1884) 14 QBD 22.
3 [1978] QB 814, [1978] 2 All ER 896.

purposes of the agency, ie the surrounding circumstances and the usual course of the business in which the agent is concerned.[4] In particular, where general words are used, they must be construed and understood in the light of the usual course of the agent's business.[5] As the Privy Council said in the case of *Ashford Shire Council v Dependable Motors*:[6] 'The extent of an agent's authority, if in doubt, must be determined by inference from the whole circumstances.' In that case, therefore, it was held that a shire engineer, not expressly authorised to do so, was acting within the scope of his authority in describing to sellers of a tractor the particular purpose for which his principal required the tractor, so as to show that he was relying on the seller's skill and judgment in making his report to his principal. Similarly, in *Nelson v Raphael*,[7] an agent appointed and authorised to hand over a car which had been purchased from his principal by a third party, was held to have authority to demonstrate to the purchaser the controls of the car. Hence, when such agent acted without due care and skill in the performance of that duty, with the result that the car was totally destroyed, the seller, the agent's principal, was not able to sue for the price of the car, since he was liable for his agent's negligence.

Writing which contains the agent's authority is of prime importance, but if there is any ambiguity about the wording of the agent's authority then, as long as the agent acts in good faith and in accordance with a reasonable construction of his authority (if there is more than one possible), he will be considered to have acted within his authority, whether or not in fact what he did was what the principal intended he should do.[8] Thus in *Boden v French*:[9]

> The principal instructed his agent to sell coal so as to get him a certain price, 15s a ton net cash. The agent sold at a price which would realise 15s 6d a ton; but he gave the purchaser two months' credit. It was held that this did not amount to a breach of the contract of agency, since the conduct of the agent could reasonably be considered by him as coming within the general terms of his agency.

Another case is *Ireland v Livingston*.[10]

> The principal asked his agent to get him 500 tons of sugar at a certain price. The agent was told that 50 tons more or less was of no importance as long as the price was right. The agent bought 400 tons at that price, which was the total amount he could obtain. It was held that the principal was bound to accept this amount, because what the agent had done, in the circumstances, could reasonably be interpreted as within the terms of his authority.

4 This sentence was quoted by Virtue J in *Royal Bank of Canada v Bauman* (1986) 46 Alta LR (2d) 68 at 79.
5 See eg *Wiltshire v Sims* (1808) 1 Camp 258; *Odell v Cormack Bros* (1887) 19 QBD 223; *Pole v Leask* (1860) 28 Beav 562; affd (1861) 33 LJ Ch 155.
6 [1961] AC 336 at 349, [1961] 1 All ER 96 at 101.
7 [1979] RTR 437.
8 The phrase 'in good faith and in accordance with a reasonable construction of his authority' was quoted by Virtue J in *Royal Bank of Canada v Bauman*, above at p 79.
9 (1851) 10 CB 886.
10 (1872) LR 5 HL 395. See also *Johnston v Kershaw* (1867) LR 2 Exch 82; *Weigall & Co v Runciman & Co* (1916) 85 LJKB 1187. Contrast *Vale of Neath Colliery Co v Furness* (1876) 45 LJ Ch 276; *Tallentire v Ayre* (1884) 1 TLR 143.

In a case which concerned the authority of a ship's agents appointed to represent the charterers' as well as the shipowner's interests, *Blandy Bros & Co Lda v Nello Simoni Ltd*,[11] the question was whether the agents could recover from the charterers expenses incurred in connection with the ship. The charterers alleged that in meeting such expenses the agents acted outside the scope of their authority. Megaw J held that in the type of contract that was involved, ie free in and out stowed, where the agents had received no specific instructions either way, the agents could reasonably pay for loading and stowage and in so doing acted within their authority. This decision was affirmed by the Court of Appeal.

C. IMPLIED AUTHORITY

The scope of implied authority. It is possible, indeed in some instances necessary, to read into the agent's express authority a certain implied authority. This may be because what has been expressly stated when the agency relationship was created does not cover the acts performed or required to be performed by the agent. It may be because the only way of construing the document which contains the agent's express authority is by inferring necessary implications. Moreover, if there is no statement which clarifies exactly what the agent's authority is, then the only way of knowing what authority can properly be attributed to the agent is by inferring a certain implied authority. This is part of an agent's actual authority, which the principal has consented, by implication, that the agent should have.[12] If the principal has not consented to his agent's having this implied authority, and has taken the necessary steps to make the outside world aware of his lack of consent, then the agent will not have such authority. Failing such lack of consent together with notice thereof to third parties, the agent's implied authority is part of the authority which the parties have agreed upon shall be exercised by the agent on the principal's behalf.[13]

This form of authority must be contrasted, therefore, with the *apparent* or *ostensible* authority possessed by some agents, resulting from conduct on the part of the principal which gives rise to an estoppel.[14] It must also be contrasted with the presumed authority of a wife or mistress, and the authority implied by the law in cases of agency of necessity.[15] The authority to be described here is an authority implied in fact from the circumstances of the parties, unless there is evidence which makes it impossible that such authority should be implied.

11 [1963] 2 Lloyd's Rep 393. See also *Stafford v Conti Commodity Services Ltd* [1981] 1 Lloyd's Rep 466, on the authority of brokers in the commodities futures market.
12 Above, p 63.
13 This paragraph was quoted by MacDonald CJTD in *North Shore Seafoods v Montague Seafoods Inc* (1994) 110 Nfld & PEIR 322 at 325–326.
14 But note the complicating factor to be discussed further below, that the principal may be bound, *either* because the agent has acted within his *implied* authority, *or* because the agent has acted with *apparent* authority. Sometimes this has led judges to use the language of estoppel or holding out, when they need only have referred to the notion of implied authority as described in the text. Such confusion, it is suggested, has resulted from the description of both types of authority as 'usual', ie as depending upon what would usually be expected of an agent of the class involved: cf *Bowstead and Reynolds* pp 105–109; Stone, loc cit, above, p 64, note [10].
15 Below, pp 134–150.

Every agent has implied authority to do everything necessary for, and ordinarily incidental to carrying out his express authority according to the usual way in which such authority is executed. For example, an agent authorised to find a purchaser for certain property is impliedly authorised to describe it and tell a prospective purchaser about the state of the property.[16] An agent authorised to make and deliver documentation relating to complete refinancing of a multiple-unit residential project and to complete the refinancing was held to be impliedly authorised to make a cash call, which the defendant investor in the project was held obliged to pay.[17] On the other hand, an agent authorised to perform certain acts, such as to find a purchaser for property and make a contract of sale in respect of it, will not be impliedly authorised to receive the purchase money.[18] An agent expressly authorised to receive payment of money is not impliedly authorised to receive anything other than cash or to make any other arrangements about payment.[19] This must be understood as subject to two qualifications. First, that there is no operative usage or custom.[20] Secondly, that the agent could not have done otherwise in the interests of his principal since the debtor was not able to pay the full amount. In the latter event the agent will not be guilty of a breach of duty if he fails to collect all the cash owed: though this will not necessarily relieve the debtor of his obligation to pay immediately, irrespective of the time for which credit was allowed by the agent, all he owes the principal.[1]

Beyond this notion of what is necessary and incidental, however, two other principles, which expand the notion of implied authority, must also be considered. Both are broad in the sense that they are of general application: they are also narrow in that they relate to, and operate only in respect of agents employed to act for a principal in connection with matters concerning a particular trade or business, or to act for the principal in the ordinary course of his trade, business or profession. The principles in question involve 'usual' authority and 'customary' authority.

Usual authority. An agent in the class or group referred to above is impliedly authorised to do what is *usual* in his trade, profession, or business for the purpose of carrying out his authority or anything necessary or incidental thereto.[2] Thus, a person employed to sell a horse was impliedly authorised to warrant its

---

16 *Mullens v Miller* (1882) 22 Ch D 194. See also *Smith v Mosher Limestone Co Ltd* (1981) 88 APR 230; *Woeller v Orfus* (1979) 106 DLR (3d) 115.
17 *Clareview Rental Project (Edmonton) Ltd v Walker* [1993] 4 WWR 284.
18 *Mynn v Joliffe* (1834) 1 Mood & R 326; *Butwick v Grant* [1924] 2 KB 483. Note the Law of Property Act 1925, s 69, see below, p 83. For the refusal of a court to hold that an agent necessarily had implied authority to endorse a cheque, see the Australian case of *Day v Bank of New South Wales* (1978) 19 ALR 32.
19 *Williams v Evans* (1866) LR 1 QB 352; *Pearson v Scott* (1878) 9 Ch D 198.
20 But note here, as in the case of receiving purchase money when not expressly authorised, there may be an 'apparent' authority: see for example *Townsend v Inglis* (1816) Holt NP 278. Compare *First Energy (UK) Ltd v Hungarian International Bank Ltd* [1993] 2 Lloyd's Rep 194 and *Gurtner v Beaton* [1993] 2 Lloyd's Rep 369, in both of which the agent did not have implied actual authority to perform the relevant acts, but was held to be invested with 'apparent' authority to do so.
1 *Gokal Chand-Jagan Nath v Nand Ram Das-Atma Ram* [1939] AC 106, [1938] 4 All ER 407.
2 It should be noted, in the light of earlier discussion above, pp 62–64, that this is defined as *usual* authority in *Bowstead and Reynolds on Agency* (16th edn) pp 104, 123, 126.

soundness.[3] A commission agent employed to make a bet for his principal is impliedly authorised to pay the bet if he lost.[4] Some agents are impliedly authorised to secure payment of debts owed to their principals.[5]

A solicitor was held to have authority to make certain representations respecting a loan since this was a transaction that was of a kind that was part of the usual business of a solicitor.[6]

The theoretical justification for this is to be found in the much-discussed judgment of Wills, J in *Watteau v Fenwick*,[7] where it was said: 'the principal is liable for all the acts of the agent which are within the authority usually confided to an agent of that character'. This will be so despite 'limitations as between the principal and the agent put upon that authority'. The principal will be liable even if he has prohibited or restricted the agent from acting in the way he has done, unless the third party had notice of the limitations. For there is a 'well established principle that if a person employs another as an agent in a character which involves a particular authority he cannot by a secret reservation deprive him of that authority'.[8]

Although this appears at first sight very similar to the doctrine of holding out an agent as having apparent authority, where again the question of notice to the third party is relevant, the two types of authority must be distinguished. The former is the result of representing that someone is an agent when the relationship has not been expressly created, or has not been intended to cover the particular transaction involved, whereas the notion of implied authority, of which usual authority is a variety, is a corollary of the express creation of the relationship of principal and agent. Apparent authority is determined by the conduct of the principal as reasonably understood by the particular third party, ie it is subjective, whereas the agent's usual authority rests upon the objective idea of what is usual in a particular trade, business, or profession. But it cannot be denied that there is a strong resemblance between the two kinds of authority, so strong that courts have sometimes used the language more applicable to one in order to describe the other.[9]

---

3 *Howard v Sheward* (1866) LR 2 CP 148. Similarly insurance brokers employed to arrange insurance on a car have authority to enter into a contract of interim insurance: *Stockton v Mason* [1979] RTR 130.

4 *Read v Anderson* (1884) 13 QBD 779.

5 *Howard v Chapman* (1831) 4 C & P 508; cf *International Sponge Importers Ltd v Andrew Watt & Sons* [1911] AC 279.

6 See *City Trust Ltd v Levy* [1988] 3 All ER 418, discussed in Stone, loc cit, above, p 64, note [10].

7 [1893] 1 QB 346 at 348, below, p 72. This statement of principle is criticised by Professor Hornby 'The Usual Authority of an Agent' [1961] CLJ 239 at pp 244–246. He considers it doubtful whether English courts would now follow it. The decision is supported by *Stoljar* pp 55–59: cf also Goodhart and Hamson 'Undisclosed Principals in Contract' (1932) 4 CLJ 320 at p 336.

8 *Edmunds v Bushell and Jones* (1865) LR 1 QB 97 at 99 per Cockburn CJ. Contrast the position of a wife forbidden to pledge her husband's credit, when the husband will *not* be liable, unless her conduct amounts to a representation setting up an agency by estoppel. Below, pp 148–149.

9 *Ryan v Pilkington* [1959] 1 All ER 689, [1959] 1 WLR 403: cf *Albemarle Supply Co v Hind & Co* [1928] 1 KB 307 at 318: cf Lord Denning, MR, dissenting, in *Burt v Claude Cousins & Co Ltd* [1971] 2 All ER 611 at 617. See also *Eusden v Hughes* (1984) 134 NLJ 584; *Waugh v HB Clifford & Sons Ltd* [1982] Ch 374, [1982] 1 All ER 1095.

Three cases, in particular, have given rise to difficulty as regards their reconciliation and the true nature of the doctrine of usual authority. They are: *Edmunds v Bushell and Jones*,[10] *Daun v Simmins*,[11] and *Watteau v Fenwick*.[12]

In the first of these cases the facts were as follows:

> The principal employed an agent to manage a business in which the drawing and accepting of bills was incidental and usual. But the principal stipulated that the agent should not draw or accept bills of exchange. The agent, disregarding his instruction, accepted a bill. It was held that the principal was liable to X, the indorsee of the bill, who took without knowledge of the principal's restriction on the agent's authority.

The language employed by the members of the court in this case is the language of estoppel. The judges all refer to the principal's holding out the agent, of apparent authority to contract as he did, of making him an ostensible principal. It is suggested, however, that another way of looking at this case is by saying that once a man is put into a position of manager of a business which normally or usually carries with it the power to transact certain kinds of legal acts, then such a manager has authority to do whatever is so normal or usual. Where the principal is disclosed, the agent will have implied, meaning in this instance usual, authority to do what is normal in such business, unless those with whom he deals know that such usual authority has been excluded by something expressly said by the true principal. If the principal is undisclosed, however, the doctrine of implied, or usual, authority may not be of such great relevance in determining the position of the parties, since other considerations may apply, though with the same, or somewhat similar effect.

Knowledge of such an exclusion of what would be normal or usual may itself be expressly given to the third party by the principal, or it may be implicit from what the principal does or the surrounding circumstances. *Daun v Simmins* is a good illustration of this. There:

> The principal, whose name appeared on the licence, employed the agent as a manager of a 'tied' house, and authorised him to buy spirits only from X. The agent bought spirits from Y. It was held that the principal was not liable to Y, because Y, as a person involved in this trade, should have known that it was usual for managers to be authorised to buy goods only from specified persons, and he knew that he was not a person from whom the agent would normally have been authorised to buy.

Here, of course, the agency was disclosed. As a consequence, the third party should have been aware that there might be restrictions on the agent's authority. In fact, because of his knowledge of the trade, the third party was considered to be endowed with knowledge of the specific restrictions that were involved. In this case, however, the language used by the court is that of implied, not apparent, authority. Thus Brett LJ said[13] that the question was whether there was

10 (1865) LR 1 QB 97.
11 (1879) 41 LT 783.
12 [1893] 1 QB 346. Contrast the approach of the Privy Council in *Miles v McIlwraith* (1883) 8 App Cas 120, below, p 73.
13 (1879) 41 LT 783 at 785.

any evidence of an implied authority to deal with the third party. The only fact from which such an implication could arise was putting the agent in as manager in the principal's name of the public-house. 'Unless the mere fact of a man being manager of a public-house is evidence that he has authority to order spirits of all the world, there was no evidence of [the agent's] authority. No evidence was given as to whether it is the practice in the trade for a manager to order spirits of all dealers so as to pledge the owner's credit.' Cotton LJ[14] stressed the fact that 'the public-house was mortgaged to persons who thereby had a hold over it, and a monopoly of supplying it with beer and spirits. No doubt, buying beer and spirits is necessary to carrying on the business of a public house; but it does not follow that a manager has authority to order beer and spirits of all the world'. It would seem reasonable to conclude that, so far from a person in the position of the agent in this case having usual authority to deal with the world at large, as third parties in other situations might expect, he was restricted in his class of suppliers and the plaintiffs in this case could be expected to know this since they were familiar with the general practice in this kind of business. In a sense, therefore, it could be said that the third party knew that the agent's authority was limited, since he could not possess any usual authority, as the agent in the *Edmunds* case could, none being inferable in the circumstances in question.

The third case is *Watteau v Fenwick*,[15] which has caused considerable discussion among writers on agency.[16]

> The principal, a firm of brewers, employed the agent as manager of a beer house. The agent's name appeared on the licence over the door. The principal forbade the agent to buy articles for the business (though doing so was within the usual course of such a manager's conduct of affairs) and said that they would supply such articles. The agent ordered articles of the kind in question from X, who later discovered the existence and name of the principal. It was held that the principal was liable to X for the price of the articles concerned.

As in the later, similar case of *Kinahan & Co Ltd v Parry*,[17] the principal was undisclosed, and the agent did something which a licensee of such premises would normally do, ie order goods of this kind from a supplier of this description. In both cases, therefore, it was held that the principal had implicitly authorised the agent to contract as he did and was liable on such contract. Though the language of apparent authority is used, it is suggested that, as the

---

14 Ibid.
15 Above. This case was distinguished on the facts on *Jerome v Bentley & Co* [1952] 2 All ER 114, where the 'agent' involved did not belong to any well-known class of agents: therefore no usual authority could be implied. The discussion of this case in the 4th edn, 1976, pp 101–102 was relied upon by Laskin CJC in *Guardian Insurance Co of Canada v Victoria Tire Sales Ltd* [1979] ILR 1–1154.
16 See *Powell* pp 76–78; Goodhart and Hamson 'Undisclosed Principals in Contract' (1932) 4 Cam LJ 320 at p 336; *Stoljar* pp 55–59; Hornby 'The Usual Authority of an Agent' [1961] CLJ 239; *Bowstead and Reynolds on Agency* (16th edn) pp 107–109, 416–419, referring to recent indications that extensions of authority should be limited, viz, *Moorgate Mercantile Co Ltd v Twitchings* [1977] AC 890, [1976] 2 All ER 641; *Kooragang Investments Pty Ltd v Richardson and Wrench Ltd* [1982] AC 462, [1981] 3 All ER 65.
17 [1910] 2 KB 389: reversed on appeal on the ground that no agency existed, [1911] 1 KB 459, which makes the case very dubious authority.

agency was undisclosed, such language is inappropriate.[18] What really happened was that the agent was endowed with all the normal powers of a principal, ie to do everything which was usual in the trade, business or profession that was in question. None the less the decision has been accepted by some writers as a case of apparent authority, and has been called 'an excellent example of a pure estoppel by conduct'.[19] Notwithstanding this, it has been attacked as wrong on grounds of reason and principle.[20] It has even been said that it is doubtful whether English courts would now follow the statement of the law of Wills J.[1] It was not followed by a Canadian court in *McLaughlin v Gentles*.[2] There:

> The plaintiff sought to recover from the defendants, who were members of a syndicate formed to explore and test mining properties, the price of goods supplied on the order of one of the defendants, C, and on his credit. At the time the goods were supplied, the plaintiff did not know that C was a member of the syndicate or was acting for others. He thought, therefore, that C was the principal. When the plaintiff sued, he did so on the basis that C was the agent of the other members, his undisclosed principals. They had not held C out as an agent: they had not heard of the plaintiff: and the fund provided by the defendants for exploring and testing had been exhausted, and C's authority to act for the defendants revoked before the plaintiff supplied any goods. In the circumstances it was held that, other than C himself, the defendants were not liable to the plaintiff.

The Ontario court followed and applied *Miles v McIlwaith*,[3] which had held that where there are general agents of an undisclosed principal with a special restriction or limitation on their authority, one who contracts with such agents as principals can only resort to the real principal subject to the limitation which has been placed upon the agent's authority, because he has not dealt with them as his agents, nor has there been any holding out of them or crediting as such, and so contracting on the faith of the authority. More recently *Watteau v Fenwick* was rejected and held to have been wrongly decided by the British Columbia Court of Appeal in *Sign-O-Lite Plastics Ltd v Metropolitan Life Insurance Co*:[4]

> The plaintiff contracted with X in 1978 for the renting of an electronic sign to be installed and maintained by the plaintiff at a mall in Calgary. This agreement was for 61 months. In it was a clause providing for automatic

18 Cf *Powell* p 76, note 1. Hence the rejection of the undisclosed agent's apparent authority in *McLaughlin v Gentles*, below.

19 Goodhart and Hamson, 4 Cam LJ 320 at p 336.

20 Ibid. Note the use of the term 'implied' by the authors who have just referred to this as estoppel. It is not surprising that this is confusing.

1 Hornby, [1961] CLJ 239 at p 246. Cf Scrutton LJ in *AL Underwood Ltd v Bank of Liverpool* [1924] 1 KB 775 at 792: '. . . you cannot rely on the apparent authority of an agent who did not profess in dealing with you to act as an agent.' See also Bingham LJ in *Rhodian River Shipping Co SA v Halla Maritime Corpn* [1984] 1 Lloyd's Rep 373 at 378–379 describing this case as 'puzzling', the argument for the plaintiff as 'fallacious' and the doctrine of the case as being one of which a court should be wary in applying.

2 (1919) 46 OLR 477. This was followed in the Supreme Court of Alberta in *Massey-Harris v Bond* [1930] 1 WWR 72.

3 (1883) 8 App Cas 120.

4 (1990) 73 DLR (4th) 541; Fridman (1991) 70 Can Bar Rev 329.

renewal for a further term of 60 months if neither party communicated a contrary intention to the other, in writing, more than 30 days before the end of the first term. Under that clause the agreement was renewed in 1984. Before then the defendant acquired ownership of X which owned and controlled the mall in question. As part of this transaction the defendant agreed to assume the 1978 agreement between X and the plaintiff. When the defendant acquired ownership of the mall it ageed with Y that Y should manage the mall as the defendant's agent. Y was given limited authority to enter into contracts on behalf of the defendant. The plaintiff knew nothing of the change of ownership of the mall, ie the plaintiff knew nothing of the existence of an undisclosed principal of Y. In 1985, after the automatic renewal of the rental agreement, Y entered into a new rental agreement with the plaintiff, intended by the parties to replace the original agreement. The plaintiff believed, as it had every reason to believe, it was dealing with a different corporate form of the same owner with which the plaintiff had originally contracted in 1978. Y had no authority to make this agreement. The agreement did not disclose that Y was acting as the agent of the defendant: nor did it provide for cancellation on 60 days' notice. When the plaintiff sued the defendant for breach of the new rental agreement, ie the agreement of 1985, not the original one of 1978, the defendant was held not liable as an undisclosed principal on the 1985 rental agreement. In arriving at this conclusion the court held that *Watteau v Fenwick* was not part of the law of British Columbia. It was a case of doubtful origin and unanimously unfavourable reputation.

A different approach, at least where the agent acts for an undisclosed principal, was suggested by Professor Conant, who wrote:[5] 'An undisclosed principal, being one whose agent poses as dealing for himself, creates no direct appearance to the third party. Thus he can never be charged with appearing to consent that his agent has a certain scope of authority.' The learned author's explanation of the cases in which the undisclosed principal has been liable, responsible, or bound by the agent's acts, despite any lack of express authority, is based not upon contractual estoppel, but upon an estoppel founded on apparent ownership, whether of a business, securities, or goods. Professor Conant, in propounding his objective theory of agency, is attempting to state an explanation that is applicable to both disclosed and undisclosed agency. He unites the situations of a disclosed and an undisclosed principal, so far as concerns their agents' authority, by the notion of estoppel based on apparent ownership. Whether or not his rejection of contractual estoppel in favour of this other kind of estoppel is well-founded, it is suggested that it is erroneous, and misleading, to apply it indiscriminately to disclosed as well as undisclosed agency. Indeed, it can be said that the various attempts to reconcile the case law in this area have gone awry because of a failure to appreciate and take into account the crucial differences between these two distinct commercial situations.

The problem stems from the fact that some of the cases have been concerned with disclosed agency, whereas others have been concerned with concealed

---

5 'The Objective Theory of Agency' (1968) 47 Nebraska LR 678 at p 686: cf Hornby, [1961] CLJ 239: *Bowstead and Reynolds on Agency* (16th edn) p 418.

agency. In the latter different considerations are applicable. The writers have examined this issue in relation to disclosed agency and have talked in terms of apparent authority when in fact there is no holding out as an agent since the third party did not know or have reasonable grounds for believing that he was dealing with an agent. What the cases considered above indicate, it is suggested, is that, where a person is employed in a position which usually carries with it the authority to transact certain kinds of legal business, such a person will still be endowed by the law with this authority, despite any undisclosed limitation which may have been made by the principal. The true explanation of this, *where the agency is disclosed*, is not apparent, or ostensible authority, ie not estoppel; it is that what would normally be expected to be the situation must be taken as being the situation, unless there are indications to the contrary arising from the conduct of the parties or the external circumstances as appreciated by anyone dealing with the agent. In such cases the usual authority of the agent continues to operate, despite the secret limitation. But this does not invest the agent with apparent authority. For his authority is not apparent: it is implied, ie it is what he would normally be entrusted with by his principal.[6]

Where the agency is undisclosed, the explanation is not in terms of either implied or apparent authority, since the third party knows nothing of any principal. It has been suggested that where, as in *Watteau v Fenwick*, an undisclosed principal is involved, it would be better to regard the agent's authority as usual authority, in so far as the agent is employed in a trade, business or profession in which a certain authority may be usual, and to regard usual authority, in such instances, not as a variety of implied authority, as previously described,[7] but as an independent type of authority.[8] As such it would involve what has been termed 'inherent agency power'.[9] This is not an easily digestible or acceptable idea; and it has been criticised.[10] The trouble is that, unless there is some sort of limitation on the power of the agent of an undisclosed principal to bind that principal, such a principal may be exposed to the prospect of unlimited responsibility (unless he can invoke the doctrines of 'identification' and 'personality' that will be discussed in due course[11]). Professor Conant's analysis is an attempt to provide such a limitation. So, too, is the notion of usual authority as an independent type of authority. There is something intrinsically undesirable, however, about proliferating the different kinds of authority with which an agent may be invested. Hence, presumably, the language of the courts in cases like *McLaughlin v Gentles*, (or *Sign-O-Lite Plastics Ltd v Metropolitan Life Insurance Co*), where an undisclosed principal was held not to be liable without

---

6 Cf *Restatement, Second, Agency*, paras 161, 194 and Reporter's Notes. In other words, a lack of consent by the principal, where he would normally have impliedly consented to the investing of the agent with the authority in question, must be manifested to the outside world if it is to be effective. In this sense, it is suggested, this authority may be said to be *actual*, despite the prohibition.
7 Above, p 64.
8 *Bowstead and Reynolds on Agency* (16th edn) pp 106–109.
9 *Restatement, Second, Agency* paras 8A, 140. See Fishman, 'Inherent Agency Power—Should Enterprise Liability Apply to Agents' Unauthorized Contracts?' (1987) 19 Rutgers LJ 1.
10 Conant (1968) 47 Nebraska LR 678 at pp 686–687.
11 Below, pp 258–264.

limit for what his agent did, by refusing to invoke the *Watteau v Fenwick* notion of usual authority. Even that exposition would put *some* boundaries upon the undisclosed principal's liability. However, it must be conceded that the logical and reasonable interpretation and application of the *Watteau v Fenwick* doctrine could lead to absurd and unreasonable results where undisclosed principals are involved. Hence, in the final analysis, it may have to be said that the notion of usual authority, although largely created and supported by cases dealing with undisclosed principals, is not truly applicable to such cases; and that, for reasons of policy, the doctrine is not properly applicable unless what the agent has done is directly connected with the business with which he has been entrusted.[12] Thus it is time that in England, as in British Columbia and Ontario, *Watteau v Fenwick* should be discarded.

The foregoing discussion, it should be stressed, pertains to situations in which the agency has been created by contract (or consent) either in advance or as a result of ex post facto ratification. They must be differentiated from cases where someone is an agent not because he has been created such by the principal, but because of the doctine of estoppel,[13] and the authority of the agent, which is apparent, also stems from what would be usual or normal in instances of this kind, *if the person believed to be an agent had actually been appointed agent by the principal*. In such cases the apparent authority of the agent seems to be a kind of usual authority: (and, therefore, is wrongly termed 'implied' authority, because of the association, already described, between implied and usual authority). But in the cases under discussion in this chapter the situation is different. The agent is *in fact*, not by virtue of estoppel, an agent. His authority is *actual*, not apparent, even though, in part it may be implied and not express. Its extent is measured in terms of what is expressly stated to be within its scope plus what is implicit. That which is implicit is that which is usual or normal. This must still govern his authority, not only as between principal and agent, but also as between principal and third party, unless and until a third party has notice that what is usual or normal has been excluded.

If this explanation is accepted, then the difficulties alleged to result from the cases discussed above can be seen to be imaginary. But it is essential to differentiate usual authority which is implied from usual authority (in a much broader, looser sense) which is apparent, and comes into operation only where the agency relationship exists or may be said to extend because of the operation of the doctrine of estoppel. Though seemingly the same, these situations are very different. Distinguished, they cause no trouble: confused, they lead to misunderstanding.

Customary authority. Where an agent is employed to act for his principal in a certain place, market, or business, then the agent is impliedly authorised to act

---

12 Cf the treatment of the issue of ratification of an agent's unauthorised acts, by the undisclosed principal, in *Keighley, Maxsted & Co v Durant* [1901] AC 240: below, pp 89–90, in particular the refusal to invoke any doctrine of usual or apparent authority: see Higgins 'The Equity of the Undisclosed Principal' (1965) 28 MLR 167 at pp 173–174.
13 Below, ch 6.

according to the usages and customs of such place, market, or business.[14] Such customary authority is a variety of usual authority, itself an illustration or variety of the agent's implied authority. Thus in *Bayliffe v Butterworth*:[15]

> The principal authorised a broker (A) to sell shares for him. A sold them to X, another broker, but failed to deliver the shares. X bought other shares, at the market price, and claimed the difference from A, who paid X and then sued his principal for the sum. There was a custom among brokers at Liverpool, where these transactions took place, for brokers to be responsible to each other on such contracts, and the principal knew about this custom. He was therefore liable to reimburse A.

Parke B put the rule in these words:[16]

> 'If there is, at a particular place, an established usage in the manner of dealing and making contracts, a person who is employed to deal or make a contract there has an implied authority to act in the usual way.'

In *E Bailey & Co Ltd v Balholm Securities Ltd*[17] brokers in cocoa and sugar were held to be agents even though, in accordance with custom, they acted in their own name and made themselves personally liable to the third party. Hence their action in closing certain accounts was not unauthorised and therefore did not involve a breach of contract. The principals were therefore liable to the brokers. So, too, in *Limako B V v Hentz & Co Inc*,[18] it was held that brokers were entitled to act as principals when dealing with clients in the particular market involved, namely, the Cocoa Terminal Market. In another instance,[19] in which a similar custom was validly asserted to govern the agency relationship, the consequence was that the agent was not liable to repay the principal money given by the principal to the agent which the agent had not paid to third parties. Hence the agent, which was an advertising agency, could recover its fees from a client in respect of advertisements placed in the press on the client's behalf, even though the client had previously given the agency money with which to pay newspapers in which the client's business had been advertised.

The custom must be known to the principal, or be so notorious that the principal cannot be heard to say that he has no knowledge of it. Moreover, the custom must be reasonable[20] and lawful.[1] If, while lawful, it is not a reasonable

---

14 See, eg *Goodey and Southwold Trawlers Ltd v Garriock, Mason and Millgate* [1972] 2 Lloyd's Rep 369: custom as to receipt of deposit on purchase of ship by ship brokers bound the principal who was held liable for the return thereof to the third party: cf what is said as to *estate agents* below, p 82. As to what is 'usage', see the judgment of Ungoed-Thomas J in *Cunliffe-Owen v Teather and Greenwood* [1967] 3 All ER 561 at 572–573.
15 (1847) 1 Exch 425.
16 Ibid at 428; cf Alderson B, ibid, at 429. See an Australian case, *Bell Group Ltd v Herald & Weekly Times Ltd* [1985] VR 613, principal bound by rules and regulations of the local Stock Exchange when he enployed a broker to buy or sell securities on the floor of the Exchange.
17 [1973] 2 Lloyd's Rep 404.
18 [1978] 1 Lloyd's Rep 400; affd [1979] 2 Lloyd's Rep 23.
19 *Press and General Publicity Services v Bilton* [1979] CLY 26.
20 *Pollock v Stables* (1848) 12 QB 765; *Reynolds v Smith* (1893) 9 TLR 494: cf below, note 7.
1 But see the curious case of *Seymour v Bridge* (1885) 14 QBD 460, where a custom of the Stock Exchange which contravened an Act of 1867 was nevertheless upheld, so as to permit indemnification of a broker and prevent his being declared a defaulter. Contrast *Perry v Barnett* (1885) 15 QBD 388.

custom then the principal will not be bound by it unless he expressly consents to be bound by it.[2] His implied assent to be bound by custom of the trade, place, or business, only operates where the custom is reasonable. This is particularly true where the custom in question is one which is in conflict with, or affects the inherent nature of the agency relationship. Such a custom would not be regarded as reasonable. For such a custom to be binding it must be specifically incorporated in the contract which creates the relationship of principal and agent. In the absence of such consent, 'although a custom of trade may control the mode of performance of a contract, it cannot change its intrinsic character.'[3] Thus in *Robinson v Mollett*:[4]

> The principal authorised his agent, a tallow broker, to buy tallow for him. The agent, in accordance with a custom in his trade, bought tallow in his own name, in larger quantities than the principal needed, and he allotted to this principal the amounts the principal required. The principal refused to accept the goods, whereupon the agent sold the tallow and sued the principal for the difference in price. It was held that the agent could not succeed. The principal was not bound by this custom of the trade of which he had no knowledge, because the effect was to make the agent a principal vis-à-vis third parties, which was inconsistent with the character of the broker.

'This mode of executing the order', said Blackburn, J[5] (who dissented on the ground that the custom was not unreasonable, but did not disagree with the principles of law involved), 'was a departure from the ordinary duty of a broker (that duty requiring the broker to establish privity of contract between the two principals)'. Moreover the way in which the agent transacted the business involved him in a conflict between his duty to his principal and his interest as a purchaser of tallow on his own account.[6] This could not be permitted by custom of the trade without the consent of the principal.[7]

In *Anglo-African Merchants Ltd v Bayley*,[8] Megaw J held that an insurance broker could not argue that he had customary authority to obtain a report from assessors on an insurance claim in respect of a policy the broker had placed for

2 *Cunliffe-Owen v Teather and Greenwood*, above, at 573. Cf *MacManus Realty Ltd v Bray* (1971) 14 DLR (3d) 564.
3 *Robinson v Mollett* (1875) LR 7 HL 802 at 816 per Mellor B; cf ibid at 828, 829 per Cleasby B, at 836, per Lord Chelmsford. If a custom changes the character of the agency relationship, it could be said that it operates in breach of the contract of agency, or in breach of an implied term of such contract. On that basis, it could further be said that such a custom was not only unreasonable but also unlawful, since a breach of contract is unlawful, according to the decision in *Rookes v Barnard* [1964] AC 1129, [1964] 1 All ER 367. For an attempt to assert a custom which conflicted with a solicitor's duty towards his client, see *Brown v IRC* [1965] AC 244, [1964] 3 All ER 119 as to the use of client's money. The aftermath of this case was the passing of the Solicitors Act 1965, s 8: (see now Solicitors Act 1974, s 33).
4 Above; cf *Nickalls v Merry* (1875) LR 7 HL 530; *Blackburn v Mason* (1893) 68 LT 510.
5 (1875) LR 7 HL 802 at 809.
6 On which see further below, pp 175–181.
7 But in *Jones v Canavan* [1927] 2 NSWLR 236 an Australian court held that, in the circumstances of that case, a custom that the agent could act for *both* parties to a transaction (normally something which cannot be done: below, pp 179–180) was reasonable and therefore valid. Cf *Kelly v Cooper* [1993] AC 205, below, p 175. Contrast *McDonnell v Barton Realty Ltd* [1992] 3 NZLR 418.
8 [1969] 2 All ER 421 especially at 429–430: cf also below, p 179.

the insured, his principal, when the instruction to obtain such a report had come from the insurers, ie, the third party, unless the broker had disclosed that he wished to be free to act in accordance with such customary practice, and the client, his principal, had agreed to his so acting, with full knowledge of what was involved in such collaboration between his agent and the insurers, the third party. Otherwise the broker would be in breach of his duty as an agent. In deciding this, Megaw J said that even if the practice was well known to persons seeking insurance, a custom would not be upheld by the courts if it contradicted the vital principle that an agent may not at the same time serve two masters, two principals, in actual or potential opposition to one another unless he had the explicit informed consent of both principals. An insurance broker was in no privileged position in this respect. This was followed by Donaldson J in *North and South Trust Co v Berkeley*,[9] in which the agent obtained an assessor's report for brokers for whom the agent had obtained insurance on goods for his original principal. This was held to be in breach of the agent's duty to his original principal: but that did not mean that the agent was compelled to disclose to such principal the confidential information revealed in the report in question, as it was not obtained in the service of that principal, nor in discharge of any duty owed to such principal by the agent.

A valid and normally applicable custom will not affect an agency relationship created by contract where the contract of agency expressly excludes such custom. In *Benham and Reeves v Christensen*,[10] the plaintiffs, estate agents, asserted that they could invoke a custom to the effect that they could erect signs on property with which they were dealing on behalf of their principal. The principal did not want such signs erected and, when they were, he refused to pay ten per cent of the agents' bill. He was not bound to pay that amount, as he had informed the agents that he did not want the signs erected, with the result that the contract between the parties contained a term to such effect thereby making the custom inoperative.

D. THE IMPLIED AUTHORITY OF CERTAIN KINDS OF AGENTS

The extent of an agent's implied authority varies considerably with the nature of the business in which he is employed, and with the trade or other customs and usages which normally govern and define the performance of his everyday employment. The illustrations given must not be taken as being the only examples of the exercise of an implied authority by the agents particularised. Nor must the agents given be regarded as the only kinds of agents who may be said to be invested with implied, in addition to express, authority.

Factors. A factor may sell the goods entrusted to him for sale in his own name[11] unless he has been instructed to sell in the name of his principal.[12] If he does sell

9 [1971] 1 All ER 980, especially at 992–993.
10 [1979] CLY 31.
11 *Baring v Corrie* (1818) 2 B & Ald 137.
12 *Stevens v Biller* (1883) 25 Ch D 31.

in his own name he may receive payment of the purchase price.[13] He may sell in the way he thinks best,[14] including on credit, as long as the credit is reasonable.[15] He may also warrant the goods sold, provided that the giving of a warranty in respect of such goods is customary.[16]

At common law he may not pledge the goods,[17] or barter them,[18] if he has been instructed to sell them. However, by so doing he may affect or extinguish his principal's title, in view of the provisions of the Factors Act 1889.[19]

Brokers. A broker may act in accordance with the usages and rules of the market in which he normally deals. For example, a broker who had been forced to follow a custom of the Leeds Stock Exchange and pay the differences on the price of shares which had to be resold because of the principal's failure to pay the broker, and the broker's consequent inability to pay the vendor of the shares, could recover this from his principal.[20] A broker could close his client's account on the failure of the client to pay the balance due for differences by the current pay day.[1] A broker could rescind the sale of bonds discovered to be not genuine.[2] A broker instructed by several principals could make one contract in his own name for the total number of shares[3] and apportion them among his principals, thereby establishing privity of contract with each principal and the jobber, even if he included in the contract shares with which he was dealing on his own account.[4]

Such usage or rule must not be illegal or unreasonable.[5] However, in *Seymour v Bridge*[6] the custom was in contravention of a statute,[7] yet the custom was upheld, apparently because it was well known.[8] It is difficult to know when a custom is unreasonable. Thus in some cases[9] a contract made by a broker in his

---

13 *Drinkwater v Goodwin* (1775) 1 Cowp 251; *Fish v Kempton* (1849) 7 CB 687.
14 *Smart v Sandars* (1846) 3 CB 380.
15 *Houghton v Matthews* (1803) 3 Bos & P 485.
16 *Dingle v Hare* (1859) 7 CBNS 145. For a case where the implied authority to warrant was accepted, see *Benmag Ltd v Barda* [1955] 2 Lloyd's Rep 354.
17 *Paterson v Tash* (1743) 2 Stra 1178.
18 *Guerreiro v Peile* (1820) 3 B & Ald 616.
19 Below, pp 290–300.
20 *Pollock v Stables* (1848) 12 QB 765. In respect of shipbrokers see, *Goodey and Southwold Trawlers Ltd v Garriock, Mason and Millgate* [1972] 2 Lloyd's Rep 369.
  1 *Davis & Co v Howard* (1890) 24 QBD 691. See also *Samson v Frazier Jelke & Co* [1937] 2 KB 170, [1937] 2 All ER 588.
  2 *Young v Cole* (1837) 3 Bing NC 724.
  3 Although a broker cannot contract in his own name: *Baring v Corrie* (1818) 2 B & Ald 137. As to cocoa and sugar brokers see, *E Bailey & Co Ltd v Balholm Securities Ltd* [1973] 2 Lloyd's Rep 404, cf *Limako BV v H Hentz & Co Inc* [1979] 2 Lloyd's Rep 23.
  4 *Scott and Horton v Godfrey* [1901] 2 KB 726.
  5 *Robinson v Mollett* (1875) LR 7 HL 802; cf as to an insurance broker settling with underwriters by setting off debts due from such broker, *Sweeting v Pearce* (1859) 7 CBNS 449; affd (1861) 9 CBNS 534.
  6 (1885) 14 QBD 460.
  7 Banking Companies (Shares) Act 1867. This Act has now been repealed by the Statute Law Revision Act 1966.
  8 Contrast *Perry v Barnett* (1885) 14 QBD 467: affd 15 QBD 388.
  9 *Cropper v Cook* (1868) LR 3 CP 194; *Scott v Godfrey* (above); *E Bailey & Co Ltd v Balholm Securities Ltd* (above).

own name has been upheld on the basis of a custom of the market allowing it: in others such a contract has not been upheld.[10]

Auctioneers. An auctioneer has implied authority to sign a contract on behalf of both vendor and purchaser,[11] but not where there has been a mistake on the part of either party.[12] Nor has he authority to receive payment except in cash.[13] Nor can he give credit.[14] Furthermore he cannot warrant the goods he sells.[15] If the sale is advertised as being subject to a reserve price[16] the auctioneer has no authority to sell at less than the reserve, so that his principal will not be liable on the sale,[17] but the auctioneer will be liable for breach of the implied warranty of authority.[18]

Shipmasters. Apart from the authority conferred on a shipmaster under the doctrine of agency of necessity,[19] such an agent is invested with a very wide implied authority, which extends to the doing of all the things that may be necessary for the due and proper prosecution of the voyage.[20] Thus, for example, he may render salvage service to ships in distress,[1] pledge his principal's credit for repairs and stores that are reasonable and necessary to obtain on credit,[2] and borrow money on the credit of the owners when communication with them is impossible and they have no solvent agent on the spot who can advance the money.[3] By statute[4] the master of a ship, or someone with the express, implied or apparent authority of the carrier to sign bills of lading, can sign such a bill, which will then be conclusive evidence of the shipment or receipt of the goods in favour of the lawful holder of the bill.

Estate agents. An estate agent instructed to find a purchaser for his principal's property ordinarily has no implied authority to delegate his representation to a

10 *Robinson v Mollett* (above).
11 *Rosenbaum v Belson* [1900] 2 Ch 267.
12 *Van Praagh v Everidge* [1903] 1 Ch 434.
13 *Williams v Evans* (1866) LR 1 QB 352.
14 Cf the similar position of brokers: *Wiltshire v Sims* (1808) 1 Camp 258.
15 *Payne v Leconfield* (1882) 51 LJQB 642.
16 For the effects of this in relation to the sale of goods, see Sale of Goods Act 1979, s 57 on which see *Benjamin's Sale of Goods* (4th edn 1992) para 2–006.
17 *McManus v Fortescue* [1907] 2 KB 1. But see *Garnier v Bruntlett* (1974) 236 Estates Gazette 867, sale by auctioneer at reserve price *after* public auction. On the situation when there were two separate auctioneers, the first having failed to achieve the reserve price, see *Barnard Marcus & Co v Ashraf* [1988] 1 EGLR 7, [1988] 18 EG 67, CA.
18 *Fay v Miller, Wilkins & Co* [1941] Ch 360, [1941] 2 All ER 18. See pp 243–249.
19 Below, p 135.
20 *Arthur v Barton* (1840) 6 M & W 138; *Beldon v Campbell* (1851) 6 Exch 886. In modern times, when communication has improved, the implied authority of shipmasters may be of less practical importance.
1 *The Thetis* (1869) LR 2 A & E 365.
2 *Gunn v Roberts* (1874) LR 9 CP 331.
3 *Arthur v Barton* (1840) 6 M & W 138.
4 Carriage of Goods by Sea Act 1992, s 4, which reverses the decision in *Grant v Norway* (1851) 10 CB 665.

sub-agent,[5] or to make a contract for the sale of the property.[6] But one employed to *sell* property at a fixed price has such authority.[7]

A question which caused much judicial debate was whether an estate agent had implied authority to receive a deposit from a prospective purchaser of the house or property the agent was employed to sell on behalf of the owner. In *Ryan v Pilkington*,[8] the Court of Appeal held that an estate agent was impliedly authorised to accept a deposit from a prospective purchaser; therefore the owner was liable. In *Burt v Claude Cousins & Co*,[9] over the dissent of Lord Denning MR, who doubted the validity of the earlier decision,[10] the majority of the Court of Appeal held that the agent had implied authority to ask for and receive such a deposit, as this was something reasonably incidental to his functions as an estate agent selling property. Moreover, the owner had put it into the power of the agent to receive the deposit, so he should be held liable for any default on the part of the latter. Subsequently, in *Barrington v Lee*,[11] the Court of Appeal, doubting the *Burt* case, without overruling it, held that, in a somewhat similar situation, the owner was not liable to the third party. But this was because the facts showed that the agent had received the deposit as *stakeholder* not as agent:[12] he had involved himself in personal liability to return the deposit to the third party on demand: and the third party had first sued the agent for the money and only proceeded against the owner when the judgment obtained against the agent could not be satisfied.[13]

The House of Lords resolved this conflict in *Sorrell v Finch*.[14] There an estate agent had taken deposits from several prospective purchasers of a house owned by the defendant who had instructed the agent to deal with it. Each such purchaser was given a receipt for his money. The receipts identified the house and purchase price and stated that the receipt was for a preliminary deposit or balance of the deposit on such house 'subject to contract'. The defendant was not mentioned in the receipt nor was any indication of the capacity in which the agent received the deposit. When the agent disappeared and a prospective purchaser sued the defendant for the return of his deposit, the House of Lords, reversing the trial judge and the Court of Appeal, held that the defendant was not liable. Although the members of the House gave different reasons for arriving at that conclusion, it would appear to be now settled that the mere employment of

5 *John McCann & Co v Pow* [1975] 1 All ER 129: below, pp 164–171.
6 *Hamer v Sharp* (1874) LR 19 Eq 108. Although if the circumstances of the case justify it, such authority may be inferred, as in *Davies v Sweet* [1962] 2 QB 300, [1962] 1 All ER 92. So, too, if he is held out as having authority: *Walsh v Griffiths-Jones* [1978] 2 All ER 1002. See also *Michael Elliott & Partners Ltd v UK Land plc* [1991] CLY para 107.
7 See the law as summarised by Russell J in *Keen v Mear* [1920] 2 Ch 574.
8 [1959] 1 All ER 689, [1959] 1 WLR 403, followed in *Goding v Frazer* [1966] 3 All ER 234.
9 [1971] 2 QB 426, [1971] 2 All ER 611.
10 Which he thought was based on *apparent* or *ostensible* authority: [1971] 2 All ER at 617.
11 [1972] 1 QB 326, [1971] 3 All ER 1231.
12 Cf *Wolf v Hosier & Dickinson Ltd* [1981] CLR 89.
13 There was an interesting sequel to this case. In *Potters v Loppert* [1973] Ch 399, [1973] 1 All ER 658 (following the old case of *Harington v Hoggart* (1830) 1 B & Ad 577) it was held that an estate agent taking a deposit as a *stakeholder* was not liable for interest on the money in question, only the return of the principal amount, since he held under a contractual, or quasi-contractual, obligation, not a fiduciary one.
14 [1977] AC 728, [1976] 2 All ER 371. See Seepersad (1978) 122 Sol Jo 479, 496. See also Fridman (1982) 20 UWOLR 23 at pp 36–41.

an estate agent to 'sell' a house does not, of itself, without some express statement or some holding out by the owner of the property endow the agent with any authority to receive a deposit from would-be purchasers, so as to make the owner liable for such money. Such an estate agent does not have implied authority, as an estate agent, to receive and accept such deposits on behalf of the owner.

Solicitors. Solicitors have implied authority to receive payment for debts they are instructed to claim by action[15] and in some instances may receive payment under a deed.[16] When undertaking the conduct of litigation for a client they may compromise or abandon the action.[17] But they have no implied authority to compromise a claim where the action has not yet begun,[18] nor to receive payment of purchase money (except as stated above),[19] nor to receive a bankruptcy notice on behalf of a client.[20]

15 *Yates v Freckleton* (1781) 2 Doug KB 623.
16 Law of Property Act 1925, s 69.
17 *Re Newen, Carruthers v Newen* [1903] 1 Ch 812; *Butler v Knight* (1867) LR 2 Exch 109; *Re Wood, ex p Wenham* (1872) 21 WR 104. As long as the compromise does not include matters collateral to the action: *Waugh v H B Clifford & Sons Ltd* [1982] Ch 374, [1982] 1 All ER 1095. Cf two Canadian cases in which the authority of a solicitor to settle an action on behalf of his client was discussed: *Scherer v Paletta* (1966) 57 DLR (2d) 532: *Propp v Fleming* (1968) 64 WWR 13. Contrast *Philipp v Southam* (1981) 9 Man R (2d) 413. But the lawyer may have *apparent* authority in this respect: *Landry v Landry* (1981) 128 DLR (3d) 570; *Pineo v Pineo* (1981) 45 NSR (2d) 576; *Revelstoke Companies Ltd v Moose Jaw* [1984] 1 WWR 52. In *Wright v Pepin* [1954] 2 All ER 52, [1954] 1 WLR 635 it was held that a solicitor authorised to take steps to put his client's affairs in order was impliedly authorised to acknowledge a mortgage, so as to defeat the Limitation Act.
18 *Macaulay v Polley* [1897] 2 QB 122.
19 *Bourdillon v Roche* (1858) 27 LJ Ch 681.
20 *Singer v Trustee of the Property of Munro* [1981] 3 All ER 215: cf as to estate agents *Woeller v Orfus* (1979) 106 DLR (3d) 115. See, generally, Fridman, 'Lawyers as Agents' (1987) 36 UNBLJ 9.

CHAPTER 5

Agency resulting from ratification

A. What ratification means

The previous chapter has described how the relationship of principal and agent can be created before anything has been done by the agent on behalf of the principal. In such instances the agent's authority to act is granted before the exercise of that authority. With 'ratification' the position is reversed. What the 'agent' does on behalf of the 'principal' is done at a time when the relation of principal and agent does not exist: (hence the use in this sentence, but not in subsequent ones, of inverted commas). The agent, in fact, has no authority to do what he does at the time he does it. Subsequently, however, the principal, on whose behalf, though without whose authority, the agent has acted, accepts the agent's act, and adopts it, just as if there had been a prior authorisation by the principal to do exactly what the agent has done. The interesting point, which has given rise to considerable difficulty and dispute, is that ratification by the principal does not merely give validity to the agent's unauthorised act as from the date of the ratification: it is antedated so as to take effect from the time of the agent's act. Hence the agent is treated as having been authorised from the outset to act as he did. Ratification is 'equivalent to an antecedent authority'.[1]

The effect of ratification will be discussed in greater detail later: for the moment it suffices to express it in the usual way, namely that its effect is to treat the parties as having been in the relationship of principal and agent before the agent acted on behalf of the principal, exactly as if they had expressly or impliedly created that relationship in the ways explained in the previous chapter. As Tindal CJ said in *Wilson v Tumman*:[2]

'That an act done, for another, by a person, not assuming to act for himself, but for such other person, though without any precedent authority whatever,

---

1 *Koenigsblatt v Sweet* [1923] 2 Ch 314 at 325 per Lord Sterndale MR. See, for example, *The Pindaros* [1983] 2 Lloyd's Rep 635; and the Canadian case of *DCH Services Ltd v Newfoundland Salvage Ltd* (1987) 61 Nfld & PEIR 68, in both of which ratification was an alternative basis for the liability of the principal; *Irving Oil v Slattery* (1983) 44 NBR (2d) 602; revsd (1984) 48 NSR (2d) 1.

Ratification is defined in the American Restatement as 'the affirmance by a person of a prior act which did not bind him but which was done or professedly done on his account whereby the act, as to some or all persons, is given effect as if originally authorised by him': *Restatement, Second, Agency*, para 82. For a discussion of ratification, and particularly the question of retroactivity, see Procaccia 'On the Theory and History of Ratification in the Law of Agency' (1978) 4 Tel Aviv U Studies in Law 9.

2 (1843) 6 Man & G 236 at p 242.

becomes the act of the principal if subsequently ratified by him, is the known and well-established principle of law. In that case the principal is bound by the act, whether it be for his detriment or his advantage, and whether it be founded on a tort or a contract, to the same effect as by, and with all the consequences which follow him from the same act done by his previous authority.'

It will be seen later that, to a large extent, the same result follows in respect of third parties who may have been affected by the agent's act. Such a third party is bound to, or can recover from the principal. The effect of ratification is to create privity of contract between the principal and a third party, just as if the agent had been acting with authority on behalf of an undisclosed or unnamed principal.[3] Since the third party, dealing with the agent, who at that time was not authorised to act, intended to contract with an agent, and through him with a principal, there is nothing illogical or detrimental in holding such a third party bound to the principal by the transaction when the principal subsequently ratifies the agent's act. All that happens is that the real intention of the parties is given effect to by the doctrine of ratification.[4]

This identity of intention on the part of both agent and third party is one of the distinguishing features of the doctrine of ratification, as compared with the more illogical, and more difficult doctrine of the undisclosed principal. Where there is an undisclosed principal, the third party (unlike the agent) always intends to transact with someone who is in fact an agent, but whom he believes is a principal; hence the appearance of another person claiming to be a party to the transaction, by virtue of the fact that he is a principal although hitherto undisclosed, can seriously affect the position of the third party. Therefore the law adopts a different attitude to such cases, and provides for different rules.[5]

---

3 *National Oilwell (UK) Ltd v Davy Offshore Ltd* [1993] 2 Lloyd's Rep 582 at 597 per Colman J. Hence an interesting suggestion has been made in respect of the decision in *Johnson Matthey & Co Ltd v Constantine Terminals Ltd* [1976] 2 Lloyd's Rep 215. This case concerned the loss of silver sent by the plaintiffs for carriage by rail to Milan. International Express collected the silver and delivered it to Constantine Terminals at a shed belonging to the London International Freight Terminal. The contract between Continental and International contained certain exceptions from liability. The silver should have been put in a secure export cage. Because this was full and no railway wagons were available the silver was placed elsewhere, and later stolen. When the plaintiffs sued Constantine and International, Donaldson J held (at 222) that the plaintiffs, the original bailors, could not rely on the sub-bailment to Constantine in order to make them liable for the theft, without also being bound by the exceptions contained in the contract between International and their sub-bailees, Constantine. In doing so, it is suggested, the learned judge was invoking the doctrine of ratification, to create privity of contract between the bailors and the sub-bailees, or something very close to that doctrine. The suggestion that ratification could be used to explain and justify this decision was rejected by Lord Goff in *The Pioneer Container* [1994] 2 AC 324 at 341, [1994] 2 All ER 250 at 261. The owner could hold a sub-bailee responsible as bailee without relying on the contract of sub-bailment: therefore his doing so did not amount to ratification of the terms of that contract if unauthorised by him.
4 *Keighley, Maxsted & Co v Durant* [1901] AC 240 at 263 per Lord Lindley.
5 See further below, pp 253–272.

B. Requirements for ratification

In *Firth v Staines*[6] Wright J gave three conditions that had to be satisfied to constitute a valid ratification. First, the agent whose act is sought to be ratified must have purported to act for the principal. Secondly, at the time the act was done the agent must have had a competent principal. Thirdly, at the time of the ratification the principal must be legally capable of doing the act in question himself. This analysis brings out the four features of ratification which are important: the principal's position; the agent's intentions; the legal quality of the act done by the agent; and the time when ratification takes place. These elements require further elaboration, discussion and illustration.

The principal's position. (a) The principal must be in existence at the time the act was done by the agent. No one can purport to act as an agent for a person who will come into existence at some future date, even if the agent can reasonably expect that his acts will be adopted. 'Ratification can only be . . . by a person in existence either actually or in contemplation of law.'[7] This means that the principal must be a live human being, or a juristic person. This latter category clearly includes limited companies, as long as such a company is in existence, not in liquidation and carrying on business of some sort. Hence in *Lawson v Hosemaster Machine Co Ltd*[8] a company which was being managed by a receiver was a company which, through a subsequent receiver, could ratify the acts of an earlier receiver.

Where a company is not yet in existence 'in contemplation of law', but is in the pangs of birth, it would seem that the common law continues to apply, and such a company will not be able to ratify a contract purported to be made on its behalf once the company has achieved legal existence.[9] In other common law jurisdictions statutes have greatly enlarged the capacity of such companies to ratify pre-incorporation contracts so as to make them liable thereon.[10] However,

---

6 [1897] 2 QB 70 at 75. This passage and the succeeding paragraph were referred to by Dea DCJ in *Edwards Real Estate Ltd v Bamtar Holdings Ltd* (1978) 7 Alta LR (2d) 52 at 53. The first few sentences of this paragraph were cited by Cameron J in *DCH Services Ltd v Newfoundland Salvage Ltd* (1987) 61 Nfld & PEIR 68 at 71.

7 Willes J in *Kelner v Baxter* (1866) LR 2 CP 174 at 184. Does this include unborn children, as to which see *Elliot v Joicey* [1935] AC 209. It certainly excluded a non-existent investment group on whose behalf the agent purported to act in *Edwards Real Estate Ltd v Bamtar Holdings Ltd* (1978) 7 Alta LR (2d) 52, and a corporation that never existed: *Westcom Radio Group Ltd v MacIsaac* (1989) 70 OR (2d) 591.

8 [1966] 2 All ER 944.

9 See *Gowers' Principles of Modern Company Law* (5th edn 1982) p 304, note 54, p 306. See *Kelner v Baxter* (1866) LR 2 CP 174; *Natal Land and Colonization Co Ltd v Pauline Colliery and Development Syndicate Ltd* [1904] AC 120; *Newborne v Sensolid (GB) Ltd* [1954] 1 QB 45, [1953] 1 All ER 708. See also Gross 'Pre-Incorporation Contracts' (1971) 87 LQR 367; Gosse 'Liability on Pre-Incorporation Contracts' (1972) 18 McGill LJ 514; Markesinis, 'The Law of Agency and Section 9(2) of the European Communities Act 1972', [1976] CLJ 112 at pp 114–124; Easson and Soberman, 'Pre-Incorporation Contracts: Common Law Confusion and Statutory Complexity' (1992) Queens LJ 414.

10 Eg, the Ontario Business Corporations Act, RSO 1990, c B16, s 21(2); Canada Business Corporations Act RSC 1985, c C-44, s 14(2). For the personal liability of the agent see RSO 1990, c B16, s 31(1)(4) and RSC 1985, c C-44, s 14(1)(4).

nothing, as yet, has been achieved in this respect. What has occurred, is the alteration of the position with respect to those acting, or purporting to act as agents, on behalf of such companies. The previous possible inability of such persons to sue on, and immunity from suit in respect of such contracts,[11] was originally changed by the European Communities Act 1972, s 9(2) which is now contained in the Companies Act 1985, s 36C.[12] What that statute provides, and how it has altered the law, will be examined in due course.[13] It must be noted here, however, that this statutory provision does not in any way affect the question of ratification after incorporation and commencement of trading by a company of a contract allegedly made on the company's behalf prior to the coming into legal existence of such company. Reform of the law in this respect is still to be achieved, even though, in consequence of the recent statute, those dealing with such a company may not be as deprived as once they were of any remedy or relief in respect of transactions entered into before the company was legally born.

(b) Not only must the principal be in existence at the time the act was done: he must also be ascertained at that time.[14] This means that the principal must either be known, or must be capable of identification. It is not necessary that he should be named but there must be such a description of him as will amount to a reasonable description of the person intended to be bound as principal.[15] For it is

11 *Newborne v Sensolid (GB) Ltd*, above, where the agent could not sue on the contract because he had not contracted an agent but had merely signed for the company which had contracted directly with the defendants: (see the discussion in *Phonogram Ltd v Lane* [1982] QB 938, [1981] 3 All ER 182); *Dairy Supplies Ltd v Fuchs* (1959) 18 DLR (2d) 408, where the agent could not be sued by the supplier of goods to a company for the price of the goods since the agent had made it clear that the supplier intended the company to be its debtor and the agent had made it clear that he was not going to be liable personally. As indicated in these cases (and others, discussed below, pp 237–242), everything turned upon the manner and capacity in which the agent contracted. Cf *Elders Pastoral Ltd v Gibbs* [1988] 1 NZLR 596.

12 Substituted for the original s 36(4) of the 1985 Act by the Companies Act 1989, s 130(4): see *Halsbury's Statutes* (4th edn reissue 1991) Vol 8, p 156. This provision applies to registered and unregistered companies incorporated in and having a principal place of business in Great Britain: Companies Act 1985, s 718(1), Sch 22; Companies (Unregistered Companies) Regulations 1985, SI 1985 680, amended by SI 1990 Nos 438, 1394, 2571: but see also s 718(4). It also applies to companies registered outside Great Britain, by the Foreign Companies (Execution of Documents) Regulations, SI 1994 No 950.

13 Below, pp 354–356.

14 *Kelner v Baxter* (1866) LR 2 CP 174 at 184 per Willes J.

15 Willes J in *Watson v Swann* (1862) 11 CBNS 756 at 771. It was objected (see Bridge, (1977) 14 JSPTL at p 151) that what is meant by 'identifiable' has not been clarified. With respect, this is unjustified comment. What Willes J meant seems clear enough: that from the description given by the agent of his principal the third party should be able to appreciate with whom he is contracting, or believes that he is contracting, so that the third party can decide whether or not he should continue with the transaction and bind himself to the indicated and 'identified' principal.

The reviewer in question also put forward the 'reasonable proposition that any disclosed principal should be able to ratify subject to cases where the third party might be entitled to object to the personality of the principal'. Again with respect, this is to miss the point. Where a principal is *undisclosed*, there might indeed be scope for some later objection on grounds of personality to the subsequent intervention of such principal (see below, pp 262–264). Where a principal is disclosed, all that would appear to be required, or indeed necessary, is that the disclosure is sufficiently detailed so that the third party can be aware of the other potential contracting party: at that stage he can decide what he wishes to do, to contract or not contract.

essential that third parties should know with whom they are contracting.[16] Thus in *Watson v Swann*:[17]

> An agent was instructed to effect a general policy of insurance on goods for a principal. He was unable to do so. Therefore he declared the goods on the back of a general policy of insurance effected for himself. The goods were subsequently lost and the principal sued on the policy. It was held that he could not recover since the policy was not expressed to be made on his behalf at the time it was taken out, therefore he could not ratify the agent's act so as to benefit from it.

It follows from this that the only person who can ratify an agent's act is the person on whose behalf the act was expressed to be done. The agent must purport to act on behalf of an identified, or indentifiable person, and under the authority of that person, before that person can ratify the agent's act. Hence, only the person under whose authorisation the agent has purported to act can take the benefit of, or be made liable under the agent's act. Thus in *Wilson v Tumman*:[18]

> A sheriff, under a writ of execution, wrongfully seized goods which were not the property of the judgment debtor. When it was sought to make the execution creditor liable for this trespass it was held that he was not liable because the execution creditor could not ratify the sheriff's act so as to become liable for the sheriff's trespass. This was because the sheriff acted in pursuance of a public duty, under the authority of the law which ordered him to seize the debtor's goods, not under the authority, and on behalf of the execution creditor.

Similarly in *Barclays Bank Ltd v Roberts*:[19]

> A sheriff's officers, in execution of a writ of possession obtained by the bank, evicted a sub-tenant who was stated by the bank's solicitors to be wrongfully in possession of the bank's premises. In fact the solicitors were incorrect. When the bank was sued by the sub-tenant it was held that there was no liability, because the sheriff's officers were not acting as agents for, and under the authority of the bank; they were acting under the authority of a writ of possession, ie, as agent of the court, not of the bank.

It is not clear whether the reviewer making these comments intended that the law should be that an agent acting without authority should indicate that there are *several* possible principals, identifying each and every one of them, without attributing his agency to any particular principal, so that any of them could later ratify. If this is what is meant, the author would not be in agreement, since to permit this would be to undermine the very nature of the doctrine of ratification as it has been developed, and would have serious practical consequences in that it would mean that a third party might never be certain with whom he was contracting (even though he might be able to escape from a contractor if he did not like the nominated or intervening principal). Either consequence, it is suggested, would be commercially, and otherwise, unsatisfactory.

16 *Watson v Swann* (1862) 11 CBNS 756 at 773; cf *Gewa Chartering BV v Remco Shipping Lines Ltd* [1984] 2 Lloyd's Rep 205 at 210 per Webster J.
17 Above.
18 (1843) 6 Man & G 236.
19 [1954] 3 All ER 107, [1954] 1 WLR 1212. For the suggestion that the requirement that the agent purported to act as agent has a different meaning in relation to ratification of a tort as compared with ratification of a contract, see Tedeschi 'Authorization of Torts' (1969) 4 Israel LR 1 at p 15.

The position is the same in the law of contract, as is shown by the leading case of *Keighley Maxsted & Co v Durant*:[20]

> X was authorised to buy wheat on the joint account of X and Y with a limit as to the price he could pay. X entered into a contract for the purchase of wheat at a price in excess of the limit on behalf of himself and Y. But he did not disclose to the seller of the wheat his intention to contract on Y's behalf as well as his own. Y later purported to ratify X's act and was subsequently sued by the seller for breach of the contract.

The point at issue was stated in these terms by Lord Davey:

> 'The question of law is whether a contract made by a man purporting and professing to act on his own behalf alone and not on behalf of a principal but having an undisclosed intention to give the benefit of the contract to a third party, can be ratified by that third party so as to render him able to sue or be liable to be sued on the contract.'[1]

The House of Lords was unanimous in saying that this could not be done. Y was therefore not liable. The rationale of the judgments is succinctly summarised by Lord Macnaghten's remark that 'civil obligations are not to be created by, or founded upon, undisclosed intentions'.[2] If a relationship of principal and agent is to exist and affect third parties, it must be based upon knowledge on the part of all concerned, and their joint intention that such a relationship should exist and affect right and liabilities.

This is a rather wide statement of the principle contained in Lord Macnaghten's remark, for, as will be seen in later chapters, the doctrine of the undisclosed principal is in complete contradiction to it and the doctrine of vicarious liability in tort also does not depend upon any knowledge of the existence of a principal on the part of the injured third party. It would, perhaps, be safer to restrict that remark to the field of contract, and to say further that, for reasons of policy, there is an important exception to the doctrine that civil obligations do not arise from undisclosed intentions, namely the anomalous doctrine of the undisclosed principal. But elsewhere in the law of agency, as will be seen, the position of a third party cannot be affected by intentions of which he has no actual knowledge, or of which he cannot reasonably be expected to know. In *Keighley Maxsted & Co v Durant*, the House of Lords refused to extend the doctrine of the undisclosed principal any further and distinguished that doctrine

---

20 [1901] AC 240. The case is really one of an agent acting for an undisclosed principal, exceeding an authority which was in fact granted, not assuming an authority which had never actually been granted: but the principle is the same. Cf also *Saunderson v Griffiths* (1826) 5 B & C 909; *Bird v Brown* (1850) 4 Exch 786. The case is strongly criticised by Stoljar *Law of Agency* pp 199–201, on the ground of being contrary to early authority and theoretically at fault. It is also criticised by Rochvarg 'Ratification and Undisclosed Principals' (1989) 34 McGill LJ 286. He concludes that ratification by undisclosed principals should be allowed.

For a more recent example, see the Canadian case of *Crampsey v Deveney* (1969) 2 DLR (3d) 161, where the Supreme Court of Canada held that children who were joint tenants with their mother of some land could not ratify her sale of the land because she had not purported to act on their behalf. See also *Trident General Insurance Co Ltd v McNiece Bros Pty Ltd* (1987) 8 NSWLR 270; affd (1988) 165 CLR 107.

1 [1901] AC at 253.

2 Ibid at 247. Cf Lord Shand at 250, Lord James at 251, Lord Davey at 256, Lord Lindley at 265.

from ratification on the ground of the difference between the intentions of the agent in the two cases.[3] However, the decision clearly lays down that, without disclosure of the intention to act as agent, there can be no later ratification by another person.

Although this case was followed and applied by the Court of Appeal in *Spiro v Lintern*,[4] it may be argued that the decision in that case suggests a way in which the rigours of the *Keighley Maxsted* rule may be overcome in appropriate circumstances. In *Spiro v Lintern*:

> The defendant (H) owned a house and told his wife to arrange for an estate agent to find a purchaser. But he did not give the wife authority to sell. Through the estate agent, the wife agreed to a sale to the plaintiff, and a written agreement of sale was entered into and signed by the plaintiff and the estate agent as agent for the vendor. H allowed the plaintiff (who had instructed an architect to undertake certain functions on his behalf in respect of the house) to carry out repairs to the house, to prevent damage by damp. He also permitted the plaintiff's gardener to work in the garden. Later, before going abroad, H gave his wife a power of attorney empowering her to complete the sale of the house. The wife transferred the house to a third party, X. The plaintiff sued for specific performance. It was held that the plaintiff could not rely on the doctrine of ratification, so as to argue that H's conduct after the wife had contracted with the plaintiff amounted to ratification of the transaction, because at the time the wife contracted she was acting for an undisclosed principal. However, the Court of Appeal, affirming the trial judge, held that the plaintiff's action succeeded by the application of the doctrine of estoppel.

What the court held was that, because the husband knew of the plaintiff's belief that the husband was bound to him (because everyone at the earlier stage of the transaction believed that the wife was the owner of the house), the husband was under a duty to disclose the true state of affairs to the plaintiff. By not making such disclosure, at any appropriate time, ie by his silence and inaction, the husband had represented to the plaintiff that the wife had authority to sell the house.[5] On the faith of that representation, the plaintiff had been induced to act to his detriment. Therefore the husband was estopped from asserting that the contract had been entered into without his authority.[6] Consequently he was bound to the plaintiff. It would seem to emerge from this decision, therefore, that an undisclosed principal who is aware that his agent has contracted with a third party, in circumstances in which such third party believes that a binding obligation has come into existence, and will bind everyone (including the undisclosed principal, even though the third party is unaware of his existence), will be estopped from raising his agent's lack of authority, and will not be able to rely on the inapplicability of the doctrine of ratification, as long as the undisclosed principal's failure to clarify the mistake of the third party has led the latter to act to his detriment. This doctrine might have made a difference, on

---

3 [1901] AC at 256 per Lord Davey.
4 [1973] 3 All ER 319, [1973] 1 WLR 1002.
5 Ibid at 326–327.
6 Ibid at 328–329.

the facts, in the *Keighley Maxsted* case itself: it will only make a difference where the facts of any given situation permit the invocation of notions of mistake, representation, estoppel, and detriment. How far this may be said to undermine the *Keighley Maxsted* doctrine is a matter of speculation. It does not repudiate the doctrine itself: quite the reverse, since the doctrine was applied in *Spiro v Lintern*.[7] At best what it does is to open up to third parties a potential method of binding an undisclosed principal in the absence of ratification, and even where ratification would be impossible as a matter of law.

(c) Before ratification can validly take place the principal must be aware of all the material facts. 'Acquiescence and ratification must be founded on a full knowledge of the facts.'[8] So in *Savery v King*:[9]

> X on Y's behalf entered into a mortgage agreement, which in fact was invalid. Afterwards Y acted in a way which showed that he was purporting to adopt the transaction. But it appeared that Y did not know the mortgage was invalid. It was held that Y's purported ratification was to no effect.

On the other hand there may be liability for some acts performed by the agent even in the absence of complete knowledge, if there was no inquiry as to the true state of affairs, and consequent assumption of the risks involved, ie if there was negligence on the part of the principal.[10] In *Marsh v Joseph*:[11]

> X's name was used by Y in fraudulent proceedings, whereby Y obtained some money. Y then told X about the use of his name, but did not inform him of the fraud. X took some of the money which Y had told him he obtained on his behalf. When later the fraud was discovered and X was sued for the return of *all* the money, it was held that X's acts, in the absence of knowledge of the fraud, did not amount to ratification; therefore he was not liable for all that had been obtained by Y. But X was liable for the money he had actually acquired through Y.

In so far as ratification is applicable in relation to liability for torts, as opposed to contractual liability, the knowledge that is required on the part of the principal is knowledge of the *acts* performed by the agent, and not necessarily knowledge of the *legal quality* of those acts, unless there is the assumption of the risk involved in acceptance of the acts. In other words, ratification in the law of tort means

---

7 Ibid at 326–327.
8 *Banque Jacques-Cartier v Banque d'Epargne de Montreal* (1887) 13 App Cas 111 at 118: cf *Briess v Woolley* [1954] AC 333 at 344, [1954] 1 All ER 909 at 912 per Lord Oaksey. This would seem to mean knowledge of all the facts known to the agent of which it was objectively necessary for the principal to be aware in order to be able to decide whether or not to affirm: *Brennan v O'Connell* [1980] IR 13.
9 (1856) 5 HL Cas 627. See also *Spackman v Evans* (1868) LR 3 HL 171. Cf a Canadian case: *Ryder v Osler, Wills, Bickle Ltd* (1985) 16 DLR (4th) 80, unsophisticated investor did not ratify wrongful acts by stockbroker of which she was ignorant. Nor did estoppel operate in the absence of such knowledge on her part.
10 *Welch v Bank of England* [1955] Ch 508 at 534, [1955] 1 All ER 811 at 822–823, per Harman J where it was held on the facts that the plaintiff's negligence, in respect of *some* transactions, did not amount to ratification (or give rise to estoppel): below, p 118.
11 [1897] 1 Ch 213.

something quite different from ratification in relation to contract. Thus in *Hilbery v Hatton*:[12]

> The plaintiff's ship was unlawfully purchased by X, the defendant's agent. Later the defendant purported to approve and ratify X's act, but the defendant did not know that the sale to X was unlawful. None the less it was held that the defendant was liable for conversion of the ship.

Since conversion can be committed unwittingly, in the sense of without knowledge of the unlawful nature of the act one is committing,[13] it would seem that the defendant in this case, by merely accepting X's act, could properly be held to have ratified it for the purposes of liability, even though there was not that 'full knowledge of the facts' or 'all the essential facts'[14] that is necessary where a contract is involved. On the other hand, where liability in tort does depend upon a state of mind, such as the intention to commit a wrongful act, then it may well be that there is no ratification of any such sort committed by an agent acting without authority, unless there is both knowledge of the surrounding circumstances which show that the agent's act was illegal and acquiescence in the agent's state of mind, as well as knowledge and acceptance of the agent's acts.

What has just been said about the meaning and relevance of ratification in relation to torts would appear also to be true in respect of criminal liability. Where mens rea is required for such liability, knowledge of the act performed by the agent is not sufficient to make the principal who ratifies liable: there must also be knowledge of the circumstances which indicate that the act is criminal.[15] Where mens rea is unnecessary, then adoption of the act may be sufficient to involve the principal in criminal liability. In this connection there is a dictum of Rowlatt J which throws some doubt upon the possibility that there can be ratification of a crime. In *Harrisons and Crossfield Ltd v London and North Western Rly Co*[16] he said that 'it may be that a person cannot ratify an act when

---

12 (1864) 2 H & C 822. Contrast *Lewis v Read* (1845) 13 M & W 834, where it was held that a principal could not be liable for an unauthorised, unlawful distraint by his agent unless he received the proceeds with full knowledge of the irregularity, or recklessly undertook the risk without inquiry. See, generally, Stoljar *Law of Agency* pp 179–182, who argues in favour of the redundancy of ratification as regards tort liability. Somewhat the same view is propounded by Tedeschi, (1969) 4 Israel LR 1 at pp 9–15. In the light of the argument that agency in contract is different from agency in tort, above, pp 36–37, this is tenable and valid. Contrast Atiyah *Vicarious Liability in the Law of Torts* ch 28, who deals with ratification as giving rise to vicarious tort liability, although in relation to the acts of a *servant* rather than an agent.

13 *Hollins v Fowler* (1875) LR 7 HL 757. Note the notion of wrongful interference with goods under the Torts (Interference with Goods) Act 1977, which has not otherwise redefined the old law: *Salmond and Heuston on the Law of Torts* (20th edn 1992) at p 95.

14 *Eastern Construction Co v National Trust Co Ltd and Schmidt* [1914] AC 197 at 213 per Lord Atkinson.

15 Contrast *R v Woodward* (1862) Le & Ca 122 with *R v Dring* (1857) Dears & B 329.

16 [1917] 2 KB 755 at 757. It would seem that ratification of a criminal act will not be possible so as to *legalise* the act: *Brook v Hook* (1871) LR 6 Exch 89: *Bedford Insurance Co Ltd v Instituto Co Ltd v Instituto de Resseguros do Brasil* [1985] QB 966, [1984] 3 All ER 766 below, pp 95–96

the ratification involves the adoption of a criminal element'. The context of the case makes it doubtful whether this remark was intended to refer to cases of crime, unconnected with tortious or other liability.[17]

(d) Lastly, there is the question of capacity. 'At the time the act was done,' said Wright J,[18] 'the agent must have had a competent principal.' This means that the principal must be qualified in law to act in the way the agent has acted. Therefore, infants, mentally incompetent, and other incapacitated persons may not be able to ratify acts purporting to be done on their behalf, in the same way that such persons may not be able to appoint agents by prior agreement before the agent performs acts on their behalf.[19] A case which illustrates this is *Boston Deep Sea Fishing and Ice Co v Farnham.*[20]

> When France was occupied in 1940 a trawler owned by a French company (X) was in an English port. An English company (Y) which had previously acted as X's agent in the course of its business, carried on trade using X's trawler. But Y had no authority to do so at the time, although they pretended to have. Y were never formally appointed managers of X's business, but they kept accounts of the takings, expenses, and profit, after deducting their commission. Y were assessed to tax in respect of their profits of their trade with X's trawler, on the footing that Y had been X's agent. By Rule 10 of the All Schedules Rules to the Income Tax Act 1918, Y would not be liable to tax unless they were 'an authorised person carrying on a regular agency' on behalf of X. It was held that the only way Y could be so authorised was by X's purported ratification, after the war. But such ratification was impossible in law because at the time of Y's purported agency X were alien enemies[1] therefore incompetent to be a principal since they could not have acted for themselves.

Furthermore, at the relevant time, the principal must have had the capacity to enter into the particular transaction which was carried out by the agent on his behalf. Hence there can be no ratification of acts which are ultra vires the

---

17 Below, p 106. Note that *R v Woodward* and *R v Dring* (in which the crime was receiving through a wife) are not inconsistent with this dictum, since they must be regarded as cases of primary, direct liability (in that the husband was or was not a party to the receiving), not cases involving vicarious liability through the acts of an agent without personal participation which, in general, is only possible where the crime is one which can be committed without any mens rea. See further, below, pp 334–341.
18 *Firth v Staines* [1897] 2 QB 70 at 75.
19 See above, p 57. Compare *Dibbins v Dibbins* [1896] 2 Ch 348 at 353, per Chitty J. This may explain, in part at least, not only the decision in *that* case, but also the decision in *Bird v Brown* (1850) 4 Exch 786: below, p 98.
20 [1957] 3 All ER 204, [1957] 1 WLR 1051 (referred to, apparently with approval, by Danckwerts LJ, in *Lawson v Hosemaster Machine Co Ltd* [1966] 2 All ER 944 at 951): cf *Kuenigl v Donnersmarck* [1955] 1 QB 515, [1955] 1 All ER 46.
 1 Applying *Sovfracht (Valuation Officer) v Van Udens Scheepvaart en Agentuur Maatschappij (N V Gebr)* [1943] AC 203, [1943] 1 All ER 76: on which see Fridman 'Enemy Status' (1955) 4 Int & Comp LQ 613.

principal. This point was of great importance in company law.[2] But it applies elsewhere. Thus in *Firth v Staines:*[3]

> A committee of a metropolitan vestry directed a sanitary inspector to serve a notice to abate a nuisance upon someone and to lay an information and take other proceedings if the notice were not complied with. Upon the non-abatement of the nuisance a summons was issued against the respondent. It was held that the respondent ought to be convicted, because by its subsequent ratification the vestry had authorised the committee to take the necessary action: and the vestry, under statute,[4] had the power so to authorise the committee.

The agent's intentions. At the time of contracting, the agent must contract as agent for a definite, identified, or identifiable, principal, who is the person who later ratifies.[5] 'If the agent, when he made the agreement', said Holroyd J in *Saunderson v Griffiths,*[6]

> 'had professed to have authority to act for A . . . then the subsequent ratification would have been a ratification of the authority which the agent assumed to have when he made the agreement. But here A never previously authorised the agent to make the agreement on his behalf, nor is he named as a party for whom the latter professed to act.'

Hence, in that case, A's purported ratification of a contract made by the agent in the name, and on behalf of A's wife and X was of no effect, and A could not sue upon it.

If Lord Macnaghten's remark about 'undisclosed intentions' is remembered, it will be seen that this requirement on the part of the agent is the same as the requirement about the identification of the principal, seen from a different standpoint. The important point to be borne in mind is that, so far as contractual obligations are concerned, it is essential that the identity of the person with whom the contract is purported to have been made should be known to the third party. Hence the position of the principal, the question whether he can validly ratify the agent's act, is determined by reference to the way the transaction appears to the third party: and this depends upon what the agent has shown his intention to be.[7]

2 *Ashbury Rly Carriage and Iron Co Ltd v Riche* (1875) LR 7 HL 653, with which contrast *Irvine v Union Bank of Australia* (1877) 2 App Cas 366.
   Note, however, that someone dealing in good faith with a company may be protected despite the company's lack of capacity or limitations on the power of directors: see now Companies Act 1985, s 35 as substituted for the original provision by the Companies Act 1989, s 108(1) and in effect from 4 February 1991 by SI 1990 No 2569. *Halsbury's Statutes* (4th edn Reissue) Vol 8, pp 153–154. See below, pp 354–355.
3 [1897] 2 QB 70.
4 Metropolis Management Act 1855, s 58.
5 *Wilson v Tumman* (1843) 6 Man & G 236; cf above, p 88: see *Rhodian River Shipping Co SA v Halla Maritime Corpn* [1984] 1 Lloyd's Rep 373; *National Oilwell (UK) Ltd v Davy Offshore Ltd* [1993] 2 Lloyd's Rep 582 at 597, Colman J. Note that the principal could only ratify to the limited extent of the scope of the insurance policy negotiated by the agent; ibid at 579–602.
6 (1826) 5 B & C 909 at 915.
7 Though the *contents* of the contract may depend on the agent's *subjective* intention: *National Oilwell (UK) Ltd v Davy Offshore Ltd* above note 5.

This explains the decision in *Keighley Maxsted & Co v Durant*, discussed above. It also explains the decision in *Re Tiedemann and Ledermann Frères*:[8]

An agent acted in X's name as principal, though intending the sale to be for his own benefit and to his own account. The third party later wanted to avoid the contract when he found out the truth, on the ground of the false pretence about the party with whom he was contracting. X purported to ratify the sale. It was held that he could do so and thus deprive the third party of his right to turn a voidable contract into a nullity.

Another aspect of this case will be mentioned later. For the moment the point to notice is that since the agent's intention appeared to the third party to be to contract as agent for X, ratification by X was possible, despite the secret, opposite intention of the agent. X could therefore obtain the advantage of a contract not intended to be made for his benefit.[9]

The legal quality of the act. The possibility of ratification depends upon the principal's personal capacity to perform the act himself at the time that the agent performs it for him.[10] The issue must also be looked at in terms of the act itself, ie whether it is one that can be ratified.

Theoretically, provided the principal is aware of the facts,[11] any act can be ratified. But it has been said that there can be no ratification of a legal nullity,[12] or, as it was put more recently, 'life cannot be given by ratification to prohibited transactions.'[13] Doubt has been expressed whether acts which amount to crimes can be ratified. The dictum of Rowlett J in *Harrison and Crossfield Ltd v London and North Western Rly Co* has already been quoted. Moreover in *La Banque Jacques-Cartier v La Banque d'Epargne de Montreal*[14] Lord Fitzgerald said:

'Acquiescence and ratification . . . must be in relation to transaction which may be valid in itself and not illegal and to which effect may be given as against the party by his acquiescence in and adoption of the transaction.'

These dicta are supported by the case of *Brook v Hook*.[15] There

The agent forged his principal's signature as the maker of a promissory note. Before the note matured the holder discovered the forgery and threatened to

8 [1899] 2 QB 66.
9 A neat converse is provided in *Trueman v Loder* (1840) 11 Ad & El 589. There an agent had acted in the past for X, who later terminated the agent's authority. This was not known to the third party, to whom the agent in the course of business sold goods, intending the sale to be on his own account, but, in the circumstances making it appear that, as before, he was acting as X's agent. It was held that, notwithstanding the secret intention of the agent, X was bound to the third party as principal to the contract.
10 Above, pp 57–59.
11 What amounts to 'awareness' is discussed above, p 91.
12 Per Maugham J in *Watson v Davies* [1931] 1 Ch 455 at 469.
13 *Bedford Insurance Co Ltd v Instituto de Resseguros do Brasil* [1984] 3 All ER 766 at 776 per Parker J.
14 (1887) 13 App Cas 111 at 118.
15 (1871) LR 6 Exch 89; and by the statement of Lord Denning MR in *Stony Stanton Supplies (Coventry) Ltd v Midland Bank Ltd* (1965) 109 Sol Jo 255, that there can be no ratification of a forged document. See also *Greenwood v Martins Bank Ltd* [1933] AC 51 in which the forgery aspect of the case was discarded in favour of estoppel; cf *Spiro v Lintern*, above, pp 90–91.

prosecute the agent. Whereupon the principal purported to ratify the agent's act. Later the principal refused to pay on the note. Was he liable?

The majority of the court thought that the attempt at ratification was void because the act sought to be ratified was illegal. Martin B, dissenting, thought that the act of forging the signature was not void in itself (though if not adopted or ratified it would have been criminal) and could be adopted or ratified. The proposition that an illegal act cannot be ratified was accepted and applied by Parker J in *Bedford Insurance Co Ltd v Instituto de Resseguros do Brasil*.[16] Because contracts of insurance were illegal under the provisions of the Insurance Companies Act 1974, ss 2(1), 83(4),[17] it was not possible for the insurance company which acted through London brokers to ratify such contracts which, originally, the brokers had neither actual nor, according to the evidence, which failed to indicate reliance on representations by the principal, ostensible authority to make.

A further difficulty is created by the distinction which has been drawn (as in *Brook v Hook*) between acts which are void ab initio and voidable acts. In the case of void acts, it is said that ratification cannot affect their nullity and so make them valid. Voidable acts, on the other hand, not being complete legal nullities before avoidance has taken place, can be ratified.[18] Indeed this may occur after the attempt to avoid them has taken place, as in *Re Tiedemann and Ledermann Frères*.[19] Assuming that this distinction and its effects are accepted as correct, the problem arises how to determine whether the act in question is properly to be regarded as void ab initio or merely voidable. This is illustrated by *Danish Mercantile Co v Beaumont*:[20]

> An action was begun by agents on behalf of a limited company, but without the company's proper authorisation. Later, in the course of the proceedings the liquidator of the company (which was now in the process of winding up) purported to ratify the commencement of proceedings. It was held that the ratification was valid and the proceedings would not be stayed on the grounds that they had been instituted without authority.

Much of the discussion in the case was concerned with the meaning and application of the word 'nullity' in the context of the doctrine of ratification.[1] What the case does recognise, however, is that there may be acts which, before

---

16 [1985] QB 966, [1984] 3 All ER 766.
17 Since replaced by the Insurance Companies Act 1982 ss 2, 14, Sch 1. A different view of the original, ie, 1974 provisions and their effect was taken in *Stewart v Oriental Fire and Marine Insurance Co Ltd* [1985] QB 988, [1984] 3 All ER 777.
18 *Brook v Hook* (1871) LR 6 Exch 89 at 99; Powell *Law of Agency* (2nd edn) p 124. The distinction is criticised by *Bowstead and Reynolds on Agency* (16th edn) pp 68–69, on the ground that the 'voidable' act would be void ab initio if there were no ratification. This seems a strange criticism which misses, indeed confuses, the point.
19 [1899] 2 QB 66. Compare *Bolton Partners v Lambert* (1889) 41 Ch D 295, discussed below.
20 [1951] Ch 680, [1951] 1 All ER 925: (approved by the House of Lords in *Alexander Ward & Co Ltd v Samyang Navigation Co Ltd* [1975] 2 All ER 424, [1975] 1 WLR 673). Cf *Warwick RDC v Miller-Mead* [1961] Ch 590, [1961] 3 All ER 542 where a council could ratify a previously unauthorised issue of a writ. Compare also *Presentaciones Musicales SA v Secunda* [1994] 2 All ER 737: below, p 98.
1 See [1951] Ch 680, at 683–687, 688–689, [1951] 1 All ER 925 at 927–29, 931.

ratification, appear to be nullities (if not exactly illegal as was the act of signing in *Brook v Hook*), but may be rendered effective by the subsequent ratification. The better view would therefore appear to be that voidable acts are capable of being given effect to by ratification (subject to what is said in the next section about time for ratification): void acts cannot ever be ratified: and the case of *Danish Mercantile Co v Beaumont* involved a voidable act.

Ratification will not be allowed if it imposes a duty on a third person who before the attempted ratification was not under such duty. Thus in *Solomons v Dawes*:[2]

> The agent without authority demanded the return of the principal's goods from the defendant. Ratification by the principal could not justify the agent's demand so as to make the defendant liable in trover, because at the time of the demand to re-deliver the defendant was under no duty to deliver without enquiring into the agent's authority.

An exception seems to exist in the case of marine insurance. Under the Marine Insurance Act 1906, s 86,[3] a contract of marine insurance which bona fide, though without authority, has been effected by one person on behalf of another, may be ratified so as to entitle the assured to recover on the policy even after the assured is aware of a loss which gives rise to recovery under the policy. This does not apply to other forms of insurance, eg fire insurance.[4]

Time for ratification. Not only must the principal have capacity to ratify: he must enjoy such capacity at the time of the purported ratification. The act of ratification must be taken at a time, and under circumstances when the ratifying party might himself have lawfully done the act which he rectifies.[5] This is of greatest importance in relation to proprietary (including contractual) rights which may have vested before ratification was attempted. As Cotton LJ said in

2 (1794) 1 Esp 81. Compare *Doe d Mann v Walter* (1830) 10 B & C 626.
3 For the previous common law see *Williams v North China Insurance Co* (1876) 1 CPD 757.
4 *Grover & Grover Ltd v Mathews* [1910] 2 KB 401. This decision has been criticised: and the suggestion is made that ratification after loss should be possible in all cases of indemnity insurance: see Brown and Menezes, *Insurance Law in Canada* (2nd edn 1991) pp 50–51, citing McGillivray and Parkington *Insurance Law* (see now 8th edn 1988, para 184; see also ibid para 370), and an American decision, *Marquesec v Hartford Fire Insurance Co* 198 F 475 (1912), cert denied 299 US 621 (1913): see also *Stocks v Reliance Insurance Co* 238 NE 2d 420 (1968). They also point to the contrary statement by Lord Campbell in *Waters and Steel v Monarch Fire and Life Assurance Co* (1856) 5 E & B 870. See also *Bowstead and Reynolds on Agency* (16th edn) p 95. In *Goldshlager v Royal Insurance Co Ltd* (1978) 84 DLR (3d) 355 an Ontario judge did not follow the *Grover* doctrine but held that in Canada the weight of authority supported the conclusion that ratification after loss was possible in a case of fire insurance (following the remarks in *MacGillivray and Parkington* (8th edn para 184). Nor did an Australian judge in *Trident General Insurance Co Ltd v McNiece Bros Pty Ltd* (1987) 8 NSWLR 270 (affirmed (1988) 165 CLR 107) in which the *Waters* case and the American decisions were preferred and followed. Cf *Hughes v NM Superannuation Pty Ltd* (1993) 29 NSWLR 653 at 665.
5 *Presentaciones Musicales SA v Secunda* [1994] 2 All ER 737 at 743 per Dillon LJ, quoting from *Bird v Brown* (1850) 4 Exch 786 at 799. However, Roch LJ, ibid at 750, thought this was not a correct statement. See further below, pp 98–99.

Bolton Partners v Lambert:[6] 'An estate once vested cannot be divested . . . by the application of the doctrine of ratification.' Thus in *Donelly v Popham*:[7]

> A naval commodore, without authority, appointed the captain of a ship. When the question of sharing in prizes taken by the ship came before the court, it was held that even if the Crown ratified the appointment of this captain, the commodore would not be able to share with the captain prizes taken before the date of ratification, for shares in those prizes would already have vested in other people.

In *Bird v Brown*:[8]

> An agent, without the authority of the vendor of goods, sent a notice of stoppage in transitu. The assignees in bankruptcy of the buyer made a formal demand of the goods, tendering payment of the freight at the same time, of the master of the ship in which the goods had arrived in port. Surrender of the goods was refused: and the goods were delivered to the agents. A similar demand was made of the agents, who relied on the stoppage and refused to surrender possession to the assignees. Subsequently, another agent of the vendor, acting under a power of attorney, ratified the stoppage, which was also later ratified by the vendor himself. It was held that this attempt at ratification came too late to divest the assignees in bankruptcy of their right to obtain possession of the goods. The transit could not artificially be extended by the operation of the doctrine of ratification.

This was followed in *Dibbins v Dibbins*:[9]

> The principal was given an option to purchase the other partner's share in a partnership which had to be exercised within three months of the death of the partner in question. His agent purported to exercise this option within the three months, but at the time he did so the principal was insane, hence the agent had no authority to act. Later the agent was authorised by an order under the Lunacy Acts to act on the principal's behalf. He thereupon purported to re-exercise the option to purchase: but by this time the three months had elapsed. It was held that it was too late, because by the date of authorisation (ie ratification) the principal had been divested of his right to purchase.

More recently this issue arose in *Presentaciones Musicales SA v Secunda*:[10]

> In April 1988 English solicitors issued a writ on the instructions of a director of the plaintiff company, incorporated in Panama. The writ claimed relief

---

6 (1889) 41 Ch D 295, at 307. Cf Danckwerts LJ in *Lawson v Hosemaster Machine Co Ltd* [1966] 2 All ER 944 at 952. See also Sheller JA in *Hughes v NM Superannuation Pty Ltd* (1993) 29 NSWLR 653 at 665, Roch LJ in *Presentaciones Musicales SA v Secunda* [1994] 2 All ER 737 at 750.

7 (1807) 1 Taunt 1.

8 (1850) 4 Exch 786: see especially Rolfe B at 799–800. For another explanation of this case see above, p 93, note 19.

9 [1896] 2 Ch 348. See also *Walter v James* (1871) LR 6 Exch 124. On the effects of insanity see below, p 407.

10 [1994] 2 All ER 737.

for alleged infringements of copyright by the first defendant. In 1991 the defendants discovered that the plaintiff company had been 'dissolved' under Panamanian company law in 1987, before the writ was issued. By the law of Panama a dissolved corporation was entitled, for three years after dissolution, to initiate and defend legal proceedings: and the directors of the corporation could initiate proceedings in the corporation's name and represent it in such proceedings. In May 1991 the three directors appointed as liquidators of the plaintiff company purported to ratify the original instructions to the English solicitors to initiate the action. A preliminary issue which arose was whether, after the expiration of the three-year limitation period, the liquidators could ratify the commencement of an action began without authority within the limitation period. The trial judge held they could. His decision was upheld by the Court of Appeal.

Dillon and Nolan LJJ considered several cases, including the two just referred to above, which it was argued supported the proposition that ratification was not possible if, at the time of ratification, the unauthorised action would have been wholly or partly statute-barred. They agreed that if a time were fixed for doing an act, whether by statute or agreement, the doctrine of ratification would not apply if it would have the effect of extending that time.[11] However, *Bolton Partners v Lambert*,[12] which, as will be seen, seems to state the opposite, was to be understood as deciding that as long as the original, unauthorised act was not a legal nullity at the time of ratification, such ratification could be operative.[13] Hence, since all the claims in this case were not statute-barred, the ratification took effect.

Roch LJ, who rejected as correct the statement in *Bird v Brown* previously quoted,[14] also agreed that ratification of an act was possible as long as the act still existed at the moment of purported ratification.[15] The impossibility of a valid ratification where the original act no longer existed was one exception to the general rule as to the retroactivity of ratification stated in *Bolton Partners v Lambert*. Another, which was referred to by Roch LJ but not the other members of the court,[16] was that, in the words of Cotton LJ previously quoted, '. . . an estate once vested cannot be divested'. That exception did not apply here because the expiry of the limitation period in the present case did not create a vested right in the defendants: if it were applicable it would merely bar the plaintiff's remedies. Hence the vested right exception, which Roch LJ considered was exemplified in *Bird v Brown*, did not apply to the case before the court.

Although *Bolton Partners v Lambert* was referred to and relied on in this modern case, it was distinguished by the court in *Dibbins v Dibbins*,[17] which was

11 Ibid at 745.
12 (1889) 41 Ch D 295: below.
13 Cf *Walter v James* (1871) LR 6 Exch 124; *Pontin v Wood* [1962] 1 All ER 294.
14 Above, note 5.
15 Above, note 10 at 751.
16 Ibid.
17 Above, note 9.

also referred to by Dillon LJ. The basis for the distinction by the court in the *Dibbins* case was that there no time limit had been fixed within which ratification would have had to take place in order to be effective. In *Bolton Partners v Lambert*:[18]

> A third party made an offer to X's agent which the agent, without authority, accepted on behalf of X. The third party later purported to revoke his offer. Later still X ratified his agent's acceptance. It was held that notwithstanding the third party's attempt at revocation he was bound by the contract with X.

This is a decision which appears at first sight to be anomalous and difficult. In the first place, it is true that an offer may be revoked at any time before acceptance by the offeree.[19] But who was the offeree? It was not the agent personally, because, as far as the third party knew, the offer was being made to the agent's principal; and irrespective of the true state of affairs between principal and agent as already seen, the position must be taken in the way in which it appears to the third party. Hence, so far as the third party was concerned, there was a binding contract the moment the agent accepted his offer. On the other hand, if the principal had never ratified the agent's acceptance of the offer, there could have been no valid contract between the third party and the principal although the third party could have sued the agent for breach of the implied warranty of authority.[20] Therefore, at one and the same time it would appear that there was a contract between the principal and the third party (ie rights had vested), and there was not such a contract.

Clearly such a chaotic situation cannot be allowed to arise. Therefore a choice has to be made between treating the acceptance by the agent as a nullity, completely void ab initio (like the forgery in *Brook v Hook*), and regarding it as a voidable act (like the sale in *Re Tiedemann and Ledermann Freres*) which can be ratified so as to give it retrospective validity. It is difficult to classify the agent's acceptance in this case with the agent's forgery in *Brook v Hook*: the one is lawful (even if unauthorised), whereas the other, being unauthorised, is criminal. Hence it would seem more reasonable to regard the agent's acceptance as an act which can be repudiated or adopted by the principal at will, and so can give rise to a binding contract, which may be taken as having come into existence before the offeror attempted to revoke. This, indeed, as already noted, was the view of this case taken by Dillon and Nolan LJJ in the *Presentaciones* case. The acceptance by the agent without authority was not without legal effect. It could not be treated as a nullity. Hence the commencement of proceedings without authority in the *Presentaciones* case was also not a nullity and could therefore be ratified.

However, as realised in *Bolton Partners v Lambert* and endorsed by Roch LJ in the recent case, there are limitations on the effectiveness of a purported ratification in such circumstances.

First, ratification will be too late to support the agent's acceptance of an offer if, in the meanwhile, proprietary rights had been affected, or if to permit the

18 (1889) 41 Ch D 295.
19 *Payne v Cave* (1789) 3 Term Rep 148. Cheshire, Fifoot and Furmston's *Law of Contract* (12th edn 1991) p 57.
20 Below, pp 243–249.

ratification to be effective would prejudice the vested rights of third parties, as is illustrated by the facts of *Dibbins v Dibbins*. This, as already seen, was also given by Roch LJ in the *Presentaciones* case as an exception to the operation of ratification in accordance with the rule stated in *Bolton Partners v Lambert*. He put this exception in these words:[1]

'. . . the putative principal will not be allowed to ratify the acts of his assumed agent, if such ratification will adversely affect rights of property in either real or personal property, including intellectual property, which have arisen in favour of the third party or others claiming through him since the unauthorised act of the assumed agent.'

Roch LJ, as already stated, did not believe this exception applied in the case before him, which concerned intellectual property, namely copyrights. But he did consider that *Bird v Brown* was an example of this exception.

Secondly the situation will be different if the third party's offer was expressly made subject to ratification. In such circumstances the offer is conditional and there is no binding contract until ratification of the agent's acceptance. This is what occurred in *Watson v Davies*.[2]

The third party's offer to sell property was made to and accepted by agents who were members of a board of a charity (the charity itself being the principal). The offer, which was made subject to ratification by the board, was later revoked. Subsequently the charity, at a meeting of *all* the members of its board, ratified the acceptance by its agents. In an action for specific performance of the contract it was held that under the circumstances it was open to the third party to withdraw his offer *before* ratification since the offer was made subject to ratification. The agents' acceptance was therefore a legal nullity. Specific performance of the alleged agreement to sell was therefore denied because there was no contract.

Bolton Partners v Lambert accordingly was distinguished, and one way out of the theoretical difficulties produced by that case was indicated. Similarly in *Warehousing and Forwarding Co of East Africa Ltd v Jafferali & Sons Ltd*:[3]

The agent offered to take a three-year lease of certain premises. In his letter he made it clear that the offer was subject to the approval of his employer's general manager. The third party wrote to the principal setting out the terms of the lease, to which the principal replied, agreeing all these terms except the length of the lease, in respect of which he asked for further consideration. The third party sent a draft lease to the principal, by which time the general manager's approval of a three year lease had been received by the agent. In an action for damages for loss of rent through breach of contract for a three-year lease, the third party claimed that the general manager's approval brought a valid lease into existence. The Privy Council held that the third party's claim failed.

1 Above at 751.
2 [1931] 1 Ch 455.
3 [1964] AC 1, [1963] 3 All ER 571. This case also throws light on the time when ratification is effective, viz, on communication thereof to the third party (except where *Bolton Partners v Lambert* applies, in which instances, presumably, ratification operates when manifested by the principal, though before knowledge of such ratification on the part of a third party).

The reason for this was that the third party had knowledge that the agent was acting subject to ratification. Hence neither party could be bound until ratification by the principal had been communicated to the third party. In this case the principal had withdrawn from the contract, by disputing its terms, before the general manager's approval had been given. It is to be noted that the Privy Court differentiated 'approval' from ratification. From what was said it would appear that an agent who contracted 'subject to approval' could bind his principal, whereas an agent who contracted 'subject to ratification' could only bind his principal if the principal subsequently ratified. In this way a very fine distinction may be drawn between the application and the exclusion of *Bolton Partners v Lambert*. Indeed, it would seem from the language of Lord Guest[4] that all that is necessary to exclude this case is if the third party 'has intimation of the limitation of the agent's authority.' If that is so, then the case of *Bolton Partners v Lambert* will only apply where a third party is in ignorance of the agent's want of authority.

Thirdly, although, following *Bolton Partners v Lambert*, the contract which is ratified is considered to have been in existence from the moment when the agent in fact made it with the third party, none the less it has been held that ratification will not entitle the principal to sue for any breach of the contract which may have occurred *before* the time for ratification.[5] This suggests that the position of the third party is not as detrimental as has sometimes been indicated.[6] For if the third party, between the time of the agent's acceptance and the principal's ratification does something which, in effect, makes the contract between the third party and the principal virtually non-existent (eg commencing to work for another employer, after having agreed to work for the principal) then the third party will be able to have all the advantages of the revocation or withdrawal of his offer, even though he cannot technically revoke or withdraw it.

Taken together, therefore, these various limitations severely restrict what would otherwise appear to be a very harsh rule, resulting from the peculiarities of the doctrine of ratification. So that it is possible to reject the view that *Bolton Partners v Lambert* is wrong, or open to reversal,[7] or the view that there is only an agreement between the third party and the agent, the principal not being bound or being able to bind the third party until he ratifies the agent's act, and to adopt, instead, the view that the case is correctly decided in principle but must be

---

4 [1963] 3 All ER 571 at 575.
5 *Kidderminster Corpn v Hardwick* (1873) LR 9 Exch 13. The American *Restatement, Second, Agency*, para 89, suggests that ratification will not be effective if it would result in an inequitable subjection of the other party to liability, eg, if the subject-matter of the contract has been destroyed between contract and ratification.
6 Eg per North J in *Re Portuguese Consolidated Copper Mines* (1890) 45 Ch D 16, at 21.
7 *Fleming v Bank of New Zealand* [1900] AC 577, at 587. Seavey ('The Rationale of Agency' (1920), 29 Yale LJ 859 at p 891), criticised the case strongly and said it was wrong. His criticism was that the case invokes the worship of the fiction of relation back as a transcendental shrine. 'It creates an offer where none was intended, and imposes upon a mistaken party an obligation not imposed upon an offeror. The English Court creates before ratification . . . a one-sided obligation created elsewhere only where it has been paid for, where protection is afforded to a dependent class, or where there is fraud.' The case is supported, however, by Stoljar *Law of Agency* pp 189–193. It is cited, with several others, in support of the retrospective effect of the principal's title, cf Danckwerts LJ in *Lawson v Hosemaster Machine Co Ltd* [1966] 2 All ER 944 at 951.

understood in the light of the other requirements of the doctrine which have been discussed.[8] In this respect it should be noted that Dillon LJ, in the *Presentaciones* case,[9] could not easily discern the logic of the dividing line between cases where ratification would be retrospective and those where ratification might come too late to be effective. However, he would not determine that *Bolton Partners v Lambert* was wrongly decided and should be overruled, although the Court of Appeal was invited to do so. In view of the way that case was interpreted and applied in the *Presentaciones* case, the first modern case in many years to raise this issue, it would appear that the decision therein will remain good law unless and until the House of Lords conclude that it has created an irrational situation, requiring careful distinguishing of the decision if cases are to be decided in any consistent way.

If a time has been fixed by the parties within which ratification should occur, ratification must take place within such time. If no time has been fixed, then, it has been said that ratification must be made within a reasonable time after acceptance by an unauthorised person, in the case of a contract accepted by an agent without authority to accept.[10] That reasonable time can never extend after the time at which the contract was to commence.[11] With this latter statement Parker J disagreed in *Bedford Insurance Co Ltd v Instituto de Resseguros do Brasil*.[12] The ratification in that case would not have been too late, even though it occurred after the date the contract was to commence, had it not been for the illegality of the contract that was purportedly ratified by the principal.[13] In view of this decision, the comments on time for ratification made by Parker J must be considered to be obiter dicta. It is therefore questionable whether the validity of the earlier remarks made by Fry LJ in the earlier case has been effectively queried. The comments by Parker J, however, seem to be supported by the decision of the House of Lords in *Alexander Ward & Co Ltd v Samyang Navigation Co Ltd*[14] in which ratification was possible of the arrestment of a ship although at the time of ratification the arrestment had been discharged. However, as Lord Hailsham explained,[15] arrestment was simply a step necessary to bring the proceedings in respect of a claim against the defendants effectively into being. Hence it was as capable of being ratified as any other steps in the proceedings even though it had served the purpose for which it was intended. Hence the situation in this case could be distinguished from that which obtains in a case concerning ratification of a contract after it was intended that the contract should commence: in which event the decision in this Scottish case may not affect the issue which arises from the remarks of Parker J in the *Bedford Insurance* case.

---

8 This was the view of *Powell* pp 141–147.
9 Above at 746.
10 *Hughes v NM Superannuation Pty Ltd* (1993) 29 NSWLR 653 at 665 per Sheller JA.
11 *Metropolitan Asylums Board Managers v Kingham & Sons* (1890) 6 TLR 217 at 218 per Fry LJ.
12 [1984] 3 All ER 766 at 776.
13 Above, p 96.
14 [1975] 2 All ER 424, [1975] 1 WLR 673, HL.
15 Ibid at 430.

C. Proof of ratification

By express acts. It is accepted that generally speaking ratification need not be expressed in writing. Any act or statement which clearly shows the intention of the principal is sufficient. But if the contract made by the agent is in the form of a deed than the principal's ratification must be by deed.[16]

A problem which has arisen is whether ratification must be in writing (not necessarily in a deed) where the agent has entered into a contract which itself must be in writing, or evidenced by some writing.[17] In *Soames v Spencer*[18] it was held that a parol ratification was good even though the agent's contract with the third party had to be in writing. This case was later said by Lord Davey[19] to be explicable on the principle that fraud will not be presumed: therefore a man who assumes to sell X's property professes to act for X. Ratification of his act, therefore, need not be in writing, because, as Bayley J said in *Soames v Spencer*, the 'original authority to sell need not be in writing'. This view is accepted by some commentators,[20] and rejected by another.[1] It is difficult to see whether the case relied on for the latter view is truly supportive or merely decides that, on the facts, there was no enforceable agreement made by the agent or there was no express ratification by the principal.

Ratification, by its very nature, must take place after the acts performed by the agent. As Lord Atkin said in *Midland Bank v Reckitt*,[2] 'a ratification in advance seems to contradict the essential attributes of ratification as generally understood'. If approval of an agent's acts is given prospectively, not retrospectively, then the relationship of principal and agent has been created either expressly, or impliedly (or possibly by estoppel), and there is no need for anything further to be done by the principal in order to produce reciprocal obligations between himself and a third party.

Nor can there be a partial ratification.[3]

By implication. It has already been seen that the relationship of principal and agent can be created, before the agent acts on behalf of the principal, by a contract or other agreement which is implied from the conduct of the parties.[4] Such a relationship may arise subsequent upon the agent's acts from conduct on the part of the principal showing clearly that he has approved and adopted what has been done on his behalf.[5]

---

16 *Oxford Corpn v Crow* [1893] 3 Ch 535.
17 As to which see now the Law Reform (Enforcement of Contracts) Act 1954; and the Law of Property (Miscellaneous Provisions) Act 1989, s 2: above, p 56.
18 (1822) 1 Dow & Ry KB 32.
19 *Keighley, Maxsted & Co v Durant* [1901] AC 240 at 254.
20 *Bowstead and Reynolds on Agency* (16th edn) pp 80, 84; *Powell* p 135.
 1 Hanbury, *Principles of Agency* (2nd edn) pp 105–106, relying on *Fitzmaurice v Bayley* (1856) 6 E & B 868; revsd (1860) 9 HL Cas 78.
 2 [1933] AC 1 at 18.
 3 *Presentaciones Musicales SA v Secunda* [1994] 2 All ER 737 at 750 per Roch LJ.
 4 Above, pp 59–61.
 5 Axelrod, 'The Doctrine of Implied Ratification—Application and Limitations' (1983) 36 Oklahoma LR 849, for an American view.

Usually the principal performs some positive, unequivocal act which indicates ratification.[6] If the principal does nothing, however, it would seem that such inactivity may constitute ratification, despite the suggestion by the Supreme Court of Canada in *Crampsey v Deveney*[7] that merely standing by without objecting would not be sufficient: and that silence was not ratification.[8] However, in *Suncorp Insurance and Finance v Milano Assicurazioni SpA*[9] Waller J stated that mere acquiescence or inactivity may be sufficient to establish ratification. He questioned whether, as expressed in *Bowstead on Agency*,[10] where silence or inactivity is known to the third party an estoppel may arise against the principal. Estoppel was not relied on in the *Suncorp* case, where, on the facts, the failure of the principal to dispute the agent's authority within a reasonable time was held to amount to ratification, although no positive act of adoption occurred.[11] Waller J preferred the way the doctrine was put in *Halsbury's Laws*:[12]

'If the principal is aware of all the material facts and appreciated that he was "being regarded as having accepted the position of principal and took no steps to disown that character within a reasonable time, or adopts no means of asserting his rights at the earliest time possible" that can amount to "sufficient evidence of ratification".'[13]

This, thought the judge, was very close to estoppel but it was still ratification. It was, in his view, a correct formulation. It should not be open to a principal, who to the outside world by his conduct, or that of his duly authorised agents, appears to have adopted a transaction to be able to prove subjectively that as a fact he had not, any more than such a principal would be able to prove subjectively that he did not intend to adopt a transaction when he does an act, such as accepting payment of money, that objectively adopts the transaction.[14]

Thus the English, but not seemingly the Canadian, view is that, in certain circumstances, the inactivity of the principal can constitute implied ratification of an unauthorised act. The view expressed in the *Suncorp* case is consistent with an earlier decision[15] in which it was held that delay in repudiating an unauthorised act can sometimes amount to ratification, and with the idea that a failure to return goods obtained by an agent may well amount to ratification, unless to demand their return would be inequitable on the part of the third party.[16]

---

6 See, for example, *Canada Trust Co v Gordon* [1978] 5 WWR 268, ratification by executors of a deceased landowner of the unauthorised acts of their agents employed by them to sell the deceased's land, by their course of dealing with the purchaser introduced to them by the agent.
7 (1969) 2 DLR (3d) 161, where the fact that the children did not object until the time came for them to sign the deed transferring the land of which they were joint tenants with their mother did not amount to ratification (perhaps especially since they were originally ignorant of their interest in the land).
8 Per Judson J in *Crampsey v Deveney* (1969) 2 DLR (3d) 161 at 164.
9 [1993] 2 Lloyd's Rep 225 at 234: cf *Michael Elliott & Partners v UK Land* [1991] CLY para 107.
10 (15th edn) art 17, p 66. See now 16th edn p 80.
11 Above, note 9 at 241.
12 (4th edn Reissue) Vol 1(2), para 83.
13 Above, note 9 at 234–235.
14 Ibid at 236. See below, note 20.
15 *Prince v Clark* (1823) 1 B & C 186.
16 *Restatement, Second, Agency*, para 99.

But the compulsory acceptance of unauthorised acts on the part of the agent will not amount to ratification. Thus in *Forman & Co Pty Ltd v The Liddesdale*:[17]

> Extra repairs were done to a ship by the order of the shipowner's agent. Such repairs were not within the scope of the agent's authority. After the repairs had been done the principal took back the ship and sold it. This was held not to be ratification of the agent's acts on the part of the principal, when sued for the repairs, because he had no choice but to retake the ship when it was ready.

The case has been regarded as like the case of 'one who has received a gratuitous service which he has no option but to accept'.[18] But the rationale of the case is better expressed, as it was in the judgment,[19] as depending on the difference between taking back the principal's own property and taking goods not previously the principal's. Thus receipt by the principal of the purchase price of his goods sold without authorisation by the agent will generally be ratification.[20] But, as already stressed, there must be complete knowledge of the facts surrounding the sale and this must be proved by the party who alleges that this has taken place. Hence in *The Bonita*[1] where a shipmaster sold the ship without authority to do so, and in circumstances which did not come within the scope of his agency of necessity,[2] the owners who received the purchase money without knowledge of the circumstances of the sale were held not to have ratified the sale.[3]

There appears to be controversy about the implied ratification of part of the acts performed by the agent. *Bowstead*[4] says that adoption of part of what the agent has done amounts to ratification of all. Powell,[5] on the other hand, suggested that there could be ratification of one of a series of acts without the principal's being forced to accept all of them. Support for this view can be found in *Harrisons and Crossfield Ltd v London and North Western Rly Co.*[6] There:

> The defendants' agent fraudently obtained tea from the plaintiffs. On discovering this the defendants prosecuted their agent for stealing, laying the property in the tea in themselves, as the result of a bailment to them by the plaintiffs through the agent. The agent was convicted. Subsequently the plaintiffs sued the defendants to recover the value of the tea. It was held that the defendants had only ratified their agent's act for the purposes of the

---

17 [1900] AC 190.
18 Hanbury, *Principles of Agency* (2nd edn) p 107.
19 [1900] AC 190 at 204. Nor would there be recovery on any quasi-contractual or restitutionary ground: see Goff and Jones *The Law of Restitution* (4th edn 1993) pp 439, 441.
20 *The Bonita* (1861) 1 Lush 252 at 265 per Dr Lushington. See eg, *Findlay v Butler* (1977) 19 NBR (2d) 473.
 1 (1861) 1 Lush 252.
 2 See below, p 135.
 3 Compare *Banque Jacques-Cartier v Banque d'Epargne de Montreal* (1887) 13 App Cas 111; *Wall v Cockerell* (1863) 10 HL Cas 229.
 4 *Bowstead and Reynolds* Article 17(4), citing in support *Wilson v Poulter* (1730) 2 Stra 859; *Brewer and Gregory v Sparrow* (1827) 7 B & C 310; *Valpy v Sanders* (1848) 5 CB 886; *Smith v Baker* (1873) LR 8 CP 350; *Keay v Fenwick* (1876) 1 CPD 745.
 5 *Powell* p 138. To the same effect would seem to be *Stoljar* pp 186–187.
 6 [1917] 2 KB 755.

prosecution: what they had done did not amount to a sufficient ratification to make them liable to the plaintiffs for the acts of their agent.

Leaving aside the point, previously considered, that it was possible that ratification of an act cannot take place when it involves the adoption of a criminal element in it,[7] the case could be, and was decided on the 'subtle' consideration that, as Rowlett J said, 'all that the defendants necessarily ratified was a bare bailment'.[8] They ratified the agent's de facto possession of the goods, not any possession under a contract of carriage. Consequently, they were not liable in the absence of proof that they were negligent, ie independently of their agent's act.

On the other hand, it is clear that a principal cannot adopt whatever is advantageous to him in the acts of his agent, while repudiating whatever is onerous: and this point may explain the difference between *Bowstead* and *Powell*; for some of the cases cited by *Bowstead* are cases where the principal was seeking to adopt and repudiate different aspects of the agent's acts. For example, in *Union Bank of Australia v McClintock*.[9]

> The agent fraudently obtained bearer drafts on the principal's bank in exchange for the principal's cheques also drawn on the bank. The agent then for his own benefit paid the drafts into the X Bank, which collected by money due on them from the principal's bank. When the fraud was discovered the principal sued the X Bank for conversion of the drafts. It was held that he could only do this if he ratified his agent's acts. But this involved accepting what the X Bank had done, which, therefore, did not amount to conversion.[10]

Moreover in a case involving express ratification[11] Roch LJ agreed that there could be no partial ratification. If this is true of express ratification, it would seem to be equally valid where ratification is implied.

D. The effect of ratification

The general principle, as already seen, is that a valid ratification produces the same result as if the agent has acted under an antecedent authority. 'Ratification, as we all know', said Harman J in *Boston Deep Sea Fishing and Ice Co v Farnham*,[12] 'has a retroactive effect'. Some limitations on this have already been

7 Above, p 92.
8 Above, note 6 at 759.
9 [1922] 1 AC 240. This was followed in the very similar case of *Commercial Banking Co of Sydney Ltd v Mann* [1961] AC 1, [1960] 3 All ER 482 (criticised by Hornby (1961) 24 MLR 271). The *McClintock* case was also followed in *Souhrada v Bank of New South Wales* [1976] 2 Lloyd's Rep 444, where an agent was held to have implied authority to pay cheques into his own account, with the result that the bank was entitled to deal with the cheques: but the bank was also protected by the application of the doctrine of ratification. It was distinguished by Laskin CJC in *Canadian Laboratory Supplies Ltd v Engelhard Industries of Canada Ltd* (1979) 97 DLR (3d) 1 at 11–13.
10 [1922] 1 AC 240 at 248 per Lord Sumner.
11 *Presentaciones Musicales SA v Secunda* [1994] 2 All ER 737 at 750: above, p 98.
12 [1957] 3 All ER 204 at 209. Cf Dankwerts LJ in *Lawson v Hosemaster Machine Co Ltd* [1966] 2 All ER 944 at 951; Lord Morris of Borth-y-Gest in *Alexander Ward & Co Ltd v Samyang Navigation Co Ltd* [1975] 2 All ER 424 at 426.

seen: and in the ensuing section further comments upon this will be discussed. For the moment it is necessary to consider how far the situation produced by subsequent ratification is comparable to the position where in fact an antecedent authority has been given to the agent.

In the first place, the relations between principal and agent appear to be the same. Thus in *Risbourg v Bruckner*:[13]

> The agent's contract with a third party was later ratified by the principal. Therefore only the third party could be sued for breach of that contract, not the agent, since, once the relationship of principal and agent was created by ratification, the agent, as in the case of a previously created agency, ceased to be a party to the contract between the principal and the third party.[14]

The rights of the agent against the ratifying principal are illustrated by *Keay v Fenwick*:[15]

> The managing owner of a ship sold it through an agent. Later all the co-owners, who had not previously authorised the sale, ratified what had been done. It was held that all the owners, not merely the managing owner, were jointly liable to the agent for his commission.

But ratification only operates in respect of *past* acts on the part of the agent. It does not authorise the agent to perform further acts in the future.[16] Nor does ratification require that the agency relationship be terminated, or notice of termination be communicated to the third party. Hence the argument of Powell[17] that the similarity between prior authorisation and subsequent ratification does not exist.

Secondly, the agent, who may have been liable to the third party for breach of implied warranty of authority,[18] ceases to be subject to such liability; and, as seen above, is no longer personally liable to the third party in any other way[19] unless expressly made a party with the principal by the contract, or other transaction involved. Furthermore, ratification may operate to turn what was an unlawful act on the part of the agent, for which he was liable to the third party, into a lawful act, for which, in consequence, there will be no liability. So in *Whitehead v Taylor*:[20]

> The agent (after his principal's death terminated his authority) distrained on X for rent due. This, in the circumstances, was wrongful. Later the principal's executor ratified the agent's act. No action for unlawful distraint could then be brought against the agent.

13 (1858) 3 CBNS 812.
14 See further below, p 216.
15 (1876) 1 CPD 745.
16 *Irvine v Union Bank of Australia* (1877) 2 App Cas 366. Note also that the conduct of the children in *Crampsey v Deveney* (1969) 2 DLR (3d) 161 not only did not amount to ratification: it did not give rise to any representation as to the authority of the mother to act as agent for the children. Compare, however, *Spiro v Lintern* [1973] 3 All ER 319, [1973] 1 WLR 1002, discussed above, pp 90–91.
17 *Powell*, pp 139–140.
18 Below, p 243.
19 *Risbourg v Bruckner*, above; *Spittle v Lavender* (1821) 2 Brod & Bing 452.
20 (1839) 10 Ad & El 210.

Thirdly, the principal and the third party are in direct relationship with each other, eg through a contract, as if there had been an antecedent authorisation of the agent's act. But this statement must be considered in the light of what has previously been said about the divesting of proprietary rights, prejudice of vested interests, and rights of action in respect of breaches of contract that occurred before the ratification; though these matters are better regarded as part of the law relating to the requirements of a valid ratification.

E. The nature of the doctrine

From what has been said in the previous sections, there are obvious difficulties in accepting the orthodox view that ratification is exactly the same as a prior authorisation. Hanbury[1] and *Bowstead*[2] seem to accept ratification as the retrospective creation of the principal–agent relationship. But Powell and Seavey did not.

Seavey,[3] stressing the notion that ratification involves a 'fiction', in that the relations between all the parties are treated 'as if' the agency has preceded what the agent has done, argued that the doctrine of ratification is not connected with the creation of agency, but is quite distinct. 'So far from being the creation of a power in an agent', he said,[4] 'ratification is the exercise of a power created in one not a principal by one not an agent, but who purports to be one'. Seavey had doubts about the logical place of ratification in the scheme of agency. He would appear to have had the agreement of Powell,[5] who considered it an anomaly with some anomalous rules, and thought that the relationship of principal and agent is not created by ratification because 'that relation depends on agreement, and a one-sided adoption by P of A's unauthorised act cannot produce an agreement'. All that ratification does is to give 'the effects of authorisation to the unauthorised act'.[6]

This view is the result of regarding ratification as a 'unilateral act of the will'.[7] But is it correct to describe ratification in this way? Admittedly, everything depends upon the will of the party who has been cited as principal. If that party chooses not to adopt the act done on his behalf, no relationship of principal and agent will result. To that extent it is true that ratification is a one-sided act. But there is also the act of the agent to be considered; for the agent, in stipulating to the third party (which he must do, as already seen) that he is acting on behalf of a principal, is also saying to that principal that he is willing to act as his agent. Ratification by that principal is therefore acceptance of the agent's offer to act as

---

1 *Hanbury* p 100.
2 *Bowstead and Reynolds* Article 20(1): cf ibid, Article 13 and comment thereon, pp 62–64.
3 *The Rationale of Agency* (1920) 29 Yale LJ 859 at pp 886–892.
4 Ibid at p 886.
5 *Powell* pp 120, 138–139.
6 *Powell* p 120: Seavey justified ratification on the ground that what the law is doing here, as elsewhere, is to fulfil the reasonable expectations of the parties, in particular the third party: (1920) 29 Yale LJ 859 at pp 887–888. Note also the other instances of 'relation back' he cited ibid at p 889.
7 Rowlett J in *Harrisons and Crossfield Ltd v London and North Western Rly Co* [1917] 2 KB 755 at 758.

his agent. Since consideration is not required for ratification any more than it is necessarily required for the prior creation of the relationship of principal and agent,[8] ratification can also be regarded as a consensual, not one-sided act, the equivalent of a prior authorisation.

On the other hand, it is quite true that there are limitations, already noticed, upon the doctrine of ratification, limitations which do not operate where the agency was created prior to the acts of the agent. This means, as Powell pointed out,[9] that the doctrine is not allowed to become inequitable. But it does not mean that the doctrine is an anomalous fiction which does not logically belong to that part of the law of agency which deals with the creation of the agency relationship. When Powell limited the effect of ratification to the authorisation of unauthorised acts he was looking at one, and only one aspect of ratification. The discussion above should show that, to a large extent, what ratification achieves is something other than simply the authorisation of unauthorised acts. Even the limitations on the doctrine (such as the principle in *Bolton Partners v Lambert* as subsequently developed) can be, indeed, as already stated, should be, regarded as determining when ratification can be valid and not what are the effects of a valid ratification. Consequently, it is suggested, there is nothing inherently illogical in treating agency resulting from ratification in conjunction with other modes of creating the agency relationship, or varieties of agency, once the rules relating to the requirements for ratification are looked at from the standpoint of determining when ratification can be valid, and not from the point of view of the effects of ratification as compared with the effects of a prior authorisation.

8 Ie in the case of consensual, but non-contractual agency: above, pp 14–19.
9 *Powell* pp 121–122.

CHAPTER 6

Agency by estoppel

In certain situations although there is no true consent between one person and another to stand in the relationship of principal and agent, vis-à-vis each other or the outside world, the law treats their relationship as one of principal and agent, giving effect to their conduct as if it amounted to the expression of consent that they should be principal and agent.[1] In fact, of course, consent is quite irrelevant to the power of the person treated as an agent to affect the position of the person treated as a principal. By the application of the doctrine of estoppel, an agency relationship comes about in the absence of true consent between principal and agent. As already argued,[2] this form of agency may be regarded as a type of agency arising by operation of law. But it merits separate treatment in that, for it to arise, special requirements must be fulfilled, quite distinct from other instances of agency by operation of law, and different policies underlie the action of the law in recognising and enforcing an agency relationship where none was previously agreed upon between the parties. In these instances the law is concerned to protect third parties who may have acted on the reasonable inference that a relationship of principal and agent existed between the parties concerned.

A. The application of estoppel to agency

Estoppel means that a person who has allowed another to believe that a certain state of affairs exists, with the result that there is reliance upon such belief, cannot afterwards be heard to say that the true state of affairs was far different, if to do so would involve the other person in suffering some kind of detriment.[3] Applied to agency this means that a person who by words or conduct has allowed another to appear to the outside world to be his agent, with the result that third parties deal with him as his agent, cannot afterwards repudiate this apparent

---

1 Professor Seavey, wrongly it is respectfully suggested, denied that agency can be created by law without the consent of the principal: 'The Rationale of Agency' (1920) 29 Yale LJ at pp 863–864. For the same reasons the present writer rejects Professor Conant's 'objective theory of agency' which would make apparent authority also stem from 'the objective consent of the principal to third parties': (1968) 47 Nebraska LR 678. See further, below, pp 120–121.
2 Above, p 19.
3 This was quoted and relied on by Gerein J in *Anderson Ventures Inc v Jarrie Farm Equipment* (1988) 60 Sask LR 25 at 31, and earlier in *Burns/Pape Associates Inc v Argus Holding Ltd* (1980) 2 Sask LR 56.

agency if to do so would cause injury to third parties; he is treated as being in the same position as if he had in fact authorised the agent to act in the way he has done.

Even in the absence of prior agreement as to authority or subsequent ratification of unauthorised acts, a person can become a principal 'by placing another in a situation in which . . . according to the ordinary usage of mankind that other is understood to represent and act for the person who has placed him so'.[4] Everything depends upon the way the principal makes the situation appear to the outside world, in the light of what is usual and reasonable to infer,[5] and upon the reliance which is placed by third parties upon the apparent authority of the person with whom they are dealing.[6] The 'principal' is said to 'hold out' as his agent the person represented as having authority to act on his behalf. The 'agent' is said to have 'ostensible' or 'apparent' authority.

The effect of this doctrine of agency by estoppel may be observed in two kinds of cases.

First of all the agent may have no actual authority at all, ie there may be no relationship of principal and agent actually in existence. By virtue of the doctrine such a relationship is created. Thus if the owner of goods allows X to have possession of the goods or the documents of title to them, and X usually deals with that class of goods, then even if there is no intention on the part of the owner to make X into his agent for the purpose of selling the goods, if X does sell them, the owner will be treated as if he had appointed X his agent, and will lose his right to the goods.[7]

Secondly, and this is the more frequent occurrence, there may be a relationship of principal and agent in existence, but the authority of the agent may be limited by the agreement between the parties. If the agent exceeds his authority the

---

4 *Pole v Leask* (1861) 8 LT 645 at p 648 per Lord Cranworth.
5 For example see *United Bank of Kuwait Ltd v Hammoud, City Trust Ltd v Levy* [1988] 3 All ER 418, where the solicitor was held out as having authority to do what was part of the ordinary business of a solicitor: cp above, p 70. See also *Alliance and Leicester Building Society v Hamptons* [1994] CLY para 112, on the ostensible authority of an unqualified employee of estate agents to give a valuation, which in fact was fraudulent, on the basis of which the plaintiffs advanced money to the purchaser of the valued property; *Granum v Northwest Territories (Minister of Personnel)* [1992] NWTR 20, 30, where over the telephone, an agent of the government told the plaintiff, being interviewed for employment, that she would be provided with housing at a certain rent: later she discovered this was not true.
6 *First Energy (UK) Ltd v Hungarian International Bank Ltd* [1993] 2 Lloyd's Rep 194 at 201 per Steyn LJ; *MacFisheries Ltd v Harrison* (1924) 93 LJKB 811.
7 *Pickering v Busk* (1812) 15 East 38 (irrespective of the Factors Act). Cf *Spiro v Lintern* [1973] 3 All ER 319, [1973] 1 WLR 1002, discussed above, p 90: *Burns/Pape Associates Inc v Argus Holdings Ltd* (1980) 2 Sask LR 56, mortgage broker acting for party seeking to obtain mortgage funds from other mortgage brokers; *Piper Group (1978) Ltd v Shearson Equities Ltd* (1987) 78 NSR (2d) 413, salesman employed by the defendant had business card describing himself as Vice-President Marketing of the company: when he signed a contract on behalf of the company, the latter was liable. Contrast *Lewin Finance Co v Jagede* [1979] CLY 14, possession of land certificate did not give rise to agency by estoppel; (with which compare *Bank of British Columbia v Andrews and Struss* [1979] 6 WWR 574); *Caledonia Inc v Tractors and Equipment (1962) Ltd* (1980) 31 NBR (2d) 32, purchase of goods in another's name did not make the party negotiating the purchase the agent of the party whose name was used; *Murphy v Luckiw Holdings (1980) Ltd* (1987) 49 Alta LR (2d) 200, giving cheque to defendant did not create agency relationship, so that no fiduciary duty arose on the part of the defendant or his father to whom the cheque was payable.

doctrine of estoppel may operate to bind the principal: for the ostensible or apparent authority of the agent can supplement his actual authority, and so broaden the scope of the relationship of principal and agent as to make it cover the unauthorised acts of the agent.[8] This is true even if, in fact, the agent is really acting for his own benefit, not for the benefit of his principal,[9] and even if he is acting *against* the interests of his principal.[10] Scrutton LJ expressed the law thus in *Lloyds Bank Ltd v Chartered Bank of India, Australia and China*:[11]

'A third party dealing in good faith with an agent acting within his ostensible authority is not prejudiced by the fact that as between the principal and his agent, the agent is using his authority for his own benefit and not for that of the principal.'

So, too, the improper exercise of a power of attorney will not affect the validity of a transaction entered into by the attorney on behalf of his principal with a third party where the attorney is acting within his apparent authority and the third party is acting in good faith.[12]

The first type of situation is clearly one in which an agency relationship is *created* by the law, when none previously existed, by the application of the

---

8 See, for example, *Swiss Air Transport Co Ltd v Palmer* [1976] 2 Lloyd's Rep 604; *Walsh v Griffiths-Jones* [1978] 2 All ER 1002; *Bank of Montreal v RJ Nicol Construction (1975) Ltd* (1981) 32 OR (2d) 225; *Russelsteel Ltd/Ltee v Consolidated Northern Drilling and Exploration Ltd* [1981] 4 WWR 113; *Lift Systems International Ltd v Bank of Montreal* (1987) 62 Sask LR 44; affd (1988) 73 Sask LR 235, comptroller of a company who embezzled the company's funds; *OG Enterprises Ltd v Grasskamper* (1983) 22 Man R (2d) 219; *Tasita Pty Ltd v Sovereign State of Papua New Guinea* (1994) 34 NSWLR 691, consul-general had ostensible authority to enter into lease so as to bind his government. Contrast *Woeller v Orfus* (1979) 106 DLR (3d) 115.

    Hence the ostensible or apparent authority of a solicitor or counsel to bind his client to a compromise of an action could exceed his implied authority to do so: see *Waugh v HB Clifford & Sons Ltd* [1982] Ch 374, [1982] 1 All ER 1095. See also *First Energy (UK) Ltd v Hungarian International Bank Ltd*, above, on the ostensible authority of the senior manager of the branch office of the defendant bank to communicate that head office approval had been given for a facility letter in connection with the granting of credit; *Gurtner v Beaton* [1993] 2 Lloyd's Rep 369, on the ostensible authority of an aviation manager to permit air taxi work although that was not part of the business of the aviation company; *Freeman v Sovereign Chicken* [1991] IRLR 408, on the ostensible authority of a representative of a Citizens Advice Bureau to enter into a settlement with employers on behalf of a dismissed employee. Contrast *Rhodian River Shipping Co SA v Halla Maritime Corpn* [1984] 1 Lloyd's Rep 373, the manager of a company who managed the affairs of the plaintiff companies had no apparent authority to commit one of them even though all three companies had the same shareholders and directors; *Re Selectmove* [1995] 2 All ER 531, collector of taxes had no ostensible authority to agree with taxpayer about payment of back taxes.

9 *Hambro v Burnand* [1904] 2 KB 10; *Trade Practices Commission v Queensland Aggregates Pty Ltd* (1982) 44 ALR 391. Unless this fact is known to the third party: *Lysaght Bros & Co Ltd v Falk* (1905) 2 CLR 421; and especially if the third party dealing with a dishonest agent knows the agent is acting in his own interest rather than that of the principal and is indeed colluding in the concealment of the facts from the principal: *Combulk Pty Ltd v TNT Management Pty Ltd* (1993) 113 ALR 214.

10 *Lloyd v Grace, Smith & Co* [1912] AC 716. See also *Canadian Laboratory Supplies Ltd v Engelhard Industries of Canada Ltd* (1979) 97 DLR (3d) 1; *Royal-Globe Life Assurance Co Ltd v Kovacevic* (1979) 22 SASR 78; *Combulk Pty Ltd v TNT Management Pty Ltd*, above.

11 [1929] 1 KB 40 at 56.

12 *Abbott v UDC Finance Ltd* [1992] 1 NZLR 405 at 414.

doctrine of estoppel to the particular circumstances. The second situation is not so much concerned with the creation of an agency relationship as with its *extension.* An agency relationship exists, having been created by agreement between the parties, but is limited by the principal in a certain way, or for a certain purpose. By the application of the doctrine of estoppel, as will be seen, the agency relationship is made to apply to acts and transactions by the agent which the principal never agreed with him that he should perform or undertake. In straddling both the creation and the extension of an agency relationship in this way, estoppel gives rise to many difficulties; and the true juristic basis of agency by estoppel has been much debated, as will be seen. While it may be descriptively correct to distinguish agency created by estoppel from agency extended by estoppel, it is suggested that these two applications of estoppel to agency do not involve any analytical differences necessitating any separate treatment.[13]

B. Requirements for estoppel

In the *Rama* case,[14] Slade J summed up the requirements for agency by estoppel by saying that there had to be: (i) a representation; (ii) a reliance on a representation; and (iii) an alteration of a party's position resulting from such reliance.[15] This can be expanded in the following way.

First there must be some statement or conduct on the part of the principal which can amount to a representation that the agent has authority to act on his behalf in the way he is acting. It was made clear by the Court of Appeal and the House of Lords in *Armagas Ltd v Mundogas SA*[16] that the relevant representation must come from the principal: it cannot come from the agent himself.[17] Ostensible authority is created by a representation by the principal to the third party that the agent has the relevant authority: and the representation, when acted upon by the third party, operates as an estoppel, precluding the principal from asserting that he is not bound. 'Ostensible authority' said Lord Atkin in *Midland*

---

13 The foregoing general account of agency by estoppel was relied upon by Halvorson J in the Saskatchewan Court of Queen's Bench in *Burns/Pape Associates Inc v Argus Holdings Ltd* (1980) 2 Sask LR 56 at 58; and by Stratton J of the New Brunswick Court of Queen's Bench in *Caledonia Inc v Tractors and Equipment (1962) Ltd* (1980) 31 NBR (2d) 32 at 40–42. See also Gerein J in *Anderson Ventures Inc v Jarrie Farm Equipment* (1988) 60 Sask LR 25 at 31.

14 *Rama Corpn Ltd v Proved Tin and General Investments Ltd* [1952] 2 QB 147 at 149–150, [1952] 1 All ER 554 at 556. See also *Freeman and Lockyer v Buckhurst Park Properties (Mangal) Ltd* [1964] 2 QB 480 at 503, [1964] 1 All ER 630 at 664, per Diplock LJ: cf also *Hely-Hutchinson v Brayhead Ltd* [1968] 1 QB 549, [1967] 3 All ER 98, below, pp 358–360.

15 This analysis of agency by estoppel was cited with approval and relied on in *Caledonia Inc v Tractors and Equipment (1962) Ltd,* note 13 above.

16 [1985] 3 All ER 795 at 804 per Goff LJ; on appeal [1986] 2 All ER 385 at 389 per Lord Keith. See also below, p 115. For an example of such representation see *Egyptian International Foreign Trade Co v Soplex Wholesale Supplies and Refson & Co* [1985] FLR 123.

17 *First Energy (UK) Ltd v Hungarian International Bank Ltd* [1993] 2 Lloyd's Rep 194 at 201 per Steyn LJ, 205 per Evans LJ, 207 per Noarse LJ: *Suncorp Insurance and Finance v Milano Assicurazioni SPA* [1993] 2 Lloyd's Rep 225 at 231 per Waller J.

Bank v Reckitt[18] 'appears to be excluded when the party averring it cannot show that any appearance of authority other than the actual authority was ever displayed to him by the principal.' Such statement or conduct must be clear and unequivocal.[19] Hence if the conduct by the principal is capable of being interpreted in a way which does not accord with the granting of authority to an agent no estoppel can arise. In *Colonial Bank v Cady*:[20]

> Executors signed blank transfers on the back of share certificates, for the purposes of settling the deceased's estate by selling the shares. The broker with whom they dealt fraudulently made them out to himself and deposited them with the bank, which took them, bona fide and without notice of the fraud, as security for advances made to the broker. It was held that the executors were not estopped from claiming back the certificates. No representation that the broker had authority to dispose of them could be construed out of the executors' conduct.

Not only were dealings of this sort by brokers out of the ordinary, and therefore not reasonably to be understood as having been authorised by his principals; the circumstances were such that the bank should have made enquiries to see whether they were justified in taking the certificates in this way.

Sometimes the fact that an agent is entrusted with certain duties in the normal course of his work may amount to an implied representation of authority to act in a certain way. This, too, was expressed clearly in *Armagas Ltd v Mundogas SA*.[1] A common, general example of the kind of representation that will give rise to an estoppel by creating ostensible or apparent authority is by permitting the agent to act in some way in the conduct of the principal's business with other persons thereby representing that the agent has the authority which an agent so acting in the conduct of the principal's business usually has.[2] 'In the commonly encountered case', said Lord Keith,[3] 'the ostensible authority is general in character, arising when the principal has placed the agent in a position which in the outside world is generally regarded as carrying authority to enter into

---

18 [1933] AC 1 at 17.
19 Cf Lerner J in *Woeller v Orfus* (1979) 106 DLR (3d) 115 at 124. For an example see *Spiro v Lintern* [1973] 3 All ER 319, [1973] 1 WLR 1002, discussed above, p 90.
20 (1890) 15 App Cas 267. Cf *Earl of Sheffield v London Joint Stock Bank* (1888) 13 App Cas 333; *Farquharson Bros v King & Co* [1902] AC 325. See also *Charrington Fuel Oil v Parvant Co* [1989] CLY 58, request by new owners of property to previous suppliers to deliver more goods to same address not a representation giving rise to estoppel creating ostensible authority.
1 [1986] AC 717, [1985] 3 All ER 795 at 804 per Goff LJ, 815 per Dunn LJ, 824 per Stephenson LJ: *Gurtner v Beaton* [1993] 2 Lloyd's Rep 369 at 379 per Neill LJ. Cf *Crabtree-Vickers Pty Ltd v Australian Direct Mail Advertising and Addressing Co Pty Ltd* (1975) 133 CLR 72 at 78 per Gibbs J.
2 Eg in *First Energy (UK) Ltd v Hungarian International Bank Ltd*, above, the position of the senior manager of the defendant's branch gave rise to just such authority; *The Raffaella* [1985] 2 Lloyd's Rep 36; cf *Gurtner v Beaton* [1993] 2 Lloyd's Rep 369 at 379–381.
3 [1986] 2 All ER 385 at 389. But sometimes it will not be right simply to inquire what is the normal or usual authority of the particular type of agent in question: actual representations may extend that authority: *Egyptian International Foreign Trade Co v Soplex Wholesale Suppliers and PS Refson Co Ltd* [1985] FLR 123, CA.

transactions of the kind in question'. For example, in *Lloyd v Grace, Smith & Co*:[4]

> A solicitor's managing clerk dealt with a client's property, and fraudulently persuaded her to sign documents which gave him all her estate. It was held that the solicitors were liable to the client, because, by allowing the clerk to deal with matters of this kind, they had represented that he had authority to get clients to agree to transfers of their property.

The fact that the agent was acting in his own interests does not affect the question. For 'the principal . . . cannot escape from liability merely because the agent may have abused the authority or betrayed his trust.'[5]

But the agent must appear to be acting in a way in which a person in his position would normally act: otherwise it will not be possible to assert that to the outside world he quite reasonably appeared to have the necessary authority.[6] Thus a coachman who pledged his master's credit for forage supplied to horses was not acting in a manner usually to be expected of a coachman: hence it could not be said that he had ostensible or apparent authority to do so.[7] So in *Farquharson Bros v King & Co*:[8]

> A clerk who pretended to have authority to dispose of timber and did so, fraudulently keeping the proceeds of the sales, was not the agent by estoppel of his employers in respect of such sales. He was not normally employed for such a purpose. Therefore the purchasers of the timber ought to have realised he had no authority to sell; and they could not keep the timber as against the clerk's employers.

But in *United Bank of Kuwait Ltd v Hammoud: City Trust Ltd v Levy*[9] the solicitor was doing something ordinary within the class of transactions to be performed by a solicitor; and in *First Energy (UK) Ltd v Hungarian International Bank Ltd*,[10] the branch senior manager was doing something normally handled by such an official.

In the *Armagas* case[11] the defendants' chartering manager fraudulently entered

---

4 [1912] AC 716: below, pp 318–319. Cf *Royal-Globe Life Assurance Co Ltd v Kovacevic* (1979) 22 SASR 78, agent employed by insurance company to effect life assurance proposals, and supplied with a receipt book of the company, made the company liable for deposits received by the agent from parties who intended to insure their lives with the company, when the agent misappropriated said money; liability based on holding out or ostensible or apparent authority. Contrast *British Bank of the Middle East v Sun Life Assurance Co of Canada (UK) Ltd* [1983] 2 Lloyd's Rep 9; *Combulk Pty Ltd v TNT Management Pty Ltd* (1993) 113 ALR 214.

5 *Hambro v Burnand* [1904] 2 KB 10 at 23 per Romer LJ. As Lord Dunedin said of this case in *Reckitt v Barnett, Pembroke and Slater Ltd* [1929] AC 176 at 185: 'the agent was doing the very business he was authorised to do, to issue letters of guarantee. He was doing very bad business and he was doing it for an improper motive.'

6 *Richardson v Cartwright* (1844) 1 Car & Kir 328; *Spooner v Browning* [1898] 1 QB 528.

7 *Wright v Glyn* [1902] 1 KB 745.

8 [1902] AC 325, distinguished by Laskin CJC in *Canadian Laboratory Supplies Ltd v Engelhard Industries of Canada Ltd* (1979) 97 DLR (3d) 1 at 15–16, as being 'simply another instance of a fraudulent agent's inability to give a good title to goods stolen from his principal.'

9 [1988] 3 All ER 418, above, p 70.

10 [1993] 2 Lloyd's Rep 194, above, p 62 note 1.

11 [1986] AC 717, [1985] 3 All ER 795; affd [1986] 2 All ER 385.

into a transaction with the plaintiff for the benefit of himself and a broker acting for shareholders in the plaintiff company. When the defendants were later sued by the plaintiff company on the contract made by the defendants' chartering manager, and for damages for the tort of deceit,[12] the Court of Appeal and House of Lords, reversing the trial judge, held that the manager had no apparent authority to make that contract: and the defendants were not estopped from denying his lack of authority. The defendants had made no express representation of such authority: nor had they impliedly done so since the chartering manager did not normally have the kind of authority which he asserted in this instance. Appointing him as a chartering manager represented that he had authority to bind the principal by those contracts which an agent in his position ordinarily had authority to make. That would embrace the making of representations by the agent concerning the subject-matter of such contracts. It did not embrace authority on the part of the agent to communicate approval by his superiors to his making a contract which, to the knowledge of the third party, the agent had no authority to make without such approval, so as to make the principal bound by such a communication.[13]

However, it is possible that, although an agent is not held out in a general way as having authority to act, he may be held out to a particular party as having such authority. Ostensible general authority may also arise, according to Lord Keith,[14] where the agent has had a course of dealing with a particular contractor and the principal has acquiesced in this course of dealing and honoured transactions arising out of it. In such situations the agent may have authority vis-à-vis a particular individual, based on past experiences and dealings: but he will not have such authority as regards the outside world in general. For that to be the case, the agent must be acting in the manner previously described, namely, in respect of acts or transactions that are usually, normally or ordinarily entrusted to such an agent in such a position.

Secondly, this representation must be made to the person who relies upon it.[15] This means that it must be made either to the particular individual who transacts business with the agent, or to the public at large in circumstances in which it is to be expected that the general public (or members of the general public) would be likely to transact business with the agent.

> 'The "holding out" must be to the particular individual who says he relied on it, or under such circumstances of publicity as to justify the inference that he knew of it and acted upon it.'[16]

---

12 Below, pp 319–322.
13 [1985] 3 All ER 795 at 804–805 per Goff LJ. Nor can an agent with authority to act or make representations confer ostensible authority on *another* agent to do the act, by a representation on which a third party relies: *Crabtree-Vickers Pty Ltd v Australian Direct Mail Advertising and Addressing Co Pty Ltd* (1975) 133 CLR 72.
14 [1986] 2 All ER 385 at 389–390. This may explain the curious Canadian case of *Timmerman's Enterprises Ltd v Painter* (1987) 42 Man R (2d) 16, where the personal defendant told the plaintiffs that they were dealing with a limited company, which had replaced the original firm with which the plaintiffs had dealt in the past.
15 Compare the law relating to deceit: *Peek v Gurney* (1873) LR 6 HL 377.
16 *Farquharson Bros v King & Co* [1902] AC 325 at 341 per Lord Lindley.

Thirdly, the representation must be made intentionally or, possibly, negligently. Clearly a deliberate representation by a person of another as his agent will bring about the application of the doctrine of estoppel. The effect of a non-wilful, perhaps negligently made, representation is more difficult to assess. It would seem that negligence in representing the true state of affairs will probably only result in an estoppel where there was a contractual or a fiduciary relationship between the representor and the person to whom the representation was made,[17] or some duty of care existed between them. Until recently it might have been argued that no such duty of care could exist unless the representation was in some way connected with the physical (as opposed to the legal) condition of goods or land, and that merely inducing a detrimental cause of conduct involving economic loss, without physical or proprietary damage, could not suffice, except where the effect of the representation was to cloak someone with the apparent indicia of title.[18] As a result of the decision in the House of Lords in *Hedley Byrne & Co Ltd v Heller & Partners*,[19] it may be that a duty to use care in the making of statements which can be interpreted as representing someone as an agent can exist more widely.[20]

Fourthly, this representation must be 'the proximate cause of leading the party into that mistake'.[1] Unless the third party has relied upon the representation there can be no allegation of estoppel. As with all instances of estoppel there must be the suffering of the 'detriment' as a result of a change in position because of faith in the representation.[2] Notice of want of authority, whether the third party was

---

17 *Nocton v Lord Ashburton* [1914] AC 932.
18 Below, pp 128–132, 281–290. Cf, the discussion in *Mercantile Credit Co Ltd v Hamblin* [1965] 2 QB 242, [1964] 3 All ER 592.
19 [1964] AC 465, [1963] 2 All ER 575. For subsequent development, see *Salmond & Heuston on Torts* (20th edn 1992) pp 214–219; *Winfield & Jolowicz on Tort* (14th edn 1994) pp 290–304.
20 It is debatable whether the Misrepresentation Act 1967, which grants a remedy in damages for an innocent, but negligent misrepresentation, could provide a remedy in a situation in which a contract is made in consequence of a misrepresentation as to the agency of a person other than the other contracting party. Even if any such liability arises, it would not seem to involve the doctrine of estoppel. On this statute and its effects, see Cheshire, Fifoot and Furmston *Law of Contract* (12th edn 1991) pp 282–285, 297, Treitel *Law of Contract* (8th edn 1994) pp 312–314, 320–322, 326.
    Note that this statute, which, as amended by the Unfair Contract Terms Act 1977, s 8, prevents the exclusion or restriction of liability for a misrepresentation by a party or his agent, does not qualify the right of a principal publicly to limit the otherwise *apparent* authority of his agent: see *Overbrooke Estates Ltd v Glencombe Properties Ltd* [1974] 3 All ER 511, [1974] 1 WLR 1335: see also below, p 126.
    On the incidence of liability under the Misrepresentation Act, s 2(1) where an agent's misrepresentation has induced a contract to which his principal is a party, see *Resolute Maritime Inc v Nippon Kaiji Kyokai* [1983] 2 All ER 1, [1983] 1 WLR 857.
 1 *Swan v North British Australasian Co Ltd* (1863) 2 H & C 175 at 182 per Blackburn J. See *Welch v Bank of England* [1955] Ch 508 esp at 534–539, [1955] 1 All ER 811 at 823–824, per Harman J.
 2 See, eg *Spiro v Lintern* [1973] 3 All ER 319, [1973] 1 WLR 1002, discussed above, p 90. The question whether 'detriment' in reliance on the misrepresentation must be shown is still debatable: see *Ajayi v R T Briscoe (Nigeria) Ltd* [1964] 3 All ER 556; *W J Alan & Co v El Nasr Export and Import Co* [1972] 2 QB 189, [1972] 2 All ER 127; *Brikom Investments Ltd v Carr* [1979] QB 467, [1979] 2 All ER 753; *P v P* [1957] NZLR 854; *Société Italo-Belge pour le Commerce et l'Industrie SA v Palm and Vegetable Oils (Malaysia) Sdn Bhd* [1982] 1 All ER 19. See generally, Fridman 'Promissory Estoppel' (1957) 35 Can BR 279; Fridman, *Law of Contract in Canada* (3rd edn 1994) pp 133–135; Cheshire, Fifoot and Furmston *Law of Contract* (12th edn 1991) pp 103–105.

actually aware of such want of authority or ought in the circumstances to have been aware of it, will mean that the third party cannot rely upon estoppel: if there is such notice, the third party cannot allege that he was misled into believing that the agency relationship existed and covered the acts of the agent.

In this respect the fact that the agent was acting in his own interests, and not for the benefit of his principal, may be extremely relevant.[3] Actual or constructive knowledge of this ought to put the third party on his guard and inform him that the agent was not acting within the scope of any authority. 'The notice found to exist defeats reliance on ostensible authority equally with actual authority.'[4] For example, if the agent pays his own debts with the principal's money this should give the third party notice that the agent had no authority to draw on his principal's account, and this, in turn, will break the connection between the principal's representation of authority and the third party's reliance thereupon.[5] Thus in *Lloyds Bank Ltd v Chartered Bank of India, Australia and China*:[6]

> The agent (an employee in a bank) fraudulently drew cheques on his principal and paid them into the defendant bank for his own benefit. The principal sued the defendant bank for conversion. It was held that the bank was liable and could not rely upon the provisions of the Bills of Exchange Act 1882, s 82[7] because the fact that such large sums of money were being paid into the account of a person in the agent's position should have put them on their guard.

The proximate cause of the defendant bank's action was not the representation of the principal that the agent had authority.[8]

Apart from the necessity at common law to inquire into the validity and extent of a representation of authority, there may be statutory obligations to make sure that there is an agency relationship which covers the acts in question.[9]

---

3 *Combulk Pty Ltd v TNT Management Pty Ltd*, above, p 113, note 9.
4 *Midland Bank v Reckitt* [1933] AC 1 at 17 per Lord Atkin. Compare Scrutton LJ in *Lloyds Bank Ltd v Chartered Bank of India* [1929] 1 KB 40 at 56 '. . . it is otherwise where the third party has notice of irregularity putting him on inquiry as to whether the ostensible authority is being exceeded.' Cf *Bank of Montreal v R J Nicol Construction (1975) Ltd* (1981) 32 OR (2d) 225.
5 *Reckitt v Barnett* [1928] 2 KB 244; revsd by House of Lords [1929] AC 176. Contrast *Danby v Coutts & Co* (1885) 29 Ch D 500.
6 [1929] 1 KB 40. Cf the unusual nature of the transaction, which should have put the third party on his guard, and therefore resulted in the principal *not* being liable, in *Hazlewood v West Coast Securities Ltd* (1975) 49 DLR (3d) 46; affd (1976) 68 DLR (3d) 172. Contrast *Lift Systems International Ltd v Bank of Montreal* (1987) 62 Sask LR 50; affd (1988) 73 Sask LR 235 where the fact that the comptroller of a company was embezzling the company's funds did not put the bank on inquiry: therefore they were not liable because the company was estopped from denying the comptroller's authority.
7 By the provisions of which a bank which collected a crossed cheque for its customer in good faith and without negligence was protected against liability where the customer has no title, or a defective title, to the cheque. This provision has now been replaced by the Cheques Act 1957, s 4.
8 [1929] 1 KB 40 at 60 per Scrutton LJ.
9 Eg Bills of Exchange Act 1882, s 25 (see also below, p 372).

C. The relevance of estoppel

The preceding discussion has been based upon the notion that it is correct to speak of agency by estoppel, which some textbook writers and judges alike assume to be correct. Several writers, however, have criticised the idea that the creation or extension of an agency relationship, by the investiture of someone with ostensible or apparent authority, is connected with estoppel.[10] Professor Stoljar, echoing the view of the American Restatement, adopted the attitude that there is no separate agency by estoppel: cases of apparent authority are only instances of a contract between agent and third party becoming a contract between principal and third party. Powell regarded the phrase 'agency by estoppel' as misleading. Estoppel does not create the relation of principal and agent; it only affects the relation of principal and third party, by preventing the principal from denying that he is liable for the acts of the agent. He differentiated estoppel and apparent authority on a number of grounds.[11]

First, the doctrine of apparent authority was established before the courts used the language of estoppel.[12] Powell, however, admitted that this was not conclusive.[13]

Secondly, estoppel is tortious in origin, apparent authority is contractual. This distinction, it is suggested, is of spurious validity in modern times. Estoppel has shaken off the shackles of tort, while the apparent authority of an agent may stem sometimes from a contract between him and the principal, but at others could be said to have no connection with contract at all.

Thirdly, estoppel does not give rise to a cause of action,[14] whereas under the

---

10 For example, Seavey 'The Rationale of Agency' (1920) 29 Yale LJ 859 at pp 873–874; *Powell* pp 68–72; *Stoljar* pp 30–36 (who rejects any divergence between contract and estoppel); Conant 'The Objective Theory of Agency: Apparent Authority and the Estoppel of Apparent Ownership (1968) 47 Nebraska LR 678 (who regards apparent or ostensible authority as being based on the objective consent of the principal to third parties, assimilating such agency to ordinary agency and rejecting any difference between contract and estoppel).

　　See also *Restatement, Second, Agency* paras 8, 27, Appendix, Vol 3, pp 41–43, which rejects the estoppel theory in favour of something approaching a 'risk' doctrine. Fishman, 'Inherent Agency Power—Should Enterprise Liability Apply to Agents' Unauthorized Contracts?' (1987) 19 Rutgers LJ 1, argues that the liability of a principal for the unauthorised contracts controls made by his agent is wider than what it could be if based on apparent authority or estoppel.

11 The arguments in the second edition differ somewhat from those in the first edition: pp 60–62.

12 Cook, 15 Harv LR 325.

13 Cf Montrose 'The Basis of the Power of an Agent is cases of Actual and Apparent Authority' (1938) 16 Can BR 757 at 787, who pointed out that the modern law of estoppel began with a case of apparent authority: *Pickard v Sears* (1837) 6 Ad & El 469.

14 *Combe v Combe* [1951] 2 KB 215, [1951] 1 All ER 767; *Tool Metal Manufacturing Co Ltd v Tungsten Electric Co Ltd* [1955] 2 All ER 657, [1955] 1 WLR 761 *Argy Trading Development Co Ltd v Lapid Developments Ltd* [1977] 3 All ER 785, [1977] 1 WLR 444. But this may be different with regard to so-called 'proprietary estoppel': *Crabb v Arun District Council* [1976] Ch 179, [1975] 3 All ER 865; *Greasley v Cooke* [1980] 3 All ER 710, [1980] 1 WLR 1306; *Pascoe v Turner* [1979] 2 All ER 945; *Lloyds Bank plc v Rosset* [1991] 1 AC 107, [1990] 1 All ER 1111: see Treitel *Law of Contract* (8th edn 1994) pp 124–136. The Supreme Court of Canada appears to have accepted this: *John Burrows Ltd v Subsurface Surveys Ltd* (1968) 68 DLR (2d) 354; *Canadian Superior Oil Ltd v Paddon-Hughes Development Co* (1970) 12 DLR (3d) 247: see also *Sohio Petroleum Co v Weyburn Security Co* (1970) 13 DLR (3d) 340; *Cull v Canadian Superior Oil Ltd* (1971) 20 DLR (3d) 360. See also *Owen Sound Public Library Board v Mial Developments Ltd* (1980) 102 DLR (3d) 685; *Reclamation Systems Inc v Rae* (1996) 27 OR (3d)

doctrine of apparent authority causes of action may arise in favour of principal or third party. Estoppel does not create a contract; or even the appearance of a contract. On the other hand, if the agent has apparent authority to make a contract, there does appear to be a contract, and the law supposes that the contract exists.[15] It is suggested, however, that if the objection is that the principal acquires no right of action under the doctrine of estoppel, this is no practical barrier, since there do not appear to be any cases in which the principal was suing the third party on the basis of an agency of this kind. All the cases are the other way round.

Fourthly, estoppel involves a substantial detriment or change of position, whereas, under the doctrine of apparent authority, the third party's change of position can be very small indeed. This seems a difference, if any, of such triviality of degree as to be unworthy of serious consideration. It does not appear that the 'detriment' relevant for estoppel is really any substantially greater than the reliance and change of position needed in cases of apparent authority. In the same way, the argument as to the difference between representations of existing fact and promises in future, and the distinction between *real* and *metaphorical* titles to goods,[16] are also neither greatly relevant nor greatly effective.

The criticisms of Powell, therefore, it is suggested, do not fundamentally shake the basic acceptance by the courts of the doctrine of estoppel as underlying the kind of agency situations referred to in this chapter. Indeed the importance and relevance of estoppel have both been expounded by Diplock LJ in what has become the leading decision on this matter, cited and relied on in subsequent cases, *Freeman and Lockyer v Buckhurst Park Properties (Mangal) Ltd*[17] a case concerned with the liability of a company for the acts of a director.[18] Not only is estoppel recognised by the courts as the explanation of this kind of agency: it is also semantically and juristically correct to employ the language of estoppel in this context, as long as it is realised that this form of agency has a narrower scope than that of the other forms. Its purpose is to protect third parties. It is not employed to regulate the relationship and position of the principal and agent, as is the case with the usual, purely consensual, or strictly contractual kind of agency. If this fundamental difference in approach and purpose of the law is appreciated, the differentiation of this kind of agency by employing the terminology and ideas of estoppel becomes intelligible and justifiable.

---

419. A different view was expressed, however, by an Ontario court in *Re Tudale Explorations Ltd and Bruce* (1978) 88 DLR (3d) 584; cf *Robichaud v Caisse Populaire de Pokemouche Ltee* (1990) 105 NBR (2d) 227 at 246–248 per Rice JA. But see *Secretary of State for Employment v Globe Elastic Thread Co Ltd* [1979] 2 All ER 1077 at 1082, per Lord Wilberforce. Cf also the discussion and arguments of Jackson 'Estoppel as a Sword' (1965) 88 LQR 84, 222. See, further, Fridman, *Law of Contract in Canada* (3rd edn 1994) pp 124–127, and cases there cited.

15 *Powell* p 70.

16 Ibid, pp 71–72. On this see *Eastern Distributors Ltd v Goldring* [1957] 2 QB 600, [1957] 2 All ER 525; *Moorgate Mercantile Co v Twitchings* [1977] AC 890 at 918, [1976] 2 All ER 641 at 658 per Lord Edmund-Davies.

17 [1964] 2 QB 480 at 530, [1964] 1 All ER 630 at 644. See also *Hely-Hutchinson v Brayhead Ltd* [1968] 1 QB 549, [1967] 3 All ER 98. The *Freeman and Lockyer* case was accepted and followed by the High Court of Australia in *Crabtree-Vickers Pty Ltd v Australian Direct Mail Advertising and Addressing Co Pty Ltd* (1975) 133 CLR 72.

18 See further, below, pp 353–362.

D. Apparent authority

The nature of apparent authority. Where the doctrine of estoppel operates to give rise to the agency relationship, or to create some, if not all of the effects of that relationship, the agent is regarded as having 'apparent' or 'ostensible' authority to act. By his exercise of this authority the agent affects the legal position of the person whose conduct has made him, the agent, appear to be a principal.

Unlike the kinds of authority which have been discussed in the preceding chapter, the agent's authority in agency by estoppel is not an actual or real authority at all.[19] That is to say it does not result from consent on the part of the principal, whether express, or implied according to the rules already discussed, that the agent should have any authority at all, or the kind of authority which he has purported to exercise.[20] The agent's authority here is the product of the principal's conduct, his representation that the agent is authorised to act on his behalf.[1] It is an authority which 'apparently' exists, having regard to the conduct of the parties. In fact it does not exist. But as a matter of law, arising out of the factual position, the agent is said to have authority.

The apparent authority must be carefully distinguished from the *implied* authority, in particular that variety of implied authority which has been called *usual* authority, which some agents may possess over and above the express authority granted them by the principal. *Implied* (including in this context *usual*) authority is the authority which in fact the agent possesses as a result of the

19 See *British Bank of the Middle East v Sun Life Assurance Co of Canada (UK) Ltd* [1983] 2 Lloyd's Rep 9 where the House of Lords negated first any implied actual authority on the part of the manager whose acts were in issue, and then any ostensible authority: cf *Rhodian River Shipping Co SA v Halla Maritime Corpn* [1984] 1 Lloyd's Rep 373. Contrast cases in which actual authority was negated but ostensible authority was found to exist: *First Energy (UK) Ltd v Hungarian International Bank Ltd* [1993] 2 Lloyd's Rep 194; *Gurtner v Beaton* [1993] 2 Lloyd's Rep 369.

  The language of Scrutton LJ in *Reckitt v Barnett, Pembroke and Slater Ltd* [1928] 2 KB 244 at 257; revsd [1929] AC 176 is very misleading. There it was said (quoting an American case referred to in *Bryant, Powis and Bryant Ltd v La Banque du Peuple* [1893] AC 170), 'the apparent authority is the real authority'. Contrast the language of Scrutton LJ with that of Russell LJ: [1928] 2 KB 244 at 257, 269–270. See also Slade J in *Rama Corpn Ltd v Proved Tin and General Investments Ltd* [1952] 2 QB 147 at 149, [1952] 1 All ER 554 at 556: 'Ostensible or apparent authority, which negates the existence of actual authority . . .'

  Cf the confusion in *The Choko Star* [1989] 2 Lloyd's Rep 42 between implied actual authority and ostensible authority, which was questioned on appeal, by Parker LJ [1990] 1 Lloyd's Rep 516 at 524 and by Slade LJ at 527.

20 The contrary view is expressed by Conant 'The Objective Theory of Agency' (1968) 47 Nebraska LR 678, especially at 681–686. His general argument is based upon the liability of an undisclosed principal for contracts or dispositions of property made by his agent. If it is once accepted that the situation of the undisclosed principal is anomalous and peculiar, and that dispositions of property raise special problems, it will follow that no satisfactory argument based on the consent of a principal to any apparent authority being exercised by his agent can be founded upon the situation of the undisclosed principal.

1 Hence in *C R Ogden & Co Pty Ltd v Reliance Fire Sprinkler Co Pty Ltd* [1973] 2 NSWLR 7, the third party was not liable to the principal when the agent had made a fraudulent misrepresentation in the course of negotiating the contract. Even though the agent acted without express instructions in this respect, the principal was bound by what he had done as he had entrusted the negotiations to the agent. Contrast the facts and the decision in *Armagas Ltd v Mundogas SA* [1986] AC 717, [1985] 3 All ER 795, CA; affd [1986] 2 All ER 385, HL.

construction of his contract of agency in the light of business efficacy, or of the normal practices and methods of the trade, business, market, place, or profession, in which the agent is employed. *Apparent* authority, on the other hand, is the authority which, as a result of the operation of the legal doctrine of estoppel, the agent is considered as possessing, in view of the way a reasonable third party would understand the conduct or statements of the principal and the agent.[2] Sometimes this is described as implied authority, on the ground that it is implied by the law, or as usual authority, on the ground that it is what a third party would expect an agent in such a position to possess in the ordinary course of events. Such use of the terms implied authority and usual authority, it is suggested, is a source of confusion.[3]

A good illustration, not of confusion actually occuring, but of a statement which could give rise to confusion, is to be found in the judgment of Lord Denning MR, in *Hely-Hutchinson v Brayhead Ltd.*[4] Speaking of the way that apparent authority can often *coincide* with actual authority, his lordship said: 'Thus, when the board appoint one of their number to be managing director, they invest him not only with implied authority, but also with ostensible authority to do all such things as fall within the usual scope of that office.'[5] Even though actual authority (including implied authority) and apparent authority are not mutually exclusive and generally co-exist and coincide,[6] the expressions implied authority and usual authority should be reserved for the kinds of authority which have been described above, since, sometimes, apparent authority exceeds actual authority (which may include implied or actual authority).[7] In *Freeman and Lockyer v Buckhurst Park Properties (Mangal) Ltd* Diplock LJ explained that an 'apparent' or 'ostensible' authority was:

'. . . a legal relationship between the principal and the contractor[8] created by a representation, made by the principal to the contractor, intended to be and in fact acted on by the contractor, that the agent has authority to enter on behalf of the principal into a contract of a kind within the scope of the "apparent" authority, so as to render the principal liable to perform any obligations imposed on him by such contract.'[9]

To the relationship that is created in this way the agent is a stranger. He need not be aware of the existence of the representation, though he often is. 'The representation, when acted on by the contractor by entering into a contract with the agent, operates as an estoppel, preventing the principal from asserting that he

---

2 Cf Slade J in the *Rama Corpn Case* [1952] 2 QB 147 at 149, [1952] 1 All ER 554 at 556.
3 Cf Montrose 'The Basis of the Power of an Agent in cases of Actual and Apparent Authority' (1938) 16 Can BR 757 at 764; Hornby 'The Usual Authority of an Agent' [1961] CLJ 239; see also Stone 'Usual and Ostensible Authority – One Concept or Two?' [1993] JBL 328, criticising the approach in *City Trust Ltd v Levy* [1988] 3 All ER 418.
4 [1967] 3 All ER 98 at 102. Compare the language of Glidewell and Staughton LJJ in *City Trust Ltd v Levy*, above, at 426–427, 428.
5 Cf Lord Denning's language when speaking of implied authority, cited above, p 64.
6 Lord Pearson in the *Hely-Hutchinson* case, above, at 108.
7 Ibid at 102 per Lord Denning MR.
8 Ie the third party contracting with the agent.
9 [1964] 1 All ER 630 at 644.

is not bound by the contract. It is irrelevant whether the agent had actual authority to enter into the contract.'

A possible connecting factor between these two kinds of authority, which may be the cause of the confusion that sometimes exists in respect of them, is the idea that, where a man is in a position in which it is *usual* for him to possess a certain authority, it will be reasonable for outside parties to act on the basis that he does have this authority.[10] This may sometimes give rise to an implied authority, and it may sometimes give rise to an apparent authority. Distinguishing between the two can be awkward. But the distinction undoubtedly exists. It is important, because, to prove the existence of implied authority, it must be shown that the acts performed by the agent were necessarily incidental to the proper performance of his agency, or that some trade, professional or other practice justified his acting in such a manner, whereas, to prove apparent authority, it is necessary to show that the principal's conduct was such as to mislead the third party, and to induce him to rely upon the existence of the agency to his detriment. Once a person is known to be an agent, then, as seen in a previous chapter,[11] he is prima facie invested with authority to do whatever is usual in the trade, business or profession in which he is employed. As long as there is some usual, or normal type of transaction or conduct which agents of his class undertake, he will be assumed to have authority to act in such a way. This usual authority, which is implied, depends upon the appointment of the agent in question as an agent. It is otherwise where the 'agent' has not in fact been appointed as such by the principal, but is believed to be an agent, on the basis of the principal's representation. In such instances the agent's authority may possibly depend upon what it is reasonable for the third party to believe it to be or to invoke, in the light of what authority such a person would possess if he in fact had been appointed an agent of the kind in question. If the third party believes he is dealing with an agent of a certain class, the authority he believes such agent to possess may well be the kind of authority it is usual for an agent of that class to possess. In such a case the apparent authority of the agent is coincident with usual authority. It differs from usual authority in the correct sense in that the principal has represented, but not authorised, the agent to be his agent. Some examples of this involve cases in which the person whose conduct was in issue was represented as being a *principal*, not an agent.[12] It is suggested that such cases cannot be used to invalidate the doctrine of usual authority, nor to justify the use of the idea of usual authority to confuse implied with apparent authority.

There is one feature which is common to both forms of authority. If the third party has notice of the fact that the agent has neither implied nor apparent authority, or ought to have been on his guard against the lack of such authority, he will not be able to rely on either doctrine to make the principal liable.[13]

10 This is stated in *Armagas Ltd v Mundogas SA*, above: cf above, pp 115–116.
11 Above, pp 69–76.
12 Eg *Watteau v Fenwick* itself: above, pp 72–76.
13 Cf Lord Atkin in *Midland Bank Ltd v Reckitt* [1933] AC 1 at 17–18. Hence the decision of the Supreme Court of Canada in *Rockland Industries Inc v Amerada Minerals Corpn of Canada Ltd* (1980) 108 DLR (3d) 513 to the effect that the clothing by the sellers of goods of their agent with authority to negotiate on their behalf involved the conclusion that the sellers should have notified the buyers of the limitations on the agent's authority: cf *Calgary Hardwood and Veneer Ltd v Canadian National Rly Co* [1979] 4 WWR 198. Similarly, in *Canadian Laboratory*

In this respect it may be important to differentiate the status of the employee who is acting, or purporting to act, as an agent. If he is in a position to negotiate contracts for his employer, it may be reasonable for a third party to conclude that he has apparent, and perhaps even actual, authority.[14] If he occupies a minor position in the organisation with which the third party is dealing, eg, a mere clerk as contrasted with a managing director, then for such conclusion to be drawn by the third party may be unreasonable: such third party ought to know that employees of that kind lack the necessary authority to transact the kind of business that is involved.[15] In this regard much attention may have to be paid to the structure and organisation of modern corporations and to the possibilities for the infliction of harm or loss by the acts of a corporation's employees. To preclude such loss or harm it may be that responsibility may have to be extended far down the line of management and control of a corporation.[16]

It was suggested by Laskin CJ that an agent by virtue of his position might be able to extend the scope of his authority by his own act, thereby making the principal liable although the principal had not specifically held out the agent as having such extended authority. Laskin CJ thought that this would depend on the situation of the agent and what he was assigned to do.[17] It is doubtful whether this suggestion can be taken very far. To admit that an agent can have such an effect upon the position of his principal would be to allow an agent to become 'self-authorising', which contradicts the essential nature of agency.[18] Although there is one Canadian case, *Berryere v Fireman's Fund Insurance Co*,[19] in which this appears to have occurred, in *Armagas Ltd v Mundogas Ltd*,[20] Lord Keith considered that even if this case had been rightly decided on its facts, having regard to the wide powers ostensibly given to the agent in that case to bind the insurance company for which he acted, the case was not authority for the general proposition that ostensible authority of an agent to communicate agreement by his principal to a particular transaction was conceptually different from ostensible authority to enter into that particular transaction. If an agent did not have ostensible authority to enter into a transaction, in accordance with what has been indicated earlier, then such an agent cannot confer authority upon himself to enter into such a transaction by indicating to the third party that the requisite assent by his principal has been given by and through the agent himself.

Supplies Ltd v Engelhard Industries of Canada Ltd (1979) 97 DLR (3d) 1 the Supreme Court of Canada were divided as to the precise date on which the third party should have realised that the agent lacked authority to deal with the goods he was buying from, and then reselling to, the third party under the guise of a fictitious other person. The damages recoverable by the agent's principal depended upon the determination of this date.

14 *Rockland Industries Inc v Amerada Minerals Corpn of Canada Ltd*, above.

15 *Canadian Laboratory Supplies Ltd v Engelhard Industries of Canada Ltd*, above, at 10 per Laskin CJC, 17 per Estey J.

16 Ibid at 24–25 per Estey J, discussing the theoretical bases for modern corporate practice and the legal consequences of corporate structure so far as agency is concerned. The learned judge concluded that a purchasing agent in a modern corporation of the kind involved in that case was a responsible officer for these purposes.

17 Ibid at 10 per Laskin CJC.

18 Fridman, 'The Self-Authorizing Agent' (1988) 13 Man LJ 1.

19 (1965) 52 DLR (2d) 603.

20 [1986] 2 All ER 385 at 391.

This is a question that has arisen in other Canadian decisions, in which a different result was reached from that in the *Berryere* case.[1] With that approach, ie negating authority, the Court of Appeal and the House of Lords concurred in *Armagas Ltd v Mundogas SA*. There the third party knew that the agent lacked authority to enter into the transaction in issue. The representation by the agent that he possessed the necessary authority in respect of this particular transaction could not be treated as a representation by the principal to that effect, even though the principal had employed the agent in a certain position, viz, chartering manager and transportation vice-president in its organisation. In those circumstances no estoppel could be raised against the agent's principal. The third party's knowledge of the agent's want of authority could not be overcome by the conduct of the agent himself in the absence of some positive, more definite, specific representation that the third party can assume that if the agent enters into a transaction not normally within his authority and requiring the principal's approval, the necessary approval has been given. As Lord Keith said,[2] such situations would be very rare and unusual. It was difficult to envisage circumstances in which an estoppel could arise from conduct only in relation to a one-off transaction, such as the one in the *Armagas* case.

No estoppel can arise where the transaction is of such an unusual nature that any reasonable person in the position of the third party would be put upon his enquiry.[3] As the *Armagas* case shows, a clearer case is where the third party definitely knows about, not merely suspects or should suspect, the agent's want of authority.[4] Thus in the Alberta case of *Jensen v South Trail Mobile Ltd*[5] the third party entered into a contract to purchase a mobile home. The contract provided that all sales had to have the final approval of an officer of the principal company. This was known by the third party, but the agent stated that he had received such approval for the purchase in question. The majority of the Appellate Division[6] held that by this statement, the agent could not confer authority upon himself; and the knowledge of the limitation on the agent's authority affected the third party's claim that the principal was estopped from denying that the agent acted with authority. In *Overbrooke Estates Ltd v Glencombe Properties Ltd*:[7]

1 *Jensen v South Trail Mobile Ltd*, below note 5; *Cypress Disposal Ltd v Inland Kenworth Sales Ltd*, below note 5.
2 Above, note 20 at 390.
3 *A L Underwood v Bank of Liverpool* [1924] 1 KB 775; *Houghton & Co v Nothard, Lowe and Wills Ltd* [1927] 1 KB 246; *Hazlewood v West Coast Securities Ltd* (1975) 49 DLR (3d) 46; affd (1976) 68 DLR (3d) 172.
4 See, eg *Wilkinson v General Accident Fire and Life Assurance Corpn Ltd* [1967] 2 Lloyd's Rep 182. Contrast *Stone v Reliance Mutual Insurance Society Ltd* [1972] 1 Lloyd's Rep 469 (declining to follow *Newsholme Bros v Road Transport and General Insurance Co Ltd* [1929] 2 KB 356). The *Stone* case was followed by the majority of the Supreme Court of Canada in *Blanchette v CIS Ltd* (1973) 36 DLR (3d) 561: but note the powerful dissent by Ritchie J denying the principal's liability.
5 (1972) 28 DLR (3d) 233. See also the divided decision of the BC Court of Appeal in *Cypress Disposal Ltd v Inland Kenworth Sales Ltd* (1975) 54 DLR (3d) 598.
6 Relying on *Russo-Chinese Bank v Li Yau Sam* [1910] AC 174.
7 [1974] 3 All ER 511.

The principal gave property to A, auctioneers, to sell. The catalogue set out the conditions of sale which included a term that the principal gave no authority to the agent to make or give representations or warranties in respect of the property. The third party asked the agent about the intentions of the Greater London Council with respect to the piece of property in question. He obtained what was in fact a 'wrong' reply. The third party bid for and bought the property. Then he discovered the truth about the Greater London Council's slum clearance programme which was going to affect the property. The question was whether the third party was bound by the contract. This depended upon the effect of the statement or warranty alleged to have been given by the agent with respect to the future intentions of the Greater London Council. It was held that the third party was bound. The principal had informed the third party of the lack of authority on the part of the agent. Therefore, the third party knew that the principal was not bound by anything that the agent had said. No estoppel could be produced out of the situation.

Much the same was the situation in *Armagas Ltd v Mundogas SA*,[8] where the agent was held to have acted without either cited or ostensible authority.

Thus once the third party knows, or ought to know, that the agent is without any authority, or has only limited authority, in respect of a certain transaction, he cannot rely on any alleged representation by the principal; and the conduct of the *agent*, ie a misrepresentation by him, cannot affect the principal's *contractual* position.[9]

In this context the fact that the agent was acting in his own interests may be extremely relevant. It may show that the third party knew, or ought to have known, that the agent had no authority to act as he did, and therefore it may make inoperative the doctrine of estoppel, as well as showing that the representation, if any, by the principal was not the 'proximate cause' of the third party's reliance and detriment. Powell,[10] with some justification, did not regard these cases as properly speaking cases of apparent authority. They are really cases where the agent by virtue of his position had some kind of actual or real authority, upon the strength of which third parties relied, only to discover afterwards that the agent had abused such authority for his own benefit, for example, by paying his own debts with cheques drawn on his principal.[11] Another case, which can be looked upon in this way, is *Hambro v Burnand*:[12]

The principal, a group of underwriters at Lloyd's, authorised the agent, another underwriter, to underwrite insurance policies in the name of the principal and the agent. The agent was a director of a company (X) and in the names of himself and the principal, the agent underwrote a policy guaranteeing the bills of X. One such bill, drawn upon X, was accepted by

8 Above, note 20.
9 Nor, as held in the *Armagas* case, could it affect the principal by the invocation of vicarious tort liability: below, pp 309–311.
10 *Law of Agency* (2nd edn) pp 78–80; cf Hanbury *Principles of Agency* (2nd edn) pp 122–127.
11 *Reckitt v Barnett* [1929] AC 176; *Midland Bank Ltd v Reckitt* [1933] AC 1: cf also *John v Dodwell & Co* [1918] AC 563.
12 [1904] 2 KB 10.

the third party, who knew nothing of the exact nature of the authority given to the agent. When the bill was not met, the third party sued the agent and his principal upon the policy of guarantee. It was held that since the underwriting of such policies was within the ordinary course of business of a Lloyd's underwriter, the agent had acted within his usual, or implied authority, and the third party could not be expected to know that in guaranteeing this particular company's bills, the agent was also acting in his own interests as a director: therefore the principal was liable to the third party.

Here, therefore, the question of notice was decided in favour of the third party. But the case shows that had it been possible to conclude that the third party knew, or should have known, of the agent's breach of duty to his principal (in acting for his own benefit as well as for the benefit of his principal without the latter's consent), the third party could not have relied upon any contention that the agent was acting within the scope of his amplified, and inferentially extended express authority.[13] If the result of notice of such facts is to limit the scope of an express or implied authority, it is easy to see how much more it is the result where the third party is attempting to assert and rely upon an apparent authority.

Extent of apparent authority. This will depend, of course, upon the representation which has been expressly made or can be implied from the position in which the agent has been placed by the principal. Therefore very little can be said by way of generalisation about this subject. More often than not, the doctrine of apparent authority is invoked not to make an agent out of someone who was never in any kind of agency relationship with a principal, but in order to assert that an agent who was appointed with a limited express authority (perhaps supplemented by the implication of some form of usual authority) has also been clothed with an additional apparent authority, in reliance upon which the third party has transacted business with the agent.[14]

Many of the cases involve dealings by the agent with property belonging to the principal; for one of the most important ways in which an agent may appear to have authority to act upon behalf of his principal, is if he is in possession of the principal's property. Hence the fact that an owner has entrusted his property to another, who deals with it in an unauthorised way, may give rise to an estoppel,[15] either at common law or under the terms of s 21 of the Sale of Goods Act 1979.[16]

---

13 If such amplification or extension could be made where to do so might have caused a conflict between the agent's duty and his interest: cf *Robinson v Mollett* (1875) LR 7 HL 802; see above, p 78.

14 See, for example, *Lloyds Bank v Chartered Bank of India, Australia and China* [1929] 1 KB 40; *A-G for Ceylon v A D Silva* [1953] AC 461; *Calgary Hardwood and Veneer Ltd v Canadian National Rly Co* [1979] 4 WWR 198; *First Energy (UK) Ltd v Hungarian International Bank Ltd* [1993] 2 Lloyd's Rep 194; *Gurtner v Beaton* [1993] 2 Lloyd's Rep 369. Contrast the decisions in *Walsh v Griffith-Jones* [1978] 2 All ER 1002, *Swiss Air Transport Co Ltd v Palmer* [1976] 2 Lloyd's Rep 604, and *Armagas Ltd v Mundogas SA* [1986] AC 717, [1985] 3 All ER 795, CA; affd [1986] 2 All ER 385, HL: above, p 116. Professor Hornby invokes the idea of usual authority to do just this: 'The Usual Authority of an Agent' [1961] CLJ 239.

15 It may also involve the operation of the Factors Act 1889 (see below, pp 290–300).

16 Below, p 281.

The ruling idea is that if the principal has clothed the agent with all the indicia of authority to act, thereby misleading third parties, and the agent thereupon deals with the goods as though he were in fact authorised to do so, then the agent will bind the principal by what he does.[17] This is similar to the more general rule that anyone who clothes another with the indicia of *title* to property will be estopped from denying that such other person had title if he deals with the property as if it were his own.[18] In the law of agency, as in the law of property generally, there is a conflict between two ideas. The first is that property owners shall not be deprived of their property against their will. The second is contained in the famous generalisation of Ashhurst J in *Lickbarrow v Mason*[19] that 'wherever one of two innocent persons must suffer by the acts of a third, he who has enabled such third person to occasion the loss must sustain it.' Opinion since 1787 has gone against the generality of this idea's application, although many attempts have been made to invoke it in different branches of the law. The most prevailing view would seem to be that the doctrine of Ashhurst J must not be carried too far: and there is no broad, general duty of care to look after one's title to property so as to avoid financial loss to others, as there is a general duty of care to look after the physical state of the property, or the way the property is handled, so as to avoid physical harm to others.[20]

Apart from statute,[1] there may be cases when the conduct of a property owner will be construed as giving apparent authority to an agent to dispose of the property, in which event the doctrine of agency by estoppel will operate, and the property owner will be bound, as long as the agent acts within the scope of such apparent authority. Powell purported to divide the cases into two main categories:[2] (i) delivery plus express authority to the agent to dispose of the property; (ii) delivery plus authority apparent from the principal's representation to the third party. Is there any real need to distinguish in this way? Both categories of cases involve an apparent authority to deal freely with the property, the only difference between them seeming to be in the fact that in the first there is a limited express authority on to which the law grafts an apparent authority, whereas in the second there never was any express authority at all. Yet in one of

---

17 See Blackburn J in *Cole v North Western Bank* (1875) LR 10 CP 354 at 372. In the Canadian case of *Crampsey v Deveney* (1969) 2 DLR (3d) 161 it was held that the silence of the principals (the children of the 'agent', with whom they were joint tenants of the property) did not amount to any representation that the 'agent' (their mother) had authority to sell the property. Contrast *Spiro v Lintern* [1973] 3 All ER 319, [1973] 1 WLR 1002, discussed above, pp 90–91.

18 See the discussion in *Central Newbury Car Auctions Ltd v Unity Finance Ltd* [1957] 1 QB 371, [1956] 3 All ER 905. Compare *Eastern Distributors Ltd v Goldring* [1957] 2 QB 600, [1957] 2 All ER 525; *Mercantile Credit Co Ltd v Hamblin* [1965] 2 QB 242, [1964] 3 All ER 592; *Lloyds and Scottish Finance Ltd v Williamson* [1965] 1 All ER 641, [1975] 1 WLR 404: discussed below, pp 279–281. But in two cases where an agent dealt with land certificates, or the equivalent, no apparent authority was held to arise: *Lewin Finance Co v Jagede* [1979] CLY 14; *Bank of British Columbia v Andrews and Struss* [1979] 6 WWR 574.

19 (1787) 2 Term Rep 63 at 70.

20 On this see *Central Newbury Car Auctions Ltd v Unity Finance Ltd* (above): *Jerome v Bentley & Co* [1952] 2 All ER 114, esp at 118 per Donovan J; *Moorgate Mercantile Co Ltd v Twitchings* [1977] AC 890, [1976] 2 All ER 641.

1 Eg Sale of Goods Act 1979 s 21(1).

2 *Powell* pp 81–93.

the cases Powell cited as coming within the second category[3] there was in fact an express, though limited authority in the agent. It would seem that there is no point in making this distinction.[4] In all cases the only problem is to determine the inference a reasonable man would have drawn from the conduct of the owner in relation to his property. In answering this question ideas already discussed are all material, that is to say, the irrelevance of secret limitations unknown to the third party, notice by the third party of want of authority on the part of the agent, and the inferences which a reasonable man would draw from his knowledge of the position of the agent and the kind of authority normally entrusted to such an agent.

Some examples will illustrate these points. Thus in *Farquharson Bros v King*[5] the agent in question, a clerk to a timber merchant, was not one who normally would have authority to sell goods for his principal, even though, in fact, he had certain authority to make sales, as well as authority to sign delivery orders. Therefore third parties were held not to be entitled to rely upon the fact that to them the agent apparently had authority to dispose of his principal's goods; and the principal was able to recover the goods from the third party.

In *Brocklesby v Temperance Permanent Building Society*:[6]

> An agent, the son of the property owner, was given the authority to borrow money for his father from the X Bank. For this purpose he was given documents which enabled him to obtain the title deeds to the property from another bank, with which they were deposited as security for a loan. The son, having obtained the deeds, deposited them with the Y Bank as security for a larger loan than the father wanted and he kept the excess for himself. Later he forged certain documents which made him appear owner of the land in question and sold the land to building societies which paid off the Y Bank. When the father sued the building societies it was held that he could recover the land but that he was bound by what his son had done to the extent that he had to pay the building societies the amount of the loan obtained from the Y Bank which the building societies had paid.

From this it would seem that the delivery of title deeds to an agent, either directly or indirectly, in circumstances in which the agent is made to appear, or would normally appear, to the outside world as the owner of such deeds, or entitled to deal with them, will give rise to an estoppel, despite whatever limitations exist in

---

3 *Brocklesby v Temperance Permanent Building Society* [1895] AC 173.

4 In *Lloyds and Scottish Finance Ltd v Williamson* [1965] 1 All ER 641 at 645, Salmon LJ seems to suggest that expressly authorising the agent in possession of goods and indicia of title to sell as principal may make the question whether the agent sold in the ordinary course of business relevant only in so far as the bona fides of the buyer was concerned. How far this justifies Powell's division is questionable.

5 [1902] AC 325. Note distinction of this case in *Canadian Laboratory Supplies Ltd v Engelhard Industries of Canada Ltd* (1979) 97 DLR (3d) 1, where the fraudulent employee who acted much like the clerk in the English case was in fact a *purchasing agent*. Cf *Armagas Ltd v Mundogas SA*, above, pp 116, 125.

6 [1895] AC 173. Cf *Marshall v National Provincial Bank of England* (1892) 61 LJ Ch 465; *Fuller v Glyn, Mills, Currie & Co* [1914] 2 KB 168. See, however, *Lewin Finance Ltd v Jagede* [1979] CLY 14; *Bank of British Columbia v Andrews and Struss* [1979] 6 WWR 574.

the agent's authority. Further illustrations are provided by *Rimmer v Webster*[7] and *Fry v Smellie*.[8] In the first:

> The agent, a broker, by the use of fraud, got the principal to execute deeds of transfer of the bonds from the principal to the agent (though it was not intended that the agent should keep the bonds, but should sell them on behalf of his principal). These transfers were registered, as required by statute. The agent then pledged the bonds with the third party, showing him the transfers as proof that he had title. It was held that the principal could not recover the bonds, because the agent had all the indicia of title: therefore no secret limitation on that title as between principal and agent could affect the transaction with the third party.

In the second case:

> The agent was authorised to borrow a sum of money on shares owned by the principal: and to effect this he was given the documents of title, including a blank transfer signed by the principal. The agent borrowed some money, giving the shares to the third party as security. When the agent failed to repay, the third party filled in his own name in the blank transfer, and obtained the shares. It was held that the principal had given the agent the indicia of title, and therefore could not dispute the title obtained by the third party.

Powell thought that this case, at any rate, was not truly a case of apparent authority, because its effect would be that, whenever an owner gave his agent a blank transfer of shares, or some similar document, the agent would be able to divest the principal of his title by the operation of the doctrine of estoppel without any further representation on the part of the principal.[9] Since, he argued, there is no similar result where other articles have been left in the possession of the agent, for example, a suite of furniture, this should not be the result in such instances, except where the document is a negotiable instrument, in which event there is a duty of care owned by the principal.

This is to ignore, or deny the effect of placing a document of this kind into the hands of an agent, in circumstances in which the agent can reasonably be taken to have complete authority to behave in the way he has done. Is there not a representation contained in the document?[10] Is that not like the case where a owner has entrusted goods to another in circumstances in which third parties can reasonably infer that the possessor of the goods is entitled to deal with them? Thus a factor, at common law, was regarded as being in a position in which it was reasonable for third parties to believe that he had authority to sell goods in his possession.[11] By the Factors Acts this was extended to make it reasonable to infer that he had authority to pledge them.[12] But a warehouseman is not in such a

---

7 [1902] 2 Ch 163: distinguished in *Jerome v Bentley & Co* [1952] 2 All ER 114.
8 [1912] 3 KB 282.
9 *Powell* pp 82–83.
10 Cf Pickford J in *Fuller v Glyn, Mills, Currie & Co* [1914] 2 KB 168 at 177.
11 *Baring v Corrie* (1818) 2 B & Ald 137.
12 Factors Act 1889, s 2. This can now be regarded as an instance of *implied* authority: below, pp 288–290.

position for nobody would reasonably infer that he had any such authority.[13] Hence everything turns upon the particular situation of the agent in the light of what the outside world would reasonably expect his authority to be. If this important aspect of the doctrine of agency of estoppel is remembered then it is not difficult to explain or understand the effect of such cases as *Fry v Smellie*, nor will it be possible to extend the effect of such cases beyond the point to which they really go. The limits of such cases are shown by *Colonial Bank v Cady*,[14] in which it was clearly stated that only where the circumstances show unequivocally that a person acting on the basis of the apparent authority of an agent was reasonably justified in assuming that such an agent could deal with the title to shares, could the scope of the agent's apparent authority cover the third party and estop the real owner.[15]

It must be borne in mind, however, that dispositions of property are not the only instances in which the doctrine of agency by estoppel, and the notion of apparent authority, are material and effective. Contractual, tortious, and criminal liability may be affected by acts committed with an 'agent's' apparent authority. In all these contexts the principles and ideas that are applicable are the same as those discussed above. The test is always what the reasonable man in the position of the third party would believe, as a result of the principal's conduct or language, was the position and authority of the agent with whom he transacted.[16]

13 *Cole v North Western Bank* (1875) LR 10 CP 354.
14 (1890) 15 App Cas 267: above, p 115.
15 The passage from 'Hence everything turns upon the particular situation . . .' to the end of this paragraph, as it appeared in the 4th edn, 1976, was cited with approval and relied upon by Van der Hoop LJSC in *Bank of British Columbia v Andrews and Struss* [1979] 6 WWR 574 at 575.
16 Conant's approach ((1968) 47 Nebraska LR 678 at 703) is based upon the ideas of 'voluntary assumption of risk and market uncertainty', ie so as to make the 'principal' liable to those affected by his activities. This is only another way of looking at the need to protect third parties, which, it is suggested, is the true basis for the doctrine of agency by estoppel or apparent authority, and does not involve the conclusion that this kind of agency is also founded upon the principal's consent.

CHAPTER 7

Agency by operation of law

The suggestion was made previously that agency by estoppel might be considered a variety of agency arising by operation of law, in that such agency does not come about by reason of any agreement between the parties but because the law treats the situation as requiring the invocation of the agency relationship, at least so far as it involves and gives rise to certain of its consequences.[1] In contrast with agency by estoppel, there are what may be termed true instances of agency by operation of law. These also, as with agency by estoppel, involve circumstances in which agreement between principal and agent is lacking. There is no consent to the agent's acting as an agent, yet, for reasons of policy, the law treats one person as the agent of another. The reasons why such relationships are considered to arise differ. The purpose of the law may be to safeguard a person who, without prior agreement, has acted as if he were an agent; to give him rights against the person on whose behalf he acted; or, possibly, to protect third persons who may have transacted business with the one who acted as an agent on his own responsibility. Whatever the true reason in any given instance, it can be stated categorically that in all these cases of agency the explanation for the existence of any agency relationship is neither the consent of the principal nor the conduct of the principal, ie neither agreement nor estoppel.

Since the agency relationship in these situations does not arise by consent of the parties, it is obvious that the authority of such agents cannot be called express authority. Nor can it be called apparent authority, because it is not to be inferred from any representation or other conduct on the part of the principal. It has sometimes been referred to as implied authority. This is erroneous and misleading. Implied authority refers to the authority which an agent has over and above the express authority which has been given to him by the principal, or in place of such express authority, if none has been given; and such implied authority arises from what is required on the grounds of 'business efficacy', reasonable and necessary inference, or what is usual or customary in the light of the usages of the trade, business, place, market, or profession in which the agent is employed, having regard to the proper fulfilment of his duties as agent. The authority of the kinds of agent to be discussed in this chapter cannot reasonably be brought within the meaning given above to the phrase 'implied authority'. The authority of these agents does not depend either upon what is necessarily incidental to the performance of an expressly created agency, or upon trade,

---

1 Above, p 19.

professional, or other usage. It really depends upon what the law 'presumes' the principal would have agreed to the agent's doing, if the principal had been free to give instructions to the agent. Sometimes the drawing of this presumption is a matter of law, and can never be prevented by the introduction of evidence showing that the principal would not have authorised the agent's acts had he been aware beforehand of what the agent was proposing to do. Sometimes, on the other hand, this presumption may be rebutted by appropriate evidence. The exact legal category into which these presumptions may fall is not relevant to the question how to describe the authority possessed by such agents. For that authority, in all these instances, is in one way or another the creature of the law, not the product of agreement between, or the conduct of the parties.

The suggestion is made, therefore, that the authority of the kinds of agent to be described in this chapter should be called 'presumed authority'. That expression has been used in connection with the agency of a wife or mistress,[2] and it is suggested that this expression can usefully and properly be employed to describe the other instances. It is proper to do so because the authority, as already argued, is really one that is *presumed* by the law: it is useful to do so because this expression clearly distinguishes the authority of the agent in these instances from both the implied authority and the apparent authority of other agents.

A. Agency of necessity

The notion of 'necessity' links certain circumstances in which, although no relationship of principal and agent exists or covers the exact situation which has arisen, the law regards what has been done by someone as having been done with the authority of some other person and therefore as his agent. Prior to the abolition of the deserted wife's agency of necessity,[3] it was difficult to state what, if any, was the common principle underlying all the cases.[4] As Professor Powell rightly indicated,[5] the term 'agency of necessity' had been used for many years as a label to cover several groups of cases which had different characteristics.[6] Since the change in the law, however, it is possible to say that by 'necessity' is meant that an unforeseen situation has arisen which carries with it sudden danger to the property, or similar interests of the person on whose behalf acts are performed. In mercantile affairs this means the force of circumstances which

---

2 *Bowstead and Reynolds on Agency* (16th edn) pp 138–140. Cf ibid at pp 137–138 regarding this presumed authority as a kind of implied authority, although it differs from implied authority in several ways. Why then refer to it as implied authority? And why reject the idea that this form of agency arises by operation of law when it is also stated that the implication of authority is a question of law?

3 Matrimonial Proceedings and Property Act 1970, s 41 (on which see Matrimonial Causes Act 1973, s 54(1)(b)); see also Matrimonial and Family Proceedings Act 1984. It has also been abolished in Ontario: Family Law Reform Act 1978, s 33(4); see below, 145.

4 Powell *Law of Agency* (2nd edn) p 426; Hanbury *Principles of Agency* (2nd edn) p 42; *Bowstead on Agency* (15th edn) p 84 (see now *Bowstead and Reynolds on Agency* (16th edn) pp 145–157).

5 *Law of Agency* p 410.

6 Perhaps for this reason Powell preferred to call the deserted wife's right to pledge her husband's credit for necessaries, a 'quasi-agency': *Law of Agency* p 426. The same appellation might fit other instances: ibid pp 428–429.

determines the course a man might take.[7] Before agency can arise out of necessity, however, even in situations which involve such 'force of circumstances', other conditions must be fulfilled.[8] These are manifested by the two classical examples of agency of necessity which were mentioned by Parke B in *Hawtayne v Bourne*.[9]

The first is where a bill of exchange was accepted for the honour of the drawee by someone not already liable on the bill. The person so accepting is then subrogated to the rights of the holder, as regards the person for the sake of whose honour he accepts and pays. The 'necessity' involved here is plain: it arises from the prospect that the person primarily liable on the bill will be placed in a difficult and dishonourable situation. This form of liability springs from the law of merchants, but the law is now contained in the Bills of Exchange Act 1882.[10]

The second is the case of the master of a ship. He was empowered to hypothecate, or even sell, the ship or the cargo in certain circumstances, and his acts, though not expressly authorised would bind the owners of the ship and/or the owners of the cargo.[11] But there must be some urgent necessity, arising from accident, for this form of agency to arise; in the absence of necessity there is no such agency.[12] By 'necessity' is meant that what is done is

'... reasonably necessary, and in considering what is reasonably necessary any material circumstance must be taken into account, eg, danger, distance, accommodation, expense, time and so forth.'[13]

It must be impossible for the master to be able to communicate with the owners of the ship or the cargo and ask for instructions[14] (which seems severely to limit the operation of this form of agency in the light of modern communications, although it may be relevant where there are numerous cargo owners). A further essential feature is that the master must act bona fide and for the benefit of the interested parties, ie the shipowners or the cargo owners.[15]

The cases establish that the shipmaster's authority of necessity is limited in the first instance by the safety of his ship and the cargo he is carrying,[16] and in the second by the impossibility of communicating with the owners of either ship or cargo.[17] The master must make quite sure that he cannot save the ship before he sells or hypothecates it, or sells or hypothecates any part of the cargo in order to

---

7 *Australasian Steam Navigation Co v Morse* (1872) LR 4 PC 222.
8 Goff and Jones *Law of Restitution* (4th edn 1994) pp 336–369; *Sims & Co v Midland Rly* [1913] 1 KB 103; *Prager v Blatspiel, Stamp and Heacock Ltd* [1924] 1 KB 566; *Condev Project Planning Ltd v Kramer Autosales Ltd* [1982] 2 WWR 445 at 456–457 per Lomas J.
9 (1841) 7 M & W 595 at 599.
10 Sections 66(1), 68(5).
11 *Tronson v Dent* (1853) 8 Moo PCC 419.
12 *The Bonita* (1861) 1 Lush 252.
13 *James Phelps & Co v Hill* [1891] 1 QB 605 at 610 per Lindley LJ.
14 *The Australia* (1859) 13 Moo PCC 132.
15 *Tronson v Dent* (1853) 8 Moo PCC 419 at 451–453. Cf Lord Simon of Glaisdale in *China-Pacific SA v Food Corpn of India* [1981] 3 All ER 688 at 698.
16 See *The Australia* (1859) 13 Moo PCC 132; *The Margaret Mitchell* (1858) Sw 382.
17 See cases cited in previous note and *The Gratitudine* (1801) 3 Ch Rob 240; *Australasian Steam Navigation Co v Morse* (1872) LR 4 PC 222.

repair the ship and continue the voyage.[18] Furthermore he must communicate with the owners of the ship or the cargo if to do so is practicable.[19] In the event of necessity he may also borrow money on the credit of his principal in order to continue the voyage.[20]

This form of agency must be distinguished from the more normal, customary agency of the master of a ship. As a result of the contract of agency he has with the shipowners, the master of a ship is invested not only with an express authority but also with implied authority, as considered earlier,[1] that does not emanate from necessity but from what is ordinarily incidental or customary in relation to the performance of his agency. That *implied* authority is distinct from the special powers the master of a ship is *presumed* by the law to possess in cases of necessity as previously described. Those powers are not implied into his contract of agency and therefore are not capable of being excluded by any express term of the contract between the master and the owners. They are granted to the master by virtue of the operation of rules of law.

But the master of a ship has no contract with the owners of cargo being carried on the ship.[2] That difference and the distinction between implied authority and authority presumed by law just mentioned became of crucial importance in recent years in connection with the need for the master of a ship to contract with salvors for the salvage of a ship in distress. In several cases the question arose whether a master who entered into such a contract could bind (a) the owners of the ship and (b) the owners of the cargo: and, if so, on what basis. It now appears that if the contract of salvage was made on behalf of the shipowners they will be bound on the ground that such a contract was within the *implied authority* of the master of the ship: but if such a contract is made on behalf of the cargo owners they will only be bound if the situation can be brought under the doctrine of agency of necessity as described above. That the master has implied authority to contract for salvage on behalf of the shipowners was decided in *The Unique Mariner*.[3] In *The Choko Star*[4] Sheen J, at first instance, held that the master had the same implied authority to enter into a salvage contract on behalf of cargo owners. But the Court of Appeal disagreed[5] and held that only if the circumstances came within the four corners of the doctrine of agency of necessity would the master have the same power as he had in respect of actions on behalf of the shipowners. Both Parker and Slade LJJ considered that it would be better if the master had the same authority in respect of shipowners and cargo

---

18 See cases previously cited and *Kleinwart, Cohen & Co v Cassa Marittima of Genoa* (1877) 2 App Cas 156; *The Staffordshire* (1872) LR 4 PC 194; *The Sultan* (1859) SW 504; *Gibbs v Grey* (1857) 26 LJ Ex 286; *Freeman v East India Co* (1822) 5 B & Ald 617.
19 See cases previously cited and *The Onward* (1873) LR 4 A & E 38; *The Hamburg* (1864) 33 LJ PM & A 116.
20 *Arthur v Barton* (1840) 6 M & W 138; *Beldon v Campbell* (1851) 6 Exch 886; *Gunn v Roberts* (1874) LR 9 CP 331.
1 Above, p 81.
2 Hence, even before the cases to be discussed, his authority to deal with cargo was an authority derived from necessity, ie presumed by the law: *Gibbs v Grey* (1857) 2 H & N 22, 26 LJ Ex 286; *Freeman v East India Co* (1822) 5 B & Ald 617.
3 [1978] 1 Lloyd's Rep 438.
4 [1989] 2 Lloyd's Rep 42.
5 [1990] 1 Lloyd's Rep 516, see Reynolds [1990] JBL 505; Brown (1992) 55 MLR 414.

owners, as proposed in the International Convention on Salvage 1989, art 6 (which was not part of English law).[6] However, they agreed that this difference represented the state of the law. Parker LJ quoted and relied on the language of Lord Diplock in *China-Pacific SA v Food Corpn of India: The Winson*,[7] although the facts of that case differed from those in *The Choko Star* in that the claim by the salvors in the former case was for expenses incurred in off-loading and storing the cargo rather than in salvaging a distressed ship as in *The Choko Star*.[8] Lord Diplock had said:[9]

'The legal nature of the relationship between the master and the owner of the cargo aboard the vessel in signing the agreement on the latter's behalf is often, though not invariably, an agency of necessity. It arises only when salvage services by a third party are necessary for the preservation of the cargo. Whether one person is entitled to act as agent of necessity for another person is relevant to the question whether circumstances exist which in law have the effect of conferring on him authority to create contractual rights and obligations between that other person and a third party that are directly enforceable by each against the other.'

Lord Diplock was referring here to the external effects or consequences of agency. He went on to state that clarity would be enhanced if agency of necessity were used only in this context and was not extended 'to cases where the only relevant question is whether a person who, without obtaining instructions from the owner of goods, incurs expense in taking steps that are reasonably necessary for their preservation is in law entitled to recover from the owner of the goods the reasonable expenses incurred by him in taking those steps'.[10] Employing the expression agency of necessity in this context, he thought, led to confusion in the case before the House of Lords since, where reimbursement was the issue, as there, it was not necessary to apply all the conditions to be fulfilled where the issue was whether a direct contractual relationship with a third party had come into existence. The language of Lord Simon of Glaisdale in the same case,[11] though to the same effect in some degree, was not completely ad idem. He thought that to confine the idea of agency of necessity to the contractual situations was justified by the fact that the law of bailment could often resolve issues between an alleged principal and an alleged agent of necessity (as it did in *The Winson*). However, he also thought that sometimes the law of agency could be more useful (for example to obviate a problem about the correlation of performance of a duty of care with a claim for reimbursement, because of an agent's entitlement to indemnity for expenses incurred reasonably for the benefit of the principal). This difference of opinion, minor though it might be, leaves the scope and role of agency of necessity in some doubt.

---

6 [1990] 1 Lloyd's Rep 516 at 524, 527.
7 [1982] AC 939, [1981] 3 All ER 688.
8 Below, p 139.
9 [1981] 3 All ER 688 at 693.
10 Ibid.
11 Ibid at 698.

The historical instances of agency of necessity just considered, ie acceptance of a bill of exchange for honour and the agency of the master of a ship in cases of emergency (together with the now defunct agency of a deserted wife) were thought to be the only instances when someone without an original agency power could plead necessity by way of justification in respect of the disposition of the property or money of another person.[12] The approach of Lord Diplock in *The Winson* suggests that agency of necessity should not properly be extended to other situations, unless they also involved the creation of contractual rights and obligations between the agent of necessity and the person on whose behalf, although without authority, that agent acted, and only as long as the relevant, classical conditions for such agency existed, viz, (1) impossibility of communication between the parties; (2) necessity as already explained; (3) bona fide acts by the agent in the interests of the one for whom the agent acted; (4) reasonable and prudent action by the agent. All other situations, as Lord Diplock indicated, should be regarded as instances of the exercise of some implied authority in addition to the agent's express authority, or of the implication of some term into a pre-existing contract between the parties in conformity with the doctrine of 'business efficacy'.

The language of Lord Simon of Glaisdale in *The Winson* could be taken as suggesting that some, if not all of these instances can, at least sometimes, properly be classified as examples of agency of necessity. Such instances are those when the alleged agent of necessity has acted in order to protect the property of the alleged principal. When the actions in question were designed to protect the personal safety of the principal, ie his health or well-being, the situation is more dubious.

Protection of property. In *The Winson*,[13] Lord Simon said:

> 'One of the ways in which an agency of necessity can arise is where A is in possession of goods the property of B, and an emergency arises which places those goods in imminent jeopardy. If A cannot obtain instructions from B as to how he should act in such circumstances, A is bound to take without authority such action in relation to the goods as B, as a prudent owner, would himself have taken in the circumstances.'

---

12 *Hawtayne v Bourne* (1841) 7 M & W 595 (agent borrowing money to pay strikers so as to prevent their injuring machinery and tools of the mine was not an agent of necessity of the mining company so as to compel that company to reimburse him); *Gwilliam v W Twist* [1895] 2 QB 84 (volunteer who drove bus when driver was drunk and incapable of driving was not an agent of necessity of the owners of the bus so as to make them liable when such driver caused injury to the plaintiff); *Beard v London General Omnibus Co* [1900] 2 QB 530. However, in *Sachs v Miklos* [1948] 2 KB 23, [1948] 1 All ER 67, at 36, 68, Lord Goddard LCJ was not against the extension of the doctrine as long as there was 'a real emergency', although he thought that the court should be slow to increase the classes of those who could be looked upon as agents of necessity in selling or disposing of other people's goods without the authority of the owners. In that case, as in *Munro v Wilmott* [1949] 1 KB 295, [1948] 2 All ER 983, it was held that there was no emergency: so, in any event, the doctrine could not be relied upon by a bailee who had disposed of the bailor's goods without instruction or authority.

13 [1981] 3 All ER 688 at 697.

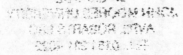

Although this usually arose where A had entered into a contract with C in relation to the goods,[14] and this issue was whether B was bound by such contract, this did not preclude the application of other incidents of agency, including the liability of B to reimburse A for the reasonable expenses incurred by the latter. Whether or not the law of bailment could apply to a given situation, the law of agency might be able to resolve the problem, especially where it related to the reimbursement of the agent.[15] However, for agency to apply, there had to be an emergency at the material time. Hence in the case in question, the doctrine of agency of necessity was inapplicable, because, at the time that the 'agents' purported to act on the principal's behalf, no such emergency had arisen. Moreover, the agents in this case had not acted solely out of the desire to protect the interests of the principals, but more from the desire to maintain their lien on the principal's property.

In that case what was involved was the actions of the salvors of a ship's cargo after the goods were removed from the ship carrying them, which had stranded on a reef.[16] Subsequent to the salvage of the cargo, the salvors had made arrangements for its storage at Manila, where the salvors had no premises of their own. They stated that this was to preserve the cargo, wheat, from the dangers of deterioration; and they claimed reimbursement on a number of grounds, including the doctrine of necessity. Their claim was successful before Lloyd J.[17] It was defeated on appeal to the Court of Appeal.[18] But it was again successful in the House of Lords, although their lordships did not uphold that claim on the basis of agency.[19] Instead the salvors were held to be entitled to be reimbursed in respect of what they had done in their capacity as bailees of the goods. Hence, it may be argued, what was said as to agency of necessity was obiter dictum and not binding. However, the language of Lord Simon in this respect is a strong affirmation of the possibility of agency of necessity in regard to the protection of another's property, at least where the essential conditions are fulfilled, although it must be considered in the light of, and in comparison with, the language of Lord Diplock in that case and the judgments in the Court of Appeal in *The Choko Star*.[20] In this regard it is useful to examine what was held in earlier cases of this type.

14 As Lord Diplock suggested was the only proper use of 'agency of necessity': ibid at 693, above, p 137. For an illustration see *White v Troups Transport* [1976] CLY 33, where police entered into a contract with a crane driver to remove the defendant's lorry jammed under a bridge. The plaintiff succeeded in his suit against the defendant for a reasonable price for his work on the basis of the agency of necessity of the police.
15 [1981] 3 All ER 688 at 697–698.
16 This fact distinguishes this case from *The Choko Star*, above, p 136. On salvage generally see Powell *Law of Agency*, pp 416–417; Goff and Jones *Law of Restitution* (4th edn 1994) ch 16; Fridman *Restitution* (2nd edn 1992) pp 281–285; *The Goring* [1987] QB 687, [1986] 1 All ER 475; revsd [1987] 2 All ER 246, CA; affd [1988] AC 831, [1988] 1 All ER 641, HL: on which see Rose, 'Restitution for the Rescuer' (1989) 9 Ox JLS 167. Salvage was regarded as a 'quasi-contract' related to the civil law concept of negotorum gestio: Brown *A Compendious View of the Civil Law and of the Law of the Admiralty* (1802) at p 122: see Tetley 'The General Maritime Law – The Lex Maritima' (1994) 20 Syracuse J of Int Law and Commerce 105 at p 132.
17 [1979] 2 All ER 35.
18 [1981] QB 403, [1980] 3 All ER 556.
19 [1982] AC 939, [1981] 3 All ER 688.
20 Above, p 136.

Carriers of goods by land were treated in a fashion similar to shipmasters in respect of the cargo they were carrying, where the goods were sold without the authority of the owners in circumstances in which there was a danger that the goods might perish. Thus in *Great Northern Rly Co v Swaffield*:[1]

> The plaintiffs were a railway company who were delivering a horse on behalf of the defendants. Owing to delays for which the railway company were not responsible, it was not possible for the horse to be delivered to its consignee as agreed. Since there was nowhere on the railway premises to keep the horse pending delivery, the plaintiffs kept it in livery stables kept by X. It was held that the defendants were liable to pay the plaintiffs the livery charges.

The reason for this was the need to look after the horse which otherwise might have perished through lack of food and care.[2] It is important to remember that there already was a contractual relationship in existence between the railway company and the defendants. In other cases, where a *stranger*, not bound by any contract with the owner, looked after a stray animal,[3] or found one by a river,[4] no liability to reimburse the stranger could be imposed on the owner. For the general principle is that benefits (or burdens) cannot be imposed on a person behind his back.[5]

Another illustration is provided by *Sims & Co v Midland Rly Co.*[6]

> The defendant railway was delivering perishable goods to the plaintiff. As the result of a strike, there was delay in the delivery and the goods began to deteriorate. The railway sold them to avoid their total loss. It was held that the railway was not liable for breach of the contract to deliver the goods.

This was also really a case of breach of the contract of carriage and not an instance of agency.[7] Both this case and *Great Northern Rly Co v Swaffield* could therefore be regarded not as involving the doctrine of agency of necessity but simply as determining the scope of the authority given to a carrier of goods in circumstances in which the goods are in danger of perishing: in other words, as limiting the liability of the carrier for failure to deliver, or for expenses incurred in the course of delivery. Looked at in this way, they were consistent with the eighteenth-century cases, referred to above, in which no agency was held to arise so as to provide the person who looked after the goods with any rights against their owner. But in *Sachs v Miklos*[8] Lord Goddard accepted these cases as

---

1 (1874) LR 9 Exch 132.
2 (1874) LR 9 Exch 132 at 138 per Pollock B.
3 *Binstead v Buck* (1777) 2 Wm Bl 1117. Contrast with this, however, *Palmer v Stear* (1962) 113 L Jo 420, when a County Court judge held that a veterinary surgeon who destroyed a dog injured in an accident was an agent of necessity. Sed quaere?
4 *Nicholson v Chapman* (1793) 2 Hy Bl 254.
5 See Fridman 'The Quasi-Contractual Aspects of Unjust Enrichment' (1956) 34 Can BR 393 at 413–414. Cf Goff and Jones *Law of Restitution* (4th edn 1994) pp 363, 369–370, who deal with such instances as cases of necessitous intervention by a stranger, not as cases of agency of necessity; Fridman *Restitution* (2nd edn 1992) pp 263, 271–281. See also Rose, loc cit, above, note 16, especially at pp 178–199.
6 [1913] 1 KB 103.
7 Ibid at 112 per Scrutton J.
8 [1948] 2 KB 23 at 35, [1948] 1 All ER 67 at 68.

providing an extension to the agency of necessity of a shipmaster where 'the goods are perishable or in a somewhat similar category, that is to say, livestock which has to be tended, fed, and watered'. However, so far as questions of rights and liabilities arising from acts of carriers are concerned, it would seem to have been of little practical importance whether their position was regarded as that of agent of necessity, or their rights and duties under the contract of carriage were looked at as including the right (or duty) to care for perishable goods, or, in extreme circumstances, to sell them, on the owner's behalf.

In *Prager v Blatspiel, Stamp and Heacock Ltd*[9] McCardie J extended the doctrine to the case where a seller of goods (not a carrier) sold the goods outside the terms of his authority. But on the facts of the case the doctrine did not apply, since the goods (fur skins) were not perishable, and could have been kept by the seller until such time as he could have communicated with his principal. There was no 'necessity' such as the doctrine requires. However, the learned judge went far towards saying that since it was designed to meet commercial convenience, the doctrine of agency of necessity was not limited to previously accepted instances, but was capable of extension to cover new ones, provided that the requirements of the doctrine are fulfilled, ie there is a 'necessity': communication with the principal is impossible: and the agent has acted bona fide and in the principal's interest.

Scrutton LJ in *Jebara v Ottoman Bank*[10] criticised the approach of McCardie J and said that the expansion of the doctrine was acceptable when the agency of necessity developed from 'an original and subsisting agency', since where an unforeseen event occurs which was not provided for in the original contract it was covered by that contract; but agency of necessity did not apply, outside the instances in which it undoubtedly applied, when there was no pre-existing agency, for example the finder of perishable chattels or animals.[11] This, as already seen, is one way of regarding the cases previously discussed. Moreover, McCardie J in *Prager v Blatspiel, Stamp and Heacock, Ltd* was really only doing what Scrutton LJ admitted was permissible, namely applying the doctrine of agency of necessity, or perhaps more correctly, something similar, to the case of a subsisting agency. Thus there would seem to have been good authority for regarding the position of a seller of goods also as not really that of an agent of necessity at all but as that of an agent, normally created, whose authority was extended by the force of circumstances to cover an unforeseen emergency.

However, the statement of Lord Goddard, quoted above, appears to conflict with this; for it regards all these cases as properly instances of agency of necessity. That statement must be considered in the context in which it was made. The facts of *Sachs v Miklos*[12] were as follows:

---

9 [1924] 1 KB 566.
10 [1927] 2 KB 254 at 271. This was accepted with approval by Vaisey J in *Re Banque Des Marchands de Moscou* [1952] 1 All ER 1269 at 1278.
11 Nor did it apply so as to create an agency on behalf of a bank dissolved by Soviet confiscatory decrees: *Re Banque Des Marchands de Moscou* [1952] 1 All ER 1269.
12 [1948] 2 KB 23, [1948] 1 All ER 67. For the power to sell in bailments for repair or other treatment, see now the Unsolicited Goods and Services Act 1971 and the Torts (Interference with Goods) Act 1977.

The defendant gratuitously stored the plaintiff's furniture. During the war the defendant was unable to communicate with the plaintiff. He wanted for other purposes the space which was occupied by the furniture and failing any instructions from the plaintiff the defendant sold the furniture. Later the plaintiff returned and demanded his property. It was held that the defendant was liable in conversion for its value.[13]

The argument that the defendant was not liable because he acted as an agent of necessity was not accepted; for it was held that there was no emergency, as in the animal cases, since the furniture was not perishable. Therefore the case was not a strong authority for saying that a gratuitous bailee can be an agent of necessity, although there was the suggestion in the judgment of the court that where the bailment was of goods in danger of perishing the bailee could be an agent of necessity. On the other hand, it must be remembered that the application of this doctrine depended upon lack of communication with the principal: and in *Sachs v Miklos* it was said that if the bailee did attempt such communication and the bailor did not reply, it could be said that the bailor may have assented impliedly to the bailee's sale of the article.[14] This would not have involved the application of agency of necessity, but would have been another instance, like the ones discussed above, of an existing contract being construed or extended so as to cover an unforeseen emergency. Lord Goddard's statement, seen in this light, was not really as strong an authority in favour of the extension of the doctrine of agency of necessity as might have been thought at first.

A later case, in which the same point arose was *Munro v Wilmott*:[15]

The defendant, without asking for payment, allowed the plaintiff to park her car in the defendant's garage. It was left there for some years, after which time the defendant found it was too inconvenient to keep it further, and was unable to locate the plaintiff to ask her to take the car away. The defendant sold the car. It was held that the defendant was liable for conversion.

Once again agency of necessity was pleaded by way of defence: once again it was held that, even if the doctrine applied to such an instance there was no emergency, no 'necessity', so that the doctrine could not be relied upon by the defendant.

Thus the case law preceding the recent *China Pacific* decision was inconclusive. Some dicta indicated support for the kind of proposition set out by Lord Simon. Others were more cautious, and preferred to restrict the doctrine of agency of necessity in relation to the protection of property to situations which closely resembled that of the shipmaster. Such statements of the law revealed an inclination to confine the doctrine within very narrow limits. The language of Lord Diplock and the decision in *The Choko Star* appear to have given greater weight to these statements. Hence the view that the doctrine of agency of necessity should be confined to cases of pre-existing agency, so that 'necessity' will elaborate or amplify the agent's rights and duties, while all other instances

13 At the higher value which it had at the date of judgment.
14 [1948] 2 KB 23 at 37, [1948] 1 All ER 67, at 68–69.
15 [1949] 1 KB 295, [1948] 2 All ER 983.

should be subsumed under the heading of restitution.[16] That would be an acceptable resolution of the issue: but it requires some development of the law of restitution, which may have occurred in Canada[17] but may not have taken place as yet in England.

Protection of the person. Whether the doctrine of agency of necessity is appropriate where someone has acted, in an emergency, to safeguard the life or health of another, lacking authority or instructions to do so, is a difficult question. Some cases suggest that at least certain persons may invoke this doctrine. For example, it has been held that some agents of a railway authority can bind their principal to pay if they get medical attendance for passengers injured in a railway accident. The liability of the railway authority depends on the position of the agent in question. Thus a stationmaster has been held not able so to bind the railway,[18] but a general manager and a railway police district sub-inspector have been held capable of doing this.[19] But this may be not so much a case of agency of necessity as the implied extension of what is the undoubted authority of certain railway agents.

There are other instances in which the doctrine of agency of necessity has been invoked to provide a remedy. In *Hastings v Semans Village*,[20] for example, a doctor who gave emergency treatment to someone injured in a car accident early in the morning was held to be the agent of necessity of the municipality which was under a statutory duty to look after the injured person because that person was an indigent. So too, in *Samilo v Phillips*,[1] the doctrine was invoked to permit the estate of a suicide to recover from the estate of the suicide's father moneys which the suicide had spent to pay off debts of the father so as to protect the health and sanity of the father in the closing years of his life. However, in these, and many other instances, in which it might be said that a stranger has intervened out of necessity to protect a threatened, disabled, or otherwise disadvantaged party, a better approach to the problem of reimbursement might be that of restitution, or unjust enrichment, rather than agency.[2]

This raises the question whether English law ought to recognise some general principle of reimbursement or legal protection akin to the Roman doctrine of negotiorum gestio.[3] There are instances where English law does appear to

---

16 Brown (1992) 55 MLR 414 at 420.

17 See the cases referred to below, notes 20, 1.

18 *Cox v Midland Counties Rly Co* (1849) 3 Exch 268.

19 *Walker v Great Western Rly Co* (1867) LR 2 Exch 228; *Langan v Great Western Rly Co* (1873) 30 LT 173.

20 (1946) 4 DLR 695; note the protection given to doctors and nurses rendering aid in an emergency under the Alberta Emergency Medical Aid Act, RSA 1980, c E-9. Such interveners will not be liable for injuries or death resulting from what they do without proof of gross negligence. Is this a type of agency of necessity?

1 (1969) 69 DLR (2d) 411: unjust enrichment or restitution was also utilised as a ground for recovery.

2 Goff and Jones *Law of Restitution* (4th edn 1994) ch 15; McCamus 'Necessitous Intervention: The Altruistic Intermeddler and the Law of Restitution' (1979) 11 Ottawa LR 297; Fridman *Restitution* (2nd edn 1992) ch 10, Rose, 'Restitution for the Rescuer' (1989) 9 Ox JLS 167; Brown loc cit, above, note 16.

3 For which see Justinian *Institutes* 3, 27: Buckland *Text Book of Roman Law* (3rd edn) ch CLXXXV.

recognise that negotiorum gestio, or something very like it, exists, and someone can be bound by acts done for his benefit although he has not authorised another to act for him. Some of these instances in the past may have come within the scope of agency of necessity. But that doctrine is wider than negotiorum gestio, since in some of the instances considered earlier a previous agency may have existed before the necessity arose, whereas in negotiorum gestio no agency relationship of any kind pre-existed the acts performed by the negotiorum gestor. Moreover, there are instances where the law does in effect recognise negotiorum gestio, such as the payment of funeral expenses on behalf of the deceased's estate,[4] which have not been recognised as cases of agency of necessity, but of restitution.[5] Since these cases do not usually affect the relations of the persons on whose behalf acts are performed with third parties it seems illogical to regard them as cases of agency of necessity.[6] They are better regarded as restitutionary relationships arising between the person on whose behalf the acts are done and the person performing these acts. Hence the law of restitution, not the law of agency, should be regarded as appropriate for dealing with these cases, as well as other instances where strangers intervene to protect property, on behalf, but without the authority of, the owner.[7] To classify these as instances where the doctrine of agency of necessity might possibly be invoked seems to extend the whole conception of agency far beyond the sphere of legal relations to which it properly belongs, and might involve the full consequences of the agency relationship, eg, vicarious liability for the torts of an 'agent', where to do so would produce startling and undesirable results.

B. Agency from cohabitation

(A) THE AGENCY OF A WIFE

Despite the abolition of the deserted wife's agency, marriage is still important in the law of principal and agent. That relationship exists between spouses (apart from express consent, estoppel, or implied contract) as long as they are living together, for the purpose of the purchase of necessaries: and the wife has the husband's authority to pledge his credit for such necessaries. Willes J in the leading case of *Phillipson v Hayter*[8] explained the rule in these words:

---

4 *Ambrose v Kerrison* (1851) 10 CB 776; Denning (1939) 55 LQR 54 at p 64. Cf a New Zealand case, *Croskery v Gee* [1957] NZLR 586. Note the duty of local authorities under the Public Health (Control of Disease) Act 1984, ss 46–48.
5 Fridman 34 Can BR 393 at pp 413–414, 417; Goff and Jones *Law of Restitution* pp 382–384; *Fridman* pp 279–281.
6 Which is the point made by Lord Diplock in *The Winson*, above, p 137.
7 *Binstead v Buck* (1777) 2 Wm Bl 1117; *Nicholson v Chapman* (1793) 2 Hy Bl 254 (considered above, p 125). Contrast *Palmer v Stear*, above, p 140 note 3. For a detailed comparative study of the situation in Anglo-American law and European legal systems see Dawson 'Negotiorum Gestio: The Altruistic Intermeddler' (1960) 74 HLR 817, 1073.
8 (1870) LR 6 CP 38 at 42. See, generally, Hardingham 'A married woman's capacity to pledge her husband's credit for necessaries'. (1980) 54 Aust LJ 661.

'What the law does infer is that the wife has authority to contract for things that are really necessary and suitable to the style in which the husband chooses to live, in so far as the articles fall fairly within the domestic department which is ordinarily confided to the management of the wife.'

To which Bovill CJ added another instance when this authority is inferred:[9]

'Or if the wife, with the concurrence of her husband carries on a separate trade, goods supplied to her for the purpose of that trade would fall within the same category.'

At the time these words were spoken a wife could not own separate property and was not personally liable on her contracts. Hence the need for some rule to protect tradesmen who dealt with a wife, and others who carried on business with her. Since the Law Reform (Married Women and Tortfeasors) Act 1935, a married woman, at least for these purposes, is treated as if she were a feme sole. It may well be, therefore, that the instance of this kind of agency given to Bovill CJ is no longer in existence. The reason for making a husband liable when his wife is engaged in trade has really gone: and there would seem to be little point in continuing with this form of liability, since wives who do engage in trade presumably do so with their own separate property, not, as then, with property provided by their husbands. However, the same argument does not apply to the case of domestic necessaries: and there is no reason for supposing that this form of agency does not exist today.[10]

Unlike the now abolished deserted wife's agency, the agency of a wife still cohabiting with her husband is not a presumption of *law*, juris et de jure: it is a rebuttable presumption of *fact*.[11] She is presumed to have his authority unless the facts show that he never gave her any such authority. This form of agency, therefore, seems to be similar to agency created by implied contract between the parties: but it is advisable to treat it separately, since, although it does not exist irrespective of the real wishes of the parties, it is much closer to agency by estoppel, which, as already seen, must itself be distinguished from agency arising from a contract to be implied between the parties. Indeed, in *Jolly v Rees*[12] Byles J (dissenting, for reasons which will later appear) approached a case of this kind

9 (1870) LR 6 CP 38 at 41.
10 But is probably diminishing in importance having regard not only to the wife's own contractual capacity but also to the statutory means available to obtain support from the husband. See, for example, the Matrimonial Causes Act 1973, s 27, amended by the Matrimonial and Family Proceedings Act 1984, ss 4, 46(1), Sch 1, para 12: *Halsbury's Statutes* (4th edn 1992 Reissue) Vol 27, pp 770–773.

In Ontario the right to pledge credit is now statutory: Family Law Act RSO 1990, c F.3, s 45(1). It applies to 'necessaries of life' and is available to 'a spouse'. This term has a wide connotation and includes those whose marriage is voidable, those whose marriage is void, but has been celebrated in good faith, and men and women who are not married, but have been co-habiting for at least five years, or are 'in a relationship of some permanence where there is a child born of whom they are the natural parents': ibid ss 1(1), 29.
11 *Jolly v Rees* (1864) 15 CBNS 628 at 640 per Erle CJ; *Debenham v Mellon* (1880) 6 App Cas 24 at 32 per Lord Selborne. Eg, it may be rebutted by proof that the husband has forbidden his wife to pledge his credit': below, p 148.
12 (1864) 15 CBNS 628.

from the standpoint that the wife had 'apparent' authority invested in her by cohabitation with her husband. However, confusion may well result if the terminology of agency by estoppel is used in this context. A wife, here, may be said to have 'presumed' authority as distinct from 'actual', 'apparent' or 'implied' authority.

Although this form of agency arises as a result of the drawing of implications from the facts, that is to say, from the exact situation between husband and wife, it is probably more correct to say that in this instance a relationship of principal and agent arises from a rule of law. It is not any real consent between the parties, whether express or implicit in their conduct, which creates an agency relationship between them. It is the operation of the law, which states that, in the absence of any conduct which would make it impossible to construe the relationship as existing between husband and wife, the wife is presumed to be her husband's agent, for the limited purpose of purchasing necessaries. This feature of this form of agency is important as showing its true nature. If this form of agency arose from some implied agreement between the parties, then the scope of the wife's authority would not necessarily be restricted in this way, but would extend to cover every act which was usual or customary in the light of the position of the parties and the purposes of the agency.[13] Though it might be argued that where principal and agent are husband and wife the 'usual' authority would only cover the purchase of necessaries (so that this is a true instance of agency arising from an agreement implied in fact not by operation of law), to restrict a wife's 'usual' authority in this way, and for such purpose, would be unjustifiable.

Requirements for such agency: (i) cohabitation. The husband and wife must be cohabiting.[14] Since the wife's agency is presumed to be authorised by her husband there must be some basis upon which this presumption may be drawn. The only basis is the fact that husband and wife are living together from which it is reasonable to infer that the wife is acting on behalf of her husband when she orders necessaries. So, if the parties are living apart, this form of agency cannot be invoked to create liability in the husband. But distinctions must be drawn between some instances of non-cohabitation and others.

First, if the parties are separated by judicial decree, whether of the High Court or a court of summary jurisdiction, the wife does not have the presumed authority to pledge her husband's credit.[15]

Secondly, at common law a wife did not have this authority if the parties were living apart by reason of her own misconduct: for example, if she were guilty of desertion[16] or committed adultery in the matrimonial home before she left it,[17] or elsewhere after she left it.[18] But she had this authority where the husband

---

13 Cf above, pp 69–76.
14 *Jolly v Rees* (1864) 15 CBNS 628.
15 *Re Wingfield and Blew* [1904] 2 Ch 665.
16 *Eastland v Burchell* (1878) 3 QBD 432 at 436 per Lush J.
17 *Atkyns v Pearce* (1857) 2 CBNS 763.
18 *Govier v Hancock* (1796) 6 Term Rep 603; *Emmett v Norton* (1838) 8 C & P 506; *Hardie v Grant* (1838) 8 C & P 512. But the husband would be bound if he held out his wife as his agent: *Norton v Fazan* (1798) 1 Bos & P 226.

connived at the adultery,[19] or condoned it and then turned her out of the house.[20] In either event notice to the tradesman of revocation of the wife's authority was ineffectual to remove from the husband liability for necessaries supplied to the wife. The 'traditional' grounds for divorce and the previous 'bars' to a successful petition have both disappeared.[1] But it may still be possible for such misconduct to affect the wife's agency.

Thirdly, what is the situation where the parties have separated by mutual consent, without any formal judicial decree? This depends upon whether there has been an agreement between the parties on the subject of maintenance. If there is, then the wife does not have this authority, unless the agreement is not kept, in which event she can pledge his credit for necessaries. There is some doubt whether it matters that the amount agreed upon by way of maintenance is not really adequate. According to Lush J in *Eastland v Burchell*:[2]

> 'where the terms are . . . that the wife shall receive a specified income for her maintenance and shall not apply to the husband for anything more, how can any authority to claim more be implied.'

In *Johnston v Sumner*:[3]

> It was agreed between husband and wife that the wife should receive £200 a year after they separated. It was held that this terminated the wife's presumed authority to bind her husband.

However, the ground of the decision seems to have been that there was no proof that the allowance was insufficient. In this respect Pollock CB[4] not only drew a distinction between a wife who leaves with and one who leaves without consent, but also said it was important to distinguish between a labouring man and others: for what was a reasonable allowance in the one instance would not be in the other. It is therefore possible to argue that the adequacy of the maintenance agreed upon is a relevant factor. But in *Negus v Forster*[5] the Court of Appeal seem to have concluded that inadequacy of income, even if combined with the husband's misconduct after the separation and maintenance agreement, was not a good ground for pledging her husband's credit: and the husband was therefore not liable for necessaries supplied to the wife, since he had duly kept up payments as required.

If there is no maintenance agreement, then she has the presumed authority described in this chapter unless the wife has other adequate means of support, whether coming from her husband or elsewhere.[6]

---

19 *Wilson v Glossop* (1886) 20 QBD 354.
20 *Harris v Morris* (1801) 4 Esp 41.
 1 Matrimonial Causes Act 1973 (as amended), which contains the law relating to divorce.
 2 (1878) 3 QBD 432 at 436.
 3 (1858) 3 H & N 261.
 4 Ibid at 267.
 5 (1882) 46 LT 675. Contrast *Biffin v Bignell* (1862) 31 LJ Ex 189 where it was held that the husband's misconduct after separation justified the wife living apart from him without his consent. Therefore she had authority to pledge his credit.
 6 *Johnston v Sumner* (1858) 3 H & N 261. Under the Matrimonial Causes Act 1973, s 35, application may be made to the court to alter the financial arrangements between the spouses or import such arrangements, where there has been a change in the wife's circumstances. This might affect what is said in the text.

(ii) A domestic establishment. The fact that the parties cohabit is insufficient unless they are living together as man and wife in circumstances which show that they are a family. This is obvious when the rationale of this kind of agency is remembered.

The leading case is *Debenham v Mellon*:[7]

> Husband and wife were the manager and manageress of an hotel where they also lived and cohabited. The wife had an allowance for clothes, but the husband forbade her to pledge his credit for them. The wife bought clothes from the plaintiff in her own name and paid the bills. Then she incurred a debt with the plaintiff who demanded payment of it from the husband. It was held by the House of Lords that the husband was not liable.

A number of points were raised in the case, but the one which is relevant here is that no presumption of agency could be drawn here because the parties were not cohabiting in a domestic establishment but in a hotel (which was the address known to the plaintiff); hence, despite the marriage and the fact of cohabitation, no authority from the husband could be presumed on the part of the wife.

Factors which deprive the wife of authority. First, if the wife orders goods or services which are not necessaries suitable to the style in which she and her husband customarily live, the husband will not be liable to pay.[8] Thus it must be shown that the goods were necessaries, of which the wife did not already have a sufficient quantity, and were not of an extravagant nature.[9] What are necessaries is, of course, a question of fact, to be proved by the person supplying the goods. The presumed authority of the wife is limited to the purchase, on credit, of such necessaries. If she exceeds this authority the husband will not be liable to the tradesman.

Secondly, since the wife's authority is only a rebuttable presumption of fact, if there is evidence on the basis of which she cannot be presumed to have this authority, the husband will not be liable as principal. Thus if the wife really contracted on her own behalf, the husband will not be liable.[10] If the wife has been expressly forbidden to pledge her husband's credit he will not be liable. This is one of the points involved in *Debenham v Mellon*. But it appears to be debatable whether there has to be notice to the tradesmen concerned that the wife had no authority. In *Lane v Ironmonger*:[11]

> The tradesman had not been told that the wife had no authority to pledge her husband's credit. The husband was held not liable.

On the other hand, in accordance with the doctrine of agency by estoppel, if the husband had previously held out his wife as having the requisite authority, it would seem that a secret prohibition to pledge his credit will not relieve the husband of liability until such time as the tradesman discovers the existence of

---

7 (1880) 6 App Cas 24. This case may justifiably be queried on this ground.
8 *Phillipson v Hayter* (1870) LR 6 CP 38 (where the goods in question were not in fact necessaries).
9 *Debenham v Mellon* (1880) 6 App Cas 24.
10 *Debenham v Mellon* (above); cf *Paquin Ltd v Beauclerk* [1906] AC 148.
11 (1844) 13 M & W 368.

such prohibition.[12] In *Jolly v Rees*[13] the effect of such a prohibition (by giving the wife an allowance) was to free the husband from liability even though the tradesman knew nothing about it. This was because there had been no conduct on the part of the husband which amounted to a holding out of his wife as an agent. Byles J dissented, however, on the ground that the wife was invested with 'apparent authority' by the mere fact of cohabitation (which the other members of the court seem to have denied); therefore *express* notice of revocation of this authority was required by the plaintiff before the husband could be relieved of liability.[14] Acceptance of this would mean that this kind of agency on the part of a wife was a variety of agency by estoppel. The better view, in the light of the other cases which have been referred to, is that, while there is a strong connection between the two forms of agency, they are distinct.

Another material factor in determining whether the wife can be presumed to have authority to bind her husband is whether the husband has given his wife a sufficient allowance to provide for necessaries. If he has, this will operate as an implied prohibition or negation of authority to pledge his credit.[15]

Thirdly, if the tradesman elects to give credit exclusively to the wife, thereby contracting with her as principal, or has chosen to extend such credit to someone else other than the husband, the husband will not be liable as principal.[16] The wife can no longer be presumed to be the agent of the husband. She is acting for herself or for another party.

(B) AGENCY OF UNMARRIED WOMEN

Marriage is not an essential prerequisite to the kind of agency that is under discussion. As long as there is cohabitation between a man and a woman in circumstances in which the outside world is allowed to think that they are man and wife, it makes no difference to the question of agency; the woman will be in the same position as a wife.[17] But it is not sufficient for the man to permit the woman to use his name.[18] Moreover, the effect of separation is different. Separation does not of itself deprive a wife of her presumed authority. The separation must involve something more, such as desertion on the part of the wife. Where the parties are not married, however, separation does immediately deprive the woman of her authority, unless the tradesman has no notice of the separation, in which event the man will be liable (presumably, here, through the

12 *Jolly v Rees* (1864) 15 CBNS 628; *Jetley v Hill* (1884) Cab & El 239.
13 (1864) 15 CBNS 628.
14 Ibid at pp 643–644.
15 *Morel Bros & Co Ltd v Earl Westmoreland* [1903] 1 KB 64; affd [1904] AC 11. See also *Jolly v Rees* (1864) 15 CBNS 628; *Debenham v Mellon* (1880) 6 App Cas 24. Or the wife may have independent means: *Biberfeld v Berens* [1952] 2 QB 770, [1952] 2 All ER 237, CA but contrast what is said in *Callot v Nash* (1923) 39 TLR 292 at 293.
16 *Jewsbury v Newbold* (1857) 26 LJ Ex 247. See also *Debenham v Mellon* (above); *Miss Gray Ltd v Cathcart* (1922) 38 TLR 562; *Callot v Nash* (1923) 39 TLR 292.
17 *Blades v Free* (1829) 9 B & C 167 at 171 per Littledale J; *Ryan v Sams* (1848) 12 QB 460. Cf the situation in Ontario under the Family Law Act, above, p 145 note 10.
18 *Gomme v Franklin* (1859) 1 F & F 465.

operation of the doctrine of agency by estoppel). Two old cases illustrate this. The first is *Munro v De Chemant*:[19]

> Goods were supplied to a woman after she had been turned away without support by the man with whom she was living. It was held that the man was liable to the supplier because the jury decided that the woman was his wife. Lord Ellenbrough made it clear that if they had not been married, the supply of necessaries after separation would not have made the man liable.[20]

In that case it was 'notorious that the parties had separated', as Patterson J said in *Ryan v Sams*.[1] There:

> The plaintiff knew that X was the defendant's mistress. But at the time he did some work for X he had no knowledge that they had separated. It was held that there was evidence on which the jury could find that the defendant's presumed authority to X still subsisted and she was his agent. Therefore the defendant was liable for the price of the work done.

Although the language of the court is in terms of 'presumed authority', it may be better to regard this as a case of agency by estoppel, although the effect is the same whichever legal rule is invoked.

C. Other instances

It can be argued that, under certain statutes, other categories of agents by operation of law have been created.[2] For example, under the Sale of Goods Act 1979[3] an unpaid seller may have the right to resell goods, even if title to such goods has already passed to the buyer who had not paid the seller. Under the Torts (Interference with Goods) Act 1977[4] a power to sell another's goods is also given. Under the Mental Health Act 1983[5] (which replaced the 1959 Act), a judge may appoint a receiver to manage the affairs of a person of unsound mind, and exercise the wide powers conferred by that statute on the judge. It is questionable, however, whether the effect of these various provisions is to create a relationship resembling that of principal and agent as understood at common law.

More to the point, however, is the possibility of a new class of agents by operation of law suggested by the treatment of the defendants in *Boardman v Phipps*[6] as 'self-appointed agents'. In that case one of the defendants had been solicitor to the trust, the beneficiaries of which were the 'principals'. But the other defendant was one of the beneficiaries and the solicitor had ceased to advise the trust at the material time. Was this really a case of agency or an

---

19 (1815) 4 Camp 215.
20 Ibid at 216.
 1 (1848) 12 QB 460 at 462.
 2 See Powell *Law of Agency*, pp 428, 429.
 3 S 48(3).
 4 S 12.
 5 Part VII.
 6 [1967] 2 AC 46, [1966] 3 All ER 721: below, pp 182–185.

application of a rigorous rule of equity applicable to fiduciaries generally, involving the extension of the notion of fiduciary, not of that of agency? Acceptance of the agency approach, it is suggested, would lead to a very wide broadening of the agency concept in contractual situations.[7] It would also raise the question: what type of *authority* is possessed by such agents. In the light of the earlier analysis of authority[8] it is difficult to see where such 'agents' would fit. However, in *Walden Properties Ltd v Beaver Properties Pty Ltd*[9] a judge of the New South Wales Supreme Court invoked the notion of a self-appointed agent in order to create liability for profits made by someone alleged to be under a fiduciary duty.

---

7 Cf Fridman 'Establishing Agency' (1968) 84 LQR 224 at pp 231–239.
8 Above, pp 19–21, 61–79, 122–132.
9 [1973] 2 NSWLR 815 at 833 per Hope JA. Contrast *William B Sweet & Associates Ltd v Copper Beach Estates Ltd* (1994) 108 DLR (4th) 85. where the idea of self-appointed agents was not applied to create a fiduciary relationship between the parties.

PART III

The obligations of agency

SUMMARY

CHAPTER 8

The agent's duties

A. Duties arising from agreement

Express and implied obligation. Agency being primarily a consensual relationship,[1] most instances of the agency relationship will arise from agreement, more particularly a contract, the express or implied terms of which govern the rights and liabilities of the parties. Where there is a contract with express terms, those terms will dictate the internal obligations of principal and agent. In the absence of any, or any relevant express terms, those obligations must be regulated by rules of law applicable to the relationship of principal and agent. Thus, once there is an agreement giving rise to an agency relationship, then, in the absence of any express, contractual terms, the agent, as a matter of law, owes certain implicit duties to his principal.[2]

Performance. Where the agency is contractual, the agent must perform what he has undertaken to perform. In most instances this amounts to the duty to carry out the contract which the agent has made with the principal. For example in *Turpin v Bilton*:[3]

---

1 Cf above, pp 14–19.
2 The American Restatement on Agency calls them 'duties of service and obedience': *Restatement, Second, Agency*, paras 377–386. The nature and terms of the contract between the parties may indicate the scope and content of their relationship: see *The Borag* [1980] 1 Lloyd's Rep 111; cf, as to an implied term in the contract, *Stansfield v South East Nursing Home Services Ltd* (1985) 277 Estates Gazette 311, duty not to act for two parties in same transaction without full knowledge and consent of both parties arose from implied term in contract of agency that estate agent would act in accordance with rules of the Incorporated Society of Valuers and Auctioneers.

   In modern times there may be duties arising under certain statutes, such as, eg, the Consumer Credit Act 1974, in connection with agents involved in arranging credit; see s 175, applying to ibid, ss 57(3), 69(6), 71(4) and 102(1) (on which see Goode *Consumer Credit Act 1974* p 236); or the Estate Agents Act 1979, s 18, in respect of information to clients of prospective liabilities (on which see *Solicitors' Estate Agency (Glasgow) v MacIver* [1991] CLY 4385).
3 (1843) 5 Man & G 455: with which contrast *Wilkinson v Coverdale*, below, note 8. But see *Menna v Guglietti* (1970) 10 DLR (3d) 132 on the duty of an insurance agent to 'service' the policy by transferring the insurance to a new vehicle. Cf as to the duty of an insurance agent when originally insured plant was being converted, *Fairview Enterprises Ltd v US Fidelity and Guarantee Co* [1979] ILR 1–1088; see also *Olanick v R Cholkan & Co Ltd* [1980] ILR 1–1282. As to failure by an insurance agent to inform the principal of the scope of a policy, see *Stockton v Mason* [1979] RTR 130; or failing to inform a principal that an insurer declined a risk and would not issue a policy, see *Reardon v Kings Mutual Insurance Co* (1981) 120 DLR (3d) 196.

The agent was appointed under a contract to insure the principal's ship. He failed to do so, the ship was lost, and the principal was therefore uninsured at the time. It was held that the agent had been guilty of a breach of contract, for which he was liable.

But the agent is not obliged to perform the undertaking if it is illegal. Nor is he obliged to carry out a transaction which, either by common law or statute, is null and void. The most important illustration of this is a gaming or wagering contract.[4] Thus in *Cohen v Kittell*:[5]

The principal employed a turf commission agent to place certain bets which the agent failed to do. The principal sued the agent, claiming the loss of the money he would have won had the bets been made. It was held that the agent was not liable.[6]

Where the agency relationship is non-contractual, that is to say it is the result of agreement but is gratuitous, then the agent is not obliged to perform the undertaking at all: and he will not be held liable for failure to do so, ie non-feasance:[7] though he will be liable for a negligent performance of the under-taking, as in *Wilkinson v Coverdale*,[8] where the agent did attend to the insurance policy, but failed to get the policy indorsed for the benefit of the principal, who was unable to claim on the insurance, hence the gratuitous agent's liability to the principal. Whether the agent, in such circumstances, is obliged to inform his principal of the intention not to perform the undertaking is a question which is difficult to answer. Powell[9] hesitantly came to the conclusion that there is a duty to inform within a reasonable time, the failure to do so giving rise to liability in negligence. But it is difficult to reconcile this with the accepted view that there is no liability for non-feasance: for to adopt Powell's view would be more or less to

---

In *Volkers v Midland Doherty Ltd* (1985) 17 DLR (4th) 343 the agent, in breach of his instructions, delayed buying shares for the principal: for the resulting loss the agent was liable. Having undertaken to act on the principal's orders he was bound to do so or else inform the principal so that the principal could make other arrangements.

4 See Gaming Act 1845, s 18; Gaming Act 1892, s 1. Cheshire, Fifoot and Furmston's *Law of Contract* (12th edn 1991) pp 326–334. See *AR Dennis & Co Ltd v Campbell* [1978] QB 365, [1978] 1 All ER 1215.

5 (1889) 22 QBD 680: distinguished by the Court of Appeal in *Fraser v BN Furman (Productions) Ltd* [1967] 3 All ER 57, [1967] 1 WLR 898, where the principal could sue the agent (insurance brokers) since the contract was not void ab initio and the third party could not have relied on any conduct of the principal to avoid it and escape their liability, as insurers, to indemnify the principal.

6 For the non-liability of the principal to reimburse the agent when he has placed bets see *Tatam v Reeve* [1893] 1 QB 44: and for the position where the principal has paid the agent for bets which have been placed and lost see *Maskell v Hill* [1921] 3 KB 157.

7 *Coggs v Bernard* (1703) 2 Ld Raym 909; *Elsee v Gatward* (1793) 5 Term Rep 143; *Balfe v West* (1853) 13 CB 466. This is accepted as the law by Stoljar *Law of Agency* pp 271–273. But see Palmer *Bailment* (2nd edn 1991) at pp 594–597.

8 (1793) 1 Esp 74. See also below, pp 160–164.

9 *Law of Agency* (2nd edn) pp 302–303; see also *Restatement, Second, Agency*, para 378 which states that a gratuitous agent must perform his promise, if the principal, relying on the promise, refrains from alternative performance, or the agent does not inform the principal so as to enable such alternative performance to be arranged. See also Reporter's Notes to para 354: Seavey 'Reliance Upon Gratuitous Promises or other Conduct' (1951) 64 HLR 913; Prosser *Selected Topics on the Law of Torts* p 380.

say that non-feasance in such circumstances amounts to mis-feasance (for which, as will shortly be seen, there is liability). It would also tend to make the English agency coincide rather more with the Roman *mandatum* than would seem to be justifiable, having regard to the general refusal of English law to accept Roman categories of contract and bailment, despite Holt CJ's efforts in *Coggs v Bernard*.

Obedience. The agent, in the performance of the undertaking, must act in accordance with the authority which has been given him. He must obey instructions contained in his express authority (as long as they are lawful); or he must act in accordance with the general nature of his business, that is to say within his implied authority; or he must act in accordance with trade, or other customs or usages,[10] where they can apply in the performance of the undertaking, that is to say when he can act within his usual or customary authority.[11] But the paramount consideration, particularly where there are neither express instructions nor usages or customs to guide the agent, is the benefit of the principal,[12] and as long as he acts for the principal's benefit, the agent in such circumstances may use his discretion.[13]

Thus, where an agent was expressly authorised to sell shares at a certain price he could not wait until they went higher.[14] A solicitor expressly told by his client not to enter a compromise could not do so even when so advised by counsel.[15] But an auctioneer conducting a sale without reserve is not bound to obey an

---

10 See *Cunliffe-Owen v Teather and Greenwood* [1967] 3 All ER 561, [1967] 1 WLR 1421, broker acting in accordance with practice of the Stock Exchange.

11 In *Golby v Nelson's Theatre and Travel Agency Ltd* (1967) 111 Sol Jo 470, a travel agent altered the flight arrangements of his principal, despite the principal's specification of the particular flight on which he wished to be booked: this was held not to be a breach of duty by the agent, who was able to claim his loss of profit when the principal repudiated the contract, and could retain the deposit given him by the principal. But it is not clear on what basis the agent's departure from express instructions was upheld. Could it be said that he was justified by the nature of the business or some professional usage? By way of contrast in *Benham and Reeves v Christensen* [1979] CLY para 31 an estate agent was not entitled to rely on the custom of such agents to erect a 'For Sale' board on the client's property, because the client had expressly asked that no such board should be erected. Hence this was a term of the contract of agency and governed the relationship.

12 Hence in *LS Harris Trustees Ltd v Power Packing Services (Hermit Road) Ltd* [1970] 2 Lloyd's Rep 65 a principal was entitled to determine the agency when the agent broke his principal's confidence by revealing certain information, even though this was done to effectuate the transaction for which the agent was employed.

13 In this respect a very interesting problem was raised in *Bonsor v Musicians' Union* [1956] AC 104, [1955] 3 All ER 518. For it was necessary to consider whether an officer of a trade union, who was the agent of all the members of the union, was acting as the agent of one particular member, when he was instrumental in obtaining the wrongful expulsion of that member from the union. It was held that he had acted improperly, ie not in accordance with his authority: therefore he was not acting for the expelled member, but only for the other members. Hence they, and the union, could be sued.

14 *Bertram v Godfray* (1830) 1 Knapp 381. Nor could an agent delay in buying shares when instructed to do so by the principal at the opening of the market, even though the agent wished to consult the salesman with whom the principal usually dealt about the wisdom of the purchase: *Volkers v Midland Doherty Ltd* (1985) 17 DLR (4th) 343. Failure to follow the principal's oral instructions was *negligence* in *Meddich & Meddich v Cullen & Harvey* (1983) 36 SASR 542.

15 *Fray v Voules* (1859) 1 E & E 839. Cf *Benham and Reeves v Christensen*, above, note 11.

instruction from the owner not to sell for less than a stated sum, since such instruction is unlawful;[16] and he must sell to the highest bidder, even if the bid is lower than the sum mentioned by the owner.[17] A broker need only carry out the sale of shares on behalf of a client in accordance with the rules of the Stock Exchange and other incidental methods of conducting such business,[18] and in making such a sale he can only sell for ready money, according to the customs of his business, unless expressly authorised to do otherwise.[19]

Care and skill. Not only must the agent act in accordance with his authority (whether express, implied, or usual): he must also perform the undertaking with due care and skill. All agents owe this duty of care to their principals, whether the agency be contractual or gratuitous.[20] A distinction may exist, however, between the standard of care to be observed by a gratuitous agent and that to be observed by one who acts under contract for reward.[1]

In the case of contractual agency, the standard of care to be observed by the agent is put in terms of the skill which an agent in his position would usually possess and exercise.[2] As long as he has behaved with normal care and skill,

16 Sale of Goods Act 1979, s 57.
17 *Bexwell v Christie* (1776) 1 Cowp 395.
18 *Hawkins v Pearse* (1903) 9 Com Cas 87: cf *Cunliffe-Owen v Teather and Greenwood*, above. But in *Laskin v Bache & Co Inc* (1971) 22 DLR (3d) 382, it was held a breach of the agent's duty, when purchasing on the Stock Exchange, to accept other certificates in lieu of the proper ones, even though a practice of the Exchange permitted this. See also *Midland Doherty Ltd v Rohrer* (1985) 20 DLR (4th) 188, stockbrokers could not claim from principal for provision of cash margins, as required under the rules of the Toronto Stock Exchange, because the stockbrokers had acted in breach of those rules by accepting letters undertaking certain obligations from a trust company.
19 *Wiltshire v Sims* (1808) 1 Camp 258.
20 They may also owe a duty of care to a third party with whom the agent is negotiating on behalf of the principal: see eg, *Chand v Sabo Bros Realty Ltd* (1979) 96 DLR (3d) 445; *Komarniski v Marien* (1979) 100 DLR (3d) 81; *Olsen v Poirier* (1978) 91 DLR (3d) 123; *Roberts v Montex Development Corpn* (1979) 100 DLR (3d) 660; *Shulist v Hurd* (1987) 51 Alta LR (2d) 69 (applying the same standard of care as that which was to be observed vis-à-vis a principal); *Patay v Hutchings* (1990) 6 RPR (2d) 121; *Fletcher v Hand* (1994) 40 RPR (2d) 52. See also *Canada Trust Co v Sorkos* (1992) 90 DLR (4th) 265, where there was no evidence of loss, therefore no liability. Contrast *Hawkhead v Sussex Realty Ltd* (1979) 13 BCLR 289 (no negligence); *B D C Ltd v Hofstrand Farms Ltd* (1986) 26 DLR (4th) 1 (no duty owed by courier to plaintiffs, the courier being an agent of the Crown); *Ingwersen v Dykstra* (1984) 4 DLR (4th) 355 (no negligent misrepresentation); *Tooton v Atkinson* (1985) 55 Nfld & PEIR 125, where a vendor's solicitor owed no duty of care to the purchaser.
 1 *Chaudhry v Prabhakar* [1988] 3 All ER 718: below, p 162: see *Thompson v Nanaimo Realty Co Ltd* (1973) 44 DLR (3d) 254: with which contrast *Avery v Salie* (1972) 25 DLR (3d) 495. For the suggestion that an agent for reward owes a higher standard of care than a gratuitous agent see *Metropolitan Toronto Pension Plan v Aetna Life Assurance Co of Canada* (1992) 98 DLR (4th) 582 at 597.
 2 See *Andrew Master Hones Ltd v Cruickshank and Fairweather* [1979] FSR 268 (patent agent); *Volk v Schreiber* (1978) 82 DLR (3d) 602 (travel agent); *Russell v Wispenski* (1987) 13 BCLR (2d) 196 (real estate agent) *Metropolitan Toronto Pension Plan v Aetna Life Assurance Co of Canada* (1992) 98 DLR (4th) 582 (Investment of pension funds).
      Whether an agent has acted negligently is a question of fact. For an illustration, when there was no negligence by a forwarding agent, see *Pringle of Scotland Ltd v Continental Express Ltd* [1962] 2 Lloyd's Rep 80. Cf *Marston Excelsior Ltd v Arbuckle, Smith & Co Ltd* [1971] 1 Lloyd's Rep 70. For an example of negligence in making an ineffective re-insurance contract, see *Everett v Hogg Robinson and Gardner Mountain Insurance Ltd* [1973] 2 Lloyd's Rep 217. For other

having regard to the nature of his business, and has acted in as reasonable a manner as could be expected from an agent employed in such an undertaking, the agent will not be liable for negligence, even if his efforts were not successful.[3] Thus where a broker was employed to buy railway stock and did so on the market in the normal course of business, buying what was usually sold as scrip, he was not liable for misfeasance when it transpired that what he had bought was not genuine.[4] Where the agent obeys his instructions, he will not be liable even if the performance of them is not in the principal's interest,[5] unless possibly he was

instances of negligence by insurance agents, see the cases cited in Baer 'Annual Survey of Canadian Law: Insurance Law' (1980) 12 Ottawa LR 610 at pp 626–629; Fridman 'Annual Survey of Canadian Law: Commercial Law' (1981) 13 Ottawa LR 571 at p 578, note 14, p 596, note 91; and see *Lawrence V Roy v Curtis Insurance Agency Ltd* [1979] ILR 1–1090; *Dorner v Royal Insurance Co* [1979] ILR 1–1142; *LB Martin Construction Ltd v Gaglardi* [1979] ILR 1–1061; *GR Young v Dominion Insurance Corpn* [1979] ILR 1–1157; *McLeod v Lunenburg Insurance Agencies* [1980] ILR 1–1171; *Helpard v Atkinson Marine and General Insurance Ltd* [1981] ILR 1–1337; *Pond v Dovell* [1981] ILR 1–1343; *Knowles v General Accident Assurance Co of Canada* (1984) 49 OR (2d) 52; *Firestone Canada Inc v American Home Assurance Co* (1989) 67 OR (2d) 471; *Markal Investments Ltd v Morley Shafron Agencies Ltd* (1990) 67 DLR (4th) 422, reversing (1987) 44 DLR (4th) 745 on the issue of causation; *Engel v Janzen* (1990) 65 DLR (4th) 760 (insurance agent advising client to cancel insurance policy while on holiday).
For an example of negligence in selecting the choice of a sub-agent, in this case someone to drive the principal's car from Toronto to Calgary, see *Hillcrest General Leasing Ltd v Guelph Investments Ltd* (1971) 13 DLR (3d) 517. See also *New Zealand Farmers' Co-operative Distributing Co Ltd v National Mortgage and Agency Co of New Zealand Ltd* [1961] NZLR 969, where an agent employed to buy 'top' rams, was guilty of negligence by buying first-class rams which were not 'top': the agent lacked the knowledge and skill which the agent had held out to the principal he possessed. Hence, also, the dictum of Russell LJ in *Hill v Harris* [1965] 2 All ER 358 at 362 as to the liability of a solicitor who failed to inspect a head-lease when negotiating a sub-lease. For other cases involving lawyers or estate agents in relation to property, see *Kenney v Hall, Pain and Foster* (1976) 239 Estates Gazette 355 (negligence in valuing property); *Lough Eske Holdings v Knight Frank & Rutley* [1991] EGCS 18, [1991] CLYS 105 (failure to advise expert valuation): contrast *Watson v Lane Fox* [1991] ECGS 8 [1991] CLY 103; *Druce Investments v Thaker* [1991] CLY para 104; *Knight Frank & Rutley v Randolph* [1991] EGCS 7, [1991] CLY 106 (in none of which was the duty of care broken); *Palmeri and Palmeri v Littleton* [1979] 4 WWR 577; *Academy Aluminum Products Ltd v McInerny Realty Ltd* (1980) 113 DLR (3d) 289; *Spiewak v 251268 Ontario Ltd* (1988) 43 DLR (4th) 554; *Kotowich v Petursson* [1994] 3 WWR 669; *Flandro v Mitha* (1992) 93 DLR (4th) 222; *Rieger v Croft & Finlay* [1992] 5 WWR 700.
3 But the agent will be liable if *his* servant was negligent: *Brutton v Alfred Savill, Curtis and Henson* (1971) 218 Estates Gazette 1417. In *Fine's Flowers Ltd v General Accident Assurance Co of Canada* (1977) 81 DLR (3d) 139 (followed in many subsequent cases, see, eg, *Bell v Tinmouth* (1987) 39 DLR (4th) 595, reversed on appeal on the issue of negligence, (1989) 53 DLR (4th) 731), Estey CJO (as he then was) purported to place the agent's liability for breach of his obligation to exercise care and skill on the basis of breach of a fiduciary duty owed by the agent to the principal. The other members of the Ontario Court of Appeal preferred the more traditional grounds of negligence and breach of contract: see Fridman (1981) 13 Ottawa LR 571 at pp 596–598. The learned Chief Justice must have been incorrect in his confusion of two distinct responsibilities on the part of an agent: compare below, pp 174–188.
4 *Lambert v Heath* (1846) 15 M & W 486; Cf *Stafford v Conti Commodity Services Ltd* [1981] 1 All ER 691, no negligence by commodity brokers in the conduct of their principal's affairs. Nor was a real estate agent negligent in telling his principal not to worry about selling his house before making an unconditional offer to buy the third party's house, because the agent would be able to sell the principal's house: *Shields v Broderick* (1984) 8 DLR (4th) 96.
5 *Bertram v Godfray* (above, note 14); *Overend, Gurney & Co v Gibb* (1872) LR 5 HL 480. He is not under any duty to protect the principal from the latter's own stupidity in this respect: *RH Deacon & Co Ltd v Varga* [1973] 1 OR 233.

under the duty, by virtue of his position, to advise the principal upon what instructions should be given.[6] Where he has no instructions then the agent must act in the interests and for the benefit of his principal.[7]

Where an agent for reward is guilty of negligence in the performance of the contract of agency, it would now seem to be accepted that his liability to the principal may be for breach of contract and in tort for negligence:[8] the older exclusion of tort liability where a contract regulated the relationship of the parties[9] has been rejected by more recent decisions.[10] In this respect, if indeed in no others, the situation of the contractual agent resembles that of the gratuitous agent. Either may now be made liable in tort for negligence, since both kinds of agency involve a duty of care which, if not fulfilled, renders the agent susceptible to tort liability.

However, the duty owed by an agent acting in pursuance of a gratuitous agency has sometimes been expressed somewhat differently from that which is owed by an agent acting under a contract for reward. That may no longer be correct.

The classical, traditional mode of expressing the gratuitous agent's obligation was that the agent must exercise the care that a reasonable man would exercise in respect of his own affairs, or, if the agent has held himself out to possess the skill necessary for a particular undertaking, then the care which is reasonably necessary for that undertaking.[11] In other words, a person who does not profess to be skilled in any particular way need only show the same sort of care he would devote if he were performing the undertaking for himself. If he assumes a skill which would normally be shown by one following the trade, business, or profession in question, then he is bound to exercise the degree of care which

6 *Keppel v Wheeler* [1927] 1 KB 577, where the agent should have informed his principal of a later, better offer from another party; cf *Jackson v Packham Real Estate Ltd* (1980) 109 DLR (3d) 277, where the liability of the agent in similar circumstances was based on breach of fiduciary duty, not negligence. Does this support the view expressed by Estey CJO referred to above, note 3? Cf *Paul S Starr & Co Ltd v Watson* [1973] 1 OR 148, when the agent ought to have exercised care and so was disentitled to commission, even though the principal accepted the offer, which was in ambiguous terms.

7 *Pariente v Lubbock* (1855) 20 Beav 588; *Harrods Ltd v Lemon* [1931] 2 KB 157.

8 *Punjab National Bank v De Boinville* [1992] 1 Lloyd's Rep 7. See also *Forskikringsaktieselskapet Vesta v Butcher* [1988] 1 Lloyd's Rep 19; *Youell v Bland Welch & Co Ltd (No 2)* [1990] 2 Lloyd's Rep 431: *Macmillan v Knott Becker Scott Ltd* [1990] 1 Lloyd's Rep 98.

9 The older view may be seen expressed in cases such as *Bagot v Stevens, Scanlon & Co Ltd* [1966] 1 QB 197, [1964] 3 All ER 577; *Clark v Kirkby-Smith* [1964] Ch 506, [1964] 2 All ER 835; and the decision of the Supreme Court of Canada in *J Nunes Diamond Ltd v Dominion Electric Protection Ltd* (1972) 26 DLR (3d) 699.

10 *Esso Petroleum Co Ltd v Mardon* [1976] QB 801, [1976] 2 All ER 5; *Batty v Metropolitan Property Realisations Ltd* [1978] QB 554, [1978] 2 All ER 445; *Midland Bank Trust Co Ltd v Hett, Stubbs and Kemp* [1979] Ch 384, [1978] 3 All ER 571; *Fine's Flowers Ltd v General Accident Assurance Co* above, note 3; *Tai Hing Cotton Mill Ltd v Liu Chong Hing Bank Ltd* [1986] AC 80, [1985] 2 All ER 947; *Caparo Industries plc v Dickman* [1990] 2 AC 605, [1990] 1 All ER 568; *Lancashire and Cheshire Association of Baptist Churches Inc v Howard & Seddon Partnership* [1993] 3 All ER 467. *Central Trust v Rafuse* (1986) 31 DLR (4th) 481; *Canadian Pacific Hotels Ltd v Bank of Montreal* (1987) 40 DLR (4th) 385; *BG Checo International v BC Hydro and Power Authority* (1993) 99 DLR (4th) 577.

11 *Moffatt v Bateman* (1869) LR 3 PC 115; *Beal v South Devon Rly Co* (1864) 3 H & C 337; *Bowstead on Agency* (15th edn) p 152; cf Palmer, *Bailment* (2nd edn 1991) pp 528–564, 598–609.

normally would be expected of someone so skilled. Thus, unless misled by the agent as to his ability, a principal who entrusts an undertaking to an agent acting gratuitously will only be able to blame himself if he has chosen an incompetent, careless person to act on his behalf. Thus in *Shiells v Blackburne*:[12]

> An agent, acting gratuitously, entered a parcel belonging to the principal with one of his own at the Customs. By a mistake on the agent's part the parcels became liable to forfeiture, and were seized. It was held that the agent was not liable to the principal since he had exercised the same care in respect of the principal's parcel as he had shown in respect of his own.

In *Wilson v Brett*[13] an agent who gratuitously rode the principal's horse to show it to others was held obliged to exercise the skill he possessed. In *Giblin v McMullen*:[14]

> X deposited Railway Debentures with a bank. The deposit was on the facts a gratuitous one. Later a cashier fraudulently misappropriated the Debentures. It was held that the bank was not liable to X, because there had been no 'gross negligence'. The bank had not failed to exercise the care of a reasonable man in his own affairs, or, in more appropriate terms, the bank had not failed to exercise the care which any bank would normally be expected to exercise in such circumstances.[15]

The use of the expression 'gross negligence', in contrast with the unqualified sort of negligence for which an agent for reward will be liable, seems unnecessarily complicated. All that it appears to indicate is that something more than lack of skill is required before a gratuitous agent is liable for misfeasance, in respect of the undertaking.[16] An agent for reward, as seen above, undertakes to possess and exercise a certain skill, measured in terms of what is to be expected from agents in his position—an objective test for liability. A gratuitous agent does not undertake to possess any such skill, he merely undertakes that he will behave as carefully as he normally behaves, leaving it to the principal to discover how carefully that is—a subjective test of liability. The agent for reward, by implication, holds himself out to be as skilful and as careful as people in his trade, business, or profession normally are: this is a standard of care which the principal can be expected to have in mind when he employs the agent. The gratuitous agent, on the other hand, does not imply that he is any more skilful or careful than he himself actually is: the standard of care to be expected from such persons fluctuates with the individual. It is for the principal to satisfy himself as to the degree of skill and care he can expect from the agent.[17] In particular, this

12 (1789) 1 Hy Bl 158.
13 (1843) 11 M & W 113.
14 (1868) LR 2 PC 317; (a case of bailment, but, seemingly, governed by the same principles). On the comparison of gratuitous agency and bailment, see Stoljar *Law of Agency* pp 273–274.
15 (1868) LR 2 PC 317, at pp 337–338 per Lord Chelmsford.
16 Cf the remarks of Ormrod LJ in *Houghland v RR Low (Luxury Coaches) Ltd* [1962] 2 All ER 159 at 160–161 (a bailment case); and the comments of Stuart-Smith LJ in *Chaudhry v Prabhakar* [1988] 3 All ER 718 at 721. On the whole subject cf Paton *Bailment* pp 100–110, 135–138; Palmer *Bailment* (2nd edn 1991) pp 528–547, 598–609, who is critical of the classical differentiation between degrees of negligence, and questions its modern validity and application.
17 Cf the distinction in Roman law between mandatum and depositum: Buckland *Text Book of Roman Law* (3rd edn 1963) pp 467–468, 514–518.

means that it is for the principal to make sure that the agent is one who will be likely to perform the undertaking; hence there is no liability on the part of a gratuitous agent for non-feasance, even though there may be liability for mis-feasance, if there has been a failure to observe the standard of care described above.[18]

The Court of Appeal may have resolved the issue of a gratuitous agent's duty of care in *Chaudhry v Prabhakar*.[19] There it was said that the standard of care, set out earlier, was an objective standard. It was not to be measured simply by the agent's honest statement that he would have acted similarly if he had been transacting the business on his own account however foolish that may be. Hence, the view of Stuart-Smith LJ that the agent's duty of care, whether the agent was acting gratuitously or for reward, was 'that which may reasonably be expected of him in all the circumstances'.[20] The relevant circumstances were to be considered in determining whether a sufficient standard of care had been observed. One of those relevant circumstances was whether or not the agent was paid. If paid the relationship was contractual and express terms might resolve the issue. Moreover a paid agent in a trade, profession or calling was required to exercise the degree of skill and diligence reasonably to be expected of a person exercising such trade, profession or calling, irrespective of the degree of skill he may possess. Where the agent is unpaid, however, the duty of care arises in tort.

> 'Relevant circumstances would be the actual skill and experience that an agent had, although, if he has represented such skill and experience to be greater than it in fact is and the principal has relied on such representation, it seems to me to be reasonable to expect him to show that standard of skill and experience which he claims to possess.'[1]

The fact that the parties were friends did not affect the existence of a duty of care though it might be a relevant circumstance in considering the degree or standard of care. However, that the parties were friends might indicate that advice or a representation was made on a purely social occasion, and that there was no voluntary assumption of responsibility necessary for liability under the doctrine first enunciated in *Hedley Byrne & Co Ltd v Heller & Partners Ltd*,[2] which laid down the basic requirements of liability for a negligent misrepresentation.[3] The facts which gave rise to these comments were as follows:

> The plaintiff knew nothing about cars. She asked the first defendant, a friend who had some knowledge of cars, although he was not a mechanic, to find her a suitable secondhand car to buy. She stipulated that it should not have been involved in an accident. The defendant found a car being offered for

---

18 *Wilkinson v Coverdale* (1793) 1 Esp 74, above, p 138. But see Palmer *Bailment* pp 339–342. The passage from 'An agent for reward' down to the end of this paragraph was cited and relied on by Andrekson J in *Modern Livestock Ltd v Elgersma* (1980) 50 CCLT 5 at 49 (where it was unnecessary to decide whether this standard had been breached). The passage from 'It is for the principal to satisfy himself' to the end of this paragraph was quoted by Walsh J in *Engine & Leasing Co v Atlantic Towing Ltd* (1992) 52 FTR 1 at 36.
19 [1988] 3 All ER 718.
20 Ibid at 721.
 1 Ibid.
 2 [1964] AC 465, [1963] 2 All ER 575.
 3 [1988] 3 All ER 718 at 722.

sale by the second defendant, a car sprayer and panel beater. The car's bonnet had been crumpled and straightened or replaced. Nevertheless the first defendant thought the car was in good condition and recommended that the plaintiff buy it, which she did. A few months later it became clear that the car had been in an accident, had been badly repaired, and was unroadworthy. The plaintiff sued both defendants. At trial the judge held that the first defendant had breached his duty to take reasonable care (the other defendant being liable for breach of an implied term that the car was of merchantable quality). On appeal this judgment was affirmed as regards the first defendant.

On the basis of the reasons referred to earlier by Stuart-Smith LJ, the friend, a gratuitous agent, owed a duty of care to exercise such care and skill as could be expected of him in all the circumstances. He knew that the plaintiff relied on him, and, since he ought to have been put on inquiry by the crumpled bonnet, and the trade of the other defendant, and should have inquired whether the car had been involved in an accident, he was in breach of that duty. Both Stuart-Smith LJ and Stocker LJ interpreted the standard of care as objective, not subjective.[4] The question was whether the reasonable man in these circumstances would have acted as the friend acted, or would have taken other steps, ie made further inquiries. On that test the friend had fallen short of what was expected of him both by the plaintiff and by the law. May LJ was doubtful of the concession made by the defendant that he owed a duty to take such care in and about the plaintiff's business as he would have done about his own affairs.[5] That doubt was based on recent developments in the law of negligence since the views of Lord Wilberforce in *Anns v Merton London Borough*.[6] To apply the 'formalities of the law of tort' to the situation in this case, a family friend looking out for a first car for a girl of 26, was not entirely attractive. To do so in this and similar cases would make social regulations and responsibilities between friends unnecessarily hazardous. However, he accepted the consequences of the concession made by the defendant, as a result of which, even between friends, when one was the gratuitous agent of the other, a duty of care could arise and its standard would be determined not by the actual qualities and abilities of the agent, but on an objective basis.[7]

Although Stuart-Smith LJ, if not the other members of the court, was prepared to treat *Chaudhry v Prabhakar* as a case of agency, it is possible to argue on the basis of what was said by all three judges that what was involved here was not an agency relationship, requiring determination of the issue by the application of the relevant principles of the law of agency, but the negligent giving of unsound advice or a negligent misrepresentation, which ought to have been resolved by the application of the relevant principles of the law of negligence, namely, the extent to which a causal statement made without responsibility among social acquaintances, given without any intent thereby to create legal relations, ie a contract, should entail legal liability. Hence the case is not a strong decision on

4 Ibid at 721, 724.
5 Ibid at 725.
6 [1978] AC 728 at 751–752, [1977] 2 All ER 492 at 498.
7 [1988] 3 All ER 718 at 725.

the issue under discussion, namely, the standard of care expected of a gratuitous agent.[8] In view of some of the statements made, especially by Stocker and May LJJ,[9] it might have been more appropriate for the court to consider the facts in light of the evolution of liability for negligent misrepresentation causing economic loss following the decision in *Hedley Byrne v Heller & Partners*.[10] On that basis, as hinted at in the *Chaudhry* case, had it not been for the defendant's admission of the existence of a duty of care, it is likely that no such duty would have been found to have arisen. To have done so would have carried the *Hedley Byrne* doctrine to extreme lengths. It might also have confused liability arising from contract with liability in tort.[11] Since 1963, when *Hedley Byrne* was decided, courts in the common law world have been struggling with the problem of determining the scope and limits of non-contractual liability for verbal negligence causing economic loss. The *Chaudhry* case purports to hold that one way to solve the difficulty is by finding, if possible, that an agency relationship was in existence between the one making the statement or giving the advice and the one who relied thereon. But the language of the court in that case indicates another difficulty: that of deciding whether the actual relationship between those parties was such as to justify a finding that one was the agent of the other where no contract or intent to create legal relations can be discovered in the circumstances.

In one sense, therefore, *Chaudhry v Prabakhar* solves one problem but creates a new one. The case may also suggest that the study of gratuitous agency can offer fertile ground for exploring the juridical basis of agency, and for deciding whether its development in specific cases should be modelled on contract, tort, trust, bailment or restitution. If such an approach were adopted it might spell the disappearance of agency as a distinct body of law, and the end of the principal–agent relationship as being meaningful. Such a result, it is suggested, would be unacceptable. Admittedly there are connections and to some degree overlap between agency and other branches of the law: but that does not mean that the time has, or will, come to declare that agency, as such, is dead, as being unnecessary or irrelevant to the modern English legal system or the realities of the commercial world. To read this into the decision in *Chaudhry v Prabhakar* is to go too far.

Non-delegation. The general rule is that the agent must perform his undertaking personally. The relationship of principal and agent is a confidential one: the principal imposes trust in the agent of his choice. Hence the obligation of the agent is to act personally, in conformity with the maxim delegatus non potest delegare, which applies here as in the law of trusts and administrative law, and for the same reasons. Unless permitted by the law or by the contract between the parties the employment of a sub-agent by the agent will be a breach of his

8 Although it is cited as a case on gratuitous agency in Palmer *Bailment* (2nd edn 1991) at pp 24, 54, 126, 541, 621, 649.
9 [1988] 3 All ER 718 at 723–725.
10 [1964] AC 465, [1963] 2 All ER 575; *Salmond and Heeuston on Torts* (20th edn 1992) pp 214–218; *Winfield and Jolowicz on Torts* (14th edn 1994) pp 290–302.
11 See the discussion in [1988] All ER Rev 18 at pp 19–20.

obligation to the principal. As Buckley J explained in the case of *Allam & Co Ltd v Europa Poster Services Ltd*:[12]

> 'The relation of an agent to his principal is normally at least one which is of a confidential character and the application of the maxim *delegatus non potest delegare* to such relationships is founded on the confidential nature of the relationship. Where the principal reposes no personal confidence in the agent the maxim has no application, but where the principal does place confidence in the agent that in respect of which the principal does so must be done by the agent personally unless either expressly or inferentially he is authorised to employ a sub-agent or to delegate the function to another. If the agent personally performs all that part of his function which involves any confidence conferred on him or reposed in him by the principal it is, in my judgment, immaterial that he employs another person to carry out some purely ministerial act on his behalf in completing the transaction.'

This was a case involving the service of a notice to terminate a licence by a company to another company. Several notices were involved since several licences were involved. Each notice was comprised in a letter served by the solicitors of the defendant company. The question so far as this part of the case was concerned was whether this service of a notice was in each instance valid. The argument of the plaintiffs was that the serving of a notice was something which could not be delegated hence the letter from the solicitors was insufficient to make the notice capable of terminating the arrangement. On this the learned judge said:

> 'The defendant company, being an incorporated company, could not in its own person serve notices determining any of these arrangements. Any incorporated company must always act through some agent or other and, therefore, this may be one of those cases in which by inference the agent is authorised by the principal to act through an agent in performance of his agency. It seems to me to be of no particular significance if an agent employed is not, for instance, the secretary of the company or one of its directors but is its solicitor. The important consideration is whether, in doing what it did, the defendant company exercised the will power and made the decisions and did all in respect of its agency under its authority from the various site owners in respect of which those site owners reposed any confidence in the defendant company.'

It should be pointed out that the defendant company was acting as the agent for the site owners who had originally granted the licensing agreement. Hence the defendant company was an agent and the question of delegation arose. In this respect the decision of the learned judge was that the way the defendant company performed its duty as an agent of the site owners was legitimate and valid.

The facts of this case and the extract from the judgment which has been cited above reveal not only the basic principles of the law in regard to delegation by an agent but also the recognition by the law that there are circumstances in which it is permissible for the agent to delegate the performance of the undertaking to another.

12 [1968] 1 All ER 826 at 832.

Thus if, as in the above case, the act done is purely ministerial, not involving confidence or the exercise of discretion, such as the affixing of a signature, or digging a grave and ringing a bell,[13] this may be done by a subordinate of the agent.[14] So, too, in a Canadian case,[15] a foreign Consul, who had been given a power of attorney under the will of a deceased person, although therefore an agent, was entitled to appoint someone else to perform the real task of the agency, namely the administration of the deceased's estate. The Consul, not being an executive officer, but an intermediary on behalf of others, felt it was reasonable to infer that the donor of the power of attorney intended that the Consul should delegate his authority. Such delegation may not occur, however when it is 'an employment to which personal skill was essential'.[16] Thus in *John McCann & Co v Pow*[17] delegation by the estate agents employed by a vendor to another firm of estate agents was not permitted, because the acts in question were not of a purely ministerial nature. In consequence the estate agents were not entitled to commission on the sale effected by the agents to whom they had improperly delegated their duty. Much more important, however, is the fact that delegation is not a breach of the agent's duty to his principal if it is within the scope of his authority, whether express, implied, or usual, or is subsequently ratified by the principal (and therefore, in accordance with the ideas already discussed, ex post facto expressly authorised), or is required by the exigencies of necessity.[18] Thus in the leading case of *De Bussche v Alt*:[19]

> The principal appointed X his agent to sell a ship in China at a certain price. X not being able to sell the ship in China at the agreed price, obtained the approval of the principal to the appointment by him of a sub-agent in Japan, to sell the ship at the price required by the principal. It was held that this was not a breach of the agent's duty.

This was a case where there was express consent to the delegation. But consent may be implied, for example, where it was obvious that the agent must act through subordinates so that delegation can be said to have been intended by the principal, eg where the agent is a corporation.[20] Or the use of subordinates may be within the usual authority of the agent, being justified by trade or other usage, in accordance with the rules of law applying to such usages which have already

---

13 *St Margaret's, Rochester, Burial Board v Thompson* (1871) LR 6 CP 445. Similarly an additional superintendent registrar of births, deaths and marriages may be an agent, although a delegate, for the purpose of the Prevention of Corruption Act 1906: *R v Barrett* [1976] 3 All ER 895, [1976] 1 WLR 946.

14 *White v Proctor* (1811) 4 Taunt 209.

15 *Re Deutsch* (1976) 82 DLR (3d) 567: but the application to appoint such an administrator was refused on other, procedural grounds.

16 *John McCann & Co v Pow* [1975] 1 All ER 129 at 132 per Lord Denning MR.

17 [1975] 1 All ER 129, [1974] 1 WLR 1643.

18 *De Bussche v Alt* (1878) 8 Ch D 286. This may also explain the view expressed in *Re Deutsch*, above. For an example of express authority to delegate see *United Real Estate Inc v Headrick* (1988) 65 Sask LR 118, contrast *S/S Steamship Co v The Alchatby* (1986) 5 FTR 253; affd (1988) 29 FTR 106n, where there was no express authority to appoint a sub-agent.

19 (1878) 8 Ch D 286.

20 No such authority could be implied in *John McCann & Co v Pow* above; nor in *S/S Steamship Co v The Alchatby*, above.

been discussed. For example, the practice of country solicitors having town agents may be cited.[1] In short, therefore, the question of delegation is bound up with the problem of the agent's authority, and is to be settled by reference to that authority.

Where delegation is allowed, then the agent will be liable to the principal for breaches of duty on the part of the sub-agent.[2] Thus the liability of the agent will not depend upon whether or not the delegation was within the scope of his authority. But that will affect the nature of the relationship between the principal and the person to whom the agent has delegated the performance of the undertaking.

The general rule is that delegation does not create any privity of contract between principal and sub-agent.[3] Hence, so far as any rights or liabilities in contract are concerned, the principal may sue and be sued only by his agent and the sub-agent may only sue and be sued by the agent.[4] For example in *Schmaling v Tomlinson*[5] the sub-agent could not recover compensation from the principal for services rendered; and in *Calico Printers' Association v Barclays Bank*[6] the principal could not recover anything from the sub-agents for their failure to insure goods of which a purchaser had failed to take delivery, to effect which

1 See *Solley v Wood* (1852) 16 Beav 370; *Robbins v Fennell* (1847) 11 QB 248. Another, more modern, illustration is the Canadian case of *Carmichael v Bank of Montreal* (1972) 25 DLR (3d) 570, in which a court took notice of, and applied a trade usage as to delegation by a 'real estate broker', ie estate agent.

2 *Mackersy v Ramsays, Bonars & Co* (1843) 9 Cl & Fin 818; *Swire v Francis* (1877) 3 App Cas 106; *Academy Aluminum Products Ltd v McInerny Realty Ltd* (1980) 113 DLR (3d) 289. See *Benjamin v Clothier* (1969) 210 Estates Gazette 29, where there was liability for deposits paid by purchasers to the sub-agent of the vendors' agents, when the sub-agent absconded: (but this case may now be wrong in view of the decision in *Sorrell v Finch* [1977] AC 728, [1976] 2 All ER 371; above, p 82). In *Edwards Real Estate Ltd v Bamtar Holdings Ltd* (1978) 7 Alta LR (2d) 52, an agent was held liable when his employee, the sub-agent, wrongfully purchased the principal's property which the agent was employed to sell.

  There may not be such liability for the negligent acts of a sub-agent (aliter, possibly, with respect to breaches of fiduciary duty, as in the *Edwards Real Estate* case) if the agent has acted with reasonable care and skill in choosing the sub-agent: Stoljar *Law of Agency* p 280, citing and comparing *Re Mitchell, Mitchell v Mitchell* (1884) 54 LJ Ch 342 and *T Cheshire & Co v Vaughan Bros & Co* [1920] 3 KB 240 at 259, per Atkin LJ. For an example of *lack* of such care, see *Hillcrest General Leasing Ltd v Guelph Investments Ltd* (1971) 13 DLR (3d) 517 (negligence in selecting agent to drive principal's car from one city to another).

3 In *United Real Estate Inc v Headrick*, above, there was held to be privity of contract between the principal and the sub-agent, resulting in the latter's being able to claim commission from the principal. Was this a case of substitution, rather than delegation? See below, p 168.

  The sub-agent will have certain rights of lien over the goods and chattels of the principal, ie *either*, those he would have had against the agent, if the agent had been the owner of the goods or chattels in question: *or*, those the agent would have had against the principal, if the agent had been in possession of the goods: *Mann v Forrester* (1814) 4 Camp 60; *Montagu v Forwood* [1893] 2 QB 350; *Mildred v Maspons* (1883) 8 App Cas 874. (For the agent's lien, see below, pp 207–211.) If the sub-agency is *unauthorised*, the sub-agent will have no lien: *Solly v Rathbone* (1814) 2 M & S 298.

4 *Lockwood v Abdy* (1845) 14 Sim 437; *Mason v Clifton* (1863) 3 F & F 899. See *Balsamo v Medici* [1984] 2 All ER 304 at 309 per Walton J. Cf *New Zealand and Australian Land Co v Watson* (1881) 7 QBD 374.

5 (1815) 6 Taunt 147.

6 (1931) 145 LT 51.

insurance the agent had been instructed. However, Powell pointed out that this is only where the agent has authority to appoint a sub-agent to perform the undertaking.[7] This, he described as 'a true case of delegation'.[8] He distinguished this from situations in which the agent is employed to create the relationship of *agent* between the principal and a third party (as for example in *De Bussche v Alt*, where what really happened was that the relationship of principal and agent was created between the principal and the sub-agent in Japan),[9] and situations in which the agent has undertaken to provide a substitute for himself.[10] In these instances the effect of the argument is that the first agent is functus officio on the appointment of the other one, who then becomes the principal's agent, with the usual rights and liabilities on the part of both principal and agent. Powell was of the opinion that these three instances of non-personal performance of the undertaking by the original agent must be carefully distinguished to avoid confusion. But it seems unnecessary to say more than: (i) where the agent is not authorised to get someone else to perform the undertaking, there is no privity of contract between principal and sub-agent;[11] (ii) where he is so authorised (for one of the reasons already discussed) the question of privity of contract between principal and sub-agent will turn upon the intention of the principal in the light of the express or implied authority he gave to the original agent; (iii) it may be said as a general guiding principal that the law leans against the creation of privity between principal and sub-agent, and requires what Wright J called[12] 'precise proof 'before the authorisation of the creation of such privity can be substituted.

On the other hand, even though there is no such privity between a principal and a sub-agent as will entitle either party to sue the other in contract for an alleged breach of duty, it may be that an action in tort would lie.[13] Recent

---

7 It is, of course, also true where the agent acts without authority in delegating: the principal will not be bound by the sub-agent's acts, and the agent will be liable to the principal for breach of duty.

8 *Law of Agency* p 308: in the first edition of his book Powell described this as the *only* true case of delegation. See also Seavey 'Subagents and Subservants' (1955) 68 HLR 658; *Restatement, Second, Agency* para 406, and Appendix Vol 3 pp 25–36.

9 See also *Calico Printers' Association v Barclays Bank* (1931) 145 LT 51 at 55 per Wright J.

10 *Schwenson v Ellinger, Heath, Western & Co* (1949) 83 Ll L Rep 79. Cf *Re Deutsch* (1976) 82 DLR (3d) 567, where such undertaking might be said to have been implicit in the relationship between the Consul and the deceased. A sub-agent of this kind will be liable to the principal as if he were the agent, eg for breach of fiduciary duty: *Guaranty Trust Co v Jerol Investments* (1977) 4 Alta LR (2d) 215. Was *De Bussche v Alt* also a case of this kind?

11 *S/S Steamship Co v The Alchatby* (1986) 5 FTR 253; affd (1989) 29 FTR 106n.

12 *Calico Printers' Association v Barclays Bank* (1931) 145 LT 51 at 55.

13 Support for this might has been derived from the decision of the House of Lords in *Junior Books Ltd v Veitchi Co Ltd* [1983] 1 AC 520, [1982] 3 All ER 201 (see the remarks of Walton J in *Balsamo v Medici* [1984] 2 All ER 304 at 310). But subsequent decisions of the House of Lords and the Court of Appeal have severely curtailed the potential scope of this case: see *Leigh and Sillavan Ltd v Aliakmon Shipping Co Ltd* [1986] AC 785, [1986] 2 All ER 145; *London Congregational Union Inc v Harriss* [1988] 1 All ER 15; *Simaan General Contracting Co v Pilkington Glass Ltd (No 2)* [1988] QB 758, [1988] 1 All ER 791; *Greater Nottingham Co-operative Society Ltd v Cementation Piling and Foundations Ltd* [1989] QB 71, [1988] 2 All ER 971; *Caparso Industries plc v Dickman* [1990] 2 AC 605, [1990] 1 All ER 568. See also *D&F Estates Ltd v Church Comrs for England* [1989] AC 177, [1988] 2 All ER 992; *Murphy v Brentwood District Council* [1991] 1 AC 398, [1990] 2 All ER 908.

developments in the law relating to bailees has shown that when goods are bailed by P to A and A then makes a sub-bailment of the goods to T (eg under a contract between A and T whereby T is to perform a certain task in respect of the goods) then T may be liable to P if the goods are lost or damaged through T's negligence, or through the negligence or wrongful act of T's servant.[14] In other words, using the language of agency, not bailment, if there is delegation by A to T, a sub-agent, or sub-contractor, and the delegation involves a bailment of the principal's goods to the sub-agent there is a sufficiently proximate relationship between the principal and the sub-agent in *tort*, even if there is no contractual relationship, to create duties and liabilities at least as between the sub-agent and the principal.

For example in *Lee Cooper Ltd v C H Jeakins & Sons Ltd*[15] the principal instructed his agent to deliver goods from London to Eire. As part of the performance of this task the agent contracted with a sub-agent for the delivery of the goods to the agent's warehouse. While on route, the goods were stolen because of the negligence of the sub-agent's servant. It was held that the sub-agent, through contracting with the agent, who was a principal for this purpose, could be liable in tort to the agent's principal, the owner of the goods. So, too, in *Morris v CW Martin & Sons Ltd*[16] where the bailee of goods to repair made a sub-bailment to the defendant, whose employee stole them. The sub-bailee (or sub-agent as he may be termed in this instance) was liable to the owner of the goods, the original principal. Similarly in *Moukataff v British Overseas Airways Corpn*[17] the sub-bailees, BOAC, who were agents of the principal's agents (his bank) for the delivery of banknotes to Kuwait, were liable to the principal when the notes were stolen by reason of the sub-bailee's neglect or the wrongdoing of the sub-bailee's servants. In contrast in *Johnson Matthey & Co Ltd v Constantine Terminals Ltd and International Express Co Ltd*[18] where a sub-bailee was prima facie guilty of negligence in respect of the silver originally entrusted by the plaintiffs to bailees, who then delivered the silver to the sub-bailees, any liability for such negligence was held to have been excluded by an exemption clause contained in the contract between the plaintiffs, the original bailors, and the bailees. Donaldson J held that the plaintiffs could not prove the bailment on which they relied for the success of their action without also referring to the terms on which the silver being bailed was received by the sub-bailees from the original bailees. Those terms included an exemption clause that qualified the duties of the sub-bailees as bailees, or sub-bailees, for reward. The language of the learned judge suggests either that there was an original privity of contract between the bailors and the sub-bailees or that, if no such privity existed originally, it was created *ex post facto* by conduct amounting to ratification. This

---

14 This subject is given extensive treatment in Palmer *Bailment* (2nd edn 1991) ch 20. In *Balsamo v Medici*, above, at 310, Walton J confined this development to cases of bailment, although counsel, relying on what is said on these pages, attempted to persuade the learned judge to apply similar developments to agency.

15 [1967] 2 QB 1, [1965] 1 All ER 280; cf *Learoyd Bros & Co Ltd and Huddersfield Fine Worsteds v Pope & Sons Ltd* [1966] 2 Lloyd's Rep 142; *British Road Services Ltd v Arthur V Crutchley & Co Ltd* [1968] 1 All ER 811; *James Buchanan & Co Ltd v Hay's Transport Services Ltd* [1972] 2 Lloyd's Rep 535.

16 [1966] 1 QB 716, [1965] 2 All ER 725, for another aspect of this case see below, pp 317–319.

17 [1967] 1 Lloyd's Rep 396.

18 [1976] 2 Lloyd's Rep 215: see also above p 85, note 3; below, pp 328.

decision seems to be anomalous, and dependent on the particular facts of the case. The majority of the cases deal with the liability of sub-bailees on the basis of tort, not contract. By such means, as previously seen, courts have been able to avoid the problem of privity. Indeed in *The Pioneer Container*[19] Lord Goff criticised the decision of Donaldson J in the *Johnson Matthey* case as being inconsistent with earlier decisions such as that in *Morris v CW Martin & Sons*. It would appear, therefore, that the decision and the reasoning in the *Johnson Matthey* case must now be considered incorrect.

The attempt to apply the tort approach to agency generally, which failed in *Balsamo v Medici*,[20] is affected by several important qualifications or conditions of such liability.

In the first place, everything seems to depend upon there being a bailment of goods as well as a delegation of the agent's duty. It would not seem that a sub-agent could be liable simply for negligence which affected the principal injuriously otherwise than through the loss of or damage to his goods. An argument to such effect was attempted by the principal in the Guyanan case of *Bart v British West Indian Airways Ltd*[21] where the 'principal' (as he may be called, though it is doubtful whether the situation was truly one of agency) complained that because of the sub-agent's negligence the principal's pools coupon was delivered late in consequence of which the principal was unable to claim the sum he would have won on the coupon. This argument was rejected by the majority of the court after an exhaustive analysis of earlier case law which showed that negligence which did not affect the goods of the principal or bailor would not be remediable.

Secondly, except where the situation involves carriage of goods by sea, in respect of which the Carriage of Goods by Sea Act 1992, s 2 has altered the law, the goods in respect of loss or damage to which there is a claim must be goods owned by the principal or bailor at the material time. Where that statute applies, a person who, as consignee of goods being transported by sea, has neither title to, nor possession of such goods may now sue, where, formerly,[1] such a person could not. This change in the law may effectively deal with the majority of situations when a sub-agency, or sub-bailment, concerns goods that are not owned or possessed by the principal or bailor. However, it is conceivable that there might be instances in which a non-owner of goods without possession of them at the time the sub-agency or sub-bailment arises could be denied any remedy against a negligent sub-agent or sub-bailee.

As previously mentioned, an attempt to apply the bailment cases to a situation of agency, not involving the bailment of goods, was made unsuccessfully in *Balsamo v Medici*.[2] There an agent delegated to a sub-agent the task of selling the

---

19 [1994] 2 AC 324 at 340–341, [1994] 2 All ER 250 at 260–261.
20 [1984] 2 All ER 304, [1984] 1 WLR 951.
21 [1967] 1 Lloyd's Rep 239.
 1 See *Margarine Union GmbH v Cambay Prince SS Co Ltd* [1969] 1 QB 219, [1967] 3 All ER 775; *Albacruz (Cargo Owners) v Albazero (Owners), The Albazero* [1977] AC 774 [1976] 3 All ER 129; *Leigh and Sillavan Ltd v Aliakmon Shipping Co Ltd* [1986] AC 785, [1986] 2 All ER 145.
 2 [1984] 2 All ER 304, [1984] 1 WLR 951. Note the importance of the agent's duty to account: below, p 173; and the absence of any such duty on the part of the sub-agent: [1984] 2 All ER 304 at 312.

plaintiff's car. The sale was made by the sub-agent, who was unaware of the existence of the principal. The agent returned to Italy before the purchaser of the car paid the total amount of the purchase price to the auctioneer who sold it. The agent instructed the sub-agent to collect the remaining money and see that it was obtained by the principal's relative, to whom the principal had instructed the agent the money should be paid. The sub-agent lost that relative's telephone number and so could not get in touch with her. An impostor later contacted the sub-agent claiming to be the person entitled to receive the money, and, without making any check of identity, the sub-agent handed the money to the impostor's representative. The principal sued the agent and the sub-agent. The agent was liable for breach of contract. The sub-agent was not liable either on the basis of any liability to account for the proceeds as a sub-agent or in negligence. Walton J held that there was no privity between principal and sub-agent. Nor could the principal sue the sub-agent in negligence as no duty of care arose as between sub-agent and principal. The principal's only right of action was in contract against the agent. He could have sued the sub-agent only as a co-contractor, which he was not, or as a joint tortfeasor with the agent, but that too was not possible. The principal could not sue the agent in contract and the sub-agent in tort in respect of the same damage. It must be noted, however, that the problem in this case appears to have arisen because the agent did not serve a third party notice on the sub-agent. Had he done so, the sub-agent could have been made liable. Since the principal was attempting to sue the sub-agent directly, the lack of privity and absence of any tort liability in these circumstances resolved the issue against the principal.

Respect of principal's title. The agent cannot deny the title of the principal to goods, money, or land possessed by the agent on behalf of the principal. The possession of the agent is the possession of the principal for all purposes, including the acquisition of title under statutes of limitation,[3] even where in fact the agent, though in ignorance of his claim, is entitled to the land,[4] unless the agent possesses not as agent but on his own behalf, in which event his possession will be personal and not for his principal.[5] This means also that the agent cannot dispute his principal's claim to goods put in his possession by the principal and held on the principal's behalf, for example, if the agent is a wharfinger, or a carrier, and the principal has given him goods to hold or deliver on his behalf.[6]

None the less, there are circumstances in which the agent will be able to refuse

---

3 *Dixon v Hamond* (1819) 2 B & Ald 310; *Lyell v Kennedy* (1889) 14 App Cas 437.
4 *Williams v Pott* (1871) LR 12 Eq 149. Where money is paid by the principal to the agent to discharge liabilities of the principal, the agent will not be a constructive trustee of such money (so as to prevent the agent's creditor from taking or keeping it) except in very special circumstances: *Neste Oy v Lloyds Bank plc* [1983] 2 Lloyd's Rep 658.
5 *A-G v London Corpn* (1850) 19 LJ Ch 314. Hence in *Zurich Insurance Co v Tippet* [1978] CLY 3, the agent claimed that he was entitled to commission and damages for loss of reputation in respect of insurance premiums collected by the agent for the principal but not yet paid over to the principal. The agent's claim failed for want of evidence. In a criminal case, *R v Brewster* (1979) 69 Cr App Rep 375, an agent who received insurance premiums on behalf of his principal could be guilty of an offence under the Theft Act 1968, when he used the money for his own purposes. The title in the money was in the principal.
6 *Betteley v Reed* (1843) 4 QB 511; *Sheridan v New Quay Co* (1858) 4 CBNS 618.

to accept the claim by his principal to property possessed by him. If a third party is entitled to the property in question the agent may set up the title of such third party (ie plead jus tertii). Thus, if the principal has wrongfully distrained X's goods and given them to the agent (an auctioneer), the latter may set up X's title against his principal when he discovers the truth.[7] At common law, this would only apply where the agent, at the time of taking possession of the property in question, had no knowledge of adverse claims in respect of it: if he had such knowledge, and none the less took possession on behalf of the principal, then he could not set up the adverse claimant's title against his principal.[8] Now, under the Torts (Interference with Goods) Act 1977,[9] the plea of jus tertii may be raised in respect of any action for 'wrongful interference with goods'.[10] Hence at common law, and under the statute this does not apply where the agent has received money on behalf of his principal.[11]

However, it would seem that if the agent receives money from his principal which belongs at law or in equity to a third party, the agent will not be accountable to that third party unless he has been guilty of some wrongful act in relation to that money. In other words, the agent is protected by reliance on the title of his principal unless he can somehow be classified as acting wrongfully. Acting wrongfully involves (i) knowingly participating in a breach of trust by the principal or (ii) intermeddling with the trust property otherwise than merely as an agent or (iii) receiving or dealing with the money knowing that his principal has no right to pay it over or to instruct him to deal with it in the manner indicated or (iv) some dishonest act relating to the money.[12] 'The law being reluctant to make a mere agent a constructive trustee' as Edmund Davies LJ said (quoting Lord Selbourne LC in *Barnes v Addy*)[13] in the case of *Carl-Zeiss Stiftung v Herbert Smith & Co (No 2)*:[14]

> 'mere notice of a claim asserted by a third party is insufficient to render the agent guilty of a wrongful act in dealing with property derived from his principal in accordance with the latter's instructions unless the agent *knows* that the third party's claim is well founded and that the principal accordingly had no authority to give such instructions.'

There is a possible exception here where the agent is under a duty to enquire into the validity of the third party's claim. Failure to enquire may constitute wrongful

---

7 *Biddle v Bond* (1865) 6 B & S 225; see also *Rogers, Sons & Co v Lambert & Co* [1891] 1 QB 318.

8 *Re Sadler, ex p Davies* (1881) 19 Ch D 86.

9 Section 8(1): see also ibid ss 7, 9: see generally, Palmer *Bailment* (2nd edn 1991) pp 259–260, 354–359; *Winfield and Jolowicz on Tort* (14th edn 1994) pp 497–515.

10 Viz, conversion, trespass, negligence and any other tort so far as it results in damage to goods or an interest in goods: Torts (Interference with Goods) Act 1977, s 1.

11 *Blaustein v Maltz, Mitchell & Co* [1937] 2 KB 142, [1937] 1 All ER 497.

12 But the agent may be liable even if he does not profit by receiving any trust property, and even if the trustee was not dishonest or fraudulent: *Royal Brunei Airlines Sdn Bhd v Tan* [1995] 3 All ER 97, and cases there cited.

13 (1874) 9 Ch App 244, at 251, 252.

14 [1969] 2 All ER 367 at 384: italics in original. For an account of the liability of *strangers* as constructive trustees, which might have some relevance to the situation of agents, see the judgment of Ungoed-Thomas J in *Selangor United Rubber Estates Ltd v Cradock (No 3)* [1968] 2 All ER 1073 at 1095–1105. See Goff and Jones *Law of Restitution* (4th edn 1993) pp 670–672.

conduct by the agent. For example, in the case from which that quotation comes, the plaintiff, an East German company, was suing the solicitors of a West German company of the same name, alleging that the property and assets possessed by the West German company really belonged to the East German company. In consequence of this the defendants were alleged to be accountable to the plaintiffs for all moneys received from the West German company for fees, costs and disbursements derived from the property in the hands of the West German company. The plaintiffs failed, on the ground, inter alia, that since the plaintiffs' claim to the property in the hands of the West German company was unsettled, there was no valid legal or equitable proprietary claim by the plaintiffs so as to set up an adverse title against the defendants as constructive trustees or to dis-enable the defendant to rely on the title of their principals, the West German company.

Should the agent find himself in difficulties on questions of title, he may interplead, and so obtain a decision of the court resolving adverse claims.[15]

Duty to account. It follows from what has been said above that the agent must pay over to his principal all money received to the use of his principal.[16] This contractual, or restitutionary duty exists even if, as already seen, there is an adverse claim to the money by someone else, including the agent, to whom the principal's debtor may owe money.[17] It exists even if the transaction in respect of which the money is received by the agent on behalf of the principal was void or illegal, as long as the contract of agency is not itself illegal.[18] Thus if a turf commission agent is employed to make bets he must pay over any winnings received by him as a result of such bets.[19] The position if the contract of agency is illegal is illustrated by *Harry Parker Ltd v Mason*.[20] There the whole arrangement between the backer and the agent was a conspiracy to deceive other backers, as well as an infringement of the Street Betting Act 1906. The backer was held to have no remedy against the agent. No duty to pay over money received for the principal arises if in fact the agent has had to repay the money to the person from whom he obtained it, for example if there was a mistake of fact, failure of consideration, or fraud (even if it is on the part of the agent himself as in *Murray v Mann*[1]).

Clearly this duty requires for its proper performance that the agent should be in a position to know what he must pay the principal, and that the principal should be able to see whether the agent has fulfilled his duty. Hence the agent is

---

15 RSC Ord 17.
16 *Blaustein v Maltz, Mitchell & Co* [1937] 2 KB 142 at 151–154, [1937] 1 All ER 497 at 502: per Slesser LJ; *Balsamo v Medici* [1984] 2 All ER 304 at 312, per Walton J; cf the view taken as to the position of the buyer of the goods in the special circumstances of *Aluminium Industrie Vaassen BV v Romalpa Aluminium Ltd* [1976] 2 All ER 552, [1976] 1 WLR 676 (on which see below, p 256). The duty to account may extend to include excess commission or 'advance' commission remaining unearned: see *Rivoli Hats Ltd v Gooch* [1953] 2 All ER 823, [1953] 1 WLR 1190; *Bronester Ltd v Priddle* [1961] 3 All ER 471, [1961] 1 WLR 1294: contrast *Clayton Newbury Ltd v Findlay* [1953] 2 All ER 826n, [1953] 1 WLR 1194n. There is some doubt whether this is based on implied contract or money had and received.
17 *Heath v Chilton* (1844) 12 M & W 632.
18 *Bousfield v Wilson* (1846) 16 LJ Ex 44; *Booth v Hodgson* (1795) 6 Term Rep 405.
19 *De Mattos v Benjamin* (1894) 63 LJQB 248.
20 [1940] 2 KB 590, [1940] 4 All ER 199.
 1 (1848) 2 Exch 538.

obliged to keep the principal's property and money separate from his own and from other people's property, to keep proper accounts, and to be ready to produce them on demand to the principal, or a proper person appointed by the principal.[2] It should be added that an agent owes a duty in equity to account to his principal.[3]

B. Duties arising from the fiduciary nature of the agency relationship[4]

In addition to those duties which are implied by the law into the agreement creating the agency relationship, there are others which stem from the fact that the agency relationship is sometimes[5] one of trust, even though not strictly a relationship of trustee and beneficiary.[6] Irrespective of any contract, or even agreement, between the parties, once the relationship of principal and agent exists, however it may arise, a complex of duties attaches to the agent.[7] These duties are equitable in character,[8] and may be lumped together under one general

2 *Gray v Haig* (1854) 20 Beav 219; *Dadswell v Jacobs* (1887) 34 Ch D 278. See *Yasuda Fire and Marine Insurance Co of Europe Ltd v Orion Marine Insurance Underwriting* [1995] 2 WLR 49 at 57 per Colman J.

3 *Makepeace v Rogers* (1865) 34 LJ Ch 396; *Navulshaw v Brownrigg* (1852) 21 LJ Ch 908; *Barry v Stevens* (1862) 35 LJ Ch 785.

4 Passages from this section were cited with approval in *Keeler & Keeler v Jack's Real Estate Ltd* (1980) 1 Sask LR 444 at 447 per Woods JA, in *Gerco Services Ltd v Astro* (1982) 48 NSR (2d) 541 at 559 per Hallett J, and in *Galaxy Realtors Ltd v Outlook Agencies Ltd* (1986) 48 Sask LR 215 at 216, 217. For a case concerning a quasi-fiduciary duty see *449576 Ontario Ltd v Bogojevski* (1984) 46 OR (2d) 161, arising from a purchaser's poor knowledge of English.

5 There is a distinction between fiduciary and non-fiduciary agents: *Bowstead and Reynolds on Agency* (16th edn 1996) pp 192–197; Shepherd *Law of Fiduciaries* (1981) at p 25; *Knoch Estate v Jon Picken Ltd* (1991) 4 OR (3d) 385 (distinguished in *Baillie v Charman* (1992) 94 DLR (4th) 403). See also *Austin v Habitat Development Ltd* (1992) 94 DLR (4th) 359.

6 Cf the treatment of the purchaser of property vis-à-vis the vendor in the same way so far as concerns profit made by the former, in *English v Dedham Vale Properties* [1978] 1 All ER 382, [1978] 1 WLR 93. For discussion of fiduciary relationships see Cooter and Freedman 'The Fiduciary Relationship; its Economic Character and Legal Consequences' (1991) 66 NYULR 1045.

7 Eg if the agent is appointed under a power of attorney: *Tim v Lai* (1986) 5 BCLR (2d) 245; cf *Powell v Thompson* [1991] 1 NZLR 597, donee of power could not pay his personal debts by using the power to advantage himself. But there must be an agency relationship: *Murphy v Luckiw Holdings (1980) Ltd* (1987) 49 Alta LR (2d) 200. Hence no duty of loyalty is owed after the termination of such a relationship: *Sears Investment Trust Ltd v Lewis's Group Ltd* [1992] RA 262. Contrast *Cineplex Odeon Corpn v Drabinsky* (1990) 30 CPR (3d) 370, where the agency agreement continued though a supply agreement has been terminated: hence a duty of loyalty was still owed. For examples of breach of fiduciary duty see *Midland Doherty Ltd v Rohrer* (1985) 20 DLR (4th) 188; *Weitzman v Hendin* (1986) 56 OR (2d) 445. An employee of the agent will make the agent liable if the employee is guilty of the breach; *Guertin v Royal Bank of Canada* (1983) 43 OR (2d) 363; affd (1984) 47 OR (2d) 799. The Contributory Negligence Act and the defence of *ex turpi causa* were held not to be available to an agent sued for breach of fiduciary duty in *United Services Funds v Richardson Greenshields of Canada Ltd* (1988) 48 DLR (4th) 98.

8 For a discussion whether the duty to obey precise instructions was *contractual* or fiduciary, and for the practical effect of the distinction in terms of the remedy available to the principal, see the Canadian case of *Laskin v Bache & Co Inc* (1971) 22 DLR (3d) 382; cf the treatment of the agent's duty of care as a kind of *fiduciary* duty by Estey CJO in *Fine's Flowers Ltd v General Accident Assurance Co of Canada* (1977) 81 DLR (3d) 139; above, p 159.

principle; namely, that the agent must not let his own personal interest conflict with the obligations he owes to his principal.[9] This general idea is manifested in various ways.

Fidelity. Where the agent is in a position in which his own interest may affect the performance of his duty to the principal, the agent is obliged to make a full disclosure of all the material circumstances, so that the principal, with such full knowledge, can choose whether to consent to the agent's acting.[10] If this is not done, then the principal (if he does not choose to ratify it) may set aside the transaction, and claim from the agent any profit the agent may have obtained from such transaction.[11]

The Privy Council, however, in *Kelly v Cooper*,[12] made it clear that the contract between principal and agent, including implied as well as express terms, governed and defined the content and scope of such relationship: and this meant that the scope of fiduciary duties owed by an agent to the principal, though originating in

On the calculation of damages for breach of fiduciary duty (ie was it like tort or breach of contract or was it sui generis, like restitution?) see *Canson Enterprises Ltd v Boughton & Co* (1991) 85 DLR (4th) 129, with which compare *Mead v Day* [1985] 1 NZLR 100; Gummow 'Compensation for Breach of Fiduciary Duty', in Youdan, ed *Equity, Fiduciaries and Trusts* (1989) Ch 2, especially pp 82–84, 85–91. The House of Lords has said that equity applies the common law principles of causation and compensation: see *Target Holdings Ltd v Redferns* [1995] 3 All ER 785 at 792 per Lord Browne-Wilkinson: but not the common law rules of remoteness of damage; ibid at 794.

Note also, in relation to estate agents, the duties imposed by the Estate Agents Act 1979, s 21, which lack any criminal or civil sanction; see also the Property Misdescriptions Act 1991.

9 *Aaron Acceptance Corpn v Adam* (1987) 37 DLR (4th) 133; *Trophy Foods Inc v Scott* (1994) 129 NSR (2d) 1. The American Restatement calls them 'duties of loyalty': *Restatement, Second, Agency*, paras 387–398. Cf Stoljar *Law of Agency* p 288, who refers to them as 'duties of economic loyalty'.

10 *Ocean City Realty Ltd v A & M Holdings Ltd* (1987) 36 DLR (4th) 94, where the agent conspired with a prospective purchaser to pay the purchaser part of the agent's commission; no commission was payable by the principal. The duty to disclose involves disclosure of everything which to the agent's knowledge might operate on the principal's judgement: the test is objective, viz, whether the reasonable agent would consider the information likely to influence the principal's behaviour: ibid. But if there is no conflict of interest and duty the agent is not obliged, even in equity, to disclose facts that would reveal the improvidence of the transaction authorised by the principal: *R H Deacon & Co Ltd v Varga* (1973) 30 DLR (3d) 653. See also *Lin v Leung* (1992) 64 BCLR (2d) 226 president of company should have disclosed appraisal of land; *Matchett v Blue Gold Drilling Ltd* (1992) 6 Alta LR (3d) 370 breach of fiduciary duty owed by participant in a joint-venture agreement.

11 For the position of The Law Society with respect to contracts of insurance made on behalf of solicitors, and the commission earned by the Law Society: *Swain v Law Society* [1980] 3 All ER 615, [1980] 1 WLR 1355; varied [1981] 3 All ER 797, [1982] 1 WLR 17; revsd [1983] 1 AC 598, [1982] 2 All ER 827, HL.

12 [1993] AC 205: with which contrast *Keppel v Wheeler* [1927] 1 KB 577 where there was no duty of confidentiality owned by the agents to other persons: and *North and South Trust Co v Berkeley* [1971] 1 WLR 470, where no term could be implied that the brokers were to be free to act for the opposing party, insurers against whom the plaintiff was claiming under a policy of insurance effected by the agents, when the agents were instructed by the insurers to obtain a report from assessors, which report the agents refused to disclose to the plaintiff, their original principal: above, p 79.

equity, could be affected by such terms.[13] The case concerned the fiduciary duty of fidelity owed by agents who, in the ordinary course of business, acted for numerous principals, several of whom might be competing and whose interests would conflict. Where an agent is carrying on such a general agency, to the knowledge of the principal who understands that the agent will be acting for other principals selling goods or property of the same description, the terms to be implied into the agency contract differed from those to be implied where an agent was not carrying on such general agency business. Estate agents belonged in the category of those carrying on the business of acting for several principals where properties were of a similar description and there would be a conflict of interest between principals each of whom would be concerned to attract potential purchasers to their property rather than to that of another. Nevertheless estate agents had to be free to act for several competing principals: if not they would be unable to fulfil their functions. It could not be said that an estate agent was contractually bound to disclose to any one of his principals information confidential to another principal: and the same was true of stockbrokers. Hence a term had to be implied into contracts with such agents (a) that they were entitled to act for other principals selling competing property, and (b) that they were to keep confidential information obtained from each of the principals.[14] On this basis, therefore, on the facts of the case in issue, the estate agents employed by the plaintiff to sell his house were not in breach of their duty in failing to inform the plaintiff of an agreement made by X with the owner of a house adjacent to that of the plaintiff to buy that house, which information was confidential to the owner of that house. Nor did the estate agents' financial interest in that sale, for which they were the agents, give rise to a breach of fiduciary duty owed to the plaintiff.

An important, though not the only, illustration of the agent's obligation to make full disclosure is provided by the situation that arises where the agent himself[15] purports to purchase the property he is engaged to sell on his principal's behalf.[16] For example, in *McPherson v Watt*:[17]

> The agent of two ladies, who wanted to sell their house, bought it in the name of his brother, so as to conceal that he was really buying it for himself. Specific performance of the contract of sale was therefore refused.

13 [1992] 3 WLR 936 at 942, quoting *New Zealand Netherlands Society Oranje Inc v Kuys* [1973] 1 WLR 1126 at 1129–1130 and *Hospital Products Ltd v United States Surgical Corpn* (1984) 156 CLR 41 at 97.
14 [1992] 3 WLR 936 at 941–942.
15 Or, as in one case, his father: *Dyck v Nodge Real Estate Ltd* (1980) 2 Sask LR 424.
16 *Palinko v Bower* [1976] 4 WWR 118; *Wood v St Jules* (1976) 69 DLR (3d) 481; *Cymar Leasing v Cross Country Realty* (1978) 5 Alta LR (2d) 278; *Edwards Real Estate v Bamtar Holdings Ltd* (1978) 7 Alta LR (2d) 52; *Keeler & Keeler v Jack's Real Estate Ltd*, above, note 4; *George W Rayfield Realty Ltd v Kuhn* (1981) 115 DLR (3d) 654; on appeal 118 DLR (3d) 192. Or the agent conceals a higher offer so that the agent can arrange a subsequent resale of the property by the original purchaser to another party: *Yorkland Real Estate Ltd v Dale* (1987) 60 OR (2d) 460.
17 (1877) 3 App Cas 254. Cf *Rothschild v Brookman* (1831) 2 Dow & Cl 188, purchase of client's stock by a broker, set aside; *Lucifero v Castel* (1887) 3 TLR 371, purchase of yacht by agent, resold to principal, agent could only recover what he paid for yacht. Cf *Regier v Campbell-Stuart* [1939] Ch 766, pretended purchase price given by agent to principal; principal could recover excess profit on ground of non-disclosure by agent. Cf *Aaron Acceptance Corpn v Adam*, above, agent was the lender under a mortgage as well as the agent charged with obtaining a mortgage loan for the principal, the borrower: no commission payable by the principal.

It is immaterial that the contract is really fair,[18] or that a long time, for example, thirteen years,[19] has passed, as long as the principal, without fault on his part, is in ignorance of what has happened.[20] Moreover, it is not possible as *Robinson v Mollett*[1] shows, to allege a trade custom which allows an agent to buy from or sell to his principal on his own behalf.[2] However, it may not involve the agent in a conflict of interest and duty to exercise a lien over his principal's goods to enforce his claims for remuneration and indemnity, when the principal has repudiated the contract.[3]

Unless he has the consent of his principal, an agent must not make use for his own personal benefit of information acquired in the course of his employment as an agent. The chief illustration of this rule is to be found in cases in which employees have had access to processes, or lists of customers of their employer, and have sought after the termination of the employment to make use of knowledge gained therefrom. In other words, the agent is not allowed to make use of such confidential information to engage in competition with the principal.[4] Thus in *Robb v Green:*[5]

---

18 *Gillett v Peppercorne* (1840) 3 Beav 78; *Aberdeen Rly Co v Blaikie Bros* (1854) 2 Eq Rep 1281; *Armstrong v Jackson* [1917] 2 KB 822.

19 *Oliver v Court* (1820) Dan 301.

20 *Oelkers v Ellis* [1914] 2 KB 139. Contrast two Canadian cases in which it seems to have been held that the agent was accountable even if he did not keep what he was doing secret from his principal: *Karst v Selinger* (1980) 4 Sask LR 113; *Lilley v Corynthian Restaurants Ltd* (1980) 7 Sask LR 110.

1 (1875) LR 7 HL 802 (above, p 78). Contrast *Macoun v Erskine* [1901] 2 KB 493; *Christoforides v Terry* [1924] AC 566, both of which cases are also of importance on the question of the duration of the agent's obligations after the termination of the relationship. See also *Keppel v Wheeler* [1927] 1 KB 577, where an agent had to inform his principal of an offer after an earlier offer had been accepted; cf *Jackson v Packham Real Estate Ltd* (1980) 109 DLR (3d) 277; *Yorkland Real Estate Ltd v Dale*, above.

2 The passage from the beginning of this paragraph to here was quoted by Wallace JA in *Aaron Acceptance Corpn v Adam* (1987) 12 BCLR (2d) 300 at 305.

3 *The Borag* [1980] 1 Lloyd's Rep 111 at 122 per Mustill J (reversed on other grounds [1981] 1 All ER 856, [1981] 1 WLR 274).

4 *International & Scientific Communications Ltd v Pattison* [1979] FSR 429; cf the general law of restraint of trade: Cheshire, Fifoot and Furmston's *Law of Contract* (12th edn 1991) pp 397–415. Hence an agent could be restrained from using such information, on the basis of fiduciary duty, even though an express term to such effect in the contract of employment was invalid as being in restraint of trade: *Investors Syndicate Ltd v Versatile Investments Inc* (1983) 42 OR (2d) 397. Cf *White Oaks Welding Supplies v Tapp* (1983) 149 DLR (3d) 159. The improper use of confidential information by a contracting party justifies termination of the contract: *Computer Workshops Ltd v Banner Capital Market Brokers Ltd* (1988) 50 DLR (4th) 118; affd (1990) 74 DLR (4th) 767.

For a curious case involving a solicitor who had an affair with his client's wife after he discovered from his client that the marriage was unhappy, see *Szarfer v Chodos* (1986) 27 DLR (4th) 388. This carries the notion of breach of fiduciary duty to extreme lengths.

5 [1895] 2 QB 315. A variation on this is to be found in *Sanders v Parry* [1967] 2 All ER 803, where the defendant, an assistant solicitor employed by the plaintiff, having come into contact with a client of the plaintiff, through his work for the plaintiff, left the employment of the plaintiff and then undertook to do all the client's legal work for seven years, to the loss of the plaintiff. This was held to be a breach of contract by the defendant. For a somewhat different example of misuse of confidential information by an agent, see *Harris Trustees Ltd v Power Packing Services (Hermit Road) Ltd* [1970] 2 Lloyd's Rep 65. Cf and contrast *North and South Trust Co v Berkeley* [1971] 1 All ER 980 above p 79.

An employer obtained an injunction and damages against an employee who, after he finished working, made use of lists of names and addresses of the employer's customers which the employee had obtained while working.

A contract of employment is not a contract *uberrimae fidei*; so the employee is not bound to disclose his own misconduct.[6] But he is obliged to disclose misconduct of other employees (even if this entails revealing what he himself has done). The employee owes this kind of duty akin to his duty not to misuse confidential information.[7] This latter duty, however, depends upon whether the agent's position was such that it gave him access to special information which he would otherwise not have obtained. So in *Nordisk Insulinlaboratorium v CL Bencard Ltd*:[8]

The principal's property was seized by the Custodian of Enemy Property on the outbreak of war. It was sold to X (who had been the principal's agent until that time). X resold it at a profit to Y. Later the principal claimed this profit from X. It was held that X was not liable.

This was not a case where the agent had acquired any special knowledge from acting in the capacity of agent. X knew nothing about the method of making insulin which was the principal's business. Hence no special fiduciary duty was owed by X to the principal.[9] An extension of this seems to have been approved by the majority of the House of Lords in *Boardman v Phipps*.[10] There it was held that knowledge as to the value of shares in a company, which the agent gained while acting as solicitor for the principals, was something like property belonging to the principal, the use of which by the agent made him accountable to the principal for profit thereby gained, even though the principal had earlier refused to use the knowledge for his own benefit. In arriving at this conclusion, the majority of the House relied heavily on the earlier decision in *Regal (Hastings) Ltd v Gulliver*[11] which was concerned with the duty of fidelity of a company director in relation to knowledge of this sort. The attitude of the House

---

6 But see *Courtright v Canadian Pacific Ltd* (1983) 5 DLR (4th) 488; affd (1985) 18 DLR (4th) 639, employee obliged to disclose possibility of criminal charges in respect of actions *before* hiring.
7 *Sybron Corpn v Rochem Ltd* [1984] Ch 112, [1983] 2 All ER 707.
8 [1953] Ch 430, [1953] 1 All ER 986.
9 [1953] Ch 430 at 445–446, [1953] 1 All ER 986 at 994; per Jenkins LJ. Cf *Mid-Western News Agency Ltd v Vanpinxteren* (1976) 62 DLR (3d) 555, again no misuse of confidential information received in the course of the principal's business; cf *Two Brothers (Kingston) Ltd v Zakos* (1986) 28 DLR (4th) 541, where the agent did not make use of information derived from his employment by the principal as an agent to place insurance on property which the agent agreed to buy. See also the curious case of *H C Misener & Son Ltd v Misener* (1977) 77 DLR (3d) 428, where the misbehaving employee was the wife of a director and had given information to her lover, from which it was alleged he had obtained a benefit. Contrast *McLeod and More v Sweezey* [1944] 2 DLR 145, where agents were liable since they were expert in mining exploration and were making claims on land which they had explored for their principals.
10 [1967] 2 AC 46, [1966] 3 All ER 721 (on which see Rider 'The Fiduciary and the Frying Pan' (1978) Conv 114). For a Canadian example, see *Sinclair v Ridout and Moran* [1955] OR 167. For an Australian case which follows the decision in *Boardman v Phipps*, see *Walden Properties Ltd v Beaver Properties Pty Ltd* [1973] 2 NSWLR 815.
11 [1967] 2 AC 134, [1942] 1 All ER 378; distinguished in *Lindgren v L & P Estates Ltd* [1968] Ch 572, [1968] 1 All ER 917.

of Lords seems to have been that agents or 'quasi agents', as the defendants were there described, must be regarded as fiduciaries, to whom the broad principles of equity apply when it comes to fidelity and making a private, personal profit out of the performance of their undertaking.[12] The Supreme Court of Canada distinguished the *Regal* case in *Peso-Silver Mines Ltd v Cropper*,[13] in which it would seem that the extent of an agent's duty (in this instance a company director) was not as broadened as it was by the House of Lords in the *Boardman* case. Later, however, in *Canadian Aero Service Ltd v O'Malley*,[14] the Supreme Court appears to have made an agent's liability more extensive, and to have included within the scope of this kind of accountability employees of a corporation who were not necessarily as senior in the corporate hierarchy as directors, as long as they were managerial. That decision has been followed and applied.[15] It was held not to be applicable where the 'agents' were the committee of a private members' golf club and had sold the club premises for their own benefit. No trust or similar relationship existed between the parties so as to enable the non-committee members to invoke this doctrine and recover the profit.[16]

The agent may not act for the principal and a third party contracting with the principal unless he has made a complete disclosure to both parties of what he was doing and they both consented.[17] This is true even in the case of a solicitor, who may act for both parties, despite the fact that their interests conflict, as long as he has obtained the informed consent of both parties to his acting. Informed consent in this context means consent that is given in the knowledge that there is a conflict between the parties and that as a result the solicitor may be disabled from disclosing to each party the full knowledge which he possesses as to the transaction or may be disabled from giving advice to one party which conflicts with the interests of the other. If the parties are content to proceed on this basis the solicitor may properly act.[18]

Although in *McPherson v Watt*[19] Lord Blackburn seems to have suggested that an agent may act for both sides up to a certain point as long as he gives

12 Fridman 'Agency and Secret Profits' (1968) 3 Manitoba LJ 17; Jones 'Unjust Enrichment and the Fiduciary's Duty of Loyalty' (1968) 84 LQR 472; Goff and Jones *Law of Restitution* (4th edn 1993) pp 656–658.
13 (1966) 58 DLR (2d) 1: cf *Aas v Benham* [1891] 2 Ch 244, distinguished by the House of Lords in the *Boardman* case. See Beck 'The Saga of Peso Silver Mines' (1971) 49 CBR 80.
14 (1973) 40 DLR (3d) 371.
15 Eg *Abbey Glen Property Corpn v Stumborg* (1978) 85 DLR (3d) 35; *Redekop v Robco Construction Ltd* (1978) 89 DLR 507; *Weber Feeds Ltd v Weber* (1979) 99 DLR (3d) 176.
16 *Evans v Anderson* (1977) 76 DLR (3d) 482: there was no trust property to which fiduciary duties could attach: hence the basis for the liability was lacking. For an extension of the doctrine of fiduciary duty not to disclose confidential information, where no agency, or contractual relationship existed between the parties, see the decision of the Supreme Court of Canada in *LAC Minerals Ltd v International Corona Resources Ltd* (1989) 61 DLR (4th) 14: contrast *Hospital Products Ltd v United States Surgical Corpn* (1984) 156 CLR 41, in which the High Court of Australia was against importing trust concepts into a commercial setting or situation.
17 *McDonnell v Barton Realty Ltd* [1992] 3 NZLR 418. Or an applicable custom is alleged and proved: *Jones v Canavan* [1927] 2 NSWLR 236: above, p 78, note 7. Contrast *MacManus Realty Ltd v Bray* (1971) 14 DLR (3d) 564.
18 *Clark Boyce v Mouat* [1993] 4 All ER 268 at 273.
19 (1877) 3 App Cas 254 at 274–5.

'disinterested and true advice',[20] this must be taken as being correct only where the agent has made clear, in accordance with what was stated above, what he is doing and its consequences. In *Clark Boyce v Mouat*,[1] where this was said to be the law, solicitors in New Zealand agreed to act for a woman seeking to mortgage her house as security for a loan to her son and for her son (whose usual solicitors had declined to act for the son in the transaction). When the parties met in the solicitors' office, the solicitors advised the mother to seek independent advice before entering into the transaction. She declined to do so and signed an authority to such effect. The transaction was explained to her: she was advised she would be the principal debtor not merely a guarantor; she was also warned that she could lose her property if the son did not keep up the mortgage payments. She signed the mortgage documents. The son's business failed: he became bankrupt: and the mother was obliged to repay the mortgage. She sued the solicitors alleging, inter alia, breach of fiduciary duty in failing to decline to act for her. The Privy Council held that no breach of fiduciary duty had occurred. To decide whether informed consent had been obtained it was necessary to see what services were required of the solicitor by the client, since, if the client had command of his faculties and was apparently aware of what he was doing when he sought the assistance of a solicitor in carrying out a particular transaction, the solicitor was under no duty, before or after accepting instructions, to go beyond those instructions by proffering unsought advice on the wisdom of the transaction. Here the mother required only of the solicitors that they should carry out the necessary conveyancing on her behalf and explain to her the legal implications of what she was doing. She was already aware of the consequences to her if her son defaulted, and she was not concerned about the wisdom of the transaction. Since the solicitors had advised her to obtain, and offered to arrange independent advice, they had performed all that was reasonably required of them before accepting her instructions.[2]

A case which illustrates what happens when an agent is neither open nor disinterested about his activities is *Fullwood v Hurley*.[3]

> The agent was employed by X, the owner of a hotel, to sell the hotel for him. P was the purchaser of the hotel, with whom the agent alleged he had made a contract for the payment of commission to him for buying the hotel on P's behalf. It was held that there was no such contract, because the agent had not disclosed to P the fact that he was already acting as the agent of X.

There are many examples of the forfeiture by an agent of his commission for failure to disclose that his course of conduct resulted in a clash between the interests of his principal and his own personal interests when acting for more

---

20 Ibid at 276 see *Davey v Woolley, Hames, Dale & Dingwald* (1982) 133 DLR (3d) 647; *Moores Sequiera* (1985) 55 N fld & PEIR 128; *Marasco v Bow Bend Trailer Park Ltd* (1982) 36 AR 54, affd (1983) 31 Alta LR (2d) 162.

1 [1993] 4 All ER 268.

2 Ibid at 274–275.

3 [1928] 1 KB 498. For the possibility of damages if the agent acts for vendor and purchaser at the same time, see *Len Pugh Real Estate Ltd v Ronvic Construction Co Ltd* (1974) 1 OR (2d) 539.

than one party.[4] However it must be proved that the agent was seeking to serve the interests of another, not the principal for whom he was obliged to act under the contract of agency.[5] Moreover, it was suggested by McEachern CJ of British Columbia, in a case involving an agent employed to find a party to lend money to his principal on a long-term loan,[6] that the agent could not be guilty of misconduct in acting in this way as long as he honestly believed that what he was doing was in the best interests of his principal. However, because, on the facts, the loan finally arranged by the agent did not result in the agent's being paid a double commission, it is suggested that these remarks are obiter dicta and are of dubious validity.

Secret profits. Another way of expressing what has been said above is that an agent may not make a secret profit out of the performance of his duties as agent. It is his duty to account for all such profit. Failure to do so will amount to a breach of his contract of agency and will disentitle the agent to his commission as well as make him liable to dismissal.[7]

What is a secret profit? The expression refers to any financial advantage which the agent receives over and above what he is entitled to receive from his principal by way of remuneration. This includes bribes given to obtain the agent's complicity in some activity not necessarily in the interests of his principal. A bribe is 'the payment of a secret commission'[8] by a third party, or the receipt by the agent of a 'secret advantage for himself from the other party to a transaction in which the agent was acting for his principal'.[9] But there need be no bribery involved in the making of a secret profit. Nor need there be corruption of the agent on the part of a third person. It is sufficient if the agent, without the complicity of a third person, secretly gains financial advantage to himself from the exercise of his authority.[10] There may be no fraud on the part of the agent.

---

4 *Henry Smith & Son v Muskett* (1977) 246 Estates Gazette 655: *Canada Permanent Trust Co v Christie* (1979) 16 BCLR 183; *Campbell v Wilroy Real Estate Ltd* (1979) 17 AR 414; *Advanced Realty Funding Corpn v Bannink* (1979) 106 DLR (3d) 137; *Comeau v Canada Permanent Trust Co* (1979) 27 NBR (2d) 126.

5 *Goodfellow v Drschiwiski* (1979) 18 AR 561: cf *The Borag* [1980] 1 Lloyd's Rep 111 (alleged that the agent was serving his own interests): reversed on other grounds [1981] 1 All ER 856.

6 *Turner v Laurentide Financial Realty Corpn* (1979) 97 DLR (3d) 429.

7 *Boston Deep Sea Fishing and Ice Co v Ansell* (1888) 39 Ch D 339; *Andrews v Ramsay* [1903] 2 KB 635; *Galaxy Realtors Ltd v Outlook Agencies Ltd* (1986) 48 Sask LR 215. Moreover, a contract entered into by the principal in consequence may be treated as void by the principal (at least as long as the third party has actual knowledge and is involved in the improper activity of the agent: *Logicrose Ltd v Southern United Football Club Ltd* [1988] 1 WLR 1256). Recovery of the money from the agent does not amount to adoption of the transaction by the principal and does not disentitle him to rescind: ibid. However, the bribe, or secret profit, was not a benefit obtained by the principal which had to be returned to the third party, on the basis of *restitutio in integrum*, when the principal rescinded the contract: ibid.

8 *Industries and General Mortgage Co v Lewis* [1949] 2 All ER 573 at 575 per Slade J.

9 *Mahesan v Malaysia Government Officers' Co-operative Housing Society Ltd* [1978] 2 All ER 405 at 408 per Lord Diplock. Cf *Anangel Atlas Compania Naviera SA v Ishikawajima-Harima Heavy Industries Ltd* [1990] 1 Lloyd's Rep 167 at 171 per Leggatt J.

10 No bribery or conflict of interest occurred, however, where an agent, a former director of a company, had accepted employment with a third party prior to the granting of an option agreement for the sale of shares by the company to the third party: *Amalgamated Industrials v Johnson & Firth Brown* [1981] CLY 18.

Nevertheless there will be liability to account for the profit received, for the contract between principal and agent is one uberrimae fidei. Thus in *De Bussche v Alt*:[11]

> The agent in Japan, to whom had been delegated the task of selling the ship at a certain price, could not find a purchaser at that price. Therefore he bought the ship himself at that price. Later he sold the ship to X at a higher price.

It was held, first of all, that the effect of the principal's consent to the delegation by his agent to the agent in Japan made such delegation valid, and created the relationship of principal and agent between the principal and the agent in Japan. Hence that agent owed the normal duties of an agent. By purchasing the ship himself he had broken one of these duties; and by later making a profit from the transaction, without telling his principal and obtaining his consent, the agent had been guilty of further wrongdoing, for which he was liable to account to the principal. In *Lavigne v Robern*[12] the Ontario Court of Appeal held that, to discourage conduct of this kind, a fiduciary who made a generous profit had to repay the entire amount of such profit, even when a certain percentage of the property sold by the fiduciary on behalf of himself and others was owned by the fiduciary. Here the subject-matter of the sale was a corporation, 50% of the shares in which were owned by the misbehaving fiduciary who arranged the sale and made the secret profit. All of this had to be disgorged, not merely the 50% representing the shareholding interest of the other owners of the corporation. This was not a case where economic initiative was to be encouraged.[13]

Even if the agent is not being paid commission for acting on the principal's behalf, he may not secretly profit from his position. In *Turnbull v Garden*:[14]

> An agent employed, but without a commission, to purchase an outfit for his principal's son, obtained discounts on the purchase, but sought to charge the principal for the full price. It was held that the principal could not be compelled to reimburse the agent more than the agent had actually spent. The agent could not make a secret profit from the transaction.

The position of agents who make secret profits was considered at length in *Boardman v Phipps*.[15] In that case the defendants were treated as having acted as agents of a trust even though not actually appointed agents, when they made a profit out of certain dealings with companies, involving a reorganisation of shares. It was held that such profit was to be yielded to the beneficiaries of the trust, even though the defendants had not acted dishonestly. In the Court of Appeal[16] Lord Denning made it clear that however an agent obtained an advantage for himself from his special position as an agent, the result was the same.

---

11 (1878) 8 Ch D 286. See also above, p 166.
12 (1984) 18 DLR (4th) 759.
13 Ibid at 762.
14 (1869) 20 LT 218.
15 [1967] 2 AC 46; see above, pp 178–179.
16 [1965] 1 All ER 849 at 856.

'It is quite clear that if an agent uses *property*, with which he has been entrusted by his principal, so as to make a profit for himself out of it, without his principal's consent, then he is accountable for it to his principal.... So, also, if he uses a *position of authority*, to which he has been appointed by his principal, so as to gain money by means of it for himself, then also he is accountable to his principal for it ... Likewise with *information or knowledge* which he has been employed by his principal to collect or discover, *or which he has otherwise acquired*, for the use of his principal, then again if he turns it to his own use, so as to make a profit by means of it for himself, he is accountable ... for such information or knowledge is the property of his principal, just as much as an invention is....'

The rationale of this liability to account was explained by Lord Denning thus:

'Once it is found that the agent has used his principal's property or his position so as to make money for himself, it matters not that the principal has lost no profits or suffered no damage.... Nor does it matter that the principal could not have done the act himself.... Nor do you have to find that the act, which brought about the profit, was done within the course of his employment.... The reason is simply because it is money which the agent ought not to be allowed to keep. He gained an unjust benefit by the use of his principal's property or his position and must account for it.'

When the case came before the House of Lords the decision of the Court of Appeal was upheld by a majority of the House on the ground that the information about the value of the shares was property belonging to the principal, the misuse of which, by the agent, albeit not a dishonest misuse, rendered the agent liable to account for any profit to the principal. It may be that the information involved in this case was of such a 'special' kind, in Lord Hodson's phrase,[17] possibly by virtue of the source of the information, viz a private company[18] or a trust holding[19] that the liability attached. Thus in *Industrial Development Consultants Ltd v Cooley*:[20]

The agent was the managing director of a company in the construction industry. He was also an architect. He was approached by the chairman of the Eastern Gas Board to come and work for them although at the time the company of which he was the director were interested in a project for the Gas Board. In his position as managing director he obtained knowledge which should have been passed on to the company. Concealing this knowledge, he obtained his release from the service of the company, basing his request on alleged ill health. The company would never have released him if they had had full knowledge of the facts. The former director thereupon went to work for the Gas Board who gained the advantage of his knowledge. It was held that the director was under a fiduciary obligation in the circumstances: that his interest and duty conflicted: and therefore he was

17 [1967] 2 AC 46 at 109.
18 Ibid at 101, 102–103 per Lord Cohen.
19 Ibid at 115, per Lord Guest.
20 [1972] 2 All ER 162, [1972] 1 WLR 443. Cf the facts of, and decision in, *Canadian Aero Service Ltd v O'Malley* (1973) 40 DLR (3d) 371.

liable to account to the company of which he was formerly managing director for all the profit he had made by his transfer of services.

Here the case was much clearer: for the agent was fully cognizant of the impropriety of his conduct, unlike the solicitor in the *Boardman* case, who genuinely believed that he was acting with the consent of his 'principals'. What is interesting, however, is that the Court, following the *Boardman* decision, regarded the information possessed by the agent as the key to his obligations as an agent. Thus the *Boardman* case can be used to extend the scope of an agent's responsibilities.

The decision of the House of Lords is capable of being used to extend the scope of an agent's liability for secret profits beyond the boundaries of prior authority. Possibly the rationale of this case is to be found not in the law of agency but in the general law of equity[1] or even in the doctrine of unjust enrichment or restitution.[2] It is clear that a similar doctrine applies to those who are not agents in the strict sense, but are in a similarly fiduciary relationship. Thus it has been held to apply to policemen and soldiers who have used their position to make a secret (and illegal) profit.[3] In *A-G v Goddard*[4] a police sergeant took bribes to conceal criminal offences. In *Reading v A-G*[5] a soldier used his uniform to get drugs and other goods illegally through police barriers: for this service he was bribed by large amounts of money. In both cases it was held that the person acting illegally had to hand over his profit to the Crown, despite the fact that the persons involved were not really 'servants' or 'agents' of the Crown,[6] nor were strictly speaking in a fiduciary relationship, and moreover, were really acting outside the scope of their authority. The rationale of the cases was that the men in question were improperly making use of their special position to profit secretly and illicitly. In this respect, therefore, an agent may not be in any special position.[7]

1 The whole attitude of the House of Lords is consistent with the decision (and the dissent) being based upon general principles of equity dating back to *Keech v Sandford* (1726) Sel Cas Ch 61.
2 For a detailed, general discussion, see Jones 'Unjust Enrichment and the Fiduciary's Duty of Loyalty' (1968) 84 LQR 472, in which the learned author discusses an important aspect of the question, namely, whether the principal's remedy is proprietary, so that he can claim everything, or only personal, which will limit the principal's claim to the profits made by the agent. See also Goff and Jones *Law of Restitution* (4th edn 1993) ch 34: and also ch 2.
  For an even wider use of the notion of fiduciary duties, leading to the disgorgement of 'secret' profits, or benefits unfairly obtained at the expense of another, to whom such a duty was owed, see the decision of the Supreme Court of Canada in *LAC Minerals Ltd v International Corona Resources Ltd* (1989) 61 DLR (4th) 14. Contrast with this the Australian decision in *Hospital Products Ltd v United States Surgical Corpn* (1984) 156 CLR 41: see above, p 179, note 16.
3 And to municipal officers, eg a Mayor, although on the facts nothing improper had taken place, according to the Supreme Court of Canada, reversing the Courts below: see *City of Edmonton v Hawrelak* (1972) 24 DLR (3d) 321: on appeal (1973) 31 DLR (3d) 498: affd (1975) 54 DLR (3d) 45.
4 (1929) 98 LJKB 743.
5 [1951] AC 507, [1951] 1 All ER 617.
6 *A-G for New South Wales v Perpetual Trustee Co Ltd* [1955] AC 457, [1955] 1 All ER 846.
7 For the situation of the Law Society vis-à-vis solicitors in England and Wales, see *Swain v Law Society* [1980] 3 All ER 615, [1980] 1 WLR 1335; varied [1981] 3 All ER 797, [1982] 1 WLR 17 where the Court of Appeal held that the society was the agent for solicitors in arranging liability insurance: therefore the society was not allowed to keep commission granted by the insurance company. This was reversed by the House of Lords [1982] 2 All ER 827.

On the other hand an agent may be distinguishable from other fiduciaries, in that if the principal knows about the profit being made by the agent, and consents to his doing so, or does not object, then the agent is entitled to keep the profit he makes, for it is no longer secret.[8] Furthermore, if the profit, though secretly made, has not been obtained as a result of any fraud practised on the principal, the making of such profit will not deprive the agent of his rights against the principal, though the agent will not be able to keep his secret profit. This is illustrated by *Hippisley v Knee Bros*:[9]

> The principal employed the agents to sell goods on commission. The agents did so, and debited the principal with the cost of printing and advertising. From the people with whom they had dealt on these matters the agents had received discounts. This was perfectly honest, and in accordance with custom in the trade. None the less, it was held that to do this was a breach of their obligations as agents, and they could not make an extra profit by debiting the principal with the discount they had obtained. However, since they had not been guilty of fraud, they were entitled to receive their commission.

In *Boardman v Phipps*[10] the House of Lords considered that the defendants, who had not acted fraudulently, deserved some compensation for their work and skill in obtaining the shares and so acquiring a profit for the principals, the beneficiaries of the trust, which the trustees were unwilling to acquire by and for themselves. On what basis this was held is not clear. In the Court of Appeal[11] there was a difference of opinion as to the validity of such 'compensation' between Lord Denning MR and Pearson and Russell LJJ, the former regarding an honest agent as entitled to something, in the discretion of the court, if he had done valuable work in obtaining the profit, the two latter judges being less inclined to approve such a policy, for which it has been suggested[12] there is some support in earlier authority.[13]

---

8 *Hippisley v Knee Bros* [1905] 1 KB 1 at 9 per Kennedy J. See *Anangel Atlas Compania Naviera SA v Ishikawajima-Harima Heavy Industries Ltd* [1990] 1 Lloyd's Rep 167, where the plaintiffs knew about the relevant payments which were held not to be bribes. But in *Brown v IRC* [1965] AC 244, [1964] 3 All ER 119, it was held that a solicitor could not allege that there was a valid custom under which he was entitled to invest his clients' money and retain the interest for himself. Although this practice appears to have been accepted in Scotland (where this case arose), and, seemingly adopted by many English solicitors, it was held by the House of Lords to be an infringement of the agency relationship, as not being based upon any consent on the part of the principal. As a result of the uncertainty produced by this case, the Solicitors Act 1974, s 37 provides for the making of rules relating to the interest on client's money.
   In *Swain v Law Society*, above, it was held by the Court of Appeal that the society could retain the commission obtained from the insurance company, as long as this commission was received *after* individual solicitors had learned the facts; on appeal see [1982] 2 All ER 827.
9 Above. Contrast *Turnbull v Garden*, above. Cf *Stubbs v Slater* [1910] 1 Ch 632, where a practice of the stock market permitted a broker to charge a small fee for arranging transfers of shares. This was not fraudulent. Cf also the dicta in *Kelly v Cooper* [1993] AC 205.
10 [1967] 2 AC 46.
11 [1965] 1 All ER 849 at 857, 864, 865.
12 Goff and Jones *Law of Restitution* (4th edn 1993) p 664, note 90.
13 But see, suggesting the contrary, *Guinness plc v Saunders* [1990] 2 AC 663, [1990] 1 All ER 652.

For a secret profit to take the form of a bribe, and therefore give rise to the civil and criminal liabilities that are involved in the giving and taking of such bribes, the profit must have come to the agent through the activity of some third party, who intentionally and secretly offers a commission to the agent for doing something, usually, but not necessarily, for the benefit of the third party. In the event that an agent has accepted a bribe from a third party, the principal has several possible remedies available to him as against both the bribed agent and the briber. This was made clear by the Privy Council in *Mahesan v Malaysia Government Officers' Co-operative Housing Society Ltd.*[14]

> The director of a housing society conspired with M for the purchase by M of land in Penang and its resale to the society at a considerable profit to the conspirators. M bought the land at the sale price of $456,000 and sold it to the society for $944,000. Between the date of purchase and the date of resale to the society, M had to evict certain squatters from the land, at a cost of $45,000. The gross profit from the arrangement was therefore $488,000 (net $433,000 after the eviction of the squatters). M gave the director of the society $122,000, representing one-quarter of M's gross profit, by way of a bribe to the director. By the time the society discovered the truth, M had escaped to India. The director was prosecuted under anti-corruption legislation and convicted. He was then sued by the society for (i) the amount of the bribe, viz $122,000: (ii) damages in the amount of $488,000, being the difference between the price paid by the society for the land and the price paid for it by M. Such damages were claimed on the basis of the director's fraudulent breach of duty. The trial judge awarded the society the amount of the bribe, but did not give the society the damages also claimed. On appeal to the Federal Court of Malaysia, the director's appeal against the judgment awarding the society his bribe was dismissed: and the society's appeal against the denial of their damages was allowed, to the extent that the society was awarded $488,000 less the sum paid to the squatters, ie, $45,000. Thus the society was awarded both the $122,000 and the net profit on the sale made by M, viz, $443,000. The director appealed to the Privy Council.

The issue was whether the society could obtain what was, virtually, the same amount of money twice over. Prior to this case it had been held that a principal could obtain from his corrupt agent the amount of the bribe he had accepted since this was a 'secret profit'. He could also sue the agent and the person giving the agent the bribe, jointly and severally, to compensate the principal for any loss or damage resulting to him from the agent's acceptance of the bribe. Such liability existed cumulatively with the agent's liability to account for the bribe.[15] The liability to pay damages was for deceit and conspiracy: and on proof that a secret commission had been paid, it was irrebuttably presumed that it was given for a corrupt motive, that it influenced the agent to the detriment of the principal, and

---

14 [1979] AC 374, [1978] 2 All ER 405: on which see Beatson and Reynolds (1973) 94 LQR 344; Tettenborn 'Bribery Corruption and Restitution—the Strange Case of Mr Mahesan' (1979) 95 LQR 68; Needham 'Recovering the Profits of Bribery' (1979) 95 LQR 536.
15 *Salford Corpn v Lever* [1891] 1 QB 168.

that it had caused damage (at least to the extent of the bribe).[16] The Privy Council decided, however, that, as against the agent and the briber, the affected principal had alternative, not cumulative, remedies: and he had to make an election which one he wished to pursue, although such election did not have to be made until the time for entry of judgment in the principal's favour on one or other of the alternative causes of action. His alternatives were between (a) claiming the amount of the bribe from the agent, as money had and received by the agent, ie, by a restitutionary claim; and (b) suing for damages for fraud in respect of the actual loss sustained by the principal in consequence of his entering the transaction in relation to which the bribe had been given.

In reaching this conclusion, the Privy Council reconciled differences of opinion that had developed between members of the Court of Appeal in England in several earlier cases:[17] and made it clear that the earlier decision in *Salford Corpn v Lever*,[18] to the effect that the principal's remedies were cumulative not alternative, was incorrect: to say this was 'flying in the face of a long line of authority',[19] which had been discussed and applied by the House of Lords in *United Australia Ltd v Barclays Bank Ltd*.[20] Thus, on the facts of the *Mahesan* case, where, in the absence of the briber, only the corrupt agent was amenable to the court's jurisdiction, the Privy Council held that, because the society was bound to elect which remedy to pursue, and would obviously have chosen to claim the greater amount by way of damages, the judgment of the Federal Court of Malaya would be varied by awarding the society only the sum of $443,000, with interest, based upon the gross profit of M less the payment to the squatters.

This judgment has been criticised on a number of grounds. For example, one critic[1] considered that the Privy Council was wrong to deny the society the right to recover both the bribe and the profit on the ground that the society would thus have received an undeserved 'windfall'. This was because, in all cases where a principal recovers a secret profit, the principal obtains a windfall. Nor should the award of bribe have been regarded as diminishing the damages actually suffered by the society because it came out of the original profit. The reason for this was that the purpose of the law was to deter agents from committing corrupt acts and making unauthorised profits, even if this might result in the apparent unjust enrichment of the principal. Moreover, the recovery of the bribe was intended by

16 *Industries and General Mortgage Co v Lewis* [1949] 2 All ER 573 at 578 per Slade J. This was applied by Havers J in *Taylor v Walker* [1958] 1 Lloyd's Rep 490 at 511–512. There the bribe in question was given by an insurance company to assessors, who were the agents of someone injured in a road accident and who was claiming compensation. It was held that the effect of this bribe, given the assessors to get them to make the injured person accept a settlement, was to avoid the settlement.
17 *Grant v Gold Exploration and Development Syndicate Co* [1900] 1 QB 233; *Hovenden & Sons v Millhoff* (1900) 83 LT 41 (applied in respect of the damages recoverable when an agent earned a finder's fee from the third party as well as acting as the agent of the plaintiff: *Wakeford v Yada Tompkins Huntingford & Humphries* (1986) 28 DLR (4th) 481, which was not a case of bribery, merely breach of fiduciary duty).
18 [1891] 1 QB 168.
19 *Mahesan v Malaysian Government Officers' Co-operative Housing Society Ltd*, above at 410 per Lord Diplock.
20 [1941] AC 1, [1940] 4 All ER 20.
 1 Tettenborn, (1979) 95 LQR 68 at p 73.

188   Chapter 8

the law to be deterrent, rather than to repair actual loss: and the recovery of
damages was not to prevent corruption. Therefore, since the two claims were of
a different nature, there was no reason why the two should not co-exist and be
available cumulatively.[2] Although this appears to be a strong argument, it is
suggested that the actual decision of the Privy Council is more reasonable and
more consistent with true principle, in that it precludes double recovery in
respect of the same 'wrong', loss or damage. Furthermore, it was only by reason
of the peculiar circumstances of the case, viz, the inability of the society to sue
M, that the agent was rendered liable for the bribe and the society's loss, rather
than for his own share in the wrongdoing, the bribe that he received. In other
situations it may well be that the principal will pursue different remedies against
different parties to the corruption. A more significant criticism is that the guilty
parties were able to deduct from their liability the amount which they had paid to
others, viz, the squatters. It is hard to justify this, unless it be on the ground that
what the wrongdoer had done was a benefit to the principal, in that otherwise the
principal might have had to pay the squatters to leave. There is authority for this,
even when the defendant's action was wrongful[3] (and a fortiori when it was
innocent).[4] However, it is still arguable that the effect was to relieve the
wrongdoer, albeit in this instance it was the agent who had only received a small
proportion of the profit, from some of his otherwise undoubted liability.

Beyond these liabilities both the common law and statute reinforce the agent's
duty and make persons who accept bribes guilty of crimes. At common law a
person who accepts or agrees to accept a bribe is guilty of conspiracy.[5] Further
criminal liability on the part of the corrupt agents is provided for in the
Prevention of Corruption Acts, 1906, 1916.[6]

2 Ibid pp 74–75.
3 *Bagnall v Carlton* (1877) 6 Ch D 371; *Lydney and Wigpool Iron Ore Co v Bird* (1886) 33 Ch D
85; *Munro v Wilmott* [1949] 1 KB 295, [1948] 2 All ER 983; *Re Simms, ex p Trustee* [1934] Ch
1: Needham (1979) 95 LQR 536 at pp 552–555.
4 *Boardman v Phipps* [1967] 2 AC 46, [1966] 3 All ER 721.
5 *R v Whitaker* [1914] 3 KB 1283.
6 See *R v Barrett* [1976] 3 All ER 895, [1976] 1 WLR 946, where the expression 'agent' in these
statutes is considered: and an additional superintendent of registrar of births, deaths and
marriages was an agent for these purposes.

CHAPTER 9

The principal's duties

A. Remuneration

Contractual duty. The most important duty of the principal is to remunerate the agent for services rendered. The obligation to pay such remuneration—the agent's 'commission'—exists only where it has been created by an express or implied contract between principal and agent. As already seen, it is possible for an agency relationship to arise from agreement between the parties and yet be gratuitous. It is a question of construction in each case whether it was the intention of the parties that the agent shall work gratuitously or whether an agreement to pay remuneration was expressly made,[1] or can be implied into the relationship.[2]

The implication of such an agreement may depend upon what is reasonable in the circumstances, particularly the language used by the parties. Where nothing is said on the subject of remuneration, the circumstances may indicate that remuneration is to be paid. As Lord Atkin said, dealing with the facts of *Way v Latilla*:[3]

> 'while there is no concluded contract as to the remuneration it is plain that there existed ... a contract of employment ... in circumstances which clearly indicated that the work was not to be gratuitous.'

If the nature of the employment, and the situation of the parties, show that payment was intended, it is immaterial that nothing has been expressly agreed. Payment will be recovered on a quantum meruit basis, ie what is reasonable in the circumstances.[4] This will be so if there is a trade or other usage or custom

---

1 See, eg *Milton Marlowe & Co v Southcut Ltd* (1979) 256 Estates Gazette 293: express agreement found. Cf *Windsor Italian Village Restaurant Ltd v Remo Valente Real Estate Ltd* (1992) 27 RPR (2d) 221, contract not clear on when commission was payable, therefore term dealing with commission was ineffective.

2 See, eg *Ellis v Pipe-Chemi (Holdings) Ltd* (1980) 258 Estates Gazette 329: no term as to payment implied: as to the implication of a term securing in advance the payment and indemnification of the agent, see *Fraser v Equitorial Shipping Co Ltd and Equitorial Lines Ltd, The Ijaolo* [1979] 1 Lloyd's Rep 103.

3 [1937] 3 All ER 759 at 762.

4 *Withy Robinson (a firm) v Edwards* (1985) 277 Estates Gazette 748. In *Lewis and Graves v Harper* (1978) 250 Estates Gazette 1287, although there was no agreement as to the rate of commission, the Court of Appeal upheld a decision that payment had been agreed on a 'commission', rather than a quantum meruit basis: cf *Hampton & Sons v Trade and General Securities* (1978) 250 Estates Gazette 451. Contrast *London Commercial and Land Co Ltd v Beazer Lands Ltd* [1990] CLY para 107, where quantum meruit not commission was awarded.

which indicates that remuneration is to be paid, in which event, the amount of remuneration may be calculated by what is customary in the trade, profession or business in which the agent is employed. If something is said by the parties about remuneration regard must be had to what they say. In *Stubbs v Slater*[5] Lord Cozens-Hardy had this to say on the subject of construing the language used by the parties:

> 'By using this Stock Exchange term "net", which asserts that the broker's commission ... is included in the charge, the defendants were not in any sense claiming a secret commission, but were merely using language appropriate to the Stock Exchange in claiming this remuneration.'

In that case the language used revealed an implied contract to pay a stockbroker remuneration in accordance with the custom of the Stock Exchange.

On the other hand, the language used may show, or be interpreted to mean, that the agent was to act gratuitously. Two old cases illustrate what this involves. In *Taylor v Brewer*[6] the agent agreed to accept 'such remuneration as should be deemed right'. It was held that the agent was not entitled to any remuneration under the agreement. In *Bryant v Flight*[7] the agent agreed to work for the principal in these terms: 'the amount of payment I am to receive I leave entirely to you'. The agent worked for six months. It was held that it must be implied into the agreement that the agent was to get something for his work, and he was able to recover on a quantum meruit. This shows that the courts will sometimes, but not always, make a contract for the parties out of the language they have used. Powell argued that *Taylor v Brewer* would be differently decided today, and the courts would enforce the payment of a reasonable remuneration where none has been fixed by the parties and there was no express intention of acting gratuitously.[8] But it still seems possible for a contract of agency to be regarded as meaning that the agent will not be entitled to claim remuneration if he has left the payment of remuneration entirely to the discretion of the principal. This is what happened in *Kofi Sunkersette Obu v Strauss & Co Ltd*:[9]

> There a sum of £50 a month was agreed upon as personal and travelling expenses, together with commission which was left to the principal's discretion. It was held that the sum of £50 a month was also intended to remunerate the agent, and no further commission was payable.

Where the parties have used express terms about remuneration then, unless the

---

5 [1910] 1 Ch 632 at 642.
6 (1813) 1 M & S 290.
7 (1839) 5 M & W 114.
8 *Law of Agency* (2nd edn) p 334. This point of view was illustrated in the majority opinion of the Manitoba Court of Appeal in *Banfield, McFarlane, Evans Real Estate Ltd v Hoffer* [1977] 4 WWR 465, but O'Sullivan JA dissented on the ground that in the absence of a contract of agency, this was no reason to allow a quantum meruit claim.
9 [1951] AC 243.

contract is void,[10] or there is no concluded agreement,[11] or the contract is vague as to the amount of remuneration to be paid, the result will be that, as Hilbery J said in *Jones v Lowe*,[12] 'there is no room for the implication of any promise ... to pay a reasonable remuneration'. As long as the express terms of the contract are valid and clear, nothing may be implied into the contract which is inconsistent with such terms.[13] This is so whether the contract provides for remuneration, as in *Cutter v Powell*,[14] or, as subsequently construed, excludes the principal's obligation to remunerate, as in *Taylor v Brewer* and *Obu v Strauss*.

Liability only where earned. Even if it has been expressly or impliedly agreed by the principal that he will pay remuneration, his duty to pay remuneration only arises where the agent has earned it. This will occur only when the agent has done what was specified in the contract, which is a matter of construction,[15] *and* the agent has been the direct, effective, or efficient cause of the event upon the occurrence which the principal has agreed to pay the agent remuneration.[16] So the agent must show not only that he has achieved what he was employed to bring about,[17] but also that his acts were not merely incidental to that result, but were essential to its happening. This, like all issues of causation is ultimately a

10 *Craven-Ellis v Canons Ltd* [1936] 2 KB 403, [1936] 2 All ER 1066. Or otherwise unenforceable: cf the Canadian case of *Deglman v Guaranty Trust Co of Canada* [1954] 3 DLR 785, which has received much judicial interpretation and application: see Angus 'Restitution in Canada since the Deglman Case' (1964) 42 CBR 529. The suggestion is that even if no contractual remedy is available, rendering of services might give rise to a *restitutionary* remedy. See Goff and Jones *Law of Restitution* (4th edn 1993) pp 404–405, 441–442, 478–482; Fridman *Restitution* (2nd edn 1992) pp 285–298, 300–305, 308–310.
11 *British Bank for Foreign Trade Ltd v Novinex Ltd* [1949] 1 KB 623, [1949] 1 All ER 155.
12 [1945] KB 73 at 77, [1945] 1 All ER 194 at 197. For an example of this, see *John Meacock & Co v Abrahams* [1956] 3 All ER 660, [1956] 1 WLR 1463.
13 *Cutter v Powell* (1795) 6 Term Rep 320.
14 Above.
15 See, eg, *Property Choice Ltd v Fronda* [1992] CLY para 88, below, p 194, note 9; cf *Fairvale Ltd v Sabharwal* below.
16 Eg, a 'sale': *HW Liebig & Co Ltd v Leading Investments Ltd* (1986) 25 DLR (4th) 161, or a lease: *Riverdale Realty Ltd v MPN Holdings Ltd* (1993) 86 Man R (2d) 306; affd (1994) 92 Man R (2d) 165. For other examples, see *NRS Realty Ltd v Thealai* (1988) 59 Alta LR (2d) 232; *Barnes v Louw* (1987) 54 Sask LR 42; *Aronovitch & Leipvic Ltd v Archibald Brokerage Ltd* (1987) 44 Man R (2d) 154; *Ain Realty Ltd v Riverbank Holdings Ltd* (1986) 46 Alta LR (2d) 161; *Re/Max Real Estate Ltd v Edmonton Wholesale Auto Auctions (1982) Ltd* (1986) 46 Alta LR (2d) 205; *Quest Real Estate Ltd v R & W Holdings Ltd* (1987) 44 Man R (2d) 308; *T-D Bank v Chan* (1987) 75 AR 137; *Central Guaranty Trust Co v Welner* (1993) 119 NSR (2d) 337; *Smalley Agencies LW v Goncalo* (1994) 93 Man R (2d) 72. Even, sometimes, if the event which would normally give rise to the obligation to pay commission occurred *after* the termination of the agent's employment. Whether this be so depends upon the terms of the contract. In *Fairvale Ltd v Sabharwal* [1993] CLY para 69 the sale had to be effected within a specified time. The agent brought about the sale: but outside the specified period. Commission could not be claimed. Contrast *Di Dio Nominees Pty Ltd v Brian Mark Real Estate Pty Ltd* [1992] 2 VR 732, where the sale was concluded after the sole agency ended but the introduction of the syndicate which, when later incorporated bought the property, took place while the sole agency was in effect.
17 Such as a transaction by which the defendant obtained financing for the purchase of a ship: *Tufton Associates Ltd v Dilmun Shipping* [1992] 1 Lloyd's Rep 71 or the appointment of the defendant as management consultant for a project *Chaskill v Marina Developments* [1991] CLY para 100. Thus if the agent is to 'arrange' a mortgage he must obtain a contract to lend money to the principal: nothing less will suffice: see *Capital Management Corpn Ltd v Hachitt Development Pty Ltd* (1971) 18 FLR 362. See also *Cooper & Co v Fairview Estates*

question of fact,[18] though certain legal principles emerge from the cases. On the question of when has the agent been the direct cause of the transaction, it is useful to refer to the words of Erle CJ in *Green v Bartlett*:[19]

'If the relation of buyer and seller is really brought about by the act of the agent he is entitled to commission although the actual sale has not been effected by him.'

In that case the agent, who was employed to sell a house at an auction, failed to get a purchaser at the auction. A person (X) who had been present at the auction asked the agent who was the owner of the house. The agent told him and X then proceeded to enter into a contract directly with the owner, the agent's principal. It was held that the agent was entitled to his commission. The same result followed in *Burchell v Gowrie Collieries*,[20] where the principal sold to X behind

(Investments) (1987) 282 Estates Gazette 1131, commission payable on completion of a lease with the tenant with whom the principal had not previously been in communication: *Preston & Partners v Markheath Securities* [1988] CLY § 60, sale was 'subject to contract' and 'subject to planning', as was obligation to pay commission; *Brodie Marshall & Co v Carpenter* (1984) 274 Estates Gazette 1149, introduction of a purchaser. As to where the contract referred to a 'sale' and the issue was whether the actual sale completed was the sale contemplated in the agency agreement, see *Lord v Trippe* (1977) 14 ALR 129.

18   Cf *Reiff Diner & Co v Catalytic International Inc* (1978) 246 Estates Gazette 743 (followed in *Sinclair Goldsmith v Minero Peru Comercial* (1978) 248 Estates Gazette 1015); *Hampton & Sons v Trade and General Securities Ltd* (1978) 250 Estates Gazette 451; *John D Wood & Co v Dantata* (1985) 275 Estates Gazette 1278; affd (1987) 283 Estates Gazette 314; *Bentley's Estate Agents v Granix* [1989] 27 EG 93; *Peter Yates & Co v Bullock* [1990] 37 EG 75; *Cobbs Property Services v Liddell-Taylor* [1990] 12 EG 104; *Ross Martin Realty v Chow Holdings Pty Ltd (No 2)* [1991] 1 Qd R 182 in all of which the agent *was* the effective cause of the transaction, with *Hoddell v Smith* (1975) 260 Estates Gazette 295; *Henry Smith & Son v Muskett* (1977) 246 Estates Gazette 655; *A A Dickson & Co v O'Leary* (1979) 254 Estates Gazette 731; *LJ Hooker Ltd v WJ Adams Estates Pty Ltd* (1977) 138 CLR 52; *Robert Bruce & Partners v Winyard Development* (1987) 282 Estates Gazette 1255 (but commission was payable on other grounds); *Anscombe & Ringland v Watson* [1991] 38 EG 230; *Bradley v Adams* [1989] 1 Qd R 256 where the agent was not.
    Note the problem where two agents are involved, ie which of them should be entitled to commission, or should both be entitled: cf *Lordsgate Properties Ltd v Balcombe* (1985) 274 Estates Gazette 493; *Hampton & Sons v Garrard Smith* (1985) 274 Estates Gazette 1139; *John D Wood & Co v Dantata*, above; *Barnard Marcus & Co v Ashraf* [1988] 18 EG 67; *Chason Ryder & Co v Hedges* [1993] 08 EG 119. Contrast a Canadian case, *Eddie Willox Agencies Ltd v Great West Life Assurance Co* (1983) 21 Man R (2d) 46, only one commission payable: any other conclusion would be impracticable and unreasonable.

19   (1863) 14 CBNS 681 at 685. Contrast *Tribe v Taylor* (1876) 1 CPD 505, where the agent was instructed to introduce a financier who would invest in the principal's business. He did so, and was paid commission on the sum lent. Later the financier invested more money in the principal's business. It was held that the agent was not entitled to commission on such investment. For criticism, see Stoljar *Law of Agency* pp 313–314.

20   [1910] AC 614 (distinguished by the majority of the High Court of Australia in *LJ Hooker Ltd v WJ Adams Estates Pty Ltd*, above, when the ultimate purchaser had agreed with a prospective purchaser introduced by the agent that they would not compete: in effect, as a result of this arrangement, the prospective purchaser introduced by the agent had become part-owner of the property sold: the agent was not entitled to commission, according to the majority of the Court (Jacobs and Murphy JJ dissenting); cf *Trotter v McSpadden* [1986] VR 329, no commission payable when contrast of sale was conditional. Contrast *Di Dio Nominees Pty Ltd v Brian Marks Real Estate Pty Ltd*, above, note 16. See also *Allan v Leo Lines Ltd* [1957] 1 Lloyd's Rep 127. Contrast *Block Bros Realty Ltd v Viktore* [1974] 2 WWR 282, where in somewhat similar circumstances the agent was not held to be the cause of the eventual sale.

the agent's back, but after the agent had discovered X, in the course of fulfilling the task of finding a purchaser for the principal, and had advised his principal not to sell to X.

It would seem, therefore, that the test is whether the agent found the purchaser[1] or, as Tindal CJ expressed the question in *Wilkinson v Martin*:[2] 'did the sale really and substantially proceed from the agent's acts?' So, in *Toulmin v Millar*:[3]

> An agent found a tenant for an estate, as he was employed to do. Later the tenant purchased the estate, without the intervention of the agent. It was held that the agent was not entitled to commission on the sale.

In *Taplin v Barrett*:[4]

> The principal employed an agent to sell a house. The agent found a prospective purchaser, X, whose terms were not accepted by the principal, who therefore put the house up for auction. At the auction X was the successful bidder who bought the house. It was held that the agent was not entitled to commission.

These cases show that 'in order to found a legal claim for commission there must not only be a causal, there must also be a contractual relation between the introduction and the ultimate transaction of sale'.[5] This explains the distinction between these cases and *Burchell v Gowrie Collieries*. There the person

1 *Murray v Currie* (1836) 7 C & P 584 per Lord Denman CJ. See *Riverside Realty v Amanda Homes Ltd* (1987) 43 Man R (2d) 581 contract 'arranged' by the agent: commission payable. Hence as long as the agent found the purchaser the fact that the mechanics of the sale were effected through another agent would seem to be immaterial; see two Canadian cases *Miller v Bell Refrigerator Co Ltd* (1966) 55 WWR 681: *Rungay v Forrester* (1967) 63 DLR (2d) 338; cf *Doyle v Mount Kidsbrom Mining & Exploration Pty Ltd* [1984] 2 Qd R 386, introducing a buyer was enough: the same was the case even where the vendor subsequently withdrew the property from the market: *Walters v John Crisp Pty Ltd* (1982) 64 FLR 299. But the situation will be different if the agents were rivals and one did, but the other did not, find the purchaser: *AA Dickson & Co v O'Leary* (1979) 254 Estates Gazette 731.

2 (1837) 8 C & P 1 at 5. Cf McPherson J in *Doyle v Mount Kidsbrom Mining & Exploration Pty Ltd* [1984] 2 Qd R 386 at 391: the question was whether the transaction which in fact occurred was brought about as a result of the agency: cf Gibbs J in *LJ Hooker Ltd v WJ Adams Estates Pty Ltd* (1977) 138 CLR 52 at 66. So no commission was payable in *Empela H Ltd v Reidy Surety Ltd* (1988) 48 Man R (2d) 305; *Re/Max Real Estate of Dartmouth Ltd v Wilron Eastern Ltd* (1988) 84 NSR (2d) 7.

3 (1887) 58 LT 96. See also *Poulter v Doggett* [1964] CLY 14, where an agent was appointed to sell or let a house. It was let to a third party with an option to purchase. Later the agent, acting for the third party, obtained his agreement to exercise the option. It was held that the agent was entitled to commission on the sale, less the commission on the lease. In contrast see *Tapley v Giles* (1986) 40 SASR 474, purchaser negotiated directly with principal, after being introduced by agent: no commission payable.

4 (1889) 6 TLR 30. Cf *Coles v Enoch* [1939] 3 All ER 327, where the third party took a lease of the principal's premises after overhearing a conversation between the agent and another person whom the agent thought, mistakenly, might be interested. The third party asked for, but failed to get, details from this other person, in whose office he was at the time of the conversation with the agent. *Held*: the agent was not entitled to commission.

5 Per Lord Watson in *Toulmin v Millar*. Even if the sale is at a different price and after a substantial interval of time, following the first introduction of the purchaser: *Century 21 C G Realty Ltd v Trickett* (1986) 47 Alta LR (2d) 137 at 139 per Kerans JA, see also *Century 21 Suburban Real Estate Ltd v Duff* (1987) 62 Nfld & PEIR 190: *First Group Real Estate Ltd v City of Edmonton* (1987) 76 AR 10, commission payable despite breach in continuity of agent's involvement in sale.

introduced by the agent as a purchaser was the one with whom the principal negotiated in the manner originally intended, even though against the agent's opinion. In *Toulmin v Millar* and *Taplin v Barrett* the immediate effect of the agent's introduction was not the negotiation of the kind of contract which would have given rise to the duty to pay the agent remuneration. The result of the agent's introduction was either a different kind of transaction or no transaction at all.[6] Another illustration of this is *Hodges & Sons v Hackbridge Park Residential Hotel Ltd*:[7]

> The agent told a Government Department about his principal's house, which he was employed to sell. The Department did not purchase the house, but acquired it compulsorily. It was held that the agent was not entitled to remuneration.

In that case there was a causal relationship between the agent's act, and the acquisition of the house by the Department: but there was no *contractual* relationship between these two events.

Irrelevance of benefit to principal. It is immaterial to the payment of remuneration that the principal has derived no benefit from the agent's acts. As long as the agent has performed what he was employed to do, and has not been at fault in failing to benefit has principal, the latter will be bound to pay the agreed remuneration. For example, in *Fisher v Drewett*:[8]

> The agent was employed to get a mortgage on the principal's property. A third party was found ready to advance the money. But the mortgage could not be made because the principal had no title. It was held that the agent was entitled to his remuneration, despite the fact that the principal had got no benefit from his act. For the agent had done what he was employed to do.

On the other hand the agent would not be entitled to his commission if he has not performed what the contract of agency required him to do before his commission was payable,[9] even if the principal prevented the agent from achieving this, as long as the principal's conduct was legitimate under the contract, eg where the principal accepted a higher offer from another purchaser[10] or the principal was

---

6 See *Lord v Trippe* (1977) 14 ALR 129 where the majority of the High Court of Australia (Barwick CJ and Mason J), over the dissent of Aickin J, held that a sale to a company other than the originally interested company was a sale within the meaning of the agency agreement, entitling the agent to commission, because the new company/purchaser was owned by the vendors who transferred the share capital to the originally intended purchaser (a manoeuvre rendered necessary by the initial refusal of the Administrator of the Northern Territory to approve the originally intended sale). Cf *Di Dio Nominees Pty Ltd v Brian Mark Real Estate Pty Ltd* [1992] 2 VR 732, above, note 16. Contrast *LJ Hooker Ltd v WJ Adams Estates Pty Ltd* (1977) 138 CLR 52, above, note 20.

7 [1940] 1 KB 404, [1939] 4 All ER 347.

8 (1878) 48 LJ QB 32.

9 As in *Property Choice v Fronda* [1992] CLY para 88, a case of sole agency where the agent failed to bring about a concluded sale: no commission was payable; so too in *Fairvale Ltd v Sabharwal* [1992] 32 EG 51, where the sale was concluded outside the period of the agency contract; see also *Pen-Mor Investment Services Ltd v Shore* (1993) 88 BCLR (2d) 53, purpose effected after agency contract expired: no commission.

10 *Henry Smith & Son v Muskett* (1977) 246 Estates Gazette 655.

entitled to reject the offer of a loan from a third party introduced by the agent, in accordance with his task of finding a lender, on the ground that the terms of such loan were unacceptable.[11] This raises the question of the extent to which the principal can prevent the agent from fulfilling his undertaking, and so deprive him of the opportunity to earn his commission.

This particular aspect of the principal's duty to pay remuneration has caused considerable difficulty in recent years in respect of the payment of commission to estate agents who have not actually completed a sale. A number of cases have laid down and illustrated the principles applicable to the problem of liability when an agent has earned his commission, or when the principal becomes liable to pay anything to his agent.[12] The solution is to be sought in the judgments delivered in the leading case of *Luxor (Eastbourne) Ltd v Cooper*[13] where, on the facts, it was held that the agent was not entitled to any commission on the sale of property because he had not completed the arrangements. What the case shows is that everything turns upon the terms of the agreement between principal and agent. The actual position depends upon: (a) the express terms of that agreement, and (b) whether any term can be implied in the absence of anything express.

11 *Fawcus v Bond Street Brokers Ltd* (1967) 111 Sol Jo 495. There must be *default* by the principal, ie wilful refusal or deceit before the agent can succeed: *Blake & Co v Sohn* [1969] 3 All ER 123, [1969] 1 WLR 1412. Cf the Australian case of *R J Mabarrock Pty Ltd v King* (1971) 1 SASR 313 and a Canadian case, *Smalley Agencies Ltd v Hill-Everest Holdings Ltd* [1992] 4 WWR 233; affd (1993) 83 Man R (2d) 240 leave to appeal to SCC refused [1993] 7 WWR lxviii note. But does this entitle the agent to commission on a contractual basis? It has been held in Canada that, even if the contract was rendered nugatory by the misrepresentation, ie wrongful act, of the principal, the agent could not sue for his commission, though he might have an action for *deceit*, since the commission had not been earned: *Bradley-Wilson Ltd v Canyon Gardens Ltd* (1965) 52 DLR (2d) 717. Similarly, in *Burns Fry Ltd v Khurana* (1985) 20 DLR (4th) 245, the agent could not claim commission on the basis of an implied term, or on the ground of unjust enrichment or restitution, where the contract provided for payment of commission 'after closing the transaction', and the principal changed his mind and would not sell after the agent found a purchaser willing to pay the principal's asking price. The non-liability of the principal is even clearer where the *agent* knew that the principal might not be able to satisfy the legitimate requirements of a third party, eg with respect to access to the property: see *Oldfield, Kirby and Gardner Real Estate Ltd v Kliewer* (1971) 18 DLR (3d) 762.
12 Canadian statutes have provisions which lay down the conditions under which an estate agent may claim his commission, thereby solving some, if not all, of the difficulty: see the Real Estate Agents' Licensing Act, RSA 1980, cR-5 (Alberta); Real Estate Act RS BC 1979, c 356 (British Columbia); Real Estate Brokers Act, RSM 1987, cR-20 (Manitoba); Real Estate Agents' Act, RSNB 1973, cR-1 (New Brunswick); Real Estate Trading Act, RS Newfd 1990, cR-2 (Newfoundland); Real Estate Brokers' Licensing Act, RSNS 1989, c 384 (Nova Scotia); Real Estate and Business Brokers Act, RSO 1990, cR-4 (Ontario); Real Estate Trading Act, RSPEI 1988, cR-2 (Prince Edward Island); Real Estate Brokers Act, SS 1986–87–88, cR-2 (Saskatchewan).

The same is also true of the situation of various Australian states. See, for example, the Estate Agents Act 1980, No 9428 (Vic): Auctioneers and Estate Agents Act 1959 No 81, ss 30, 31 (Tas): Auctioneers and Agents Act 1971, s 70 (Queensland); Auctioneers and Agents Act 1941, No 28 ss 42, 42AA; Real Estate and Business Agents Act 1978 (Western Australia); Agents Ordinance 1968 (ACT); Land and Business Agents Act 1979 (Northern Territory) (most, if not all of which have been subject to amendment from time to time). See also the New Zealand Real Estate Agents Act 1976 No 9, s 62.

Curiously enough, no attempt was made in the English Estate Agents Act 1979 to legislate along similar lines.
13 [1941] AC 108, [1941] 1 All ER 33.

If there is an express or an implied term in the contract that the principal will not interfere with the agent's execution of his authority, by himself, getting a purchaser for the property, or otherwise making it impossible for the agent to perform his undertaking and so earn his commission, then the principal will be liable if he breaks that term, and the measure of damages will be the amount of commission involved.[14] If no such term is in the contract, then the principal can negotiate and sell himself and will not be liable for commission. This is what happened in *Bentall, Horsley and Baldry v Vicary*,[15] where the contract contained no 'express words at all indicating a prohibition against a sale by the [principal] himself'.[16]

If there is an express agreement to pay the agent his commission *before* the principal derives any benefit from the agent's acts, in the form of a binding contract between himself and the third party, then the principal will be liable for the commission when the agent has done the stipulated task. These contracts are not contracts of employment, in that the agent is not obliged to do anything. But, if the agent wishes to earn his payment, he must bring about the happening of an event.[17] What the event is depends upon the terms of the agreement between principal and agent. If the principal wishes to protect himself, then he must see to it that he will only be bound to pay commission if the agent finds a 'purchaser' for the property, so that his liability to pay commission will only arise when a 'purchaser' is found.[18] On the other hand, if the agent wishes to protect himself against loss of commission, then he will obtain a commission contract 'containing special terms such as to impose an obligation on the vendor actually to sell through the particular agent to the potential purchaser introduced by that agent. Contracts containing such terms, though not perhaps usual, are possible.'[19] Alternatively the agent can get the principal to agree that the agent shall be entitled to commission whether or not his efforts to sell have been successful. Such an agreement would have to be very clearly expressed, and in the construction of it the law will lean heavily against finding that such were its terms. Two reasons are given for this. The first is that commission is paid out of the purchase price and so there ought therefore to be a purchase. The second is the possibility that the principal may employ several agents and there can only be, or ought only to be, one commission.

What is the position in the absence of any express term? Can the courts imply

---

14 In *Shackleton Aviation Ltd v Maitland Drewery Aviation Ltd* [1964] 1 Lloyd's Rep 293 and *Marcan Shipping (London) Ltd v Polish SS Co* [1989] 2 Lloyd's Rep 138, the agent unsuccessfully argued that a term could be implied. In *Alpha Trading Ltd v Dunnshaw-Patten Ltd* [1981] QB 290, [1981] 1 All ER 482, the agent was successful: see below, pp 197–198. See, however, *Sinclair Goldsmith v Minero Peru Comercial* (1978) 248 Estates Gazette 1015, where the agent were rewarded on a quantum meruit basis, cf *Debenham Tewson & Chinnocks v Rimington* [1990] 34 EG 55.
15 [1931] 1 KB 253. In the Canadian case of *Knowlton Realty Ltd v Mace* (1979) 106 DLR (3d) 667 a term to such effect was *implied*; See also *Del Bro Real Estate Ltd v Goldstein* (1991) 76 Man R (2d) 57.
16 Per McCardie J at 258.
17 *Luxor (Eastbourne) Ltd v Cooper* [1941] AC 108 at 124, [1941] 1 All ER 33 at 44 per Lord Russell.
18 [1941] AC 108 at 126, [1941] 1 All ER 33 at 45 per Lord Russell. This has given rise to special problems in relation to estate agents, the cases on which are discussed below, pp 411–421.
19 Ibid at 54, 139, per Lord Wright.

any term which will make the principal liable to pay commission even though the agent has not sold the property for him? This was the precise problem raised in *Luxor v Cooper* itself, and in *Alpha Trading Ltd v Dunnshaw-Patten Ltd*.[20] In the *Luxor* case,[1] it was argued that, where the contract said that the agent was to get his commission on *completion* of the contract, a term could be implied to the effect that the principal could not prevent the completion of the transaction so as to deprive the agent of the agreed commission. Such a term was too wide. It would have to be modified by saying that the principal could reject for 'reasonable cause' an offer made through the agent. But 'reasonable' cause was too vague. Therefore, so wide or vague a term could not necessarily be implied into the contract.[2] Any implied term of that kind would be unreasonable or void for uncertainty.[3] Such a term would have to be expressly agreed.[4] The reasons why such a term could not be implied were explained by Lord Wright.[5] What would happen if there were several agents, or if the principal changed his mind? He would still be bound to pay commission, which was clearly unreasonable. There was also the consideration that in such contracts the agent takes upon himself the risk that nothing will emerge despite his efforts. As Lord Simon said:[6]

'The agent is promised a reward in return for an event, and the event has not happened. He runs the risk of disappointment, but if he is not willing to run the risk he should introduce into the express terms of the contract the clause which protects him.'

The difficulties involved in implying a term that would, in a sense, guarantee payment of the agent's commission, are illustrated by the cases in which attempts to achieve such implication were unsuccessful.[7] However, in the *Alpha Trading* case,[8] the necessary term was implied.

Agents were employed to find a buyer for 100,000 tonnes of cement at $49.50 per tonne. On this sale the agents were to receive a commission of $1.50 per tonne, as well as other payments. A buyer was introduced by the agents to the principal, who entered into a contract with the third party for the sale of the correct quantity of cement at the agreed price. The third party, the buyer, supplied a letter of credit, and the principal, the seller, gave a performance bond: but the principal, being unable or unwilling to complete

20 [1981] QB 290, [1981] 1 All ER 482.
1 [1941] AC 108, [1941] 1 All ER 33.
2 Ibid at 38–39; 115–118 per Lord Simon.
3 Ibid at 64–65, 155 per Lord Romer.
4 Ibid at 39, 118 per Lord Simon.
5 Ibid at 53–56, 138–142.
6 [1941] AC 108, [1941] 1 All ER 33 at 120–141; cf Lord Russell at 125, 44; Lord Wright at 141, 55.
7 See above, p 196 note 14, below, p 393.
8 [1981] QB 290, [1981] 1 All ER 482; cf *George Moundreas & Co SA v Navimplex Centrala Navala* [1985] 2 Lloyd's Rep 515 where a term was implied. Contrast *Marcan Shipping (London) Ltd v Polish SS Co* [1988] 2 Lloyd's Rep 171; affd [1989] 4 CLR 5, where no term could be implied because there was an express term that the principal would pay commission in accordance with market principles. See also, a Canadian case, similar to the *Alpha Trading* case, *Knowlton Realty Ltd v Mace* (1979) 106 DLR (3d) 667; contrast *Carsted v Gass* (1981) 116 DLR (3d) 550 which turned on the *express* terms of the agreement between principal and agent: no commission was payable when the principal failed to complete.

the transaction, the contract of sale was never implemented, and the third party was released from the obligation to pay the purchase price. The agents sued for the agreed commission, or, alternatively, for damages for breach of an implied term that the principal would not break the contract with the third party and so deprive the agents of their commission. At the trial of the action, it was held that a term could be implied, for breach of which the principal was liable. The Court of Appeal upheld that judgment.

The distinction between this case and many others (including the *Luxor* case) was that, apparently for the first time, according to Brandon LJ,[9] the question arose in the context of a refusal by a principal to complete a contract actually negotiated by the agent. Hence the issue was whether some dicta of Lord Wright in the *Luxor* case[10] could be applied, so as to permit the implication of a term: or whether to do so would conflict with the decision of the House of Lords in *L French & Co Ltd v Leeston Shipping Co Ltd*,[11] where a term could not be implied to the effect that the principal would not dispose of the business asset from which the agent derived his commission. Brandon LJ distinguished this case[12] on the ground that it revolved around the freedom of a person to deal with his property as he chooses, which was very different from the situation involved in the *Alpha Trading* case, where it could not be said that a principal could break his contract with a third party so as to deprive the agent of his commission. Applying the test of 'the officious bystander', the requisite term could be implied. As Templeman LJ said,[13] it was necessary 'to imply a term which prevents a vendor ... from playing a dirty trick on the agent with impunity after making use of the services provided by that agent in order to secure the very position and safety of the vendor ... a term which prevents the vendor from acting unreasonably to the possible gain of the vendor and loss of the agent'. The term to be implied in such circumstances was that 'the vendors will not deprive the agents of their commission by committing a breach of the contract between the vendors and the purchaser which releases the purchaser from its obligation to pay the purchase price'.

The state of the authorities was subsequently summarised by Bingham LJ in *Marcan Shipping (London) Ltd v Polish SS Co*[14] as follows:

'(1) If A, the agent, acting on behalf of P, the principal, has negotiated a contract with TP, a third party, under which A is entitled to payment of commission periodically during the performance of the contract, a term is not to be implied into the agency contract between P and A that P will not, in a manner involving no breach of contract, make a further agreement with TP which will prevent the first contract running its full course and so deprive A of the commission he would otherwise have received . . .[15]

---

9 Above, note 8 at 487. Note also the point that there was no difference between 'estate agent' cases and other instances of agency.
10 [1941] AC 108 at 141–142, [1941] 1 All ER 33 at 55–56.
11 [1922] 1 AC 451: below, p 393.
12 *Alpha Trading Ltd v Dunnshaw-Patten Ltd* [1981] 1 All ER 482 at 489–490.
13 Ibid at 491; *Marcan Shipping (London) Ltd v Polish SS Co* [1989] 2 Lloyd's Rep 138 at 140 per May LJ.
14 [1989] 2 Lloyd's Rep 138 at 143.
15 Citing *French & Co Ltd v Leeston Shipping Co Ltd* [1922] 1 AC 451.

(2) If A, acting on behalf of P, has negotiated a contract with TP under which A is entitled to payment of commission when the contract is performed, it may not be proper to imply a term that P will not break his contract with TP and thus deprive A of the commission A would otherwise have received.'[16]

The case from which this passage is taken was not like (1) because there was a breach of contract in the *Marcan* case (the ship to be bought was not ready by the due date so the buyers cancelled the contract); it was not like (2) because the breach here was by TP whose agent A, the plaintiff, was not. The question in this case, therefore, was: if A acting on behalf of P has negotiated a contract with TP under which A is entitled to commission when the contract is performed and TP has agreed with A that the commission may be deducted from the contract price otherwise payable to TP is a term to be implied into that second agreement that TP will not fail to perform the contract and thus deprive A of the commission he would otherwise have received? Bingham LJ and the other members of the Court of Appeal had no hesitation in answering that question 'No'. No such term could be implied into the agreement under the well-known test of business efficacy, nor if the question were asked whether the parties must obviously have intended to include such a term.[17]

However, according to the House of Lords in the *Luxor* case, there were two instances, when, possibly irrespective of an express or implied term, the agent was entitled to something, even if he had not completed the contract beneficially to his principal. The first was where the contract stated that he was to be paid commission for introducing the principal to a purchaser for a stipulated price.[18] The second was where the agent was entrusted with the disposal of property, and spent time and money, unsuccessfully, on such task.[19] Thus in *Prickett v Badger*[20] quantum meruit was allowed for work done by an agent, even though nothing was gained by the principal. This case was criticised by the House of Lords in the *Luxor* case, and said to rest on the special facts. It was, in fact, really a case of wrongful dismissal of the agent.[1] So that, although there was no express term about payment if the agent did not complete the sale, nevertheless a new contract to pay a reasonable sum for work actually done could be implied into the original contract making the principal liable thereunder. A similar case, also considered

---

16 Citing the *Alpha Trading* case, above, note 8.
17 Above, note 14 at 143–144; nor under the test of necessity: ibid at 142.
18 Above, note 10 at 40–41, 120 per Lord Simon.
19 Ibid.
20 (1856) 1 CBNS 296. This is now a case of questionable authority. But see *Debenham Tewson & Chinnocks plc v Rimington* [1990] CLY para 108, where the agent who did not succeed in achieving a sale was awarded £15,000 in quantum meruit for work done on the principal's behalf.
1 Contrast *Fisher v Drewett* (1878) 48 LJ QB 32 (above p 194), where the agent's remedy was on the contract of agency for the agreed commission, because the principal had not dismissed him but had made it otherwise impossible for the agent to achieve anything for the principal. On the other hand, in *Bradley Wilson Ltd v Canyon Gardens Ltd* above, p 195, note 11, the court suggested that the agent's correct remedy, when there was a wrongful prevention of the opportunity to earn commission, was damages for deceit, based on misrepresentation by the principal, and not in contract for commission. Contrast the view as implied in *Blake & Co v Sohn* [1969] 3 All ER 123, [1969] 1 WLR 1412 that the agent's remedy would be for his commission, ie in contract.

by the House of Lords to be one of wrongful dismissal,[2] is *Inchbald v Western Neilgherry Coffee Co*:[3]

> The agent was employed to sell shares in a company. Under the contract he was to receive his commission when all the shares were allotted. Some shares were sold by the agent, and then the company was wound up, thus making it impossible for the agent to continue. It was held that the agent was entitled to damages for breach of contract calculated on the basis that all shares would have been allotted.

It was not commission that the agent recovered but damages for preventing him from earning his commission. But this must not be taken as meaning that, whenever a business closes down voluntarily, there will be liability to agents who thereby have been prevented from earning commission. That will depend upon whether something is expressly said about the length of the agent's service or whether some term can be implied to such end.[4]

Remuneration irrecoverable. Even if there is an agreement to pay remuneration, and the agent has obtained what the principal wanted, there may be no liability to pay the agreed remuneration. This will be so where the transaction on which the agent was employed was illegal.[5] This is the corollary of the proposition that the agent is not obliged to perform the undertaking if it is illegal.[6] The same applies in respect of an agency connected with a gaming or wagering transaction.[7] But the liability to pay remuneration depends upon whether the agent knew the undertaking was illegal. Hence in *Haines v Busk*:[8]

> Commission was recoverable by a broker for procuring freight, even though the charterparty arranged by the broker was illegal. This was because although to make it legal the charterer had to obtain certain licences (which he had not done), the broker did not have to obtain the licences but was entitled to rely upon the charterer's doing so.

Similarly, the agent may be unable to receive remuneration when he has acted in breach of his duties under the contract of agency, or is otherwise guilty of misconduct. Thus, if the agent has acted in an unauthorised way, for example, by

2 See *Luxor v Cooper* above, at 56, 148 per Lord Wright.
3 (1864) 17 CBNS 733.
4 See *Luxor v Cooper* [1941] AC 108 at 142–144, [1941] 1 All ER 33 at 56–57; per Lord Wright, and cases there cited. Cf *Alpha Trading Ltd v Dunnshaw-Patten Ltd* [1981] QB 290, [1981] 1 All ER 482 and the cases cited above, p 197, note 8. See also below, pp 393–394.
5 For an illustration of a transaction in which the principal *unsuccessfully* argued that payment of the commission was illegal, on the basis of a statutory instrument regulating rents, see *Brecker, Grossmith & Co v Canworth Group Ltd* [1974] 3 All ER 561. But the transaction was illegal, under the Accommodation Agencies Act 1953, in *Crouch and Lees v Haridas* [1972] 1 QB 158, [1971] 3 All ER 172. Where an agreement to pay commission was illegal under a statute, a later agreement by way of a compromise to pay a lesser sum was also illegal, and therefore unenforceable: *Metlege v Ryan* (1980) 113 DLR (3d) 248.
6 See above, p 156.
7 Gaming Act 1845; Gaming Act 1892. But if the transaction, eg speculation in futures, is not illegal in that it is not a wagering contract, because the brokers stood to gain or lose nothing by the rise or fall of the market, commission (and indemnity) will be payable: *Jackson Securities Ltd v Cheesman* [1986] 4 NSWLR 484.
8 (1814) 5 Taunt 521.

selling property by private contract instead of by auction as agreed, he cannot recover commission (even though there may be a custom permitting him to recover his commission) as long as such custom is not known to the principal.[9] But he can recover commission if the custom is known to the principal, and therefore can be taken as having been assented to by the principal (ie is part of the agent's authority, as already explained).[10] The agent will not be able to claim remuneration if he is guilty of negligence in the performance of his duty,[11] or has made a secret profit out of the transaction,[12] or has otherwise failed to observe the obligations laid down by the fiduciary nature of the relationship, as in *Salomons v Pender*[13] where the agent sold his principal's land to a company of which he was both shareholder and director. It was held that he was not entitled to commission.[14] But the agent will be able to make the principal liable to pay remuneration even though he has acted wrongfully if it is possible to sever the wrongful part of his behaviour from the rest. Thus in *Hippisley v Knee Bros*[15] where the agent was getting a discount on the cost of the goods and services required to perform the undertaking, the full price of the goods and services was not recoverable from the principal, but since the agents had not been guilty of fraud in the performance of their duty, and had acted in the honest belief that in accordance with trade custom they were entitled to keep such discount, they were not deprived of their commission.

B. Indemnity

The principal's duty to indemnify his agent against losses, liabilities and expenses incurred in the performance of the undertaking may be expressly stated in the contract of agency. But it is more usually implied. Hence the extent of this liability depends upon the nature of the agreement between the parties, and the

---

9 *Marsh v Jelf* (1862) 3 F & F 234.

10 *Lansdowne v Somerville* (1862) 3 F & F 236, cf above, pp 76–79.

11 *Dalton v Irvin* (1830) 4 C & P 289; cf above, pp 158–164.

12 *Andrews v Ramsay* [1903] 2 KB 635. But note what was said in *Phipps v Boardman* [1965] 1 All ER 849 at 857 per Lord Denning MR and not approved by Pearson and Russell LJJ, ibid at 864, 865, as to recovery in the absence of dishonesty and bad faith: contrast the contrary view in *Guinness plc v Saunders* [1990] 2 AC 663, [1990] 1 All ER 652; above, p 185. *Andrews v Ramsey* was distinguished in *Stansfield (a firm) v South East Nursing Home Services* (1985) 277 Estates Gazette 311, where the agent was not in breach of duty but would have been entitled to commission in any event. Cf *Robinson Scammell & Co v Ansell* [1985] CLY 23, agent in breach of duty but acting in good faith in fulfilling his duty under the contract of agency entitled to commission.

13 (1865) 3 H & C 639; cf *Edwards Real Estate Ltd v Bamtar Holdings Ltd* (1978) 7 Alta LR (2d) 52, non-disclosure by agent resulted in no payment of commission.

14 Cf above, pp 174–188. But if there was no conflict of interest, and the agent was acting for the benefit of his principal, even though accepting a double commission, he will be entitled to be paid by the principal: *Turner v Laurentide Financial Realty Corpn (Western) Ltd* (1979) 97 DLR (3d) 429.

15 [1905] 1 KB 1; cf above, p 185. Cf the Canadian case of *Rosart Real Estate Co Ltd v Horvath* (1961) 29 DLR (2d) 205 at 208, where it was said that an agent who acts in good faith, even though in breach of duty, may recover his commission as long as the breach was not material to the matter in issue; cf *Turner v Laurentide Financial Realty Corpn*, above; cf the cases cited above, note 12. Contrast *Re/Max Moncton Inc v Smith* (1987) 84 NBR (2d) 113.

kind of business in which the agent is employed. In *Adams v Morgan & Co*,[16] for example, the business carried on by the agent for the principal was such that it could be implied that the principal would indemnify his agent in respect of payments of super tax. Such liability may be excluded by the contract, if any, between the parties. Where there is no contract, or no term excluding such liability, the principal's liability will depend upon the nature of the authority granted to the agent.

Thus, the agent in order to make his principal liable to indemnify him in this way, must have acted within his express, implied, or usual authority. For example, in *Barron v Fitzgerald*:[17]

> The agent was employed to effect insurance on the principals' lives. He was given authority to do so in the names of the principals, or in his (the agent's) own name. He did so in the name of himself and X, and then claimed indemnity. It was held that the principals were not liable, since the agent had exceeded his authority.

On the other hand in *Bayliffe v Butterworth*:[18]

> The principal authorised his agent, a broker in Liverpool, to sell shares for him. The agent sold them to X, another broker, but failed to deliver them. X bought the shares, at the market price, and then claimed the difference in price from the agent, who paid X and sued his own principal for indemnity. It was held that the principal was liable, because there was a custom among the brokers in Liverpool to be responsible to each other on such contracts. The principal knew of this custom. Hence the agent in paying X was acting within the scope of his usual authority.

However, there is no duty to indemnify an agent who has acted unlawfully, or in breach of his duty, or negligently.[19] Thus in *Duncan v Hill*:[20]

> A broker incurred liabilities namely the sale at a loss of stock carried over on the instructions of his principal until the next settlement of their accounts, because the broker had become insolvent before the next date of settlement. It was held that the principal was not liable to indemnify the broker against such loss, since it was caused not in the course of authorised transactions but because of the broker's own default in becoming insolvent.

But in *Thacker v Hardy*:[1]

---

16 [1924] 1 KB 751, distinguished in *Re Hollebone's Agreement* [1959] 2 All ER 152. For the failure of the argument that an agent who signed a contract disclosing his agency was not entitled to indemnity, see *Perishables Transport Co Ltd v Spyropoulos (London) Ltd* [1964] 2 Lloyd's Rep 379. See also *Fraser v Equitorial Shipping Co Ltd and Equitorial Lines* [1979] 1 Lloyd's Rep 103.
17 (1840) 6 Bing NC 201.
18 (1847) 1 Exch 425.
19 See *Thacker v Hardy* (1878) 4 QBD 685 at 687 per Lindley J.
20 (1873) LR 8 Exch 242.
1 (1878) 4 QBD 685; with which compare an Australian case, *Jackson Securities Ltd v Cheesman* [1986] 4 NSWLR 484, above, p 200, note 7. Contrast *Universal Stock Exchange Ltd v Strachan* [1896] AC 166.

A broker was employed to speculate for his principal. It was agreed that the principal was to be paid the differences between the prices of the stock bought and sold. In pursuance of this authority, the broker incurred liability on personal contracts for the purchase and sale of stock. It was held that, since the Stock Exchange recognised such transactions as real contracts, and not as gaming or wagering contracts, the principal was liable to indemnify the agent.

Similarly in the case of *New Zealand Farmers' Co-operative Distributing Co Ltd v National Mortgage and Agency Co of New Zealand*,[2] an agent was held not to be able to recover expenses which were incurred through his lack of knowledge and skill as regards the transaction in respect of which the agent was employed, namely the purchase of 'top' rams.

2 [1961] NZLR 969: contrast *Fraser v Equitorial Shipping Co Ltd and Equitorial Lines* [1979] 1 Lloyd's Rep 103, when the damage to the principal's property was not caused by the agent's negligent inspection, hence the agent was not deprived of his indemnity.

CHAPTER 10

Remedies

A. Remedies available to principal

Dismissal. Upon discovering the agent's misconduct the principal may dismiss him without giving any notice and without being liable to pay the agent any compensation. The agent's misconduct, for example fraud, can be relied upon by the principal in an action by the agent for wrongful dismissal, even if the fraud was discovered only *after* the dismissal.[1] In such circumstances the principal has a complete defence to a claim for damages, compensation or indemnity.[2]

Actions. In addition to being able to dismiss the agent in the way described above, or after the termination of the agency by passing of time, notice, or otherwise, the principal may bring a number of different actions against the agent, depending upon what the agent has done or omitted to do.

Thus, if a gratuitous agent has been guilty of fraud, negligence, or other wrong,[3] in the performance of the agency, the principal will have the appropriate action in tort, eg, for negligence.[4] If the agency is contractual, then, where the agent has been guilty of fraud or negligence,[5] the principal's remedy will be an action in tort, for the appropriate wrong, or an action for breach of contract.[6] The measure of damages in an action for breach of contract is calculated in accordance with the general rules laid down in *Hadley v Baxendale*[7] and

---

1 *Boston Deep Sea Fishing and Ice Co v Ansell* (1888) 39 Ch D 339 at 357 per Cotton LJ, 364 per Bowen LJ.
2 Ibid, at 364–365 per Bowen LJ; cf *Andrews v Ramsay & Co* [1903] 2 KB 635.
3 Eg, breach of fiduciary duty, where damages may be recovered: *Len Pugh Real Estate Ltd v Ronvic Construction Co Ltd* (1974) 1 OR (2d) 539: *Lin v Leung* (1992) 64 BCLR (2d) 226; *Baillie v Charman* (1992) 94 DLR (4th) 403, see above, p 180.
4 For the duty that is relevant or appropriate in gratuitous agency, see above, pp 160–164.
5 For the circumstances in which an agent will be considered negligent, see above, pp 158–160.
6 For some examples, see *Kenney v Hall, Pain and Foster* (1976) 239 Estates Gazette 355, negligent valuation of property by an estate agent; *LB Martin Construction Ltd v Gaglardi* [1979] ILR 1–1061, negligence by insurance agent in representing that insurance had been placed when it had not; *Faruk v Wyse* [1988] 44 EG 88, estate agents representing a barmaid as an employee of a cricket club authorised to enter an agreement on its behalf, for which the agents were liable for the full rental value of the property during the material period when it could have been let to a responsible corporate tenant (which was the intention of the principal in employing the agents).
7 (1854) 9 Exch 341.

subsequent decisions.[8] It should be noted, however, that, where the agent has been involved in the taking of a bribe, or, possibly, some equally corrupt activity, the principal will have to elect whether to sue the agent (or the other guilty party) for the recovery of the bribe or any profit made through the corruption, by way of an action for money had and received, or to sue the agent or other party, in tort, for damages for fraud and conspiracy.[9]

Where an agent has failed to hand over property received by him for and on behalf of his principal, the latter can bring an action for conversion, or for money had and received, whichever is appropriate in the circumstances.[10] In order to enable the principal to discover what the agent has in his possession that should be handed over to the principal, the latter has an action for an account, by which the agent must disclose all that he has received on the principal's behalf, including secret profit.[11] Mention should also be made of the possibility of a proprietary action in contrast with the personal actions of conversion or money had and received. Such an action, enabling the principal to trace property in the hands of the agent which rightfully belongs to the principal, holds certain advantages for the principal, eg, in the event of the agent's bankruptcy, or the agent's mixing the principal's property, especially money, with his own, when

8 See Cheshire, Fifoot and Furmston's *Law of Contract* (12th edn 1991) pp 595–609. Note the possibility of damages for nervous shock or emotional distress being awarded in such an action: *Jarvis v Swans Tours Ltd* [1973] QB 233, [1973] 1 All ER 71 (breach of contract by travel agents). See also *Jackson v Horizon Holidays Ltd* [1975] 3 All ER 92, [1975] 1 WLR 1468 which was strongly criticised by the House of Lords in *Woodar Investment Development Ltd v Wimpey Construction (UK) Ltd* [1980] 1 All ER 571, [1980] 1 WLR 277. Cf *Elder v Koppe* (1974) 53 DLR (3d) 705.

In *Osman v J Ralph Moss Ltd* [1970] 1 Lloyd's Rep 313, the agent who misled his principal and obtained car insurance with a firm that went into liquidation, was liable for loss of premiums and for fines paid by the principal.

9 *T Mahesan S/O Thambiah v Malaysia Government Officers' Co-operative Housing Society Ltd* [1979] AC 374, [1978] 2 All ER 405: discussed above, pp 166–168. Note the right of the principal to recover a bribe or secret profit made by the agent *and* to rescind a transaction entered into with a third party as a consequence of the agent's misconduct: *Logicrose Ltd v Southend United Football Club Ltd* [1988] 1 WLR 1256.

10 It has been held that overpayment of commission or 'advance' commission which had not yet been earned, could be recovered by a principal from an agent, on the basis of an implied agreement to refund such unearned money, or on the basis of money had and received: see *Bronester Ltd v Priddle* [1961] 3 All ER 471, [1961] 1 WLR 1294; *Rivoli Hats Ltd v Gooch* [1953] 2 All ER 823, [1953] 1 WLR 1190; *Clayton Newbury Ltd v Findlay* [1953] 2 All ER 826n, [1953] 1 WLR 1194n.

11 *Boston Deep Sea Fishing and Ice Co v Ansell* (1888) 39 Ch D 339 at 364 per Bowen LJ. See *Bowstead on Agency* pp 159–162. See, eg, *James & Co Scheepvaarten Handelmij BV v Chinecrest Ltd* [1979] 1 Lloyd's Rep 126, where it was held that an agent could not counterclaim for damages or set off their claim, but had to bring a cross-action: *International & Scientific Communications Ltd v Pattison* [1979] FSR 429, where the principal's delay in suing deprived them of an action for an account (but not an action for damages for passing-off); *Vita Credit Union Ltd v Stotski* [1981] ILR 1–1356, where the agreement between the parties was valid notwithstanding the policy of the Manitoba Public Insurance Corporation which the parties had endeavoured to circumvent, since what they had done had not infringed anything in the Manitoba Public Insurance Corporation Act, or the Regulations made thereunder. Cf *Bowstead and Reynolds on Agency* (16th edn 1996) pp 225–259. Note the agent's duty to keep separate and accurate accounts and the possible consequences of a failure to do so, or to produce appropriate records: *Bowstead and Reynolds* above, pp 253–255.

the doctrine of tracing can be applied.[12] But the availability of a proprietary action may depend upon whether the agent can be treated as a constructive trustee of the property for the principal rather than being merely a debtor.[13]

Prosecutions. Where an agent's misconduct takes the form of a criminal offence, such an acceptance of a bribe, or misappropriation of the principal's property, the principal, besides his remedy in damages, such as an action for conspiracy or conversion, or his restitutionary claim, can also institute the appropriate criminal proceedings, under, for example, the Prevention of Corruption Acts.[14]

B. Remedies available to agent

Action. Since the principal's obligation to pay remuneration arises from a contract between himself and the agent, failure to pay the agreed remuneration is a breach of contract, for which the agent may sue. The position where no amount has been fixed by the parties has already been discussed,[15] where it was seen that the agent may claim on a quantum meruit, unless he must be considered to have agreed to work gratuitously.[16]

The obligation on the part of the principal to indemnify the agent may be enforced by action based on a breach of the express, or more usually implied contract which gives rise to such obligations.

It would seem from the decision in *Georgiades v Edward Wolfe & Co*[17] that the obligation to pay commission (and presumably also the obligation to indemnify the agent) cannot be enforced by registering the principal's debt to the agent as a Class C (iii) land charge[18] upon the property with which the agent is dealing on behalf of the principal.

Set off. If the principal brings an action against the agent, for breach of duty, etc, the agent may reply to the principal's claim by setting off against such claim the amounts alleged to be due to the agent by way of remuneration or indemnity.[19]

---

12 Goff and Jones *Law of Restitution* (4th edn 1993) ch 2; Fridman *Restitution* (2nd edn 1992) pp 417–433.
13 *Bowstead and Reynolds on Agency* (16th edn, 1996) pp 201–205, 487–490.
14 Archbold, *Pleading, Evidence and Practice in Criminal Cases* (1994) Vol 2, paras 31–160-31-169; above, p 188.
15 Above, pp 189–191. Note *Hampton & Sons v Trade and General Securities Ltd* (1978) 250 Estates Gazette 451, where the agreed scale of commission, not quantum meruit, was the correct amount due to the agent.
16 *P Withy Robinson (a firm) v Edwards* (1985) 277 Estates Gazette 748, a case of quantum meruit. But in the absence of an express or implied term that permits remuneration, no restitutionary action may be possible, if the principal decides not to complete a transaction brought into being by the agent: *Burns Fry Ltd v Khurana* (1985) 20 DLR (4th) 245: see also above, p 195.
17 [1965] Ch 487, [1964] 3 All ER 433.
18 Under the Land Charges Act 1925, s 10(1) (repealed by and replaced by s 2(4) of the Land Charges Act 1972).
19 But the agent cannot set off, or counterclaim, such a claim to an action for an account: he must bring a cross-action: *James & Co Scheepvaarten Handelmij BV v Chinecrest Ltd* [1979] 1 Lloyd's Rep 126.

Lien. If the principal has not discharged his obligation of paying remuneration or indemnity and the agent is in possession of goods belonging to the principal, then, subject to the considerations to be mentioned below, the agent is entitled to exercise a lien on such goods and retain possession of them until such time as the principal has satisfied the due claims of the agent.[20]

Agents may have either general or particular liens. A general lien is a right in respect of the general balance of an account, or in respect of debts or obligations incurred independently of the goods or chattels which are the subject of the right. A particular lien is a right in respect of obligations incurred in connection with goods or chattels subject to the right. The law disfavours general liens, since they give too wide a power over the goods and chattels of another. Therefore the lien exercisable by an agent is usually a particular lien, unless there is an express or implied agreement between principal and agent giving rise to a general lien. Such a general lien may be implied from trade or other custom or usage, for example, in the case of solicitors,[1] factors,[2] bankers,[3] and stockbrokers.[4]

Acquisition of lien. For him to be able to exercise a lien, an agent must first of all have lawful possession of the goods which were the subject of the lien. This involves two things: possession and legality of possession. In *Taylor v Robinson:*[5]

> The agent bought goods from X for his principal. The goods were retained by X, the rent for them being paid by the principal. Then the agent, without authority, took the goods away from X and kept them at his own premises. The principal became bankrupt and the question arose whether the agent had a lien on the goods. It was held that he had not, because, under the circumstances, the principal still retained the possession of them which he had acquired through X by paying rent for the goods to remain on X's premises.

In *Madden v Kempster*[6] it was held that an agent who gained possession of a bill by misrepresentation did not thereby acquire a lien over it. His possession was wrongful.

Possession of the goods must have been obtained by the agent in his capacity of agent and not otherwise. As Jervis CJ said in *Dixon v Stansfield:*[7]

---

20 See eg *Fraser v Equitorial Shipping Co Ltd and Equitorial Lines Ltd* [1979] 1 Lloyd's Rep 103, when a right to a lien was implied into the contract, because of the need to provide security for the agent who was personally liable on sub-contracts made to fulfil the purposes of the agency. But the contract with the agent may be inconsistent with the exercise of a lien by the agent, as in *Ariston Products Pty Ltd v Egan* (1977) 3 ACLR 418, a case involving an accountant.
1 *Cowell v Simpson* (1809) 16 Ves 275. See also the Solicitors Act 1974, s 73, on which see *Bowstead and Reynolds on Agency* p 341.
2 *Baring v Corrie* (1818) 2 B & Ald 137.
3 *London Chartered Bank of Australia v White* (1879) 4 App Cas 413.
4 *John D Hope & Co v Glendinning* [1911] AC 419. Note also, the maritime lien of a shipmaster on the ship and its freight for his wages, etc: see the Merchant Shipping Act 1970, s 18: *Bowstead and Reynolds on Agency*, pp 341–342. See also the Supreme Court Act 1981, s 20(2).
5 (1818) 2 Moore CP 730; cf *Bryans v Nix* (1839) 4 M & W 775. See also, Palmer *Bailment* (2nd edn 1991) pp 944–950).
6 (1807) 1 Camp 12.
7 (1850) 10 CB 398 at 418.

'A man is not entitled to a lien simply because he happens to fill a character which gives him such a right, unless he received the goods, or has done the act in the particular character to which the right attaches.'

Hence in *Lucas v Dorrien*[8] a banker did not acquire a lien over a lease which had been *casually* left in his possession. In *Dixon v Stansfield*:[9]

A factor acted as such for a principal on various occasions. On one such occasion he was instructed to take out an insurance policy on certain cargo. This he did, and then claimed a lien on the policy in respect of *other* services performed as a *factor*, for which he was owed payment. It was held that he could not exercise such a lien, because the policy had not come into his possession in his capacity as factor, but in respect of a transaction when he was not performing factorial duties.

Moreover, the goods in question must have been delivered to the agent for a purpose connected with the lien.[10] Thus in *Brandao v Barnett*:[11]

The agent of P deposited P's exchequer bills with a bank, and then instructed the bank to obtain the interest on the bills and then exchange them for others. When the agent became bankrupt, and the question arose whether P or the bank were entitled to possession of the bills, it was held that the bank could not exercise any lien over them in respect of the balance due on the agent's account, because the bills were deposited with the bank for a special purpose not connected with the alleged lien.

Notwithstanding what is said above, a lien will not be acquired over goods if there is an express or implied agreement between principal and agent which is inconsistent with the exercise of a lien.[12] To have such effect, the agreement must be clearly inconsistent with the existence of any lien. In *Re Bowes*,[13] a memorandum was deposited with a life policy at a bank, charging such policy with overdrafts up to a stated amount. It was held that this agreement excluded the banker's general lien on the policy. But in *Fisher v Smith*[14] an agreement that an insurance broker's account should be settled monthly did not amount to an agreement excluding the broker's lien on policies in his hands in respect of unpaid premiums. The habits of business of the parties showed that the lien was meant to continue to exist.

Dicta by Mustill J in the recent case of *The Borag*[15] suggest that the exercise of a lien by the agent over his principal's property will not constitute a conflict of interest between the agent's duty to respect his principal's property and title[16] and

8 (1817) 7 Taunt 278.
9 (1850) 10 CB 398.
10 Cf *Dixon v Stansfield* (see above, note 7).
11 (1846) 12 Cl & Fin 787; cf *Wylde v Radford* (1863) 33 LJ Ch 51.
12 *Brandao v Barnett* (1846) 12 Cl & Fin 787 at 807 per Lord Campbell.
13 (1886) 33 Ch D 586.
14 (1878) 4 App Cas 1. Note that the broker in this case was a sub-agent, so that the case illustrates how, in some instances, a sub-agent may exercise a lien over the *principal's* goods: cf *Bowstead and Reynolds on Agency* pp 352–354.
15 [1980] 1 Lloyd's Rep 111; reversed on other grounds [1981] 1 All ER 856, [1981] 1 WLR 274.
16 Above, p 171.

the agent's self-interest in obtaining his remuneration or an indemnity. That case was concerned with the alleged rights of the managers of a ship under an agreement for its management to arrest the ship so as to enforce the managers' right in respect of money said to be owed them by the owners of the ship. With respect to this, the learned judge said:[17]

'It is by no means an easy question whether a ship's agent or manager can ever properly enforce a monetary claim by arresting his principal's vessel, while the relationship of principal and agent remains in existence. It may well be that the answer depends on the particular circumstances of the case.'

However, he went on to state that 'the exercise by the agent of remedies over his principal's goods is not ruled out merely because an agent is under a general obligation not to prefer his own interests to that of his principal'.[18] Hence the agent's right to exercise a lien over the principal's goods for remuneration and indemnity. No case was cited to the judge to suggest that the relationship of principal and agent must be terminated before such a lien could be legitimately exercised. On the other hand, the judge went on to say:[19]

'common sense suggests that where the agency is of a continuing nature, it will not usually survive the exercise by the agent of rights inconsistent with those of the principal over goods which are the very subject-matter of the agency; and this would appear to indicate that the principal's conduct must at least be of a repudiatory nature, even if not formally treated by the agent as such, before the agent can exercise his remedy of self-help.'

The same approach appeared to be material to a case of arresting a ship, although, in the circumstances of the instant case it became unnecessary for the judge to have to determine this, or to remit the case to the umpire for resolution on the facts. So far as the general law of agency is concerned, however, the remarks of Mustill J are important with respect to the reconciliation of the apparent conflict or inconsistency between the agent's right to help himself to obtain what is his due from the principal and the principal's right to have the integrity of his property respected by the agent, and not to be deprived of possession of his goods, etc, by reason of the agent's conduct.

Loss of lien. An agent will lose his lien if he agrees to act, or does act in a way that is inconsistent with the existence of a lien that would otherwise arise.[20] This amounts to a waiver of his right of lien. Where there is agreement such waiver is express. But it may also be implied from the conduct of the agent, as in *Weeks v Goode*,[1] where an agent from whom a lease had been claimed refused to deliver up possession of the lease, basing his refusal on a ground other than lien. Or it may be implied from the fact that the agent has taken some other security for his claims, provided that this amounts to acting inconsistently with the exercise of a

17 [1980] 1 Lloyd's Rep 111 at 122.
18 Ibid.
19 [1980] 1 Lloyd's Rep 111 at 122.
20 See *Re Lawrance* [1894] 1 Ch 556.
 1 (1859) 6 CBNS 367.

lien. An interesting case is *Re Morris*.[2] There it was held that a solicitor was under a duty to give notice to his client that he intended to retain his lien on the client's papers in respect of his costs, if he wished to retain his lien despite the fact that he had taken security for his costs, at least in circumstances in which the taking of such security was inconsistent with the continued existence of the lien. On the facts of the case it was held that the solicitor had not acted inconsistently with his lien. Hence the solicitor could still exercise such lien, although he had taken security. But it was said obiter by Kennedy LJ that this duty on the part of a solicitor arose on the taking of *any* security, whether or not inconsistent with the continuance of a lien.[3]

An agent will lose his lien if he parts with possession of the goods, provided that this is done freely and without any accompanying act which shows that he intended to continue to exercise his lien. Thus in *Sweet v Pym*:[4]

> The agent delivered goods, which were subject to a lien, on board ship for delivery to his principal. It was held that his lien was lost because he had put the goods on the account and at the risk of the principal.

But an agent will not lose his lien if he has been induced by fraud to deliver up the chattel to his principal,[5] nor if the circumstances show that he did not mean to surrender his lien.[6] For example, in *Albemarle Supply Co v Hind*[7] (which though not strictly speaking a case of agency, yet illustrates the point under discussion):

> X hired taxis from Y, under a hire purchase agreement. For the purposes of repairs and refuelling, X let a garage have the taxis in their possession on the understanding that X was allowed to take the taxis out of the garage's possession every day, for business purposes, and to return them every night. It was held, inter alia, that notwithstanding this parting with possession, the garage still retained its lien on the taxis.

An agent who has acquired a lien on goods will not continue to enjoy such right if the principal discharges his obligations to him. But his lien still continues even though the principal's obligation becomes statute-barred[8] or the principal becomes bankrupt or insolvent.[9] Moreover, the agent's lien will continue, once it has attached to certain goods, even though the principal subsequently sells the goods or otherwise deals with them. In other words, the agent's lien, once exercised, is valid against all other persons claiming an interest in the goods.[10] Two points should be noted. First, the agent's lien must have attached *before* the principal deals with the goods, for the agent can only exercise his lien over goods in respect of which the principal can validly create a lien in favour of the agent

---

2 [1908] 1 KB 473.
3 Ibid, at 481.
4 (1800) 1 East 4.
5 *North Western Bank Ltd v Poynter* [1895] AC 56.
6 *Watson v Lyon* (1855) 7 De G M & G 288.
7 [1928] 1 KB 307.
8 *Curwen v Milburn* (1889) 42 Ch D 424.
9 *Re Capital Fire Insurance Association* (1883) 24 Ch D 408.
10 *West of England Bank v Batchelor* (1882) 51 LJ Ch 199.

as against third parties.[11] Secondly, where the agent can exercise his lien, his rights will be confined to the rights of the principal in the goods at the time the lien was exercised. Therefore the interests of third parties, in the form of rights and equities, will have priority over the agent's lien.[12] But this will not be so (a) if there is a statutory provision giving the agent his lien free of such third-party rights and equities,[13] or (b) where the agent is exercising his lien upon money or negotiable instruments, provided that at the time he exercised his lien the agent has no knowledge of third-party rights, ie defects in the principal's title.[14]

Other remedies. Where the agent has so contracted on behalf of the principal that the agent is personally liable for the price of goods bought in the agent's own name,[15] there are two ways in which the agent is protected against the possible failure on the part of the principal to reimburse or indemnify him. First, the property in the goods remains in the agent until the principal has paid him, or until the agent allows and intends the property in the goods to pass to the principal.[16] Secondly, the agent has the same right of stoppage in transitu against the principal as an unpaid seller has against the buyer.[17]

Where adverse claims are made upon an agent in respect of goods or money in his possession the agent may interplead,[18] even if this means calling into question his principal's title.[19]

Finally, where there is any disagreement or uncertainty about the state of the accounts between principal and agent, which cannot be dealt with by an action at law, the agent can bring an action in equity for the taking of any account.[20]

11 *Richardson v Goss* (1802) 3 Bos & P 119; *Barry v Longmore* (1840) 12 Ad & El 639; *London and County Banking Co Ltd v Ratcliffe* (1881) 6 App Cas 722.
12 *A-G v Trueman* (1843) 11 M & W 694; *A-G v Walmsley* (1843) 12 M & W 179; *Peat v Clayton* [1906] 1 Ch 659.
13 Eg under the Factors Act 1889: see pp 290–300 below.
14 *Brandao v Barnett* (1846) 12 Cl & Fin 787; *Misa v Currie* (1876) 1 App Cas 554; *Jeffryes v Agra and Masterman's Bank* (1866) LR 2 Eq 674.
15 For circumstances in which the agent is personally liable see below, pp 231–243. Cf the availability of a lien in the similar circumstances of *Fraser v Equitorial Shipping Co Ltd and Equitorial Lines Ltd* [1979] 1 Lloyd's Rep 103, which involved *other* contracts, not purchases of goods, in respect of which the agent was personally liable.
16 See *Jenkyns v Brown* (1849) 14 QB 496.
17 Sale of Goods Act 1979, ss 38(2), 44–46. See *Imperial Bank v London and St Katharine Docks Co* (1877) 5 Ch D 195 (note in that case the effect of a custom of the trade that the broker should be liable to the seller for the price of the goods if his principal did not pay). For the right of stoppage in transit see Fridman *Sale of Goods in Canada* (4th edn 1995) pp 324–331; *Benjamin's Sale of Goods* (4th edn 1992) pp 721–739.
18 RSC Ord 17.
19 *Ex p Mersey Docks and Harbour Board* [1899] 1 QB 546.
20 Contrast *Padwick v Stanley* (1852) 9 Hare 627 with *Padwick v Hurst* (1854) 18 Beav 575.

The effects of agency

SUMMARY

CHAPTER 11

Contracts by agents

A. Introduction

Different kinds of principal. A 'named' principal is one whose name has been revealed to the third party by the agent. In such instances the third party knows that the agent is contracting as an agent, and knows also the person for whom the agent is acting.

A 'disclosed' principal is one whose existence has been revealed to the third party by the agent, but whose exact identity remains unknown. The third party knows that the agent is contracting as an agent, but he is unaware of the name of th principal.

When a principal is named or disclosed the third party knows that he is not contracting with the agent personally, but with another person through the agent. Hence for the purposes of this chapter no distinction need be drawn between them and they will both be included under the heading of 'disclosed' principals.

Where the principal is 'undisclosed', neither the identity of the principal nor the fact that the agent is acting on behalf of someone else, is revealed to the third party with whom the agent contracts. In such instances, the third party believes that he is contracting personally with the agent, and only after the contract has been made, if at all, does the third party become aware that there ever was an agency relationship in existence and capable of affecting his position.

A 'foreign' principal (who may be 'named', 'disclosed' or 'undisclosed') is a principal who does not reside or carry on business in England or Wales.

Relevance of the distinctions. One important ground for the above differentiation may be put succinctly for the moment by stating that the class into which the principal falls may affect the issue of the personal liability of the agent, and may also determine whether the principal is excluded from the benefits and burdens of a contract made by the agent with the third party.

Another vital matter is the content of the agent's powers. Where the agent has been acting for an undisclosed principal and where the agent has been acting without authority but later has his acts ratified by the principal, the third party may find himself bound contractually to someone other than the party with whom he has contracted.[1] However, whereas in cases of ratification the third

1 Cf above, pp 84–110; below, pp 253–272.

party always intends to contract with a named (or at least disclosed) principal through an agent (despite the agent's lack of authority), where an agent is acting for an undisclosed principal the third party may not be intending to contract with anyone except the person with whom he is contracting (despite the fact that such person is really an agent for someone else all the time).[2]

The difference between these two cases really lies in the intention of the *agent*.[3] The conduct of the third party is induced by the representation of the agent, hence the intention of the third party is the product of the agent's intentions. If the agent intends to act on behalf of an undisclosed principal, and so purports to act on his own behalf and in his own name, then he may or may not be able to affect the position of such principal by the contract he makes.[4] If he intends to bind another person, and purports to do so, though without having the requisite authority, then he will be able to produce a change in the position of such a person, provided his acts are capable of being ratified and are in fact ratified. The requirements for a valid ratification have been discussed elsewhere[5] and it was there seen that the person on whose behalf the agent acted must be identified to the third party, or at least must be capable of being identified by him.[6] Since an undisclosed principal is never identified in this way, it follows that such a principal cannot validly ratify his agent's unauthorised act.[7]

Thus, the power of an agent to affect the legal position of an undisclosed principal is less than that of an agent for a disclosed principal, in that the former can only act effectively within the scope of his actual authority,[8] whereas an agent for a disclosed principal can transact outside the scope of such authority in such a way as to affect his principal, provided that the principal subsequently ratifies the agent's unauthorised transaction.

B. Where the agent acts for a disclosed principal

A. EFFECTS AS BETWEEN PRINCIPAL AND THIRD PARTY

Contractual liability

The basic rule. It is axiomatic that where the agent has made a contract with a third party on behalf of a disclosed principal who actually exists and has authorised the agent to make such contract, the principal can sue and be sued by the third party on such contract. A direct contractual relationship is thereby created between principal and third party by the acts of the agent, who is not,

---

2 Below, pp 258–264.
3 *Keighley, Maxsted & Co v Durant* [1901] AC 240 at 256 per Lord Davey. The case is discussed above, pp 89–90.
4 Below, pp 258–266.
5 Above, ch 5.
6 Above, p 87.
7 Cf Powell *Law of Agency* (2nd edn) pp 125–126.
8 Above, pp 61–64.

himself, a party to that relationship.[9] This, indeed, is the very purpose and rationale of agency.

The importance of authority. The agent must have been acting with authority in making such contract. The earlier analysis of the concept of authority revealed the different ways in which an agent may be invested with the power to contract on behalf of a principal. The previous discussion may be summarised here by saying that, for a direct contractual relationship to result from the conduct of an agent, it must be shown that the principal expressly authorised the agent to make the contract; *or* the agent, in making such contract, was acting within the scope of some implied authority, eg that it was necessary or usual or customary for an agent in his trade, business or profession to make such contracts;[10] *or* the agent was a wife of mistress and the circumstances were such that she had authority to contract;[11] *or* the principal had held out the agent as having authority to make such contract;[12] *or* the agent was not authorised to make such contract but his action was subsequently ratified, and such ratification was valid;[13] *or* the making of such contract was within the scope of the authority of an agent of necessity.[14]

Exclusion of liability. The converse of what is said above is that the principal is not bound by (and cannot sue upon) any contract made by the agent outside the scope of such *actual, apparent,* or *presumed* authority, whatever the derivation of the relevant type of authority. For example, an insurance company was not bound by a contract to grant a policy entered into by a local agent who had neither express nor implied authority to make such contract.[15] A stockbroker who sold stock on credit, although in good faith and on behalf of his principal, did not bind his principal by such contract, since he was not expressly authorised to make such a sale, nor was it within his implied authority as being usual or customary.[16]

9 See, eg, *Stockton v Mason* [1979] RTR 130, where the broker who arranged car insurance with an insurance company was held not liable for negligence: instead the Court of Appeal held that a valid interim policy of insurance had been made by the broker on behalf of the plaintiff's father, and this covered the plaintiff so that the insurers could be made liable to indemnify the plaintiff in respect of his liability to a third party when the plaintiff drove his father's car with the consent of his father. See also *Foalquest v Roberts* [1990] 21 EG 156, [1990] CLY § 101, agent not personally liable on 'contract to pay commisson to a 'middleman' on the sale of an office building to the principal.
   For Canadian illustrations of the agent's non-liability on a contract negotiated on behalf of his principal, see *Aurora Importing & Distributing Ltd v Saguenay Shipping Ltd* (1989) 29 OAC 301; *Wm Roberts Electrical & Mechanical Ltd v Kleinfeldt Construction Ltd* (1986–87) 20 CLR 206; *Westcom Radio Group Ltd v MacIsaac* (1989) 70 OR (2d) 591 (agent making a pre-incorporation contract for a non-existent corporation); *Steeves v MacLellan (SJ) Travel Ltd* (1994) 134 NBR (2d) 447; *Wilson's Truck Bodies v Teehan* (1990) 100 NBR (2d) 345; *Timmerman's Enterprises Ltd v Painter* (1987) 42 Man R (2d) 16.
10 For examples, see above, pp 69–79.
11 Above, pp 144–150.
12 Above, pp 122–132.
13 Above, ch 5.
14 Above, pp 134–144.
15 *Linford v Provincial Horse and Cattle Insurance Co* (1864) 34 Beav 291; *Comerford v Britannic Assurance Co Ltd* (1908) 24 TLR 593. Cf *Wilkinson v General Accident Fire and Life Assurance Corpn Ltd* [1967] 2 Lloyd's Rep 182, where the principal's powers were limited, so as to preclude any authority in the agent to grant the kind of insurance policy claimed by the third party.
16 *Wiltshire v Sims* (1808) 1 Camp 258.

This, indeed, is only one aspect of the way in which a principal is not bound by any unauthorised act on the part of his agent.[17]

An agent who lacks actual authority to make a contract on behalf of the principal may nonetheless have apparent authority to do so.[18] In *First Energy (UK) Ltd v Hungarian International Bank Ltd*[19] the plaintiffs knew that the actual authority of the senior manager in charge of the Manchester branch of the Bank had been terminated. However, this did not mean that his authority to communicate decisions by the head office was also terminated. Therefore the Court of Appeal held that the manager had ostensible or apparent authority to tell the plaintiffs that office approval had been given for the granting of a loan facility to the plaintiffs.

However, if the third party dealing with the agent not only has notice of the agent's lack of actual authority but also knows or is aware of facts from which the agent's want of apparent or ostensible authority can be inferred, the situation will be different. In such circumstances the third party cannot hold the principal liable on a contract made by the agent. When a third party may be said to have the requisite notice of lack of actual or apparent authority is obviously an issue of prime importance.[20]

Notice. Clearly, if the third party has actual notice of such want of authority, the principal will not be bound. The same result will follow if the third party has constructive notice, ie, if he had the opportunity of discovering that the agent had no authority to contract, and should have availed himself of such opportunity, but did not. In what circumstances, therefore, will the third party be considered to have such constructive notice?

Generally speaking, the fact that the agent is acting in his own interests does not of itself mean that the third party has constructive notice of the agent's want of authority.[1] However, it may amount to 'notice of irregularity', putting the third party on inquiry as to whether the agent's apparent authority is being exceeded.[2] For an agent to benefit himself is a suspicious circumstance, and it is the duty of the third party to inquire more fully into the agent's authority where there are suspicious circumstances, such as occurred in *Lloyds Bank v Chartered Bank of India*.[3]

There may be a statutory duty to enquire into the agent's authority. For example, under the Bills of Exchange Act 1882, s 25:

---

17 See eg *McGowan & Co Ltd v Dyer* (1873) LR 8 QB 141, where an agent who got X to pay his debts to his principal under the belief that X were paying their own debts, did not bind his principal. Cf *Kabel v Ronald Lyon Espanola SA* (1968) 208 Estates Gazette 265, where an agent persuaded a third party to enter into an illegal transaction and obtained a deposit from him even though the agent had no authority to receive such deposit: the principal was not liable to reimburse the third party.

18 On apparent authority based on 'holding out' by the principal see above, ch 6.

19 [1993] 2 Lloyd's Rep 194: above, p 113 note 8.

20 Cf the discussion above, pp 126–128.

 1 *Hambro v Burnand* [1904] 2 KB 10 (above, p 127).

 2 *Lloyds Bank v Chartered Bank of India* [1929] 1 KB 40 at 56 per Scrutton LJ: (he uses the word 'ostensible').

 3 [1929] 1 KB 40 (for the facts of which see above, p 119): cf *Earl of Sheffield v London Joint Stock Bank* (1888) 13 App Cas 333.

'A signature by procuration operates as notice that the agent has but a limited authority to sign, and the principal is only bound by such signature if the agent in so signing was acting within the actual limits of his authority.'[4]

In such circumstances the third party cannot neglect to investigate the true state of the agent's authority, and then seek to make the principal liable.

When the agent's authority has been put into writing, for example where it is contained in a power of attorney, the third party must discover the scope of that authority by reading the document; and he cannot hold the principal bound by a contract made by the agent in excess of his authority, if he could have found out about that excess merely by looking at the writing, but neglected, or deliberately chose not to do so.[5] In *Jacobs v Morris*:[6]

> The agent borrowed money from the third party. He said, falsely, that under his power of attorney he had authority to borrow money and he offered to show the power of attorney to the third party who did not look. It was held that the principal was not bound by bills of exchange signed by the agent on the principal's behalf, and given as security for the loans.

There may be some trade or other usage or custom, known to the third party, or one that should be known by the third party, under which the authority of the agent is restricted, so that he has no authority to make the contract in question (in the absence of express authorisation overriding the usage or custom). Unless there has been such express authorisation by him the principal wil not be bound by any such contract.[7]

Deeds.[8] When an agent contracts by deed the principal will not be able to sue or be sued on such a contract unless he is described in the deed as a party to it, and the deed is executed in his name.[9] Thus in *Schack v Anthony*:[10]

> The master of a ship executed in his own name, and by deed, a charterparty, expressing himself as acting as agent for the owners. Notwithstanding this description, the owners could not sue for the freight, since they were not parties to the deed.

However, there are circumstances in which the principal is not deprived of any remedy.

---

4 See also below, p 372.
5 Note, however, the provisions of the Powers of Attorney Act 1971, s 10(1): above, p 65.
6 [1902] 1 Ch 816.
7 On trade usage or custom see above, pp 76–79. The old decision in *Grant v Norway* (1851) 10 CB 665, dealing with the effect of a custom that shipmasters had no authority to sign bills of lading in respect of goods not yet shipped has been reversed by the Carriage of Goods by Sea Act 1992, s 4: above, p 81.
8 See also above, pp 64–66.
9 *Chesterfield and Midland Silkstone Colliery Co Ltd v Hawkins* (1865) 3 H & C 677; *Re International Contract Co Pickering's Claim* (1871) 6 Ch App 525.
10 (1813) 1 M & S 573; cf *Berkeley v Hardy* (1826) 5 B & C 355, which now might be decided differently, by virtue of the Law of Property Act 1925, s 56(1): below.

The common law rule excluding a principal from participation in a contract entered into by a deed has been eroded by equitable and statutory developments. In equity, if the agent entered into the deed in his own name, but as trustee for the principal, the principal may enforce his rights under the deed by an action in which the agent is joined as a party, either as plaintiff or defendant. The general equitable principle of enforcing the rights of a cestui que trust by direct action on his part is brought into operation. So, too, is the idea that circuity of actions should be avoided, ie one action by the agent against the third party on the deed, and a second by the principal against the agent on the contract of agency (or the trust relationship). In *Harmer v Armstrong*,[11] for example:

> The agent was appointed to make an agreement with X about the purchase of certain copyrights. This agreement was made by a contract under seal, the agent contracting as agent and trustee for the principal. Later the agreement was rescinded by X, and the copyrights were sold to Y. When the principal sued his agent and X for specific performance of the original contract, it was held that this could be decreed, since the agent held as trustee for the principal, and all the necessary parties were before the court.

Secondly, by statute, ie, the Powers of Attorney Act 1971, s 7(1), as amended by the Law of Property (Miscellaneous Provisions) Act, 1989, s 1, Sch 1, para 7(1), it is provided that the donee of any power of attorney, if he thinks fit, may execute any instrument with his own signature or do any other thing in his own name, by the authority of the donor of the power; and such instrument executed or thing done will be as effective in law, to all intents, as if it had been executed or done by the donee of the power with the signature and seal or in the name of the donor.

The effect of this provision, as it originally appeared in the Law of Property Act 1925, was said not to be clear.[12] The question still remains: what is its effect? Plainly it does not involve the conclusion that any principal can sue and be sued on any deed made by any agent. For it only applied to agents appointed under, and acting in pursuance of, a power of attorney, and it may only apply where the agent has authority to act in his own name.[13] Moreover, in *Harmer v Armstrong*[14] it was recognised that the common law rule still remained, so that there were some principals who could not sue on a contract under seal made by their agent, unless the equitable principle discussed above could be brought into operation.

Powell[15] suggested that the section may mean (a) that the principal can sue and

---

11 [1934] Ch 65, [1933] All ER Rep 778: cf generally, the law relating to the question of rights under a contract by beneficiaries who are not parties to such contract; see Cheshire, Fifoot and Furmston's *Law of Contract* (12th edn 1991) pp 452–461. In this respect the law may be different in Canada, where it was said by Laskin JA (as he then was) in the Ontario Court of Appeal in *Zamikoff v Lundy* (1970) 9 DLR (3d) 637 at 648, that the original common law still applied, following the decision of the Supreme Court of Canada in *Porter v Pelton* (1903) 33 SCR 449. Cf Fridman *Law of Contract in Canada* (3rd edn 1994) pp 184–185.

12 Powell *Law of Agency* (2nd edn) pp 178–179.

13 The point is disputable: *Bowstead on Agency* (15th edn) pp 326–327 (but see *Bowstead and Reynolds on Agency* (16th edn) pp 586–587); cf Powell *Law of Agency* at p 178.

14 Above, note 11.

15 *Law of Agency* at p 179.

be sued on a deed executed in the agent's name as long as he is named in the deed as a party or (b) that the agent cannot sue or be sued upon a deed executed in the agent's name, provided that he indicates in the deed that he executes it as an agent for a principal. The first, he suggested, may not have added much to the previous law, since as already seen there was a method whereby a principal could sue on a deed made by his agent, viz, if it was executed in his name and he was described as a party to it. The second possible result of the section Powell rejected (although it brings the law relating to deeds into line with the law about other written contracts).[16] He did so for two reasons: (1) because at common law an agent who made a contract by deed in his principal's name possibly could not have sued on the deed,[17] (2) because the legislature could have used more appropriate words for such a result.[18]

However, it is suggested that the language of the section is by no means as doubtful of effect as Powell argued. In the circumstances to which it applies, namely where the agent acts under a power of attorney, and where he acts in the way set out in the section 'by the authority of the donor of the power',[19] then the result is the same as if the agent had acted in the way required by the common law in order that the principal may sue and be sued on the deed, even though the agent has made the deed in his own name, and with his own signature and seal. On this reasoning, the principal may therefore sue and be sued on such a deed: and, if the effect of the common law doctrine was (and is) that the agent could also sue,[20] and be sued[1] on the deed, then the result under the Powers of Attorney Act is that where the section applies, the agent is in the same position, even though the principal also may sue on such a deed.

A further relevant statutory provision is contained in s 56(1) of the Law of Property Act 1925. Under this, a person may take an immediate or other interest in land or other property, or the benefit of any condition, right of entry, covenant, or agreement over or respecting land or other property, although he may not be named as a party to the conveyance or other instrument. In *Beswick v Beswick*[2] the majority of the House of Lords held that this did not affect the general common law under which a person who was not a party to a contract could not sue upon it. All this enactment did was to enable interests in land to pass under a conveyancing instrument to a person who was not himself a party to such instrument. Two members of the House of Lords were prepared to accept that s 56(1) had a broader effect, as long as (a) the claimant was specifically granted something by the donee in the instrument; (b) the agreement was under seal; (c) the agreement was inter partes. At the very least, therefore, the effect of this provision, as interpreted by the House of Lords, is that a principal may acquire

---

16 On which see below, pp 231–243.
17 *Law of Agency* at p 179 citing *Frontin v Small* (1726) 2 Ld Raym 1418.
18 Like the words used in the Bills of Exchange Act 1882 s 26(1): below, p 374.
19 Presumably *express* or *implied* authority.
20 Though this is a matter of some doubt: see Powell *Law of Agency* p 179.
 1 *Combes's Case* (1613) 9 Co Rep 75a; *Cass v Rudele* (1692) 2 Vern 280; *Appleton v Binks* (1804) 5 East 148; *Hancock v Hodgson* (1827) 4 Bing 269.
 2 [1968] AC 58, [1967] 2 All ER 1197.

an interest in *land* meaning 'tenements or hereditaments',[3] under a deed to which his agent was a party but he was not. In such circumstances the principal may sue upon the document.

Effect of contract by agent. Except when the circumstances exclude the operation of the basic rule stated earlier, the general result of an agent's making a contract between his principal and a third party is that the agent ceases to play any role in the relationship thus created, and the rights and liabilities of principal and the third party are determined irrespective of any rights and liabilities on the part of the agent. This statement must be considered in the light of the position where either principal or third party has attempted to discharge his debt to the other by payment to the agent. Its application may also be limited by the effect of certain relationships between the agent and the third party.

Settlement with the agent. First there is the question, how is the relationship between the principal and the third party affected by payments[4] made by either to the agent? Can payment by one of them to the agent discharge the one paying from his liability to the other, to whom payment was owed and should have been made? Generally speaking, of course, payment to the agent is really irrelevant to the dealings between the principal and the third party. But there are instances in which the party paying the agent will get a good discharge from his liability.[5]

Payment of agent by principal. If the third party has so conducted himself as to make the principal believe that the agent has discharged his (the principal's) liability to the third party, whereupon the principal pays the agent, the third party will not be able to make the principal liable to pay him, even if the principal's liability to him has not, in fact, been discharged by the agent. Everything depends upon whether the third party has acted so as to produce this belief on the part of the principal, for example, if he has given credit to the agent.[6] For instance in *MacClure v Schemeil*:[7]

> The agent bought goods, apparently on his own account, on terms that cash was to be paid. The seller did not press for payment, and the agent had not

---

3 Real Property Act 1845, s 5, which was held by Lords Reid, Hodson and Guest as being still operative in respect of the construction of the words 'land or other property' in s 56(1) of the 1925 Act.

   The only Canadian province with a similar statute is Prince Edward Island. In *Keoughan v Holland* [1948] 1 DLR 605, an argument in favour of a third party beneficiary was raised on the basis of the provision, but failed, as it later did in England: Fridman *Law of Contract in Canada* (3rd edn 1994) pp 200–201.

4 Or other form of settlement made with the agent.

5 This is especially true where the principal is undisclosed: see below, p 270.

   Note also the issue raised by a payment by the principal to the agent whether this can create a constructive trust, giving the principal rights against a creditor of the agent, eg a bank to which the agent is indebted. In *Neste Oy v Lloyds Bank plc* [1983] 2 Lloyd's Rep 658 Bingham J was loath to introduce the intricacies and doctrines connected with trusts into everyday commercial transactions: ibid at 665. Hence his conclusion that the relations between principal and agent were those of creditor and debtor, save for one payment, in respect of which, for particular reasons (ibid at 665–666), a constructive trust did arise.

6 *Robinson v Read* (1829) 9 B & C 449.

7 (1871) 20 WR 168. See also *Hopkins v Ware* (1869) LR 4 Exch 268.

paid at the time the principal gave him the money for the goods. It was held that this payment to the agent discharged the principal.

However, mere delay on the part of the third party in enforcing payment from the agent or the principal will not necessarily be sufficient.[8] 'There must be a change of position between the principal and agent caused by the conduct of the seller.'[9] The general principle, and the underlying reason for it, were expressed in this way by Parke B in the leading case of *Heald v Kenworthy*:[10]

'If the conduct of the seller would make it unjust for him to call upon the buyer for the money, as for example, where the principal is induced by the conduct of the seller to pay his agent the money on the faith that the agent and seller have come to a settlement on the matter, or if any representation to that effect is made by the seller, either by words or conduct, the seller cannot afterwards throw off the mask and sue the principal.'

In *Heald v Kenworthy*[11] it was held that the principal was still liable to pay the third party, even though he had already paid the agent. The same was held in *Irvine & Co v Watson & Sons*.[12] There:

The plaintiff sold oil to the defendant through the defendant's agent. Although the plaintiff knew of the existence of a principal, he did not know the principal's name. He did not insist upon payment of the price before delivering the oil. This was not usually done, but there was no custom of the trade to the contrary. The defendant, who did not know that the plaintiff had not been paid, settled with his agent, who later became insolvent. Thereupon, the plaintiff sued the defendant. It was held that the defendant was liable. Since there was no invariable custom to insist on prepayment the plaintiff, by not seeking for payment from the agent before delivery, had not done anything to induce in the defendant the belief that the agent had paid for the goods.

In that case the narrower ground of representation by conduct put forward in *Heald v Kenworthy* was reaffirmed,[13] despite the earlier statement of Blackburn J in *Armstrong v Stokes*[14] that the underlying reason for refusing to allow the third party to sue the principal was the much broader one that it would be unjust to the principal that he should have to pay. Another possible basis for refusing to allow an action against the principal is that the state of the account between the principal and the agent must not be altered to the prejudice of the principal.[15] But the idea which would seem to govern (at least where the principal is disclosed[16]) is that of estoppel, ie representation by conduct on the part of the third party

8 See, eg *Davison v Donaldson* (1882) 9 QBD 623.
9 Ibid at 629 per Jessel MR.
10 (1855) 10 Exch 739 at 746; cf Alderson B at 747.
11 Above, note 10.
12 (1874) 5 QBD 414. Stoljar *Law of Agency* pp 213–216, refers to this as the 'absolute' liability of the principal. But it is not completely absolute.
13 (1880) 5 QBD 414 at 417 per Bramwell LJ. See also *Restatement, Second, Agency*, para 183.
14 (1872) LR 7 QB 598 at 610, relying on earlier cases.
15 *Thomson v Davenport* (1829) 9 B & C 78 (disclosed but unnamed principal).
16 For the position of undisclosed principals see below, pp 258–270.

inducing a belief that he has been paid. Hence in *Wyatt v Marquis of Hertford*,[17] where the third party gave a receipt for payment to the agent, without money actually having been paid by the agent, it has held that the principal could not afterwards be sued by the third party, when he had settled with the agent on the faith of the receipt.

Payment of agent by third party. Just as the principal may be discharged from further liability to the third party by payment to the agent in settlement of his account, so, conversely, the third party may be absolved from further liability to the principal upon settlement of the account with the agent. The general rule is that payment to an agent will never discharge the third party. But there are circumstances in which this general rule is inapplicable.

In the first place, if the agent had authority to receive payment on behalf of the principal, then, in effect, payment to the agent is payment to the principal, in accordance with the general principles of agency, and the third party will be held to have discharged his liability to the principal. 'Authority' here, bears the meaning which has already been explained and discussed.[18] If the agent is expressly authorised to receive payment, the position is straightforward. If he is authorised to receive it in a certain way, eg in cash, and he in fact accepts payment in some other way, the question whether such a payment to the agent discharges the third party depends for its answer upon whether or not there was a trade, or other usage applicable to the contract of agency, under which the agent's authority impliedly extended to cover the receipt of payment in such way.[19] For example, in *Williams v Evans*[20] it was held that an auctioneer was not impliedly authorised by custom, to receive payment in the form of a bill of exchange for goods sold in an auction. In *Hine Bros v SS Insurance Syndicate Ltd*[1] it was held that an insurance broker was not authorised by any custom to accept payment by a bill of exchange in respect of a claim under a policy. However, even if the agent is neither expressly nor impliedly authorised to receive payment otherwise than by cash, if the principal has held out the agent as being authorised to receive payment in some alternative way, payment by the third party to the agent in such way will be a good discharge. The same would be true if the principal subsequently ratified the agent's receipt of payment in some unauthorised way. The general principles of 'holding out' and 'ratification'[2] apply here as elsewhere. Even if the agent is not expressly authorised to receive payment, he may be impliedly authorised, by custom, to do so (either in cash or in any way),[3] or the principal may have held him out as authorised to receive

---

17 (1802) 3 East 147: see also *Smyth v Anderson* (1849) 7 CB 21.
18 Above, pp 64–68, 122–132.
19 If the agent is authorised to receive money, but extends credit instead of taking cash, he may be estopped from denying he has received cash, or he may be treated as if he had received it: *Trading and General Investment Corpn SA v Gault Armstrong & Kemble Ltd* [1985] CLY para 28.
20 (1866) LR 1 QB 352, cf *Catterall v Hindle* (1867) LR 2 CP 368. But payment by cheque is now so common that it may be that this is no longer true: cf Stoljar *Law of Agency* p 81.
 1 (1895) 72 LT 79.
 2 Above, chs 5 and 6.
 3 For customary authority, see above, pp 76–79.

payment (either in cash or in any other way).[4] In either event, payment to the agent will discharge the third party.

Secondly, if the agent has received payment, though unauthorised to do so, and has paid the money over to the principal, the third party will be discharged.[5] But if the agent has not paid the money over to the principal then, in the absence of any authority of any kind in the agent to receive payment, the third party will not be discharged from his liability to the principal.[6]

Thirdly, if the agent is entitled to a lien on goods belonging to his principal,[7] and, in pursuance of his authority, sells the goods to a third party, who pays the agent, or otherwise settles with him, then the third party will be held to have discharged his liability to the principal to the extent of the value of the agent's lien. In other words, where the agent has a lien over the principal's goods in respect of a debt owed to him by the principal, the third party who buys the goods can set off the principal's debt to the agent against the debt he (the third party) owes the principal. In the leading case of *Hudson v Granger*:[8]

> The principal sold goods to a third party through an agent (who was a factor). The principal owed money to the agent, who, therefore, had a lien on the goods before they were sold. The factor went bankrupt, whereupon the third party settled his debt, for the price of the goods, with the factor's assignees in bankruptcy. When sued by the principal for the price of the goods, the third party was able to rely on this settlement as a good defence.

Lastly, by way of a general principle, the third party will be discharged by payment to, or settlement with, the agent, if the principal, by his conduct, has led the third party to believe that the agent is contracting as principal. This will be the result if the principal has allowed the agent to appear to the outside world as the owner of the goods which he is selling.[9] However, this point really ought to be discussed in connection with the position of an undisclosed principal, to which further reference should be made.[10]

Effect on principal of relationship between agent and third party

Agent sued or given exclusive credit by third party. If the third party, with knowledge of the existence of a principal,[11] chooses to pursue his remedies, or enforce his rights against the agent, rather than the principal, can he afterwards

---

4 The fact that on previous occasions the principal had in fact authorised the agent to receive payment may not be sufficient evidence for such a 'holding out' on a subsequent occasion: *Linck, Moeller & Co v Jameson & Co* (1885) 2 TLR 206. Cf *International Sponge Importers Ltd v Andrew Watt & Sons* [1911] AC 279 with *Butwik v Grant* [1924] 2 KB 483.
5 This would be regarded as ratification which has already been mentioned in the preceding paragraph.
6 *Linck v Jameson* (above, note 4); *Crossley v Magniac* [1893] 1 Ch 594.
7 Above, pp 207–211.
8 (1821) 5 B & Ald 27.
9 *Ramazzotti v Bowring* (1859) 7 CBNS 851: where this question was sent back for a new trial.
10 Below, pp 270–272.
11 For the position where the principal is undisclosed, see below, p 267.

change his mind and make the principal liable? The third party may wish to do this, because the agent is incapable of satisfying the debt. In what circumstances, if ever, is the principal free of liability?

For the principal to be discharged, it is essential that the agent should have contracted with the third party in such a way as to be personally liable on the contract.[12] Only where the agent is himself a party to the contract, and can be charged with liability under it, can efforts by the third party to enforce the contract against the agent, before attempting to enforce it against the principal, have any effect upon the principal's liability. In such circumstances, if the third party sues the agent to judgment, he will be barred from suing the principal, even if the judgment against the agent remains unsatisfied.[13] Thus in *Priestly v Fernie*:[14]

> The master of a ship signed a bill of lading in his own name, thereby becoming personally liable on it. The third party sued on the bill and obtained judgment against the master, which judgment was unsatisfied. It was held that the third party could not sue the owner of the ship (the principal) on the same bill.

The reason for this is that the third party, by suing to judgment, is deemed to have elected conclusively to hold the agent, rather than the principal liable on the contract.[15] Such election, it would appear, may be shown in other ways.[16] But the conduct of the third party must be clear and unequivocal, otherwise there will be no election. So, in *Calder v Dobell*,[17] where the third party invoiced the goods to the agent (though he knew the goods were being bought for a named principal) and later called on the agent to pay, threatening him with legal proceedings, this was not considered to be necessarily a sufficient election to discharge the principal from liability in a subsequent action. The question was said by Bovill CJ to be one of fact and the evidence must show a clear intention to exonerate the principal. Even proving the agent's bankruptcy will not necessarily amount to

---

12 On this see below, pp 231–243.

13 Lord Cairns in *Kendall v Hamilton* (1879) 4 App Cas 504 at 514–518.

14 (1865) 3 H & C 977. Cf *Kendall v Hamilton* (above).

15 The doctrine of election and its application are criticised in Reynolds *Election Distributed* (1970) 86 LQR 318. His general point is that the cases may be explained on different grounds, not involving election at all, and that the third party's rights against the agent and principal are or should be *cumulative* and not *alternative*. See also Sargent and Rochvarg 'A Reexamination of the Agency Doctrine of Election' (1982) 36 U of Miami LR 411 which criticises the application of election to undisclosed principals, but accepts its relevance where a principal is partially disclosed, so as to encourage full disclosure: ibid at pp 432–437. See also Phillips 'Agency: Elections and Reflections' [1993] Juridical Rev 133.

   Note also the distinction between election and waiver: it is only election if one or the other party can be held liable: if their liability is joint and several the action of the plaintiff in choosing between them is waiver: *Fowler v St Stephens College* [1991] 3 NZLR 304: above, p 11.

16 Eg by giving exclusive credit to the agent: see *Addison v Gandassequi* (1812) 4 Taunt 574: *Paterson v Gandasequi* (1812) 15 East 62: on which see Reynolds (1970) 86 LQR 318 pp 331–333. Cf also the position of a husband where the tradesman chooses to give credit to the wife: above, p 49.

17 (1871) LR 6 CP 486.

such an election.[18] Nor will commencing proceedings.[19] In a case which was concerned with undisclosed principals, *Clarkson, Booker Ltd v Andjel,*[20] it was said that a decision to sue an undisclosed principal (and the same would presumably apply to a decision to sue an agent) would only constitute an election if it was taken with full knowledge of all the relevant facts and was a truly unequivocal act, which depended on a review of all the relevant circumstances. Suing to judgment is therefore probably the most convincing way of proving an election, though, as Russell LJ said in the case just referred to,[1] that is more than election, though frequently referred to as election.

However, even an act which otherwise would amount to a valid election, will not count as such unless the third party knew that the agent was acting for a principal, and knew the name of the principal, ie the principal must be disclosed and named.[2] If this were not so then: (a) on the one hand the third party would never really have a chance to elect, for he would not be able to appreciate the worth of such liability, if he knew that someone else was liable but did not know who it was: and (b) on the other hand, an undisclosed principal might sometimes be in the position of not being liable to the third party although the third party was liable to him.

Agent debtor of third party. What is the position of the third party in respect of his liability to the principal where the agent owes money to the third party? Can the third party set off such debt against his liability to the principal? This can clearly be done if the agent has authority to receive payment[3] and to deduct his debt to the third party from the amount the third party owned the principal. By authority here is clearly meant express or implied authority. But it may also include *apparent* authority. For it seems to be the law that, where the principal holds out the agent as having authority to deduct his debt to the third party from the amount the third party owes the principal, the third party may set off his debt from the agent against his debt to the principal. This may only apply where the principal has induced the third party to believe that the agent is acting as a principal and not as an agent, that is to say, where the principal is undisclosed. It is more appropriate, therefore, to consider this in connection with the position of the parties where the agent deals on behalf of an undisclosed principal.[4] All that need be said for the moment is that the availability of such a set-off to the third party seems to depend upon the application of the doctrine of estoppel,[5] and such

18 *Curtis v Williamson* (1874) LR 10 QB 57. Nor will pursuing a claim in arbitration against the agent: *Pyxis Special Shipping Co Ltd v Dritsas and Kaglis Bros Ltd* [1978] 2 Lloyd's Rep 380.
19 Cf the decision in respect of the converse situation in *Pyxis Special Shipping Co Ltd v Dristas and Kaglis Bros Ltd, The Scaplake* [1978] 2 Lloyd's Rep 380, where Mocatta J held that a third party who commenced proceedings first against the principal was later not barred from suing the agent: no election had occurred. But commencement of proceedings was held to be the clearest evidence of the exercise of election in *Chestertons v Barone* (1987) 282 Estates Gazette 87, a case involving an undisclosed principal: see also p 267.
20 [1964] 3 All ER 260 at 266 per Willmer and Davies LJJ.
1 Ibid, at 268; but see *Fowler v St Stephens College*, above, at 308. See further, below, p 267.
2 *Thompson v Davenport* (1829) 9 B & C 78; *Paterson v Gandassequi*, above, note 16; *Dunn v Newton* (1884) Cab & El 278. On undisclosed principals, see below, pp 253–272.
3 Above, pp 224–225.
4 Below, pp 267–270.
5 *Cooke & Sons v Eshelby* (1887) 12 App Cas 271 at 278 per Lord Watson.

set-off will not exist where the third party had *actual* notice of the existence of a principal.[6] Constructive notice will not be enough,[7] despite the fact that, in respect of the termination of an agent's apparent authority, constructive notice of such termination may well be sufficient.[8]

Agent guilty of misconduct. Suppose that the agent has been fraudulent, or guilty of misrepresentation, or non-disclosure, whereby the third party was induced to contract with the principal. Does this affect the third party's liability to the principal?[9]

The general principle seems to be that, if the third party could set up such fraud or other misconduct against the principal, if the principal himself had been guilty of it, then he may do so where the agent was the guilty party, even if the principal did not know what the agent was doing,[10] as long as the agent was acting within the scope of his authority. Hence, even though the agent was not expressly authorised to make a certain misrepresentation (whether fraudulent or innocent) or to refrain from disclosing certain information, nevertheless, if the agent made such misrepresentation or concealed such information, and he appeared to the third party to have authority to behave in this way, the principal will be bound by what his agent has done, and the third party will have the appropriate remedy.[11] For example in *Refuge Assurance Co Ltd v Kettlewell*:[12]

> The holder of an insurance policy was induced by the insurance company's agent to continue to pay premiums by the false representation that after a time she would receive a free policy. It was held that, although this statement was made without the knowledge of the company, the company was liable to refund the premiums.

Another possible remedy is the refusal of specific performance of the contract to the principal.[13]

---

6 *Semenza v Brinsley* (1865) 18 CBNS 467; *Kaltenbach v Lewis* (1885) 10 App Cas 617. See, generally, Derham 'Set-off and Agency' (1985) 44 CLJ 384, especially in relation to situations where the principal is *not* undisclosed, and the action is brought by the agent, pp 402–407.

7 *Greer v Downs Supply Co* [1927] 2 KB 28.

8 Below, pp 404–406.

9 For the possible liability of the principal in tort to the third party see pp 319–322.

10 If the principal knew what the agent was doing there may be an express or implied authorisation by him in which event he would be clearly liable: but see *Cornfoot v Fowke* (1840) 6 M & W 358. See further below, pp 319–322.

11 But note the situation where the *agent* misrepresents, or otherwise purports to *extend* his authority: above, pp 125–128.

12 [1909] AC 243. For a case not involving fraud by the agent see *British Workman's and General Assurance Co Ltd v Cunliffe* (1902) 18 TLR 502.

13 *Wilde v Gibson* (1848) 1 HL Cas 605. *Mullens v Miller* (1882) 22 Ch D 194; *Archer v Stone* (1898) 78 LT 34. Cf the Australian case of *CR Ogden & Co Pty Ltd v Reliance Fire Sprinkler Co Pty Ltd* [1975] 1 Lloyd's Rep 52, where the third party was not bound to the principal because of the agent's fraudulent misrepresentation. In *Warren v Henry Sutton & Co* [1976] 2 Lloyd's Rep 276, the majority of the Court of Appeal (Lord Denning MR dissenting) held that the agent's negligent misrepresentation meant that the third party, an insurance company, was not liable on the policy of insurance issued in consequence of such misrepresentation: but the principal was able to sue the agent for negligence. However, Lord Denning held that the cause of the principal's loss was his *own* breach of duty to the third party *and* his agent, in not disclosing certain information about the party in respect of whom the insurance was to be issued. Sed quaere.

It is now clear that even though the agent was not acting for the benefit of his principal, the latter will still be bound by the agent's fraud or other misconduct.[14] If the agent was not in fact fraudulent, although the statement he made was (unknown to him) untrue, and the fact that he was making a false statement was not known to the principal, then the principal will not be bound by the agent's mis-statement.[15] However, under the Misrepresentation Act 1967, s 2(1) it would appear that there would now be liability in the absence of fraud, eg, for negligence, where the principal would have been liable 'had the misrepresentation been made fraudulently'. It has been held, under this provision, that a principal can be liable for his agent's misrepresentation even though there has been no shared responsibility of the kind required to make the principal liable where there has been fraud.[16] But the agent may not be sued under this provision, since he is not a party to the contract and the 1967 Act was aimed at the position of the parties. The Act was designed to fill a gap existing at common law. At common law the agent was already subjected to ordinary liabilities in fraud and negligence: therefore no purpose was to be served by creating an entirely new absolute liability.[17]

Misconduct by an agent figured prominently in a number of cases, previously referred to,[18] in which a wife signed a guarantee or a mortgage as a result of persuasion or request by her husband, and, in consequence, made herself liable for the payment or repayment of money. When the creditor or mortgagee sued the wife, she sought to avoid liability on the ground that she had signed as a consequence of some wrongdoing on the part of the husband, such as undue influence or misrepresentation. Agency principles were applied in some of these

---

14 *Lloyd v Grace, Smith & Co* [1912] AC 716. This has now taken the place of earlier statements such as those in *Udell v Atherton* (1861) 7 H & N 172; *Barwick v English Joint Stock Bank* (1867) LR 2 Exch 259; *British Mutual Bank Co Ltd v Charnwood Forest Rly Co* (1887) 18 QBD 714. See pp 317–319.

15 *Armstrong v Strain* [1951] 1 TLR 856; affd [1952] 1 KB 232, [1952] 1 All ER 139, and see below, pp 319–322. Unless it could be argued that the agent was acting negligently and would be guilty of the tort of negligence in making the untrue statement, which would render the principal vicariously liable in tort; below, pp 315–319. The possible tort liability of the agent involves the scope and effect of the decision in *Hedley Byrne & Co v Heller & Partners* [1964] AC 465, [1963] 2 All ER 575.

There are Canadian cases in which the agent has been held liable for a negligent misrepresentation to a third party; *Dodds v Millman* (1964) 45 DLR (2d) 472 (where the principal could not be sued because the contract between the principal and the third party provided for the exemption of the principal); *Bango v Holt* (1971) 21 DLR (3d) 66; *Chand v Sabo Bros Realty Ltd* (1979) 96 DLR (3d) 445; *Olsen v Poirier* (1978) 91 DLR (3d) 123; *Komarniski v Marien* (1979) 100 DLR (3d) 81; *Roberts v Montex Development Corpn* (1979) 100 DLR (3d) 660; *Hofstrand Farms Ltd v The Queen in Right of British Columbia* (1982) 131 DLR (3d) 464; *Fletcher v Hand* (1994) 40 RPR (2d) 52 (where an agent acting for a vendor was liable to the purchaser for negligence). Contrast *Bank of Montreal v Young* (1967) 60 DLR (2d) 220, where the agent was acting in a *personal* capacity, therefore was not liable for negligence in relation to investment advice (nor was the bank liable for his acts, because the agent, a bank manager, had no actual, usual or apparent authority to recommend or effect investments for clients of the bank).

16 *Gosling v Anderson* (1972) 223 Estates Gazette 1743.

17 *Resolute Maritime Inc v Nippon Kaiji Kyokai* [1983] 2 All ER 1.

18 Above, p 17.

instances,[19] on the basis that the debtor who arranged for the signature of the wife (or, in one case, his parents) was the agent of the creditor, the bank or finance company that was providing the money in respect of which the wife made herself (or in the case of the parents, themselves) liable.

Prior to 1985, in consequence of the decision of the Privy Council in *Turnbull & Co v Duval*,[20] which was relied on and followed by the Court of Appeal in *Chaplin & Co Ltd v Brammall*,[1] it was considered that the creditor was unable to claim from the surety or mortgagor by reason of a general equitable principle concerning the breach of a duty owed by creditors to sureties. Agency was not thought to be relevant.[2] Hence, even if the person obtaining the consent of the surety or mortgagor could not properly be considered to be the agent of the creditor, the misconduct of that person would preclude any claim by the creditor against the surety or mortgagor. The real question in such cases was whether the assent of the surety or mortgagor had been obtained by undue influence, misrepresentation or some other improper conduct that could render the transaction void or voidable at the option of the surety or mortgagor.

Between 1985 and 1992, as explained by Lord Browne-Wilkinson in *Barclays Bank plc v O'Brien*,[3] the decisions were all based on agency theory, ie, that the principal debtor had acted in breach of duty to his wife, the surety, and that, if the principal debtor was acting as the creditor's agent, but not otherwise, the creditor could not be in any better position than its agent, the husband. However, as he went on to state, some cases since 1985 held that, even in the absence of agency, if the debtor had been guilty of undue influence or misrepresentation, the creditor might not have been able to enforce the surety contract, if the creditor had actual or constructive notice of the debtor's conduct.[4] In the *O'Brien* case, Lord Browne-Wilkinson preferred to base the correct principle on which the courts should act as being the proper application of the doctrine of notice.[5] However, in *CIBC Mortgages plc v Pitt*,[6] the judgment in which was given on the same day as that in the *O'Brien* case, Lord Browne-Wilkinson seems to be saying that the surety would not be liable either on the basis of the creditor's notice of the husband's undue influence or on the ground that the husband was, in a real sense, acting as the creditor's agent in procuring the wife's agreement.

That approach would seem to be appropriate. It has been seen that the relationship of principal and agent does not always exist where the facts might indicate that it does.[7] A borrower of money who seeks to get his wife, or someone else, to act as surety for repayment is not necessarily the agent of the creditor

---

19 Viz, *Kingsnorth Trust Ltd v Bull* [1986] 1 All ER 423 (where the husband was guilty of fraudulent misrepresentation); *Midland Bank plc v Shephard* [1988] 3 All ER 17 (where there was neither fraudulent misrepresentation nor undue influence); *Bank of Credit and Commerce International SA v Aboody* [1992] 4 All ER 955 (where there was no unfair dealing).

20 [1902] AC 429.

1 [1908] 1 KB 233.

2 *Barclays Bank plc v O'Brien* [1993] 4 All ER 417 at 427 per Lord Browne-Wilkinson.

3 Ibid.

4 See *Avon Finance Co Ltd v Bridger* [1985] 2 All ER 281; *Coldunell Ltd v Gallon* [1986] 1 All ER 429; *Midland Bank plc v Shephard*, above; *BCCI v Aboody*, above.

5 [1993] 4 All ER 417 at 428.

6 [1993] 4 All ER 433 at 441.

7 Above, pp 12–14.

who has required that a surety be found. Should an agency be found to exist between the debtor and surety, it would be correct to apply the principles set out earlier as regards the effect of the agent's misconduct on the rights of the principal. But if, as is more often the case, it would be incorrect to call the debtor the agent of the creditor, some other basis for denying the creditor a right to sue the surety must be found. The equitable doctrine that seems to have been approved in the *O'Brien* and *Pitt* cases, ie about notice of wrongdoing, is one that is applicable to wives, cohabitees, and sons, as Lord Browne-Wilkinson pointed out.[8] If the relationship between the debtor and the surety is not familial or quasi-familial, if they are 'strangers', then it would seem that the debtor's misconduct will only be material if the debtor was in fact and law the agent of the creditor.

B. EFFECTS AS BETWEEN AGENT AND THIRD PARTY

Liability of the agent

Contractual liability

In certain circumstances an agent will be personally liable on a contract which he has negotiated for and on behalf of a principal. The possibilities of such liability differ according to the nature of the contract.

Where the contract is under seal. If the agent contracts by deed, then it is clear that, irrespective of the position of the principal,[9] the agent will be personally liable as long as he is a party to the deed and has executed it in his own name: and this will be true even if he is described as acting for someone else as principal.[10] Where s 7 of the Powers of Attorney Act 1971 operates, then, as already suggested,[11] it may still be possible for the agent to be personally liable on the deed, even if the principle is also liable.

Where the contract is in writing. The situation with respect to contracts that are in writing, but not expressed in a deed, is different. First of all, it must be stated that it is always possible for the agent to contract personally, so as to make himself liable on the contract.[12] Whether he has done so is a matter of the agent's intention.[13] To determine such intention involves the construction of the contract.[14] The agent's liability, however, does not depend upon whether the

8 [1993] 4 All ER 417 at 431.
9 Above, pp 219–222.
10 *Appleton v Binks* (1804) 5 East 148.
11 Above, p 220.
12 *Sika Contracts Ltd v BL Gill and Closeglen Properties Ltd* [1980] CLY 21; *Owl Construction Ltd v McKee* (1987) 62 Nfld & PEIR 162; *Rooke v Hoffmann* (1987) 18 OAC 226: cf *Re A-G of Canada and Théorêt* (1989) 61 DLR (4th) 289, a decision under art 1715 of the Civil Code of Lower Canada.
13 *Public Trustee v Taylor* [1978] VR 289.
14 *Sika Contracts v BL Gill & Closeglen Properties*, above. See *Foalquest v Roberts* [1990] 21 EG 156 (agent not personally liable).

principal is named, or known to the third party. Indeed in one case,[15] where there was no identification of the correct principal, the agent was not held to be personally liable, because such was not his intention. What may be relevant is the knowledge of the third party as to the agent's intention. If there is no evidence that the third party thought that the agent was contracting personally, then the agent will not be so liable.[16] Nor will it matter that the principal is insolvent.[17] The true test is the intention of the agent. Hence, as long as the agent has revealed that he intends to be personally liable on the contract, it will not matter that the principal is also liable, unless the third party gives exclusive credit to the principal. This is one aspect of the issue of election. Wherever the agent has also made himself personally liable on the contract, the continuance of such liability will depend upon whether the third party has declared his intention of making the principal or the agent liable on the contract. Hence, in each case, it must be determined whether the agent has contracted personally, and, if so, whether the third party has elected to make the principal liable to the exclusion of the agent.[18]

Contracting personally

No authority. The fact that the agent has no authority to make a contract, but makes it nevertheless, even if fraudulently, will not make the agent liable on the contract.[19] Though no fraud was involved, and the case was a somewhat special one, the general point may be illustrated by reference to *Paquin Ltd v Beauclerk*:[20]

> A married woman bought goods on credit from a tradesman. She was living with her husband and had no separate property. The goods were necessaries. Nothing having been said about whether or not she was contracting as agent for her husband, or whether she had authority to contract as his agent, it was held by an evenly divided House of Lords, that the woman was not personally liable, since, under the circumstances, she must be taken as having contracted as an agent.

---

15 *Don Greenwood Garages v Stevenson & McNaught* [1981] CLY 26; *4 Seasons Electrical Mechanical Contractors of Canada (1979) Ltd v Apex Realty Properties Ltd* (1993) 90 Man R (2d) 239. Contrast *Blackwood Hodge Atlantic Ltd v Connolly* (1977) 25 NSR (2d) 621, ignorance of existence of principal, agent personally liable. The identity of the other contracting party may be vital, in which event the agent may not be able to sue (which would suggest he could not be made liable: below p 249): *Gewa Chartering BV v Remco Shipping Lines Ltd* [1984] 2 Lloyd's Rep 205 at 210 per Webster J.
16 *The Santa Carina* [1977] 1 Lloyd's Rep 478; *Lambert Scott Architects Ltd v 413643 Alberta Ltd* (1993) 140 AR 85; *Village Green Landscaping Ltd v Murphy* (1994) 115 Nfld & PEIR 68. Contrast *Liddell v Van-City Electric Ltd* (1994) 91 BCLA (2d) 331; *Fracflow Consultants Ltd v White* (1994) 113 Nfld & PEIR 192 (agent personally liable).
17 *The Santa Carina*, above.
18 On election see above, p 226, below, p 242.
19 *Lewis v Nicholson* (1852) 18 QB 503.
20 [1906] AC 148; cf the similar problem which arose in *Fick & Fick Ltd v Assimakis* [1958] 3 All ER 182, [1958] 1 WLR 1006.

However, if the agent has no authority to contract as agent, he will be personally liable to the third party for breach of the implied warranty of authority.[1]

No principal. The agent will always be personally liable, whether contracting as agent or not, where in fact the agent is really the principal.[2] There must be evidence to show that the agent was the principal, otherwise such liability to the third party will not ensue.[3] If the agent contracts as agent on behalf of a principal who turns out to be fictitious, ie, someone who does not exist, never has existed, and will not exist in the future, the agent will not necessarily be personally liable. In such situations it does not automatically follow that the agent intended to contract personally, despite the statement by Byles J in *Kelner v Baxter*[4] that 'persons who contract as agents are generally personally responsible where there is no other person who is responsible as principal'. There must be some evidence that the agent intended to involve himself personally in the contract. The decision in *Kelner v Baxter*[5] may well have proceeded on the basis that those signing the contract accepting goods delivered by the plaintiff were not doing so as agents, notwithstanding their use of language to indicate that they were acting on behalf of a projected, but as yet unformed and unregistered company.[6] Moreover, the goods were delivered and consumed: which might have made a difference to the question of liability.[7] In the Australian case of *Black v Smallwood*,[8] specific performance was refused of a contract for the sale of land

---

1 Below, pp 243–249. Reference to the previous few paragraphs as they appeared in the third edition was made by Jones J at first instance in *Fidelity Realty Ltd v Rockingham Realty Ltd* (1976) 9 APR 54 at 67–68: on appeal to the Nova Scotia Court of Appeal (1977) 17 NSR (2d) 527 the decision of Jones J was reversed on grounds other than agency; and by Daigle J in *Rejean Lemieux Inc v Levesque* (1984) 52 NBR (2d) 103 at 110.

2 Below, pp 251–252. For an interesting case involving some rather special facts, see *Browne & Sons Ltd v Smith* [1964] 2 Lloyd's Rep 476. See also *Lunenburg Country Press Ltd v Demore* (1978) 26 NSR (2d) 179, political candidate liable for newspaper advertisements inserted although his party had forbidden him to advertise; *Northrup v Taylor* (1980) 31 NBR (2d) 185, agent purchasing house in his own name, principal failed to complete. Cf *Owl Construction Ltd v McKee* (1987) 62 Nfld & PEIR 162, agent contracting as owner for extension to principal's property: agent liable for unpaid money, not the principal; *Rooke v Hoffmann* (1987) 18 OAC 226, husband liable when wife refused to accept offer for property registered in the wife's name: the husband was liable either as principal or as agent for his wife.

3 *Carr v Jackson* (1852) 7 Exch 382.

4 (1866) LR 2 CP 174 at 185, where the agents who contracted on behalf of a projected, but non-existent company were held to be personally liable (see now the Companies Act 1985, s 36c(4) discussed below). It was held that the company could not ratify the contract after the company was formed, above, p 86.

5 With which contrast the Ontario case of *Westcom Radio Group Ltd v MacIsaac* (1989) 70 OR (2d) 591, where the agent was not personally liable in similar circumstances, on the basis of s 21(1) of the Ontario Business Corporations Act 1982 (now RSO 1990 cB.16). But in *Power v Nathan* [1981] 2 NZLR 403, the plaintiff's intention was to bind the agent personally: hence the agent was liable.

6 Fridman 'Personal Liability of Agent' (1966) 116 NLJ 1605.

7 Contrast *Newborne v Sensolid (GB) Ltd* [1954] 1 QB 45, [1953] 1 All ER 708 where an *executory* contract was not enforceable by the 'agent' who signed it.

8 [1966] ALR 744, discussed in Fridman (1966) 116 NLJ 1605. This was followed in Canada in *Wickberg v Shatsky* (1969) 4 DLR (3d) 540 and *General Motors Acceptance Corpn of Canada Ltd v Weisman* (1979) 96 DLR (3d) 159 and in New Zealand in *Hawke's Bay Milk Corpn Ltd v Watson* [1974] 1 NZLR 236.

signed by the directors of a company which had not been incorporated. The directors were held not to be personally liable on the ground that they were acting as agents at the time (even though the principal was not in existence). The distinction between this case and *Kelner v Baxter* was said by Dryer J of the Supreme Court of British Columbia in *Wickberg v Shatsky*[9] to lie in that in *Kelner v Baxter* the decision was that in the circumstances the writing disclosed an intention that the defendants should be bound, whereas this was not the case in *Black v Smallwood*. Hence in the Canadian case, where there was no intention that the 'agents' should be personally liable,[10] the plaintiff could not sue for breach of contract (though he had an action, for nominal damages only, for breach of warranty of authority).[11] Thus the very broad, general statement of Byles J cited above must be read subject to a very considerable qualification.

Where an agent is contracting on behalf of a company that has not yet been formed or incorporated (as contrasted with other instances where the principal does not exist at the time the agent contracts) the situation is now dealt with by legislation.[12] The European Communities Act 1972, s 9(2) was passed when the United Kingdom entered the European Community in order to give effect to art 7 of the First Company Law Directive. The provisions of the 1972 Act were replaced by those of the Companies Act 1985, s 36(4). This stated:

'Where a contract purports to be made by a company, or by a person as agent for a company, at a time when the company has not yet been formed, then subject to any agreement to the contrary the contract shall have effect as a contract entered into by the person purporting to act for the company or as agent for it, and he shall be personally liable on the contract accordingly.'

The 1985 Act was replaced by a new provision, s 36C(1), inserted in place of the earlier one by the Companies Act 1989, s 130. This now provides:

'A contract which purports to be made by or on behalf of a company at a time when the company has not been formed, has effect, subject to any agreement to the contrary, as one made with the person purporting to act for the company or as agent for it, and he is personally liable on the contract accordingly.'

This more recent language does not appear to make any fundamental difference in or to the intent and effect of the original legislation. The result of the earlier version of the legislation was that what was previously only possibly an inference, ie of the personal liability of the agent, became a rule of law, unless excluded by the circumstances.

---

9 (1969) 4 DLR (3d) 540 at pp 542–543.
10 Cf the earlier Saskatchewan case of *Dairy Supplies Ltd v Fuchs* (1959) 18 DLR (2d) 408, where the third party dealing with the agent of an unformed company intended that the company would be his debtor, and the agent made it clear he was not going to be personally liable. The agent was immune from responsibility.
11 On which see below, pp 243–249: for a Canadian case in which the agent for an unformed company was liable on this basis see *Delta Construction Co v Lidstone & Pierney* (1981) 82 APR 70. Contrast *AE LePage Ltd v Kamex Developments Ltd* (1977) 78 DLR (3d) 223; affd (1979) 105 DLR (3d) 84.
12 Cf above, pp 86–87.

The meaning of the original enactment, which would seem to be the same as that of the more recent version, was considered by the Court of Appeal in *Phonogram Ltd v Lane*.[13] From what was said there it would appear that even if the agent signs the contract as agent for the company, in other words with the kind of qualification added to his signature that, as will be seen,[14] may otherwise have the effect of excluding his personal liability, it cannot be inferred that there is any 'agreement to the contrary' within the meaning of the provision. Lord Denning MR was of the opinion that the words 'subject to any agreement to the contrary' really mean 'unless otherwise agreed'. If there were an express agreement that the person signing was not to be liable, the section would not apply. Unless there is a clear exclusion of personal liability, however, the section should be given its full effect.[15] Hence, as in the case in question, where a person purports to contract on behalf of a company not yet formed, then however he expresses his signature he himself will be personally liable on the contract. Oliver LJ made it clear that whatever subtle distinctions may have arisen at common law, eg, in cases such as *Kelner v Baxter*[16] and *Newborne v Sensolid (GB) Ltd*,[17] such distinctions have been rendered irrelevant by the provision of the Act in any case where a contract is either with a company or with the agent of a company.[18] As Shaw LJ pointed out,[19] the whole purpose of the section was to provide a remedy where one did not previously exist at common law, ie, where an agent entered into a contract for a company whose incorporation was contemplated but which had not yet been effected (except, possibly, it may be added, where the agent had concealed the fact of the non-existence of the company when an action for breach of warranty of authority might have been granted).[20]

In the *Phonogram* case, the agent was held to be personally liable, under the provisions of the section. He had argued that the section should be construed in accordance with the French text of EEC Council Directive 68/151, which had led to the enactment of the section. Therefore the section was limited to a contract purporting to be made on behalf of a company in the course of formation. Hence it did not apply to the company in this case, a company to manage a pop music group, in respect of which the parties had entered into a contract whereby the plaintiff would finance the group, under which agreement the plaintiff had already advanced half the promised sum, which he was claiming back from the defendant, the agent who had signed the contract 'for and on behalf of' the projected company. This argument failed because the court held that the section

---

13 [1982] QB 938, [1981] 3 All ER 182. See also *Rover International Ltd v Cannon Films Ltd (No 3)* [1989] 3 All ER 423 and *Cotronic UK Ltd v Dezonie* [1991] BCLC 721, discussed in Gower *Modern Company Law* (5th edn 1992) pp 308–309. These do not directly consider these statutory provisions, but they appear to confirm the views in the *Phonogram* case as to the voidness of a contract with an unformed company.
14 Below, pp 239–240.
15 [1981] 3 All ER 182 at 187.
16 (1866) LR 2 CP 174.
17 [1954] 1 QB 45, [1953] 1 All ER 708.
18 *Phonogram Ltd v Lane* [1981] 3 All ER 182 at 188.
19 Ibid, at 187–188.
20 Below, pp 239–240.

had to be construed in accordance with it own terms, which followed the spirit and intent of the directive, as the United Kingdom was obliged to do. Secondly, it was argued that, to bring the section into operation, there had to be a representation that the company was already in existence, as this was what was meant by the word 'purported'. This argument was also rejected, on the ground that a contract 'purported' to be made on behalf of an unformed company even though both parties knew that the company had not been formed and was only about to be formed. No representation was necessary. Thirdly, the defendant argued that only a company could be the 'person' who purported to contract on behalf of the unformed company, within the meaning of the section: therefore the company of which the defendant was the director, and to which, for administrative reasons, the plaintiff's cheque had been made payable, was the person who had purported to contract on behalf of the unformed company, and therefore the person who was liable under the section. This argument was rejected, on the ground that the company in question had not entered into the contract to repay the money advanced, so that this company was not the 'person' who had 'purported' to contract as agent for the unformed company.

To the extent to which the judgments in this case clarify the meaning and scope of the current statutory provision, the uncertainties which have been pointed out in various comments on the original 1972 provision[1] may be said to have been removed. However, criticism has been made of the way in which the legislature enacted the spirit and intent of the EEC Directive which was the progenitor of the statute. The main cause for complaint would appear to be that the statute did not go far enough, and did not enact what had been suggested by an earlier Committee,[2] namely, that a company should have power to ratify a pre-incorporation contract, which would have removed the necessity for making the agent personally liable.[3] To achieve such liability, an express novation of the contract under seal would appear to be necessary. However, in light of the way the Court of Appeal interpreted the statutory provision, it would seem that the more immediate practical problems have been removed in these instances:[4] since the agent will more often than not be personally liable. The only way he can escape or avoid such liability is where he makes an express contract with the third party that he, the agent, will not be liable whatever the outcome of the contract.

The situation differs again where an agent contracts for an unincorporated group, or an association with a numerous or fluctuating membership, on the ground that identification of the principal would be difficult, if not impossible: hence somebody accessible must be affixed with responsibility and legal liability. For example, in *Bradley Egg Farm Ltd v Clifford*:[5]

---

1 Markesinis 'The Law of Agency and Section 9(2) of the European Communities Act, 1972' [1976] CLJ 112 at pp 125–127; Prentice 'Section 9 of the European Communities Act' (1973) 89 LQR 518 at pp 531–533.
2 Jenkins Committee, Cmnd 1749, para 42.
3 Collier and Sealy [1973] CLJ 1 at pp 6–7; Farrar and Powles 'The Effects of Section 9 of the European Communities Act, 1972 on English Company Law' (1973) 36 MLR 270 at p 277; Gower *Modern Company Law* (5th edn 1992) p 310.
4 Note, however, other criticisms raised by Gower op cit at pp 309–310.
5 [1943] 2 All ER 378. Cf *Stoljar* pp 260–261.

The executive council of an unincorporated poultry society were held to be personally liable for the damage caused by a servant of the society who performed a contract negligently. Since there was no principal on whose behalf the council members could act (the society being unincorporated) only those members would be liable. Other members of the society were not liable.[6]

In view of the importance of the parties' intentions, evidence may be introduced to show that the agent did not intend to contract personally, despite the fact that the principal he named does not exist. However, if the contract is written, parol evidence may not be introduced to rebut the presumption and to show that the agent was not contracting personally.[7] The only evidence that may be introduced to disprove the intention to contract personally is that which is contained in the terms of the contract itself or the surrounding circumstances. For example, if the third party contracted with the steward of a club on terms which showed that he intended to be paid from club funds, and in no other way, then the committee which authorised the steward to contract will not be liable.[8] However, once the agent has given evidence purporting to identify the principal for whom he alleged that he was acting, he cannot afterwards attempt to claim that someone else is the principal, if his original evidence is false. In other words, an agent who fails to disclose the true principal, so as to enable the third party to sue such principal, will himself be personally liable to the third party, just as if he had contracted on behalf of a fictitious principal.[9]

Intention of agent. Apart from these two particular situations, the general rule is that an agent will be personally liable on the contract he has made, even where he is described in the contract as acting on behalf of someone else as principal, if the intention of the parties to the contract was that the agent should be personally liable.[10] The rule was expressed in these words of Park J in *Spittle v Lavender*:[11]

'... where the principal is known the agent is not liable ... though it is true that an agent may under certain circumstances render himself liable in all events. But it is not merely because he calls himself agent that he can become liable, he must so frame the undertaking as to make his additional engagement clear beyond dispute.'

6 [1943] 2 All ER 378 at 386 per Scott LJ.
7 *Kelner v Baxter* above; cf *Public Trustee v Taylor* [1978] VR 289 at 293 per Kaye J.
8 *Steele v Gourley and Davis* (1887) 3 TLR 772 (aliter if he gave credit to the committee).
9 *Hersom v Bernett* [1955] 1 QB 98, [1954] 3 All ER 370.
10 For some examples, see *The Santa Carina* [1977] 1 Lloyd's Rep 478; *Sabb Inc v Shipping Ltd* [1976] 2 FC 175; affd [1979] 1 FC 461; *Wilson's Truck Bodies v Teehan* (1990) 100 NBR (2d) 345; *Steeves v MacLellan (SJ) Travel Ltd* (1994) 134 NBR (2d) 447 (agent contracting as agent, not bound personally); *Salsi v Jetspeed Air Services Ltd* [1977] 2 Lloyd's Rep 57; *Pyxis Special Shipping Co Ltd v Dritsas and Kaglis Bros Ltd* [1978] 2 Lloyd's Rep 380; *Limako BV v H Hentz & Co Inc* [1979] 2 Lloyd's Rep 23; *Jugoslavenska Linijska Plovidba v Hulsman (t/a Brusse & Sippel Import-Export), The Primorje* [1980] 2 Lloyd's Rep 74; *Sika Contracts v B L Gill & Closeglen Properties* [1980] CLY 21; *Fidelity Realty Ltd v Rockingham Realty Ltd* (1976) 9 APR 54; affd (1977) 17 NSR (2d) 527; *Blackwood Hodge Atlantic Ltd v Connolly* (1977) 25 NSR (2d) 621; *McNulty Cartage Ltd v McManus* (1980) 29 NBR (2d) 332; *Liddell v Van-City Electric Ltd* (1994) 91 BCLR (2d) 331 (agent contracting as principal, therefore bound personally).
11 (1821) 2 Brod & Bing 452 at 455.

In *The Swan*,[12] the law was put concisely by Brandon J in these words:

'Where A contracts with B on behalf of a disclosed principal C the question whether A and C are liable on the contract or only C depends on the intention of the parties. That intention is to be gathered from (1) the nature of the contract, (2) its terms, and (3) the surrounding circumstances ... The intention for which the court looks is not the subjective intention of A or of B. Their subjective intentions may differ. The intention for which the court looks is an objective intention of both parties, based on what two reasonable businessmen making a contract of that nature, in those terms and in those surrounding circumstances, must be taken to have intended.'

In that case the defendant (JDR) owned a ship called the *Swan* which he hired to JDR Ltd (the company). The company instructed the plaintiff to repair the ship, the instructions being given orally and on notepaper of the company signed by the defendant as director of the company. The plaintiff's account was sent to the company which could not pay. The question was whether the defendant was personally liable on the contract to repair the ship. It was held that the defendant contracted as agent for the company. But when a shipowner discussed repairs of his ship with a repairer, it was natural for the repairer to assume that the owner would accept personal liability for such repair unless the contrary were made clear. Since the exclusion of the defendant owner's liability was not clear, he was personally liable. By way of contrast, in *The Santa Carina*,[13] where the parties were both members of the Baltic Exchange, the agent was held not to have contracted personally. There, at the request of the defendants, the plaintiffs, a company which supplied bunkers to vessels at ports throughout the world, supplied bunkers to the *Santa Carina* at Penang. The plaintiffs forwarded the invoices to the defendants. The latter denied liability on the invoices, on the ground that their request had been made on behalf of their principals, the time charterers of the ship; and that, although the plaintiffs did not know the identity of the principals, they did know that the defendants acted as agents. On appeal from a judgment of Mocatta J, who had found for the plaintiffs, the Court of Appeal held that, since on the facts the plaintiffs knew that the defendants were agents, the onus was on the plaintiffs to introduce evidence to enable an inference to be drawn that the defendants were personally liable. Failing such evidence, the agents were not personally bound by the contract.

Various matters have a bearing upon the ascertainment of the relevant

---

12 [1968] 1 Lloyd's Rep 5 at 12: this case is discussed in Reynolds 'Personal Liability of an Agent' (1969) 85 LQR 92 at pp 92–103. See also *Format International Security Printers v Mosden* [1975] 1 Lloyd's Rep 37, on the personal liability of a stamp dealer.

   The Swan was followed and applied in *Wm Roberts Electrical and Mechanical Ltd v Kleinfeldt Construction Ltd* (1986–87) 20 CLR 206, where the agent was *not* liable because there was nothing in the contract to inform the third party that the contract was with the agent. The third party knew of the principal who was disclosed at all times.

13 [1977] 1 Lloyd's Rep 478: cf *A E LePage Ltd v Kamex Development Ltd* (1977) 78 DLR (3d) 223; affd (1979) 105 DLR (3d) 86. But in *Aitkin Transport Pty Ltd v Voysey* [1990] 1 Qd R 570, which follow *The Santa Carina*, the agent, who carried on a business through a company, which was not referred to in the contract for the hire of cranes had not discharged the onus of rebutting the presumption of personal liability on the contract.

intention.[14] If the contract is wholly in writing, everything depends upon the true construction, having regard to the nature of the contract and the surrounding circumstances, of the document or documents in which the contract is contained.[15] If the contract is partly oral and partly in writing, the intention depends on the true effect, having regard again to the nature of the contract and the surrounding circumstances, of the oral and written terms taken together.[16] What this means, it is suggested, in the light of earlier authorities, is that it is necessary to pay attention to three important factors.

The first is the nature of the signature. The question to be decided is whether the signature is *descriptive* or *representative*.[17] If the agent's signature is qualified by some words which show the representative character of the person signing, then the agent will not be personally liable. The following phrases have been held to be descriptive and to show that the agent was contracting personally: 'on behalf of the creditors' (the agent's clients);[18] 'as solicitor to the assignees';[19] 'consignee and agent on behalf of X' (where this appeared in the description of the agent in the contract, but he signed his own name without qualification);[20] 'as purchaser';[1] 'as charterer'.[2] Where, as in *Parker v Winlow*[3] the agent signs without any qualification at all, he will be personally liable.[4] On the other hand,

---

14 But the insolvency of the principal has no relevance: *The Santa Carina*, above, at 482 per Lord Denning MR. Nor has the payment of commission to the agent: *Limako BV v H Hentz & Co Inc* [1979] 2 Lloyd's Rep 23.

15 *Bridges & Salmon Ltd v The Swan (Owners), The Swan* [1968] 1 Lloyd's Rep 5 at 12 per Brandon J: but in *Public Trustee v Taylor* [1978] VR 289 at 293 Kaye J stated that it was not permissible to go outside the contents of the documents. Cf *Transcontinental Underwriting Agency v Grand Union Insurance Co* [1987] 1 FTLR 35, where an agent who signed a retrocession agreement could sue on the agreement and hold the proceeds for his principal. Such action could be brought by the agent unless the contrary appeared from the wording of the agreement.

16 [1968] 1 Lloyd's Rep 5 at 12 per Brandon J; cf Lord Denning MR in *The Santa Carina*, above, at 481.

17 *Universal Steam Navigation Co v J McKelvie & Co* [1923] AC 492. For criticism of this distinction see Stoljar pp 251–256; cf Reynolds (1969) 85 LQR 92 13, at pp 95–97. It would seem that an agent can sign in two capacities, on behalf of his principal *and* personally, even though only one signature appears on the document: *Ontario Marble Co Ltd v Creative Memorials Ltd* (1963) 39 DLR (2d) 149: cf *Holtz v G & G Parkdale Refrigeration Ltd* (1981) 117 DLR (3d) 185 with which contrast *JDF Builders v Albert Pearl (Management) Ltd* (1975) 49 DLR (3d) 422; affg (1973) 31 DLR (3d) 690. If he signs the contract in his own name, as owner of property on which work is to be done, even if he is not the owner, he, not the principal, the owner, will be liable: *Owl Construction Ltd v McKee* (1987) 62 Nfld & PEIR 162. Note, however, the suggestion that if an agent signs for a company he is obliged to inform the third party of the intention to rely on the limited liability of such corporation: *Hampstead Carpets Ltd v Ivanovski* (1981) 12 Sask LR 173.

18 *Hall v Ashurst* (1833) 1 Cr & M 714.

19 *Burrell v Jones* (1819) 3 B & Ald 47.

20 *Kennedy v Gouveia* (1823) 3 Dow & Ry KB 503.

1 *Public Trustee v Taylor* [1978] VR 289.

2 *Pyxis Special Shipping Co Ltd v Dritsas and Kaglis Bros Ltd* [1978] 2 Lloyd's Rep 380. Or as 'owner': *Owl Construction Ltd v McKee*, above.

3 (1857) 7 E & B 942: even though the contract was made with the agents as agents for a named principal. This case was doubted by Lord Cave in *Universal Steam Navigation Co v J McKelvie & Co* [1923] AC 492 at 495.

4 See also *Paice v Walker* (1870) LR 5 Exch 173, where agents who acted on behalf of *foreign* principals and added 'as agents for X' to their signature were also personally liable (doubted by Lord Cave: [1923] AC 492 at 495 and by James and Mellish Lord Justices in *Gadd v Houghton* (see below)). See also *Sika Contracts v BL Gill & Closeglen Properties* [1980] CLY 21.

the following phrases accompanying the agent's signature have been held to exclude the agent's personal liability: 'on account of X';[5] 'broker';[6] 'sold to my principal';[7] 'for and on behalf of X as agents';[8] 'on account of my principal X'.[9] In the last case, where agents, not being personally liable on the contract, were held not to be liable for a criminal offence committed in connection with the contract, Lord Goddard summed up the position by saying:[10]

> 'the cases show that what you have to find is whether in the contract the person signing as seller or buyer . . . is signing as principal or . . . as agent.'

Brandon J summarised the effect of these cases in these words:[11]

> 'When it is stated in the contract that a person makes it "as agent for" or "on account of" or "on behalf of" or simply "for" a principal, or where words of that kind are added after such person's signature, he is not personally liable . . . When such words are not used but the person is merely stated to be an agent, or the word "agent" is just added after his signature, the result is uncertain, because it is not clear whether the word is used as a qualification or merely as a description . . . In general it would seem that in such a case the person does not avoid personal liability, although there may be exceptions to this general rule depending on the other terms of the contract or the surrounding circumstances. When a person contracts as agent for a company and does nothing more than add the word "director" or "secretary" after his signature, it seems that he does not avoid personal liability.'

In other words, while the signature may be a determining factor, it may also leave the question still open, in which event reference must be made to the contract as a whole or to the surrounding circumstances.

Thus there may be evidence which shows that, although the written contract appears to relieve the agent of personal liability, or appears to make the agent personally liable, no such intention was in the minds of the parties. It is a question of interpretation of the contract by admissible evidence. But parol evidence may not be introduced, if its effect is to *contradict* the written contract: it may only be introduced to *amplify* the contract, by showing the real intention

---

5 *Gadd v Houghton & Co* (1876) 1 Ex D 357: a case of foreign principals (contrast previous note). This was not followed by Mocatta J in *Jugoslavenska Linijska Plovidba v Holsman (t/a Brusse & Sippel Import-Export)* [1980] 2 Lloyd's Rep 74, when the various telexes between the parties were looked at and indicated that the agents were not contracting as agents for the Indonesian government (a foreign principal) but as principals.

6 *Fairlie v Fenton* (1870) LR 5 Exch 169 (where the agent could not *sue* on the contract): cf *Aurora Importing & Distributing Ltd v Saguenay Shipping Ltd* (1989) 29 OAC 301 (agent could not be sued for damage to goods en route to Toronto by rail, after signing a contract of carriage on behalf of the principal).

7 *Southwell v Bowditch* (1876) 1 CPD 374.

8 *Universal Steam Navigation Co v J McKelvie & Co* [1923] AC 492. See also, *Brandt & Co v Morris & Co Ltd* [1917] 2 KB 784, where an opposite conclusion was reached. That case, however, is authority for the proposition that a signature without qualification renders the agent personally liable, even if he is known to be acting as an agent: see *The Santa Carina* [1977] 1 Lloyd's Rep 478 at 481 per Lord Denning MR.

9 *Lester v Balfour Williamson Merchant Shippers Ltd* [1953] 2 QB 168, [1953] 1 All ER 1146.

10 Ibid at 1148, 175.

11 *The Swan* [1968] 1 Lloyd's Rep 5 at 13.

of the parties, eg that the agent's signature was understood by the parties as being the signature of the principal.[12] As Montague Smith J said in *Calder v Dobell*:[13]

'Evidence is admissible to show that the person contracting was acting for a principal, because the admission of such evidence does not contradict the written contract.'

Such evidence was admitted in that case, but it was not allowed in *Higgins v Senior*,[14] even though the third party knew that the agent was contracting on behalf of someone else when he made the contract. The test may be whether the effect of such evidence is to *add* rather than to *substitute* a principal, for such evidence 'in no way contradicts the written agreement. It does not deny that it is binding on those whom, on the face of it, it purports to bind, but shows that it also binds another.'[15] Thus in *Abdul Karim Basma v Weekes*:[16]

Parol evidence was admitted to satisfy the Statute of Frauds and to show that although the written agreement made no mention of the principal, all the parties knew that the apparent purchaser of certain property was acting as agent for a principal, who could be identified by the introduction of the evidence.

It has further been suggested that parol evidence may be introduced, where the contract is in writing, to show that the agent should not be made personally liable, since it was agreed orally that he should not, despite the fact that he contracted personally. This appears from *Wake v Harrop*,[17] where it was considered that such evidence would raise an equitable defence, based on fraud or at least mistake. However, two judges, Baron Bramwell[18] and Willes J,[19] thought that such a defence would be good *in law*, not merely in equity, so that, as a matter of law, parol evidence was admissible to relieve the agent of personal liability in such cases. But this seems to conflict with what has already been said above. Moreover, it is possible that *Wake v Harrop* itself is no longer a good authority, even for the narrower proposition.[20]

---

12 Cf *The Santa Carina*, above.
13 (1871) LR 6 CP 486 at 496.
14 (1841) 8 M & W 834.
15 Ibid at 844, per Parke B. See eg the Canadian case of *Automobiles Renault Canada Ltd v Maritime Import Autos Ltd* (1962) 31 DLR (2d) 592, where extrinsic evidence was admitted to solve the ambiguity of the agent's signature and identify the principal, the company of which the agent was general manager; cf *Holtz v G & G Parkdale Refrigeration Ltd* (1981) 117 DLR (3d) 185, and the cases cited therein.
16 [1950] AC 441, [1950] 2 All ER 146; cf Lord Evershed MR in *Davies v Sweet* [1962] 1 All ER 92 at 96. This may provide one rationalisation or justification of the decision in *The Swan* [1968] 1 Lloyd's Rep 5. *Basma v Weekes* was followed in *Alliance Acceptance Co Ltd v Oakley* (1988) 48 SASR 337, where the agent who contracted for a loan in his own name was personally liable although the lender knew that he was acting as an agent.
17 (1861) 6 H & N 768; affd (1862) 1 H & C 202.
18 (1861) 6 H & N 768 at 775.
19 (1862) 1 H & C 202 at 208.
20 In the light of *Universal Steam Navigation Co v J McKelvie & Co* [1923] AC 492 at 503. This case was said to be authority for the proposition that the exclusion of the agent's liability 'must be apparent elsewhere in the document': *The Santa Carina* [1977] 1 Lloyd's Rep 478 at 481 per Lord Denning MR.

The third and last factor to be considered is custom. Evidence may be introduced to show that, by custom or usage of the trade or business in which the agent is engaged, the agent is to be held personally liable on the contract he has made, despite the fact that the agent has *not* contracted personally. But such custom or usage must not be repugnant to or inconsistent with the written contract.[1] It can only be introduced to explain or supplement the contract by the addition of a term, as long as it is 'not inconsistent with any term of the contract', as Brett J said in *Hutchinson v Tatham*.[2] There:

> A charterparty was signed by agents with the following description, 'as agent for principals'. The name of the principals was not disclosed. Although the agents were clearly not intending to be bound personally by their signature, it was held that evidence was admissible to prove a custom to the effect that if they failed to disclose their principals' name within a reasonable time they could be personally liable.[3]

Similarly, evidence of such customs in particular trades was admitted in *Pike v Ongley*,[4] in *Fleet v Murton*,[5] and in *Limako BV v Hentz & Co Inc*.[6] But in *Barrow v Dyster*,[7] where brokers made a contract by which they agreed, inter alia, to act as arbitrators if there was a dispute between their principal and the third party, it was held that evidence of a custom making them personally liable on the contract could not be admitted. Such a custom was inconsistent with the express term relating to their function as arbitrators. However, even if a trade custom can affect the situation, it must be proved that such a custom exists. Hence in *The Santa Carina*,[8] no custom was alleged or proved whereby a broker on the Baltic Exchange was personally liable: therefore the plaintiffs were unable to assert any customary liability on the part of the agents.

Election. The personal liability of the agent will depend, not only on whether he has contracted personally but also upon whether the third party has elected to give exclusive credit to the principal; in other words, even if the agent has rendered himself personally liable on the contract, he will be relieved of such liability if the third party chooses to look to the principal exclusively for

---

1 Cf *Robinson v Mollett* (1875) LR 7 HL 802 (see above, p 78).
2 (1873) LR 8 CP 482 at 487. Hence there must be evidence that the third party contracted with the agent in the knowledge that the allegedly applicable customs, or conditions, of the trade were intended to be terms of the contract which the agent was negotiating; failing such information on the part of the third party, they could not be bound: see *Salsi v Jetspeed Air Services Ltd* [1977] 2 Lloyd's Rep 57.
3 See the discussion of this case in *Hersom v Bernett* [1955] 1 QB 98, [1954] 3 All ER 370.
4 (1887) 18 QBD 708.
5 (1871) LR 7 QB 126.
6 [1979] 2 Lloyd's Rep 23.
7 (1884) 13 QBD 635.
8 [1977] 1 Lloyd's Rep 478. Contrast *Stott v Merit Investment Corpn* (1988) 48 DLR (4th) 288, where it was held that there was a practice in the industry, viz, dealing in securities, that the registered representative was personally responsible for the creditworthiness of the client: ibid at 293 per Finlayson JA. Hence the agent, a salesman, could be liable, which made the third party's forbearance to sue consideration for an agreement whereby the agent undertook to pay a certain sum towards the third party's losses.

satisfaction under the contract. This depends upon factors which have already been examined in connection with the liability of the principal.[9]

The clearest illustration of the third party's intention to hold the principal exclusively liable is suing the principal to judgment.[10] But there may be other acts on the part of the third party which will have the same effect. However, it is essential that both principal and agent should be personally liable on the contract,[11] that the third party has full *actual* knowledge of the true facts,[12] that the third party should act within a reasonable time, before the state of accounts between principal and agent is altered[13] and that the third party elects unequivocally, showing that he intends to relieve the agent of liability. This last is a question of fact,[14] which involves all the relevant circumstances.[15]

Where the contract is oral. If the agent has contracted orally, the question whether or not the agent is personally liable is a question of fact, dependent on the circumstances.[16]

Implied warranty of authority[17]

Where the agent has not contracted personally, but has contracted as agent, the agent cannot be made personally liable *on the contract*. But, if the agent in fact had no authority to contract, he will still be liable personally to the third party

9 Above, pp 226–227. Note the critical discussion in Reynolds (1970) 86 LQR 318, the effect of which is summarised above, p 226, note 15.
10 *Kendall v Hamilton* (1879) 4 App Cas 504; *London General Omnibus Co Ltd v Pope* (1922) 38 TLR 270. For the position where proceedings are *started*: see *Scarf v Jardine* (1882) 7 App Cas 345; *Pyxis Special Shipping Co Ltd v Dritsas and Kaglis Bros Ltd* [1978] 2 Lloyd's Rep 380, which suggests that everything depends upon whether the agent is prejudiced thereby. See also, *Clarkson Booker Ltd v Andjel* [1964] 2 QB 775, [1964] 3 All ER 260; *Chestertons v Barone* (1987) 282 Estates Gazette 87, indicating that commencing proceedings is the clearest evidence of election. Cf *Fowler v St Stephens College* [1991] 3 NZLR 304 at 308, where it is said that there is no need for a party to obtain judgment for there to be election.
11 *Addison v Gandassequi* (1812) 4 Taunt 574; *Fowler v St Stephens College*, above, at 309.
12 *Dunn v Newton* (1884) Cab & El 278.
13 *Smethurst v Mitchell* (1859) 1 E & E 622.
14 *Calder v Dobell* (1871) LR 6 CP 486 at 491 per Bovill CJ.
15 *Clarkson Booker Ltd v Andjel* (above). For a case which, at first instance, was *wrongly* treated on one of election, an error corrected on appeal, see *Barclays Bank Ltd v Williams* (1971) 115 Sol Jo 674.
16 *Jones v Littledale* (1837) 6 Ad & El 486; *Long v Millar* (1879) 4 CPD 450; *The Swan* [1968] 1 Lloyd's Rep 5 at 12 per Brandon J. This paragraph was cited and presumably approved by Hart J of the Supreme Court of Nova Scotia in *Wolfe Stevedores (1968) Ltd v Joseph Salter's Sons Ltd* (1970) 11 DLR (3d) 476 (which was distinguished by Dubé J at first instance in *Sabb Inc v Shipping Ltd* [1976] 2 FC 175, upheld on appeal [1979] 1 FC 461).
17 See eg *Grace Shipping Inc v C F Sharpe & Co (Malaya) Pte Ltd* [1987] 1 Lloyd's Rep 207. On the nature of this warranty and its operation where the agent has no actual or ostensible authority, see the decision of Mocatta J in *V/O Rasnoimport v Guthrie & Co Ltd* [1966] 1 Lloyd's Rep 1, especially at 7–16. Note the extended critical discussion of this case by Reynolds (1967) 83 LQR 189. See also Leigh 'Breach of Warranty of Authority' in Fridman *Studies in Canadian Business Law* (1971) pp 342–367. It has been held that agents of the Crown cannot be held liable for breach of warranty of authority: *Dunn v Macdonald* [1897] 1 QB 401; affd ibid at 555; *The Prometheus* (1949) 82 Ll L Rep 859. This is now questionable in view of changes in Crown immunity: *Peaker v Canada Post Corpn* (1989) 68 OR (2d) 8 at 21: below, p 383.

who has contracted with him on the faith of his representation of authority. The nature of his liability will depend upon the agent's state of mind. If the agent has contracted with knowledge that he had no authority to do so, this will amount to fraud, and he will be liable for deceit,[18] irrespective of any liability on the part of the principal based on the apparent authority of the agent. But the agent will still be liable even without proof of fraud, for breach of the implied warranty of authority and this liability exists whether the 'agent' is acting negligently, or in good faith and under the honest, but mistaken belief that he is contracting with the authority of another person, not on his own behalf as principal. Liability for breach of the implied warranty of authority is strict.[19] However, the damages recoverable may depend on the characterisation of the self-styled agent's conduct, ie whether he was fraudulent, negligent or completely innocent.[20]

The doctrine of Collen v Wright. The principle is that everyone who professes to act as an agent on behalf of somebody else impliedly warrants that he has authority to make the contract which has been made, unless he expressly disclaims such authority or the third party otherwise knows that the agent lacks such authority.[1] In other words where the third party is misled by the agent's misrepresentation of authority (however innocent), the self-styled agent will be personally liable to the third party.[2] This liability was firmly stated to exist by the decision in *Collen v Wright:*[3]

> X professed to act as agent for G, and made a lease of G's farm to the plaintiff. It was held that X's personal representatives were liable to the plaintiff because X had impliedly warranted that he had G's authority to

---

18 *Polhill v Walter* (1832) 3 B & Ad 114.
19 *Salter v Cormie* (1993) 108 DLR (4th) 372.
20 *Wickberg v Shatsky* (1969) 4 DLR (3d) 540 at 544. In *Scott v Kirkby-Bott* [1977] CLY 11 the plaintiff was awarded damages representing what he had lost in the way of resigned directorships and surrendered share options as a result of his reliance on the defendant's representation that he was acting on behalf of an unnamed principal. If the plaintiff has suffered no loss the 'agent' will not be liable: *Siculiana Holdings Inc v J Goia Holdings Inc* (1994) 42 RPR (2d) 143. See also *Farley Health Products Ltd v Babylon Trading Co* (1987) Times, 29 July: discussed below.
1 For a case in which it was necessary to determine *where* the warranty was made or given, see *The Piraeus* [1974] 2 Lloyd's Rep 266.
2 This will not extend to an innocent misrepresentation which does not affect the agent's authority, eg that certain chattels were included in the contract the agent had authority to make for the principal: *Jones v Still* [1965] NZLR 1071. Nor was there liability under *Hedley Byrne v Heller* because the agent professed no special skill. Such a situation could probably now be covered by the Misrepresentation Act 1967, s 2(1): on which see Cheshire, Fifoot and Furmston's *Law of Contract* (12th edn 1991) pp 282–285.
3 (1857) 8 E & B 647. However, the vigorous dissent of Cockburn CJ should be noted. In *Black v Smallwood* [1966] ALR 744, the High Court of Australia left open the possible liability of the defendants in damages for breach of warranty of authority, since damages were not being claimed: such damages were obtained in two Canadian cases: *Wickberg v Shatsky* (1969) 4 DLR (3d) 540; *Delta Construction Ltd v Lidstone & Pierney* (1981) 82 APR 70. Contrast cases where such a claim was not pleaded, so that no such liability was possible: *A E LePage Ltd v Kamex Developments Ltd* (1977) 78 DLR (3d) 223; affd (1979) 105 DLR (3d) 84; *General Motors Acceptance Corp of Canada Ltd v Weisman* (1979) 96 DLR (3d) 159. Cf *Peaker v Canada Post Corpn* (1989) 68 OR (2d) 8, where the agency relationship was not pleaded: hence the action would not lie.

make the lease. It was further held that the damages payable by the defendants included the plaintiff's costs of a fruitless claim for specific performance of the lease which he had brought against G.

This decision recognised that whatever its precise legal character there was some kind of relationship between the parties that could substantiate an action upon the plaintiff's discovery of the truth.[4] The juridical nature of this liability has been the subject of much speculation.

A case in which this occurred is *Yonge v Toynbee*.[5] The facts were as follows:

Solicitors acting for a principal in defending an action did not know that their principal had become insane. They continued with the litigation, thereby involving the third party in costs. When they discovered the principal's insanity the solicitors discontinued the proceedings. It was held that since the principal's insanity terminated the solicitors' authority,[6] they had impliedly warranted that they had authority by continuing the proceedings, when in fact they had no such authority, and they were therefore liable for the third party's costs, by way of damages for breach of such warranty.

It was stressed in this case that the agent's liability did not depend upon any wrong or omission on the part of the agent. Buckley LJ considered that his liability depended upon an implied contract.[7] But it is difficult to find any ordinary, or usually understood contractual relationship between the agent and the third party. Indeed where the agent does not contract personally, but as an agent (thereby not becoming a party to the contract),[8] he may still be liable for breach of the implied warranty of authority, whether he acts knowing that he has no authority, ie fraudulently, or careless as to whether he has authority, ie negligently, or honestly believing that he has authority, ie innocently. In none of these cases can it be said that the agent makes a personal contract with the third party. Whatever relationship exists between these parties does not seem to arise out of agreement between them. It cannot legitimately be considered to be contractual, as the High Court of Australia pointed out in *Black v Smallwood*.[9] Swinfen Eady J[10] acknowledged this when he stressed the importance of the fact that the agents were solicitors, who presumably should have taken more care

---

4 Cheshire, Fifoot and Furmston's *Law of Contract* (12th edn 1991) pp 65, 496–497, refers to the situation as an early example of a 'collateral contract': on which see Wedderburn 'Collateral Contracts' [1959] Camb LJ 58. That the agent's liability will be contractual in some circumstances seems to have been rejected by Barwick CJ and Kitto, Taylor and Owen Justices of the High Court of Australia in *Black v Smallwood*, above.
5 [1910] 1 KB 215.
6 Below, p 398. Note the affects of the Enduring Powers of Attorney Act 1985 where the donor of such a power subsequently becomes subject to mental incapacity.
7 [1910] 1 KB 215 at 228. Cf Mocatta J in *V/O Rasnoimport v Guthrie & Co Ltd* [1966] 1 Lloyd's Rep 1 at 12–13.
8 Above, pp 237–242.
9 Above, note 3.
10 [1910] 1 KB 215 at 233–234. But the same approach was adopted in a case of bills of lading issued by agents of shipowners: *V/O Rasnoimport v Guthrie & Co Ltd* above; cf also the situation, involving shipowners, in *Grace Shipping Inc v C F Sharpe & Co (Malaya) Pte Ltd* [1987] 1 Lloyd's Rep 207.

about discovering whether they had authority to act, and could be regarded by virtue of their office as owing some kind of duty not only to their clients but also to third parties litigating with their clients.

This suggests that liability under the doctrine of *Collen v Wright* was an early form of liability for negligent misrepresentation. However, until the decision of the House of Lords in *Hedley Byrne v Heller*[11] no such liability for purely economic loss existed in the absence of a contract or a fiduciary duty.[12] Since that decision it can be argued that, where the self-styled agent was negligent, liability for negligent misrepresentation is appropriate, just as where the self-styled agent is fraudulent an action for deceit will lie.

Another suggestion that has been made is that the self-styled agent's liability is based on estoppel, arising from a detriment suffered in reliance on the misstatement, and similar to, though different in effect from, agency by estoppel.[13] However, this would involve the conclusion that a contractual relationship giving rise to an action thereon can be created by estoppel, which is very dubious.[14]

Nor can it be argued that the doctrine can now be subsumed under the Misrepresentation Act 1967, s 2(1). This gives an action for damages 'where a person has entered into a contract after a misrepresentation'. The provision speaks of liability if there would have been liability if the misrepresentation had been made fraudulently. However, it has been held that only a principal, not an agent, is liable under the Act.[15] Hence, if there is no principal, and the misrepresentation is as to the existence of a principal, it seems unlikely that the Act can be considered to be the basis on which the doctrine of implied warranty of authority can be justified.

In *Farley Health Products Ltd v Babylon Trading Co.*[16] Sir Neil Lawson concluded that the action was *sui generis*. But it was closer to a claim for damages for misrepresentation and to the types of claim allowed in *Anglia Television Ltd v Reed*[17] (in which a claim was allowed for pre-contractual and post-contractual expenditures which had been wasted when the defendant broke his contract by refusing to perform his contractual obligation). Hence it was difficult to justify the application of contract or tort principles to measure the

---

11 [1964] AC 465, [1963] 2 All ER 575.
12 *Nocton v Lord Ashburton* [1914] AC 932.
13 Above, ch 6. See Fridman 'Promissory Estoppel' (1957) 35 Can BR 279. Cf the discussion of this type of liability in terms of estoppel by Mocatta J in *V/O Rasnoimport v Guthrie & Co Ltd* [1966] 1 Lloyd's Rep 1 at 13–18.
14 See Cheshire, Fifoot and Furmston's, *Law of Contract* (12th edn 1991) pp 100–101; Fridman, *Law of Contract in Canada* (3rd edn 1994) pp 121–128. Cf some Canadian cases: *Zeismann v WPW Developments Ltd* (1976) 78 DLR (3d) 619; *Byrne v Napier* (1975) 62 DLR (3d) 589; *Stairs v New Brunswick* (1978) 20 NBR (2d) 553; *Gilbert Steel Ltd v University Construction Ltd* (1976) 67 DLR (3d) 606 (which is still good law: *Transamerica Life Insurance Co of Canada v Canada Life Assurance Co* (1995) 25 OR (3d) 106 at 116); but note the dicta to the contrary in *Re Tudale Explorations Ltd and Bruce* (1978) 88 DLR (3d) 584, and the curious remarks by Lord Wilberforce in *Secretary of State for Employment v Globe Elastic Thread Co Ltd* [1979] 2 All ER 1077 at 1082.
15 *Resolute Maritime Inc v Nippon Kaiji Kyokai* [1983] 2 All ER 1: above, p 229.
16 (1987) Times, 29 July. It is unfortunate that there is not a fuller report of the case.
17 [1972] 1 QB 60: see Cheshire, Fifoot and Furmston's *Law of Contract* (12th edn 1991), pp 596–597.

damages in cases of breach of the implied warranty of authority. In that case goods were ordered by a person purporting to act as agent for a company which had ceased to exist. Both the company and the agent were sued for breach of contract. It was held that the correct basis for assessment of damages against the agent was an award to reimburse the plaintiff for (1) the money wasted in manufacturing, packing and shipping the goods not paid for and (2) the costs thrown away by the plaintiff claiming against the non-existent principal. This latter award, it will be noted, was similar to the award made in *Collen v Wright*. The learned judge held that the right measure of damages was the loss caused, which could also be described as expenditure wasted as the result of an untrue representation.[18]

From this it might appear that the doctrine of *Collen v Wright* might now be thought of as being analogous to liability for misrepresentation. However, the reference to *Anglia Television Ltd v Reed* also indicates some analogy with contractual liability (as Buckley LJ seems to have suggested in *Yonge v Toynbee*). In short, therefore, the true nature and basis of this anomalous liability is as uncertain and unclear as it has been since 1857.

Deception of third party. Whatever the true basis of this liability on the part of the agent, it is clear that it depends upon the fact that the third party has been misled. If he has not been misled, the agent will not be liable to him.[19] The third party will not be misled if the agent, in fact, has admitted that he had no authority, which information the third party disregarded. This occurred in *Halbot v Lens*,[20] where the agent told the third party he had no authority to sign a contract on the principal's behalf. Subsequently, therefore, the agent could not be made liable for breach of an implied warranty of authority: for in all the circumstances there was no such warranty. Nor will the third party be misled where he knew or ought to have known by virtue of his appreciation of trade or other usages or customs, that the agent was not warranting his authority. Thus in *Lilly, Wilson & Co v Smales, Eeles & Co*:[1]

> A shipbroker signed a charterparty 'by telegraphic authority as agent.' By custom of the trade, such a signature merely meant that, if the telegram he received were correct, then he had authority to sign the charterparty. Therefore it was held that this signature did not amount to a warranty of authority, as the third party knew: hence the shipbroker was not liable for a mistake in the telegram.

But in *Suart v Haigh*[2] there was a similar signature which ran 'by telegraphic authority of X'. X was Y's agent, and the shipbroker was making the charterparty on *Y*'s behalf. It was held that the shipbroker was liable for breach of the implied warranty that he had Y's authority to act on his behalf, since the custom did not cover any further relationships than those which might exist between the agent and the person whose name was appended to the authority.

18 Cp the discussion of causation in *Wickberg v Shatsky* (1969) 4 DLR (3d) 540: above, p 234.
19 Cf Lord Denning MR in *Hely-Hutchinson v Brayhead Ltd* [1967] 3 All ER 98 at 104.
20 [1901] 1 Ch 344.
 1 [1892] 1 QB 456.
 2 (1893) 9 TLR 488.

If all the facts are known to the third party, and the question whether the agent has authority is one of law, to be determined from those facts, the third party is presumed to know the law, and cannot therefore hold the agent liable if he has no authority.[3] In other words, in such circumstances, there cannot be said to be any reliance by the third party upon any representation on the part of the agent. The third party is really relying upon his own interpretation of the facts.

Scope of liability. It should be noted that no action is given to the alleged 'principal' against the self-styled 'agent'. This is because no representation has been made to him, nor has he suffered any detriment from the 'agent's' acts. If the 'principal' has been sued by the third party (who has lost), it will be the third party who pays costs. These will be recoverable from the 'agent' in the action for breach of warranty. So, too, will any damages which the third party could have recovered from the principal, if in fact the agent had had authority, but the principal had refused to perform the contract.[4] For these are the natural and probable consequences of the agent's wrongful act. However, if the contract which the 'agent' purported to make is one which needed to be in writing and this is lacking, presumably there will be no liability for breach of warranty of authority—even if an act of part performance can be proved by the third party.[5]

This form of liability, according to some cases, exists even where the agent, who professes to have authority, does not make a contract on behalf of his principal, but proposes to perform some other undertaking on his behalf. Thus in *Firbank's Executors v Humphreys:*[6]

> Directors of a company, of which all the issuable debenture stock had been issued, gave X a certificate for debenture stock in lieu of cash owed to him by the company. It was held that the directors were liable to X for breach of the implied warranty that they had authority to issue such stock.

In *Starkey v Bank of England,*[7] X a stockbroker transferred stock with the approval of the Bank, although the person who sold the stock had forged a

---

3 *Wilson v Miers* (1861) 10 CBNS 348. No cause of action lies where the misrepresentation is an error of law not a misrepresentation of fact: *Peaker v Canada Post Corpn* (1989) 68 OR (2d) 8 at 21 per Gray J where the authority of Canada Post was statutory: hence the alleged misrepresentation was a matter of law.

4 *Randell v Trimen* (1856) 18 CB 786; *Godwin v Francis* (1870) LR 5 CP 295. Hence, in *C H Rugg & Co Ltd v Street* [1962] 1 Lloyd's Rep 364, in an action for breach of this implied warranty, the third party could recover what he had paid to his sub-purchaser by way of settlement of an action for non-delivery brought against him, and the costs of this action. Note that the third party may have a restitutionary right of recovery against the principal if the latter has received money from the 'agent' which the 'agent' received from the third party: Goff and Jones *Law of Restitution* (4th edn 1993) p 477. This may depend upon the fact that the 'principal' was unaware of what the 'agent' had done and the source of the money, and upon whether the money had been utilised to pay off debts of the 'principal', in which event something akin to subrogation is involved: see the Canadian case of *Hazelwood v West Coast Securities* (1975) 49 DLR (3d) 46; affd (1976) 68 DLR (3d) 172; cf below, p 302.

5 This is based on cases decided under the Statute of Frauds, later contained in the Law of Property Act 1925, s 40, which has now been repealed and replaced by the Law of Property (Miscellaneous Provisions) Act 1989, s 2, Sch 2: see *Warr v Jones* (1876) 24 WR 695; *Rainbow v Howkins* [1904] 2 KB 322. Contrast *Fay v Miller, Wilkins & Co* [1941] Ch 360, [1941] 2 All ER 18.

6 (1886) 18 QBD 54; cf *Weeks v Propert* (1873) LR 8 CP 427.

7 [1903] AC 114.

signature to a power of attorney under which he was allowed to sell it. The Bank were held liable to the original holder of the stock, and it was held that X was liable to indemnify the Bank against the loss which they had thereby incurred.

These cases have been criticised,[8] but whatever the basis of the liability in question, it could be argued that they are not unreasonable extensions.[9]

Rights of the agent

General rule. It has earlier been pointed out that the normal, general, effect of the making of a contract by the agent on his principal's behalf is that the agent is not a party to the relationships created by such contract.[10] He cannot be sued by the third party on the contract he has made for his principal, nor can he sue the third party on such contract. However, just as there are some instances in which the agent may be personally liable on the contract made for his principal,[11] so there are instances in which the agent may personally sue the third party.

Agent personally liable. The most important instance is where the agent is personally liable on the contract, for it is only reasonable and just that an agent from whom a remedy for breach of contract can be sought by the third party should himself be able reciprocally to enforce the contract. But it is essential here (as where the agent's liability is in question)[12] that the agent has contracted personally.[13]

Thus in *Bowen v Morris*:[14]

> The mayor of a corporation, on behalf of himself and the rest of the corporation, signed a contract of sale, one of the terms of which was that the corporation might have the power of re-sale on default by the buyer. Another term was that the mayor was to receive a deposit on the sale. It was held that the mayor could not sue for breach of contract by the buyer, because he had acted merely as agent, despite the words used in the signature.

Similar results followed in *Fairlie v Fenton*,[15] where the agent signed the contract describing himself as 'broker', thus showing that he was not contracting personally and in *Repetto v Millar's Karri and Jarrah Forests Ltd*,[16] where the master of a ship, who had signed a bill of lading as agent for the owner of the ship, was held to be unable to sue on a charterparty for freight due under it.

---

8 See 3 LQR 251; 18 LQR 364.
9 Cf Powell *Law of Agency* (2nd edn) p 258, note 6.
10 Above, pp 216–217, 222.
11 Above, pp 231–243.
12 Ibid.
13 *Joseph v Knox* (1813) 3 Camp 320; cf *Transcontinental Underwriting Agency v Grand Union Insurance Co* [1987] 1 FTLR 35. *Stoljar* p 251, denies that the right to sue and the liability to be sued are 'symmetrical' obligations. This does not seem to accord with what is said in the cases. The passage from '*General rule*' to 'contracted personally' was quoted by Ritter J in *Petrifond Midwest Ltd v Esso Resources Canada Ltd* (1994) 150 AR 16 at 28.
14 (1810) 2 Taunt 374.
15 (1870) LR 5 Exch 169; contrast *Paice v Walker* (1870) LR 5 Exch 173 and see above, p 239.
16 [1901] 2 KB 306; see especially Bigham J at 310.

On the other hand, in cases like *Cooke v Wilson*[17] and *Short v Spackman*,[18] where the facts showed that the agent, while contracting on behalf of a disclosed principal, was none the less contracting personally, it was held that the agent could sue the third party for breach of contract, even if, as in *Short v Spackman*, the principal wrongfully repudiated what the agent had done (which had been within his authority), and renounced the contract made on his behalf. In *Texas Instruments v Europe Cargo*[19] a seller of goods agreed that title to the goods would pass to the buyer at the time the goods were delivered to the carrier. The seller made the contract of carriage with the carrier. It was held that the seller acted as the agent of the buyer in making this contract. But he was a party to the contract. Hence, when the goods were lost or damaged the seller could sue the carrier. Everything, therefore, turns upon this difficult question: has the agent contracted personally?

Agent's special interest. This necessity for contracting personally, in order to give the agent a right to sue on his own behalf, is absent where the agent has some special property in the subject-matter of the contract, or a lien upon it, or some beneficial interest in the completion of the contract.

Certain kinds of agents, such as factors and auctioneers, have a special property in the goods which are the subject-matter of the agency for the purpose of protecting their own interests in the agency. In consequence the law allows them to sue in their own name and on their own behalf on contracts made in respect of the goods.[20] For example, in *Williams v Millington*[1] an auctioneer was held able to sue for the price of his principal's goods which had been sold to the third party, who knew that the auctioneer was selling on behalf of somebody else. Lord Loughborough pointed out that an agent could sue on the contract made for his principal where he had possession of the goods coupled with an interest in them, or a special property in them with a lien for the charges of the sale and his commission. More recently in *Chelmsford Auctions Ltd v Poole*[2] this was followed and applied to a similar case where the agent's commission had been paid out of a deposit given to the agent, an auctioneer, by the third party, the purchaser of the goods. The agent was held able to sue the third party for non-payment after the agent had paid off the principal, ie, the owner of the goods auctioned.

Brokers, however, have no such interest, or property in the goods with which they deal: hence, failing the personal liability of a broker upon the contract he has made on behalf of his principal, he will not be able to sue the third party. To this there is one exception. For it appears that insurance brokers are in a special position, and irrespective of the nature of the contracts made by them, they may sue upon them.[3]

---

17 (1856) 1 CBNS 153.
18 (1831) 2 B & Ad 962.
19 [1990] CLY para 440.
20 Hence Stoljar's argument, *Law of Agency* pp 250–251, that no general rule can be derived from the peculiar position of factors and auctioneers.
1 (1788) 1 Hy Bl 81.
2 [1973] QB 542, [1973] 1 All ER 810.
3 *Provincial Insurance Co of Canada v Leduc* (1874) LR 6 PC 224.

Agent the principal. The agent may also sue in his own name, and on his own behalf, if, in fact, he really is the principal. The reason for the failure to disclose the fact that he is the principal may well be the desire to get brokerage fees.[4] It should be noted that in such instances the principal is *not* undisclosed. An agency relationship is acknowledged by the agent: what is not disclosed is the true name of the principal—that is the agent himself. But the principal may be named as well as disclosed,[5] or the principal may be disclosed but unnamed.[6] In either event the agent can sue, provided that the identity of the principal was immaterial to the making of the contract by the third party and the agent has notified the third party before suing that he is the real principal, or that the third party, after discovering that the agent is really the principal, has performed, in part at least, his side of the contract. The law was expressed in this way by Alderson B in the case of *Rayner v Grote:*[7]

> 'In many cases, such as for instance, the case of contracts in which the skill or solvency of the person who is named as principal may reasonably be considered as a material ingredient in the contract, it is clear that the agent cannot then show himself to be the real principal and sue in his own name.'

The same would apply 'in all executory contracts if wholly unperformed, or if partly performed without the knowledge of who is the real principal'. But in *Rayner v Grote*, in which goods were sold by an agent who was really the principal, the agent was held able to sue in his own name for non-acceptance of part of the goods, because the buyer had accepted and paid for part of them after finding that the agent was really the principal.[8]

Schmaltz v Avery[9] and *Harper & Co v Vigers Bros*[10] were both cases in which the exact identity of the person who was the principal of the agent signing a charterparty was immaterial. In any event, the charterparty would have been made. Hence in both cases the agent (who really was the principal) was held able to sue on the charterparty. But in *Sharman v Brandt*[11] an agent acting on his own behalf, but purporting to act on behalf of someone else (unnamed), was considered by some of the judges not to have contracted with the third party at all, since the identity of the principal was concealed from the third party.[12] Prior to the enactment of section 9(2) of the European Communities Act 1972 (which has now been replaced by the Companies Act 1985, s 36C(1), inserted by the

---

4 *Harper & Co v Vigers Bros* [1909] 2 KB 549. Moreover, concealing the fact that he is buying as principal may prevent agitation of the market and ensure adequate supplies: cf *Stoljar* p 256.
5 As in eg *Rayner v Grote* (1846) 15 M & W 359.
6 As in eg *Harper & Co v Vigers Bros* (above).
7 (1846) 15 M & W 359 at 365, applied by Webster J in *Gewa Chartering BV v Remco Shipping Lines Ltd* [1984] 2 Lloyd's Rep 205.
8 (1846) 15 M & W 359 at 360. Contrast *Gewa Chartering BV v Remco Shipping Lines Ltd*, above, where the identity of the other party was considered material by the defendant, when the plaintiff, the agent, sued, unsuccessfully.
9 (1851) 16 QB 655.
10 [1909] 2 KB 549.
11 (1871) LR 6 QB 720 (discussed by Pickford J in *Harper & Co v Vigers Bros* [1909] 2 KB 549 at 562).
12 The case was actually decided on the lack of a note or memorandum of the contract as required by the Statute of Frauds (but not any longer under the Law Reform (Enforcement of Contracts) Act 1954).

Companies Act 1989, s 130[13]) in *Newborne v Sensolid (GB) Ltd*[14] an agent who professed to contract on behalf of a company, not yet in existence, could not himself sue when the attempt by the company, after registration, to ratify his contract was unsuccessful. Since the agent had not acted personally or on his own behalf, while concealing his true character as principal, but had always behaved as an agent, he was not permitted to act as a principal and as a party to the contract. In similar circumstances, now, it would seem that the agent could now sue, as long as the statute was applicable to the situation.[15]

Conduct of principal and third party. Even though the agent may sue in his own name, and on his own behalf, his rights of action may be affected by what has transpired between his principal and the third party. Just as settlement between agent and third party may affect the principal's right to sue the third party,[16] so settlement, either in part or in toto between the principal and the third party will affect the agent's right to sue.[17] But the agent's rights will not be affected by anything the principal chooses to do, where the agent has a lien on the subject-matter of the contract. For in such circumstances, the agent's right to sue the third party has priority over the principal's,[18] unless the contract itself, or the agent's conduct, led the third party to believe that settlement with the principal would protect him in the event of his being sued by the agent personally.[19] For example in *Grice v Kenrick*:[20]

> An auctioneer sold goods to X on behalf of Y. Y owed X money, and it was agreed between them before the sale that the debt should be set off against the price of any goods X might buy. The auctioneer did not know of this agreement, and he let X take away the goods, thinking that X would pay for them, while X took them believing that the debt owed by Y would cover the cost. The auctioneer paid Y for the goods on account, then he learned of the agreement between X and Y. He then gave Y the balance of the proceeds of the sale (which exceeded the price of the goods bought by X). Later he sued X for the price of the goods. It was held that since he had paid Y *after* he learned of the agreement between X and Y, and since his charges had been paid before the auction, the settlement between X and Y could be set up as a good defence to the auctioneer's action against X.

Another defence open to the third party if sued by the agent is that of setting off against the agent's claim any debts due from the *agent* to the third party, even

---

13 Above, p 234.
14 [1954] 1 QB 45, [1953] 1 All ER 708. Contrast *Kelner v Baxter* (1866) LR 2 CP 174 and *Hersom v Bernett* [1955] 1 QB 98, [1954] 3 All ER 370; in both of which the agent was *liable*, despite the fact that he had not acted personally.
15 Above, pp 234–236: cf Markesinis 'The Law of Agency and Section 9(2) of the European Communities Act, 1972' [1976] CLJ 112 at p 126. Contrast the view of Prentice 'Section 9 of the European Communities Act' (1973) 89 LQR 518 at p 532.
16 Above, pp 224–225.
17 *Atkinson v Cotesworth* (1825) 3 B & C 647.
18 *Drinkwater v Goodwin* (1775) 1 Cowp 251; *Robinson v Rutter* (1855) 4 E & B 954.
19 *Coppin v Walker* (1816) 7 Taunt 237; *Coppin v Craig* (1816) 7 Taunt 243.
20 (1870) LR 5 QB 340.

though such debts could not be set off against the principal if the principal himself had been suing on the contract made on his behalf.[1]

C. Where the agent acts for an undisclosed principal[2]

The doctrine of the undisclosed principal[3]

Scope. An undisclosed principal is one of whose existence the third party is unaware, so that the third party does not know that the person with thom he is dealing is anybody's agent. As far as he is concerned, the agent is really a principal, dealing on his own behalf, and in his own name, with the third party. There is no duty on a third party to inquire whether there is an undisclosed principal. In contracting with the person physically or metaphorically before him, the third party undertakes the risk that such person has been authorised to act as the agent of another, without revealing the existence of such principal. He may find, in consequence, that instead of contracting with one person he has contracted with another.

This anomalous doctrine has been heavily criticised as being 'unsound', 'inconsistent with elementary principles' and 'unjust'.[4] However, its origin, while uncertain, seems of reasonable antiquity, substantial solidity and eminent judicial respectability.[5] Under it, a person who is not overtly a party to a contract may acquire rights and be subjected to liabilities under it. In other words, an undisclosed principal, in much the same way as one who is disclosed, can sue and be sued in his own name on any contract duly made on his behalf, as long as the agent acted within the scope of his authority in so contracting.[6] That this basic

---

1 *Gibson v Winter* (1833) 5 B & Ad 96. As will be seen later these matters are also relevant where the agent has acted on behalf of an undisclosed principal.

2 This section, as it appeared in the fourth edition, was relied on by Bouck J in *Kootenay Savings Credit Unions v Tundy* (1987) 17 BCLR (2d) 203 at 215–216.

3 See Goodhart and Hamson 'Undisclosed Principals in Contract' (1931) 4 Camb LJ 320; Müller-Freienfels 'The Undisclosed Principal' (1953) 16 MLR 299; Ferson 'Undisclosed Principals' (1953) 22 U Cin LR 131; Higgins 'The Equity of the Undisclosed Principal' (1965) 28 MLR 167; Stoljar *Law of Agency* ch 10. See also Weinrib 'The Undisclosed Principle of Undisclosed Principals' (1975) 21 McGill LJ 298; Geva 'Authority of Sale and Privity of Contract: The Proprietary Basis of the Right to the Proceeds of Sale at Common Law' (1979) 25 McGill LJ 32 at pp 32–38; Schiff, 'The Undisclosed Principal: An Anomaly in the Laws of Agency and Contract' (1983) 88 Commercial LJ 229; Barnett 'Squaring Unilateral Agency Law with Contract Theory' (1987) 75 Calif LR 1969.

See also Reynolds 'Practical Problems of the Undisclosed Principal Doctrine' [1983] CLR 119, who suggests that, in view of the way the law has emerged in respect of the relations between the parties when a principal is undisclosed (there being various differing situations that may be possible) the undisclosed principal situation and the unnamed (but disclosed) principal situation are very close together and should be governed by much the same prima facie rule, viz, that the agent is prima facie liable as well as the principal.

4 *Stoljar* p 203.

5 *Stoljar* pp 204–211: contrast Pollock 3 LQR 359: 12 LQR 204; 14 LQR 2.

6 *Sin Yin Kwan v Eastern Insurance Co Ltd* [1994] 1 All ER 213 at 220; see also *Edmunds v Bushell and Jones* (1865) LR 1 QB 97; *Watteau v Fenwick* [1893] 1 QB 346 (on which see the comments of Bingham J in *Rhodian River Shipping Co SA v Halla Maritime Corpn* [1984] 1 Lloyd's Rep 373 at 378–379: and the British Columbia decision in *Sign-o-Lite Plastics Ltd v Metropolitan Life Insurance Co* (1990) 73 DLR (4th) 541; above p 73). However, the authority

and simple rule is subject to many qualifications will emerge later. Fundamentally, however, it represents the attitude of the law.

Clearly this anomalous doctrine emerged and was recognised and accepted by the common law by reason of its commercial utility.[7] As the cases that will be considered láter reveal, it may sometimes be to the advantage of a contracting party to conceal the fact that he is the true principal to the transaction. It is indeed 'a very ordinary practice', as an Australian judge once described it,[8] for an agent to act for an undisclosed principal. The principles have been developed to enable contracts for the sale of goods to be made in favour of undisclosed principals, and undisclosed principals to obtain the title to goods, although concurrent rights may be given at the same time to the known party who was in fact acting as agent.[9]

So much is this so that in *Boyter v Thomson*[10] the House of Lords held that under s 14(5) of the Sale of Goods Act 1979, where a buyer bought goods from an agent acting for an undisclosed principal, the buyer was entitled to sue the undisclosed seller for breach of the implied conditions set out in s 14(2) and (3) in respect of the unseaworthiness of the boat that was the subject-matter of the sale. Section 14(5) applied the preceding provisions of subsections (2) and (3) to a sale by a person who in the course of business is acting as agent for another just as they applied to a sale by a principal in the course of business (except where 'that other' is not selling in the course of a business and either the buyer knows that fact or reasonable steps are taken to bring it to the notice of the buyer before the contract is made).

The purpose of the provision in s 14(5) was to deal with the prior situation wherein no sale of goods by private individuals was subject to any implied condition of fitness even where such individuals sold through auctioneers or agents, a situation that could cause hardship where buyers relied on the agent's reputation.[11] In *Boyter v Thomson* the seller, the undisclosed principal, argued that by reason of s 14(5) where an agent acted for an undisclosed principal only the agent would be liable for a breach of s 14(2) or (3). This was because if s 14(5) extended beyond the liability of agents acting for undisclosed principals, s 14(5) would overlap with the provisions of s 14(2) and (3).[12] That argument was rejected by the House of Lords, on the ground that, if correct, it would render wholly superfluous the provision of s 14(5) commencing with the word 'except'. Where an agent acted for an undisclosed principal, one of whose existence the buyer is unaware, the buyer could not know the business of the unknown principal. But the provisions of the exception in s 14(5) clearly presupposed a

---

must exist at the time the agent acted. Hence an undisclosed principal cannot ratify an unauthorised act by his agent: *Keighley, Maxsted & Co v Durant* [1901] AC 240 (although there is the possibility of an estoppel in certain circumstances: above, pp 90–91); Goodhart and Hamson (1931) 4 Camb LJ 320 at pp 335–336; Higgins (1965) 28 MLR 167 at pp 172–175.

7 Cp *Siu Yin Kwan v Eastern Insurance Co Ltd* [1994] 1 All ER 213 at 220 per Lord Lloyd of Berwick.
8 *Mooney v Williams* (1906) 3 CLR 1 at 8 per Griffith CJ.
9 *Maynegrain Pty Ltd v Compafina Bank* [1982] 2 NSWLR 141 at 152 per Hope JA.
10 [1995] 3 All ER 135.
11 Ibid at 137 per Lord Jauncey of Tullichettle.
12 Ibid at 137–138.

principal, whose existence was known to the buyer prior to the contract of sale. To agree with the argument of the undisclosed principal in this case would mean (a) giving no effect to the language of the subsection; (2) creating statutory alterations to normal common law rules as to (a) the sole liability of a disclosed principal on a contract made by an agent on behalf of such principal and (b) the liability of an undisclosed principal to be sued on any contract made on behalf of such principal. Consequently s 14(5) applied to any sale by an agent on behalf of a principal, whether disclosed or undisclosed, where the exception did not arise on the facts.[13]

In *Maynegrain Pty Ltd Compafina Bank*[14] the Court of Appeal of New South Wales held that the doctrine of the undisclosed principal applied where a bailee of goods in a warehouse attorned to a party who, as it turned out, was the agent of an undisclosed principal. The attornment operated as an attornment to the principal, even though the identity of the principal was not known. Hence that court held that the undisclosed principal could sue a party alleged to be guilty of conversion of the goods. The Privy Council reversed the decision[15] on the ground that the agent had consented to the third party's dealing with the goods in question, hence there could be no conversion as against the undisclosed principal, because, applying the doctrine of undisclosed principals, the consent of the agent was the consent of the principal, and dealing with goods with the consent of the owner, ie the principals, cannot be conversion.

These two, very different cases show how the doctrine of the undisclosed principal can play an important role in the determination of issues relating to ownership or liability. If the agent of the undisclosed principal is acting within the scope of his authority, his acts will bind the principal, thereby enabling the principal to acquire ownership or rendering the principal liable for breach of contract. However, the language of Lord Templeman giving the advice of the Privy Council in the *Maynegrain* case suggests that even if the agent acted without authority the undisclosed principal will be bound or affected by the agent's acts. Lord Templeman said:[16]

> 'At the hearing of this appeal it was submitted on behalf of Compafina [the plaintiff claiming for conversion of its goods] that ANZ [the bank that gave permission for the loading of the goods on board ship that was the act of conversion] was an agent without actual or ostensible authority from their principal Compafina to give consent to the loading of the Bellnes [the ship in question]. But this ground of complaint by Compafina against ANZ cannot affect Maynegrain [the warehouse where the goods were stored prior to being loaded on board ship] because Compafina was an undisclosed principal when ANZ consented to the loading of the Bellnes.'

This passage could be interpreted to mean that an undisclosed principal will be bound by an unauthorised act on the part of the agent. As will be seen later,[17] if

13 Ibid at 138.
14 Above.
15 [1984] 1 NSWLR 258.
16 Ibid at 266.
17 Below, pp 264–266.

this is what Lord Templeman was intending to convey by the words quoted above he was contradicting well-established law.

Pervasive as the doctrine is, it will not always be relevant and invoked. In the *Romalpa* case (*Aluminium Industrie Vaassen BV v Romalpa Aluminium Ltd*[18]), aluminium foil was sold by Romalpa to AIV under a contract that stated, inter alia, that ownership of material delivered by AIV would only be transferred to the purchaser when the purchaser met all that was owing AIV no matter on what grounds. The material was to be stored in such a way that it could be identified as the property of AIV and an assignment of future unascertained property, ie, manufactured goods processed from the material, was provided as surety for AIV until full payment was made, but a right was given Romalpa to sell the finished product with a transfer to AIV of all claims against purchasers from Romalpa. When Romalpa went into receivership AIV was owed £122,000: Romalpa had £35,000 in a separate account: and was in possession of £50,000 worth of unsold material provided by AIV. The action concerned the right to the sum of £35,000. Mocatta J and the Court of Appeal held that this money belonged to AIV.

One of the several issues raised in this case involved agency. It was argued by AIV that, because of the retention of title clause and the other relevant provisions of the contract with Romalpa referred to above, Romalpa were the agents of AIV who were undisclosed principals. Hence money received by Romalpa from the sale of the material, when processed, rightly belonged to AIV on general agency principles that have previously been discussed, or Romalpa were in a fiduciary situation vis-à-vis AIV, which could trace the proceeds of the sale of any materials delivered by AIV to Romalpa. Although it was held that, by reason of the particular terms of this contract, there was an obligation on Romalpa to surrender the money in question to AIV, it was also held that, in selling the finished, manufactured product to purchasers from them Romalpa were not acting as agents for an undisclosed principal, ie AIV, but were themselves acting as principals.[19] However, the situation of Romalpa with respect to AIV was akin to that of agents. Hence the money belonged to AIV. What the Court of Appeal was doing in this case, it would seem, was treating Romalpa at one and the same time as agents for certain purposes and as principals for others. Subsequent cases have revealed that the facts and the decision in the *Romalpa* case were peculiar to that case, and may not support any general principle or rule where a retention of title clause is included in a contract of sale of goods.[20] In particular, it does not seem that, in later cases, any attempt was made to found liability on the basis of agency as between the seller of goods retaining title therein and the buyer. In this context, at any rate, the doctrine of the undisclosed principal has not been permitted to affect questions of title to goods and claims to their proceeds. One comment can be made: namely that it appears somewhat incongruous to treat the unpaid seller in such circumstances as an undisclosed principal of a buyer who has not yet paid the purchase price for the goods while at the same time regarding that buyer as not acting as the agent of the unpaid seller when selling those goods or their product to third parties.

---

18 [1976] 2 All ER 552: above, pp 25, 173.
19 Ibid at 563–564 per Roskill LJ.
20 Above, p 25, note 1 for the cases in question.

Basis. Obviously, the development of the doctrine of undisclosed principals is quite at variance with the general approach of the law to contractual rights and liabilities. Ordinary agency, ie where the principal is disclosed, can be reconciled with the common law doctrine, that only parties to a contract can acquire rights and liabilities under it, on the ground that the principal is really a party to the contract (either in substitution for, or in addition to the agent): the agent may be regarded as being only an instrument, by whose hand and act the principal contracts. Since the third party does not know of the existence of the undisclosed principal, the same cannot be said of this form of agency. The fiction of the identity of principal and agent is inapplicable in this context.[1]

Consequently, other rationalisations and explanations have been suggested not to bury the undisclosed principal, but, as Professor Stoljar said,[2] 'to save and sustain him'. According to Ames,[3] the undisclosed principal is to be treated as a cestui que trust, the relationship between agent and undisclosed principal being that of trustee and beneficiary, and of equitable origin. Though the fiduciary nature or aspect of the agency relationship is clearly established, there seems little point in trying to explain what is really a common law relationship in terms which have an equitable flavour. What similarity there is between the position of an agent and that of a trustee ought not to be carried too far. Professors Goodhart and Hamson suggest that the undisclosed principal is an implied assignee of the agent.[4] Stressing the similarity between assignment and the position of an undisclosed principal, they consider that the doctrine is 'best considered as a primitive and highly restricted form of assignment'.[5] Professor Stoljar[6] strongly criticised this idea and, in line with his general views about the agency relationship, preferred to talk in terms of the transmission of rights.

1 Contrast Seavey 'The Rationale of Agency' (1920) 29 Yale LJ 859 at pp 877–880, referring to the doctrine as a sort of common law equity. Professors Goodhart and Hamson (1931) 4 Camb LJ 320 at pp 346–352, deny that there is a contract between the undisclosed principal and the third party. On the other hand Professor Müller-Freienfels bases the doctrine on the ground that consideration moves from the undisclosed principal to the third party; (1953) 16 MLR 299 at pp 305–312. Compare the 'consent' theory of contract that is used to explain the doctrine of the undisclosed principal by Barnett, loc cit above, note 3. Other, earlier American writers have suggested that the doctrine is based on the idea of 'benefit' to the principal or 'reliance' by the third party: Stoljar, *Law of Agency*, pp 230–231.
2 *Law of Agency* p 228. The main theories are set out and discussed by Rochvarg, 'Ratification and Undisclosed Principals' (1989) 34 McGill LJ 286 at 298–314. The purpose of his discussion is to argue in favour of allowing undisclosed principals to ratify unauthorised acts by their agents.
3 'Undisclosed Principal—His Right and Liabilities' (1909) 18 Yale LJ 443, criticised by Seavey (1920) 29 Yale LJ 859 at pp 879–880 on the ground that the principal is a *master* as well as cestui que trust. For other criticisms see *Stoljar* pp 228–230. The *equitable* approach, however, has been revived and re-explained by Higgins, above, p 253, note 3. Note, however, the remarks by Ungoed-Thomas J in *Pople v Evans* [1968] 2 All ER 743 at 749, that there is no trust relationship between any of the parties (ie principal, agent, or third party) which can be recognised as between the third party and the principal or agent.
4 (1931) 4 Camb LJ 320 at pp 351–352: cf Seavey (1920) 29 Yale LJ 859 at p 859, where it is said that the undisclosed principal *is in no better position* than an assignee. This article was described as 'influential' by Lord Lloyd in *Siu Yin Kwan v Eastern Insurance Co Ltd* [1994] 1 All ER 213 at 220. As to the possibility of the acceptance of the doctrine to avoid circuity of actions, see Diplock LJ in *Freeman & Lockyer v Buckhurst Park Properties (Mangal) Ltd* [1964] 1 All ER 630 at 644.
5 (1931) 4 Camb LJ 320 at p 352.
6 *Law of Agency* pp 231–233.

All these varied, and imaginative theories do not completely explain this strange, peculiarly English doctrine. Perhaps the most satisfying attitude to adopt is that the idea of the undisclosed principal is an anomaly, introduced into and accepted by the common law for reasons of mercantile convenience, and rigorously controlled by the law, so far as its scope and effects are concerned, lest this unusual relaxation of the strict attitude of the common law with regard to personal contracts be allowed to cause undue subversion.[7] The way such control has occurred must now be examined.

Position of the undisclosed principal

Rights and duties

Generally speaking, there is no difference between an undisclosed principal and one who is disclosed. That is to say, he can sue and be sued in his own name on any contract duly made on his behalf, as long as the agent intended to act on the principal's behalf in entering into the contract, and as long as the contract does not expressly or by implication exclude the principal's right to sue and his liability to be sued.[8] Hence the general position must be qualified.

Identification. The first qualification involves a consideration of the circumstances in which evidence may be introduced to prove the existence of, and identify the undisclosed principal, so as to enable him to sue or be made liable. On this there are decisions which appear to be inconsistent.[9] Sometimes parol evidence may be admitted for such purpose and sometimes it may not. In *Humble v Hunter*:[10]

> The agent described himself in a charterparty as 'owner' of a ship. It was held that parol evidence was not admissible to show that he had contracted as agent for someone else. Therefore the undisclosed principal could not sue on the charterparty.

Lord Denman[11] said that this was because 'the agent contracts as principal'. But this always happens in the case of an undisclosed principal and if Lord Denman's reason were accepted, it would seem to follow that never would such a principal be able to sue. A leading case in which Lord Denman's approach was not applied

---

7 This sentence, and the preceding paragraphs were cited and relied upon by Lander LJSC in the British Columbia case of *Vancouver Equipment Corpn v Sun Valley Contracting Ltd* (1979) 16 BCLR 362 at 367.
8 *Siu Yin Kwan v Eastern Insurance Co Ltd*, above, at 220. Cf Hope JA in *Maynegrain Pty Ltd v Compafina Bank* [1982] 2 NSWLR 141 at 149–150 (reversed an appeal to the Privy Council on the facts and in relation to tort liability: [1984] 1 NSWLR 258). Any defence the third party may have against the agent, eg based on the agent's fraud, is available against the principal: cf above, pp 228–231.
9 Landon 61 LQR 130; 62 LQR 20: cf also Müller-Freienfels 'The Undisclosed Principal' (1953) 16 MLR 299 at p 316.
10 (1848) 12 QB 310: cf *Formby Bros v Formby* (1910) 102 LT 116 where the agent was described as 'proprietor'.
11 (1848) 12 QB 310 at 315.

is *F Drughorn Ltd v Rederiaktiebolaget Trans-Atlantic*.[12] There the agent described himself in the charterparty as 'charterer'. It was held that the undisclosed principal could be identified by parol evidence. Lord Haldane[13] drew a distinction between property and contract. Where property rights were involved, then an undisclosed principal could not be identified by extrinsic evidence: but where contractual rights were involved then such evidence could be admitted because what is really involved is an explanation of the intentions of the party described in the contract. An illustration of this is *Danziger v Thompson*[14] where the agent was described in a lease as 'tenant'. Evidence was admissible to show that he was acting for a principal, who could therefore be made liable for the rent. By way of contrast, in the New Brunswick case of *Jones v Young*,[15] where a husband signed an agreement for the purchase of a house, evidence was not admitted to show that he was acting as agent for his wife, the alleged undisclosed principal. Other English cases also provide instances of the court's refusal to admit such evidence to establish agency in cases dealing with a lease[16] or the provision of a block of rooms in a hotel.[17] In a British Columbia case, *Vancouver Equipment Corpn v Sun Valley Contracting Ltd*,[18] the issue did not involve property, but contractual rights, and the alleged undisclosed principal was excluded. Leave was sought to substitute a new company as plaintiff in an action originally commenced in the name of an older, dormant company. The latter had been replaced by the newer company. The new company was not permitted to allege that it was the undisclosed principal of the older company, as the defendants believed that they had contracted only with the older company.

Such decisions tend to suggest that courts may be more and more unwilling to admit evidence that would identify an undisclosed principal. This provides modern support for the approach adopted in *Humble v Hunter*, despite earlier statements, such as that of Scott LJ in *Epps v Rothnie*[19] that *Humble v Hunter* was no longer good law. However, it should be noted that these more recent decisions did not necessarily rely on *Humble v Hunter* to arrive at their conclusion to exclude the evidence and refuse recognition to an alleged undisclosed principal. Moreover, there has been no suggestion that what was held or suggested in the *Drughorn* case was incorrect. Indeed in *Siu Yin Kwan v Eastern Insurance Co Ltd*[20] the *Drughorn* case was cited as good authority for the proposition that even if the agent is named expressly or by implication in terms that suggest that the

---

12 [1919] AC 203: ie there was no implied representation: see also *Sorrentino Fratelli v Buerger* [1915] 3 KB 367.
13 [1919] AC 203 at 206.
14 [1944] KB 654, [1944] 2 All ER 151. See the discussion of Lord Haldane's language at 656–657, 152, per Lawrence J.
15 (1978) 21 NBR (2d) 480, where, in fact, the question of agency turned out to be immaterial.
16 *Lyons v Haddadeen* [1979] CLY 15.
17 *Kuoni Travel v Hotel Management International* [1979] CLY 16.
18 (1979) 16 BCLR 362.
19 [1945] KB 562 at 565, [1946] 1 All ER 146 at 147–148: cf the *Drughorn* case [1919] AC 203 at 209 per Lord Shaw. Contrast Gresson P in the New Zealand case of *Fawcett v Star Car Sales Ltd* [1960] NZLR 406 at 421–423. Stoljar, however, says that little or nothing is left of the rule in *Humble v Hunter*: *Law of Agency* p 223. He refers to it as 'a sledgehammer rule' ibid p 224. In this he would seem to be incorrect.
20 [1994] 1 All ER 213 at 221–222.

agent is in fact the principal, this will not necessarily prevent the undisclosed principal intervening to show that he is the true principal. As Lord Lloyd said: if courts are too ready to construe written contracts as contradicting the right of an undisclosed principal to intervene, it would go far to destroy the beneficial assumption in commercial cases. In the *Siu Yin Kwan* case a claim was brought against the owners of a vessel, A Ltd, when two crew members were drowned in a typhoon in a Hong Kong bay. The judgments against A Ltd were never satisfied because A Ltd was in liquidation. The plaintiffs then sued the insurance company which had effected a policy of insurance to cover the vessel's crew. That policy had been effected by RI Ltd, shipping agents, appointed by A Ltd to be that company's general agents. RI Ltd was the proposer under the policy and no mention was made of the fact that the employer was A Ltd not RI Ltd, although the insurance company was aware from previous dealings relating to the vessel in question that RI Ltd were shipping agents not the owners of the vessel. By virtue of the provisions of a Hong Kong Ordinance, the plaintiffs claimed that A Ltd's rights as the employer to be indemnified by the insurance company under the workmens' compensation insurance policy had been transferred to and vested in the estates of the deceased crew members (whose personal representatives were the plaintiffs). The insurance company argued inter alia that no valid contract of indemnity had been effected because the insured, RI Ltd, was not the employer and the actual employer, A Ltd, was not named. Hence A Ltd could not claim under the policy therefore the plaintiffs could derive no rights under the Hong Kong Ordinance. The insurance company succeeded at trial and on appeal to the Hong Kong Court of Appeal. The Privy Council reversed this decision holding, inter alia, that there was nothing in the proposal form, or the policy, that expressly or by implication excluded A Ltd's right to sue as undisclosed principal. It was also held that the personality of the contracting party was not of such significance as would preclude the right of A Ltd to claim under the policy.[1]

In arriving at its conclusion with respect to the issue of identity, following the decision in the *Drughorn* case, the Privy Council did not find it necessary to decide to what extent, if at all, *Humble v Hunter*[2] (and *Formby Bros v Formby*[3]) should still be regarded as good law.

If indeed *Humble v Hunter* is still good law it gives rise to the problem of reconciling the approach of Lord Denman in that case with the approach in some subsequent cases. The answer may lie in the language of the Privy Council in the *Siu Yin Kwan* case indicating that everything turns on the terms of the contract.[4] Thus the description employed by the agent in making and signing the contract may (but not necessarily *must*) show that he impliedly contracts that there is no

1 Below, pp 262–264.
2 Above, note 10.
3 Above, note 10.
4 [1994] 1 All ER 213 at 220. See, eg, some Canadian cases where the agent was held to have contracted so as to exclude a principal: *Wilson's Truck Bodies v Teehan* (1990) 100 NBR (2d) 345; *Fracflow Consultants Inc v White* (1994) 113 Nfld & PEIR 192; *Lambert Scott Architects Ltd v 404577 Alberta Ltd* (1993) 142 AR 241; and cases where the agent was held to have contracted an agent: *4 Seasons Electrical Mechanical Contractors of Canada (1979) Ltd v Apex Realty Importers Inc* (1993) 90 Man R (2d) 239; *QNS Paper Co v Chartwell Shipping Ltd* [1989] 2 SCR 683.

principal.[5] If the agent contracts as 'owner' or 'proprietor' such a contract may be implied: if he contracts as 'charterer' or 'tenant' it may not. This is similar to Lord Haldane's distinction between property and contractual rights and would seem to be at the basis of it.[6] Where the description used by the agent in making the contract is so ambiguous that it is capable of being interpreted as showing either that the agent contracts as principal or that he contracts as agent, then parol evidence is admissible, since, in such circumstances, the admission of the evidence would explain the contract, not vary or contradict it, and would not produce a result that was inconsistent with the terms of the contract.[7] Hence where the contract makes it plain on the face of the document that the party signing is the party who is the principal, there would be no room for admission of evidence to establish another principal.[8] An alternative formulation of this is to say that evidence of the existence of an undisclosed principal is inadmissible where the circumstances indicate that the other contracting party believed, and had reasonable grounds for believing, that he was contracting only with the signatory of the document and not, either actually or possibly, with someone else whose identity had not been disclosed. Such was the decision not only in the *Vancouver Equipment Corp* case,[9] but also in the New Brunswick decision in *Storey v Atlan Industries Ltd*.[10] There the purchaser of a swimming pool was held able to sue the defendant personally, although he claimed that he had contracted on behalf of an undisclosed principal, one of his corporations. The purchaser was under the belief that he was contracting only with the defendant himself, not with one of the defendant's corporations. This determined the issue, and the agent could not escape liability by transferring it to an undisclosed principal. This was a case of the liability of such a principal to be sued, not his right to sue: but the approach and the principles to be applied would appear to be the same.

However, if the contract made by the agent is such that it can be construed as containing an *express* term that the agent is really the principal then there can be no right in any other (undisclosed) principal.[11] For example, in *United Kingdom*

---

5 Powell *Law of Agency* (2nd edn) p 155; Goodhart and Hamson 'Undisclosed Principals in Contract' (1931) 4 Camb LJ 320 at pp 342, 345–346.

6 [1919] AC 203 at 207 per Lord Sumner. In the New Zealand case of *Murphy v Rae* [1967] NZLR 103, the expression 'vendor' in the contract for sale of land did not exclude evidence that the husband who was selling the land was a joint owner with his wife, the undisclosed principal: see Fridman 'Establishing Agency' (1968) 84 LQR 224 at pp 239–244. But in *Jones v Young* (1978) 21 NBR (2d) 480 the husband purchaser was held to be the owner: evidence could not be admitted to prove his alleged agency for his wife. Here, however, the spouses were not joint owners, and the question was whether the husband could deny his alleged ownership by establishing that of his wife in his place.

7 Powell *Law of Agency* pp 156–157. This rule has been described as 'probably more odd in its application than irrational in its theory': Goodhart and Hamson 'Undisclosed Principals in Contract' (1931) 4 Camb LJ 320 at p 327. But it is consistent with general contractual theory and practice: cf Cheshire, Fifoot and Furmston's *Law of Contract* (12th edn 1991) pp 123–125.

8 *Kuoni Travel v Hotel Management International* [1979] CLY 16, where the contract was made with the hotel, not with the managers of the hotel who were alleged to be undisclosed principals.

9 Above, note 18.

10 (1982) 36 NBR (2d) 317. Cf *Wilson's Truck Bodies v Zeehan*, above; *Fracflow Consultants Inc v White*, above; *Lambert Scott Architects Ltd v 404577 Alberta Ltd*, above.

11 Cf *Hersom v Bernett* [1955] 1 QB 98, [1954] 3 All ER 370. The whole question is connected with the ascertainment of the personal liability of the agent.

Mutual Steamship Assurance Association v Nevill:[12]

> Contributions under an association's articles and a policy of insurance were only obtainable from members of the association. The defendant was part owner of a ship with his agent (who was a member of the association). When the defendant was sued for a contribution, it was held that he could not be made liable since he was not a member of the association, and his agent must therefore have contracted as principal.[13]

The position was summarised by McNair J in *Finzel, Berry & Co v Eastcheap Dried Fruit Co*[14] in these words:

> 'It is clear law today that a person who has concluded a contract in his own name may prove by parol evidence that he was acting for an undisclosed principal unless he has contracted in such terms as to show that he was the real and only principal, and that it was really a question of the construction of the particular contract which determined whether parol evidence was admissible to prove that some person other than the party named in the written contract was, in fact, the true principal.'

Personality. Even though, on the principles discussed above, the undisclosed principal is identifiable, none the less he may be unable to sue the third party. As Scrutton LJ said in *Greer v Downs Supply Co:*[15]

> 'When a person claims as an undisclosed principal the question sometimes arises whether the contract was made with the agent for reasons personal to the agent which induced the other party to contract with the agent to the exclusion of his principal or any one else.'

In that case the facts were as follows:

> X sold goods to the defendant (to whom he owed money). X was in fact the plaintiff's agent though this agency was not disclosed to the defendant. X used the plaintiff's headed notepaper, etc, but he said it was his. It was held that the defendant did not have actual notice of the plaintiff's existence as principal (though he might have had constructive notice). The plaintiff was not an undisclosed principal, for the defendant had not contracted with him. Personal reasons (namely X's debt to the defendant) made the defendant contract with X personally. Hence the defendant was not liable to the plaintiff on the contract.

---

12 (1887) 19 QBD 110. Reference may also be made to *Bart v British West Indian Airways* [1967] 1 Lloyd's Rep 239, especially at pp 243–249, 284–287.
13 Note that the contract to which the agent was a party was under seal. But in Canada it has been held that the fact that the contract was under seal will not prevent a party from suing an undisclosed principal: *Kootenay Savings Credit Unions v Tundy* (1987) 22 BCLR (2d) 201; but contrast *Margolius v Diesbourg* [1937] SCR 183, even though the party executing the contract did so in fact as the agent of the person sought to be made liable; cf *Winnett v Heard* (1928) 62 OLR 61.
14 [1962] 1 Lloyd's Rep 370 at 375.
15 [1927] 2 KB 28 at 35. This was followed, in a very similar situation, by the Ontario Court of Appeal in *Campbellville Gravel Supply Ltd v Cook Paving Co Ltd* (1968) 70 DLR (2d) 354.

The same inability to sue the third party may arise where the contract is one in respect of which the agent cannot assign his rights, eg, a contract to paint a portrait.[16] Since the third party is relying on the personal skill (or solvency) of the agent, it will be unfair to the third party to permit somebody else to be introduced as a party to the contract as an undisclosed principal.[17] If the identity of the person with whom the third party is contracting is material to the making of the contract, then the failure to disclose the fact that the agent is acting on behalf of a principal will deprive the principal of the right to sue on the contract. In *Said v Butt*:[18]

> The principal wanted a ticket for a theatre. He knew that the management would not sell him a ticket, so he sent an agent to purchase one in his own name. When the principal arrived at the theatre with the ticket he was refused admittance. He sued for breach of contract. It was held that no contract had been made with the principal because the manager would not have contracted had he known for whom the agent was acting. Hence the principal could not sue.

But in *Dyster v Randall & Sons*[19]—in which the contract was for the sale of land, though the agent did not reveal the identity of the principal, but contracted on his own behalf—it was held that the identity of the person contracting with the third party was not material: therefore a valid contract was made with the principal who could sue for specific performance.[20] So, too, in *Siu Yin Kwan v Eastern Insurance Co Ltd*[1] the Privy Council would not accept the insurance company's argument that a contract of indemnity insurance was a personal contract in the same sense as a contract to paint a portrait. No case had ever decided or suggested that a contract of insurance was an exception to the general rule that an undisclosed principal may sue on a contract made by an agent within his actual authority.[2] Nor was there any suggestion that marine insurance was an exception to that supposed exception. There was no sufficient ground to distinguish between contracts of marine insurance and contracts generally.

Where the undisclosed principal is being *sued*, it does not appear to have been settled whether he can raise and rely upon the issue of personality. On the one

---

16 *Siu Yin Kwan v Eastern Insurance Co Ltd* [1994] 1 All ER 213 at 223.
17 Cf *Rayner v Grote* (1846) 15 M & W 359 at 365 per Alderson B; relied on, to negate the agent's right to sue, by Webster J in *Gewa Chartering BV v Remco Shipping Lines Ltd* [1984] 2 Lloyd's Rep 205 at 210. The third party is under no duty to inquire whether there is a principal, *Fish v Kempton* (1849) 7 CB 687; *Re Henley, ex p Dixon* (1876) 4 Ch D 133; *Toners Garage Ltd v Brentwood Motors Ltd* (1988) 91 NBR (2d) 239. Nor does he have to establish his lack of means of knowledge of such principal: *Borries v Imperial Ottoman Bank* (1873) LR 9 CP 38. On this whole subject see 4 Camb LJ 320 at pp 338–345.
18 [1920] 3 KB 497: discussed by Goodhart and Hamson 'Undisclosed Principals in Contract' (1931) 4 Camb LJ 320 at pp 349–351: see also *Archer v Stone* (1898) 78 LT 34; cf *Smith v Wheatcroft* (1878) 9 Ch D 223; cf *Collins v Associated Greyhound Racecourses Ltd* [1930] 1 Ch 1: discussed in Goodhart and Hamson (1931) 4 Camb LJ 320 at pp 352–356.
19 [1926] Ch 932.
20 Cf *Nash v Dix* (1898) 78 LT 445, where the agent contracted on his own behalf, though with the intention of reselling to someone to whom the third party would not have sold the property. The identity of the contracting party was held to be immaterial.
1 [1994] 1 All ER 213 at 223.
2 Indeed the contrary was established by *Browning v Provincial Insurance Co of Canada* (1873) LR 5PC 263.

hand it could be said that this should be permitted, since otherwise undisclosed principal and third party are not being treated equally by the law. On the other hand it might be said that since the third party contracted with the agent as principal because, or as a result, of the concealment of the agency relationship on the express or implied instructions of the principal, it would be inequitable to permit the undisclosed principal to raise this defence if he is sued on the resultant contract.[3] On this latter approach, it might then be argued that the principal can raise the 'personality' issue when the agent has concealed the agency relationship against express instructions. The whole question, it is suggested, remains open.

If the undisclosed principal has been guilty of fraud, though this was unknown to the agent, the contract may be revoked at the suit of the third party.[4] The contrary view would lead to the undisclosed principal's obtaining the fruits of his own fraud, or the agent's obtaining an unjustified enrichment resulting from the undisclosed principal's fraud, as Megaw J explained in *Garnac Grain Co Inc v Faure and Fairclough Ltd.*[5] Equally, if the agent has been guilty of any fraud, misrepresentation or failure to disclose any material fact, then, if this would have operated as a defence in an action brought by the agent, it will equally be available as a defence to an action brought by an undisclosed principal.

The agent's authority

As long as the agent is acting within the express authority given him by his undisclosed principal, there will be no difficulties (in the absence of the materiality of the principal's personality). Problems emerge when the agent is acting beyond such authority.

The earlier discussion of usual authority,[6] and especially the case of *Watteau v Fenwick,*[7] revealed that there were conceptual and practical difficulties about applying the notion of implied authority to the situation where a principle is undisclosed. Even harder to rationalise and harmonise with the position where an agency is undisclosed is the notion of apparent authority in relation to

---

3 Hence in a Canadian case, *Hal H Paradise Ltd v Apostolic Trustees of the Friars Minor* (1966) 55 DLR (2d) 671 where an agent acted with the express written authority of the undisclosed principal, the ignorance of the third party of the identity and existence of the undisclosed principal was immaterial where the third party wanted to enforce a contract against the principal, when the contract was within the scope of the express authority of the agent. This case was approved and followed by Bouck J in *Kootenay Savings Credit Union v Tundy* (1987) 17 BCLR (2d) 203, varied on reconsideration (1987) 22 BCLR (2d) 201.

4 For a case where the undisclosed principal was guilty of conduct lacking in commercial morality but not fraud, see *N Yorke Transfer Ltd v Wallace Construction Specialties Ltd* (1992) 106 Sask R 62.

5 [1965] 1 All ER 47n at 49. The learned judge left open the solution when the undisclosed principal was guilty of an *innocent* misrepresentation. This decision was reversed by the Court of Appeal on different grounds: [1965] 3 All ER 273. Diplock LJ was of the opinion that the judgment of Megaw J was correct on the facts in issue at the trial (ibid at 286–287), but it did not fall to be decided on the view taken on appeal as to the interpretation of the facts. The House of Lords affirmed the Court of Appeal, without discussing the point now under consideration: [1967] 2 All ER 353.

6 Above, pp 69–76.

7 [1893] 1 QB 346.

undisclosed principals.[8] It is difficult, if not impossible, to reconcile all the cases, and in particular the case of *Watteau v Fenwick*, whether the case is regarded as one involving implied, in the sense of usual, authority or apparent or ostensible authority. As seen in an earlier chapter,[9] that decision would make an undisclosed principal liable for acts of an agent, even though that agent acted not only without authority but in defiance of an express prohibition on the part of the principal. The case and its doctrine have been described as 'fallacious' in a more recent English decision.[10] As long ago as 1919 the Ontario Court of Appeal refused to hold that an undisclosed principal could be liable without limit, i.e. by unauthorised acts by the agent:[11] and would not accept *Watteau v Fenwick* as good law. The same approach was adopted by the British Columbia Court of Appeal in 1990, by which it was held that *Watteau v Fenwick* was not part of the law of that Province.[12] Despite the suggestions that an undisclosed principal is liable because he has made the agent appear to be an owner,[13] it would appear that the better view is that neither implied nor apparent authority can apply where an agent acts for an undisclosed principal. Moreover, as previously noted, an undisclosed principal cannot validly ratify an unauthorised contract made by the agent so as to entitle the principal to sue on it.[14] All this would seem to indicate that an undisclosed principal will only be bound by or be able to claim under a contract entered into by an agent acting with express authority.

However, the remarks of Lord Templeman giving the advice of the Privy Council in *Maynegrain Pty Ltd v Compafina Bank*[15] call this into question. What was said there seems to mean that even though the agent for an undisclosed principal acted without actual or ostensible authority the principal will still be bound by what that agent does, since the agent was acting for the undisclosed principal. The facts of that case involved a situation in which the agent consented to dealing with goods belonging to the undisclosed principal that would otherwise have been conversion of the goods. Hence it may be that Lord Templeman was restricting his statement to cases where the third party would have been liable in tort to the undisclosed principal had it not been for the acts of the agent. The learned judge may not have intended what he said to mean that an undisclosed principal would be liable on a contract made by the agent acting without actual or ostensible authority. If Lord Templeman intended his words to have that wider import, then his language contradicts the conclusion arrived at above based upon earlier decisions in England and elsewhere.

Indeed if that is the meaning of what Lord Templeman said the potential liability of an undisclosed principal would be virtually limitless. There would be

---

8 Conant, 'The Objective Theory of Agency' (1968) 47 Nebraska LR 678: see also Fishman, 'Inherent Agency Power—Should Enterprise Liability Apply to Agents' Unauthorised Contracts' (1987) 19 Rutgers LJ 1.
9 Above, pp 72–76.
10 *Rhodian River Shipping Co SA v Halla Maritime Corpn* [1984] 1 Lloyd's Rep 373 at 378–379 per Bingham J.
11 *McLaughlin v Gentles* (1919) 51 DLR 383; above, p 73.
12 *Sign-o-Lite Plastics Ltd v Metropolitan Life Insurance Co* (1990) 73 DLR (4th) 541: above, p 73.
13 Conant, loc cit above, note 8 at p 686.
14 *Keighley Maxsted v Durant* [1901] AC 240: above, p 89.
15 [1984] 1 NSWLR 258 at 266: above, p 255.

grave danger in empowering an agent to act without disclosing the fact of agency. In view of the attitude of the House of Lords in *Keighley Maxsted v Durant* and the more recent condemnation of *Watteau v Fenwick*, it is difficult to accept that Lord Templeman was intending to adopt and espouse the view that undisclosed principals can be bound by actions performed by their agents acting without express, i.e., actual, authority.

Effect of dealings with agent

Except in so far as the undisclosed principal is excluded from the contract made by the agent with the third party for the reasons given above, such a principal is in the same position as one who is disclosed. It was seen earlier in this chapter,[16] that the relationship existing between a disclosed principal and the third party may be affected by the principal's settlement of his account with the agent, by the third party's suing or otherwise giving credit to the agent, or by a debt owed to the third party by the agent. How far do these acts affect the position of an undisclosed principal?[17]

Dealings by principal: settlement with agent. If the principal settles his account with the agent before the third party discovers the existence of the principal, then, according to the decision in *Armstrong v Stokes*,[18] the third party cannot later sue the principal when the latter's existence is made known. In that case the agent was one who sometimes acted as agent, sometimes as principal, and the third party never inquired whether any principal existed. Blackburn J decided the issue on the basis that to have made the principal pay twice would have been unjust. However, this was criticised in *Irvine & Co v Watson & Sons*[19] where Blackburn J's principle was said to be too wide. That case, like *Heald v Kenworthy*[20] which it followed, concerned a *disclosed* principal. And it is possible, therefore, that the idea that a third party is only prohibited from suing the principal where his own conduct has induced the principal to change his position, is only applicable where the third party knows of the existence of the principal. Where the relationship of principal and agent is unknown to the third party, anything which occurs as between the principal and agent before the third party discovers that such a relationship exists, should be irrelevant to the question of the liability of the principal to the third party. This will be so whether the principal has paid the agent, thereby affecting the state of the accounts between them,[1] or the principal is owed money by the agent.[2] Such cases would seem to deny the proposition that the question of the principal's liability must be

---

16 Above, pp 222–225.
17 Cf Müller-Freienfels 'The Undisclosed Principal' (1953) 16 MLR 299 at pp 312–316.
18 (1872) LR 7 QB 598 relying on dicta in *Kymer v Suwercropp* (1807) 1 Camp 109 and *Thomson v Davenport* (1829) 9 B & C 78. See the discussion in Higgins 'The Equity of the Undisclosed Principal' (1965) 28 MLR 167 at pp 175–178. Cf the discussion by Reynolds, 'Practical Problems of the Undisclosed Principal Doctrine' [1983] CLP 119 at 133–135.
19 (1874) 5 QBD 414; above, p 223; see 4 Camb LJ 320 at pp 335–338.
20 (1855) 10 Exch 739.
 1 *Thomson v Davenport* (1829) 9 B & C 78.
 2 *Waring v Favenck* (1807) 1 Camp 85.

settled by whether it is just to make the principal pay again. It is likely, therefore, that *Armstrong v Stokes*, the only case, apparently, in which the undisclosed principal was relieved of liability, is not a good authority today.

Dealings by third party: election. Where an agency is disclosed, if the third party elects to sue the agent or otherwise to give the agent exclusive credit, he cannot subsequently make the principal liable.[3] But as long as the principal remains undisclosed, the third party is not free to elect. Hence the doctrine of election can only operate *after* the third party discovers the existence and identity of the principal, at which time a conclusive choice by the third party to sue the agent will free the principal and vice versa.[4] As seen earlier, it is not enough that the third party acted with full knowledge of all the relevant facts. He must have performed some truly unequivocal act revealing that he had abandoned his rights against the other, whether agent or principal.[5] Giving credit to the agent might be indicative of an election. Instituting proceedings against the principal might also be such an act. Indeed it might be the clearest evidence of the exercise of an election.[6] One test is whether the third party when suing the agent was intending to preserve his rights against the principal. Hence, once a *final* judgment has been obtained, an election will have occurred. But it must be final—thereby excluding a judgment signed in default of the agent's appearance which was not final under the appropriate Rules of Court.[7] And it must not have been obtained by fraud, eg as a result of a conspiracy between the agent and the undisclosed principal.[8]

Set-off. Another situation which can give rise to difficulty is where the third party wishes to set off against a claim by the undisclosed principal a personal debt

3 Where the third party sues the agent and obtains a judgment, it was said by Gibbs and Mason Justices of the High Court of Australia, in *Marginson v Ian Potter & Co* (1976) 136 CLR 161 at 169, that the liability of the undisclosed principal *merges* in the judgment so then obtained: relying on, and citing, *Priestly v Fernie* (1865) 3 H & C 977; *Kendall v Hamilton* (1879) 4 App Cas 504; and an Australian case, *Petersen v Moloney* (1957) 84 CLR 91.
4 The converse is also true in that the third party is only liable to be paid by the principal if the agent has not already done so. Hence, where an agent began proceedings and then was adjudicated bankrupt, and his trustee in bankruptcy elected not to proceed with the suit, the undisclosed principal was able to bring a new action and was not barred by any plea of res judicata: *Pople v Evans* [1969] 2 Ch 255, [1968] 2 All ER 743.
5 *Clarkson Booker Ltd v Andjel* [1964] 2 QB 775, [1964] 3 All ER 260 (where the third party was suing the *agent*, after having commenced proceedings against the originally undisclosed principal): followed in *Chestertons (a firm) v Barone* (1987) 282 Estates Gazette 87: *Cyril Lord Carpet Sales Ltd v Browne* (1966) 111 Sol Jo 51, where the *Clarkson Booker* case was distinguished.
6 *Chestertons (a firm) v Barone*, above, obiter by the Court of Appeal, where agreeing to accept commission from the agent of an undisclosed principal was not sufficient to establish an election. Cp *Fowler v St Stephens College* [1991] 3 NZLR 304 at 308.
7 *Morgan v Lifetime Building Supplies Ltd* (1967) 61 DLR (2d) 178, a decision of the Court of Appeal of Alberta; *Kootenay Savings Credit Unions v Tundy* (1987) 17 BCLR (2d) 203 (where obtaining judgment was election although the third party was ignorant of the existence of the undisclosed principals); see, however, subsequent proceedings (1987) 22 BCLR (2d) 201 where the plaintiffs were held able to sue the undisclosed principals, shareholders of a company.
8 *Swanton Seed Service Ltd v Kulba* (1968) 68 DLR (2d) 38, a decision of Bastin J, Manitoba Queen's Bench.

which is owed to him by the agent.[9] The third party is entitled to set up against the undisclosed principal any defence which would be available to him against the agent.[10] This would seem to suggest that the third party may indeed set off any debts owed to him by the agent, which he could have set off against a claim by the agent himself. This appears to be the law. However, it must be considered in the light of several determining factors.

In the first place, the agent must have acted within the scope of his authority. For example in *Baring v Corrie*:[11]

> A broker sold goods without disclosing the name of his principal. This was outside the scope of his authority.[12] It was held that the buyer could not set off a debt due to him from the broker as a defence in an action by the principal demanding the return of the goods.

Secondly, there is the question of notice of the existence of a principal. The right to set off in this way is only available if the agent's debt accrued before the third party knew that there was in fact a principal. If the debt, which would otherwise be available for setting off, comes into existence *after* the existence of the principal has been disclosed to the third party, it cannot be set off against the principal. In such circumstances, there is no longer any reason to charge the principal with a liability to the third party which has been incurred by his agent with the knowledge of the third party that he was dealing with an agent.[13] It should be remembered that, in respect of the existence of an undisclosed principal, the kind of notice that is required in order to be effective is actual notice. As was seen in *Greer v Downs Supply Co*,[14] constructive notice will be insufficient to affect the position of the third party.

This leads to the really important point. Does the third party's right to set off a debt due from the undisclosed principal's agent depend upon estoppel, or is it available in all cases? The suggestion has been made in some cases[15] that the right of set-off only exists where

> 'the agent has been permitted by the principal to hold himself out as the principal and ... the person dealing with the agent has believed that the agent was the principal and has acted on that belief.'[16]

---

9 Derham 'Set-off and Agency' [1985] CLJ 384. See also, Reynolds, loc cit above, note 18.
10 *Browning v Provincial Insurance Co of Canada* (1873) LR 5 PC 263. Similarly if the defence would be available against the undisclosed principal it ought to be available against the agent: *Garnac Grain Co Inc v Faure and Fairclough Ltd* [1965] 1 All ER 47n; revsd [1965] 3 All ER 273; affd [1967] 2 All ER 353; cf above, p 264. As to the availability of a defence to the undisclosed principal, see *Collins v Associated Greyhound Racecourses Ltd* [1930] 1 Ch 1.
11 (1818) 2 B & Ald 137.
12 Abbott CJ said: '. . . the broker . . . is not trusted with the possession of the goods and he ought not to sell in his own name. The principal, therefore, who trusts a broker ought to expect that he will not sell in his own name.' (1818) 2 B & Ald 137 at 143.
13 *Mildred, Goyeneche & Co v Maspons* (1883) 8 App Cas 874 (discussed by Reynolds, loc cit pp 129–131); *Kaltenbach v Lewis* (1885) 10 App Cas 617. Cf the Canadian case of *Armstrong v Oliver Ltd* [1933] 2 WWR 462.
14 [1927] 2 KB 28: for the facts see above, p 262.
15 And is criticised by *Bowstead and Reynolds on Agency* (16th edn) pp 441–443: cf Reynolds, loc cit pp 122–125.
16 *Cooke & Sons v Eshelby* (1887) 12 App Cas 271 at 275 per Lord Halsbury LC.

For, as Lord Watson said, in the same case:[17]

> 'It would be inconsistent with fair dealing that a latent principal should by his own act or omission lead a purchaser to rely upon a right of set-off against the agent as the real seller, and should nevertheless be permitted to intervene and deprive the purchaser of that right at the very time when it had become necessary for his protection.'

Hence this rule rested upon the doctrine of estoppel. And everything depended upon the third party's knowledge and belief about the existence of a principal for whom the person with whom the third party was negotiating was acting. Thus in *Montagu v Forwood*:[18]

> The principal employed agents to collect contributions in respect of general average loss. The agents were not brokers, so they employed the third party (who were Lloyd's brokers) to do the job. These brokers believed that the agents were in fact the principal. The agents owed the brokers some money. It was held that the debt could be set off against the principal's claim.

But in the leading case of *Cooke & Sons v Eshelby*:[19]

> The agents acting in their own name, sold cotton to X. They were in fact selling on behalf of an undisclosed principal. X knew that sometimes the agents sold for principals, and sometimes for themselves. But X did not know who was the principal in this particular contract. It was held that X could not set off a debt owed by the agents in an action brought by the undisclosed principal, for the principal had not held out the agents as principals.

This was because the peculiar circumstances of the agents' business known to X made it just as likely that they were acting on someone's behalf as on their own. It was the agent's conduct, not the principal's, which was the cause of X's belief that the agents were principals.

However, it could be said that in all instances where the principal is undisclosed, the principal has held out the agent as principal.[20] Hence there is no special need for any doctrine of estoppel to operate, so that in all cases the third party may exercise a right of set off (subject to the question of notice discussed above).[1] At any rate this is true where the agent has authority not to disclose that he is acting as an agent. Where he has no such authority, but does in fact conceal the existence of an agency relationship, then it may be necessary to resort to the doctrine of estoppel to subject the principal to the agent's personal liability.[2]

---

17 Ibid, at 278–279.
18 [1893] 2 QB 350 (applied, to a slightly different effect, in *Lloyds and Scottish Finance Ltd v Williamson* [1965] 1 All ER 641). See Goodhart and Hamson 'Undisclosed Principals in Contract' (1931) 4 Camb LJ 320 at pp 332–333. Contrast *Kaltenbach v Lewis* (1885) 10 App Cas 617.
19 (1887) 12 App Cas 271.
20 Cf Powell *Law of Agency* (2nd edn) pp 176–177. But note the problem of holding out in relation to undisclosed principals, adverted to above.
 1 Cf *Rabone v Williams* (1785) 7 Term Rep 360n; *George v Clagett* (1797) 7 Term Rep 359 (discussed at length by Derham, loc cit above note 9 at pp 387–402).
 2 This would seem to be a converse of the notion of 'agency by estoppel'.

Perhaps, therefore, the terminology of estoppel should be reserved for such instances: and in all other cases where the agent in acting as principal has followed express instructions, or has implied authority to do so, it can be said that there is a right of set-off, unless, as in *Cooke v Eshelby*, it was the agent's own ambiguous position that produced the belief that there was no principal.[3]

Settlement with agent. A similar problem is raised by the third party's settlement with the agent before discovering the existence of an undisclosed principal. Will this discharge the third party from further liability to the principal? It would seem that, since the existence of the agency relationship is concealed from the third party (either with or without the authority of the undisclosed principal), the third party is entitled to treat the agent as principal, and settle with him, as long as he had no actual notice that any other principal exists. Hence, if settlement with the agent would have discharged the third party, if the agent really had been the principal, then it will operate as a discharge as against the real, undisclosed principal.[4] But everything depends here, as in the case of set-off, upon whether the third party's belief came from the agent's own personal position, as ordinarily understood by the third party, or from the position of the agent resulting from the authority given to him by the principal.

Thus in *Ramazotti v Bowring*[5] the issue of whether the principal had held out his clerk as proprietor of brandy which had been sold to the third party was sent back for a new trial. In *Drakeford v Piercy*[6] it was held that the plea of payment to the agent was insufficient, unless the agent was a factor, or had been authorised by the undisclosed principal to act as principal or to receive payment.

Position of the agent. Since the agent contracts personally where his principal is undisclosed, it is clear that, in accordance with the general rules considered above,[7] the agent, as well as the undisclosed principal may sue and be sued upon the contract.[8] Indeed, if the third party intended to contract with the agent, the latter may be precluded from setting up an undisclosed principal and thereby avoiding his personal liability.[9]

The liability of the agent to be sued may depend upon the third party's election upon his discovery of the existence of a principal. Once the third party knows there is a principal, he can choose between each of the two parties who are liable

---

3 It was admitted by the principal in *Campbellville Gravel Supply Ltd v Cook Paving Co Ltd* (1968) 70 DLR (2d) 354, that if he could sue, as an undisclosed principal, the third party could set off a debt owned by the agent to him, and no question of estoppel arose. In the event, the principal was held unable to sue: cf above, p 262.

4 *Coates v Lewes* (1808) 1 Camp 444.

5 (1859) 7 CBNS 851.

6 (1866) 7 B & S 515.

7 See above, pp 231–242, 249–253.

8 *Short v Spackman* (1831) 2 B & Ad 962; *Hersom v Bernett* [1955] 1 QB 98, [1954] 3 All ER 370. This sentence was cited by De Graves J in *Smith v Lasko* [1986] 5 WWR 716 at 720 (reversed on other grounds [1987] 5 WWR 412). The rights and obligations of principal and agents are not joint, but, subject to the superior right of the principal, alternative: Hope JA in *Maynegrain Pty Ltd v Compafina Bank* [1982] 2 NSWLR 141 at 150.

9 *Storey v Atlan Industries Ltd* (1982) 36 NBR (2d) 317: above, p 261.

to him. The factors determining the decision of the question whether the third party has made his election have already been considered and it is unnecessary here to say more than that the position is exactly the same as it is where the principal is disclosed at the time the contract is made, and the agent has so contracted as to make himself personally liable.[10]

The right of the agent to sue in his own name on a contract made on behalf of an undisclosed principal is subject to certain qualifications.

First, if the principal himself sues the third party, or has otherwise intervened, by way of prohibiting the agent from suing, or settling with the third party, then the agent cannot sue. The general rule is that the right of the principal prevails over that of his agent and the right of the agent to enforce the contract is destroyed by the intervention of the principal in the exercise of his own right.[11] In *Atkinson v Cotesworth*:[12]

> The commander of a ship (the agent of the owners) made a charterparty in his own name. The owners received the agreed freight from the charterer. It was held that the agent could no longer maintain an action for the freight.

But this will not prevent the agent himself from suing where he has a lien (or other interest) over the goods which are the subject-matter of the contract: for then he is protecting his own personal advantage under the contract both against the principal and the third party.[13]

Secondly, the third party can set up against the agent any defence which would have been available against the undisclosed principal.[14] But a right of set-off will not be available unless, probably, the action is brought by the agent on behalf of the principal.[15] A debt due to the third party from the agent himself, however, may be set off if the agent sues on his own behalf, and possibly also if he sued on his principal's behalf, whether or not such debt was contracted before the third party discovered the principal's existence. This is suggested in *Gibson v Winter*,[16] but is rejected as unsound by the *American Restatement on Agency*[17] on the reasonable ground that to admit such a wide right of set-off would be inconsistent with the principle that the third party should be put in the same position as if he had been sued by the principal. Hence the right to set off a debt

---

10 Above, pp 225–227. See *Clarkson Booker Ltd v Andjel* [1964] 2 QB 775, [1964] 3 All ER 260, for full discussion. Hence a default judgment obtained against the principal was a bar to a subsequent action against the agent in *M & M Insulation Ltd v Brown and E A Brown Homes Ltd* (1967) 60 WWR 115, a decision of a county court in British Columbia. On the agent's right to set off a personal claim against the third party if the agent is sued by such party, see Derham, loc cit above, p 268, note 9 at pp 407–414.

11 *Maynegrain Pty Ltd v Compafina Bank* [1982] 2 NSWLR 141 at 150 per Hope JA, quoting *Salmond & Williams on Contracts* (2nd edn 1945) p 423.

12 (1825) 3 B & C 647.

13 *Robinson v Rutter* (1855) 4 E & B 954. With respect to the validity of an agent's lien even as against the interest of his principal, see the remarks of Mustill J in *The Borag* [1980] 1 Lloyd's Rep 111 at 122: above, p 208.

14 Even fraud, where the agent is innocent of any fraud: *Garnac Grain Co Inc v Faure & Fairclough Ltd* [1966] 1 QB 650, [1965] 1 All ER 47; revsd [1966] 1 QB 650, [1965] 3 All ER 273; affd [1968] AC 1130, [1967] 2 All ER 353; above, p 264.

15 *Atkyns and Batten v Amber* (1796) 2 Esp 491; Derham, loc cit pp 401–407.

16 (1833) 5 B & Ad 96.

17 Para 371 comment c; and by Powell, *Law of Agency* p 274; Derham, loc cit p 406, note 35.

due from the agent may depend upon (a) whether the agent is suing on his own behalf or (b) whether the debt accrued while the principal was still undisclosed.

D. Where the agent acts for a foreign principal[18]

Until late in the nineteenth century there was a presumption that an agent for a foreign principal contracted *personally* unless a contrary intention appeared plainly from the contract.[19] The status of this presumption was a matter of some question: since, while in form a presumption of fact, it was sometimes referred to as a matter of law.[20] Its basis was, or was alleged to be, commercial usage or custom. Any presumption that the agent had no authority whatsoever to make the foreign principal party to a contract in this country (which meant that in all cases the agent was personally liable)[1] seems to have disappeared by the last quarter of the nineteenth century.[2] Two cases in 1917 revealed a more flexible attitude on the part of the courts, indicating that the earlier presumption had been a mere presumption of fact, if that, so that the position of the agent was to be determined by reference to the terms of the contract, the nationality or domicile of the principal being relevant only if there was doubt or ambiguity. In *H O Brandt & Co v H N Morris & Co*[3] it was held that the agents were contracting parties and could therefore sue the third party for non-delivery of goods required by the foreign principal. In *Miller, Gibb & Co v Smith and Tyrer Ltd*[4] it was held that the foreign principals were intended to be liable, therefore a custom of the trade that the agents were to be liable was excluded by the terms of the contract.

More modern statements to this effect can be found in the judgment of Pritchard J in *J S Holt and Moseley (London) Ltd v Sir Charles Cunningham & Partners*[5] where the question of the agent's personal liability or not was a matter of intention, to be ascertained from the facts as found in evidence, the nationality and whereabouts of the principal being no more and no less than one of the facts to which the court will give appropriate weight. This was echoed by Roskill J in *Maritime Stores Ltd v H P Marshall & Co Ltd*[6] where the agent was held personally liable for a variety of reasons, only one of them being that the principal was foreign. Similarly in *Rusholme Bolton and Roberts Hadfield Ltd v*

---

18 For the definition of 'foreign principal' see above, p 215. See, generally, Hudson 'Agents for Foreign Principals' (1966) 29 MLR 353: Hill 'The Commission Merchant at Common Law' (1968) 31 MLR 623 at pp 637–639.

19 *Elbinger AG für Fabrication von Eisenbahn Material v Claye* (1873) LR 8 QB 313 at 317 per Blackburn J; *Armstrong v Stokes* (1872) LR 7 QB 598 at 605 per Blackburn J.

20 Ibid.

1 *Paterson v Gandasequi* (1812) 15 East 62; *Thomson v Davenport* (1829) 9 B & C 78.

2 *Gadd v Houghton* (1876) 1 Ex D 357 (discussed above, p 240); *Ogden v Hall* (1879) 40 LT 751. Cf Stoljar *Law of Agency*, pp 238–248.

3 [1917] 2 KB 784, which was cited and relied upon by Lord Denning MR in *The Santa Carina* [1977] 1 Lloyd's Rep 478 at 480.

4 [1917] 2 KB 141.

5 (1949) 83 Ll L Rep 141 at 145.

6 [1963] 1 Lloyd's Rep 602 at 608; applied, in relation to the liability of shipping agents, in *Wolfe Stevedores (1968) Ltd v Joseph Salter's Sons Ltd* (1970) 11 DLR (3d) 476.

Read & Co (London) Ltd[7] Pearce J held that agents who made a contract under instructions from an Australian principal were personally liable for non-acceptance of goods.

In the light of these and other modern cases,[8] it was suggested that the presumption may be confined to 'confirming houses'.[9] Some discussion has centred around the possible confusion in the nature of 'agency' in such situations, and the mistaken treatment of the relationships arising where an agent acted for a foreign principal.[10] But the decision of the Court of Appeal in *Teheran-Europe Co v S T Belton Ltd*[11] seems to deny any such possibilities, while clarifying the present position. In that case agents in England acted for an unnamed principal, which was a Persian company. A point arose as to the fitness of the goods purchased on behalf of the principals, who wished to sue on the contract, alleging breach of implied conditions. Although the principals lost on this contractual issue, it was held that they had a right to sue. The court accepted the view that the foreign character of the principal was only one factor to be taken into consideration, even where the principal was undisclosed, or unnamed, as well as foreign. Hence there was no longer any business usage making the contract one personal to the agent, and excluding the foreign principal. Nor could the contract in question be construed as limiting rights of action upon it to the agent. All the members of the court adverted to the changes which had taken place in commercial usage in the past century, as affecting the way commercial men intended their contracts to be construed when dealing with foreign parties.

More recently still, in *The Santa Carina*,[12] which involved a foreign principal, the Court of Appeal approached the issue of the agent's liability from the standpoint of determining whether the third party knew of any facts from which he could reasonably conclude that the agent was not contracting personally. In the absence of any evidence to this effect, it was held that the agent was not liable, since the third party believed that he was contracting with a principal, and intended so to contract. Nor was there any custom on the Baltic Exchange which affected the question. Moreover, the insolvency of the principal did not alter the situation. These decisions make it clear that the liability of the agent who acts for a foreign principal is to be determined in exactly the same way as that of an agent who acts for an English, ie not foreign, principal. It would seem, therefore, that

---

7 [1955] 1 All ER 180, especially at 183. Contrast *Lester v Balfour Williamson* [1953] 2 QB 168, [1953] 1 All ER 1146.

8 *Cox v Sorrell* [1960] 1 Lloyd's Rep 471, not itself a case concerning a confirming house, but an agent exporting cattle for foreign principals, who was held personally liable for loading charges: *Anglo-African Shipping Co of New York v Mortner* [1962] 1 Lloyd's Rep 610; *Sobell Industries Ltd v Cory Bros & Co* [1955] 2 Lloyd's Rep 82.

9 Stoljar *Law of Agency* p 242. Contrast Hudson (1966) 29 MLR 353 at pp 361–365. See also, generally, Hill 'Confirming House Transactions in Commonwealth Countries' (1972) 3 J of Maritime Law and Commerce 307; *Bowstead on Agency* (15th edn) pp 436–437.

10 Hill (1968) 31 MLR 623 at pp 637, 639–641.

11 [1968] 2 QB 545, [1968] 2 All ER 886 (overruling the dictum of Blackburn J in *Elbinger v Claye*, above, note 19), especially at 889, per Lord Denning MR 892–893 per Diplock LJ, 895, per Sachs LJ. See, on this case, Reynolds 'Practical Problems of the Undisclosed Principal Doctrine' [1983] CLP 119 at pp 126–127. See also *Maynegrain Pty Ltd v Compafina Bank* [1982] 2 NSWLR 141 at 150 per Hope JA.

12 [1977] 1 Lloyd's Rep 478: above, p 238; Reynolds, loc cit pp 120–121.

the queries raised in recent years have been put to rest, even though it might still be argued that a satisfactory solution would be to hold the agent liable as well as the principal.

It is to be noted that the foreign principal cannot sue or be sued on the contract unless the agent had authority to establish privity of contract: but the agent's authority, as already seen, is a question of fact.

CHAPTER 12

Dispositions of property by agents

During the course of the continuance of the agency relationship, the agent has the power to affect the proprietary rights of the principal in a variety of ways: the agent may acquire money or other property on behalf of the principal; or the agent may dispose of the principal's money or other property. Therefore it is necessary to discuss how, and in what circumstances, dealings by the agent with money or property entrusted to him by the principal, or by a third party, can affect the legal position of the principal. Since, in most cases, the purpose of the creation of the agency relationship is to empower the agent to deal with money, goods or land, on behalf of the principal (usually by the making of contracts in connection with such money, goods or land), the effect of the agency relationship on title to property, especially goods, is one of the most important and significant features of the law of agency.

Three matters call for consideration: first, the rights of the principal against the agent in respect of property of any kind in the possession of the agent; secondly, the rights of the principal against third parties who have come into possession of the principal's property as a result of the agent's conduct; thirdly, the rights, if any, of third parties in respect of money or property given to the agent to pay or give to such third parties.

A. Rights of principal against agent

Title to property. It has already been seen[1] that generally the agent may not deny his principal's title to property in the possession of the agent as agent. The agent's possession is that of the principal for most purposes.[2] However, under the Torts (Interference with Goods) Act 1977[3] the agent, in an action for wrongful interference, is entitled to show in accordance with rules of court that a third party has a better right than the principal as respects all or any part of the interest claimed by the principal or in right of which he sues; and the rule of law sometimes called jus tertii to the contrary has been abolished.[4] It should also be noted that where the agent is employed to purchase property on behalf of his

---

1 Above, p 171.
2 Including the Limitation Act: see *Lyell v Kennedy* (1889) 14 App Cas 437.
3 Section 8: see *Salmond and Heuston on the Law of Torts* (20th edn 1992) p 114: cf Palmer *Bailment* (2nd edn 1991) pp 259–260, 354–359: above, p 172.
4 Note, however, the agent's right to interplead in certain circumstances: above, p 173.

principal and does so in his own name, then, upon conveyance or transfer of the property to the agent, he is considered to be trustee of it for the principal.[5]

Account. The agent is also liable to account for and pay over to the principal all money received from third parties on behalf of, and to the use of the principal. It is not open to the agent to plead that a third party is claiming the money[6] or that the agent himself has a claim against the third party.[7] Nor does it matter that the money was received by the agent as a result of a void transaction such as a wager,[8] or an illegal contract (the illegality of which has been waived by the third party's payment)[9]—unless the agency itself was illegal.[10]

But there are circumstances in which the agent will not be liable to pay to the principal money received by the agent for the principal's use, and, indeed, will be bound to repay the money to the third party from whom he received it. This will occur, for instance if the agent has obtained the money wrongfully, by duress[11] or fraud,[12] or there has been a mistake of fact resulting in the payment, or failure of consideration (provided that the agent contracted personally or had notice of the third party's claim to repayment before the time arrived to pay the money over to his principal).[13]

Rights of action. The principal can sue the agent for the property or money, by bringing an action for account, or, where appropriate, in tort, or for breach of contract (if a contract existed between the parties), or by an action for restitution or unjust enrichment if there is no contract between the parties. All these remedies are available where the property in question is still in the hands of the agent. If the agent has wrongfully dealt with the property on his own behalf, some of these remedies may not be appropriate. The agent may be liable for the tort of 'wrongful interference', in which the principal, generally speaking, will

---

5 *Austin v Chambers* (1837–8) 6 Cl & Fin 1; *James v Smith* [1891] 1 Ch 384. Cf the Queensland case of *Lincoln Contractors Pty Ltd v Hardy* (1976) Australian Digest Supplement 342, where the trust relationship precluded an estate agent from paying himself his commission out of money received from the prospective purchaser, after the contract was rescinded for the principal's default, despite the provisions of a statute which empowered such an agent to draw his commission, etc, from a trust account kept pursuant to the statute.

6 *Blaustein v Maltz, Mitchell & Co* [1937] 2 KB 142, [1937] 1 All ER 497. Contrast the situation with respect to *goods*: above. However, the problem of the agent is different if he received the money as a *stakeholder*, ie, if the facts show that the money was received by the agent on such terms, as in *Wolf v Hosier & Dickinson Ltd* [1981] CLR 89.

7 *Heath v Chilton* (1844) 12 M & W 632.

8 *De Mattos v Benjamin* (1894) 63 LJ QB 248.

9 *Bousfield v Wilson* (1846) 16 M & W 185.

10 *Booth v Hodgson* (1795) 6 Term Rep 405; *Harry Parker Ltd v Mason* [1940] 2 KB 590, [1940] 4 All ER 199.

11 *Snowdon v Davis* (1808) 1 Taunt 359. Indeed, the agent will be liable to repay the third party, even if he has already paid over the money to the principal: Goff and Jones, *Law of Restitution* (4th edn 1993) pp 754–755.

12 *Murray v Mann* (1848) 2 Exch 538.

13 *Holland v Russell* (1863) 4 B & S 14; *Gurney v Womersley* (1854) 4 E & B 133; *Gowers v Lloyds and National Provincial Foreign Bank* [1938] 1 All ER 766. See generally, Goff and Jones *Law of Restitution*, pp 750–755, for the general rule and the exceptions when the agent may not rely on the defence of payment over to a claim for repayment by the third party. See also Fridman *Restitution* (2nd edn 1992) pp 464–466.

be able to recover damages, not specific restitution, if the principal's goods have been dealt with improperly.[14] But what if it is the principal's money that has been affected? And what if the agent has purchased other property with the proceeds of the sale of the principal's goods, or by the use of the principal's money? Has the principal any right to the goods thus obtained by the agent? And if the agent has taken the principal's money, or money obtained by the sale of the principal's goods, and mingled it with his own, or used it in conjunction with his own money to purchase other goods, what remedies will be available to the principal.[15]

Here the problem has been that at common law it was necessary to be able to identify one's own property in order to recover it from someone wrongfully withholding it.[16] As long as the property could be identified, even though it had been changed into some other kind of property, the original owner, ie the principal, could sue the agent for its return. This was decided in *Taylor v Plumer*:[17]

A broker misappropriated his principal's money and bought stock and bullion. It was held that the principal could claim the stock and bullion, notwithstanding it had been money which he had entrusted to the agent.

Lord Ellenborough explained the result by saying:[18]

'It makes no difference in reason or in law what other form different from the original the change may have been made, whether it be into that of promissory notes for the security of the money which was produced by the sale of the goods of the principal ... or into other merchandise ... for the product of or substitution for the original thing still follows the nature of the thing itself, as long as it can be ascertained to be such and the right only ceases when the means of ascertainment fail.'

However, such 'means of ascertainment' will fail 'when the subject is turned into money and mixed and confounded in a general mass of the same description'. Thus the principal's common law remedy in rem (as opposed to his personal claim for damages) against the agent only exists as long as there is an identification between the property given the agent and the property actually in the hands of the agent. Where there was no such means of identification the common law gave no remedy. Instead, an equitable remedy in rem, a charging order, was made available to the principal, by means of which he could proceed

---

14 Torts (Interference with Goods) Act 1977, ss 1(a), 2(2), 5: unless the agent still has the goods in his possession or control: ibid, s 3.
15 See also Maudsley 'Proprietary remedies for the Recovery of Money' (1959) 75 LQR 234. The problems of legal and equitable proprietary claims are dealt with at length in *Goff and Jones* ch 2; *Fridman* ch 12.
16 Scott 'The Right to "Trace" at Common Law' (1966) 7 Univ of WAALR 63.
17 (1815) 3 M & S 562. Cf also *Re Hammond, ex p Brooke* (1869) 20 LT 547; *Re J Leslie Engineers Ltd* [1976] 2 All ER 85, [1976] 1 WLR 292. However the nature of, and ratio decidendi in, this celebrated case have recently been the subject of much discussion, which throws the whole matter into some confusion: see Goode 'The Right to Trace and its Impact in Commercial Transactions' (1976) 92 LQR 360, 528, especially at pp 367–371; Khurshid and Matthews 'Tracing Confusion' (1979) 95 LQR 78.
18 (1815) 3 M & S 562 at 575.

against the funds or property in the agent's hands, even where those funds or that property did not completely represent the principal's money or the proceeds of the use of the principal's money or goods.[19]

These remedies will be available to the principal not only as against the agent himself but also against the agent's trustee in bankruptcy, who really represents the agent, and is in the same position as the agent if the agent becomes bankrupt.[20]

B. Rights of principal against third parties

The principal's remedies. Whether the principal can recover money or property which has come into the hands of a third party as a result of a wrongful, ie unauthorised act by the agent involves the question considered above in respect of the principal's rights against the agent.[1]

The principal may have (i), an action for wrongful interference, giving rise to a judgment for damages against the third party, where the property dealt with by such third party has been goods;[2] (ii) an action in respect of money which is still identifiable,[3] or in respect of a cheque;[4] (iii) an action for money had and received, ie, restitution or unjust enrichment, as long as the third party acted wrongfully, ie with notice of the agent's lack of authority, and the money retained its original form.

However, the right of the principal to follow his property and recover it specifically depends at common law upon the identification of the money or property in the hands of the third party with the money or property entrusted by the principal to the agent.[5] This, as already seen, is particularly important in respect of money entrusted to the agent. Subject to the position of a bona fide purchaser for value without notice of the agent's lack of authority (and certain other cases),

'A man's money is property which is protected by law ... If it is taken from the rightful owner ... without his authority he can recover the money from any person into whose hands it can be traced. ...'[6]

---

19 See *Frith v Cartland* (1865) 34 LJ Ch 301; *Broadbent v Barlow* (1861) 30 LJ Ch 569. See also Goode (1976) 92 LQR 360 especially pp 528–541, 553.

20 *Scott v Surman* (1742) Willes 400; *Re Strachan, ex p Cooke* (1876) 4 Ch D 123; and see *Taylor v Plumer* (above n 17). See also Factors Act 1889, s 12(2).

1 However, it has been suggested that the principal's right to claim from a third party the proceeds of a sale by the agent to such third party is proprietary, not contractual, and is distinct from the situation with respect to the agent: Geva 'Authority of Sale and Privity of Contract: The Proprietary Basis of the Right to Proceeds of Sale at Common Law' (1979) 25 McGill LJ 32.

2 Torts (Interference with Goods) Act 1977, s 1: 'goods' include all chattels personal other than things in action and money: ibid s 14(1). Note however the exceptions discussed below, pp 279–300, where the third party is innocent of any deliberate wrong-doing.

3 Eg, if in a box or a bag: presumably this money would qualify as 'goods'.

4 For conversion (ie now 'wrongful interference') of cheques, see *Salmond and Heuston on the Law of Torts* (20th edn 1992) pp 105–106. See *Lloyds Bank Ltd v E B Savory & Co* [1933] AC 201. Note however the Bills of Exchange Act 1882, ss 54, 55, 88, 90: Cheques Act 1957, s 4.

5 Eg *Fox v Martin* (1895) 64 LJ Ch 473 (blank transfer and share certificate); *Re European Bank Ltd, ex p Oriental Commercial Bank Ltd* (1870) 5 Ch App 358 (overdue bills). See also the references in notes 15, 16, above, p 277.

6 *Nelson v Larholt* [1948] 1 KB 339 at 342, [1947] 2 All ER 751 at 752 per Denning J.

If the money or property cannot be traced, since the original money or the proceeds of the sale of the property has or have been mingled with the third party's own money, then at common law no right in rem existed. But an equitable remedy in rem may be available to the principal as it is to beneficiaries under a trust, even where the third party has drawn out of his account, and spent some of the money.[7] However, whether the rules which apply to third parties who take from those in a *fiduciary* relationship, such as executors of a will, also apply generally to agents who wrongfully dispose of the principal's money or of money obtained by misappropriation of the principal's property, is a matter of some argument.[8]

Denial of recovery by principal. There are circumstances in which a principal who might otherwise have the right to recover his specific property from a third person who has taken it from the agent will not be entitled to do so. The principal's right to recover his property may be affected by (i) the authority given to the agent to dispose of property; (ii) the doctrine of estoppel, ie the agent's apparent authority; (iii) the Factors Act, ie the implied authority of one particular class of agents, namely, mercantile agents.[9]

Unauthorised dispositions

The first type of situation arises where the principal has authorised the agent to dispose of his property but has not authorised the particular disposal, or mode of disposal, undertaken by the agent. Can the principal argue that, as the agent has acted outside the scope of his authority, the transaction is one which can be upset by the principal? The answer would seem to be that the principal will be bound by what the agent has done, as long as the person taking from the agent does so in good faith, without knowledge of the agent's want of actual authority to do what he has done.

This is illustrated by the case of *Lloyds and Scottish Finance Ltd v*

---

7 Cf *Devaynes v Noble, Clayton's Case* (1816) 1 Mer 529, 572; *Re Hallett's Estate, Knatchbull v Hallett* (1880) 13 Ch D 696; *Sinclair v Brougham* [1914] AC 398; *Banque Belge Pour L'Etranger v Hambrouck* [1921] 1 KB 321; *United Australia Ltd v Barclays Bank Ltd* [1941] AC 1, [1940] 4 All ER 20; *Re Diplock, Diplock v Wintle* [1948] Ch 465, [1948] 2 All ER 318 (in the House of Lords, *Ministry of Health v Simpson* [1951] AC 251, [1950] 2 All ER 1137); Maudsley, 'Proprietary Remedies for the Recovery of Money' (1954) 75 LQR 234; Oakley 'The Prerequisites of an Equitable Tracing Claim' [1975] CLP 64; Goff and Jones *Law of Restitution* (4th edn 1993) pp 83–93; Fridman *Restitution* (2nd edn 1992) pp 431–433. See also Goode (1976) 92 LQR 360. The rule in *Clayton's Case* was held not to be binding and applicable in Ontario; *Re Ontario Securities Commission and Greymac Credit Corpn* (1985) 51 OR (2d) 212; affd (1986) 55 OR (2d) 673; for New Zealand, see *Re Registered Securities Ltd* [1991] 1 NZLR 545. Note the criticism and restriction of *Clayton's case* by the English Court of Appeal in *Barlow Clowes International Ltd v Vaughan* [1992] 4 All ER 22.

8 Above, pp 23–27.

9 Another pertinent doctrine, sales in market overt, was abolished by the Sale of Goods (Amendment) Act 1994 s 1.

For a discussion of the problem with special reference to motor vehicles, see Davies 'Sales law and the negotiability of motor vehicles: a legal conundrum' (1995) 15 Legal St 14.

Williamson.[10] There the principal gave a car to the agent, a motor car repairer and dealer, with instructions to obtain offers to buy it. Later, the principal authorised the agent to sell the car at whatever price he could obtain for it. The agent, in fact, represented to the defendant that the car was his to sell. As a result the defendant entered into a complex transaction with the agent, involving the sale of the car to the defendant (for resale to a third person), so that a debt owed by the agent to X could be partly paid off by the defendant, ie by his paying the purchase price for the car to X on the agent's behalf. The defendant and X acted in good faith throughout. When the principal discovered the truth he sued the defendant in conversion. It was held by the Court of Appeal that the defendant obtained a good title to the car and the principal could not recover anything. The argument that the sale by the agent was not in the ordinary course of his business as a mercantile agent (which, as will be seen, might have been relevant under the Factors Act) was not relevant in this sort of situation because there was no doubt as to the bona fides of the defendant, the buyer from the agent. The Court of Appeal made it clear that the reason for the principal's loss of title, and consequent loss of any right of action, was not estoppel, ie holding out of the agent as having authority to sell, but the express authorisation of the agent to sell the car. Hence the buyer from the agent obtained a real title: not a title arising from estoppel, which, as will be seen, has sometimes been called metaphorical.

In the light of what will emerge later in the discussion of estoppel, it would seem to be important to differentiate unauthorised dispositions by an agent who has been authorised to deal with property, but has done so improperly, from completely unauthorised dispositions of property, which may involve estoppel or the Factors Act. The former are instances of express authority, effective under the ordinary doctrine of agency to deprive the principal of his property. The latter are instances of apparent or implied authority, involving either the common law doctrine or estoppel or the statutory provisions which enlarged that doctrine in a way which will be examined in due course. Moreover, the situations considered in this section do not involve, as those in the ensuing sections do, the necessity for examining the conduct of the principal in order to decide whether he has misled the third party buying the property (or under the Factors Act taking the property by way of pledge). As will be seen, the doctrine of estoppel, and the application of the Factors Act, depend upon a certain construction being placed upon the words or acts of the principal. Where the principal has in fact authorised a particular kind of disposition of his property, as in the case discussed above, it is unnecessary to consider whether he is to be estopped from raising his original title, or whether the transaction is one within the Factors Act. This is clear from the *Williamson* case, even though, at one point,[11] Salmon LJ spoke of the principal in that case doing what he could to induce any person buying the car

10 [1965] 1 All ER 641, [1965] 1 WLR 404. A similar situation, giving rise to the same answer, occurred in a Canadian case in the Court of Appeal of Novia Scotia, *Durham v Asser* (1968) 67 DLR (2d) 574, where a car was delivered to a mercantile agent to sell at a stated price; the sale at a higher price was within the agent's authority even though the agent failed to account for what he received and did other unauthorised acts. Contrast *Mercantile Credit Co Ltd v Hamblin* [1965] 2 QB 242, [1964] 3 All ER 592, in which the owner never gave the alleged agent any actual authority to dispose of her car, and the question therefore had to be considered whether the agent obtained any *apparent* authority, giving rise to an estoppel: see below.
11 [1965] 1 All ER 641, at 645.

from the agent to believe that the agent was the owner of the car by authorising him to sell as owner. The essential point would seem to be not the inducement of third parties, but the authorisation of the sale. In the situations to be considered in the ensuing sections, it will be seen that the principal has never authorised the agent to dispose of his property by a sale.

Estoppel

If the principal has clothed the agent with all the indicia of title, or authority to act in respect of the title, thereby misleading third parties, and the agent thereupon deals with the goods as though he were in fact authorised to do so, then the agent will bind the principal by what he does.[12] In other words, the third party will acquire a good title to the property as against the principal, who will be estopped from setting up his own title and the agent's lack of authority to dispose of such title to the property. Such an estoppel may arise at common law, or by virtue of s 21(1) of the Sale of Goods Act 1979 which provides that:

> 'Subject to this Act,[13] where goods are sold by a person who is not their owner, and who does not sell them under the authority or with the consent of the owner, the buyer acquires no better title to the goods than the seller had, unless the owner of the goods is by his conduct precluded from denying the seller's authority to sell.'[14]

This section is not confined to dealings by one purporting to be an agent. The scope is wider, but it can cover the agency relationship. It was discussed in two cases which, while not themselves dealing specifically with the agency relationship, throw light upon the question now under discussion, in so far as they consider this section of the Sale of Goods Act, which is parallel to the general idea of apparent authority to deal with goods and the effects of such authority. Therefore the discussion of this section shows how the notion of investing someone with the indicia of title can be applied in the field of agency.

The first case is *Central Newbury Car Auctions Ltd v Unity Finance Ltd*,[15] in which the facts were as follows:

---

12 But he must be an agent. Hence the dispute as to whether the organisation known as HP Information Ltd was the agent of the plaintiffs, the original owner of the car let on hire purchase and subsequently sold to an innocent third party, in *Moorgate Mercantile Co Ltd v Twitchings* [1977] AC 890, [1976] 2 All ER 641. Cf above, p 13, note 11.

13 Ie the provisions in ss 22–26 (less s 22(1) which was repealed by 1994 c32 s 1), and, as provided for in the Sale of Goods Act 1979, the provisions of the Factors Act 1889. See also s 26 of the Sale of Goods Act 1893, which was preserved by the Sale of Goods Act 1979, s 63(2), Schs 3 and 4.

14 There must be a *sale*. The provision will not apply if the non-owner (agent) has only agreed to sell the goods: *Shaw v Metropolitan Police Comr* [1987] 3 All ER 405, [1987] 1 WLR 1332.

15 [1957] 1 QB 371, [1956] 3 All ER 905. This was applied by Forsyth J of the Alberta Supreme Court in *Mortimer-Rae v Barthel* (1979) 105 DLR (3d) 289, to preclude an estoppel where paintings were bought from the owner of an art gallery who had received such paintings on consignment from the true owners. Contrast two more recent Canadian cases in which estoppel succeeded and the owner lost his title: *Canaplan Leasing Inc v Dominion of Canada General Insurance Co* (1990) 69 DLR (4th) 531; *HOJ Franchise Systems Inc v Municipal Savings & Loan Corpn* (1994) 110 DLR (4th) 645.

The plaintiffs who were dealers in motor cars allowed X, a rogue, to have possession of a Morris car, under the impression that X was honest, and was purchasing the car on hire-purchase terms, arranged for him by the plaintiffs. X left with the plaintiffs, as part exchange for the Morris a Hillman car, which they believed was his, but was only his on hire-purchase terms. The Morris car was still registered in the name of A, the last owner before the plaintiffs and A's name was in the registration book, which was given to X with the car. Later X went to the first defendants, pretended to be A, and sold the Morris to them. They in turn let it to the second defendants, both defendants acting innocently and in good faith. When the plaintiffs discovered the truth they sued the defendants for conversion. The defendants pleaded that by permitting X to have possession of the car and the registration book, without sufficient enquiry being made, the plaintiffs were estopped from denying X's authority to sell the car.

As already stated this is not a case of agency at all. The alleged representation by the plaintiffs did not make X appear to be an *agent* but an *owner*. X did not contract with the first defendants as one who had authority from the plaintiffs to deal with the goods on their behalf, but as one who was *himself* entitled to deal with the goods in question. However, the problem of divestment of title by estoppel against the true owner was discussed at some length, and in view of the relevance of that problem to agency that discussion is of some importance.

Hodson LJ and Morris LJ decided against the defendants, holding that the plaintiffs' conduct did not give rise to an estoppel. Hodson LJ said:[16]

'The mere handing over of a chattel to another does not create an estoppel and there will be no estoppel unless the doctrine of ostensible ownership applies, as for example when the owner gives the recipient a document of title, or, as has often been said, invests him with the indicia of ownership.'

Morris LJ put it thus:[17]

'If the owner of a car gives mere possession of it to another (not being a mercantile agent or a purchaser)[18] he does not hold out or represent that other person as being entitled to sell.'

Did the handing over of the registration book make any difference? It did not because that book was *not* a document of title. It did not identify the owner of the car, it merely stated who was registered with the appropriate council as the person liable to pay the road fund licence tax.[19] So that it could not be assumed that the possessor of a car's registration book was the owner of the car.[20]

Hence the doctrine of investing someone with the indicia of ownership did not apply. The doctrine itself was the subject of some consideration. It had been

16 [1957] 1 QB 371 at 388, 914, [1956] 3 All ER 905.
17 Ibid at pp 396, 919.
18 Factors Act 1889; Sale of Goods Act 1979, s 25.
19 [1957] 1 QB 371, [1956] 3 All ER 905: at 387–388, 914 per Hodson LJ, 396–397, 919–920, per Morris LJ; *Joblin v Watkins and Roseveare (Motors) Ltd* [1949] 1 All ER 47.
20 [1957] 1 QB 371, [1956] 3 All ER 905: at 398, 920 per Morris LJ, 390, 915 per Hodson LJ.

suggested[1] that one who 'enabled' another to occasion loss to a third person must sustain that loss. But the idea of 'enabling' was too wide, because it opened the way to a very broad doctrine of estoppel.[2] Nor could it be said that any negligence on the part of the plaintiffs would give rise to an estoppel: for negligence to have that effect it must be negligence involving the breach of a duty of care[3] ('owed either to the whole of the public, or at any rate that section of it who might become purchasers of motor cars').[4] No such duty was owed here. To create a duty of care against negligently giving possession of a car and its registration book to someone who has no authority to sell, but who wrongly purports to sell, would mean to assert that the owner owes a duty to the whole world.[5]

This the majority of the Court of Appeal were unwilling to do. Instead they would only allow estoppel where one person had armed another with the power to go into the world as the absolute owner of property.[6] Since the registration book was not a document of title, giving it to X was not either a grant of power to him as absolute owner, or clothing him with apparent authority to sell. Thus they refused to base loss of title upon negligence, for there seemed to be no general duty of care in respect of title to property. The duty on owners was more specifically phrased. It was a duty not to grant, invest or clothe others with apparent absolute ownership, or authority to dispose of goods: and the question whether this had, or had not been done in any particular case would seem to depend upon the nature of the goods or documents allowed to come into the hands of the intermediary. Negligence was really irrelevant, for estoppel was not necessarily based on negligence. 'It cannot be' said Morris LJ[7] 'that ownership is lost on the basis of enduring punishment for carelessness'.

1 In *Lickbarrow v Mason* (1787) 2 Term Rep 63 at 70 per Ashhurst J.
2 See *Farquharson Bros & Co v King & Co* [1902] AC 325 at 332 (Lord Halsbury), 335 (Lord Macnaghten), 343 (Lord Lindley); *Jerome v Bentley* [1952] 2 All ER 114; *Central Newbury Car Auctions Ltd v Unity Finance Ltd* [1957] 1 QB 371 at 388–389, [1956] 3 All ER 905 at 915–916 per Hodson LJ. See, too, the remarks of Lord Wilberforce in *Moorgate Mercantile Co Ltd v Twitchings* [1976] 2 All ER 641 at 645, with respect to the need to show something more than inaction or silence to establish an estoppel.
3 *Swan v North British Australasian Co Ltd* (1863) 2 H & C 175 at 182 per Blackburn J; *Mercantile Bank of India Ltd v Central Bank of India Ltd* [1938] AC 287, [1938] 1 All ER 52. See, also, *Mercantile Credit Co Ltd v Hamblin* [1964] 3 All ER 592 at 602, 607, per Pearson, Salmon LJJ; *Moorgate Mercantile Co Ltd v Twitchings* [1976] 2 All ER 641 at 645–646 per Lord Wilberforce, 658–660 per Lord Edmund-Davies, 663 per Lord Fraser. Note however the suggestion by Lord Edmund-Davies, ibid at 660, that perhaps the existence of a legal duty is not a sine qua non of estoppel by conduct, referring to a suggestion in Cross *Evidence* (4th edn 1974) p 305.
4 [1957] 1 QB 371 at 389, [1956] 3 All ER 905 at 915 per Hodson LJ.
5 Ibid at 917, 392–393 per Morris LJ. Cf the majority decision (Lords Wilberforce and Salmon dissenting) that no such duty was owed by HP Information Ltd to finance companies to take care to prevent frauds in connection with hire-purchase agreements with respect to the registration of such agreements, in the *Twitchings* case. Cf *Debs v Sibec Developments Ltd* [1990] RTR 91 no duty of care owed by owner to report loss of vehicle to police; *Thomas Australia Wholesale Vehicle Trading Co Pty v Masac Finance Australia Ltd* (1985) 3 NSWLR 452, no duty of care owed by owner. Contrast *Leonard v Ielasi* (1987) 46 SASR 495.
6 *Abigail v Lapin* [1934] AC 491 at 499. For example *Rimmer v Webster* [1902] 2 Ch 163 at 173; *Fuller v Glyn, Mills, Currie & Co* [1914] 2 KB 168. The effect of delivery of a motor vehicle to a dealer was a question of fact, provided there was some evidence to support an estoppel: *Raffoul v Esanda Ltd* (1970) 92 WNNSW 971 at 976 per Jacobs and Mason JJA.
7 [1957] 1 QB 371 at 394, [1956] 3 All ER 905 at 918. Note also his point about the negligence of the *purchaser*: ibid. But see comments of Lord Edmund-Davies in the *Twitchings* case [1976] 2 All ER 641 at 658–660 with respect to negligence as constituting a set-off.

Denning LJ dissented.[8] After saying that estoppel was based upon representation or conduct which made it unfair or unjust to allow the person guilty of such representation or conduct to claim back, from an innocent purchaser, property let out of his possession, he discussed what conduct was sufficient to produce that result. He agreed that carelessness in respect of the custody of the goods or the indicia of title to them, would not suffice, nor would consent to another person's possession of the goods, or the indicia of title to them:[9]

'... unless he [ie the owner] deposits them with an agent or broker so as to clothe him with apparent authority to dispose of them.'[10]

But this alleged exception seems really to beg the whole question. Whether the person disposing of the goods is made to appear to have authority to dispose of them on somebody else's behalf, or to be the owner, seems immaterial. In both instances, for the purposes of estoppel, the test is the same, namely, what would the reasonable man regard as the power of the person with whom he deals. It is not really relevant to the third party's position to distinguish between people appearing to act for themselves or on behalf of others—except possibly with regard to the question of notice of want of authority, or lack of power to dispose of the goods. But the issue of notice, it is suggested, is the same whether agency is or is not involved in the circumstances. These may be such as to put the third party on his guard, even where the person with whom he deals appears to be owner, and is not even admitting to be acting on behalf of another.

However, Denning LJ went on to distinguish between parting with *the possession* of goods and parting with the *property* in them. The cases showed that

'if a man intends to part not only with the possession of goods but also with the property in them or the power of disposing of them—*or behaves as if he had that intention by arming the recipient with all the documents necessary to that end*—he is not entitled to recover them from an innocent purchaser.'[11]

On the facts of the case before the court, he came to the conclusion that the plaintiffs intended to part with all their property in the car when they gave it to X.[12] This was emphasised by the handing over of the registration book which,

---

8 In 1975, in the Court of Appeal in *Moorgate Mercantile v Twitchings* [1975] 3 All ER 314 at 321 he still maintained that the majority in the *Central Newbury Car* case came to the wrong decision.
9 [1957] 1 QB 371 at 380–381, [1956] 3 All ER 905 at 910.
10 Ibid at 381, 910. Cf his remarks in *Moorgate Mercantile Co Ltd v Twitchings* [1975] 3 All ER 314 at 323–324: '... when a man, by his words or his silence, or acquiescence, leads another to believe that he is not the owner and has no interest in the goods, whereupon the other buys them or sells them to an innocent purchaser. It is held that the true owner cannot afterwards assert they were his. The title to the goods is transferred to the buyer. ...'
11 [1957] 1 QB 371 at 382, [1956] 3 All ER 905 at 911, italics supplied. The italicised words are most important to the effects of agency.
12 Ibid at 383, 911. The intention was to part with it to the finance company arranging the hire-purchase terms, not to X: but that was immaterial.

according to Denning LJ, was 'the best evidence of title'.[13] The plaintiffs must have known that when they handed both car and log book to X they were arming him with complete dominion over it.[14] Hence it was unjust and unfair to allow the plaintiffs, as original owners, to go behind the innocent purchaser's assumption that X was the owner of the car and registration book. Moreover, the original owner ought to have foreseen that by his conduct in parting with the property a stranger might try to dispose of it for his own benefit. 'The original owner owed a duty to any person to whom the stranger might try to dispose of this.'[15] As Lord Wright had said:[16]

> 'The duty may be . . . to the general public of whom the person is one . . . the identity may be ascertainable only by the event, in the sense that he has turned out to be the member of the general public actually reached and affected by the conduct, negligence, representation or ostensible authority.'

Here there was no representation, there was conduct.[17] But such conduct, in Denning LJ's opinion, produced an estoppel.

It is interesting to note that the effect of the decision is twofold. First, a registration book is not relevant to determining questions of title, including the issue of apparent authority to dispose of goods. Secondly, the majority of the Court of Appeal came down against the idea that there could be negligence in respect of title to goods, in the same way as there can be negligence in respect of the physical conditions of goods. As Lord Wilberforce put it in *Moorgate Mercantile Co Ltd v Twitchings*:[18] 'English law has generally taken the robust line that a man who owns property is not under any general duty to safeguard it and that he may sue for its recovery any person into whose hands it has come.' In view of the statements by the House of Lords in this case, it seems clear that the common law will not create such a duty unless it arises independently, on some other legal basis, as for example where a negotiable instrument is involved.[19] Hence such decisions as *Jerome v Bentley & Co*,[20] where Donovan J came to the conclusion that estoppel could not be applied to deprive the owner of title to a ring entrusted to a rogue to sell, for the learned judge held that the rogue had no

---

13 Ibid at 384, 912, cf the same judge in *Pearson v Rose and Young Ltd* [1951] 1 KB 275 at 289, [1950] 2 All ER 1027 at 1033; *Bishopsgate Motor Finance Corpn Ltd v Transport Brakes Ltd* [1949] 1 KB 322, [1949] 1 All ER 37; and in *Bentworth Finance Ltd v Lubert* [1967] 2 All ER 810 at 811, where he called it 'very good evidence of title'.
14 [1957] 1 QB 371 at 385, [1956] 3 All ER 905 at 912.
15 Ibid.
16 *Mercantile Bank of India Ltd v Central Bank of India Ltd* [1938] AC 287 at 304, [1938] 1 All ER 52 at 62; quoting and commenting on Blackburn J in *Swan v North British Australasian Co Ltd* (1863) 2 H & C 175 at 182.
17 Sed quaere. Can there not be a representation by conduct? See above, pp 114–119.
18 [1976] 2 All ER 641 at 645.
19 *Wilson and Meeson v Pickering* [1946] KB 422, [1946] 1 All ER 394; *Campbell Discount Co Ltd v Gall* [1961] 1 QB 431, [1961] 2 All ER 104; see Fridman, 24 MLR 502. Cf also the comments on this in *Branwhite v Worcester Works Finance Ltd* [1968] 3 All ER 104 at 112–113, per Lord Morris, 117 per Lord Upjohn, 120 per Lord Wilberforce. But see the decision of the Court of Appeal in *Mercantile Credit Co Ltd v Hamblin* [1964] 3 All ER 592 at 602–605 per Pearson LJ, 606–607 per Salmon LJ. See also the decision of the House of Lords in *Saunders v Anglia Building Society* [1971] AC 1004, [1970] 3 All ER 961.
20 [1952] 2 All ER 114.

authority to deal with the ring at all, although the facts would seem to indicate that to the reasonable man, who was a stranger to the relationship, the rogue did have such authority (however limited it may have been as between the owner and the rogue). The reason for such unwillingness to extend the scope of estoppel may well be that to do so would deprive the Factors Act of content, ie there would be no point in those Acts giving a factor a wide implied authority if *any* person (not necessarily a 'mercantile agent' within the meaning of that Act) could be placed in a similar condition simply by his being entrusted with the goods or documents.[1] This may be the reason why 'there are very few cases of actions for conversion in which a plea by estoppel by representation has succeeded'.[2]

The second important case to be discussed, where such a plea *did* succeed, was *Eastern Distributors Ltd v Goldring*,[3] which shows how an apparent authority to dispose of goods can arise, so as to estop the real owner from asserting the agent's lack of authority.

> X the owner of a Bedford van wished to buy a Chrysler car from Y, a motor dealer. He entered into an agreement with Y, under which, in order to further a pretence to enable X to buy the car when he had not the necessary money, X signed, in blank, proposal forms and memoranda for hire-purchase agreements on both vehicles. Y completed the documents and sent them to the plaintiffs, the hire-purchase company, which, in good faith, accepted the proposal in respect of the van but rejected that in respect of the car. Y's authority was limited to acting only if *both* vehicles were dealt with by the plaintiffs. Nevertheless, Y sold the van to the plaintiffs, who sent the counterpart of the agreement to X. After some time, when X had been allowed to have the Chrysler car by Y, but had not paid anything under the hire-purchase agreement in respect of the van, Y told X that the whole transaction had been cancelled. X, who thought that he was the lawful owner of the van, which he had continued to possess throughout, thereupon sold the van to the defendant from whom the plaintiffs now claimed it.

The main and most relevant point in the case was whether s 21 of the Sale of Goods Act applied, so as to involve the passing of property in the van to the plaintiffs when they dealt with Y. If this were so, then X would have had no title in the van to pass to the defendants. It was held by the Court of Appeal (in a

---

1 *Johnson v Crédit Lyonnais Co* (1877) 3 CPD 32 at 36 per Cockburn CJ. Cf the statement by Lord Wilberforce in the *Twitchings* case [1976] 2 All ER 641 at 646 that the provisions of that statute and others should warn us that the duty of care should not be stretched so widely as to make it a universal duty on the party of property owners to safeguard others against loss.

2 *Mercantile Bank of India Ltd v Central Bank of India Ltd* [1938] AC 287 at 302, [1938] 1 All ER 52 at 60 per Lord Wright. But two Australian judges thought that it would be 'easy' to envisage circumstances in which the true owner who had left a vehicle with a motor vehicle dealer would be precluded from denying the dealer's authority to sell: per Jacobs and Mason JJA in *Raffoul v Esanda Ltd* (1970) 92 WNNSW 971 at 976: sed quaere? Estoppel succeeded in *Canaplan Leasing Inc v Dominion of Canada General Insurance Co* (1990) 69 DLR (4th) 531: but the owner *intended* that the 'dealer' should sell, although the dealer sold to the 'wrong' person.

3 [1957] 2 QB 600, [1957] 2 All ER 525 (distinguished in *Mercantile Credit Co Ltd v Hamblin* [1965] 2 QB 242, [1964] 3 All ER 592).

judgment given by Devlin J) that the section did apply, therefore the plaintiffs were entitled to the return of the van.

The question was, what was the effect of X's dealings with Y? X never really sold the van to Y, so Y could not really sell it to the plaintiffs. But X's relationship with Y raised the issue of Y's power to dispose of the van. The way the common law dealt with this sort of situation was not by the application of the doctrine of estoppel, but by the application of the idea (based on 'mercantile convenience') that good title was acquired by a buyer who bought in good faith from a man who apparently had been given by the true owner the right to dispose of the goods. This was not a title by estoppel; it was like the acquisition of title to a negotiable instrument or goods bought in market overt. Unlike title by estoppel, said the court, such a title was good against the whole world.[4] Thus it was through the doctrine of 'apparent authority' that the buyer acquired a good title. The most important example of such authority was the factor.

> 'The nature of whose position was to be taken as giving him an *implied authority* to sell goods entrusted to him: he was able to pass a good title to a buyer, even if, by reason of a special limitation put by the principal upon his powers he had no actual authority to do so.'[5]

This was affected by the Factors Acts which codified and amplified the common law.[6] The Factors Act did not apply to the present case, since Y did not have possession of the van. But

> 'there are other ways besides the possession of goods in which a man can be clothed with apparent ownership or apparent authority to sell.'[7]

The doctrine of apparent authority did not apply at common law if nothing more than possession was shown. There had to be other evidence of holding out.[8] This principle or doctrine was concurrent with the Factors Acts and it applied where the agent was armed

> 'with some indicia which made it appear that he was either the owner or had the right to sell.'[9]

This would apply

> 'to any form or representation or holding out of apparent ownership or the right to sell.'[10]

And this was embodied in s 21 of the Sale of Goods Act, which expressed the old principle that apparent authority to sell is an exception to the maxim nemo dat

---

4 [1957] 2 QB 600 at 607, [1957] 2 All ER 525 at 529 (cf *Lloyds and Scottish Finance Ltd v Williamson* [1965] 1 All ER 641, [1965] 1 WLR 404). But the position of a purchaser for value without notice of the 'title by estoppel' was left in doubt.
5 Ibid at 608, 530; italics supplied.
6 Ibid at 608–610, 530–531, referring to *Fuentes v Montis* (1868) LR 3 CP 268 at 276 per Willes J. The latter case was affd in LR 4 CP 93.
7 [1957] 2 QB 600 at 610, [1957] 2 All ER 525 at 531.
8 Ibid citing *Martini v Coles* (1813) 1 M & S 140 at 150 per Bayley J; *Boyson v Coles* (1817) 6 M & S 14.
9 [1957] 2 QB 600, at 610, [1957] 2 All ER 525 at 531.
10 Ibid.

quod non habet,[11] so that if the owner of goods is precluded from denying authority, the buyer will in fact acquire a better title than the seller. The Court of Appeal doubted whether this principle was really part of the law of estoppel, although it had been called 'common law estoppel'.[12] However, whatever it was,[13] the effect of the principle was 'to transfer a real title and not merely a metaphorical title by estoppel'.[14] How far the principle extended was uncertain and the Court of Appeal did not want to discuss that. In particular the court was unwilling to discover whether the principle covered the exercise of every sort of apparent authority in relation to the sale of goods or whether it was confined to apparent authority to sell. The principle covered the facts of the case before the court, which was sufficient.

Several features of this case require comment. In the first place, it is suggested that the judgment confuses *apparent* and *implied* authority. For, as is evident from the passages referred to, what the court did was to treat the *implied authority* of a *factor* or other *mercantile agent*[15] to sell goods, which is derived from his position as factor, etc, as the exemplar, or most common application, of the doctrine of the *apparent authority* of *anybody* to sell goods, which arises from the particular circumstances of any given case, ie does not depend upon the pursuance of a particular occupation. However, the position of the *factor* or other mercantile agent is a special one.[16] It arises from his particular business, and what the owner-principal can be taken to have agreed to, at the time of giving the factor, etc, possession of the goods.[17] But the apparent authority to dispose of property which is exercised by non-mercantile agents is not derived from the pursuance of any particular business, nor from any implied consent on the part of the owner, nor from the possession of the goods. It is based on the idea that X has clothed Y with the indicia of ownership or authority to dispose of ownership.[18]

11 Ibid at 611, 532; cf ibid at 607, 529.
12 *Lowther v Harris* [1927] 1 KB 393.
13 The court distinguished it from 'equitable estoppel' which applied chiefly in relation to the sale of land, and possibly did not bind a purchaser for value without notice: [1957] 2 QB 600 at 607, [1957] 2 All ER 525 at 529. Cf Lord Edmund-Davies in *Moorgate Mercantile Co Ltd v Twitchings* [1976] 2 All ER 641 at 658.
14 [1957] 2 QB 600 at 611, [1957] 2 All ER 525 at 532; cf Pearson LJ in *Mercantile Credit Co Ltd v Hamblin* [1964] 3 All ER 592 at 601. In the *Twitchings* case, above, Lord Edmund-Davies differentiated the effects of the statute, by virtue of which the buyer acquired a good title to goods, from what he called 'a *Mercantile Credit Co Ltd v Hamblin* right to plead an estoppel'.
15 Below, pp 290–299.
16 Above, pp 40–42, 79–80.
17 At least now, after the passing of the Factors Acts. Before that legislation it may be that factors, and other mercantile agents, could be said to have had an *apparent* rather than an *implied* authority to sell goods not their own. The publicity given to the position of factors, etc by the Factors Acts, it is suggested, would indicate that their authority to sell is now *implied* (by something like custom or trade usage?): therefore there is need for a change in the description of that authority.
18 *Eastern Distributors Ltd v Goldring* [1957] 2 QB 600 at 610, [1957] 2 All ER 525 at 531; cf the *Central Newbury Cars* case [1957] 1 QB 371 at 388, [1956] 3 All ER 905 at 914, per Hodson LJ (cited above, p 282); or on negligence where a duty of care is owed: see above, p 285. Note Lord Denning's contention, *Moorgate Mercantile Co Ltd v Twitchings* [1975] 3 All ER 314 at 321, that 'estoppel by negligence' is a misleading phrase. It is only one aspect of 'estoppel by conduct'. Contrast cases such as *Lloyds and Scottish Finance Co Ltd v Williamson* [1965] 1 All ER 641, [1965] 1 WLR 404 above, p 280, where the agent's authority is *express*, ie real, not implied or apparent.

Hence, it is suggested, the principles contained in the Factors Act can rightly be said not to involve the doctrine of estoppel, since the mercantile agent, by virtue of his position, can pass what the Court of Appeal called 'a real title', which will bind not only the principal and his privies, but the whole world. But the principle of *apparent authority*, which is distinct from the implied authority contained now in the Factors Act (but formerly created and circumscribed by the common law), does involve the doctrine of estoppel, as the Court of Appeal recognised in the *Central Newbury Cars* case. For it treats someone with no real title to goods as able to confer title to another: such title must be what the court in the *Goldring* case called 'a metaphorical title by estoppel'. It is respectfully suggested, therefore, that the Court of Appeal in that case were really dealing with the deprivation of an owner's title by estoppel resulting from the holding out of another person as his agent with apparent authority to dispose of goods: and the effect of the case is to decide that such a title by estoppel (at least in the case of sale of *goods*) is valid against the whole world.[19] If this suggestion is not accepted, then it would appear that there is a conflict between these two decisions of the Court of Appeal.

Comparison of the facts of these two cases produces perplexity. The principal's loss of title is based on his arming the agent with the indicia of title or authority to sell. In the *Central Newbury Cars* case, giving the 'agent' possession of both car and registration book was held to be insufficient. Yet, in the *Goldring* case, the 'agent' did not have possession of either car or registration book. All he had were certain documents which 'enabled him to represent to the plaintiffs that he was owner of the Bedford car and had the right to sell it'.[20] It is suggested that it is very strange to find that possession of documents (without the vehicle) can found an estoppel, when possession of the vehicle and the registration book cannot. Since the whole idea of apparent authority has repeatedly been said to be founded on commercial convenience, it is surprising to find that innocent dealers can transact with impunity with documents relating to a vehicle, without enquiring into the genuineness of the claim of the person having the documents that he can deal with the vehicle, but cannot transact, without doing so to their detriment, with the vehicle itself, even where there is some additional fact, ie the registration book, which might reasonably indicate that the possessor of the vehicle has the right (ie the power) to deal with the title to the vehicle. Admittedly, there are arguments against the easy deprivation of the true owner's title by the acts of rogues, who acquire possession of the vehicle and the registration book. Yet it might be thought that similar arguments apply to the case of rogues who obtain the true owner's signature to documents such as those in the *Goldring* case. On the other hand, the argument that a person who negligently signs documents thereby should be estopped from denying the authority of the

19 There is a possible distinction between goods and land, which explains why the Court of Appeal did not want to utilise the doctrine of estoppel in this case, [1957] 2 QB 600 at 607, [1957] 2 All ER 525 at 529. But it is suggested that estoppel is at the root of the cases, even though they are justified, as the Court of Appeal said, on the ground of mercantile convenience.
20 [1957] 2 QB 600 at 611, [1957] 2 All ER 525 at 532. Contrast the view taken of the facts in *Mercantile Credit Co Ltd v Hamblin* [1965] 2 QB 242, [1964] 3 All ER 592.

person to whom he gave the documents, might well apply to persons who negligently part with possession of vehicles together with registration books.[1]

The Factors Act

Reference has already been made to 'mercantile agents', and to the power of such agents to affect the principal's legal position through the exercise of an implied authority which may be more extensive than the actual authority entrusted to them by the principal. Here it is proposed to discuss in greater detail the provision of the Factors Act 1889, under which this implied authority and the power it involves, arises.[2]

The Act applies to 'mercantile agents', the meaning of which expression has already been discussed.[3] In respect of such agents the Act amplifies and does not derogate from the powers exercisable by an agent at common law.[4] The Act (without affecting the doctrine of apparent authority) defines situations in which certain agents, without express authority to do so, may be impliedly authorised to dispose of the title to goods really belonging to their principals.[5]

The most important provision of the Factors Act relates to the power of a mercantile agent to affect the title of his principal as a result of dispositions made of the principal's goods by such an agent. By s 2(1) of the Act:

> 'Where a mercantile agent is, with the consent of the owner, in possession of goods or of the documents of title to goods, any sale, pledge, or other disposition of the goods, made by him when acting in the ordinary course of business of a mercantile agent, shall, subject to the provisions of this Act, be as valid as if he were expressly authorised by the owner of the goods to make the same: provided that the person taking under the disposition acts in good faith, and has not at the time of the disposition notice that the person making the disposition has not authority to make the same.'

1 The difficulties resulting from fraudulent dealings with property, which involve one of two innocent parties in suffering loss, viz the original owner or the purchaser from the rogue, were considered in the Twelfth Report of the Law Reform Committee (1966, Cmnd 2958). The possibility of apportionment of loss between the innocent parties was discussed and rejected: paras 8–12. In the meantime, the special instance of transactions with motor vehicles which are being bought on hire purchase is dealt with by Part III of the Hire-Purchase Act 1964 (preserved with some terminological changes, by the Consumer Credit Act 1974, s 192, Sch 4); *Benjamin's Sale of Goods* (4th edn 1992) paras 7-086–106.
2 See also, Fridman *Sale of Goods* (1966) pp 112–116: Fridman *Sale of Goods in Canada* (4th edn 1995) pp 128–134; *Benjamin's Sale of Goods* (4th edn 1992) paras 7-033–056; Twelfth Report of Law Reform Committee (1966, Cmnd 2958) paras 17–25.
3 Above, pp 40–42.
4 Section 13. *Note* that the Factors Act is preserved by the Sale of Goods Act 1979, s 21(2).
5 It should be noted that, whatever the Act says as to the effect that exceeding express authority on the part of the agent may have upon the position of third parties, the Act does not authorise the agent to exceed his actual authority, or exempt him from liability for such excess: s 12(1).

It has been held, in Canada, that a purchaser from a mercantile agent under these provisions will take precedence over prior encumbrances placed by the agent himself over the goods: *Sheriff of Vegreville v St Bernard de Lafond Savings & Credit Union Ltd* (1982) 42 AR 192. Also that retail financiers of sales, as well as ordinary consumer purchasers are within the scope of this protection under the Act: *Allis-Chalmers Credit Corpn of Canada Ltd v Lem's Manufacturing Co* (1983) 45 AR 175.

This section requires elaboration, illustration, and comment.

Mercantile agents. It only applies to 'mercantile agents'. Such an agent is

'a mercantile agent having in the customary course of his business as such agent authority either to sell goods or to consign goods for the purpose of sale, or to raise money on the security of goods' (s 1(1)).[6]

The exact scope of this definition is not clear. Whether someone is a mercantile agent is really a question of fact, as long as the person in question, in the customary course of his business, usually has authority to do the things specified in the section.[7] This means, at the very least, that the person in question must sell goods on behalf of others and not himself.[8] But an agent can be a mercantile agent even if he only acts for one principal, and for one transaction,[9] ie even if he is not engaged in any commercial business, as long as he is given goods with the authority to sell, or dispose of, in accordance with the terms of the section, at the times the goods are given him, and not afterwards.[10]

Possession. The agent must have possession of goods, or the documents of title to goods. The Act states that

'A person shall be deemed to be in possession of goods or of the documents of title to goods, where the goods or documents are in his actual custody or are held by any other person subject to his control or for him or on his behalf' (s 1(2)).

But such possession, in order to bring into operation the provisions of the Act, must be possession as a *mercantile agent*, ie with one of the kinds of authority specified in s 1(1). This was held to be the law by Chapman J in *Astley Industrial Trust Ltd v Miller*[11] following more recent dicta in the Court of Appeal as against

---

6 References to sections, unless otherwise indicated, are references to sections of the Factors Act 1889.
7 Contrast *Wood v Rowcliffe* (1846) 6 Hare 183 at 191 with *Weiner v Harris* [1910] 1 KB 285. Cf the discussion in the Canadian case of *Consolidated Motors Ltd v Wagner* (1967) 63 DLR (2d) 266, which was concerned with a car dealer repossessing a car under a recourse agreement. See also three other Canadian cases: *Re Funduk & Horncastle* (1973) 39 DLR (3d) 94; *Terra Power Tractor Co v Chapman* (1977) 2 Alta LR (2d) 247; *Bank of Nova Scotia v Tissington* (1981) 31 AR 332, where differing results ensued.
8 *Belvoir Finance Co Ltd v Harold G Cole & Co Ltd* [1969] 2 All ER 904, [1969] 1 WLR 1877.
9 *Lowther v Harris* [1927] 1 KB 393; cf *St John v Horvat* (1994) 113 DLR (4th) 670. Not if the transaction is one for the sake of convenience between friends: *Budberg v Jerwood* (1934) 51 TLR 99.
10 *Heap v Motorists' Advisory Agency Ltd* [1923] 1 KB 577 at 588 per Lush J. The English cases 'establish the proposition that a person who is not engaged in any commercial business whatsoever may be a mercantile agent within the Act simply by that person being appointed agent of another to act as a mercantile agent customarily acts': per Aikins J of the Supreme Court of British Columbia in *Thorsen v Capital Credit Corpn* (1962) 37 DLR (2d) 317 at 327.
11 [1968] 2 All ER 36: cf also *Belvoir Finance Co Ltd v Harold G Cole & Co Ltd* [1969] 2 All ER 904, [1969] 1 WLR 1877. Cf *Consolidated Motors Ltd v Wagner* (1967) 63 DLR (2d) 266: *Sheriff of Edmonton v Kozak* (1966) 54 WWR 677; *Bank of Montreal v Young* (1977) 3 Alta LR (2d) 11; *Bank of Nova Scotia v Tissington* (1981) 31 AR 332. On this, see Twelfth Report of the Law Reform Committee (1966, Cmnd 2958) para 18.

an earlier decision of Channell J.[12] Hence in that case a self-drive car hire firm did not have possession of a vehicle, which they were buying on hire purchase, in the capacity of mercantile agents. So, too, in an earlier case, delivering furniture to an agent for displaying in a showroom, without giving the agent authority to sell, did not amount to giving the agent possession under the Act, since the agent was not a mercantile agent.[13]

Delivery of goods to someone who would normally be a mercantile agent, but without giving the agent any one of the kinds of authority in s 1(1) of the Act, will not amount to giving the agent the required possession. Thus delivering a vehicle to a garage proprietor for *repair* only, not for sale, did not bring the agent within the Act.[14] To enable the Act to operate there must be a consent to the possession of the goods by a mercantile agent as a mercantile agent.[15]

> 'That means that the owner must consent to the agent having them for a purpose which is in some way or other connected with his business as a mercantile agent.'[16]

'Goods' under the Act includes 'wares and merchandise' (s 1(3)), but excludes stocks and shares, negotiable instruments and the like. 'Documents of title' includes:

> 'any bill of lading, dock warrant, warehousekeeper's certificate and warrant or order for the delivery of goods, and any other document used in the ordinary course of business as proof of the possession or control of goods,

Note that the onus of proving that the agent was in possession as a mercantile agent is on the party seeking the protection of the Act: *Stadium Finance Ltd v Robbins* [1962] 2 QB 664, [1962] 2 All ER 633; *Dalgleish v IAC Ltd* (1977) 2 Alta LR (2d) 261; *Bank of Nova Scotia v Tissington* (1981) 31 AR 332. Once this is discharged, the original owner then must prove that such possession was not with his consent: *Bank of Nova Scotia v Tissington*, above.

12 In *Turner v Sampson* (1911) 27 TLR 200 at 202, Channel J said that whether possession had been obtained as a mercantile agent did not depend upon the *actual* authority of the mercantile agent, but upon what authority such an agent had in the ordinary course of his business, ie his customary authority. But it would seem from dicta of Denning LJ in *Pearson v Rose and Young Ltd* [1950] 2 All ER 1027 at 1032 and Willmer LJ in *Stadium Finance Ltd v Robbins* [1962] 2 All ER 633 at 638, that the better view (accepted, as stated above, in the recent cases) is that the express, not implied, authority given to the mercantile agent will determine this issue. The other members of the Court of Appeal in the *Robbins* case decided the case on a different ground, viz, that the sale of a car without the ignition key or registration book was not a sale in the ordinary course of his business as a mercantile agent: see below, p 299.

13 *Brown & Co v Bedford Pantechnicon Co Ltd* (1889) 5 TLR 449. Nor did giving an agent a car to obtain offers, without also giving him the ignition key or registration book, *Stadium Finance Ltd v Robbins* [1962] 2 All ER 633 at 638 per Willmer LJ. Cf *Traders Group Ltd v Gouthro* (1969) 9 DLR (3d) 387, dealer in possession of a car bought for his personal use: not in possession as a mercantile agent.

14 *Staffs Motor Guarantee Ltd v British Wagon Co Ltd* [1934] 2 KB 305, [1934] All ER Rep 322; *McManus v Eastern Ford Sales Ltd* (1981) 128 DLR (3d) 246. Cf also *Cole v North Western Bank* (1875) LR 10 CP 354, where the warehousing of goods with a warehouseman who was also a broker did not give him possession within the Act.

15 *Oppenheimer v Frazer and Wyatt* [1907] 1 KB 519 at 529 per Channell J; *Pearson v Rose and Young Ltd* [1951] 1 KB 275 at 288, [1950] 2 All ER 1027 at 1032 per Denning LJ; *Dalgleish v IAC Ltd* (1977) 2 Alta LR (2d) 261.

16 Ibid. This means consent to the agent's having possession, not necessarily to the sale, so that even if a sale required the prior approval of the owner, the transaction would still be within the Act: *Sheriff of Edmonton v Kozak* (1966) 54 WWR 677.

or authorising or purporting to authorise either by endorsement or by delivery, the possessor of the document to transfer or receive goods thereby represented' (s 1(4)).

The expression 'any other document' has caused difficulty, especially in relation to the registration book of a vehicle.[17] The general trend of the decisions is against treating the registration book as a document of title.[18] However, one question which has been raised is whether a vehicle without a registration book is 'goods' within the meaning of the Act. In *Pearson v Rose and Young Ltd*:[19]

> P gave a car dealer who was a mercantile agent (A) possession of his car to sell. Later A, by a trick, kept possession of the registration book of the car, having formed the intention of selling the car for his own benefit. He later sold the car with its registration book to X who bought in good faith, from whom eventually it came to the defendants.

When P sued the defendants for the return of the car, it was held by the Court of Appeal that the Factors Act did not apply, therefore P could recover the car. This was because, although P had consented to A's having possession of the *car*, he did not consent to A's having possession of the registration book.[20] Since, for the Act to apply, the sale would have to be 'in the ordinary course of business';[1] and since the sale of a car without its registration book was not a sale in the ordinary course of business, because the price of the car would be substantially reduced thereby: therefore, the sale by A would not affect P's title. This was the reasoning of Somervell LJ.[2] Denning LJ adopting the view that the registration book was the best indicia of title,[3] said that for the Factors Act to operate the agent would have to have consent to the possession of the car and the registration book, because a sale without a registration book was not a sale in the ordinary course of business. 'Goods' in the Act meant the car together with the registration book.[4] This point *seems* to have been adopted by Vaisey J, who considered that in

---

17 Cf the discussion in *Central Newbury Car Auctions Ltd v Unity Finance Co Ltd* [1957] 1 QB 371, [1956] 3 All ER 905.

18 *Joblin v Watkins and Roseveare (Motors) Ltd* [1949] 1 All ER 47; *Bishopsgate Motor Finance Corpn v Transport Brakes Ltd* [1949] 1 KB 322, [1949] 1 All ER 37; *Pearson v Rose and Young Ltd* [1951] 1 KB 275, [1950] 2 All ER 1027; *J Sargent (Garages) Ltd v Motor Auctions (West Bromwich) Ltd* [1977] RTR 121; *Beverley Acceptances Ltd v Oakley* [1982] RTR 417. In Canada it has been held that a sale without a certificate of registration is a sale in the ordinary course of his business by a mercantile agent, so as to enable him to pass title under the Factors Act: *Durham v Asser* (1968) 67 DLR (2d) 574, a decision of the Nova Scotia Court of Appeal. Cf *Astley Industrial Trust Ltd v Miller* [1968] 2 All ER 36 which was concerned with the sale of a new, not second-hand car: hence the failure to give a log book did not take the transaction out of the ordinary course of business, since the log book was with the registration authority for registration and taxation of the car.

19 [1951] 1 KB 275, [1950] 2 All ER 1027.

20 On the question of 'consent', see below, pp 294–296.

1 Below, pp 298–299.

2 [1951] 1 KB 275 at 283–284, [1950] 2 All ER 1027 at 1029; cf as to the 'price' point, ibid at 289, 1033 per Denning LJ. Contrast *Folkes v King* [1923] 1 KB 282.

3 [1951] 1 KB 275 at 289–290, [1950] 2 All ER 1027 at 1033: cf above, p 285.

4 [1951] 1 KB 275 at 290, [1950] 2 All ER 1027 at 1033.

selling a car without a registration book, the agent would be acting as if he sold a car with only three wheels.[5]

The proposition that a vehicle is not 'goods' within the Act unless the registration book is included with the vehicle has been criticised on a number of grounds. Thus, if a registration book is not a document of title, the possession of the registration book would seem to be irrelevant to the question whether the agent has possession of the vehicle. If a registration book is a 'document of title' within the Act,[6] then it makes s 2(1) read 'in possession of goods *and* of the documents of title' (instead of 'or').[7] Moreover, as Goodhart argued,[8] can the vehicle be transferred if the registration book is lost; what happens if there are duplicates of registration books; is the sale of a car without its registration book within the Sale of Goods Act? Powell criticised the reasoning of Denning LJ (and possibly, by implication, that of Vaisey J) on the grounds that whether the mercantile agent can pass good title to the vehicle without the registration book is irrelevant to the definition of 'the intrinsic character of goods' for the purpose of s 2(1).[9]

In this respect it is interesting to note that in *Stadium Finance Ltd v Robbins*,[10] two members of the Court of Appeal were prepared to hold that a car without its ignition key was none the less 'goods' within the meaning of the Factors Act (as was a car without its registration book), since the word 'goods' must include all chattels of which physical possession is possible, notwithstanding that they are not easily moveable without wheels or an ignition key, or are subject to difficulties in satisfying a purchaser in the absence of a registration book.[11]

Consent. The third requirement of s 2(1) is that the mercantile agent should be in possession of the goods, etc, 'with the consent of the owner'. In normal cases of bailment the consent of the owner will be rightfully obtained.[12] Moreover, from the fact of possession it is possible to conclude that such possession was obtained with the consent of the owner. Indeed the Act provides that:

> 'For the purposes of the Act the consent of the owner shall be presumed in the absence of evidence to the contrary' (s 2(4)).[13]

Moreover, the Act deals with two special points about consent. Thus:

> 'Where a mercantile agent has, with the consent of the owner, been in possession of goods or of documents of title to goods, any sale, pledge, or

---

5 Ibid at 291, 1034. For a contrary view, see below. For a case in which delivery of the log book with the car was essential, though in relation to another matter, see *Bentworth Finance Ltd v Lubert* [1968] 1 QB 680, [1967] 2 All ER 810.
6 Which was possibly Denning LJ's view.
7 Hanbury *Principles of Agency* (2nd edn) p 112.
8 67 LQR 7.
9 *Law of Agency* (2nd edn) pp 228–229.
10 [1962] 2 QB 664, [1962] 2 All ER 633.
11 Ibid at 639 per Danckwerts LJ.
12 This will not be so if the transaction was illegal, eg in breach of statutory regulations dealing with hire purchase: see *Belvoir Finance Co Ltd v Harold G Cole & Co Ltd* [1969] 2 All ER 904, [1967] 1 WLR 1877, where the fact that the alleged mercantile agent was in possession of the vehicle sold to the defendant under illegal hire-purchase agreements was one of the grounds for refusing to allow the operation of the Factors Act.
13 See, eg *Stadium Finance Ltd v Robbins*, above. But note the shifting of the onus of proof referred to above, p 292, note 11.

other disposition, which would have been valid if the consent had continued, shall be valid notwithstanding the determination of the consent: provided that the person taking under the disposition has not at the time thereof notice that the consent has been determined' (s 2(2)).[14]

Furthermore, by the next sub-section, s 2(3):

'Where a mercantile agent has obtained possession of any documents of title to goods by reason of his being or having been, with the consent of the owner in possession of the goods represented thereby, or of any other documents of title to the goods, his possession of the first-mentioned documents shall, for the purposes of this Act, be deemed to be with the consent of the owner.'

The real problems in connection with this part of the Act have arisen in cases in which the consent of the owner to the agent's possession has been obtained by deceit practised by the agent. Does it matter, for this purpose, whether the agent has been guilty of what used to be called larceny by a trick or obtaining by false pretences? In the former, the owner parts with *possession*: in the latter the owner parts with *property* or the power to deal with property (in both cases of course as a result of fraud).[15] There was considerable difference of opinion on this. Some judges thought that if the agent had been guilty of larceny, the Factors Act did not apply because there was no true consent to the agent's possession.[16] Others thought that the criminal law distinction had no place in the operation of the Factors Act.[17] The latter view now seems to have been adopted by the Court of Appeal, obiter, in *Pearson v Rose and Young Ltd*.[18] The whole point is that the purpose of the Act was to protect innocent purchasers from agents who have been put in the position of being able to deal with goods as if they had authority to do so, as a result of some conscious act of the real owner. The *act* of the owner is the important feature, *not* the owner's real state of mind. Hence, whether he intended to pass possession or property is immaterial to the Factors Act.[19]

One point should be noted. The consent in question in s 2(1) of the Factors Act, must be the consent of the *owner*. This was held in a Canadian case[20] to mean the

---

14 See *Moody v Pall Mall Deposit and Forwarding Co Ltd* (1917) 33 TLR 306. This provision overruled the decision in *Fuentes v Montis* (1868) LR 3 CP 268; affd LR 4 CP 93.
15 Cf Fridman 'Property in the Law of False Pretences' (1957) 20 MLR 464. On the question of mistake in such instances, in so far as it may be material, since the Theft Act 1968 see Glanville Williams 'Mistake in the Law of Theft' [1977] CLJ 62.
16 *Oppenheimer v Frazer and Wyatt* [1907] 2 KB 50 at 71 per Fletcher Moulton LJ; *Oppenheimer v Attenborough & Son* [1908] 1 KB 221 at 232 per Kennedy LJ; *Lake v Simmons* [1926] 2 KB 51 at 72–73 per Atkin LJ. See also the same case in House of Lords [1927] AC 487 at 509–510 per Lord Sumner; *Heap v Motorists' Advisory Agency Ltd* [1923] 1 KB 577.
17 *Folkes v King* [1923] 1 KB 282 at 296–297 per Bankes LJ at 305 per Scrutton LJ.
18 [1951] 1 KB 275 at 284–286, [1950] 2 All ER 1027 at 1030–1031, per Somervell LJ: at 287–288, 1031–1032, per Denning LJ.
19 It should be noted that conviction of the offender, whatever the offence, will not now revest title in the original owner, since the repeal of s 24 of the Sale of Goods Act 1893 by the Theft Act 1968, s 33(3), Sch 3, Part III. The changes brought about in the criminal law by this latter Act could probably have rendered the distinction of no relevance in the law relating to mercantile agents in any event: see eg, the definition of 'appropriate' in the Theft Act 1968, s 3(1).
20 *Sheriff of Vegreville v St Bernard de Lafond Savings & Credit Union Ltd* (1982) 42 AR 192.

legal owner in that instance the credit union which held a chattel mortgage on the vehicle in issue. When the vehicle was sold to a dealership it was held that the dealer did not become the legal owner for this purpose. Therefore a sale by the dealer was not protected under the Act. In *Lloyds Bank Ltd v Bank of America National Trust and Savings Association*[1] it was argued that the Act did not apply. There:

> A company pledged bills of lading with a bank as security for bills of exchange and advances. The bank handed the bills of lading back to the company on terms contained in trust receipts. The company was to sell the goods, in trust for the bank. Instead the company pledged the bills of lading with X, who took in good faith and without notice of the bank's rights. The bank sued X for the bills of lading.

It was argued that the bank was not owner of the bills, since the bank was only a pledgee. But it was held that the Factors Act did apply, since the company had obtained consent to the possession of the bills of lading, not from the *sole* 'owner' of the goods or the bills, but from someone with whom the company's right of ownership had become divided. Thus the mercantile agent, it would appear, can have an interest in the property and yet be in possession of it with the 'owner's' consent.[2]

Protected dispositions. The fourth point to consider under the section is the meaning of the words 'any sale, pledge or other disposition of the goods'.[3] Such dispositions are protected under the Act. The power to affect the owner's title by making a pledge of the goods was given to mercantile agents by the Acts. Indeed the Acts were enacted to revise the decision in *Paterson v Tash*[4] against the possession of such a power by a factor. However, several provisions of the Act are relevant to the question of pledging. They read as follows:

> 'The expression "pledge" shall include any contract pledging, or giving a lien or security on goods, whether in consideration of an original advance or of any further or continuing advance or of any pecuniary liability' (s 1(5)).

This includes second pledges[5] and pledges where the advance is made to a third

---

1 [1938] 2 KB 147, [1938] 2 All ER 63 (applied in *Beverley Acceptances Ltd v Oakley* [1982] RTR 417).

2 See [1938] 2 KB 147 at 161, [1938] 2 All ER 63 at 70, per Greene MR.

3 On what is meant by the phrase 'or other disposition' reference may be made to a case decided under the similar provisions of the Sale of Goods Act; *Worcester Works Finance Ltd v Cooden Engineering Co Ltd* [1972] 1 QB 210, [1971] 3 All ER 708; on which see Preston 'Dispositions under Section 25(1) of the Sale of Goods Act 1893' (1972) 88 LQR 238.

   A constructive delivery of goods may suffice under provisions of the Sale of Goods Act dealing with sales, etc, by sellers or buyers in possession: *Garner's Motor Centre (Newcastle) Pty LW v Natwest Wholesale Australia Pty Ltd* (1987) 163 CLR 236. Presumably it would be equally effective under the Factors Act. Cf below, p 300, note 3.

4 (1743) 2 Stra 1178. See also *Fuentes v Montis* (1868) LR 3 CP 268 at 277. See *Pulkownik v Public Trustee and Acaben Pty Ltd* [1979] 1 NSWLR 716.

5 *Portalis v Tetley* (1867) LR 5 Eq 140.

party by the pledgee, at the mercantile agent's request.[6] It does not include entrusting goods to an auctioneer for sale, even if the auctioneer advances money.[7]

> 'A pledge of the documents of title to goods shall be deemed to be a pledge of the goods' (s 3).

> 'Where a mercantile agent pledges goods as security for a debt or liability due from the pledgor to the pledgee before the time of the pledge, the pledgee shall acquire no further right to the goods than could have been enforced by the pledgee at the time of the pledge' (s 4).

Moreover

> 'Nothing in this Act ... shall prevent the owner of goods pledged by an agent from having the right to redeem the goods at any time before the sale thereof, on satisfying the claim for which the goods were pledged, and paying the agent, if by him required, any money in respect of which the agent would by law be entitled to retain the goods or the documents of title thereto or any of them, by way of lien as against the owner, or from recovering from any person with whom the goods have been pledged any balance of money remaining in his hands as the produce of the sale of goods after deducting the amount of his lien' (s 12(2)).[8]

And by s 5:

> 'Where goods are pledged by a mercantile agent in consideration of the delivery or transfer of other goods, or of a document of title to goods, or of a negotiable security, the pledgee shall acquire no right or interest in the goods so pledged in excess of the value of the goods, documents, or security when so delivered or transferred in exchange.'

The purpose of all these provisions is to regulate the title of the pledgee, and the interest and liabilities of the owner, by restricting the extent to which the mercantile agent can deprive the owner of his goods or documents of title to goods. Much of this really brings in the question of *consideration*, for the interest and claim of the pledge are governed by the consideration given for the pledge (s 5), whether it is present or past (s 4). In this respect it is important to notice that s 5 also makes it clear that pledges and other dispositions under s 2(1) must be for valuable consideration. The section begins by saying:

---

6 *Sheppard v Union Bank of London* (1862) 7 H & N 661. But a pledge of the principal's chattel will not be protected if it is pledged with *other* chattels: *Kaltenbach v Lewis* (1885) 10 App Cas 617; *Thoresen v Capital Credit Corpn* (1962) 37 DLR (2d) 317 at 341–346. See also *Industrial Acceptance Corpn v Whitehall Finance Corpn Ltd* (1966) 57 DLR (2d) 670.
7 *Waddington & Sons v Neale & Sons* (1907) 96 LT 786.
8 For an illustration of the effect of this provision (in relation to a statutory provision dealing with records of a particular pawn) see *Pulkownik v Public Trustee and Acaben Pty Ltd* [1979] 1 NSWLR 716. The Factors Act provision was subject to the provision in the New South Wales Pawnbrokers Act 1902–1974, s 14(3). Without a duplicate record the true owner could not redeem the diamonds pledged by his agent without authority. Note also s 12(3) of the 1889 Act on the owner's right to recover where the agent has *sold* the goods.

'The consideration necessary for the validity of a sale, pledge, or other disposition of goods in pursuance of this Act, may be either a payment in cash, or the delivery or transfer of other goods or of a document of title to goods, or of a negotiable security, or of any other valuable consideration.'

Hence in *Waddington & Sons v Neale & Sons*[9] the delivery of goods by the agent to an auctioneer for sale did not come within the Act, since the advances made by the auctioneer could not be considered as valuable consideration. It should be noted, however, that by virtue of s 1(5) and s 4 the consideration under s 5 may be a *past* or antecedent consideration, although, if it is, then the rights of the pledgee will be limited by s 4.

Nature of disposition. The disposition by the mercantile agent must be made by him 'when acting in the ordinary course of business of a mercantile agent'. This has nothing to do with the authority given to the agent by the owner 'in the customary course of his business' referred to in s 1(1).[10] It means

' "acting in such a way as a mercantile agent acting would act": that is to say, within business hours, at a proper place of business, and in other respects in the ordinary way in which a mercantile agent would act, so that there is nothing to lead the pledgee to suppose that anything wrong is being done, or to give him notice that the disposition is one which the mercantile agent had no authority to make.'[11]

This is clear since the Act is designed to create authority where none has been expressly given to the agent by the owner.

Thus in *Oppenheimer v Attenborough*:[12]

A diamond merchant gave a diamond broker diamonds to show potential purchasers. The broker pledged the diamonds to X. It was not within the usual authority of a diamond broker to pledge diamonds. Nevertheless X obtained a good title under the Act.

But where a diamond broker asked a friend to pledge the owner's diamonds without authority from him to pledge, this was not protected because this was not in the ordinary course of business of a mercantile agent.[13] However, by s 6 of the Act:

'For the purposes of this Act an agreement made with a mercantile agent through a clerk or other person authorised in the ordinary course of business

---

9 (1907) 96 LT 786.
10 *Oppenheimer v Attenborough & Son* [1908] 1 KB 221.
11 Ibid at 230–231 per Buckley LJ. A sale in a town other than that in which the agent normally carried on his trade may still be a sale in the customary course of his business: see *Consolidated Motors Ltd v Wagner* (1967) 63 DLR (2d) 266. So was a sale of a van with a forged transfer of ownership: *St John v Horvat* (1994) 113 DLR (4th) 670. But the sale of an entire stock-in-trade, viz, an entire art gallery including paintings, was not a sale in the ordinary course of business in this statutory sense: *Mortimer-Rae v Barthel* (1979) 105 DLR (3d) 289.
12 See above. See also *Weiner v Harris* [1910] 1 KB 285.
13 *De Gorter v Attenborough & Son* (1904) 21 TLR 19. Note also *Biggs v Evans* [1894] 1 QB 88 (unusual mode of payment took the transaction outside the ordinary course of the agent's business).

to make contracts of sale or pledge on his behalf shall be deemed to be an agreement with the agent.'

Therefore if the disposition is made by such 'a clerk or other person' it will be protected under the Act.

In *Pearson v Rose and Young Ltd*[14] the sale of a second-hand vehicle without the registration book was held not to be a sale in the ordinary course of business. Nor was the sale of a car without the ignition key (which would have opened the compartment where the registration book was kept).[15] On the other hand, a sale of a car to someone who had no business premises, when the sale took place in Warren Street in London, in and around which there was a well-established market for such dealings in used cars, was held, in *Newtons of Wembley Ltd v Williams*,[16] to be a sale in the ordinary course of business of a mercantile agent.

Finally, the section requires that the person taking under the disposition by the agent should act in good faith and without notice at the time of the disposition of the agent's want of authority. 'Notice' here probably means actual knowledge of the facts, not 'constructive' notice. But if the circumstances of the particular case are such as would lead a reasonable businessman to believe that the agent is exceeding his authority or acting in bad faith, that will amount to notice and lack of good faith on the part of the third party.[17] For example the charging of a high rate of interest on a pledge may show that the pledgee suspected the agent's bona fides.[18] Dealing with a car without the registration book may also put the buyer on his guard.[19] It should be noted that the onus is probably on the third party to prove good faith and lack of notice.[20] If two or more persons deal together with the agent, bad faith or notice by one will deprive both of the protection of the Act.[1]

Other provisions. Three other sections of the Factors Act require mention. By s 7 a consignee of goods from an agent, who is apparently the owner of them, has his lien on the goods protected as if the agent were in fact owner. By ss 8 and 9 of the Act,[2] a seller or buyer of goods, in possession of them, or the documents of

14 [1951] 1 KB 275, [1950] 2 All ER 1027, criticised above, pp 293–294. But note the decision in *Astley Industrial Trust Ltd v Miller* [1968] 2 All ER 36, where a sale of a *new* car without the registration book was *not* outside the ordinary course of business; and the Canadian case of *Durham v Asser* (1968) 67 DLR (2d) 574: above, p 293, note 18.
15 *Stadium Finance Ltd v Robbins* [1962] 2 QB 664, [1962] 2 All ER 633.
16 [1964] 2 All ER 135, [1964] 1 WLR 1028; affd by the Court of Appeal [1965] 1 QB 560, [1964] 3 All ER 532. On this case see Cmnd 2958, paras 21–23.
17 *Gobind Chunder Sein v Ryan* (1861) 15 Moo PCC 230.
18 *Janesich v Attenborough & Son* (1910) 102 LT 605.
19 *Pearson v Rose and Young Ltd* [1951] 1 KB 275 at 289, [1950] 2 All ER 1027 at 1033, per Denning LJ. Cf *Stadium Finance Ltd v Robbins* [1962] 2 All ER 633 at 639 per Willmer LJ.
20 *Heap v Motorists' Advisory Agency Ltd* [1923] 1 KB 577 at 590 per Lush J.
 1 *Oppenheimer v Frazer and Wyatt* [1907] 2 KB 50.
 2 And see Sale of Goods Act 1979, ss 24, 25 (which excludes buyers under a conditional sale agreement which is a consumer credit agreement within the Consumer Credit Act 1974). But note the saving of the Factors Act by the Sale of Goods Act 1979, s 21(2). See the discussion of these provisions in the Twelfth Report of the Law Reform Committee (1966, Cmnd 2958) paras 19–25, where the repeal of the Factors Act provisions was recommended and s 25(2) of the 1893 Sale of Goods Act was recommended for amendment.

title to them, whether in possession after a sale, or after an agreement to sell and whether or not property has passed, can dispose of the goods, etc, by sale, pledge, other disposition, or agreement for sale, pledge, or other disposition, to any person receiving the goods, etc, in good faith and without notice of any previous sale, lien or other right of the original seller.[3] In the case of a sale by a seller in possession, such disposition will have the same effect,

> 'as if the person making the delivery or transfer were expressly authorised by the owner of the goods to make the same' (s 8).

In the case of a buyer in possession it will have the same effect

> 'as if the person making the delivery or transfer were a mercantile agent in possession of the goods or documents of title with the consent of the owner'. (s 9).[4]

Several problems have arisen in connection with these sections including (i) the nature of the possession required by the seller,[5] (ii) the consent required,[6] (iii) whether the buyer has bought or agreed to buy.[7] But these matters do not properly belong to the law of agency, rather to the general law of sale of goods.[8]

---

3 A 'seller' for the purpose of s 9 does not have to be the owner: but he must at least be a person with the general property in the goods in order to let the buyer from him acquire a good title: *National Employers Mutual General Insurance Association Ltd v Jones* [1990] AC 24, [1987] 3 All ER 385. Hence, where the seller's possession was derived from the unlawful possession of a thief, the section did not apply: if *Elwin v O'Regan* [1971] NZLR 1124; *Brandon v Leckie* (1972) 29 DLR (3d) 633.

  As to delivery by an owner to a buyer from a seller under these provisions, without first a delivery to the seller and then a delivery to the buyer, see *Four Point Garage Ltd v Carter* [1985] 3 All ER 12, where no distinction was drawn: the buyer was protected. A constructive delivery will suffice for the purpose of s 9: according to the majority of the High Court of Australia in *Gamer's Motor Centre (Newcastle) Pty Ltd v Natwest Wholesale Australia Pty Ltd* (1987) 163 CLR 236.

4 This provision has been criticised on the ground that it leads to the discussion of 'hypotheticals': see *Newtons of Wembley Ltd v Williams* [1965] 1 QB 560, [1964] 2 All ER 532 (on which see Rutherford and Todd 'Section 25(1) of the Sale of Goods act 1893: The Reluctance to Create a Mercantile Agency' [1979] CLJ 346); Twelfth Report of Law Reform Committee (1966, Cmnd 2958) paras 21–23. It was recommended that the buyer in possession should not have to be acting as if he was a mercantile agent for his transaction to be valid, and that a buyer under a voidable (and avoided) title should not be a buyer in possession.

5 See s 1(2): *Eastern Distributors Ltd v Goldring* [1957] 2 QB 600, [1957] 2 All ER 525: *City Fur Manufacturing Co Ltd v Fureenbond (Brokers) London Ltd* [1937] 1 All ER 799; *Pacific Motor Auctions Pty Ltd v Motor Credits (Hire Finance) Ltd* [1965] AC 867, [1965] 2 All ER 105 (approved by the Court of appeal in *Worcester Works Finance Ltd v Cooden Engineering Co* [1972] 1 QB 210, [1971] 3 All ER 708).

6 *Cahn v Pockett's Bristol Channel Steam Packet Co* [1899] 1 QB 643; *London Jewellers Ltd v Attenborough* [1934] 2 KB 206; *Du Jardin v Beadman Bros Ltd* [1952] 2 QB 712, [1952] 2 All ER 160.

7 *Helby v Mathews* [1895] AC 471; *Belsize Motor Supply Co v Cox* [1914] 1 KB 244; *Marten v Whale* [1917] 2 KB 480; *Lee v Butler* [1893] 2 QB 318; *London Jewellers Ltd v Attenborough* [1934] 2 KB 206. In this respect note the exclusion contained in the Sale of Goods Act 1979, s 25(2): above, note 1. Note also the matters raised in the cases referred to above, note 2.

8 See Fridman *Sale of Goods* pp 121–128: Fridman *Sale of Goods in Canada* (4th edn 1995) pp 137–146; *Benjamin's Sale of Goods* (4th edn 1992) paras 7-057–085.

C. Rights of third party against the agent and the principal

Against the agent

An agent will be directly or personally liable to the third party, if property belonging to the principal, but held in the agent's possession for the principal, is assigned or charged by the principal to or in favour of the third party. This is the ordinary case of assignment and the agent will be bound to pay the third party on receipt of notice of the assignment or charge.[9] There must be a specific fund in the hands of the agent:[10] and the third party's right to the money will be subject to any lien or set-off the agent may have against the principal at the time he received notice of the assignment.[11]

Similar liability on the part of the agent occurs if the principal directs the agent to pay the third party from money held by the agent to the use of the principal: provided that the agent thereupon contracts with the third party to pay him,[12] or otherwise agrees with the third party,[13] or promises him that he will pay him.[14] But if the agent's promise to the third party is conditional on the receipt of money from the principal, the agent is only liable to pay on receipt of the money.[15] If there is no agreement with the third party, the agent is not liable to pay,[16] eg if he offered to pay on a condition to which the third party would not agree.[17] But once the agent has agreed to pay the third party, revocation or determination of his authority to pay will not affect his liability.[18]

The law seems to have been taken further by Barry J in *Shamia v Joory*.[19] There P was owed money by A and directed A to give some of it to P's brother T, by way of gift. A sent T a cheque which was improperly drawn and had to be returned. A then promised to give T a new cheque but failed to do so. It was held that T could sue A for the money. Here there was no contract between A and T (since the contract was expressly negatived by the learned judge). There was simply assent by A (expressed to both P and T) to pay the money to T. On the basis of early authorities,[20] Barry J held that a fund existed in the hands of A over which P had power of disposal, which gave rise to an obligation on A's part to pay over in accordance with P's instructions.

The case has been criticised by several writers. Some of this criticism is that the case does not go far enough in that it requires an assent by the agent to make

---

9 *Webb v Smith* (1885) 30 Ch D 192; *William Brandt Sons & Co v Dunlop Rubber Co* [1905] AC 454.
10 *Citizens' Bank of Louisiana v First National Bank of New Orleans* (1873) LR 6 HL 352.
11 *Roxburghe v Cox* (1881) 17 Ch D 520.
12 *Griffin v Weatherby* (1868) LR 3 QB 753.
13 *Walker v Rostron* (1842) 9 M & W 411. Compare the situation where the agent has received money from the third party, as a *stakeholder*, which he must repay to the third party: *Potters v Loppert* [1973] Ch 399, [1973] 1 All ER 658.
14 *Robertson v Fauntleroy* (1823) 8 Moore CP 10.
15 *Stevens v Hill* (1805) 5 Esp 247.
16 *Barlow v Browne* (1846) 16 M & W 126.
17 *Baron v Husband* (1833) 4 B & Ad 611.
18 *Robertson v Fauntleroy* (above): *Walker v Rostron* (above).
19 [1958] 1 QB 448, [1958] 1 All ER 111.
20 *Walker v Rostron* (above); *Griffin v Weatherby* (above). See also *Williams v Everett* (1811) 14 East 582; *Lilly v Hays* (1836) 5 A & E 548; *Liversidge v Broadbent* (1859) 4 H & N 603.

him accountable to the third party, whereas, it is argued, it should be enough that the instructions have been given to create an obligation, possibly of a quasi-contractual kind or maybe arising from the general law of agency, to pay over to the third party.[1] On the other hand there is criticism that the case is incorrectly decided since it conflicts with earlier decisions holding a promise to hold the debt to someone else's use as a bare promise without any consideration and because the law is thereby circumventing the doctrine of assignment of choses in action, as well as the distinction between assignment and attornment.[2] It has also been criticised on the ground that the third party here was a donee rather than a creditor of the principal, and the earlier cases were concerned with claims by creditors rather than donees.[3] Certainly the decision is an odd one, in that it is a case of first impression which as one commentator[4] has pointed out revives an old and troubled area of the law and does not really settle the true situation. If it is correct then it certainly extends the law to cover situations not otherwise comprehended within previous authorities, and by so doing enlarges the scope of the remedies available to a third party as against both the principal and the agent.

The agent will not be liable to the third party if the principal has directed his agent to pay the third party and the agent has not paid.[5]

Against the principal

The principal will be liable to the third party for money or property of the third party which is received by the agent either while acting actually or apparently within the scope of his authority and misapplied by the agent.[6] Similarly the principal will be liable for money or property of the third party which the agent has acquired while acting wrongfully or in an unauthorised way, as long as the money has been applied for the benefit of the principal.[7] This is of particular importance where directors of a company have borrowed money when to do so was ultra vires.[8]

---

1 Stoljar *Law of Quasi-Contract* pp 84–86.
2 Goff and Jones *Law of Restitution* (4th edn 1993) pp 573–575; Fridman *Restitution* (2nd edn 1992) p 260.
3 Davies 'Shamia v Joory: A Forgotten Chapter in Quasi-Contract' (1959) 75 LQR 220, for a detailed investigation of the law.
4 Davies (1959) 75 LQR 220.
5 *Williams v Everett* (1811) 14 East 582.
6 *Swire v Francis* (1877) 3 App Cas 106.
7 *Marsh v Keating* (1834) 1 Bing NC 198 (contrast *Jacobs v Morris* [1902] 1 Ch 816). See also *Reid v Rigby & Co* [1894] 2 QB 40; *Bannatyne v MacIver* [1906] 1 KB 103; *Reversion Fund and Insurance Co v Maison Cosway Ltd* [1913] 1 KB 364; *B Liggett (Liverpool) Ltd v Barclays Bank Ltd* [1928] 1 KB 48; *Re Cleadon Trust Ltd*]1939] Ch 286, [1938] 4 All ER 518; *Hazlewood v West Coast Securities Ltd* (1975) 49 DLR (3d) 46; affd on appeal (1976) 68 DLR (3d) 172.
8 See Fridman 'The Quasi-Contractual Aspects of Unjust Enrichment' (1956) 34 Can BR 393 at p 419, note 115 and cases there cited. See also, Goff and Jones *Law of Restitution* (4th edn 1993) pp 622–638; Fridman *Restitution* (2nd edn 1992) pp 412–414. The liability, under the doctrine of restitution, is by way of subrogation. *Quaere*: has this been affected by s 35(1) of the Companies Act 1985 (as inserted by the Companies Act 1989, s 108) under which acts done by a company may not be 'called in question' on the ground of lack of capacity because of the contents of the company's memorandum.

CHAPTER 13

Torts committed by agents

A. Preliminary considerations

Agents, servants and independent contractors. It has been argued that agents are a distinct class of those persons who act for others, and that servants and independent contractors, while also persons who act for others, must be considered as subject to different rules of law, in so far as the relationships of master and servant and employer and independent contractor have different effects in law from the agency relationship.[1]

The differences in question are more clearly revealed in relation to the law of contract. Only agents (in the sense in which that term is used in this work) can affect the legal position of those for whom they act (ie principals) by creating legal relations between their principals and third parties, as a result of contracts made by agents with such third parties, or dispositions of property made by the agent.[2] Neither servants, nor independent contractors, by virtue of their employment in such capacities, can achieve the like result. However, both servants and independent contractors can affect, to some extent, the legal position of those for whom they act, in that, by certain acts of servants and independent contractors, masters and employers can be made tortiously liable to third parties injured or damnified by the acts in question. It is this feature of the master-servant, and employer-independent contractor relationships which makes them similar to the relationship of principal and agent, and has produced the previously discussed difficulties and confusion.

Since the purpose of this book is to state and discuss the law of agency, it would not appear to be relevant to consider the vicarious tort liability of masters and those who employ independent contractors. However, it is necessary to say something about such liability because, in the first place, it has been suggested that for the purposes of the law of tort the distinctions between agents, servants and independent contractors which are operative in other branches of the law are not relevant.[3] As a corollary of this, it has also been suggested that the test of the

---

1 Above, pp 31–37.
2 See chs 11 and 12 for the effects of such contracts and dispositions of property.
3 Street *Law of Torts* (9th edn 1993) p 488 (except where deceit and liability for motor vehicles are concerned: ibid pp 489–490: on which see below pp 312, 319). A contrary view is expressed and discussed by Professor Conant 'Liability of Principals for Torts of Agents: A Comparative View' (1968) 47 Nebraska LR 42 at pp 43, 65. Note, also, that Atiyah *Vicarious Liability in the Law of Torts* treats liability for servants in Part II and liability for agents in Part III. See also Estes 'Cinderella's Slipper: Agency' (1977) 10 John Marshall Journal of Practice & Procedure 225, on changes in the American view that derived from Holmes J: above, p 8 note 11.

principal's liability for the torts of his agent is the same as that which determines the master's liability for the torts of his servants. These two suggestions, when coupled with what is said in cases concerning liability for damage caused by vehicles being driven by someone not the owner at the time the damage was caused,[4] seem to indicate the possibility that, in the context of the law of tort, the term 'agent' bears a special meaning, different (since more comprehensive) from that which it has in relation to, for example the law of contract. In other words, in discussing agency in relation to tortious liability, the idea that an agent is one who has power to effect legal relations between his principal and third parties,[5] must be taken to mean 'legal relations' in the sense of liabilities in tort, as well as contractual and proprietary rights and duties.[6] This would therefore include within the scope of agency *anybody* who, by his acts, can give rise to tortious liability on the part of another, in addition to, or in substitution for himself.

Obviously this is a question that must be considered before it is possible to state the exact nature of the principal's liability in tort for the acts of his agent. Therefore it is necessary to discuss, in general terms,[7] the nature of the master's and employer's liability for the torts of servants and independent contractors, the special case of vehicles, and to consider them in relation to the general nature of the principal's liability for the torts of his agent.

Vicarious liability generally. The rules relating to the liability in tort of masters and employers of independent contractors lay down the following. A master is liable for the torts his servant commits in the course of his employment. A person who employs an independent contractor is not liable for the acts of such contractor unless the employer is under a duty to act, and he has employed the contractor to act for him, in which case he would be liable only for injuries or damage resulting from the wrongful (usually *negligent*) performance of the contract in pursuance of which the contractor undertakes the performance of the

Note also the argument that, with respect to *professional employees*, the liability of the employer may be based not upon agency and vicarious liability but upon the breach of a duty (contractual *or* tortious) owed directly by the employer to the injured third party; cf *Cassidy v Ministry of Health* [1951] 2 KB 343, [1951] 1 All ER 574; *Aynsley v Toronto General Hospital* (1970) 7 DLR (3d) 193. This is especially relevant in relation to the liability of hospitals for what goes on therein: see *Yepremiam v Scarborough General Hospital* (1980) 28 OR (2d) 494, on which see Fridman 'Hospital Liability for Professional Negligence' (1980) 4 Legal Medical Q 80; cf the remarks of Linden J of the High Court of Ontario in relation to the liability involved with respect to an anaesthetist employed by a dentist: *Kennedy v CNA Assurance Co* (1978) 88 DLR (3d) 592. In respect of such liability see Whipps, 'A Hospital's Personal and Non-Delegable Duty to Care for Its Patients—Novel Doctrine or Vicarious Liability Disguised?' (1989) 63 Aust LJ 182: cf Anderson and Clausing, 'The Expansion of Hospital Liability in Illinois: The Use and Abuse of Apparent Agency' (1988) 19 Loyala of Chi LJ 1197.

4 Eg *Ormrod v Crosville Motor Services* [1953] 2 All ER 753, [1953] 1 WLR 1120: see further below, pp 312–315.

5 Above, p 11.

6 Thus Seavey says: 'It is possible to make the term "agency" so broad as to include every situation where A has a power to affect the rights, privileges, immunities, etc of B.' *The Rationale of Agency* (1920) 29 Yale LJ 859 at 864, note 16. Again: 'A servant is an agent having power to subject his principal to liability for torts not involving representations, as well as such other powers as the principal may have given him', loc cit at p 866.

7 For details see *Salmond and Heuston on Torts* (20th edn 1992) pp 445–464, 474–480, and the cases there cited; *Atiyah* pp 171–285, 327–378.

employer's duty. The distinction between these two instances of liability lies in this: that a master will be liable for any wrong his servant commits, as long as it can be shown to be connected with the performance of his actual[8] or apparent[9] duties as a servant, even where the mode of performance employed by the servant to fulfil those duties has been prohibited by the master;[10] whereas, an employer of an independent contractor will only be liable for wrongs committed by the independent contractor in the performance of his contractual duty.

This difference is one of breadth. In the case of servants the courts have been prepared to extend the idea of 'course of employment' to cover a large number of instances in which it could be argued that what the servant was doing was not in any way expressly or impliedly authorised by the master—the reason being one of policy, namely, that, since the master put the servant in a position in which he could do a class of acts, he must be answerable for anything the servant does in the process of performing one of that class of acts, however the servant chooses to do it. But, in the case of independent contractors the law has taken a more restrictive attitude to the employer's liability, and has confined it to wrongs which can be said to come 'within the four corners'[11] of what the contractor was employed to do.[12]

On the other hand the principal's liability for the torts of his agent is confined to what the agent does within the scope of his authority.[13] The authority in question may be express or implied: it may be acquired by subsequent ratification if the act was originally unauthorised; it may be an apparent, or ostensible authority. In other words, the liability of a principal for the torts of his agent is exactly the same as his liability in respect of the contracts made by his agent. As long as the agent is acting within the proper exercise of the powers granted him by the principal, he will make his principal liable if he commits a tort.

The approach of the common law to the problems involved in this kind of situation, where an employer (whether master or principal) has employed an employee (whether servant or agent), has been characterised by Lord Wilberforce as follows:[14]

---

8 Eg *Bayley v Manchester, Sheffield and Lincolnshire Rly Co* (1873) LR 8 CP 148.

9 Eg *Poland v John Parr & Sons* [1927] 1 KB 236.

10 Eg *Limpus v London General Omnibus Co* (1862) 1 H & C 526. Note also, the possibility of ratification: above, pp 84–110: Atiyah pp 310–323.

11 To quote a phrase from another context: *Bryant, Powis and Bryant v La Banque du Peuple* [1893] AC 170 at 177 per Lord MacNaghten.

12 For examples, see *Honeywill and Stein Ltd v Larkin Bros (London's Commercial Photographers) Ltd* [1934] 1 KB 191; *Balfour v Barty-King* [1957] 1 QB 496, [1957] 1 All ER 156; *Walsh v Holst & Co* [1958] 3 All ER 33, [1958] 1 WLR 800; *Salsbury v Woodland* [1970] 1 QB 324, [1969] 3 All ER 863.

13 See further below, pp 315–319. Note that Professor Conant (1968) 47 Nebraska LR 42 objects to the use of this concept in this context, since it is based upon the consent of the principal, which is inapplicable to the commission of torts. In this respect he is repeating and relying on his argument elsewhere (47 Nebraska LR 678) to which reference has been made earlier: p 14. Rejection of Professor Conant's major thesis renders inapplicable his objections to the description of a principal's vicarious tort liability in terms of the scope of an agent's authority.

14 *Kooragang Investments Pty Ltd v Richardson and Wrench Ltd* [1981] 3 All ER 65 at 68. For a different approach to the issue see Sykes, 'The Economics of Vicarious Liability' (1984) 93 Yale LJ 1231; Sykes 'The Doctrine of Vicarious Liability: An Economic Analysis of the Scope of Employment Rule on Related Legal Doctrines' (1988) 101 HLR 563.

'The manner in which the common law has dealt with the liability of employers for acts of employees ... has been progressive: the tendency has been toward more liberal protection of innocent third parties. At the same time recognition has been given by the law to the movement which has taken place from a relationship, akin to that of slavery, in which all actions of the servant were dictated by the master, to one in which the servant claimed and was given some liberty of action.'

As explained in the same passage the problem has been that in modern times employees supplement their wages by independent use in their own interest of the skills, and even the tools, which they use in their employment. Such activities may be legitimate or surreptitious. In the light of these realities, as Lord Wilberforce referred to them,[15] the problems associated with vicarious liability, viz, problems of authority and the course of employment, must be approached.

In the case in which these remarks were made, *Kooragang Investments Pty Ltd v Richardson & Wrench Ltd*,[16] it was made clear that, where the principal's liability was alleged to be based upon an act performed by an agent within the scope of his *actual* authority (not his ostensible or apparent authority—in which respect the situation would have been wholly different), the injured party had to prove that the principal (or master) authorised the act in question. It was not sufficient to show that the act performed by the agent (or servant) was an act within the class of acts which the agent or servant was authorised to do on the principal's or master's behalf. In this case an employee[17] negligently prepared inaccurate valuations of property. Although he was employed by the defendants to prepare such valuations, in this instance he had done so not on behalf of his normal employers, the defendants, but on behalf of another company, a client of the defendants, of which the employee in question had become a director. In these circumstances the Privy Council held that he was not acting for the defendants, since he had not been authorised by them to prepare the erroneous valuations.

In reaching this conclusion, the Privy Council relied upon three sets of cases to negate the plaintiff's suggested broad proposition that, as long as an agent or servant was doing an act of the same kind as those which it was within his authority to do, the principal or master could be liable.[18] These related to: (i) situations where a servant, without authority, has invited another person to drive his master's vehicle; (ii) situations where a servant, without authority, has invited another person on to the vehicle, and such person suffers injury; (iii) situations where the servant has embarked on an unauthorised detour, a 'frolic of his own'.[19] In and by all these instances, involving the use of motor vehicles, the

15 Ibid.
16 Above.
17 Nothing appears to have turned on the precise classification of the employee whose acts were in question.
18 Above, note 14 at 70.
19 But these cases, as Lord Wilberforce acknowledged, had given rise to fine distinctions: and some instances can be found in which principals or masters have been held liable notwithstanding the allegations that the agent or servant acted without authority: see, eg, *Ilkiw v Samuels* [1963] 2 All ER 879, [1963] 1 WLR 991; *Rose v Plenty* [1976] 1 All ER 97, [1976] 1 WLR 141; see Finch, 'Express Prohibitions and Scope of Employment' (1976) 39 MLR 575; Manchester 'Injuries to Unauthorised Passengers' (1976) 126 NLJ 447: see further below.

contention of the plaintiffs was contradicted. Hence, the Privy Council concluded, it was not possible to assert any general principle of law by which the defendants could be made responsible.

Liability for independent contractors and agents compared. In the first place it is important to notice that the liability for independent contractors is really liability for improper performance by the *employer himself* of the duty upon him.[20] His liability does not depend upon the nature of powers entrusted to the independent contractor, for he has not really given the contractor any powers. He has merely employed the contractor to perform something for him, not to represent him legally, but to act in a certain way, eg build a bridge or a road. Hence the employer's liability here results from the contractor's misfeasance in the course of performing a *contract*, not in the course of exercising powers.

There appears to be similarity with the position of the agent, since agents too, are usually[1] appointed by contract so that the agent's torts could be regarded as improper performances of his contract of agency. But the difference lies in the effects of the contract. The agent's contract transfers legal powers: the contract with the independent contractor transfers the task of performing obligations which are previously on the employer.[2] Therefore, it is submitted, it is possible to regard the two forms of liability as juristically different. A principal will be liable for everything done within the scope of the agent's authority, whether or not the employment of an agent was a reasonable thing to do in relation to the work to be done. But, it is only where the employer cannot be said to have discharged the obligations the law imposes on him by the employment of an independent contractor, that the employer will be liable for the torts committed by such contractor in the course of fulfilling the employer's obligations for him. If the employment of a contractor is a sufficient discharge of the employer's duty, then he will not be liable for any wrongs committed by the contractor.

For example, under the Occupiers' Liability Act 1957:[3]

'Where damage is caused to a visitor by a danger due to the faulty execution of any work of construction, maintenance or repair by an independent contractor employed by the occupier, the occupier is not to be treated without more as answerable for the danger if in all the circumstances he had acted reasonably in entrusting the work to an independent contractor and had taken such steps (if any) as he reasonably ought in order to satisfy

---

20 *Salmond and Heuston on Torts* (20th edn 1992) p 475. See, generally, on this Glanville Williams 'Liability for Independent Contractors' [1956] CLJ 180; *Atiyah* pp 327–378.
1 But not always. See also *Atiyah* pp 346–348, on the illogicality of the distinction between independent contractors and agents.
2 See *Davie v New Merton Board Mills* [1959] 1 All ER 346 at 357 per Lord Morton, ibid per Lord Reid, 368 per Lord Tucker.
3 Section 2(4)(b). Contrast the liability of a master for breach of the duty of care he owes his servants, where he has delegated the performance of that duty to an independent contractor, who has been negligent, discussed in *Davie v New Merton Board Mills* [1959] AC 604, [1959] 1 All ER 346; but see now the Employer's Liability (Defective Equipment) Act 1969. Note that Lord Simonds drew attention to some inconsistency in the cases dealing with an employer's liability for torts committed by an independent contractor: [1959] 1 All ER 346 at 355; cf *Atiyah* pp 350–378.

himself that the contractor was competent and that the work had been properly done.'

This refers only to the employment of an independent contractor: it does not cover agents or servants.

This distinction it is suggested, is clear: for the wrongs of an agent, even if not expressly authorised, a principal will be liable,[4] but for the wrongs of an independent contractor an employer of such contractor will not always be liable. The reason behind this distinction, it is suggested, lies in the supposed nature of the two relationships in question—the one, a relationship in which a *duty* is *sometimes* fulfilled by one person on behalf of another, the other, the agency relationship, is *always* a relationship in which a *power* is exercised by one person on behalf of another.

Liability for servants and agents compared. Next, it is important to compare the principal's liability for the torts of his agent, with that of a master for the torts of his servant. The former depends upon 'scope of authority': the latter upon 'course of employment'. Can these two notions be distinguished? Or are they co-extensive? It is this problem which has caused the confusion about the true relationship of agents to servants.[5]

Sometimes the language of the judges has equated the two ideas. In *Lloyd v Grace, Smith & Co,*[6] Lord MacNaghten said:

'The expressions "acting within his authority", "acting in the course of his employment" and the expression "acting within the scope of his agency" as applied to an agent, speaking broadly, mean one and the same thing.'

In *Navarro v Moregrand Ltd,*[7] Denning LJ talked about an agent's acting 'within the course of his employment', ie with actual authority, whether express or implied, or ostensible authority whether for his master's benefit or not. He went on to draw a distinction between the position of principals and agents in contract and tort. The principal, he said, was only responsible in *contract*

'for things done within the actual or ostensible authority of the agent: but he is responsible in tort for all wrongs done by the servant or agent in the course of his employment, whether within his actual or ostensible authority or not. The presence of actual or ostensible authority is decisive to show that his conduct is within the course of his employment, but the absence of it is not decisive the other way.'

This equation of 'scope of authority' with 'course of employment' was not adopted by Denning LJ in the later case of *Ormrod v Crosville Motor Services Ltd.*[8] There he seemed to distinguish between servants and agents, and he did not suggest that their position was the same generally, but he went on to say that, in

4 Provided the acts come within the agent's implied or apparent authority: below, pp 315–319.
5 See, also, *Atiyah* Part V, the general title of which is 'The Course of Employment', but which, in several chapters, deals with 'The Scope of Authority'.
6 [1912] AC 716 at 736.
7 [1951] 2 TLR 674 at 680. There are a number of earlier cases which appear to suggest the same identification.
8 [1953] 2 All ER 753 at 754: below, p 313.

respect of liability for injuries caused by careless use of a vehicle, an agent meant anyone who with the owner's consent drove the vehicle on the owner's business, or for the owner's purposes (which really made it immaterial to determine whether the driver of the vehicle was a servant or an agent).

The two notions were further differentiated by him, as Master of the Rolls, in *Heatons Transport Ltd v Transport and General Workers' Union*.[9] But the House of Lords, when that case reached them,[10] made it clear that there was really no distinction. In the words of Lord Wilberforce:[11]

> 'No new development is involved in the law relating to the responsibility of a master or principal for the act of a servant or agent. In each case the test to be applied is the same: was the servant or agent acting on behalf of and within the scope of the authority conferred by, the master or principal? ... Usually a servant, as compared with an agent, has a wider authority because his employment is more permanent and he has a larger range of duties and he may have to exercise discretion in dealing with a series of situations as they arise. The agent in an ordinary case is engaged to perform a particular task on a particular occasion and has authority to do whatever is required for that purpose but has no general authority. That is the explanation of the reasoning in the [*Wigan*] case[12] and in *Lucas v Mason*[13] ... Those two cases do not show that for the purpose of determining the responsibility of the master for the acts of a servant and that of the principal for the acts of an agent different tests are to be applied. They only show that the application of the same test may produce different results.
>
> But there are cases in which an agent who is not a servant does have authority of considerable generality. He may be elected or appointed to some office or post for a substantial period and he may have to perform acts of several classes on behalf of the principal and he may have to exercise a discretion in dealing with a series of situations as they arise. The position of such an agent and the scope of his authority are very similar to those of a servant.'

The same approach is also implicit in the language and tenor of the judgment of the Privy Council in the more recent case of *Kooragang Investment Pty Ltd v Richardson and Wrench Ltd*.[14]

The precise nature of the relationship between course of employment and scope of authority was further considered by the Court of Appeal and the House of Lords in *Armagas Ltd v Mundogas SA*,[15] with particular reference to the tort of deceit which was involved in that case. What was said indicates that whatever may be true with respect to torts in general, the tort of deceit entails somewhat different considerations where vicarious liability is concerned. The alternative argument in favour of liability raised by the plaintiffs was that the defendant's

---

9 [1972] 2 All ER 1214 at 1246: they were comparable, but different in their effects.
10 [1973] AC 15, [1972] 3 All ER 101.
11 Ibid at 109.
12 (1869) 21 LT 122.
13 (1875) LR 10 Exch 251.
14 [1981] 3 All ER 65: above, p 306.
15 [1985] 3 All ER 795, CA; affd [1986] 2 All ER 385, HL: above, p 116.

chartering manager and transportation vice-president made a fraudulent mis-representation on which the plaintiff relied; that misrepresentation was made in the course of the manager's employment; therefore the defendant was liable vicariously for the manager's deceit.

As seen earlier, the Court of Appeal and House of Lords held that the representation by the manager was not made with the authority of his employer. It had not been authorised expressly. Nor was there a holding out by the employer that would operate to invest the manager with any ostensible or apparent authority.[16] In relation to alleged tort liability it was urged that as long as the manager was performing the kind of task which he usually performed on his employer's behalf, viz, arranging charters, it did not matter that he had no actual or apparent authority to make the kind of arrangement with the plaintiff that was negotiated. That argument was rejected, at least where the tort said to have been perpetrated was the tort of deceit. The reason given by Goff LJ was as follows:[17]

> '...where the servant's wrong consists of a misrepresentation on which the plaintiff relies, if that misrepresentation is not within the ostensible authority of the servant, the plaintiff is placing reliance on a statement by the servant which ... either does not fall within the class of acts which a person in his position is usually authorised to perform or is a statement made in circumstances where the plaintiff has notice that the authority is limited.'

The plaintiff is therefore placing his reliance exclusively on the servant: hence the policy of the law is that the unauthorised act should not be imputed to the master, who ought not to be vicariously liable for the servant's wrong.[18] Dunn LJ based his conclusion on the point that deceit involved a holding out and at least an implied representation that the servant was acting within the scope of his authority. This meant whether the servant was acting within his actual authority and whether in holding himself out the servant was acting within the scope of his ostensible authority. 'The scope of the ostensible authority defines the course of employment':[19] The judgment of Stephenson LJ also indicates that, to define the course of an agent's employment it is necessary to examine what, if any, ostensible authority he possesses based on representations made by the principal.[20] Dunn and Stephenson LJJ were critical of the dicta of Denning LJ in *Navarro v Moregrand.*[1] Goff LJ thought that his conclusion was not inconsistent with those dicta.[2]

The House of Lords were more inclined to the view of Dunn and Stephenson LJJ in this regard than towards that of Goff LJ. The remarks of Denning LJ might have some validity in relation to torts other than those concerned with fraudulent misrepresentation, but they had no application to deceit where the essence of the employer's liability is reliance by the injured party on actual or ostensible

16 Above, pp 116–117, 125–126.
17 [1985] 3 All ER 795 at 810.
18 Ibid.
19 Ibid at 818.
20 Ibid at 825–829.
 1 Ibid at 818, 829.
 2 Ibid at 810.

authority.[3] Earlier in his speech Lord Keith stated that the attempt by the plaintiff to distinguish the agent's course of employment from the scope of his actual or apparent authority had no validity in this category of case. After referring to Lord Macnaghten's equation of the two expressions as meaning one and the same thing, he said:[4]

> 'The essential feature for creating liability in the employer is that the party contracting with the fraudulent servant should have altered his position to his detriment in reliance on the belief that the servant's activities were within his authority, or, to put it another way, were part of his job, this belief having been induced by the master's representations by way of words or conduct.'

Hence just as the agent's own representation of authority could not clothe him with authority to make a contract on behalf of his principal when he had no such power,[5] so the agent's representation as to his authority could not make the principal vicariously liable for the tort of deceit when the agent had no actual authority to make such a representation and the principal had said or done nothing to convey that impression to the third party, the plaintiff in this case (and, as stated later by Lord Keith,[6] what the servant was purporting to do is not within the class of acts that an employee in his position is usually authorised to do).

Deceit may provide special problems:[7] however, in general, it appears to be conceded judicially as well as by commentators on the law,[8] that for vicarious tort liability it is unnecessary to differentiate agents from servants.[9] The main, if not only, difference seems to arise where what is involved is an act which is not within the actual authority of the agent or servant but is said to fall within his apparent or ostensible authority.[10] In this respect, especially where the act was performed for the benefit of the agent or servant rather than for the principal or master, it may be important to determine whether the tortfeasor was an agent or a servant at the time when he committed the material act. If the relevant act is alleged to have been performed by the servant or agent acting within apparent or ostensible authority it will not suffice to allege that the servant perpetrated the act while doing something that can loosely be described as coming within the course of his employment. Some more positive representation emanating from the principal will be required where the cause of action is founded on a fraudulent misrepresentation by the employee.[11] Such particularity will not be necessary,

---

3 [1986] 2 All ER 385 at 393 per Lord Keith.
4 Ibid.
5 Above, p 117.
6 Above, note 3 at 394.
7 Below, pp 319–322.
8 Seavey, 'The Rationale of Agency' (1920) 29 Yale LJ 859 at p 866, quoted above, p 304, note 6. But note the more modern American approach referred to above, p 303, note 3. Cf *Bowstead and Reynolds on Agency* (16th edn) pp 498–502.
9 Note, however, the Crown Proceedings Act 1947, s 1.
10 Cf Lord Wilberforce in *Kooragang Investments Pty Ltd v Richardson and Wrench Ltd*, above, note 14 at 69.
11 Cf the views of Conant (1968) 47 Nebraska LR 42 at 49–52 who treats separately (a) torts committed in the transaction of the business of the agency with a third party and (b) liability for misrepresentations by the agent: pp 53–64 (in this respect anticipating the decision in the *Armagas* case).

312   *Chapter 13*

however, where the act in question constituted some other tort, such as trespass or negligence, where representations are irrelevant. The irrelevance of the status of the person performing some task on behalf of another is pre-eminently illustrated by cases concerned with liability for negligence in driving a motor vehicle.

Motor vehicle cases.[12] Cases which deal with liability for injuries resulting from the careless use of vehicles show that the law seems to make no distinction between agents and servants for these purposes but

> 'puts an especial responsibility on the owner of a vehicle who allows it out on the road in charge of someone else, no matter whether it is his servant, his friend or anyone else. If it is being used wholly or partly on the owner's business or for the owner's purposes, then the owner is liable for any negligence on the part of the driver.'

This statement of the law in *Ormrod v Crosville Motor Services Ltd*[13] really goes back to the judgment of DuParcq LJ in *Hewitt v Bonvin*[14] where it was said that:

> 'The driver of a car may not be the owner's servant and the owner will be nevertheless liable for his negligent driving if it be proved that at the material time he had the authority, express or implied, to drive on the owner's behalf. Such liability depends not on ownership, but on the delegation of a task or duty.'

Prior to the case of *Morgans v Launchbury*, in 1972[15] the cases established the following points. Ownership of a vehicle which is being driven by another at the material time may give rise to a prima facie inference of agency, but this could be displaced by evidence that a driver was using the vehicle for his own and not the owner's purposes. This was a question of fact: and only if there were the necessary connection between ownership and the purpose for which the vehicle was being used would the owner be vicariously liable.[16] Eveleigh J said in *Nottingham v Aldridge*,[17] ownership was not the test: the test was whether the agent was doing something in 'a genuinely representative capacity', ie as an agent to whom the task had been delegated.

---

12 See, generally, Kodilinye 'The Rule In Barnard v Sully in the Commonwealth' (1977) 26 ICLQ 487: Kodilinye 'Vicarious Liability of Vehicle Owners in the Commonwealth Caribbean' (1977) 6 AALR 18.
13 *Ormrod v Crosville Motor Services Ltd* [1953] 2 All ER 753 at 755 per Denning LJ. This was confirmed by Pearson LJ in *Norton v Canadian Pacific Steamships Ltd* [1961] 2 All ER 785 at 790. But there must be some relationship such as service or agency if there is to be vicarious liability. In that case the porters were in no such relationship with the shipowners, who, in fact, provided bogies for carrying passengers' luggage. Hence the shipowners were not liable for a negligent porter who caused an injury with such a bogie.
14 [1940] 1 KB 188 at 194–195.
15 [1973] AC 127, [1972] 2 All ER 606.
16 *Rambarran v Gurrucharran* [1970] 1 All ER 749, [1970] 1 WLR 556 a decision of the Privy Council on appeal from Guyana, applying a New Zealand case, *Manawatu County v Rowe* [1956] NZLR 78, and an Australian case *Jennings v Hannon* (1969) 89 WNNSW (Pt 2) 232.
17 [1971] 2 QB 739 at 746–752. See the discussion of this case by Lord Lowry in *Smith v Stages* [1989] 1 All ER 833 at 846–847.

Thus the owner was liable if he stayed in the car but allowed someone else to drive it;[18] if he were not in the car but delegated to another the task of looking after it;[19] if he were not in the car but it was being used wholly or partly on his business or for his purposes, as in *Ormrod v Crosville Motor Services Ltd*[20] where the owner let someone have his car to drive to Monte Carlo where it was proposed that the owner and driver should use it for a joint holiday. But the owner escaped liability when he lent the vehicle to a third person to be used for purposes in which the owner had no interest or concern.[1] So in *Klein v Caluori*,[2] a friend borrowed the defendant's car without the defendant's consent. He then informed the defendant. The defendant instructed the friend to return it. While the friend was returning the car, by his negligence there was an accident. The question was whether the defendant was liable. It was held that he was not, since the friend was not an agent. He had never taken the car with the consent of the defendant, and the return journey was only to discharge the friend's duty to return the car and not otherwise for the defendant's purposes.

Thus, in respect of vehicles, the term agent (though at the same time contrasted with the term servant)[3] seemed to mean anyone who, with the owner's consent, drove the car on the owner's business or for the owner's purposes.[4] When the case of *Launchbury v Morgans* came before the Court of Appeal,[5] Lord Denning MR attempted to propound a special rule in motor vehicle cases. The facts in that case were as follows:

> A wife owned a car which was registered and insured in her name. It was regarded by husband and wife as 'our car'. The husband arranged with the wife that if he were ever too drunk to drive, he would either get someone to drive him home or call the wife to do so. On one occasion, the husband was in that state and he asked his friend to drive the car. There was an accident,

18 *Wheatley v Patrick* (1837) 2 M & W 650; *Samson v Aitchison* [1912] AC 844; *Pratt v Patrick* [1924] 1 KB 488; *Trust Co Ltd v De Silva* [1956] 1 WLR 376. Even if the defendant is not the owner but a passenger who has contributed towards the cost of the trip: *Scarsbrook v Mason* [1961] 3 All ER 767. This, it is suggested, goes a long way to break down the old distinction between agents and independent contractors. The case was distinguished on the facts in *Bown v Chatfield* [1963] CLY 2348.
19 *Parker v Miller* (1926) 42 TLR 408.
20 [1953] 2 All ER 753, [1953] 1 WLR 1120: see Brook-Smith 'Liability for the Negligence of Another' (1954) 70 LQR 253. Hence in *Carberry v Davies* [1968] 2 All ER 817, [1968] 1 WLR 1103 the owner was liable for the negligence of his servant while driving a lorry in the evenings for the purpose of taking the owner's son around as arranged with the owner. Here the car was being driven on the owner's behalf and with his authority. See also *Vandyke v Fender* [1970] 2 QB 292, [1970] 2 All ER 335; on which see *Smith v Stages*, above at 846–847.
1 *Ormrod's* case [1953] 2 All ER 753 at 755; see *Hewitt v Bonvin* [1940] 1 KB 188. Hence in *Carberry v Davies*, above, the owner might not have been liable if the arrangement to drive his son around in the evening had been made with the lorry driver by the *son*, not the owner himself. Cf also the decisions in *Rambarran v Gurrucharran* [1970] 1 All ER 749, [1970] 1 WLR 556 and *Manawatu County v Rowe* [1956] NZLR 78. See also *Nottingham v Aldridge*, above.
2 [1971] 2 All ER 701 [1971] 1 WLR 619.
3 *Ormrod's* case (above) per Denning LJ.
4 *Ormrod's* case [1953] 2 All ER 753, [1953] 1 WLR 1120. Or with the consent and for the purposes of other passengers in the car: *Scarsbrook v Mason*, above. Note the peculiar decision of the Supreme Court of British Columbia in *Usher v Goncalves* (1969) 9 DLR (3d) 15 that consent may be *implied* even where it has been expressly refused!
5 [1971] 2 QB 245, [1971] 1 All ER 642.

the result of the friend's negligence, and in the accident the husband was killed and the plaintiffs were injured. The question was whether the wife was liable. The House of Lords reversing the Court of Appeal held that she was not. The husband was not the agent of the wife at the time since it must be shown that the driver was using the car for the *owner's* purposes under delegation of some task or duty. Nor was the friend the wife's agent in driving the husband (despite the arrangement made between husband and wife as to what was to happen when the husband was drunk).

In the Court of Appeal Lord Denning attempted to propound a view that in the case of motor vehicles, the law was not restricted to holding an owner liable on the normal principles of master and servant or principal and agent. It would suffice if the vehicle were being used wholly or partly on the owner's business or in the owner's interests: and permission by the owner for a person to drive the car might be sufficient to impose liability for that person's negligent driving of the car. This was not accepted by the House of Lords.[6] Their Lordships preferred to confine vicarious liability to the traditional principles. In the words of Lord Pearson:[7]

'The principle by virtue of which the owner of a car may be held vicariously liable for the negligent driving of a car by another person is the principle qui facit per alium, facit per se. If the car is being driven by a servant of the owner in the course of the employment or by an agent of the owner in the course of the agency, the owner is responsible for negligence in the driving. The making of the journey is a delegated duty or task undertaken by the servant or agent in pursuance of an order or instruction or request from the owner and for the purposes of the owner. For the creation of the agency relationship it is not necessary that there should be a legally binding contract or agency, but it is necessary that there should be an instruction or request from the owner and an undertaking of the duty or task by the agent. Also the fact that the journey is undertaken partly for purposes of the agent as well as for the purposes of the owner does not negate the creation of agency relationship. ... I think there has to be an acceptance by the agent of a mandate from the principle through neither the acceptance nor the mandate has to be formally expressed or legally binding.'

The attempt by Lord Denning to incorporate into English common law what has been done by the common law and statute in the United States[8] and by statute in other jurisdictions, eg Canada,[9] and Australia,[10] under which the owner of a motor vehicle may be liable irrespective of who is driving as long as the driver is a

6 [1973] AC 127, [1972] 2 All ER 606.
7 Ibid at 613–614.
8 *Morgans v Launchbury*, above, at 610 per Lord Wilberforce; cf Fridman 'The Doctrine of the Family Car: A Study in Contrasts' (1976) 8 Texas Tech LR 323 at pp 325–334.
9 See, eg, Highway Traffic Act, RSA 1980, c H–7 s 181 (Alta); Motor Vehicle Act, RSBC 1979, c 288, s 79 (BC); Motor Vehicle Act, RSNS 1989, c 293, s 248(3) (NS) (but see ibid, s 253(2) where a vehicle is stolen); Highway Traffic Act, RSO 1990, c H-8 s 192(1) (Ont); see Fridman (1976) 8 Texas Tech LR at pp 334–342.
10 See Fleming *Law of Torts* (8th edn 1992) p 388. Even if the driver is a thief there may be vicarious liability in Australia; ibid.

member of the owner's family or is driving with the owner's consent, met with no success. The House of Lords said that if any change in the law was to take place it must be done by legislation and not through the medium of decisions by the courts.[11]

Thus the present situation is that there are no special rules in regard to motor vehicles and that in relation to liability for the negligent use of such a vehicle there is in fact no differentiation between agents and servants.

B. Position of the principal

The general rule. A principal is jointly and severally liable with his agent[12] for any tort committed[13] by the agent while acting within the scope of his authority[14] and the authority exercised by the agent may be either actual[15] or apparent, ie it may be express, implied, usual, or ostensible.[16]

Hence the principal will be liable if he has expressly authorised the agent to commit a tort, or has subsequently ratified what the agent has done.[17] He will be liable if the implied authority (or usual authority) of the agent extends to cover the acts committed by the agent.[18] He will be liable if the apparent authority of the

11 For criticism see Fridman (1976) 8 Texas Tech LR at pp 342–360.
12 Unless the agent is personally immune from suit. Cf *Broom v Morgan* [1953] 1 QB 597, [1953] 1 All ER 849: in respect of which see now the Law Reform (Husband and Wife) Act 1962, which removed the immunity of spouses in tort. Or the agent is innocent of fraud and merely purported to pass on instructions from his principal: *Goldsbro v Walker* [1993] 1 NZLR 394 as 398 and cases there cited.

    Hence a release of the principal will also release agents, such as directors of a company guilty of negligence: *New Zealand Guardian Trust Co Ltd v Brooks* [1995] 1 WLR 96. Contrast *Kuwait Asia Bank EC v National Mutual Life Nominees Ltd* [1991] 1 AC 187, where there was no vicarious liability for breaches of duty by directors of a bank.
13 Hence the suggestion that an agent who *did nothing* could not make his principal liable vicariously for the 'neglect': *O'Donnell v Lumberman's Mutual Casualty Co* [1979] ILR 1–1057. This must be wrong: cf the decision of McFarlane J of British Columbia in *G R Young Ltd v Dominion Insurance Corpn* [1979] ILR 1–1157, failure to notify third party, the insured, made the insurance agent *and* his principal liable for negligence.
14 This was applied by the Ontario Court of Appeal to hold a municipality liable for the negligence of a public utilities commission created for the municipality, in *Fenn v City of Peterborough* (1979) 104 DLR (3d) 174. The PUC was the statutory agent of the municipality.
15 Hence the discussion in *Kooragang Investments Pty Ltd v Richardson and Wrench Ltd* [1982] AC 462, [1981] 3 All ER 65, above, p 306, of the question whether the employee had been authorised expressly to make the valuations: and the decision that such authorisation could not be inferred from the fact that the acts done, viz, valuations, were of a class which the employee was authorised to do on the employer's behalf.
16 See, for example, *Uxbridge Permanent Building Society v Pickard* [1939] 2 KB 248, [1939] 2 All ER 344, discussed and explained by the Privy Council in *Kooragang Investments Pty Ltd v Richardson and Wrench Ltd* [1981] 3 All ER 65 at 70–71; and considered by Lord Keith in *Armagas Ltd v Mundogas SA* [1986] 2 All ER 385 at 393. But note the objections raised by Professor Conant, above p 276, note 13.
17 *Hilbery v Hatton* (1864) 2 H & C 822. On the subject of authorisation and ratification of torts, cf Tedeschi 'Authorization of Torts' (1969) 4 Israel LR 1 which rejects causation and agency (by ratification) as grounds of vicarious liability.
18 *Bank of New South Wales v Owston* (1879) 4 App Cas 270; *Edwards v Midland Rly Co* (1880) 6 QBD 287; *Hern v Nichols* (1700) 1 Salk 289. See *Nelson v Raphael* [1979] RTR 437, authority of agent selling a car extended to demonstration of use of car; therefore owner-vendor liable for negligence of agent in course of such demonstration.

agent extends to the performance of the acts giving rise to the liability, which will not be the case where the agent, not the principal, makes the representation of authority on which the third partly relies, that representation being fraudulent.[19] Here there are two important points to consider. One is the question of prohibition by the principal: the other is the question whether the act done in pursuance of the apparent authority has to be for the principal's benefit in order to make the principal liable. Consideration of these matters reveals how the position of principal and agent has come to resemble that of master and servant.

Prohibited acts. Originally the law took the view that an agent who had been expressly forbidden to do a certain act could not involve his master in tort liability if he did the act, even if he appeared to the outside world to have authority to do the act in question.[20] At this time, no distinction was being drawn between agents and servants, for the whole law was in its infancy. Later the position of agents was clarified, and agents were distinguished from servants (even though the exact nature of the distinction was not made clear), at least for the purposes of contractual liability. As far as tort was concerned, their position tended to be identified.[1] But a distinction does seem to have arisen between agents and servants in respect of the effect of a prohibition. Thus in *Limpus v London General Omnibus Co*,[2] a prohibition against racing given to the driver of an omnibus did not oust the omnibus company's liability for the negligence of their servant, the driver. But in *Stevens v Woodward*,[3] a prohibition given by the defendant to a clerk (who was possibly an agent not a servant—even though nothing is clearly stated) against using the defendant's private lavatory took the use of the lavatory outside the scope of the clerk's authority:[4] hence the defendant was not liable for damage resulting from the clerk's use of the lavatory.

Later cases on prohibition really deal with the position of servants. There do not seem to be any cases dealing with the position of agents as such. But the suggestion is made that a distinction can be drawn between agents and servants. For the position of servants is such that the capacity for imposing liability on their masters by the commission of torts should not be limited by any secret, unpublished, unpredictable prohibition by the master. The attitude of the law—which changed between 1790[5] and 1862[6]—is based upon the peculiar position of

---

19 *Armagas Ltd v Mundogas SA*, above. In *Montreal Bank v Young* (1967) 60 DLR (2d) 220, the bank was not bound by the fraud of their manager, since the bank had no statutory power to advise on investments, therefore the giving of such advice could not be within the apparent authority of the manager. See also the South Australian case of *Royal-Globe Life Assurance Co Ltd v Kovacevic* (1979) 22 SASR 78, insurance agent defrauding party who desired insurance: insurance company liable.
20 *Southern v How* (1618) Cro Jac 468; *Fenn v Harrison* (1790) 3 Term Rep 757.
 1 *Stevens v Woodward* (1881) 6 QBD 318 at 320 per Grove J; *Dyer v Munday* [1895] 1 QB 742 at 748 per Rigby LJ.
 2 (1862) 1 H & C 526.
 3 Above, note 1.
 4 Nor was its use incidental to the ordinary duties of the clerk's employment; per Grove J at 621.
 5 See *Fenn v Harrison* (1790) 3 Term Rep 757 at 762 per Buller J; cf *McKenzie v M'Leod* (1834) 10 Bing 385 at 387 per Park J.
 6 *Limpus v London General Omnibus Co* (1862) 1 H & C 526 at 539 per Willes J.

servants, the generality of the tasks entrusted to them, and their great potentiality for causing injury in the performance of those tasks. Hence, possibly, the decision of the Court of Appeal in *Rose v Plenty*,[7] where the employer was held liable for an injury to a passenger on the milk delivery van, although the passenger, a young boy, was there against the express instructions of the employer. It is true that the passenger was there to help the employee: but there was a precise and express prohibition of such assistance that had been given by the employer to all employees. So far as concerns agents, ie those who have been given certain legal powers to act upon and discharge, it seems to be more reasonable to accept the idea that, as with contractual liability, the liability of the principal should be effected by any prohibition or limitation that exists on the exercise of the powers entrusted to the agent, unless the existence of such prohibition or limitation is relevant to the determination of the agent's apparent authority, in which event the principal's liability would depend upon whether the third party has notice of the prohibition or limitation.

A case which illustrates this, even though it is not exactly a case of tort, is *Navarro v Moregrand.*[8] There:

> The landlords of certain premises gave X authority to let flats for them. X told the plaintiff who wanted the tenancy of one of the flats, that he would have to pay £225, which in effect was an illegal premium. In an action under the Landlord and Tenant (Rent Control) Act 1949, s 2(5) by the plaintiff against the landlords (and X) for the recovery of the £225, the county court judge held that when X asked for the premium the plaintiff had clear notice that X was exceeding his apparent or ostensible authority, and therefore he was not entitled to make the landlords liable for X's act. In the Court of Appeal this decision was reversed.

Denning LJ, as already seen, regarded the case in the light of the question 'was the agent acting within the course of his employment?' And he came to the conclusion that he was 'doing his employer's business, though doing it wrongly, and for his own benefit.'[9] Somervell LJ, however, preferred to approach the case from the standpoint of the agent's apparent authority and he held that, if there was any limitation on that authority, it was not known to the plaintiff.[10] Therefore the landlords were liable.[11]

Benefit to the principal. When the principal's *contractual* liability is concerned, the fact that the agent was acting for his own benefit, and not for the principal's, will not affect a third party who relies upon the apparent authority of the agent, unless the fact that the agent was acting for his own benefit could have amounted to notice or warning that the agent in reality had no authority.[12] What is the position in respect of the tort liability of the principal in such circumstances?

7 [1976] 1 All ER 97, [1976] 1 WLR 141: on which see Finch (1976) 39 MLR 575; Manchester 'Injuries to Unauthorised Passengers' (1976) 126 NLJ 447.
8 [1951] 2 TLR 674.
9 Ibid at 681.
10 Ibid at 679.
11 For the approval of the view of Somervell LJ and disapproval of the view of Denning LJ, by the Court of Appeal and the House of Lords in *Armagas Ltd v Mundogas SA*, above, see p 310.
12 Above, pp 119, 127.

In *Barwick v English Joint Stock Bank*,[13] the bank was held liable for the fraud of its manager, as a result of which the plaintiff was induced to supply goods to X, and look to the bank for payment of X's cheque (which was dishonoured). Willes J laid down as a general rule that

> 'the master is answerable for any such wrong of the servant *or* agent as is committed in the course of service *and for the master's benefit*, though no express command or privity of the master be proved.'[14]

Willes J was (a) distinguishing between servants and agents; and (b) assimilating their position in that the act, to impose liability, had to be for the master's or principal's benefit, not for the servant's or the agent's. In other words an agent, who, like a servant went on 'a frolic of his own'[15] and did a wilful act, involving fraud or negligence, outside the scope of his authority, would not make his principal liable for the consequences.

The idea of the servant's personal 'frolic' was applied in the courts in such a way as to show that there were many instances in which a servant could still make his master liable, although at first sight it looked as if he was not really acting in the course of his employment. In fact, the eventual result was that anything which seemed to come within the performance of the servant's duties, however improper his performance may have been, was held to be done within the course of the servant's employment, whether it was forbidden, illegal or tortious.[16] Gradually, therefore, 'the course of a servant's employment' was given a very broad, liberal, interpretation. At the same time, the notion that the agent

---

13 (1867) LR 2 Exch 259.
14 Ibid at 265–266 (italics supplied).
15 *Joel v Morison* (1834) 6 C & P 501 at 503 per Parke B; cf *Coleman v Riches* (1855) 16 CB 104; *Allen v London and South Western Rly Co* (1870) LR 6 QB 65.
16 See *Seymour v Greenwood* (1861) 7 H & N 355; *Limpus v London General Omnibus Co* (1862) 1 H & C 526; *Bayley v Manchester, Sheffield and Lincolnshire Rly Co* (1873) LR 8 CP 148; *Dyer v Munday* [1895] 1 QB 742; *Smith v Martin and Kingston upon Hull Corpn* [1911] 2 KB 775; cf *United Africa Co Ltd v Saka Owoade (1954)* [1955] AC 130, [1957] 3 All ER 216; *Sze Hai Tong Bank Ltd v Rambler Cycle Co Ltd* [1959] 3 All ER 182 at 186 per Lord Denning. See, also the remarks of Stephenson LJ in *Stone v Taffe* [1974] 3 All ER 1016 at 1022.
   This has now come to include theft by the servant: see *Morris v C W Martin & Sons Ltd* [1966] 1 QB 716, [1965] 2 All ER 725. But not necessarily an assault by the servant, unless such assault has been authorised in the course of the servant's employment; compare, eg, *Pettersson v Royal Oak Hotel Ltd* [1948] NZLR 136 (employer held liable), with *Warren v Henlys Ltd* [1948] 2 All ER 935; *Deaton's Pty Ltd v Flew* (1949) 79 CLR 370; *Keppel Bus Co Ltd v Sa' ad bin Ahmad* [1974] 2 All ER 700, [1974] 1 WLR 1082; *Auckland Workingmen's Club and Mechanics Institute v Rennie* [1976] 1 NZLR 278 (employer *not* liable). See Rose 'Boozers Barmen and Businessmen' (1976) 39 MLR 720; Rose 'Liability for an Employee's Assaults' (1977) 40 MLR 420. In relation to servants generally see *Atiyah* pp 191–202.
   In the United States there are conflicting decisions on whether an employer could be liable vicariously for a rape committed by an employee. In one case a city was held liable for a rape committed by a policeman on a woman stopped for erratic driving: *Mary M v City of Los Angeles* 814 P 2d 1345 (1991): cp *Simmons v United States* 805 F 2d 1363 (1986). In another a school board was not liable for a rape committed by a public school teacher: *John R v Oakland Unified School District* 769 P 2d 948 (1989); cp *Rabon v Guardmark* 571 F 2d 1277; cert den 439 US 866 (1978). The subject is discussed in Weber '"Scope of Employment" Redefined: Holding Employers Vicariously Liable for Sexual Assaults Committed by Their Employees' (1992) 76 Min LR 1513.

must act for his principal's benefit, was applied in some cases,[17] and approved in others.[18]

Thus the two instances of liability drew apart. But the decision of the House of Lords in *Lloyd v Grace, Smith & Co*[19] (where a solicitors' clerk perpetrated a fraud on a client for his own benefit, and the solicitors were held liable), rejected and refuted the language of Willes J, and seems to have drawn together again the position of principals and that of masters. This idea, that an agent can make his principal liable for acts done within the scope of his apparent liability, even if for his own personal benefit, was underlined and even possibly extended by the Court of Appeal in *Uxbridge Permanent Benefit Building Society v Pickard*,[20] where the defrauded plaintiffs were not even the clients of the defendant solicitor. And everything seems to depend upon whether the acts of the agent come within his 'ostensible' authority.[1] What is comprehended and understood by this expression in the context of vicarious tort liability must now be viewed in light of the discussion in *Armagas Ltd v Mundogas SA*.[2]

Some particular problems[3]

Deceit. If the agent, without the knowledge of the principal, but acting within the scope of his authority,[4] commits the tort of deceit, the principal will of course be

In Canada this problem has sometimes been dealt with by holding a defendant liable in negligence that results in a third person assaulting the plaintiff (but these instances are not really cases of vicarious liability): see *S(J) v Clement* (1995) 122 DLR (4th) 449: cp *Jane Doe v Toronto Police* (1990) 72 DLR (4th) 580.

17 Eg *British Mutual Bank Co Ltd v Charnwood Forest Rly Co* (1887) 18 QBD 714; *George Whitechurch Ltd v Cavanagh* [1902] AC 117.

18 Eg *Mackay v Commercial Bank of New Brunswick* (1874) LR 5 PC 394 at 410–412; *Swire v Francis* (1877) 3 App Cas 106; *Houldsworth v City of Glasgow Bank* (1880) 5 App Cas 317 at 326 per Lord Selborne; *Thorne v Heard and Marsh* [1895] AC 495 at 502 per Lord Herschell LC; *Ruben v Great Fingall Consolidated* [1906] AC 439 at 446 per Lord Davey.

19 [1912] AC 716. Cf *United Africa Co v Saka Owoade (1954)* [1955] AC 130, [1957] 3 All ER 216 and *Morris v C W Martin & Son Ltd*, above. Cf *Royal-Globe Life Assurance Co Ltd v Kovacevic* (1979) 22 SASR 78, above, p 316, note 19. See also Conant (1968) 47 Nebraska LR 42 at pp 55–59, for a discussion of the English and American cases.

20 [1939] 2 KB 248, [1939] 2 All ER 344; discussed, explained, and distinguished (on the ground that the *Pickard* case was concerned with apparent or ostensible authority, whereas the case before the Privy Council involved the question whether or not there was any *actual* authority to make the valuations) in *Kooragang Investments Pty Ltd v Richardson and Wrench Ltd* [1982] AC 462, [1981] 3 All ER 65: above, p 306. See also *Briess v Woolley* [1954] AC 333 at 348–349, [1954] 1 All ER 909 at 915; per Lord Reid.

1 [1939] 2 KB 248 at 258, [1939] 2 All ER 344 at 351 per MacKinnon LJ.

2 [1985] 3 All ER 795, CA; affd [1986] 2 All ER 385, HL: above pp 309–311. If the act is for the agent's benefit alone this might not suffice to put the third party on notice of want of authority. That point did not arise for discussion in the *Armagas* case: but see [1985] 3 All ER 795 at 810 per Goff LJ. Nor was it discussed in *Heaton's Transport v Transport & General Workers' Union* [1973] AC 15, [1972] 2 All ER 1214: above p 280.

3 Whether there should be vicarious liability for punitive damages assessed against a servant or agent is a vexed issue in the United States: Parlee 'Vicarious Liability for Punitive Damages: Suggested Changes in the Law Through Policy Analysis' (1984–85) 68 Marquette LR 27. In view of the decision in *Rookes v Barnard* [1964] AC 1129, [1964] 1 All ER 367, limiting the scope of such damages, this may not be a problem in England: but it might in Canada or Australia, where the law seems more favourably disposed towards the award of such damages in various tort actions.

4 In this regard note the decision in *Armagas Ltd v Mundogas SA*, above, on when an agent fraudulently misrepresenting that he has authority to act on behalf of the principal may be said to be acting within the scope of his authority.

liable.[5] Deceit involves the making of a false statement of fact with knowledge that it is false, or recklessly in disregard of whether it is true or false, with the intention that it shall be acted upon by the plaintiff, who does act upon it and suffers damage.[6] Thus it does not matter what the principal knows or says, as long as the agent has been guilty of the wrongful act, with the requisite wrongful state of mind.[7]

The question has arisen whether the principal will be liable if the ingredients of the tort of deceit (ie a false statement and knowledge that the statement was false) are split between principal and agent.

In *Cornfoot v Fowke*:[8]

> The agent, employed to let a house, told the tenant that there was nothing wrong with the house. The principal knew that there was something wrong with it: there was a brothel next door. But the principal did not know that the agent was making any statement about the house. It was held that this was not fraud on the part of the principal. Therefore the lease could not be rescinded, and the tenant was bound to perform.

But if the principal knew the agent was innocently going to make a fraudulent statement, and had in fact concealed the truth from him, the position would be otherwise. In *Ludgater v Love*,[9] the principal was held liable when his son innocently represented, with his authority, that sheep to be sold were in good condition, when the principal knew that they were suffering from rot. For this was just as if the innocent agent had been told to make a false statement.

Some later dicta suggest that the division of the essential ingredients of deceit between principal and agent made no difference to the question of the principal's liability as long as there was a misstatement somewhere. The principal and agent were one, and it did not matter which of them made the incriminated statement and which of them possessed the guilty knowledge.[10] On the other hand, the

---

5 But see the comments by Professor Conant (1968) 47 Nebraska LR 42 at pp 59–61, as to the effect of an exculpatory clause in a contract limiting a principal's liability, or excluding it completely for misrepresentations by his agent. See *Pearson & Son Ltd v Dublin Corpn* [1907] AC 351, especially at 354 per Lord Loreburn. Whether this would exclude tortious liability, quite apart from the principal's possible contractual liability, is a matter of debate.

6 *Derry v Peek* (1889) 14 App Cas 337 at 374 per Lord Herschell.

7 *Hern v Nichols* (1700) 1 Salk 289; *Udell v Atherton* (1861) 7 H & N 172; *Lloyd v Grace, Smith & Co* [1912] AC 716; *Uxbridge Permanent Benefit Building Society v Pickard* [1939] 2 KB 248, [1939] 2 All ER 344; cp *Jessett Properties Ltd v UDC Finance Ltd* [1992] 1 NZLR 138 (evidence pointed to negotiator seeking to defraud unregistered mortgagee in his capacity as agent for the lessor of the property). In *Briess v Woolley* [1954] AC 333, [1954] 1 All ER 909: the agent began to make fraudulent misrepresentations *before* he was authorised to act for the principal (a company of which he was managing director). The company was liable, because the misrepresentation continued to be made *after* the director had been authorised to conclude the contract in question.

   If the agent is privy to an act of deceit *against the principal*, the agent's knowledge is *not* imputed to the principal: *United Dominions Trust (Ireland) Ltd v Shannon Caravans Ltd* [1976] IR 225.

8 (1840) 6 M & W 358. See Conant (1968) 47 Nebraska LR 42 at pp 63–64, for a discussion of this problem: cf *Atiyah* pp 272–273.

9 (1881) 44 LT 694.

10 *Pearson & Son Ltd v Dublin Corpn* [1907] AC 351 at 354 per Lord Loreburn. See also *London County Freehold and Leasehold Properties Ltd v Berkeley Property and Investment Co Ltd* [1936] 2 All ER 1039 at 1047 per Slesser LJ 1050 per Romer LJ: criticised by Devlin J in 53 LQR 344.

importance of *knowledge* by the principal that false statements were being made was rejected by Atkinson J in *Anglo-Scottish Beet Sugar Corpn Ltd v Spalding UDC*[11] (a case where *mistake* was relied upon by the third party, not fraud), and by the Court of Appeal in *Gordon Hill Trust Ltd v Segall*,[12] relying on *Cornfoot v Fowke*.[13] The earlier cases were really ones where either (a) the agent knew a false statement was being made,[14] or (b) the principal knew through *another* agent that the false statement was being made, ie the principal was the guilty party all along, in having knowledge, or means of knowledge, that deceit was being perpetrated.[15] Hence there was no real innocence on the part of principal *and* agent in those cases. It was finally decided by Devlin J and the Court of Appeal, in *Armstrong v Strain*[16] that an innocent agent who unwittingly made a false representation could not make his innocent principal (who knew the statement was false but did not know the representation was being made) liable for deceit.[17]

It has been suggested that the result of this decision was unsatisfactory, in that it left the third party with no, or no effective, remedy.[18] The difficulties may have been removed, in part if not altogether, by the Misrepresentation Act 1967, s 2(1), which renders it unnecessary to establish a common law duty of care,[19] if there would have been liability if the misrepresentation had been made fraudulently, in the absence of proof that the party making the representation had reasonable grounds for believing, and did believe, that the facts were true. This applies to misrepresentations that lead to the making of a contract.[20] It has been held that there is no need to establish shared responsibility, as decided in *Armstrong v Strain*, in an action under this provision.[1]

---

11 [1937] 2 KB 607, [1937] 3 All ER 335; cf *Turvey v Dentons (1923) Ltd* [1953] 1 QB 218, [1952] 2 All ER 1025; *Purity Dairy Ltd v Collinson* (1966) 58 DLR (2d) 67; *Storthoaks Rural Municipality of v Mobil Oil Canada Ltd* (1975) 55 DLR (3d) 1 at 7–9. In all these cases claims for the recovery of money paid under a mistake were successful, despite the fact that one agent of the payee knew that the payment was not exigible when another agent, who requested and obtained the payment, was ignorant of such fact.
12 [1941] 2 All ER 379.
13 (1840) 6 M & W 358.
14 *Pearson & Son Ltd v Dublin Corpn*, above.
15 *London County Freehold and Leasehold Properties Ltd v Berkeley Property and Investment Co Ltd* [1936] 2 All ER 1039.
16 [1951] 1 TLR 856; affd [1952] 1 KB 232, [1952] 1 All ER 139. Quaere whether the principal really was innocent in this case.
17 Hence the distinction between an innocent agent who acted only as a conduit and purported to do no more than pass on instructions from his principal and one who passed on what he had been told inaccurately or adopted it as his own or added to it: *Goldsbro v Walker* [1993] 1 NZLR 394 at 398 per Cooke P (a decision under the New Zealand Fair Trading Act 1986).
18 Hanbury *Principles of Agency* (2nd edn) p 138: Powell *Law of Agency* (2nd edn) pp 206–207.
19 Under *Hedley Byrne & Co Ltd v Heller & Partners* [1964] AC 465, [1963] 2 All ER 575, and subsequent decisions.
20 Only a party to the contract may be sued under this provision, ie the principal, not the agent who made the misrepresentation: *Resolute Maritime Inc v Nippon Kaiji Kyokai* [1983] 2 All ER 1: above, p 229. Note that misrepresentations within this section must satisfy the requirement of the Statute of Frauds Amendment Act, s 6, below, note 2: *UBAF Ltd v European American Banking Corpn* [1984] 2 All ER 226 at 229–230 per Ackner LJ because of the phrase that the person making the representation is liable only if he 'would be liable . . . had the misrepresentation been made fraudulently'.
1 *Gosling v Anderson* (1972) 223 Estates Gazette 1743.

Since the Misrepresentation Act relates only to misrepresentations that induce the making of a contract, there may still be some distinction between fraudulent and negligent misrepresentations in respect of shared responsibility,[2] unless the doctrine of *Armstrong v Strain* can be held inapplicable to negligent misrepresentations not within the 1967 Act, as long as a duty of care exists between the relevant parties.[3]

Defamation. A principal, of course, will be liable for libels or slanders published by his agent, in accordance with the general principles of liability already discussed.[4] Similarly, if the principal publishes a libel or slander through an 'innocent' agent, ie one who does not know that he is publishing something defamatory, the principal will presumably be liable. But one problem has arisen. If the agent is 'innocent', in the sense that he believes that he is protected by privilege in the publishing of the alleged defamatory statement, and the principal has the necessary malice to take the publication outside the protection of the law of privilege, will both or either be liable?

Before 1964 there was some conflict in the cases. In *Smith v Streatfield*[5] it was held by Bankes J that the malice of the writer of a statement (the principal) destroyed the privilege of the publisher (the agent). This was followed by Uthwatt J in *Smith v National Meter Co*[6] where insurers, the agents of their employers, were held liable, even though they were not actuated by malice, since their employer did have the necessary malice. But in *Longdon-Griffiths v Smith*[7] where the trustees of a Friendly Society made a report defamatory of the plaintiff, it was held by Slade J that the malice of one trustee could not affect the privilege of the others. This decision of Slade J was approved, and the earlier case of *Smith v Streatfield* overruled, by the Court of Appeal in *Egger v Viscount Chelmsford*.[8] The plaintiff complained of a libel contained in a letter written by

---

2 Note that by the Statute of Frauds Amendment Act 1828, s 6, no action can be maintained against a principal in respect of any misrepresentation as to the character, conduct, credit, trade or other dealings of another person to the extent that such other person may obtain credit, money or goods, unless such representation is *in writing signed by the principal*; see *Swift v Jewsbury and Goddard* (1874) LR 9 QB 301 (discussed in *UBAF Ltd v European American Banking Corpn* [1984] 2 All ER 226 at 231–234 per Ackner LJ: where a signature by a duly authorised agent on behalf of a limited company satisfied this requirement). This does not apply where the representation is *negligent* as opposed to fraudulent: *Anderson & Sons Ltd v Rhodes (Liverpool) Ltd* [1967] 2 All ER 850, especially at 862–865 per Cairns J; *UBAF Ltd v European American Banking Corpn*, above at 239.

3 For debate on this prior to the 1967 Act, see Unger, 1 MLR 149; Wright, 15 Can BR 716 at pp 721–722; *Powell* pp 206–207, discussing *Efploia Shipping Corpn Ltd v Canadian Transport Co Ltd, The Pantanassa* [1958] 2 Lloyd's Rep 449, a case involving an action for breach of warranty.

4 But not if the publication is by an agent of a corporation to the corporation itself, through its being published to *another* agent of the corporation, according to Lord Denning MR in *Riddick v Thames Board Mills Ltd* [1977] QB 881, [1977] 3 All ER 677: on which see Jolowicz, [1977] CLJ 237.

5 [1913] 3 KB 764.

6 [1945] KB 543, [1945] 2 All ER 35.

7 [1951] 1 KB 295, [1950] 2 All ER 662.

8 [1965] 1 QB 248, [1964] 3 All ER 406. For an earlier case, where Winn J anticipated this conclusion, see *Meekins v Henson* [1964] 1 QB 472, [1962] 1 All ER 899.

the assistant secretary of a dog club on behalf of the committee. The letter was defamatory, but the occasion was privileged. However, five members of the committee acted with malice, although the others and the assistant secretary did not. It was held that the committee members innocent of malice were not affected by the malice of their co-principals, and the innocent agent, the assistant secretary, was not deprived of the protection of the defence of qualified privilege. Each principal, and the agent, was invested with an independent and individual privilege, which could not be defeated except by his own personal malice. The question has therefore been answered in what is suggested to be a reasonable and fair way.

Corporations. It is clear that corporations, such as incorporated companies, can be held liable for torts committed by their agents, in the same way as natural persons who are principals.[9] This has been carried to the extent of making a corporation liable for a tort (defamation) of which malice was an essential ingredient: it was held that, if the agent were malicious, then the principal would be liable for the tort in question.[10]

The tort must have been committed by the agent within the scope of his authority. Hence at common law the question was raised whether a corporation could be liable for a tort committed by its agent, if the corporation had no power to authorise the agent to do the kind of act in the course of doing which he committed the tort.

If the corporation-principal expressly authorised the act which amounts to a tort, or the performance of which necessarily and incidentally involves the commission of a tort, then the corporation was held to be liable, irrespective of any qualification of the legal powers of the corporation. In *Campbell v Paddington Corpn*:[11]

> The defendant corporation, in pursuance of a resolution passed at a meeting of the council, caused a stand to be erected across the highway where a procession was to pass. This obstructed the plaintiff's view from his flat, which he was letting out on hire to someone who wished to see the procession. It was held that the plaintiff could recover for the loss of the hire resulting from the failure to let the flat because of the obstruction. The fact that the corporation did not have the legal power to erect the stand was irrelevant: because they had in fact ordered the stand to be built.

Here, therefore, the court took the view, which had been put forward in the similar case of *Mill v Hawker*[12] by Kelly CB, that if unlawful acts were ultra vires corporations would never be liable in tort because they would not be liable for torts committed or authorised by them. Moreover, this liability was not vicarious in the sense that it is based on the acts of agents acting *for* the corporation. It was really *direct* liability on the part of the corporation for acts it has done itself *through* its agents.[13]

9 On the liability of the Crown see, below, ch 20.
10 *Citizens' Life Assurance Co v Brown* [1904] AC 423.
11 [1911] 1 KB 869. See especially ibid at 875 per Avory J, 878 per Lush J.
12 (1874) LR 9 Exch 309 at 324.
13 *H L Bolton Engineering Co v T J Graham & Sons Ltd* [1957] 1 QB 159 at 172, [1956] 3 All ER 624 at 630, per Denning LJ.

This justification of the liability of corporations which *expressly* authorised the commission of tortious acts, or of a course of conduct leading to the commission of a tort, did not necessarily apply where the tort or conduct in question was said to come within the scope of the agent's *implied* authority. There any liability could be said to be truly vicarious. If the corporation did not legally have the power to authorise expressly what the agent did, how could it be said that the corporation could have authorised it impliedly, so as to produce such vicarious liability. Hence if the agent did something outside the scope of his express authority, which he could not have been required to do by the corporation, since it was ultra vires the corporation to empower him in such a way, what he did would not have been done within the scope of his authority, and the corporation would not be liable for his acts.

With certain rare and limited exceptions,[14] the cases concerned acts by servants rather than agents.[15] These appear to have decided that if the servant in question was employed to do the act in question, or employed to do something that necessarily or incidentally involved him in doing the act in question, the corporation could be held liable vicariously. But if the servant's employment could not be taken to comprehend or include the doing of the act in question there was no liability.[16]

The uncertainty, and the academic dispute it engendered,[17] may now have been resolved by the provisions of s 35(1) of the Companies Act 1985, as substituted by s 108 of the Companies Act 1989:

> 'The validity of an act done by a company shall not be called into question on the ground of lack of capacity by reason of anything in the company's memorandum.'

This may amount to what has been called[18] the 'virtual abolition of ultra vires', a result that has been achieved in other common law jurisdictions by legislation.[19] There appears to be consensus that, whatever the intent of this provision as regards the dealings of a company with third parties, its consequence may be that when the agent, or servant, of a company commits a tort connected with his or

---

14 *Bank of New South Wales v Owston* (1879) 4 App Cas 270. *Shaw, Savill and Albion Co v Timaru Harbour Board* (1890) 15 App Cas 429. Cf *Montreal Bank v Young* (1967) 60 DLR (2d) 220. Cf *Denaby and Cadeby Main Colleries Ltd v Yorkshire Miners' Association* [1906] AC 384.

15 Although they sometimes discuss liability for agents: see, eg, *Moore v Metropolitan Rly Co* (1872) LR 8 QB 36.

16 Contrast *Goff v Great Northern Rly Co* (1861) 3 E & E 672; *Moore v Metropolitan Rly Co* (1872) LR 8 QB 36; *Lambert v Great Eastern Rly Co* [1909] 2 KB 776; *Percy v Glasgow Corpn* [1922] 2 AC 299 with *Eastern Counties Rly Co v Broom* (1851) 6 Exch 314; *Roe v Birkenhead, Lancashire and Cheshire Junction Rly Co* (1851) 7 Exch 36; *Poulton v London and South Western Rly Co* (1867) LR 2 QB 534; *Lucas v Mason* (1875) LR 10 Exch 251; *Walker v South Eastern Rly Co* (1870) LR 5 CP 640; *Allen v London and South Western Rly Co* (1870) LR 6 QB 65; *Edwards v London and North Western Rly Co* (1870) LR 5 CP 445; *Ormiston v Great Western Rly Co* [1917] 1 KB 598.

17 See Goodhart *Essays in Jurisprudence and Common Law* ch 5; *Salmond and Heuston on the Law of Torts* (19th edn 1987) pp 480–481.

18 *Gower's Principles of Modern Company Law* (5th edn 1992) p 175.

19 Eg Ontario Business Corporations Act, RSO 1990 c B–16, s 17(3).

her employment it will not matter whether the act in question could have been lawfully authorised by the company.[20]

C. Position of the agent

Personal liability. As a general rule, an agent who commits a tort will be personally liable for his wrong, even if it was done with the authority of his principal (express, implied or apparent) and for the principal's benefit.[1] He cannot plead the authority of his principal by way of defence, even though he does not know that what he is doing is tortious, eg the infringement of a copyright.[2] He will not be liable if his unlawful act was originally unauthorised and became lawful upon subsequent ratification by his principal, for example a distraint legalised by the principal's ratification of the agent's act.[3] Furthermore, the agent will not be personally liable if he himself was innocent of deceit, even though the principal knew that the agent was making a misstatement.[4] Nor will the agent be liable, even though the principal would be in respect of the agent's acts, if the agent is personally immune from liability.[5]

Vicarious immunity. Whether the agent can rely on an immunity of his principal, is a matter of some difficulty. If the principal is generally immune from tort liability, for example, an ambassador, or a trade union or trade union member,[6] the agent probably cannot avail himself of such immunity. But if the principal would not have been liable if sued, because he himself did not have the

---

20 *Salmond and Heuston on Torts* (2nd edn 1992) at p 422; *Street on Torts* (9th edn 1993) at p 566, note 18; Gower, above at pp 175–177.
 1 *Stephens v Elwall* (1815) 4 M & S 259; *McCullagh v Lane Fox & Partners* [1994] 08 EG 118, estate agent making statements that were untrue (but no loss occurred so the agent was not liable). Cf the Canadian case of *Dodds v Millman* (1964) 45 DLR (2d) 472, where an agent was liable for a negligent misstatement made to encourage the sale of the principal's property: cf *Bango v Holt* (1971) 21 DLR (3d) 66: Conant (1968) 47 Nebraska LR 42 at pp 61–63. Contrast *Montreal Bank v Young* (1967) 60 DLR (2d) 220, where the manager had no authority to make the statement and so acted outside the course of his business: hence, there being no fraud, he was not liable for any negligence, no duty being owed by him.
   Note the problem of the liability of the director of a company who may have been guilty of negligence, discussed in Fridman 'Personal Tort Liability of Company Directors' (1992) 5 Canterbury Law Review 41, based on *Trevor Ivory Ltd v Anderson* [1992] 2 NZLR 517. See also *Scotia McLeod Inc v Peoples Jewellers Ltd* (1996) 26 OR (3d) 481 at 490–493.
 2 *Baschet v London Illustrated Standard Co* [1900] 1 Ch 73.
 3 *Hull v Pickersgill* (1819) 1 Brod & Bing 282.
 4 *Eaglesfield v Londonderry* (1878) 38 LT 303. The same will be true where the agent publishes a defamatory statement either not knowing it is defamatory, as long as he is the innocent 'disseminator': cf *Emmans v Pottle* (1885) 16 QBD 354 and *Vizetelly v Mudie's Select Library Ltd* [1900] 2 QB 170: or with knowledge that it is defamatory but without malice, and on a privileged occasion: *Egger v Chelmsford*, above, p 322: (note that *Atiyah* p 402 regards this as an example of vicarious immunity: sed quaere).
 5 Which was the case where the agent (in this instance a servant) was the husband of the plaintiff: *Broom v Morgan* [1953] 1 QB 597, [1953] 1 All ER 849: see now the Law Reform (Husband and Wife) Act 1962.
 6 Trade Union and Labour Relations Act 1974, ss 13, 14, as amended by the Trade Union and Labour Relations (Amendment) Act 1976, the Employment Acts 1980–1990: see now the Trade Union and Labour Relations (Consolidation) Act 1992, ss 219–221, 226.

right to do the act in question, the position of the agent seems more difficult to determine. Powell[7] thought that the agent is liable if he has the necessary state of mind, even though the principal does not, eg malice (or knowledge of untruth); but the agent is not liable if the principal had the right to do the act, as long as the agent acted with authority. The first point seems to be substantiated in principle by the cases of defamation and deceit (where the converse held true, ie innocent agent, guilty principal).[8] The second seems substantiated in principle by the cases on the effect of ratification.[9]

If the principal has contracted with a third party in such a way as to exclude or limit his tortious liability, the question has been raised, whether, in the absence of any relevant statutory provisions,[10] an agent acting under contract with the principal can avail himself of the benefit, ie the immunity provided for in the principal's contract. The technical problems have been that the agent was not a party to such contract, nor had he provided consideration for it.[11] An early decision of the House of Lords, *Elder, Dempster & Co Ltd v Paterson, Zochonis & Co Ltd*,[12] was interpreted to mean that 'where there is a contract which contains an exemption clause, the servants or agents who act under that contract have the benefit of the exemption clause. They cannot be sued in tort as independent people, but they can claim the benefit of the contract made with their employers on whose behalf they were acting': *Mersey Shipping and Transport Co Ltd v Rea Ltd*.[13] However, the *Elder Dempster* case was not easy to decipher. Despite the suggestion that it provided an example of the way in which someone not a party to a contract might none the less derive some benefit under it, if expressly or impliedly it was made for his benefit and he has an interest in its performance,[14] the idea that this decision could support any doctrine of 'vicarious immunity from liability for torts'[15] was rejected on more than one occasion. It was specifically rejected by Bankes LJ in *Mersey Shipping and Transport Co Ltd v Rea Ltd*;[16] by Jenkins and Morris LJJ in *Adler v Dickson*;[17] by the majority of the High Court of Australia in *Wilson v Darling Island*

---

7 *Law of Agency* (2nd edn) p 279. See also *Atiyah* pp 401–404.
8 Above, pp 319–322.
9 *Hull v Pickersgill* (1819) 1 Brod & Bing 282; cf *Sykes v Sykes* (1870) LR 5 CP 113.
10 See eg, Carriage by Air Act 1961, Sch I, art 25A as amended by the Carriage by Air and Road Act 1979, s 1, Sch 1, which does confer such immunity upon an agent, if he proves that he acted within the scope of his employment. Note also the limitation as to the time within which an action may be brought against an agent: Carriage by Air Act 1961, s 5(1).
11 Cf *Dunlop Pneumatic Tyre Co Ltd v Selfridge & Co Ltd* [1915] AC 847 at 853, per Lord Haldane. The pertinence of the 'privity' doctrine is questioned by Fleming *Law of Torts* (8th edn 1992) at pp 294–295.
12 [1924] AC 522.
13 (1925) 21 Lloyd's Rep 375 at 378, per Scrutton LJ.
14 *Smith v River Douglas Catchment Board* [1949] 2 KB 500, [1949] 2 All ER 179; *White v Warrick & Co Ltd* [1953] 2 All ER 1021; *Adler v Dickson* [1955] 1 QB 158, [1954] 3 All ER 397: in all of which Denning LJ, as he then was, propounded this suggestion. See also Devlin J in *Pyrene Co Ltd v Scindia Steam Navigation Co Ltd* [1954] 2 QB 402, [1954] 2 All ER 158. See generally Dowrick 'A Jus Quaesitum Tertio by way of contract in English Law' (1956) 19 MLR 374; Guest 'Bills of Lading and a Jus Quaesitum Tertio' (1959) 75 LQR 312; Furmston 'Return to *Dunlop v Selfridge*' (1960) 23 MLR 373.
15 *Collins & Co v Panama Rly Co* 197 Fed Rep (2d) 893 (1952); 66 HLR 530.
16 (1925) 21 Lloyd's Rep 375.
17 [1955] 1 QB 158 at 195, 199, [1954] 3 All ER 397 at 409, 413.

Stevedoring and Lighterage Co Ltd[18] and by the United States Supreme Court in *Herd & Co v Knawill Machinery Corpn*.[19] It waś not applied in *Cosgrove v Horsfall*[20] nor in *Adler v Dickson*[1] in neither of which could it be inferred that the principal had contracted for exemption in such a way as to cover his agents.[2]

Eventually, in *Scruttons Ltd v Midland Silicones Ltd*[3] the majority of the House of Lords (Lord Denning dissenting[4]) held that there was no doctrine of third party benefit or immunity under a contract to which such third party was not a contracting party nor gave any consideration. The *Elder Dempster* case was criticised and limited in its effect: and the dictum of Scrutton LJ referred to above, as to the effect of the *Elder Dempster* case, was disapproved. As a result, in the *Scruttons* case, where there was no express term in the principal contract covering the agent, and no such term could be implied, the agent was not covered.

However, in *New Zealand Shipping Co Ltd v AM Satterthwaite & Co Ltd*,[5] the majority of the Privy Council[6] applied the speech of Lord Reid in the *Scruttons* case, and held that the appropriate term in a bill of lading could be construed as meaning that the principal had contracted as the agent of his agents (the stevedores) who ultimately handled the cargo; and that the transaction involved a 'unilateral contract', which was accepted by the stevedores, and for which consideration was provided by them, when they undertook the work of dealing with the goods the damage to which was in issue.[7] A subsequent Privy Council decision, *Port Jackson Stevedoring Pty Ltd v Salmond & Spraggon (Australia) Pty Ltd, The New York Star*[8] was concerned with the application of a clause involving a limitation period on claims for damage to goods, rather than a

18 [1956] 1 Lloyd's Rep 346.
19 Referred to by Diplock J in [1959] 2 All ER 289 at 292.
20 (1945) 175 LT 334.
 1 Cf *Genys v Matthews* [1965] 3 All ER 24, [1966] 1 WLR 758; *Gore v Van der Lann* [1967] 2 QB 31, [1967] 1 All ER 360.
 2 Contrast the position in *The Kirknes* [1957] P 51, [1957] 1 All ER 97: where the principal had contracted so as to give his agent the benefit of immunity, namely by contracting as the agent of his (the principal's) agent. But there were other reasons for not protecting the agent.
 3 [1962] AC 446, [1962] 1 All ER 1 (followed by the Supreme Court of Canada in *Canadian General Electric Co Ltd v Pickford and Black Ltd* (1970) 14 DLR (3d) 372): see Battersby 'Exemption Clauses and Third Parties' (1975) 25 U Tor LJ 371: (1978) 28 U Tor LJ 75.
 4 He put forward the approach that such a clause might make the one contracting party volens as regards a risk created by the negligence of the agent, the stevedores: cf *Bowstead on Agency* (15th edn) p 492, pointing out (a) that the protection would be narrower than the contractual protection; (b) that this approach was rejected by Lord Simon of Glaisdale, dissenting, in the *Satterthwaite* case, below. For an application of the *delict*, ie *tort*, approach, see *Circle Sales and Import Ltd v The Ship Tarantel* [1978] 1 FC 269 (a Canadian case).
      Note also the view of La Forest J in *London Drugs Ltd v Kuehne and Nagel International Ltd* (1993) 97 DLR (4th) 261 at 265–319, suggesting that in certain circumstances, eg those in the case in question, the employee, ie agent, owed no distinct duty of care to the plaintiff, hence was not liable.
 5 [1975] AC 154, [1974] 1 All ER 1015, distinguished in *Herrick v Leonard & Dingley Ltd* [1975] 2 NZLR 566.
 6 Viscount Dilhorne and Lord Simon of Glaisdale dissented.
 7 Cf Coote 'Pity the Poor Stevedore' [1981] CLJ 12. This would make it unnecessary to invoke agency where it is probably inappropriate, forced and fictitious: cp Fridman 'The Abuse and Inconsistent Use of Agency' (1982) 20 U of Western Ontario LR 23 at pp 27–30.
 8 [1980] 3 All ER 257, [1981] 1 WLR 138.

limitation upon the amount of money that could be claimed in the eventuality of such damage. The same doctrine was applied. On the basis of what had been found and held in courts below, the Privy Council held that the requisite agency was established to give the stevedores the protection of the clause. However the Privy Council also stated that the significance of the *Satterthwaite* case lay in the finding that, in the normal situation involving the employment of stevedores by carriers, accepted principles enabled and required the stevedores to enjoy the benefit of contractual provisions in the bill of lading.[9] So far as this particular commercial transaction is concerned, therefore, it would appear that English courts have outflanked, if not undermined completely, the earlier decisions in the *Elder, Dempster* and *Scruttons* cases.[10] In Canada, after some conflicting decisions involving stevedores and warehousemen, in which the English doctrine was applied,[11] and employees of a tenant, when it was not,[12] the Supreme Court of Canada appears to have accepted and recognised that there were circumstances in which employees were entitled to benefit from a limitation of liability clause in a contract between their employer and a customer. In *London Drugs Ltd v Kuehne and Nagel International Ltd*,[13] Iacobucci J, speaking for a majority of the court, two members of which did not share those views, stated that for employees to obtain that benefit the following requirements had to be satisfied:

(1) the limitation of liability clause must, either expressly or impliedly, extend its benefit to the employees (or employee) seeking to rely on it;
(2) the employees (or employee) seeking the benefit of the limitation of liability clause must have been acting in the course of their employment *and* must have been performing the very services provided for in the contract between their employer and the plaintiff (customer) when the loss occurred.

Though this was an extension of the previous law, the learned judge was careful to point out that (a) it depended on the intention of the parties; (b) it was similar to the recognised agency exception of earlier decisions; (c) it was limited in scope.[14]

---

9 Ibid at 261 per Lord Wilberforce.
10 An alternative approach is to apply the law of *bailment*: see *Johnson, Matthey & Co Ltd v Constantine Terminals Ltd* [1976] 2 Lloyd's Rep 215; see above, p 169. Contrast *Southern Water Authority v Carey* [1985] 2 All ER 1077 where sub-contractors were not permitted to rely on an exemption clause in the contract between the owner and the general or main contractors.
11 *Ceres Stevedoring Co Ltd v Eisen und Metall AG* (1976) 72 DLR (3d) 660; *Circle Sales and Import Ltd v The Ship Tarantel* [1978] 1 FC 269; *Marubeni America Corpn v Mitsui OSK Lines Ltd* (1979) 96 DLR (3d) 518 (on appeal (1982) 124 DLR (3d) 33, which was affd (1986) 28 DLR (4th) 641); *Miles International Corpn v Federal Commerce and Navigation Co, The Federal Schelde* [1978] 1 Lloyd's Rep 285. Contrast *Calkins & Burke Ltd v Far Eastern SS Co* (1976) 72 DLR (3d) 625.
12 *Greenwood Shopping Plaza Ltd v Beattie* (1980) 111 DLR (3d) 357, distinguished in *Dyck v Manitoba Snowmobile Association Inc and Wood* [1981] 5 WWR 97; affd (1982) 136 DLR (3d) 11, a case involving a snowmobile race, not carriage of goods and their disposition by stevedores. The case was distinguished, for reasons not relevant here, in *Crocker v Sundance Northwest Resorts Ltd* (1989) 51 DLR (4th) 321.
13 (1992) 97 DLR (4th) 261 at 366–367.
14 Ibid at 367–368. See Fridman *Law of Contract in Canada* (3rd edn 1994) pp 586–588.

Liability in conversion. One particular tort that has caused some difficulty is conversion. Even if the agent acts innocently, believing that he is entitled to deal with goods as belonging to his principal, and by the authority of his principal, he will be liable for conversion to the true owner, if his principal is not the true owner. It would appear from the cases that this depends upon the agent's having possession of the goods, and disposing of the possession of them, in such a way as to amount to an assumption of the right to deal with the property in the goods.[15] But the innocent agent will not be liable for conversion where he has not had possession or control of the goods with which he had dealt, or has not dealt with the property in the goods (merely passing possession),[16] or has not dealt with the goods in such a way as to amount to a repudiation of the true owner's title.[17] The distinction seems to be between obtaining an independent possession and passing such possession to another, which grounds liability, however innocent the act, and merely acting as a 'conduit pipe',[18] which is an interfering *act*, without the interfering *intention*. This does not ground liability if the agent acts innocently. Thus if the agent acts merely ministerially, he will not be liable, but if he acts 'in a character beyond that of mere agents'[19] he will be.

D. Joint and several liability of principal and agent

Who may be sued. Since, generally speaking, principal and agent are jointly and severally liable for torts committed by the agent,[20] the injured party may sue either principal or agent (where neither is excused from liability or immune from suit), or he can sue both principal and agent jointly. At common law judgment against either principal or agent, even if unsatisfied, barred any action against the other.[1] This was changed by the Law Reform (Married Women and Tortfeasors) Act 1935, which has been amended more recently by the Civil Liability (Contribution) Act 1978.[2] Either principal or agent can be sued first: and then another action can be brought against the one not originally sued.[3] However, if the injured party releases *either* the principal *or* the agent by deed[4] or by accord

---

15 *Hollins v Fowler* (1875) LR 7 HL 757; *Cochrane v Rymill* (1879) 40 LT 744; *Barker v Furlong* [1891] 2 Ch 172; *Consolidated Co v Curtis & Son* [1892] 1 QB 495. Nor will it matter whether the sale was 'under the hammer' or was the result of a 'provisional bid': *R H Willis & Son v British Car Auctions Ltd* [1978] 2 All ER 392, [1978] 1 WLR 438.
16 *National Mercantile Bank v Rymill* (1881) 44 LT 767; *Union Credit Bank Ltd v Mersey Docks and Harbour Board* [1899] 2 QB 205.
17 *Alexander v Southey* (1821) 5 B & Ald 247; *Lee v Bayes* (1856) 18 CB 599.
18 *Consolidated Co v Curtis & Son* [1892] 1 QB 495. Cf the remarks relating to fraud or other misrepresentation of Cooke P in *Goldsbro v Walker* [1993] 1 NZLR 394 at 398: above, p 315, note 12.
19 *Hollins v Fowler* (1875) LR 7 HL 757 at 797 per Lord Cairns LC.
20 Above, p 315.
 1 *Brinsmead v Harrison* (1872) LR 7 CP 547.
 2 Sections 3, 9(2), Sch 2, which applies to tortfeasors and those guilty of a breach of contract or trust; ibid, s 6(1). It also applies to successive actions, but this may deprive the plaintiff of costs; ibid, s 4.
 3 Note what is said, preceding note, as to costs in such successive actions.
 4 *Duck v Mayeu* [1892] 2 QB 511.

and satisfaction,[5] this will operate as a release of *both* principal *and* agent.[6] The effect will not be achieved by a mere contract with either principal or agent not to sue the particular wrongdoer with whom the contract was made.[7]

Contribution. The 1935 Act also altered the law dealing with contribution between joint tortfeasors. The case of *Merryweather v Nixan*[8] decided that there could be no contribution between joint tortfeasors. Why this should have been so is not clear.[9] Indeed, notwithstanding this decision, there were instances of common law rights to indemnification of a principal by an agent and vice versa.[10] However, the law now provides, in the language of the 1978 Act,[11] replacing that of the 1935 Act, that '. . . any person liable in respect of any damage suffered by another person may recover contribution from any other person liable in respect of the same damage (whether jointly with him or otherwise)'.

Some of the problems which arose under the 1935 Act have now been settled by the 1978 Act, following recommendations by the Law Commission.[12] Thus, 'liable in respect of any damage' means that the person who suffers damage (or anyone representing his estate or dependants) is entitled to recover compensation from the person alleged to be liable in respect of the damage, whether the basis of liability is tort, breach of contract, breach of trust, or anything else.[13] This makes the law wider in scope than it was under the 1935 Act, which referred only to 'tortfeasors'.[14] Contribution may be sought even if the party by whom it is claimed 'has ceased to be liable in respect of the damage in question since the time when the damage occurred, provided that he was so liable immediately before he made or was ordered or agreed to make the payment in respect of which contribution is sought'.[15] This means that if a party has discharged his liability or payment or compromise, he will be able to recover contribution. This is reinforced by another provision[16] which relates to those who have made or agreed to make payments in bona fide settlement or compromise of claims made against them (including payments into court) where it was not clear whether or not they would have been liable to pay damages if the matter had gone to trial, as

5 *Thurman v Wild* (1840) 11 Ad & El 453.
6 *New Zealand Guardian Trust Co Ltd v Brooks* [1995] 1 WLR 96.
7 *Duck v Mayeu* (above). See also *Gardiner v Moore* [1969] 1 QB 55, [1966] 1 All ER 365.
8 (1799) 8 Term Rep 186.
9 See per Lord Goddard in *Carmarthenshire County Council v Lewis* [1955] AC 549 at 560, [1955] 1 All ER 565 at 568. See the comments on Lord Goddard as historian of the Common Law by Lord Diplock in *Bremer Vulkan Schiffbau und Maschinenfabrik v South India Shipping Corpn Ltd* [1981] 2 WLR 141 at 148.
10 Culminating in the important case of *Lister v Romford Ice and Cold Storage Co Ltd* [1957] AC 555, [1957] 1 All ER 125 (a case involving a servant) which made clear the existence of the right to indemnity: see *Fenn v City of Peterborough* (1979) 104 DLR (3d) 174 at 220; see *Atiyah* pp 421–426. For the after-effects of that case, ibid, pp 426–427.
11 Civil Liability (Contribution) Act 1978, s 1(1). Note that this refers to liability under English law: and it is immaterial whether any issue arising in the action was or would be determined (in accordance with the rules of private international law) by reference to a country outside England and Wales: ibid s 1(6).
12 *Report on Contribution* 1977, Law Commission No 79.
13 Civil Liability (Contribution) Act 1978, s 6(1).
14 Law Reform (Married Women and Tortfeasors) Act 1935, s 6(1)(c).
15 Civil Liability (Contribution) Act 1978, s 1(2).
16 Ibid, s 1(4).

long as they would have been liable if the factual basis of the claim against them could have been established.[17] Similarly, contribution can be recovered from someone who has ceased to be liable in respect of the damage in question since the time when the damage occurred, unless this was because of the expiry of a period of limitation or prescription which extinguished the right on which the claim against him in respect of the damage was based.[18] This means that if he ceased to be liable because the claim against him by the injured party has been dismissed for want of prosecution, contribution can still be recovered from him:[19] but if he ceased to be liable because time had run out under the law relating to limitation, contribution could not be recovered.[20] In this context, a judgment given in any action brought in any part of the United Kingdom by or on behalf of a party suffering damage against anyone from whom contribution is being sought is conclusive in proceedings for contribution as regards any issue determined by that judgment in favour of the person from whom contribution is being sought.[1] The court has wide powers with respect to the amount recoverable by way of contribution: it may award whatever is found to be 'just and equitable having regard to the extent of that person's responsibility for the damage in question'.[2] The court can exempt from liability to make contribution, or grant a complete indemnity.[3] But contribution may be reduced or limited where there is a limitation on damages recoverable in respect of an injury or wrong under statute or by agreement: or there is contributory negligence recognised and taken into account under the Law Reform (Contributory Negligence) Act 1945[4] or the Fatal Accidents Act 1976; or there is a corresponding limitation or reduction under the law of any country outside England and Wales.[5]

The more recent Act has not affected some of the limitations on the statutory right of a principal or agent to contribution or indemnity from the other.[6] Thus the

---

17 Resolving a problem which emerged in *Stott v West Yorkshire Road Car Co Ltd* [1971] 2 QB 651, [1971] 3 All ER 534.
18 Civil Liability (Contribution) Act 1978, s 1(3).
19 *Hart v Hall and Pickles Ltd* [1969] 1 QB 405, [1968] 3 All ER 291.
20 *George Wimpey & Co Ltd v British Overseas Airways Corpn* [1955] AC 169, [1954] 3 All ER 661; cf *County of Parkland No 31 v Stetar* (1974) 50 DLR (3d) 376.
 1 Civil Liability (Contribution) Act 1978, s 1(5).
 2 Ibid s 2(1). The question of 'responsibility' has involved difficulties under the 1935 Act; is it based on *causation* or *fault*? See, eg, *Weaver v Commercial Process Co Ltd* (1947) 63 TLR 466; *Collins v Hertfordshire County Council* [1947] KB 598, [1947] 1 All ER 633. See also *The Miraflores and The Abadesa* [1967] 1 AC 826, [1967] 1 All ER 672 (considered in *Fitzgerald v Lane* [1988] 2 All ER 961 at 967–970 per Lord Ackner in relation to apportionment under the Law Reform (Contributory Negligence) Act 1945; *Baker v Willoughby* [1970] AC 467, [1969] 3 All ER 1528.
 3 Civil Liability (Contribution) Act 1978, s 2(2).
 4 See *Fitzgerald v Lane*, above.
 5 Civil Liability (Contribution) Act 1978, s 2(3).
 6 Indeed it is expressly provided that the right of contribution under the Act does not supersede an express contractual right to contribution (as distinct from indemnity): ibid s 7(3). Nor will the Act affect any express or implied contractual or other right to indemnity or any express contractual provision regulating or excluding contribution which would be enforceable apart from the Act: ibid.
  On the effect of such contracts of indemnity where the agent has intentionally committed a criminal act, see *Gardner v Moore* [1984] AC 548, [1984] 1 All ER 1100; or a tortious act, unless such act is not obviously tortious or has been induced by the principal's fraudulent statement, see *WH Smith & Sons v Clinton* (1908) 99 LT 840.

wrongdoing party (whether principal or agent) cannot recover anything from the innocent one who has been led by the others into the commission of the tort. For example, this would be the situation if the principal caused the agent to commit a wrong innocently, eg conversion,[7] or the agent acted in breach of duty, and this brought tort liability upon his principal. Indeed, in the latter instance the principal will be entitled to complete indemnity from the agent, either under the statute,[8] or, possibly the better view, at common law, by reason of the agent's breach of contract.[9] The difference between the two forms of indemnity lies in this: under the statute the question is one for the discretion of the court,[10] whereas at common law the right to indemnity is absolute, flowing from the breach of contract. This allows for no distinction between wilful wrongdoing of the agent (when full indemnity should be given),[11] and negligent acts by the agent (where the imposition of full liability on the agent may be unreasonable).[12]

7 *Adamson v Jarvis* (1827) 4 Bing 66. Cf the situation with respect to an agent sent out in an uninsured vehicle: *Gregory v Ford* [1951] 1 All ER 121, the correctness of which has been doubted: *Atiyah* p 426; *Vandyke v Fender* [1969] 2 QB 581 at 593, [1969] 2 All ER 1291 at 1298 per Paull J (on appeal [1970] 2 QB 292, [1970] 2 All ER 335).
8 According to Denning LJ, in *Jones v Manchester Corpn* [1952] 2 QB 852, [1952] 2 All ER 125.
9 *Lister v Romford Ice and Cold Storage Co Ltd* [1957] AC 555, [1957] 1 All ER 125; *Vandyke v Fender* [1969] 3 All ER 1291, especially at 1298. In *Harvey v RG O'Dell Ltd* [1958] 2 QB 78, [1958] 1 All ER 657, McNair J confined the case to instances where the agent (or servant) was actually doing the kind of thing he was employed to do, and thus was guilty of the breach of an implied term in his contract as to his care and skill in the performance of his duty.
10 See above, note 2.
11 As in the New South Wales case of *Davenport v Railways Comr* (1953) 53 SRNSW 552. Cf the 1978 Act, s 7(3), above, note 6.
12 As in the *Lister* case, above. But see *Sims v Foster Wheeler Ltd* [1966] 2 All ER 313, [1966] 1 WLR 769: *Atiyah* pp 429–430.

CHAPTER 14

Crimes committed by agents

Personal liability of agent and principal. As with torts, criminal acts by an agent can give rise to two different sorts of liability. The first is the direct, personal liability of principal and agent with respect to such acts. The second is the vicarious liability of a principal. As will become evident in due course, the way the criminal law has dealt with the latter of these varieties of liability reveals certain similarities as well as certain major differences between the effects of the agency relationship in the criminal law and its effects in the law of torts.

The position of the agent is clear. He will be personally liable if he is guilty of the crime in question, ie has committed the actus reus with the requisite mens rea (where required).[1] If the agent is innocent, though he has been used by the guilty principal to undertake conduct which is criminal, such as make a false statement, not knowing it to be false, though the falsity is known to the principal who obtains goods thereby,[2] then the principal is guilty, but the agent is not.

The position of the principal[3] is more involved. In general he will only be liable if he is a party to the criminal conduct, by personal participation, instruction, or authorisation of the agent to commit it on his behalf, connivance at what the agent

---

1 In this respect reference should be made to cases in which agents receiving money from principals or third parties, and dishonestly dealing with the money on their own behalf, have sometimes been convicted of appropriate offences, such as theft, breach of trust, etc, and sometimes not. The question of guilt has turned upon the terms of the arrangement between the parties, viz, did it involve contract, trust, etc, and upon whether the resulting relationship between them was merely that of debtor and creditor or something more, giving rise to duties, the breach of which could involve criminal liability: see the following English cases; *R v Hall* [1973] QB 126, [1972] 2 All ER 1009 (a travel agent); *R v Hayes* (1976) 64 Cr App Rep 82 (an estate agent) (seemingly incorrect, according to *R v Mainwaring* (1981) 74 Cr App Rep 99 at 107: and see *R v Cording* [1983] Crim LR 175); *R v Brewster* (1979) 69 Cr App Rep 375 (an insurance agent); and the following Canadian cases: *R v McKenzie* (1971) 21 DLR (3d) 215 (taxi driver employed by taxi owner); *R v Legare* (1978) 78 DLR (3d) 645 (securities broker); *R v Lowden* (1981) 59 CCC (2d) 1 (travel agent). In the last case there was a difference of opinion between the members of the Alberta Appellate Division, one of them, Moir JA, adopting the attitude that the payment of money to the agent for the purchase of travel tickets only created a relationship of debtor and creditor and could not therefore create any possible criminal liability when the money was improperly used by the agent. The agent's conviction was upheld, on other grounds, by the Supreme Court of Canada: *Lowden v R* (1983) 139 DLR (3d) 257.

For the correct way to punish a guilty estate agent, see *R v Allen* (1976) 64 Cr App Rep 297.

2 *R v Butcher* (1858) Bell CC 6. See also Glanville Williams *Criminal Law, The General Part* (2nd edn 1961) pp 349–353.

3 Ie, a principal who is a natural person. For the situation when the principal is a corporation, viz, a juristic artificial person, see below, pp 341–345.

did,[4] or standing by while it is committed.[5] That is to say the principal is liable if he did the act himself, or he expressly authorised the act or he subsequently ratified[6] the doing of the act. But the question which has arisen is whether a principal can be held criminally liable for crimes committed by his agent where there is no such express authorisation or subsequent ratification. Does the doctrine of liability for acts done by the agent within his implied or apparent authority, which is operative in the law of torts, apply in the criminal law? Or is there any similar doctrine applicable in the criminal law? In answering these questions it is necessary to look both at the common law, and at statutory crimes.

Vicarious liability. At common law there were two instances in which, without proof of personal mens rea, or actual guilty conduct, a *master* could be held liable for crimes committed by his *servant*. These were public nuisance[7] and libel (particularly if published in a newspaper).[8] Here there was liability even in the absence of any express command or authorisation by the master, and it would seem that there would be similar liability on the part of a *principal* if the person committing the nuisance or publishing the libel were his *agent*, even if acting without express authority. One point must be noted: by the Libel Act 1843, s 7, if the publisher of a newspaper can show that the libel was published without his authority and without lack of care or caution on his part, he will be free from criminal liability.[9] These anomalous instances of common law vicarious liability for criminal acts are neither of great practical importance, nor of theoretical interest, in that they do not throw much light on the nature and extent of an innocent principal's liability for the crimes of his agent.

More important are the statutory exceptions that have been created to the common law rule.[10] As Lord Diplock pointed out in *Tesco Supermarkets Ltd v Nattrass*:[11]

'Save in cases of strict liability where a criminal statute, exceptionally, makes the doing of an act a crime irrespective of the state of mind in which it is done, criminal law regards a person as responsible for his own crimes

---

4 *Dickenson v Fletcher* (1873) LR 9 CP 1.
5 *Howells v Wynne* (1863) 15 CBNS 3. Or if the principal is really the guilty party, using an innocent agent as a tool. In *R v Huggins* (1730) 2 Ld Raym 1574 the common law was stated thus: 'It is a point not to be disputed but that in criminal cases the principal is not answerable for the act of his deputy, as he is in civil cases; they must each answer for their own acts, and stand or fall by their own behaviour.' See Smith and Hogan *Criminal Law* (7th edn 1992) pp 170–171; cf *Canadian Dredge and Dock Co Ltd v R* (1985) 19 DLR (4th) 314 at 335 per Estey J.
6 As in *Bedford Insurance Co Ltd v Instituto de Resseguros do Brasil* [1985] QB 966.
7 *R v Stephens* (1866) LR 1 QB 702. But see the comments on this case by Field J in *Chisholm v Doulton* (1889) 22 QBD 736 at 740.
8 *R v Almon* (1770) 5 Burr 2686; *R v Gutch, Fisher and Alexander* (1829) Mood & M 433. But see *R v Holbrook* (1878) 4 QBD 42: below, note 9.
   In *Canadian Dredge and Dock Co Ltd v R* (1985) 19 DLR (4th) 314 at 324 Estey J referred also to absolute liability offences, below, and contempt of court.
9 This defence may apply even if the libel is published elsewhere than in a newspaper: *R v Holbrook* (1878) 4 QBD 42 at 66 per Mellor J.
10 On this see generally Edwards *Mens Rea in Statutory Offences* (1955) ch X: Glanville Williams *Criminal Law, The General Part* ch 7; Smith and Hogan pp 171–177; Glanville Williams *Textbook of Criminal Law* (2nd edn 1983) ch 43.
11 [1971] 2 All ER 127 at 155. Presumably his Lordship forgot, or chose to neglect as they are of comparative unimportance, the instances previously mentioned in the text.

only. It does not recognise the liability of a principal for the criminal acts of his agent: because it does not ascribe to him his agent's state of mind. Qui peccat per alium peccat per se is not a maxim of the criminal law.'

It is necessary, first of all, to point out the importance of strict liability in certain offences created by statute, that is to say, liability that can exist without proof of any criminal intent, mens rea. Whether a statute imposes strict liability on someone who infringes it innocently is a matter of construction, and was said by Atkin J in *Mousell Bros Ltd v London and North-Western Rly Co*[12] to depend on six points: (1) the object of the statute, (2) the nature of the duty, (3) the words used, (4) the person on whom the duty was imposed, (5) the person by whom in ordinary circumstances the duty would be performed, (6) the person on whom the penalty was imposed. According to Professor Glanville Williams:[13]

> 'the construction of a statute as imposing vicarious liability is generally a much more drastic operation than the creation of strict liability'.

One point seems certain: it will not be possible to construe a statute as creating vicarious liability, unless it is possible to construe it as creating strict liability. It is, therefore, a question of construction whether the statute imposes vicarious liability upon an innocent principal for his agent's acts (whether themselves innocent or guilty seems irrelevant, if the statute creates strict liability for such acts). As Lord Goddard said in a case involving master and servant:[14]

> 'A master who is not *particeps* in the offence can only be liable criminally for the act of his servant if the statute which creates the offence does so in terms which impose an absolute prohibition. Where the prohibition is absolute no question of knowledge or intent arises, the state of mind of the perpetrator is immaterial. But this does not mean that where an Act forbids something a master is liable if his servant does the act forbidden. It has to be decided as a matter of construction whether the Act imposes a liability on the master for the act of his servant.'

Again, in *James & Son Ltd v Smee*,[15] Slade J restricted the doctrine of vicarious liability to 'acts which the law absolutely prohibits'.

Construction of statutes. The question, when does an Act 'absolutely' prohibit certain conduct, is, therefore, the first problem which arises in respect of the criminal liability of a principal for infringement of statutes by an agent. On this several points must be noted.

---

12 [1917] 2 KB 836 at 845: at 843 per Lord Reading CJ. See also *Coppen v Moore (No 2)* [1898] 2 QB 306 at 312 per Lord Russell CJ; *Pearks, Gunstone and Tee v Ward* [1902] 2 KB 1 at 11 per Channell J. For an illustration of the problems involved, see the decision of the House of Lords in *Sweet v Parsley* [1970] AC 132, [1969] 1 All ER 347, where mens rea was required for an offence under the Dangerous Drugs Act 1965: hence lack of knowledge precluded guilt.
13 *Criminal Law, The General Part* p 269. In his *Textbook of Criminal Law* (2nd edn 1983) pp 927–937, he distinguishes between express statutory exceptions to the rule against vicarious liability and implied statutory exceptions.
14 *Gardner v Akeroyd* [1952] 2 QB 743 at 749, [1952] 2 All ER 306 at 310; cf *Bradshaw v Ewart-Janes* [1983] 1 All ER 12 at 14–15 per Lord Lane LCJ, quoting Bristow J in *Howker v Robinson* [1973] QB 178 at 181, [1972] 2 All ER 786 at 788–789.
15 [1955] 1 QB 78 at 95, [1954] 3 All ER 273 at 280: a dissenting judgment, but the principles are not different from those employed by the majority of the court.

First, it is still the most important question whether the statute clearly prohibits the conduct, irrespective of the state of mind of the principal.

> 'There is a presumption ... that mens rea ... is an essential ingredient in every offence but that presumption is liable to be displaced either by the words of the statute creating the offence or the subject-matter with which it deals, and both must be considered.'[16]

If there is such absoluteness of prohibition, then there will also be vicarious liability for the acts of an agent. This is justified on the ground that vicarious liability is 'a necessary doctrine for the proper enforcement of much modern legislation'[17] and 'because it can fairly be said that by such sanctions citizens are induced to keep themselves and their organisations up to the mark'.[18]

Secondly, if the statute enacts that something shall not be 'caused', 'suffered' or 'permitted' then it has been held that knowledge that the act is being committed, or at least wilful disregard of whether or not it is being committed, must be proved. In the absence of such knowledge or disregard, there will be no liability, direct or vicarious.[19]

Thirdly, where a statute uses the word 'knowingly' in the creation of the offence, it may be that guilt of the offence in question cannot be concluded without proof that the criminal knew what his agents were doing. Devlin J in *Roper v Taylor's Central Garages (Exeter) Ltd*[20] after discussing the question of proof where no express phrase is used in the statute, went on to say:

> 'All that the word "knowingly" does is to say expressly what is normally implied, and if the presumption that the statute requires mens rea is not rebutted, I find difficulty in seeing how it can be said that the omission of the word "knowingly" has as a matter of construction the effect of shifting the burden of proof from the prosecution to the defence.'

It has been said that the presence of the word 'knowingly' in the statute will not necessarily mean that the guilty mind must be proved and that everything

---

16 *Sherras v De Rutzen* [1895] 1 QB 918 at 921 per Wright J. For examples of such liability see: *Cundy v Le Cocq* (1884) 13 QBD 207; *Grade v DPP* [1942] 2 All ER 118; *R v Sorsky* [1944] 2 All ER 333. Cf *McNab v Alexanders of Greenock Ltd* 1971 SLT 121, on strict liability under the Trade Descriptions Act 1968.

17 *Gardner v Akeroyd* [1952] 2 QB 743 at 751, [1952] 2 All ER 306 at 311 per Lord Goddard CJ. He added that it was not a doctrine to be extended. Cf the point that in relation to the attribution of the acts of the servant or agent of a company to the company so as to make the latter liable (below, pp 342–345) regard must be had to 'the terms and policies of the substantive rule': per Lord Hoffman in *Meridian Global Funds Management Asia Ltd v Securities Commission* [1995] 3 WLR 413 at 423.

18 *Reynolds v G H Austin & Sons Ltd* [1951] 2 KB 135 at 149, [1951] 1 All ER 606 at 611, per Devlin J: cf ibid at 150, 612; *James & Son v Smee* [1955] 1 QB 78 at 93, [1954] 3 All ER 273 at 279 per Parker J. It is interesting to note that in *Hall v Farmer* [1970] 1 All ER 729, [1970] 1 WLR 366 it was held that an employer could not rely upon the mistake of his servant or agent to justify the defence of mistake available in respect of offences under the Weights and Measures Act 1963, by virtue of s 26(1)(a) of that Act.

19 For example see *Somerset v Wade* [1894] 1 QB 574; *Harding v Price* [1948] 1 KB 695, [1948] 1 All ER 283; *Lovelace v DPP* [1954] 3 All ER 481, [1954] 1 WLR 1468; *James & Son Ltd v Smee* [1955] 1 QB 78, [1954] 3 All ER 273. Generally see *Edwards* chs IV–VII; *Smith v Hogan* pp 124–127.

20 [1951] 2 TLR 284; cf also *Harding v Price* [1948] 1 KB 695 at 702, [1948] 1 All ER 283 at 285 per Humphreys J.

depends on the purpose of the Act.[1] However, in *Vane v Yiannopoullos*[2] the House of Lords, in respect of an enactment on licensing, creating a new offence, held that the word 'knowingly' involved proof of knowledge, ie guilt on the part of the master or principal. This suggests that the trend is in favour of proof of a guilty mind except where precluded by earlier interpretation of a statutory provision.

Fourthly, in a number of cases in which the offence in question has been 'aiding and abetting' or 'attempting', it has been held that there would be neither strict nor vicarious liability in the absence of knowledge of the essential fact or facts.[3] The result would otherwise be manifestly unjust nor would it really fulfil the purposes of strict or vicarious liability in crime, namely, to promote the observance of the law. As Devlin J said,[4] in another context:

'... where the punishment of an individual will not promote the observance of the law either by that individual, or by others whose conduct he may reasonably be expected to influence, then, in the absence of clear and express words, such punishment is not intended.'

Application of statutes. Thus it is by no means easy to determine whether any particular enactment creates vicarious liability on the part of an innocent principal. However, should it be decided that such liability has been created by the statute[5] a further question arises: namely, whether the circumstances show the agent's act or omission was one for which the principal should be held responsible. It is in this respect that the problem of 'authority' or 'employment', as the test of liability, has arisen.

There appear to be two views which, at different times, have been propounded on the subject of vicarious liability in crime.[6] On the one hand, there is the attitude that liability depends upon whether a task has been 'delegated' to the agent. On the other there is the apparently older attitude that a principal is liable for crimes committed by his agent acting 'within the scope of his authority', which amounted to the same thing as the master's liability for crimes committed by his servant acting 'in the course of his employment'.[7] At different times Lord

1 *Allen v Whitehead* [1930] 1 KB 211 at 230 per Lord Hewart CJ. See *Edwards* ch III; *Smith v Hogan* pp 120–122. For example, knowledge of the general nature of the wrongdoing was sufficient without proof of knowledge of the exact goods being 'smuggled' in *R v Hussain* [1969] 2 QB 567, [1969] 2 All ER 1117.
2 [1965] AC 486, [1964] 3 All ER 820. Cf *Ross v Moss* [1965] 2 QB 396, [1965] 3 All ER 145; see also below, p 339, on the subject of delegation.
3 See *Johnson v Youden* [1950] 1 KB 544, [1950] 1 All ER 300; *Ferguson v Weaving* [1951] 1 KB 814, [1951] 1 All ER 412; *Gardner v Akeroyd* [1952] 2 QB 743, [1952] 2 All ER 306. Cf *Smith and Hogan* pp 142–143.
4 *Reynolds v G H Austin & Sons Ltd* [1951] 2 KB 135 at 150, [1951] 1 All ER 606 at 612: cf Lord Goddard in *Gardner v Akeroyd*, above, 751, 311.
5 Thereby dispensing with personal actus reus on the part of the principal: cf Glanville Williams *Criminal Law, The General Part* pp 218, 269.
6 See *Edwards* pp 220–234.
7 Cf above, pp 308–312, where these two expressions are considered and compared in relation to liability in tort. See also *Smith v Hogan* pp 172–176, distinguishing 'the delegation principle' from 'where the servant's act is his master's act in law'. Glanville Williams *Textbook of Criminal Law* (2nd edn 1983) pp 958–966, prefers to analyse the situation in terms of the 'personal verbs' to be found in the statutes, eg, 'sale', 'using', 'driving'.

For discussion of these two expressions in the context of criminal liability, see *Canadian Dredge and Dock Co Ltd v R* (1985) 19 DLR (4th) 314 at 329–331 per Estey J.

Goddard put both of these attitudes forward as the basis of such liability. Thus, in one report of *Barker v Levinson*,[8] he said:

> 'The master is responsible for a criminal act of the servant if the act is done within the general scope of the servant's employment.'

In *Gardner v Akeroyd*[9] he said:

> 'The master will be liable notwithstanding that the sale was affected by his servant and without his knowledge, provided only that the sale was in the course of the servant's employment.'

But this expression of the principal's liability did not go unnoticed. In *Navarro v Moregrand Ltd*,[10] Denning LJ, after quoting the All England Report of Lord Goddard in *Barker v Levinson*, said:

> 'If that were correct it would equate the master's criminal responsibility with his civil responsibility, which would be an innovation against which I would issue a caveat.'

The learned judge pointed out that in the Law Reports' version of Lord Goddard's judgment the principle was stated thus:

> 'if a master chooses to delegate the conduct of his business to a servant who does an act in the course of conducting the business which is absolutely prohibited the master is liable.'[11]

The 'delegation' attitude was expressed by Lord Goddard in the earlier case of *Linnett v Metropolitan Police Comr*:[12]

> '[The principle underlying these decisions[13]] does not depend upon the legal relationship existing between master and servant or between principal and agent: it depends on the fact that the person who is responsible in law . . . has chosen to delegate his duties, powers, and authority to another.'

The distinction between these two tests, 'scope of authority' and 'delegation of duty' is shown by *Barker v Levinson*[14] itself. The facts were:

> The manager of a block of flats employed a rent collector. On one occasion he gave express authority to the collector to grant a lease in respect of a certain flat. But the collector was only allowed to do this if he considered the prospective tenant satisfactory. Without the knowledge of the manager, the

---

8 [1950] 2 All ER 825 at 827; contrast the report in [1951] 1 KB 342.
9 [1952] 2 QB 743 at 749, [1952] 2 All ER 306 at 310.
10 [1951] 2 TLR 674 at 681.
11 [1951] 1 KB 342 at 345.
12 [1946] KB 290 at 294–295, [1946] 1 All ER 380 at 382. Once again there are variations in the language cited in the different reports.
13 On the Lunacy Acts, the Food and Drugs Act, and 'other Acts in which convictions have been upheld of persons knowingly permitting certain acts, without any actual knowledge of them, the acts having been knowingly permitted by a servant or manager and that knowledge having been imputed to the master or principal' [1946] KB 290 at 294, [1946] 1 All ER 380 at 382.
14 [1951] 1 KB 342, [1950] 2 All ER 825; cf *Navarro v Moregrand Ltd* [1951] 2 TLR 674 at 681, per Denning LJ.

collector demanded and received a premium of £100 as a condition of granting a lease. There was no evidence that the manager received any part of the premium.

In a prosecution against the manager under the Landlord and Tenant (Rent Control) Act 1949, s 2, for requiring the payment of an illegal premium, it was held that he was not liable for the illegal act of the rent collector. This was because the rent collector had no express or implied authority to do what he did, since the business of managing the flats had not been left to him. The result might have been different if he had been 'a general agent in respect of those flats'.[15] Denning LJ in *Navarro v Moregrand Ltd* pointed out that had this been a civil case the manager would have been held liable for the rent collector's acts,[16] but in the criminal courts he was not liable because he had not authorised the agent, either expressly or impliedly, to take a premium.

For this reason, the apparent attempt by Lord Goddard in *Barker v Levinson* to equate the two tests of delegation and acting within the scope of employment[17] would appear to be unfounded, since it makes the principal's criminal liability too wide. In addition, that equation can be criticised on the ground that the cases show how the two different tests have been differently applied, with differing results.[18] In particular, in the 'licensing' cases[19] the test of delegation has been applied to create liability, even where 'knowledge' is required, the knowledge of the agent to whom a task has been delegated being imputed to the principal.[20] But it is clear that there must have been delegation by the principal to someone. A principal will not be liable criminally for the acts of someone 'over whom he had no control and for whom he had no responsibility'.[1]

Is the applicable test, therefore, one of delegation? It is favoured by Professor Edwards,[2] and, apparently, regarded as correct by Professor Glanville Williams,[3]

---

15 [1951] 1 KB 342 at 345, [1950] 2 All ER 825, at 827 per Lord Goddard; cf ibid at 346, 827, per Byrne J. The servant in this case was not acting within the general scope of his employment: an expression of the older attitude.
16 [1951] 2 TLR 674 at 681.
17 In [1950] 2 All ER 825 at 827: 'In other words if a master chooses to delegate the conduct of his business to a servant, then, if the servant in the course of conducting the business, does an act which is absolutely prohibited, the master is liable, *which is really only another way of saying the act done must be within the general scope of the servant's employment*.'
18 *Edwards* pp 229–232.
19 Glanville Williams *Criminal Law, The General Part* pp 270–273: Glanville Williams *Textbook of Criminal Law* (2nd edn 1983) pp 953–958.
20 *Linnett v Metropolitan Police Comr* [1946] KB 290 at 296, [1946] 1 All ER 380 at 383; per Humphreys J. See *Vane v Yiannopoullos* [1964] 3 All ER 820 at 823, 828, per Lords Reid and Evershed: followed and enlarged upon by Lord Parker CJ in *R v Winson* [1969] 1 QB 371, [1968] 1 All ER 197 (after some earlier comment in *Ross v Moss* [1965] 2 QB 396, [1965] 3 All ER 145). *R v Wilson* was itself followed in *Howker v Robinson* [1973] QB 178, [1972] 2 All ER 786, criticised by *Smith and Hogan* pp 173–174.
1 *Reynolds v G H Austin & Sons Ltd* [1951] 2 KB 135 at 145, [1951] 1 All ER 606 at 609, per Lord Goddard: cf *James & Son Ltd v Smee* [1955] 1 QB 78 at 91, [1954] 3 All ER 273 at 278 per Parker J.
2 *Mens Rea in Statutory Offences* pp 232–234.
3 In *Criminal Law, The General Part* pp 278–285, quoting cases which generalise from the 'licensing' cases. Seemingly he is of the same view in his *Textbook of Criminal Law* (2nd edn 1983) pp 953–958. For other views on the test, see Pace, 'Delegation—A Doctrine in Search of a Definition' [1982] Cr L Rev 627.

who says that the principles of strict and vicarious responsibility are fast becoming entangled with each other. Powell, on the other hand,[4] preferred to base the principal's liability for the crimes of his agent on the idea of 'authority', so that a principal would then be liable for his agent's criminal acts only when he would be liable for his agent's torts. But this is to adopt the view criticised by Denning LJ and others. On the basis that the liability for an agent's torts is very similar to that for a servant's torts,[5] this would involve very broad criminal liability on the part of an innocent principal. Though the courts have created such liability where the statute in question was definitely enacting strict liability of broad scope,[6] yet it is also clear that they are against unnecessarily strict imposition of criminal liability on innocent principals who have not had the opportunity of controlling or limiting their agents' acts.

In the light of the decisions in *Vane v Yiannopoullos*,[7] and *R v Winson*[8] it would seem that the 'delegation' test has now received eminent judicial approval, so as to make it possibly the decisive method of determining when a principal comes within the scope of a statute creating strict criminal responsibility.

While it is true that these cases were specifically concerned with delegation in relation to a licensing offence, some remarks of Lord Parker CJ, in the latter case,[9] in the wake of the earlier House of Lords decision, suggest that the doctrine of delegation is of wider relevance and import. What Lord Parker said was:

> 'When an absolute offence has been created by Parliament, then the person on whom a duty is thrown is responsible, whether he is delegated or whether he has acted through a servant; he is absolutely liable regardless of any intent or knowledge or mens rea. The principle of delegation comes into play, and only comes into play, in cases where, though the statute uses words which import knowledge or intent such as in this case "knowingly" or in some cases "permitting" or "suffering" and the like, cases to which knowledge is inherent, nevertheless it has been held that a man cannot get out of the responsibilities which have been put on him by delegating those responsibilities to another.'

Indeed after referring to earlier authorities, Lord Parker ended by citing the judgment of Lord Goddard in the *Linnet* case, saying that it set out 'the doctrine of delegation which does form part of our law, and no one in the House of Lords has said that it does not'.[10] This suggests the possible supremacy of the 'delegation' test, approved and applied, implicitly even if not explicitly, by the House of Lords in *Tesco Supermarkets Ltd v Nattrass*[11] (in order to permit a company to take advantage of a statutory defence to a statutory offence).

---

4 *Law of Agency* (2nd edn) p 290.
5 See the discussion above, pp 308–312.
6 Eg *Slatcher v George Mence Smith Ltd* [1951] 2 KB 631, [1951] 2 All ER 388; *Quality Dairies (York) Ltd v Pedley* [1952] 1 KB 275, [1952] 1 All ER 380.
7 [1965] AC 486, [1964] 3 All ER 820.
8 [1969] 1 QB 371, [1968] 1 All ER 197, followed in *Howker v Robinson* [1973] QB 178, [1972] 2 All ER 786.
9 [1968] 1 All ER 197 at 202.
10 Ibid at 204.
11 [1972] AC 153, [1971] 2 All ER 127.

On this view, therefore, there is a difference between the criminal and tortious liability of principals for the acts of their agents. That this is reasonable follows from the different aims of the criminal law and the law of torts. The one seeks to punish or at least to ensure obedience to the law, which means that it is not advancing those aims to cast the net of vicarious criminal liability too widely, whereas the latter seeks to compensate for harm done, thereby making it more reasonable to impose a wider form of vicarious liability.

Liability of corporations

Corporations in criminal law. The vicarious liability of a corporation for the crimes of its agent merits special treatment.[12] The position of corporations in the criminal law was anomalous for a long time because of procedural as well as substantive difficulties. Many of these defects have been cured by statute, or by the development of the doctrine of the vicarious *tort* liability of corporations, which has been accepted as applying in the field of criminal law. However, there still remain two important limitations on the criminal liability of corporations. First, certain crimes cannot physically be attributed to corporations without absurdity, eg rape, bigamy, perjury.[13] Secondly, there are some crimes the punishment for which cannot be inflicted on a corporation, for example, an offence for which the only penalty is community service.[14] Since the only possible punishment is a fine, a corporation can only be convicted of offences punishable by a fine, which includes most offences.[15]

Given that the crime in question is one for which a corporation can be convicted, the question is raised: in what circumstances can a corporation be held liable? Since a corporation can only act by, and therefore can only be made liable for, the acts of its agents or servants, it is necessary to determine the agents for whose acts a corporation will be criminally liable. This suggests that the liability is vicarious. However, there are circumstances in which the corporation will be *directly* as well as *vicariously* liable. There are situations in which the acts of the agent are really the corporation's acts (and the liability is direct though based on the agent's acts): and there are situations in which the agent's act is his own act, for which the corporation may be vicariously liable, in the true and strict sense of the expression.

---

12 See generally Glanville Williams, *Criminal Law, The General Part,* ch 22; Glanville Williams *Textbook of Criminal Law* (2nd edn 1983) ch 44; *Smith v Hogan* pp 178–185; Welsh 'The Criminal Liability of Corporations' (1946) 62 LQR 345; *Gower's Principles of Modern Company Law* (5th edn 1992) pp 193–197; Macey 'Agency Theory and the Criminal Liability of Organizations' (1991) 71 Boston ULR 315. On unincorporated associations see *Smith v Hogan* p 176; *A-G v Able* [1984] QB 795, [1984] 1 All ER 277.
13 *R v ICR Haulage Ltd* [1944] KB 551 at 554, [1944] 1 All ER 691 at 693. But a corporation could be charged with incitement to commit such crimes, or possibly aiding and abetting their commission.
14 *Meridian Global Funds Management Asia Ltd v Securities Commission* [1995] 3 WLR 413 at 419 per Lord Hoffman.
15 Smith and Hogan, pp 182–183. This would seem to include manslaughter: *R v ICR Haulage Ltd* [1944] KB 551, [1944] 1 All ER 693 (overruling *R v Cory Bros & Co* [1927] 1 KB 810. See also *R v P&O European Ferries Ltd* (1990) 93 Cr App Rep 72.

Direct liability. When is a corporation *directly* responsible for a crime committed through its agents? This depends on the position of the agent whose acts are in question. If that agent can be said *to be* the corporation, then the corporation will be directly liable. This is what Professor Glanville Williams[16] calls the alter ego doctrine, and what Gower calls, the *organic* theory.[17] It was put thus by Lord Haldane in *Lennard's Carrying Co Ltd v Asiatic Petroleum Co Ltd*:[18]

> 'A corporation is an abstraction. It has no mind of its own any more than it has a body of its own: its active and directing will must consequently be sought in the person of somebody who for some purposes may be called an agent, but who is really the directing mind and will of the corporation, the very ego and centre of the personality of the corporation. That person may be under the direction of the shareholders in general meeting: that person may be the board of directors itself. ... The fault or privity[19] is the fault or privity of somebody who is not merely a servant or agent for whom the company is liable upon the footing respondeat superior, but somebody for whom the company is liable because his action is the very action of the company itself.'

Thus the *act* that is guilty, as well as the *mind* that is guilty, producing criminal liability, must be the act and mind of someone who is 'really the directing mind and will of the corporation'. As Denning LJ said in the case of *H L Bolton Engineering Co Ltd v T J Graham & Sons Ltd*:[20]

> 'A company may in many ways be likened to a human body. It has a brain and nerve centre which controls what it does. It also has hands which hold the tools and act in accordance with directions from the centre. Some of the people in the company are mere servants and agents who are nothing more than hands to do the work and cannot be said to represent the mind or will. Others are directors and managers who represent the directing mind and will

16 *Criminal Law, The General Part* pp 857–859. It is referred to as such by Nourse LJ in *El Ajou v Dollar Land Holdings plc* [1994] 2 All ER 685 at 695.
17 *Gower's Principles of Modern Company Law* (5th edn 1992) pp 193–197. In *Canadian Dredge and Dock Co Ltd v R*, below, it is referred to as the doctrine of 'identification'; see also *Scotia McLeod Inc v Peoples Jewellers Ltd* (1996) 26 OR (3d) 481 at 482–493.
18 [1915] AC 705 at 713: see also *Daimler Co Ltd v Continental Tyre and Rubber Co (Great Britain) Ltd* [1916] 2 AC 307 at 340 per Lord Parker. Lord Haldane's language was approved in *Tesco Supermarkets Ltd v Nattrass* [1972] AC 153, [1971] 2 All ER 127. See also *El Ajou v Dollar Land Holdings plc* [1994] 2 All ER 685 at 695–696 per Nourse LJ, 699 per Rose LJ, 705 per Hoffmann LJ. It was also cited, and its consequences in England and Canada discussed, in *Canadian Dredge and Dock Co Ltd v R* (1985) 19 DLR (4th) 314 at 325–331. The contrasting position in the United States is considered *ibid* pp 331–333. The situation in Australia and New Zealand, where the English doctrine is followed, is discussed ibid pp 333–335.
19 Of the company within the meaning of a statute in that case: cf *The Lady Gwendolen* [1965] 2 All ER 283 especially at 294–295 per Willmer LJ.
20 [1957] 1 QB 159 at 172, [1956] 3 All ER 624 at 630 (followed by the Divisional Court in *John Henshall (Quarries) Ltd v Harvey* [1965] 2 QB 233, [1965] 1 All ER 725: and see *The Lady Gwendolen*, above, at 295, per Willmer LJ). This statement, too, was approved and applied by the House of Lords in the *Tesco* case, above. *Note* how the anthropomorphic language recalls the 'realist' theory of corporations, put forward by Maitland in his *Introduction to Gierke's Political Theories of the Middle Ages.*

of the company and control what it does. The state of mind of these managers is the state of mind of the company and is treated by the law as such.'

Where the law required a guilty mind as a condition of a criminal offence, the guilty mind of the directors or the managers would render the company itself guilty.[1]

Estey J of the Supreme Court of Canada put it in this way in *Canadian Dredge and Dock Co Ltd v R:*[2]

'The identity doctrine merges the board of directors, the managing director, the superintendent, the manager or anyone else delegated by the board of directors to whom is delegated the governing executive authority of the corporation, and the conduct of any of the merged entities is thereby attributed to the corporation.'

The doctrine and the language of Viscount Haldane were discussed at length by Lord Hoffman, delivering the opinion of the Privy Council, in *Meridian Global Funds Management Asia Ltd v Securities Commission*.[3] There it was said that, to determine when, and for whose acts a company was liable, reference was to be made to what were called 'the rules of attribution'.[4] It was a necessary part of corporate personality that there should be rules by which acts were attributed to the company. Rules of attribution were a matter of interpretation or construction of the relevant substantive rule, ie, the particular statutory provision that was the subject of consideration in the particular instance.[5] The difference this made was illustrated by reference to the *Tesco* case[6] and *Re Supply of Ready Mixed Concrete (No 2)*.[7] In the former the company was not liable: in the latter it was.[8] However, despite his use of the language of 'attribution', Lord Hoffman did not reject or discard Lord Haldane's notion of the 'directing mind and will' of a corporation. What he was anxious to point out was that any difficulties caused by that phrase have been caused by concentration on the phrase rather than on the purpose for which it was used by Lord Haldane.[9] 'It will often be the most appropriate description of the person designated by the relevant attribution rule, but it might be better to acknowledge that not every such rule has to be forced into the same formula.'[10] The question was one of construction rather than metaphysics.[11]

---

1 [1957] 1 QB 159 at 172, [1956] 3 All ER 624 at 630. Hence the company were not liable in the *Tesco* case, because the manager of one of several hundred supermarkets could not be identified with the company. But the company was held liable for contempt in entering into a restrictive arrangement in breach of an undertaking by the company to the Restrictive Practices Court in *Re Supply of Ready Mixed Concrete (No 2)* [1995] 1 AC 456; and a company was held to be in breach of a duty to give notice under a provision of the New Zealand Securities Amendment Act 1988 in *Meridian Global Funds Management Asia Ltd v Securities Commission* [1995] 3 WLR 413.
2 (1985) 19 DLR (4th) 314 at 336–337.
3 [1995] 3 WLR 413 at 418–423.
4 Ibid at 418.
5 Ibid at 419.
6 *Tesco Supermarkets Ltd v Nattrass* [1972] AC 153, [1971] 2 All ER 127.
7 [1995] 1 AC 456.
8 Above, note 1.
9 Above, note 3 at 422.
10 Ibid, at 422–423.
11 Ibid, at 423.

It would appear, therefore, that, notwithstanding the remarks of Lord Hoffman, the Haldane doctrine, as it may be called, still governs the way courts approach the issue of direct criminal liability on the part of a corporation.

In the past, by the application of this doctrine, a corporation could be made liable for conspiring to defraud, through the acts of its managing director;[12] for making a false statement by a transport manager thereby infringing Defence Regulations,[13] for publishing false returns of purchase tax through a sales manager and general manager.[14]

The person committing the act, the agent in question, must have been acting within the scope of his authority. This seems to involve all the familiar rules and situations already discussed in relation to vicarious tort liability. To such an extent has this been taken that in *Moore v I Bresler Ltd*[15] the corporation was held liable when the agent in question had acted in his own interests and *with the intent of defrauding the corporation*. Not surprisingly, this decision, and the principle it seems to enunciate, have been heavily criticised, on the ground that the tortious doctrine of vicarious liability has no place in the criminal law, even where it is transmuted into the idea of *direct* action by the corporation *through* a representative organ or agent.[16] To quote Estey J again:[17]

'Where the corporation benefited or was intended to be benefited from the fraudulent and criminal activities of the directing mind, the *rationale* of the identification rule holds. Where the delegate of the corporation has turned against his principal, the *rationale* fades away.'

The fact that the crime involves a guilty state of mind does not prevent criminal liability on the part of the corporation.[18] The guilty mind of the agent will be enough, as long as he was acting within the scope of his authority.[19] If the crime is a statutory one for conviction of which no mens rea is required to be proved,[20]

---

12 *R v ICR Haulage Ltd* [1944] KB 551, [1944] 1 All ER 691; cf *Canadian Dredge and Dock Co Ltd v R*, above (corporation liable for conspiracy to defraud by 'bid-rigging' of dredging contracts done by the general manager, president or vice-president in charge of dredging operations). But not for conspiring with the sole officer of the corporation responsible for its acts and intentions: *R v McDonnell* [1966] 1 QB 233, [1966] 1 All ER 193.

13 *DPP v Kent and Sussex Contractors Ltd* [1944] KB 146, [1944] 1 All ER 119.

14 *Moore v I Bresler Ltd* [1944] 2 All ER 515. But not for aiding and abetting the commission of a road offence, where the requisite knowledge was that of an employee who was not a responsible officer of the company, being employed only to weigh laden vehicles: *John Henshall (Quarries) Ltd v Harvey*, above. Cf the *Tesco* case, above.

15 [1944] 2 All ER 515.

16 *Glanville Williams*, above, note 4 p 859. Welsh 62 LQR 345 at p 360. See also the discussion of this issue, and the case of *Moore v I Bresler Ltd* by Estey J in *Canadian Dredge and Dock Co Ltd v R*, above, at pp 342–352. On the facts the issue did not arise: but Estey J appears to have questioned the extension of the *Moore* case to a situation where one or more of the directing minds acted entirely for his own benefit and diverted his principal efforts to defraud the company: ibid at p 356.

17 (1985) 19 DLR (4th) 314 at 356.

18 See the cases cited notes 12–14 above, and *Triplex Safety Glass Co Ltd v Lancegaye Safety Glass (1934) Ltd* [1939] 2 KB 395, [1939] 2 All ER 613 (criminal libel).

19 Eg *Chuter v Freeth and Pocock Ltd* [1911] 2 KB 832; *Mousell Bros Ltd v London and North-Western Rly Co* [1917] 2 KB 836.

20 Above, pp 335–341. Note, however, the 'passing on' defence under some statutes: Glanville Williams *Textbook of Criminal Law* pp 980–981: *Smedleys Ltd v Breed* [1974] AC 839, [1974] 2 All ER 21.

then the corporation can certainly be convicted as a result of the acts of its agents, even where the statute does not create vicarious liability.[1]

Vicarious liability. Apart from this *direct* liability through the acts of agents there is also the ordinary well-established kind of vicarious liability for the crimes of agents, which raises the kind of problems that have already been discussed in this chapter. For such liability the agent need not be a *directive* agent, it will be sufficient if he is *executive*. But the liability of the corporation will depend upon whether the crime is one for which vicarious liability is imposed, such as common law public nuisance,[2] or a statutory offence[3] and whether the acts of the agent come within the appropriate test of such vicarious liability.[4]

---

1 Eg *Pearks, Gunston and Tee Ltd v Ward* [1902] 2 KB 1.
2 *R v Great North of England Rly Co* (1846) 9 QB 315.
3 Above, pp 335–337.
4 Above, pp 337–341.

CHAPTER 15

Agency and evidence

In two important ways the knowledge of an agent may be relevant to the legal position of his principal. What he knows about a certain situation may be made public by him in the form of a statement on which reliance may be placed by way of evidence. The question will then arise whether the statement of the agent is in any way effective as against the principal in any litigation in which the principal is involved. Secondly, what the agent knows may be attributable to the principal, in so far as, legally speaking, the agent represents the principal. Here, as elsewhere, the agent is facing two ways and operating in two directions. He can bind his principal not only by what he does in respect of third parties or strangers to the principal-agent relationship, but also by what he acquires, in this instance in the form of knowledge, from such third parties or strangers. To this extent there is some connection between the position of agents in relation to evidence and the position of agents with regard to the question of notice of some fact on the part of the principal. Hence the discussion of these two, otherwise possibly unrelated, matters in the present chapter.

A. Admissions by an agent[1]

Admissions by a party against his interest, whether in civil or criminal cases, are evidence of the truth of such admissions, even though such statements out of court would be otherwise objectionable as hearsay.[2] This exception to the rule against the admissibility of hearsay evidence is based on the idea that 'what a party himself admits to be true may reasonably be presumed to be so'.[3] For this reason admissions by a party's agent will not only be relevant, but also be admissible evidence.[4] However, the agent must have been acting within the scope of his authority, whether express, implied, apparent or presumed, at the time of admission was made. This is really a corollary of the whole idea of the

---

1 Morgan 'Rationale of Vicarious Admissions' (1929) 42 HLR 461 and *Restatement, Second, Agency*, paras 284–289. See also *McCormick on Evidence* (3rd edn 1984) pp 787–790.
2 *Cross and Tapper on Evidence* (8th edn 1995) pp 642–662, especially as regards agents at pp 650–653.
3 *Slatterie v Pooley* (1840) 6 M & W 664 at 669 per Parke B.
4 *The Prinses Juliana, Esbjerb (Owner) v Prinses Juliana (Owners)* [1936] P 139, [1936] 1 All ER 685.

vicarious liability of the principal in substantive law.[5] Thus in *Kirkstall Brewery Co v Furness Rly Co*:[6]

> In an action by the owner of a parcel of money which had been lost, it was held that the stationmaster's statement that the money had been stolen by a railway servant was admissible.

This was because the stationmaster had authority to arrest, and therefore to assist the police. Hence the making of a statement about the theft was within the scope of his authority.

Professor Hanbury[7] draws a distinction between authority to *act* and authority to *speak*[8] and says that although the latter is derived from the former, it cannot be exactly co-extensive with it, being narrower in scope. In most cases, however, the two will coincide. But it seems unnecessary to draw any such distinctions, since an admission by an agent, to be admissible, must be connected with, and come within, his authority to act.[9] This is shown by the requirements that the statement, to be admissible evidence, must have been relevant to the particular transaction on which the agent was employed, and must have been made by him in the course of his performance of that transaction. Thus, a letter written by the master of a ship relating to goods which were being carried by charterparty in the master's ship, was admissible in an action against the owner's of the ship.[10] An admission by a wife carrying on business on behalf of her husband, relating to the state of accounts between her husband and persons supplying goods for the business was evidence against the husband.[11]

There are other qualifications which restrict the effectiveness of statements by an agent. Thus an admission is only evidence in respect of the transaction about which it was made; it cannot affect the principal in so far as *subsequent* transactions are concerned.[12] Furthermore, the agent must have been acting for his principal at the time of the admission. So an admission by a solicitor that his

---

5 Morgan (1929) 42 HLR 461 at p 463. Hence in *Edwards v Brookes (Milk) Ltd* [1963] 3 All ER 62, [1963] 1 WLR 795, it was necessary to decide whether a depot manager and a representative were agents qualified to make statements on behalf of the company by which they were employed, in order to permit the admission of their statements as evidence against the company on a criminal charge.

6 (1874) LR 9 QB 468.

7 *Principles of Agency* (2nd edn) pp 223, 224.

8 See also *Fairlie v Hastings* (1804) 10 Ves 123.

9 Hence the problem of deciding whether the agent who made an admission in a letter was *instructed* or otherwise authorised by the principal to make such statement: cf *Wagstaff v Wilson* (1832) 4 B & Ad 339; *R v Downer* (1880) 43 LT 445 with *Marshall v Cliff* (1815) 4 Camp 133 and *Roberts v Lady Gresley* (1828) 3 C & P 380. See also, on the question whether the witness was an agent for this purpose, *R v Turner* (1975) 61 Cr App Rep 67 (barrister was agent); *R v Evans* [1981] Crim LR 669 (clerk of solicitor not an agent). In *Maxwell v IRC* [1959] NZLR 708 the New Zealand Court of Appeal found it impossible to determine whether an accountant had authority because there was no evidence of what was usual or customary when an accountant was employed to act in income tax matters.

10 *British Columbia Saw Mill Co v Nettleship* (1868) LR 3 CP 499; cf *Peto v Hague* (1804) 5 Esp 134; *The Prinses Juliana*, above, note 4. See also the Civil Evidence Act 1968: *Cross and Tapper on Evidence* pp 600–616.

11 *Anderson v Sanderson* (1817) 2 Stark 204.

12 *Helyear v Hawke* (1803) 5 Esp 72; *Blackstone v Wilson* (1857) 26 LJ Ex 229.

client owed the plaintiff money, made in the course of a casual conversation, not in the furtherance of the client's business, was not admissible against the client.[13] It was merely loose conversation not made in an admission of any fact in the case.[14] Therefore, if the agent is not engaged upon the principal's business at the time the admission is made it will not be evidence against the principal. This means that he must be the principal's agent, and he must be acting within the scope of his authority at the time of the admission.[15] However, if the principal has expressly referred someone to the agent for the purpose of obtaining information, for example instructing a litigant to deliver interrogatories to an officer of a corporation,[16] then the principal will be bound by an admission by the agent, even if such an admission was not expressly, or otherwise, authorised.[17] It is also essential that the statement be against the interest of the principal.[18] Thus in *Lucas v De la Cour*:[19]

> A partner when making a contract said that the subject-matter of the contract was his sole property. It was held that this was admissible *against* his co-partners, who could not sue on the contract.

The final requirement is that the admission is to a third party. A statement to the principal, for example in the form of a report made by the agent to the principal, cannot be received in evidence as an admission.[20]

B. Notice to an agent

Notice of certain facts may have important consequences on the principal's rights and liabilities. For example, in dealing with the agent of another person the question of the extent of *that* agent's authority may depend upon notice, for example in relation to the Factors Act,[1] or in respect of rights of set-off.[2] Hence it is important to determine in what circumstances notice to the agent will affect the principal's position. Before dealing with the common law position, it is necessary to point out that, where a purchase of property for valuable consideration can be

---

13 *Petch v Lyon* (1846) 9 QB 147; *Parkins v Hawkshaw* (1817) 2 Stark 239.
14 (1846) 9 QB 147 at 153 per Lord Denman.
15 *Barnett v South London Tramways Co* (1887) 18 QBD 815; *The Prinses Juliana, Esbjerb (Owners) v Prinses Juliana (Owner)* [1936] P 139, [1936] 1 All ER 685.
16 *Welsbach Incandescent Gas Lighting Co v New Incandescent (Sunlight Patent) Gas Lighting Co* [1900] 2 Ch 1.
17 *Williams v Innes* (1808) 1 Camp 364; *Hood v Reeve* (1828) 3 C & P 532.
18 This is also true where the principal makes an admission: *Corke v Corke and Cooke* [1958] P 93, [1958] 1 All ER 224: statement by wife that she was *not* guilty of adultery was inadmissible.
19 (1813) 1 M & S 249.
20 *Langhorn v Allnutt* (1812) 4 Taunt 511; *Re Devala Provident Gold Mining Co* (1883) 22 Ch D 593. Cf the suggestion of Lord Denning MR with respect to publication of a defamation by an agent to his principal (a corporation) in *Riddick v Thames Board Mills Ltd* [1977] QB 881, [1977] 3 All ER 677: above, p 292. See, however, the Civil Evidence Act 1968, s 2: *Cross and Tapper on Evidence* pp 600, 606, 609, 613. A statement to the principal may be admissible as indicative of the speaker's state of mind: *PWA Corpn v Gemini Group Automated Distribution Systems Inc* (1993) 103 DLR (4th) 609 at 641.
1 Above, p 299.
2 *Dresser v Norwood* (1864) 17 CBNS 466.

prejudicially affected by notice of any fact, instrument, or thing, the Law of Property Act 1925, s 199 provides that he will have the required notice if it has come to the knowledge of his counsel, solicitor, or other agent, acting as such,[3] or would have come to the knowledge of such person if such inquiries and inspections had been made as ought reasonably to have been made.[4]

Notification and knowledge. So far as the common law position is concerned, a distinction has been drawn[5] between notification and knowledge. The difference seems to be this. If *notification* is in question, notification to the agent is only notification to the principal if the agent had authority to receive the notice, and at the time of its receipt was acting as agent, and the notice related to something material to the transaction performed by the agent. But if *knowledge* is relevant, then the knowledge must relate to the transaction under which the agent can bind the principal and the agent must be under a duty to communicate the information to the principal.

However, the word 'notice' is used without any distinction in the cases.[6] Furthermore, it is suggested that the alleged distinction is not of great value or importance, since the requirements stated to be necessary before notification to, or knowledge by, the agent will affect the principal, seem to coincide. In respect of both notification and knowledge much seems to turn upon the manner and content of the agent's notice. If the facts are materially connected with the performance of the undertaking, so that the proper exercise of his authority will be affected by his notice of the facts, then notice to the agent will operate as notice to the principal. There is really no valid distinction in the cases between notification within the exercise of the agent's authority and knowledge acquired in connection with the particular transaction on which the agent was engaged. There would be a difference if knowledge acquired by the agent *at any time* (not necessarily when engaged on his principal's business) would affect the principal.[7] But the cases show the general rule to be that the knowledge of the agent must be acquired by him in connection with the principal's business, if it is to affect the principal.[8] Hence, it is submitted, the effect of notification to and knowledge by the agent involve the same essentials.[9] These may be summarised as follows.

---

3 *Re Cousins* (1886) 31 Ch D 671 on the same provision of the Conveyancing Act 1881, s 3.

4 *Maxfield v Burton* (1873) LR 17 Eq 15.

5 Powell *Law of Agency* (2nd edn) pp 236–237. See also *Restatement, Second, Agency* paras 9–11, 268–282. Cf Stoljar *Law of Agency* p 83, note 81: *Bowstead on Agency* (15th edn 1985) pp 412–414. It is suggested ibid at 414 that this distinction is also very important where the agent is acting fraudulently.

6 But see *Blackley v National Mutual Life Association of Australasia Ltd* [1972] NZLR 1038.

7 As in *Turton v London and North Western Rly Co* (1850) 15 LTOS 92; *Dresser v Norwood* (1864) 17 CBNS 466.

8 *Hiern v Mill* (1806) 13 Ves 114; *Wyllie v Pollen* (1863) 32 LJ Ch 782; *Société Générale de Paris v Tramway Union Co* (1884) 14 QBD 424; *Re David Payne & Co Ltd, Young v David Payne & Co Ltd* [1904] 2 Ch 608; *Halifax Mortgage Services (formerly BNP Mortgages) Ltd v Stepsky* [1995] 4 All ER 656. Or be fresh in his mind while performing his principal's business: *Fuller v Benett* (1843) 12 LJ Ch 355.

9 The contrary view is expressed in *Bowstead on Agency* (15th edn) p 413. See now *Bowstead and Reynolds on Agency* (16th edn) pp 529–531.

When notice to an agent is effective.[10] First, the agent must acquire the notice in question in the course of his employment. Hence in *Tate v Hyslop*:[11]

> A solicitor employed by an underwriter knew about a fact which was material to an insurance policy, but had not told the underwriter. When the underwriter sought to end the policy on the ground of non-disclosure it was held that he could do so. Disclosure to the solicitor was insufficient, for it was not part of the solicitor's employment to receive notices or be given knowledge of such matters.

So if the agent of a company acquires notice of some relevant fact, but not while acting for the company,[12] or in circumstances in which the agent in question is not an agent for the particular purpose with which the notice is concerned,[13] then the notice of the agent will not affect the company.

Whether the notice was received in the course of the agent's employment will depend largely upon the scope of the agent's authority, express, implied, or otherwise.[14] Hence an insurance broker did not have authority to bind his principal by notice of a material fact,[15] though he would have authority to bind the insurer.[16] A corollary of this is that at the time of receipt of the notice the agent must have been acting as agent. Hence if the agent acquires the knowledge before the agency began the principal will not be bound:[17] so too if the agent is acting fraudulently, against the interest of his principal, his knowledge of the fraud will not affect his principal.[18] This is what happened in *Newsholme Bros v Road Transport and General Insurance Co Ltd*[19] where the insurance agent put untrue answers in an insurance proposal form. His fraud, if he knew the answers were untrue, prevented his knowledge from being the company's knowledge. But this case has been more recently not applied in England, where it has been

---

10 See the analysis by Hoffman LJ in *El Ajou v Dollar Land Holdings plc* [1994] 2 All ER 685 at 702–704, discussed in *Halifax Mortgage Services (formerly BNP Mortgages) Ltd v Stepsky* [1995] 4 All ER 656 at 669–670. See also *Christopher v Galyer* (1995) 3 Int ILR 174.

11 (1885) 15 QBD 368.

12 *Société Générale de Paris v Tramways Union Co*, above; *Re Fenwick* [1902] 1 Ch 507.

13 *Powles v Page* (1846) 3 CB 16. See *Burton Group Ltd v Smith* [1977] IRLR 351, where a trade union was held not to be the agent of an employee, for the purpose of receiving from the employer notice of the date of termination of the employee's contract with the employer.

14 Cf *Townsends Carriers Ltd v Pfizer* (1977) 33 P & CR 361, a notice to exercise an option was valid, although given *by* a subsidiary company of the lessee *to* a subsidiary company of the landlord, because the parties had previously allowed these subsidiaries to conduct their business. Hence the requisite authority could be inferred or implied: cf *Jones v Phipps* (1868) LR 3 QB 567.

15 *Blackburn, Low & Co v Vigors* (1887) 12 App Cas 531. See also *Wilkinson v General Accident Fire and Life Assurance Corpn Ltd* [1967] 2 Lloyd's Rep 182.

16 *Biggar v Rock Life Assurance Co* [1902] 1 KB 516.

17 *Jessett Properties Ltd v UDC Finance Ltd* [1992] 1 NZLR 138 at 143. But there are exceptions to these: see *Taylor v Yorkshire Insurance Co Ltd* [1913] 2 IR 1; *Blackburn, Low & Co v Vigors*, above at 537–538 per Lord Halsbury LC.

18 Cf *United Dominions Trust (Ireland) Ltd v Shannon Caravans Ltd* [1976] IR 225: knowledge of agent defrauding his principal, not imputed to the latter.

19 [1929] 2 KB 356. See the discussion in *Bowstead* p 414, and p 417 note 23, where reference is made to decisions in other common law jurisdictions in which the rigours of this doctrine, producing an unfair result, have been evaded. See also Merkin, 'Transferred Agency in the Law of Insurance' (1984) 13 Anglo-Am LR, No 3 p 33.

distinguished by reference to the duty of the agent to fill in proposal forms,[20] or in Canada.[21]

Secondly, the knowledge must be relevant to the transaction in respect of which the agent is employed. Thus, knowledge by a solicitor employed to transfer a mortgage that there were incumbrances on the property *subsequent* to the mortgage, was not imputed to his principal since it was not relevant to the transfer of the mortgage.[1] In *Halifax Mortgage Services (Formerly BNP Mortgages) Ltd v Stepsky*[2] solicitors acting for a husband and wife applying for a loan from the plaintiff to be secured by a remortgage on their home learned of the true purpose of the loan, viz, to pay off the previous mortgage and discharge the husband's business debts. Later the solicitors were instructed to act on behalf of the plaintiff as lender in the transaction. The solicitors did not inform the plaintiff that the loan was not, as the plaintiff believed, for the joint benefit of husband and wife. The husband defaulted on the loan; the plaintiff obtained an order for possession of the home. The wife appealed and the trial judge and the Court of Appeal dismissed her appeal, holding that the knowledge of the solicitors of the true purpose of the loan could not be imputed to the plaintiff. The solicitors had acquired that knowledge only when they acted for the husband and wife. Once they had that knowledge it remained with them and could not be treated as coming to them again when they were instructed to act for the plaintiff.

Thirdly, there must be a duty on the agent to communuicate the notice to his principal.[3] This again is connected with the scope of the agent's authority, for the communication of facts may be part of the performance of the undertaking he has been authorised to execute. For example it is not part of the duty of an insurance broker to communicate material facts to the principal, ie the insurance company. He has no authority to bind his principal by notice of such facts.[4] But the master of a ship was under a duty to communicate the fact of damage to the ship to the owner.[5] Hence in *Proudfoot v Montefiore*:[6]

> The agent deliberately did not tell his principal immediately of the loss of the principal's cargo. Before receipt of the agent's letter, the principal insured the goods. It was held that the principal could not claim the

---

20 *Stone v Reliance Mutual Insurance Society Ltd* [1972] 1 Lloyd's Rep 469.
21 *Blanchette v CIS Ltd* (1973) 36 DLR (3d) 561, a decision of the Supreme Court of Canada. Cf *Berryere v Fireman's Fund Insurance Co* [1961–65] ILR 663. See also a New Zealand case, *Blackley v National Mutual Life Association of Australasia Ltd* [1972] NZLR 1038.
    If notice is given to an agent in reliance on the agent's ostensible or apparent authority to receive it, the principal will be estopped from denying its receipt: *Jessett Properties Ltd v UDC Finance Ltd* [1992] 1 NZLR 138 at 143. But this seems to conflict with other cases in which the agent was not able to *extend* his authority by his own acts: compare above, pp 125–127.
1 *Wyllie v Pollen* (1863) 32 LJ Ch 782. See also *Re Holland, ex p Warren* (1885) 1 TLR 430.
2 [1995] 4 All ER 656.
3 Under the Consumer Credit Act 1974, s 175, such a duty is *deemed* in the case of the receipt of a notice as agent of the creditor or owner under a 'regulated agreement'. The duty, described as 'contractual', is to transmit the notice to the creditor or owner 'forthwith'. This applies to consumer credit agreements and consumer hire agreements: ibid, s 189(1). For discussion, see Goode *Introduction to the Consumer Credit Act 1974* pp 236–237.
4 *Blackburn, Low & Co v Vigors* (1887) 12 App Cas 531.
5 *Gladstone v King* (1813) 1 M & S 35.
6 (1867) LR 2 QB 511.

insurance money, on the ground that the policy was void for non-disclosure of a material fact, ie the loss of the cargo.

Here the agent was under a duty to communicate the facts to his principal, and failed to do so. This did not prevent the operation of the agent's notice on the principal's position. However, the principal will not be bound by the notice of his agent, even if the agent is under a duty to communicate such notice to the principal, if the third party knows that the agent is not going to tell the principal what the facts are.[7]

Nor was the knowledge of an agent for both lender and borrower imputed to the lender, despite the agent's duty to communicate that knowledge to the lender. The agent was under a duty to the borrower not to disclose such information to the lender without the borrower's consent. The agent's duty to the lender was superseded by a duty to tell the lender that he, the agent, could no longer act for the lender because of a conflict of interest, and he was not free to pass on information as to the real purpose of the intended loan (viz, to buy shares in the family business not pay off a mortgage and other debts for the joint benefit of husband and wife, the borrowers). That information had come into the agent's possession as solicitor for the borrower. In consequence of this lack of knowledge of the true purpose of the loan, the lender was not put on inquiry, and had no constructive notice of misrepresentation or undue influence on which the wife relied to set aside the mortgage given in return for the loan.[8]

7 *Sharpe v Foy* (1868) 4 Ch App 35.
8 *Halifax Mortgage Services (formerly BNP Mortgages) Ltd v Stepsky* [1995] 4 All ER 656.

CHAPTER 16

Agency in company law

Companies as principals. The fact that companies are juristic personalities, distinct from the natural persons who promote and organise them,[1] makes the law of agency of particular importance to company law. The personification of a company makes it capable of acquiring rights and of being subject to duties, whether contractual, proprietary, or otherwise and, since the artificial entity which is the company can act only by and through human beings,[2] the company must be treated as a principal, or as a master, and those through whom it acts as agents or servants. It is the position of companies as principals which is the subject of this chapter.

The trend of the law has been to assimilate as far as possible the legal position of a company as a principal to that of a natural person who by agreement or otherwise has entered into the agency relationship with another natural person. For example, former differences as regards the appointment of agents have been revised.[3] Recent developments reveal that what were differences between juristic and natural persons in regard to the extent to which they could be bound by the acts of their agents have been, to some extent, eradicated.

Prior to changes in the law enacted in 1989,[4] two important doctrines marked the difference between the situation where a natural person and that where a juristic person, a company, was a principal. The first was the doctrine of ultra vires, whereby a company's power to act was restricted by its constitution. The second was the doctrine of constructive notice. According to this, anyone who dealt with a company was deemed to have read and understood what were referred to as the 'public documents' of the company, which included its memorandum and articles of association, ie its constitutional documents.[5] This was important because those documents might reveal that the person with whom the outside party was dealing lacked any, or had only a limited, authority to act. In relation to the issues of the implied, usual or apparent authority of a company's agents the doctrine of constructive notice was vital.

---

1 *Salomon v Salomon & Co Ltd* [1897] AC 22: see *Gower: Principles of Modern Company Law* (5th edn 1992) ch 5; Schmitthoff 'Salomon in the Shadow' [1976] JBL 305, for some qualifications.
2 Or other companies: but that complicating factor need not be considered for the purposes of this chapter.
3 Above, p 57.
4 Below: see also above, p 87. But the pre-1989 law will apply to transactions, if any still subsist, entered into before the coming into force of the legislation, viz February 1991: SI 1990 No 2569.
5 *Gower* at p 170.

The doctrine of ultra vires. Historically, the courts drew a distinction between acts ultra vires the company and acts ultra vires the agent in question. This can be illustrated by two cases on ratification. In *Ashbury Rly Carriage and Iron Co v Riche*[6] the directors of a company entered into a contract on the company's behalf which was not within the scope of the company's Memorandum of Association. It was held that this contract could not be ratified because it was ultra vires and therefore void.[7] But in *Irvine v Union Bank of Australia*[8] a contract was entered into by directors on the company's behalf beyond their powers under the company's Articles of Association, but within the scope of the company's Memorandum. It was held that this contract could be ratified by the company since it was one which could legally be made by the company, and the directors' original lack of authority could be cured by ratification. At common law, therefore, a company could never be held liable on a contract made by an agent if such contract were ultra vires the company: the authority of the agent, whether express, implied, or apparent, was irrelevant in such context.

To comply with the First Council Directive on Companies issued by the European Economic Communities[9] the first inroad on the older common law was made by s 9 of the European Communities Act 1972, following the admission of the United Kingdom to the Communities. This was replaced by s 35 of the Companies Act 1985.[10] Those provisions did not abolish the ultra vires doctrine but gave a third party dealing with a company (but not the company) the possibility of relief under certain circumstances. The provisions of the 1985 Act were subjected to much criticism on various grounds.[11] In consequence, as a result of further scrutiny, the provisions of s 35 of the 1985 Act were replaced by newer provisions by the Companies Act 1989, s 108(1).[12] The new s 35 of the 1985 Act[13] now states:

'(1) The validity of an act done by a company shall not be called into question on the ground of lack of capacity by reason of anything in the company's memorandum.'

This new section has been welcomed as an improvement on its predecessor and as making it clear that neither the company nor a third party can any longer invoke strict ultra vires.[14] But criticism has been made of the provisions of subsections (2) and (3) of this section, by which members of a company can bring proceedings to restrain acts beyond the company's capacity (with certain

---

6 (1875) LR 7 HL 653. Cf *Re Jon Beauforte (London) Ltd* [1953] Ch 131, [1953] 1 All ER 634.
7 On the ratification of void transactions, see above, pp 95–97.
8 (1877) 2 App Cas 366.
9 No 68/151 EEC: *Gower's Principles of Modern Company Law* (4th edn 1979) at p 178.
10 For details see the 6th edn of this work, 1990, at pp 323–324.
11 Farrar and Fowles 'The Effect of Section 9 of the European Communities Act 1972 on English Company Law' (1973) 36 MLR 270; Prentice 'Section 9 of the European Communities Act' (1973) 89 LQR 518; Collier and Sealy [1973] CLJ 1; *Gower* (4th edn) at pp 178–179, 184–190.
12 *Gower's Principles of Modern Company Law* (5th edn 1992) pp 172–177.
13 But the provisions of this section are restricted by the Charities Act 1960, s 30B(1) and the Companies Act 1989, s 112(3) in respect of charity companies, and by the Companies Act 1989, s 322A dealing with the invalidity of transactions to which directors or their associates are parties: Companies Act 1985, s 35(4) as substituted by the Companies Act 1989, s 108(1): see *Gower* (5th edn) pp 181–184.
14 *Gower* p 175.

exceptions) and directors have a duty to observe limitations on their powers contained in the memorandum (requiring ratification for acts beyond the company's capacity to be by special resolution, which, however, will not affect the liability of the directors).[15]

The problem of authority. As well as the problem of whether an act was ultra vires there was also the question whether the act executed by the agent was within the scope of that agent's authority. Acts within the agent's express authority raised only the issue of ultra vires. Where it was alleged by the third party that the act in question was within the scope of the agent's implied (including usual) or apparent (or ostensible) authority[16] there was the added complication of notice of the agent's want of express authority to perform the act. Until changes made by the Companies Act 1989[17] this involved the issue of constructive notice of documents required to be lodged with the Registrar of Companies, which included the Memorandum and Articles of Association of the company.[18] Under this doctrine, even if the third party had no actual knowledge of limitations on the agent's authority, if such limitations could be spelled out from such documents the third party was affixed with constructive notice of them.[19] Anyone who dealt with a company was presumed to have read and understood such documents according to their proper meaning.[20] This applies also to special resolutions of the company.[1] In turn this doctrine was qualified by the so-called rule in *Royal British Bank v Turquand*[2] which applied where the documents were ambiguous as to whether the agent had the requisite authority. Nonetheless the doctrine of constructive notice removed much of the protection provided to a third party by the doctrines of implied, usual and apparent authority. Some inroads were made on this situation by the European Communities Act 1972, later contained in the Companies Act 1985, s 35. To greater effect, however, is the Companies Act 1989, by s 142(1) of which a new s 711A is added to the Act of 1985. Under this new provision:

'(1) A person shall not be taken to have notice of any matter merely because of its being disclosed in any document[3] kept by the registrar of companies (and this available for inspection) or made available by the company for inspection.'

However, this will not affect the question whether a person is affected by notice of any matter by reason of a failure to make such inquiries as ought reasonably to be made.[4]

---

15 Ibid at pp 176–177.
16 For the meaning of these expressions, see above, pp 68–76, 122–132.
17 Below.
18 See now Companies Act 1985, ss 2, 7, 10.
19 *Mahony v East Holyford Mining Co* (1875) LR 7 HL 869.
20 *Griffith v Paget* (1877) 6 Ch D 511.
1 *Irvine v Union Bank of Australia* (1877) 2 App Cas 366.
2 (1856) 6 E & B 327: below, p 358.
3 This includes any material which contains information: Companies Act 1985, s 711A(2). But certain matters are excluded: ibid, s 711A(3).
4 Ibid, s 711A(2).

The effect of this is to abolish the doctrine of constructive notice. However, by way of making other alterations to the common law rules, the 1989 Act (by s 108(1)) also added a new section, s 35A, which deals with the powers of directors to bind the company. By this provision:[5]

> '(1) In favour of a person dealing with a company in good faith, the power of the board of directors to bind the company, or authorise to do so, shall be deemed to be free of any limitation under the company's constitution.'

A person deals with a company if he is a party to a transaction or other act to which the company is a party.[6] Such a person will not be regarded as acting in bad faith by reason only of his knowing that an act is beyond the powers of the directors acting under the company's constitution.[7] Good faith is presumed unless the contrary is proved.[8] Limitations on the powers of directors include limitations resulting from a resolution passed at a general meeting of any class of shareholders or from an agreement between members of the company or any class of shareholders.[9] It is to be noted that even if the act will bind the company, the directors, or any other person, can be liable for exceeding their powers.[10]

These provisions only cover acts executed by or under the authority of the board of directors. Hence if something is done by a single director or some other person purporting to act on behalf of the company but without the authorisation of the board of directors these provisions will not apply. In such situations the applicable rules will be those of the common law, but excluding the doctrine of constructive notice. Thus, while the law relating to transactions by an outsider with a company has been simplified, this is more true of the law dealing with transactions with the board of directors of a company. Where, as is more usually the case, the outsider deals with a single director, or an employee other than a director, or with a company which has no legally constituted board of directors, it will remain necessary to examine the common law (bearing in mind that the outsider no longer may be affixed with constructive notice of any limitations on anyone's authority that may be contained in the 'public' documents, ie those kept by the registrar).

Hence it is necessary to look at the common law (as altered by the abolition of the doctrine of constructive notice) regarding acts performed by an agent of a company alleged to be within the agent's implied (including usual) authority or his or her apparent (or ostensible) authority.[11]

---

5 Which does not apply to charitable companies, governed by the Charities Act 1960, s 30B(1), Companies Act 1989, s 112(3). Nor to transactions with directors within s 322A of the 1985 Act. Note also s 35A(4) dealing with the rights of members of a company to bring proceedings to restrain directors from doing things beyond their powers (unless such acts are done in fulfilment of a legal obligation arising from a previous act of the company): on which see *Gower* at p 176.
6 Companies Act 1985, s 35A(2)(a).
7 Ibid, s 35A(2)(b).
8 Ibid, s 35A(2)(c).
9 Ibid, s 35A(3)(a)(b).
10 Ibid, s 35A(5).
11 *Gower* pp 188–192; *Palmer's Company Law* (25th edn 1992) Vol I, paras 3-310–3-317.

Agent with implied authority. As previously seen, an agent may not only have an express authority to act in a certain way: the scope of his authority may be extended by what is to be inferred from the conduct of the parties and the circumstances of the case.[12] It may also be further extended by the application of the idea that, unless expressly restricted, every agent, by implication, has the *usual* authority to act in the way the particular kind of agent which he is, would ordinarily act. This applies to the agents of a company.[13] Hence a person who deals with such an agent is entitled to transact with the agent on the terms of such agent's usual authority: and if he does so, the company will be bound by what the agent has done.

However, such a party will not be able to make the company liable if he has *actual* knowledge that the agent lacked authority or possessed only a limited authority.[14] It is actual knowledge that will now be necessary. Moreover, such knowledge may be evident not only from the public documents but from others, such as a resolution of the board of directors imposing a limit on the size of commitment authorised to be entered into by a director.[15] But, in view of the statutory provisions regarding notice by reason of a failure to make inquiries that ought reasonably to have been made,[16] a company may not be bound if the circumstances are such that the party dealing with the company's agent should have been put upon inquiry as to whether the agent in question had the usual authority of agents in his position.[17] Under the previous law, in such circumstances, the party dealing with the company was in the position of someone who had not availed himself of an opportunity to discover the true state of the agent's authority. Should such party not have been able to discover the agent's lack of authority, even if he had availed himself of the opportunity to do so, then, under the old law, the company would not have been bound.[18]

---

12 *Freeman and Lockyer v Buckhurst Park Properties (Mangal) Ltd* [1964] 1 All ER 630 at 647 per Diplock LJ; *Hely-Hutchinson v Brayhead Ltd* [1967] 3 All ER 98 at 102 per Lord Denning MR.
13 Professor Hornby has argued that although managing directors of a company *as a class* may have a usual authority, there is no usual authority attributable to the *office* of managing director: 'The Usual Authority of An Agent' [1961] CLJ 239 at pp 247–248. See, however, Campbell 'Contracts with Companies' (1980) 76 LQR 115 at pp 119–124, on the division between primary and other functions of officers of companies, and the extent to which they may be said to confer *usual* authority. In the *Hely-Hutchinson* case, above at 102, Lord Denning MR, it is submitted, is guilty of providing confusion when he suggests that the usual authority of a managing director of a company is apparent authority. His reference to the possible coincidence between apparent and actual authority in this passage reveals that he is really referring to such usual authority as *implied* authority as that expression has been expounded in earlier pages of this book.
14 *Howard v Patent Ivory Manufacturing Co, Re Patent Ivory Manufacturing Co* (1888) 38 Ch D 156.
15 *Palmer*, Vol I, para 3.311.
16 Companies Act 1985, s 711A(2): above, p 355.
17 *A L Underwood v Bank of Liverpool* [1924] 1 KB 775; *B Liggett (Liverpool) Ltd v Barclays Bank* [1928] 1 KB 48; *Houghton & Co v Nothard, Lowe and Wills* [1927] 1 KB 246 (in the House of Lords on another ground: [1928] AC 1); *Kreditbank Cassel GmbH v Schenkers Ltd* [1927] 1 KB 826 at 841 per Scrutton LJ; *Rama Corpn Ltd v Proved Tin and General Investments Ltd* [1952] 2 QB 147, [1952] 1 All ER 554.
18 *Mahony v East Holyford Mining Co Ltd* (1875) LR 7 HL 869. Possibly even if the agent's act amounted to a fraud, or a forgery: below, p 361. But to the contrary Dawson and Toohey JJ in *Northside Developments Pty Ltd v Registrar-General* (1990) 170 CLR 146 at 193–201, 207–208.

The strictness of these principles was modified by something which is still relevant in the circumstances now under consideration, ie where the new s 35A of the Companies Act 1985 does not apply. The third party dealing with the company was, and is still, entitled to rely upon the fact that what has been done by the agent has been authorised by the company in accordance with the internal procedure of the company as required by the constitution. The party dealing with the company need not concern himself with 'the indoor management' of the company.[19] This is the effect of the famous rule in *Royal British Bank v Turquand*,[20] according to which:

> 'persons contracting with a company and dealing in good faith may assume that acts within its constitution and powers have been properly and duly performed and are not bound to inquire whether acts of internal management have been regular.'[1]

This rule allows the party dealing with the company to rely upon the agent's authority to act, except in so far as the third party actually knows that the agent has no authority to act. This may happen where he was himself an agent of the company, as in *Morris v Kanssen*,[2] and knew the other agents were acting invalidly. But the rule relates not so much to the existence of an authority in the agent as to the valid creation of an authority by acts of the company which are necessary for the creation of such authority. The party dealing with the company is entitled to assume that the company has acted in accordance with its internal rules of management in order to authorise, expressly or impliedly, the agent: but, he is not entitled to assume that, even if the company had acted properly, the result of the acts would have been to invest the agent with an express or implied authority. That question turns upon the issue of notice and it is in this respect that the rule in *Turquand*'s case is limited by actual knowledge of want of authority, but no longer by the doctrine of constructive notice of such want of authority.

Agent with apparent authority. What is said above relates to the exercise by the agent in question of the *usual* authority of such agents. There is no obligation

---

19 *Mahony v East Holyford Mining Co Ltd* (1875) LR 7 HL 869 at 898 per Lord Hatherley.
20 (1856) 6 E & B 327; *Gower* at pp 186–188; *Palmer* Vol I, para 3.312. See also Campbell (1980) 76 LQR 115–136. He coins the term *potential* authority, to describe the nature of an agent's authority under this rule: ibid p 116. For another interesting and detailed discussion of this case and its subsequent development, see Nock 'The Irrelevance of the Rule of Indoor Management' (1966) 30 Conv NS 123, 163. See also Shapira 'Rule of Turquand's Case Revisited' (1976) 7 NZULR 142, which was written as a critical analysis of the rule following the decision of the New Zealand Court of Appeal, upholding the decision of Wilde CJ, in *Broadlands Finance Ltd v Gisborne Aero Club Inc* [1974] 1 NZLR 157; affd [1975] 2 NZLR 496, a case which seems to have involved 'apparent authority' of officers of an incorporated club.
1 *Morris v Kanssen* [1946] AC 459 at 474, [1946] 1 All ER 586 at 592 per Lord Simonds (quoting Halsbury's Laws of England (2nd edn) 423): note, however, his Lordship's use of the expression 'ostensible agency': ibid, pp 475, 592. For conflicting views as to whether the rule is an application of the law of agency or is founded on estoppel, see *Northside Developments Pty Ltd v Registrar-General*, above. That case and the exposition of the rule by Lord Simonds in *Morris v Kanssen*, above, were relied on by Sheller JA in *Hughes v NM Superannuation Pty Ltd* (1993) 29 NSWLR 653 at 665–666, in which the learned judge held that the rule did not apply to decide whether notice of termination of a fund had been validly given.
2 [1946] AC 459, [1946] 1 All ER 586.

on the party dealing with a company to go behind the exercise of such usual authority (unless it has been limited by the public documents), and discover whether the proper formalities have been observed.[3] Where such party is trying to make the company liable on a contract made by the agent not within the scope of an authority which such agent would usually have, the position would seem to be different. Here everything depends upon the operation of the doctrine of estoppel. The party dealing with the company is not trying to set up any *implied* authority of the agent in question: he is trying to show that the person with whom he dealt had *apparent* authority to act as he did. This means that there is some representation as a result of conduct by the company, including, possibly, the director himself with whom the party in question was dealing,[4] upon which such party relied when he contracted, believing that the agent was acting within the scope of his actual authority when all the time it only 'appeared' as if the agent had such actual authority.

Since the doctrine of constructive notice is now abolished, it is no longer necessary to consider what was a vexed issue under the older law.[5] If a party dealing with the company believed the agent with whom he was dealing had authority not from a reading of the public documents of the company but from a representation by the agent, it was queried whether anything contained in those documents, if he had read them, would have made it appear that the agent had the requisite authority so that the company could be estopped from denying that he had such authority. The better view was that the doctrine of constructive notice was purely negative: it did not operate against the company but only in its favour, in other words, it operated against the person who had failed to inquire and not in his favour.[6] Under the current law it is only if the party dealing with the company has *actual* knowledge of the contents of the relevant documents, and

---

3 *Biggerstaff v Rowatt's Wharf Ltd* [1896] 2 Ch 93; *Dey v Pullinger Engineering Co* [1921] 1 KB 77; *British Thomson-Houston Co Ltd v Federated European Bank Ltd* [1932] 2 KB 176; *Clay Hill Brick and Tile Co Ltd v Rawlings* [1938] 4 All ER 100. See the remarks of Willmer LJ on these cases in *Freeman and Lockyer v Buckhurst Park Properties (Mangal) Ltd* [1964] 1 All ER 630 at 638. See also, below, on the subject of the position where in fact the purported agent was not really an agent at all.

4 *Hely-Hutchinson v Brayhead Ltd* [1967] 3 All ER 98 at 102, 108 per Lord Denning MR, Lord Pearson; see also the earlier discussion in *Freeman and Lockyer v Buckhurst Park Properties (Mangal) Ltd* [1964] 2 CB 480, [1964] 1 All ER 630, especially the judgment of Diplock LJ at 646 (but note the decision that an agent cannot confer apparent authority on himself, in the absence of a representation from the principal, in *Armagas Ltd v Mundogas SA* [1985] 3 All ER 795; affd [1986] 2 All ER 385: above pp 116, 125). A director cannot by his conduct achieve this, in any event, if the director has resigned before he made the representation: see the South African case of *Rosebank Television and Appliance Co v Orbit Sales Corpn Ltd* [1969] 1 SALR 300.

5 *Biggerstaff v Rowatt's Wharf Ltd* [1896] 2 Ch 93; *Houghton & Co v Nothard, Lowe and Wills Ltd* [1927] 1 KB 246; *Kreditbank Cassel GmbH v Schenkers* [1927] 1 KB 826; *British Thomson-Houston Co Ltd v Federated European Bank Ltd* [1932] 2 KB 176; *Clay Hill Brick and Tile Co v Rawlings* [1938] 4 All ER 100; *Rama Corpn v Proved Tin and General Investments Ltd*, below. But see Willmer LJ in *Freeman and Lockyer v Buckhurst Park Properties (Mangal) Ltd* [1964] 1 All ER 630, at 638–639. See also Stiebel 'The Ostensible Power of Directors' (1933) 49 LQR 350 at pp 352–354; Montrose 'The Apparent Authority of an Agent of a Company' (1934) 50 LQR 224 at pp 230–240; Campbell 'Contracts with Companies' (1979) 75 LQR 469–482.

6 See *Rama Corpn v Proved Tin and General Investments Ltd* [1952] 2 QB 147 at 149, [1952] 1 All ER 554 at 556 per Slade J; Campbell (1959) 75 LQR 469 at pp 473, 479–480; *Gower* at p 191.

those documents, or some other aspect of the company's conduct of its affairs, make it appear that the agent had the authority in issue,[7] will it be possible for the party dealing with the company to allege that the agent had apparent authority to bind the company by what he did.

An important decision on the scope of apparent authority in relation to companies is *Freeman and Lockyer v Buckhurst Park Properties (Mangal) Ltd.*[8] There a person who had provided half the capital of a company to purchase an estate acted as if he were managing director, to the knowledge of the board of the company which had been formed to achieve that purpose. He and the other subscriber (with a nominee of each) were the directors, four being a quorum under the articles of association. In the course of his conduct as if he were managing director, the person in question employed on behalf of the company a firm of architects and surveyors for certain purposes connected with the estate to be purchased by the company. This firm claimed from the company for their fees in respect of such work. The Court of Appeal, after considering the earlier cases in detail, held that the company was liable on the basis of estoppel, ie that the person acting as managing director had apparent authority to bind the company. In employing the plaintiffs he acted within the ordinary ambit of the authority of a managing director of the company, and the plaintiffs' failure to examine the articles of association and enquire whether the person with whom they contracted was the properly appointed managing director did not prevent their relying on estoppel. Diplock LJ summed up the position by stating the conditions which had to be fulfilled to entitle someone contracting with a company to enforce against a company a contract entered into on behalf of the company by an agent who had no actual authority to do so.[9]

> 'It must be shown: (a) that a representation that the agent had authority to enter on behalf of the company into a contract of the kind sought to be enforced was made to the contractor [ie the person contracting with the company]; (b) that such representation was made by a person or persons who had "actual" authority to manage the business of the company either generally or in respect of those matters to which the contract relates; (c) that he (the contractor) was induced by such representation to enter into the contract, ie that he in fact relied on it; and (d) that under its memorandum or articles of association the company was not deprived of the capacity either to enter into a contract of the kind sought to be enforced or to delegate authority to enter into a contract of that kind to the agent.'[10]

No agency. The above pertains to the situation where the person with whom the third party was dealing was in fact an agent of the company, the only question

7 See eg *Mercantile Bank of India Ltd v Chartered Bank of India, Australia and China and Strauss & Co Ltd* [1937] 1 All ER 231: possibly also the *Biggerstaff* and *British Thomson-Houston Co Ltd cases*: see *Rama Corpn v Proved Tin & General Investments Ltd* [1952] 2 KB 147 at 165–166, [1952] 1 All ER 554 at 556 per Slade J.

8 [1964] 2 QB 480, [1964] 1 All ER 630, which was referred to by Lord Denning MR, and Lord Pearson in *Hely-Hutchinson v Brayhead Ltd* [1967] 3 All ER 98 at 101–102, 108.

9 [1964] 1 All ER 630 at 646.

10 Condition (d) will only apply now if the third party knows of or is put on inquiry as to limitations in the company's constitution: *Palmer*, Vol I, para 3.314. See also ibid, para 3.316.

being whether what he did was within the scope of some kind of authority. But it may be that this person was never validly appointed as an agent of the company. Does this mean that the party dealing with the non-agent cannot invoke the rules as to implied authority and apparent authority which have been discussed above? Here again the rule in *Turquand*'s case is relevant, since the validity of an agent's appointment may depend upon the fulfilment of certain formalities. Hence the party dealing with the non-agent is entitled to assume that the 'indoor management' of the company has been carried on properly, in the absence of knowledge of any irregularity, or the presence of suspicious circumstances such as would put that party on inquiry. Thus, in the absence of notice, once the so-called agent has been given the appearance of being an agent by representation of the company that agent will be considered to have the usual authority of agents of the kind he is represented to be, or he will have such apparent authority as he has been held out to have.[11]

Forgeries. It must further be questioned whether any of the above applies when the agent in question has made a forged document with which he transacted, ie whether the company will be bound by such document. It has been suggested in some cases[12] that the company will not be liable since 'an act of forgery is a nullity and outside any actual or ostensible authority'.[13] However, a principal can be estopped by the forgery of his agent:[14] the decision in *Lloyd v Grace, Smith & Co*[15] shows that a fraudulent act done for the agent's own benefit may still bind the principal; and the cases which purport to decide the question in relation to companies really did not involve that question at all since they can be explained on the ground of the absence of usual or apparent authority or of the presence of suspicious circumstances.[16] Hence the opinion has also been expressed that the fact that the transaction was a forgery or fraudulent, will not affect the operation of the rules previously discussed.[17]

The agents of a company. Lastly, in relation to this context, an important question remains: who can be considered 'agents' of a company for the purposes of the common law rules discussed above? Clearly, directors come within their scope.[18] But what other officers of a company can be held to have a 'usual'

---

11 *Mahony v East Holyford Mining Co Ltd* (1875) LR 7 HL 869; *Biggerstaff v Rowatt's Wharf Ltd* [1896] 2 Ch 93; *Clay Hill Brick and Tile Co Ltd v Rawlings* [1938] 4 All ER 100.
12 *Ruben v Great Fingall Consolidated* [1906] AC 439; *Kreditbank Cassel GmbH v Schenkers* [1927] 1 KB 826; *South London Greyhound Racecourses Ltd v Wake* [1931] 1 Ch 496. Cf *Northside Developments Pty Ltd v Registrar-General* (1990) 170 CLR 146 per Dawson and Toohey JJ: above, p 357, note 18.
13 *Slingsby v District Bank Ltd* [1931] 2 KB 588 at 605 per Wright J.
14 *Greenwood v Martins Bank Ltd* [1933] AC 51.
15 [1912] AC 716: above, p 319.
16 *Uxbridge Permanent Benefit Building Society v Pickard* [1939] 2 KB 248 at 258, [1939] 2 All ER 344 at 351, per MacKinnon LJ.
17 Stiebel (1933) 49 LQR 350 at pp 355–358; *Gower* at p 192, note 30; Campbell (1980) 76 LQR 115 at pp 130–136. The contrary view is expressed in *Palmer* Vol I, para 3.317; cf above, note 12.
18 A director is a general agent of a company: *Harmond Properties Ltd v Gajdzis* [1968] 3 All ER 263, [1968] 1 WLR 1858. But he loses his status of agent once he resigns: *Rosebank Television and Appliance Co v Orbit Sales Corpn Ltd* [1969] 1 SALR 300.

authority, or can be considered to be in such a position in relation to the company that it would be reasonable for anyone dealing with them to believe that they had 'apparent' authority to transact business? This, of course, is a point which is relevant to the duty of a person dealing with the company to inquire in suspicious circumstances: for the position of the agent in relation to the business being transacted might lead the third party to suspect irregularity. Thus, a bank manager has been held not to be an agent with the usual authority to draw bills of exchange.[19] In *Panorama Developments (Guildford) Ltd v Fidelis Furnishing Fabrics*,[20] the Court of Appeal held that a company secretary had 'ostensible' authority[1] to sign contracts connected with the administrative side of a company's affairs, such as ordering cars to meet customers. Hence the company was bound by hiring agreements made by the secretary with the plaintiffs even though the cars were really for his own purposes. As Lord Denning MR pointed out[2] a company secretary was now a much more important person, an officer of a company with extensive duties and responsibilities. He was no longer a mere clerk, but had a wide 'ostensible' authority.[3]

Liability of the agent. It should be noted that even if the party dealing with the agent has no claim against the company he may have an action against the directors or other agents with whom he has dealt. Such may be the case where the agent had no authority when an action may be for breach of the implied warranty of authority,[4] or in respect of any wrong the agent may have committed.[5]

19 *Kreditbank Cassel GmbH v Schenkers Ltd* [1927] 1 KB 826; cf *Houghton & Co v Northard, Lowe & Wills* [1927] 1 KB 246, appealed on other grounds [1928] AC 1.
20 [1971] 2 QB 711, [1971] 3 All ER 16.
 1 Should this really have been a reference to *implied* authority: cf the earlier discussion, above, pp 70, 122, 357.
 2 [1971] 3 All ER 16 at 19.
 3 For the view that almost every employee of a trading company need have apparent authority to bind the company in some transactions, see *Gower* pp 190–196.
 4 Above, pp 243–249. Cf *Hely-Hutchinson v Brayhead Ltd* [1968] 1 QB 549, [1967] 3 All ER 98, where the plaintiff would have had such a remedy against the director if the latter had not bound the company by his implied authority to act as he did.
 5 See *Palmer* Vol I, para 8.605. See also the Companies Act 1985, s 35A(5).

CHAPTER 17

Partnership and agency

A. Introduction

The essential difference between the position of companies and that of partnerships in relation to the law of agency lies in the fact that a company is a juristic person distinct from the people by whom it is created, organised and administered, whereas a partnership[1] has no such distinct juristic personality.[2] The chief result of this, for present purposes, is that each partner is personally liable for all the obligations incurred by the partnership,[3] and each partner is regarded in certain circumstances as an agent of all the other partners.[4] This means that partnership is, in many respects, a special application of agency. It is the purpose of this chapter to discuss certain important aspects of this special form of agency, in so far as the Partnership Act 1890 exemplifies or affects the general principles of the law of agency. For the sake of convenience, the relevant sections of the Act, and the cases thereunder, may be considered under three headings: (i) the creation of the relationship, (ii) the scope of the relationship, and its effects, (iii) the termination of the relationship.

B. Creation of the agency relationship by partnership

Two sections of the 1890 Act contain passages which are relevant to this matter. Section 5 begins:

'Every partner is an agent of the firm and his other partners for the purpose of the business of the partnership ...'

This indicates that a partner is only agent for his partners when he is acting on behalf of the firm, not when he acts on his own behalf:[5] and it will be seen later that the remainder of the section deals with the question of whether a partner is

---

1 Except in special instances which are not relevant here.
2 *Lindley and Banks on Partnership* (17th edn 1995) pp 32–33; *Underhill on Partnership* (12th edn 1986) p 12.
3 Partnership Act 1890 ss 9–12. *Pollock on Partnership* (15th edn) pp 41–50; *Underhill* ch 4; *Lindley and Banks*, Part 3, chs 12, 13.
4 Partnership Act, ss 5, 6, 7.
5 *British Homes Assurance Corpn Ltd v Paterson* [1902] 2 Ch 404. See Partnership Act 1890, ss 6 and 7.

acting on behalf of the firm. Thus, the creation of a partnership[6] involves the creation of the agency relationship.

One other section also affects this, for even though a person has not actually become a partner, he may be liable as a partner, ie as a principal, if he has represented himself, or suffered himself to be represented as a partner. By s 14(1):[7]

> 'Every one who by words spoken or written or by conduct represents himself, or who knowingly suffers himself to be represented, as a partner in a particular firm, is liable as a partner to any one who has on the faith of such representation given credit to the firm, whether the representation has or has not been made or communicated to the person so giving credit by or with the knowledge of the apparent partner making the representation or suffering it to be made.'

This is one instance of what has been called in this book 'agency by estoppel'.[8]

Two points call for special mention. In the first place this 'holding out' is very relevant where there is a change in the constitution of the firm, and s 36 of the Act provides that a person dealing with a firm after such change is entitled to treat all apparent members of the old firm as still being members of the firm until he has notice of the change.[9] Secondly, by the Business Names Act 1985[10] if a partnership is carrying on a business under a name which does not consist of the surnames of all partners who are individuals and the corporate names of all partners who are bodies corporate (with certain permissible additions[11]), the partnership must state the names and addresses for service of documents relating to the business of each partner on all business letters, written orders for goods or services to be supplied to the business, invoices and receipts issued in the course of the business, and written demands for payment of debts arising in the course of the business. In any premises where the business is carried on, or to which customers of the business or suppliers of goods or services to the business have access, the partnership must display a notice containing such names and addresses in a prominent position so that it can easily be read by customers or suppliers.[12] Failure to satisfy these requirements may lead to the failure of an action brought by the partnership to which the Act applies on a contract made while the partnership was in breach, unless the court thinks that it is just and equitable to allow such action.[13] However, this will not prevent an action by the *other* party.[14]

---

6 For details of which see *Lindley and Banks* pp 71–127; *Underhill* pp 15–28.
7 This does not apply to liability in tort: *Smith v Bailey* [1891] 2 QB 403.
8 Above, pp 111–132. See *Lindley and Banks* pp 94–107: *Underhill* pp 71–72; *Pollock* pp 52–55.
9 See *Pollock* pp 95–99; note also s 14(2): see below, p 370.
10 Sections 1(4), 4(1)(a).
11 Ibid, s 1(2); eg forenames or initials of individual partners.
12 Ibid, s 4(1)(b).
13 Ibid, s 5(1)(a).
14 Ibid, s 5(2).

C. Scope and effects of the relationship

Authority. A partner's authority may be express, ratified, implied, or apparent, in the same way as any agent's authority. Express authority and ratification need no further comment. A partner's implied authority is dealt with in s 5 and s 8 of the Act. Section 5, after beginning with the words already quoted above, continues:

'and the acts of every partner who does any act for carrying on in the usual way business of the kind carried on by the firm of which he is a member bind the firm and his partners, unless the partner so acting has in fact no authority to act for the firm in the particular matter, and the person with whom he is dealing either knows that he has no authority, or does not know or believe him to be a partner.'

This means that the other partners will be bound by acts done by a partner within the scope of his *usual* authority, unless (i) there was an express prohibition against such act, and (ii) the third party has notice of such prohibition, or (iii) the third party does not know the person with whom he is dealing is a partner (*or* does not believe he is a partner).[15]

Two points should be mentioned. In the first place, what is the *usual* authority of a partner? This depends upon, and must be determined by, 'the nature of the business and . . . the practice of persons engaged in it'.[16]

Secondly, what is the position of *dormant* partners, ie those who do not appear to the outside world as partners? The position of such partners appears to be somewhat like that of undisclosed principals. Will such people be liable for the acts of the real partners?[17]

Several distinctions must be drawn. The first is between undisclosed principals who carry on business by partners or agents, and persons who simply share the profits of a business carried on by others on their own account, ie as principals only, and not as agents for those who share the profits.[18] The former are dormant partners who are liable as principals in the ordinary way. The latter are not principals at all, therefore the law of undisclosed principals is irrelevant to such a relationship. Secondly, a distinction must be drawn between the express authority given by a dormant partner, for the execution of which he will always

---

15 Powell *Law of Agency* (2nd edn) p 77, note 1, asked whether the section required knowledge and belief: it is suggested that the 'or' is disjunctive. On the application of this section see *Mann v D'Arcy* [1968] 2 All ER 172, [1968] 1 WLR 893, in which it was held that it was in the usual course of business for one partner to enter into partnership with another person in the *same* business, at least where such partnership was temporary and directly served the interests of the main partnership: aliter if it is a partnership in *another* business: see also *Clarke v Newland* [1991] 1 All ER 397. Note also the comments about 'elderly cases' dealing with the ordinary authority of a solicitor in *United Bank of Kuwait v Hammoud* [1988] 3 All ER 418: above, p 46.

16 *Lindley on Partnership* (14th edn) 1979 at p 256. See now *Lindley and Banks* pp 302–305. Thus in *Mercantile Credit Co Ltd v Garrod* [1962] 3 All ER 1103, it was within the usual authority of a partner in a garage business to sell a car to a finance company so that the car could be let out on hire-purchase terms. For other examples, see *Pollock* pp 31–33. Note that the act must be on the firm's behalf: above, note 5.

17 Montrose 'Liability of Principal for Acts Exceeding Actual and Apparent Authority' (1939) 17 Can BR 695 esp at pp 699–794.

18 *Lindley and Banks* pp 88–90 referring to *Cox v Hickman* (1860) 8 HL Cas 268.

be liable, and the implied authority given by such a partner. In respect of acts within such implied authority, there is some doubt.[19]

In this respect a further distinction must be drawn between partnerships composed of *two* persons and partnerships composed of more than two.[20] Thus, if the partnership consists of three people, one of whom is concealed, s 5 of the Act should apply: and since the third party either *knows* or *believes* that the person with whom he is dealing is a partner, that partner will bind all the others, even if he is exceeding his actual authority, as long as he is acting within his usual authority and there is no knowledge that he has no actual authority to act. If the partnership consists of only two partners, one of whom is concealed, then it might be thought that, since the third party does not know or believe that the person with whom he is dealing is in fact a partner,[1] the dormant partner will not be liable under s 5 where the active partner has exceeded his actual authority. This is the view most favoured by some writers.[2] But in *Watteau v Fenwick*,[3] which did not in fact concern a partnership, the opposite conclusion was reached, and was said to be the same whether the principal was a dormant partner or not.[4] The law of partnership, on such a question, it was said, was nothing but a branch of the general law of principal and agent. But the better view, it is submitted, would seem to be that a dormant partner is not liable in quite the same way, for quite the same reasons, for unauthorised acts, as is an ordinary undisclosed principal.[5]

On the subject of notice, it is necessary to refer to s 8 of the Act, which reads:

> 'If it has been agreed between the partners that any restriction shall be placed on the power of any one or more of them to bind the firm, no act done in contravention of the agreement is binding on the firm with respect to persons having notice of the agreement.'[6]

This is sufficiently explicit not to require further comment.[7]

Effect of partner's acts. The effect of the relationship, so far as concerns contracts made by a partner, is to some extent shown by the previous discussion. As long as the partner is acting within the scope of his express or implied authority, he will make his other partners liable on the contract he made, unless (i) his authority is limited and the third party has notice of such limitation; or (ii) the other partner was a dormant partner, when the closing part of s 5 may apply;[8]

---

19 *Underhill* pp 55–56; *Pollock* p 30–31.
20 Montrose (1939) 17 Can BR 695 at p 700.
 1 But note the provisions of the Business Names Act 1985: above, p 364.
 2 *Underhill* p 56; Montrose (1939) 17 Can BR 695. *Lindley on Partnership* (13th edn 1971) p 160 also adopted this view. In the 14th edn 1979, nothing is said on this point, except for some expression of doubt as to the correctness of *Watteau v Fenwick*, below: see now *Lindley and Banks* p 301, note 12.
 3 [1893] 1 QB 346, discussed above, pp 72–76.
 4 [1893] 1 QB 346 at 348–349 per Willes J.
 5 *Powell* p 77; Montrose (1939) 17 Can BR 695 at p 704. See also Hornby 'The Usual Authority of an Agent' [1961] CLJ 239 at p 244.
 6 See *Cox v Hickman* (1860) 8 HL Cas 268 at 304 per Lord Cranworth.
 7 But note Professor Montrose's distinction between the use of 'authority' in s 5 and 'power' in s 8, (1939) 17 Can BR 695 at p 704.
 8 See above.

or (iii) the partner contracting was not doing so on behalf of the firm. Apart from what is said in s 5,[9] s 6 speaks specifically of what binds the firm, and says it is:

> 'An act or instrument relating to the business of the firm and done or executed in the firm's name, or in any other manner showing an intention to bind the firm.'[10]

This section refers to acts 'by any person thereto authorised, *whether a partner or not*'. Section 7 goes further and makes the point clear:

> 'Where one partner pledges the credit of the firm for a purpose apparently not connected with the firm's ordinary course of business, the firm is not bound, unless he is in fact specially authorised by the other partners.'

But this will not affect the personal liability incurred by an individual partner. This section really relates to the *apparent* authority[11] of partners[12] and it shows that to bind his other partners, the partner contracting must act with an appearance of authority, ie, in this context, usual authority.

A person will also be liable for the acts of another, if he held himself out as a partner, and the firm has been granted credit.[13]

It should be noted that in respect of contractual liability all parties are jointly (*not* severally) liable and this means that each partner is liable for the *total* amount of the debt, while judgment against one partner even if unsatisfied, discharges the others.[14] But the position of a deceased partner's estate is different, in that it is severally liable.[15]

However, 'a person admitted as a partner into an existing firm does not thereby become liable to the creditors of the firm for anything done before he became a partner'.[16] Nor is a firm liable for what the new partner did before he joined it.[17]

Torts. The liability of the firm, and the partners therein, for the torts of a partner is dealt with in s 10:

> 'Where by any wrongful act or omission of any partner acting in the ordinary course of the business of the firm, or with the authority of his co-partners, loss or injury is caused to any person not being a partner in the firm, or any penalty incurred, the firm is liable therefor to the same extent as the partner so acting or omitting to act.'

This is only the enactment of the ordinary rule of the law of agency in respect of

---

9 '. . . an agent . . . for the purpose of the business of the partnership.'
10 See *Re Briggs & Co, ex p Wright* [1906] 2 KB 209, assignment of debt due to the firm.
11 Above, pp 122–132.
12 *Lindley and Banks* pp 357–361.
13 Section 14(1) of the 1890 Act.
14 *Kendall v Hamilton* (1879) 4 App Cas 504. See also *Scarf v Jardine* (1882) 7 App Cas 345.
15 Partnership Act 1890, s 9.
16 Ibid, s 17(1). See *Lindley and Banks* pp 389–392; *Pollock* pp 57–61. Note however the possibility that the new partner may be liable by express agreement: *Rolfe v Flower* (1865) LR 1 PC 27.
17 *Lindley and Banks* pp 388–389.

the tortious liability of the principal.[18] Section 12, however, makes every partner jointly *and severally* liable for everything for which the firm, while he is a partner therein, becomes liable under s 10. This, therefore, means that the situation in respect of *contractual* liability, considered above, does not apply to tort.

The special case of misappropriation by a partner of money or property received from a third person is dealt with in s 11, which reads:

> 'In the following cases, namely,
> (a) Where one partner acting within the scope of his apparent authority receives the money or property of a third person, and misapplies it; and
> (b) Where a firm in the course of its business receives money or property of a third person, and the money or property so received is misapplied by one or more of the partners while it is in the custody of the firm,
> the firm is liable to make good the loss.'[19]

This covers two kinds of cases. Under paragraph (a) the liability of the firm is based upon the fact that the partner in question binds his partners because they 'held him out to the world as a person for whom they were responsible'.[20] But the receipt of the money by one partner must be the receipt of the money by the firm.[1] The firm will not be liable where the money received and misapplied by the defaulting partner was received in carrying out a contract entered into with him individually, not as a member of the firm.[2] Moreover, the receipt and misapplication must be by the same partner. Under paragraph (b) the firm is liable because it has 'in the ordinary course of its business obtained possession of the property of other people, and has then parted with it without their authority'.[3] Here the firm having once become responsible is liable for misapplication by any partner.[4] But the firm will not be liable for mere receipt of money subsequently misapplied if the partner committing the fraud was acting on his own and separate account, even though membership of the firm enabled the partner to commit the fraud,[5] at least if the firm did not have custody of the money or property[6] and knew nothing of the recipt and misapplication.[7]

---

18 Above, pp 315–319. See *Lindley and Banks* pp 332–340; *Blyth v Fladgate* [1891] 1 Ch 337; *Hamlyn v Houston & Co* [1903] 1 KB 81. For a general discussion, see Atiyah *Vicarious Liability in the Law of Torts* ch 11. On the inapplicability of this provision where a personal duty was owed to a partner, see *Meekins v Henson* [1964] 1 QB 472, [1962] 1 All ER 899. In *Mercantile Credit Co Ltd v Garrod* [1962] 3 All ER 1103, liability for fraud was based on s 5, not on s 10. It is open to question whether s 10 would have applied: see Fridman 'The Liability of Partners' (1963) 113 LJ 527.

19 *Lindley and Banks* pp 340–351; *Atiyah* pp 119–120.

20 *Earl of Dundonald v Masterman* (1869) LR 7 Eq 504 at 517 per James VC.

 1 *Lindley and Banks* p 342: see *Rhodes v Moules* [1895] 1 Ch 236; cf *Cleather v Twisden* (1884) 28 Ch D 340.

 2 *British Homes Assurance Corpn Ltd v Paterson* [1902] 2 Ch 404. See *Lindley and Banks* p 343.

 3 *Lindley and Banks* p 347; *Clayton's Case* (1816) 1 Mer 572; *Blair v Bromley* (1846) 5 Hare 542.

 4 *St Aubyn v Smart* (1868) 3 Ch App 646; *Plumer v Gregory* (1874) LR 18 Eq 621.

 5 *Tendring Hundred Waterworks Co v Jones* [1903] 2 Ch 615; *Bishop v Countess of Jersey* (1854) 2 Drew 143.

 6 *Marquise De Ribeyre v Barclay* (1857) 23 Beav 107.

 7 *Jacobs v Morris* [1902] 1 Ch 816; see *Lindley and Banks* pp 343–345, 349–351. Possibly these limitations explain the point raised by *Atiyah* p 120, that the ordinary 'course of employment' doctrine does not apply to partners.

The provisions of s 12 relating to joint and several liability apply also to cases under s 11. It should also be noted that by s 13[8] the firm is not liable for trust property improperly employed in the business or on the account of the partnership by a partner who is not a trustee. But this does not affect the liability of a partner who has notice of a breach of trust;[9] nor does it prevent such property from being followed and recovered from the firm if still in its possession or under its control.[10]

Admissions and notice. Two further sections relate to the effects of the partnership relationship in the law of evidence, and apply the usual rules of agency.[11] Section 15 enacts that an admission or representation made by a partner concerning the partnership affairs, and in the ordinary course of its business, is evidence against the firm.[12] Such an admission is not conclusive.[13] In particular, an admission or representation by a partner as to the extent of his authority to bind the firm will not of itself affect the firm.[14] Nor will the firm be bound unless the admission was made in the ordinary course of the particular business, that is, within the partner's express or implied authority.[15]

Section 16 deals with notice, and provides that notice to any partner who habitually acts in the partnership business of any matter relating to partnership affairs operates as notice to the firm, except in the case of a fraud on the firm committed by or with the consent of that partner.[16] This means that there must be actual notice, since the doctrine of constructive notice is seemingly not applicable to commercial transactions.[17] The partner must probably have been a member of the firm at the time he received the notice.[18] The notice must probably have been received in the course of acting on the partnership business.[19] But this excludes cases where the partner is acting fraudulently, or outside his powers, or is under no duty to notify the firm of what he has done.[20]

D. Termination of the relationship

It is unnecessary here to consider the ways in which a partnership may be dissolved, or the circumstances in which a partner may leave the firm.[1] The

---

8 *Lindley and Banks* pp 352–357.
9 *Blyth v Fladgate* [1891] 1 Ch 337.
10 On the subject of tracing, see above, pp 275–278.
11 On which see above, pp 346–348.
12 *Lindley and Banks* pp 306–307. Note also the Civil Evidence Acts 1968, 1972, 1995.
13 *Wickham v Wickham* (1855) 2 K & J 478.
14 *Ex p Agace* (1792) 2 Cox Eq Cas 312; *Jacobs v Morris* [1902] 1 Ch 816. Contrast the situation with regard to directors of companies: *Hely-Hutchinson v Brayhead Ltd* [1968] 1 QB 549, [1967] 3 All ER 98.
15 *Hollis v Burton* [1892] 3 Ch 226.
16 See *Lindley and Banks* pp 307–310.
17 Cf *Greer v Downs Supply Co* [1927] 2 KB 28.
18 *Williamson v Barbour* (1877) 9 Ch D 529 at 535 per Jessel MR.
19 Above, p 350.
20 *Williamson v Barbour* (1877) 9 Ch D 529.
 1 Partnership Act 1890, ss 25, 26, 32–35. *Lindley and Banks* Part 5.

subject for discussion here is the effect upon the liability of a partner of his leaving the partnership.[2]

In the first place, where a person is held to be a partner by estoppel[3] it is provided that:

> 'Where after a partner's death the partnership business is continued in the old firm's name, the continued use of that name or of the deceased partner's name as part thereof shall not of itself make his executor's or administrator's estate or effects liable for any partnership debts contracted after his death.'[4]

This is amplified more generally by s 36(3), by which the estate of a partner who dies or becomes bankrupt or retires from the firm (in the last instance if he was not known to be a partner by the person dealing with the firm), is not liable for partnership debts contracted after the date of the death, bankruptcy, or retirement respectively.[5] Hence death and bankruptcy terminate the liability of a partner unless he still 'appears' to be a member of the firm, in which event anyone dealing with the firm without notice of the change will still be able to make all the 'apparent' members liable.[6] But in this respect the provisions of the Business Names Act 1985[7] might be extremely relevant.

In the case of a retired partner, the provisions of s 14(1) and of s 36(1) are also relevant, in that if he has still held himself out to be a partner he will continue to be liable, unless he was a dormant partner who 'may retire from a firm without giving notice to the world'.[8] Moreover, by s 38, where the partnership has been dissolved, the authority of partners to bind the firm continues, so far as may be necessary to wind up the affairs of the partnership and to complete transactions begun but unfinished at the time of dissolution,[9] unless the partner has become bankrupt.[10]

Mental incapacity on the part of a partner, at least if not known to the outside world, will not affect his liability or his power to bind the firm.[11] As to revocation of a partner's authority by the other partners, the position is not clear. But it would seem that if there is a limitation on a partner's authority which is known to the third party, the firm will not be bound by such partner's act.[12]

Thus it can be seen that, so far as concerns the *future* liability of a partner who has ceased to be a member of the firm, notice to third parties may or may not be required, depending on the reason why he has ceased to be a partner.

So far as concerns the liability of a former partner for *past* debts or obligations

2 On this see generally, *Lindley and Banks* pp 410–436.
3 Section 14(1). See further above, p 364.
4 Section 14(2).
5 Cf the position in the law of agency generally: below, pp 396–399.
6 Section 36(1). As to what is notice see s 36(2).
7 Above, p 364.
8 *Heath v Sansom* (1832) 4 B & Ad 172 at 177 per Patterson J.
9 See *Goldfarb v Bartlett and Kremer* [1920] 1 KB 639.
10 Though if he holds himself out as a partner he may still be liable, s 38. On this section, see *IRC v Graham's Trustees* 1971 SC 1, 1971 SLT 46; *Welsh v Knarston* 1972 SLT 96.
11 *Lindley and Banks* p 395.
12 Section 8.

of the firm incurred before he left the partnership, the relevant sections of the Act are s 17(2) and s 17(3). By s 17(2):

'A partner who retires from a firm does not thereby cease to be liable for partnership debts or obligations incurred before his retirement.'

There may be some other reason why such a partner should no longer be liable, such as his death, in some circumstances.[13] Moreover, by s 17(3) a retiring partner will be discharged from existing liabilities by an agreement to that effect between himself and the members of the new firm and the creditors. This agreement may be express or implied.[14] There must be a novation, but there need not be the introduction of a new partner[15] and dealings by a creditor with the new firm, when he knows of the change of constitution, will probably raise the inference of a novation.[16]

One final matter should be mentioned. While the partnership relationship subsists, the duties of the partners inter se resemble the duties of an agent to his principal and vice versa. But certain sections of the Partnership Act 1890, specially state or affect those duties. Thus there is no right to remuneration.[17] But there is a right to indemnity and a duty to contribute towards the losses of the firm;[18] there is also a duty to render accounts[19] and a duty not to compete with the firm.[20] There is also liability for secret profits.[1] In other words, broadly speaking, each partner owes a duty of fidelity to the other partners and the firm.[2]

13 See *Lindley and Banks* pp 399, and the references there cited.
14 *Lindley and Banks* pp 422–433.
15 *Thompson v Percival* (1834) 5 B & Ad 925.
16 *Rolfe v Flower* (1865) LR 1 PC 27.
17 Section 24(6).
18 Section 24(1) (2).
19 Section 28.
20 Section 30.
 1 Section 29.
 2 See above, pp 174–181 on the duty of fidelity owed by agents.

CHAPTER 18

Negotiable instruments

Relevance of statute. Generally speaking, the position of principal and agent in respect of negotiable instruments is dealt with by the rules relating to their contractual liability which have previously been considered. However, where an agent deals with a bill of exchange, either as drawer, indorser or acceptor,[1] there are certain provisions of the Bills of Exchange Act 1882 which require special mention in so far as they affect the law of agency.[2]

Principal and third party. Section 23 provides that no person is liable as drawer, indorser or acceptor of a bill[3] who has not signed it as such. This would seem to suggest that for a principal to be liable as drawer, indorser or acceptor he must sign it himself, and that the signature of an agent is insufficient. Other provisions of the Act qualify this. Thus by s 91(1):

'Where, by this Act, any instrument or writing is required to be signed by any person, it is not necessary that he should sign it with his own hand, but it is sufficient if his signature is written thereon by some other person by or under his authority.'

This safeguards the effect of signature by an agent who signs *with the principal's* name. But such a signature will only be effective to bind the principal if the agent making use of the principal's name had authority to do so. Any such signature which is unauthorised will not bind the principal, except to the extent to which any unauthorised acts bind a principal.[4] In this respect two other provisions of the Act are relevant. First, by s 25:

'A signature by procuration operates as notice that the agent has but a limited authority to sign, and the principal is only bound by such signature if the agent in so signing was acting within the actual limits of his authority.'

Hence, anyone who deals with a bill so signed may acquire no rights under it.[5] An attorney's signature is a signature of procuration: hence the principal will

---

1 For the explanation of these terms see *Jacobs on Bills of Exchange* (4th edn) p 76. For other examples of negotiable instruments see *Jacobs* pp 20–24.
2 All statutory references in this chapter are to the 1882 Act, unless otherwise stated.
3 Ie a bill of exchange: s 2. The expression 'bill of exchange' is defined in s 3(1).
4 Ie as long as they are within the agent's implied or apparent authority and the third party has no notice of any want of express authority: see generally above, pp 68, 70, 122, 124.
5 *Reid v Rigby & Co* [1894] 2 QB 40; *Morison v Kemp* (1912) 29 TLR 70. Cf an Ontario case, *Sniderman v McGarry* (1966) 60 DLR (2d) 404, on the similar provisions of the Canadian Statute.

only be liable if the power of attorney authorises such a signature.[6] Secondly, by s 24:

'... where a signature is forged or placed thereon without the authority of the person whose signature it purports to be, the forged or unauthorised signature is wholly inoperative, and no right to retain the bill or to give a discharge therefor or to enforce payment thereof against any party thereto can be acquired through or under that signature, unless the party against whom it is sought to retain or enforce payment of the bill is precluded from setting up the forgery or want of authority.

Provided that nothing in this section shall effect the ratification of an unauthorised signature not amounting to a forgery.'

The result of this section is that a forged[7] or unauthorised signature by the agent cannot make the principal liable, unless either: (i) the principal is *precluded*, ie estopped[8] from saying that the signature was forged or unauthorised; or (ii) the signature was unauthorised but *not* forged, and the principal has subsequently ratified the agent's act;[9] or (iii) since s 24 is 'subject to the provisions of the Act', if any of the *statutory* estoppels operate against the principal.[10]

The requirement that the bill should be signed personally by the principal is also qualified by s 23(2), by which the signature of the name of a firm is equivalent to the signature by the person so signing of the names of all the persons liable as partners in that firm. This deals with partnerships.[11] The position in respect of corporations is dealt with in s 91(2) which provides that where a signature is required, 'it is sufficient if the instrument or writing be sealed with the corporate seal. But nothing in this section shall be construed as requiring the bill or note of a corporation to be under seal'. This means that a company can, but need not, make a bill under its seal. It can also make, accept or indorse a bill of exchange through an agent who has done any of these acts 'in the name of, or by or on behalf or on account of the company', provided that such a person was acting under the authority of the company.[12] Thus, provided that the company had

---

6 *Midland Bank v Reckitt* [1933] AC 1. See, generally, *Byles on Bill of Exchange* (26th edn 1988) pp 68–71, 274–277.

7 See *Robinson v Midland Bank Ltd* (1925) 41 TLR 402; *Kreditbank Cassel GmbH v Schenkers* [1927] 1 KB 826.

8 *Jacobs* p 80, note (9); cf *Byles* p 275. Contrast Powell *Law of Agency* (2nd edn) p 181, note 4. For estoppel see above, pp 281–290.

9 Cf above, ch 5.

10 See ss 7(3), 54(2), 55(2). If the bill is paid by a bank ss 60, 80 and 82 will also apply, as will the Cheques Act 1957, s 4. For a Canadian case involving the forgery of the drawer's signature by an employee of the drawer, see *Canadian Pacific Hotels Ltd v Bank of Montreal* (1987) 40 DLR (4th) 385, where the Supreme Court of Canada, reversing the Ontario Court of Appeal, held that the bank was not protected from liability by reason of the drawer's negligence. A sophisticated bank customer, in this instance a commercial organisation, was under no duty of care to maintain an adequate system of internal accounting controls to prevent loss through forgery. Nor could such duties, if they were to exist, be limited to sophisticated commercial customers. They could only arise as a matter of implication as terms of the contract between banker and customer. This could not be done on any ground (in the absence of an express verification agreement). See also *Citizens Trust Co v Hong Kong Bank of Canada* (1992) 85 DLR (4th) 762, an instance of a forged cheque made payable to the plaintiff on which the bank stopped payment; the bank was held liable.

11 *Byles* pp 61–62.

12 Companies Act 1985, s 37: *Byles* pp 46–53.

power to make, indorse or accept bills, and the agent in question had the necessary authority,[13] the company can be made liable on bills of exchange through the signature of its agent.

Leaving aside these special instances, it would appear that a principal is not liable unless his own name appears on a signature, whether signed by himself or not.[14] If the agent signs his, ie *the agent's* name it may nevertheless happen that *the principal*, and not the agent, will be liable on the bill. For this to result it is necessary for the agent to sign his name in such a way as to indicate that he signs for or on behalf of a principal or in a representative character. The mere addition to the agent's signature of words describing him as an agent, or as filling a representative capacity, will not achieve this result. This is provided by s 26(1). The problem of determining whether the agent is made personally liable by his own signature is one already discussed in connection with the general law of contract.[15] It was seen that it is a difficult factual problem. But the 1882 Act does help to some extent by providing that:

> 'In determining whether a signature on a bill is that of the principal or that of the agent by whose hand it is written the construction favourable to the validity of the instrument shall be adopted' (s 26(2)).[16]

In the case of acceptance by agency, the presumption most favourable to the instrument would be that the signature was that of the principal: otherwise the acceptance would be void.[17] By s 17(1) the acceptance of a bill is the signification by the drawee of his assent to the order of the drawer. This means that only the drawee of a bill can accept it.[18] Hence the signature by an agent as acceptor of a bill drawn on his principal might be construed as the signature of the principal.

One further aspect of the principal's liability should be noted. It applies to negotiable instruments generally, not merely to bills of exchange. Where an agent, without authority, deals with and transfers such an instrument for valuable consideration, and with a third party who acts in good faith without notice of the agent's want of authority, the transfer will be valid as against the principal, in favour of the third party, the holder in due course.[19] This is really only another illustration of the general idea that a principal can be estopped from denying his agent's authority to dispose of property.[20] But in the case of negotiable instruments it seems that an estoppel will be much more easy to raise against a principal, since it is considered that the maker of a negotiable instrument owes a duty of care to subsequent holders in due course who have given consideration for the instrument

---

13 On these matters see above, ch 16.
14 Subject to s 24.
15 Above, pp 239–240. See also below, p 375.
16 See also s 31(5): 'where a person is under obligation to endorse a bill in a representative capacity, he may endorse the bill in such terms as to negative personal liability.' See *Byles* pp 105, 211.
17 *Byles* p 65, note 27.
18 *Davis v Clarke* (1844) 13 LJQB 305; *Re Barnard, Edwards v Barnard* (1886) 32 Ch D 447; *Odell v Cormack Bros* (1887) 19 QBD 223. The only exception is *acceptance for honour*: s 65(1): see the discussion of 'agency of necessity', above, p 135.
19 Section 29(1).
20 Above, pp 281–290.

on the faith of the agent's authority to negotiate it.[1] The special position of such instruments has required that estoppel should be more readily available against negligent principals.[2] This is made more explicit by the provisions of s 90 of the Act that

> 'A thing is deemed to be done in good faith, within the meaning of this Act[3] when it is in fact done honestly, whether negligently or not.'

Hence it has been decided that negligence, in discovering the truth about the agent's want of authority, does not affect the good faith of the third party, or the question of his notice of that want of authority.[4]

Agent and third party. The agent's personal liability on a bill he has signed has already been mentioned. It is clear that he must sign it with his own name (s 23). But his liability will depend upon whether he has signed it 'for or on behalf of a principal or in a representative character' (s 26(1)). If he has, then he will not be personally liable, unless the bill is drawn on him in his own name.[5] If he has not, then even the addition of 'words describing him as an agent, or as filling a representative character' will not exempt him from personal liability, unless the bill is drawn on the principal.[6]

Much, therefore, turns on this question of the nature of the agent's signature. This, as seen in another context,[7] is a difficult question of fact. Hence all that can be done here is to refer to some cases which illustrate the way in which the courts have approached this problem.[8]

---

1 *Wilson and Meeson v Pickering* [1946] KB 422, [1946] 1 All ER 394; *Central Newbury Car Auctions Ltd v Unity Finance Ltd* [1957] 1 QB 371, [1956] 3 All ER 905. Contrast the position there in respect of chattels. See also *Mercantile Credit Co Ltd v Hamblin* [1964] 2 QB 242, [1964] 3 All ER 592.

2 For illustrations and discussion see *Jones v Gordon* (1877) 2 App Cas 616; *Earl of Sheffield v London Joint Stock Bank Ltd* (1888) 13 App Cas 333; *London Joint Stock Bank v Simmons* [1892] AC 201.

3 Ie, for our purposes, for s 29(1).

4 *Raphael v Bank of England* (1855) 17 CB 161; *Venables v Baring Bros & Co* [1892] 3 Ch 527: *Jones v Gordon* (1877) 2 App Cas 616.

5 *Nicholls v Diamond* (1853) 9 Exch 154; *Mare v Charles* (1856) 25 LJQB 119; *Jones v Jackson* (1870) 22 LT 828. Powell thought that he would not be liable, since the Act: nor would the principal because the bill would not be drawn on him: *Law of Agency* (2nd edn) p 251. But what about the effect of s 26(2)? For the use of this provision (in s 52(2) of the Canadian Bills of Exchange Act 1985) to create liability on the part of the agent, see *Canadian Imperial Bank of Commerce v Vopni* (1978) 86 DLR (3d) 383. See also *Dubé v Gray* (1980) 32 NBR (2d) 709; *Bank of Nova Scotia v Radocsay* (1981) 125 DLR (3d) 651.

6 *Okell v Charles* (1876) 34 LT 822; *Dermatine Co Ltd v Ashworth* (1905) 21 TLR 510. Where a cheque bore the printed name of a company and was signed by its president, the latter was personally liable, since the signature gave no indication of the capacity in which he signed: *Holtz v G & G Parkdale Refrigeration Ltd* (1981) 117 DLR (3d) 185. But this was overruled by the Ontario Court of Appeal, in a case where the facts were similar to those in *Holtz*, two years later: see *Allprint Co v Erwin* (1982) 136 DLR (3d) 587.

7 Above, pp 239–240.

8 See *Landes v Marcus and Davids* (1909) 25 TLR 478; *Chapman v Smethurst* [1909] 1 KB 927; *Elliott v Bax-Ironside* [1925] 2 KB 301; *Britannia Electric Lamp Works Ltd v Mandler & Co Ltd and Mandler* [1939] 2 KB 129, [1939] 2 All ER 469.

However, the agent may involve himself in a personal liability if he signs a bill without authority to do so. He may be liable for deceit, if he were fraudulent, or for breach of the implied warranty of authority if he were not fraudulent.[9]

---

9 Above, pp 243–249. Cf *West London Commercial Bank Ltd v Kitson* (1883) 12 QBD 157. See also *Rolfe Lubell & Co v Keith and Greenwood* [1979] 2 Lloyd's Rep 75. Note also his possible liability in negligence.

CHAPTER 19

Agency in the conflict of laws

'Foreign' agencies. In a previous chapter mention was made of the rules applicable when an agent in England acts for a foreign principal.[1] It was seen there that the position of principal and agent depended entirely upon the nature of the contract made by the agent and the intention of the parties in respect of privity of contract between the principal and the third party. That is the situation where the agent's contract with the third party is governed by English law and where, presumably, the contract of agency itself is one which is governed by English law, even though a foreign principal is involved. However, the contract of agency may not be an 'English' contract or the agent may not contract, or otherwise exercise his authority in accordance with English law or the agent may perpetuate acts which could possibly involve his principal in liability, in circumstances in which English law will not govern the rights and liabilities of the parties. It is therefore necessary to see what the English conflict of laws says about the position of principal, agent and third party in such circumstances. In this respect, a preliminary distinction, which is made by the text-writers,[2] following the leading cases,[3] is between the effects of the contract of agency as between principal and agent, and its effect in respect of third parties.[4]

The contract of agency. At common law, where the relationship of principal and agent was created by contract, the law applicable to that contract was the 'proper law of the contract', ie the law with which the contract had the most connection.[5] That is no longer the situation. By virtue of the Contracts (Applicable Law) Act 1990, the governing law of such contracts is now the law contained in the EEC Convention on the Law Applicable to Contractual Obligations ('the Rome Convention').[6] The older law will still apply to

---

1 Above, p 272.
2 Dicey and Morris *Conflict of Laws* (12th edn 1993) Vol 2, pp 1452–1453, 1458; Hanbury *Principles of Agency* (2nd edn) pp 77–79.
3 *Maspons y Hermano v Mildred* (1882) 9 QBD 530; affd (1883) 8 App Cas 874; *Chatenay v Brazilian Submarine Telegraph Co* [1891] 1 QB 79. And see Millett J in *Maclaine Watson & Co Ltd v International Tin Council* [1987] 3 All ER 787 at 796.
4 For the different approach of Continental systems, and the nature and effects of the 1978 Hague *Convention on the Law of Applicable to Agency*, see Hay and Müller-Freienfels, 'Agency in the Conflict of Laws and the 1978 Hague Convention' (1979) 27 Am J Comp L1.
5 For the doctrine of the 'proper law' of a contract, see *Dicey and Morris* (11th edn 1987) ch 32, (12th edn 1993) pp 1187–1190. Cheshire and North's *Private International Law* (11th edn 1987) ch 18. See also the previous edition of this work, at pp 346–348 and the cases there cited.
6 *Dicey and Morris* (12th edn 1993) Vol 2, p 1453: SI 1991 No 707.

contracts of agency entered into before 1 April 1991, as it will in Australia and Canada.[7]

The Rome Convention governs such matters as the formal validity of the contract; the terms of the agent's appointment; his liability to be removed; his remuneration; and similar matters. It will also determine, as between principal and agent, the agent's authority. It is possible that, under the law of some European countries, eg, Belgium, Italy, special mandatory rules to protect agents on termination of the agency contract may be applied, even if the contract expressly provides that it is to be governed by English law and is subject to the jurisdiction of an English court.[8]

Although the Convention will apply to an agency relationship which is created by express or implied contract, it has been doubted whether it will apply to a relationship created by an instrument such as a power of attorney, which is not in any sense a contract.[9]

Under the Convention the parties are free to choose the law to govern the contract (subject to certain general constraints). Where the applicable law has not been chosen, art 4 of the Convention will apply. By this it becomes necessary to determine the party who is to effect the performance which is characteristic of a contract between principal and agent, which may be that of the agent. Such presumption may be disregarded if it appears from the circumstances that the contract is more closely connected with another country than it is with the country whose law is indicated by the presumption.[10]

Transactions with third party. The Rome Convention will apply to the contract, if any, between the agent and a third party.[11] It will also apply to the relationship between the agent and the third party and to the formal validity of any contract concluded by the agent with such party.[12] But the rights and liabilities of the principal as regards third parties will be governed, in general, by the law applicable to the contract concluded between the agent and the third party.[13] Under the common law that is the proper law of the transaction which the agent executes.[14] For example, if it is a contract then the position of the parties as to privity of contract, liability, payment, set-off, transfer of property, and so on, is governed by the proper law of that contract made by the agent with the third party. As Lord Lyndhurst said in *Pattison v Mills*:[15]

> 'If I, residing in England, send down my agent to Scotland, and he makes contracts for me there, it is the same as if I myself went there and made them.'

---

7 *Dicey and Morris* at p 1187. See, eg, *Presentaciones Musicales SA v Secunda* [1994] 2 All ER 737 at 748–749, where the contract of agency dated from 1988.
8 *Dicey and Morris* at 1456.
9 Ibid at p 1456.
10 Ibid at p 1455.
11 Ibid at p 1454.
12 Ibid at p 1456. For earlier law see *Kahler v Midland Bank Ltd* [1950] AC 24, [1949] 2 All ER 621.
13 *Dicey and Morris*, rule 199, at p 1458: *Presentaciones Musicales SA v Secunda* [1994] 2 All ER 737 at 748–749 per Roche LJ.
14 *Maclaine Watson & Co Ltd v International Tin Council* [1987] 3 All ER 787 at 796 per Millet J.
15 (1828) 1 Dow & Cl 342 at 363.

In that case an English principal employed a Scottish agent to make a contract in Scotland with a third party. The contract was valid by Scots but not by English law. It was held that the contract was governed by Scots law. In *Maspons y Hermano v Mildred*:[16]

A Spanish principal acted through a Spanish agent in making a contract in England with an English merchant. The agent disclosed the fact that he was acting as an agent but did not disclose his principal's name. It was held that the rights and liabilities of the principal and the third party inter se were governed by English law.

A further illustration is provided by the leading case of *Chatenay v Brazilian Submarine Telegraph Co*.[17] There:

A Brazilian principal executed in Brazil a power of attorney in Portuguese, by which an English agent was authorised to buy and sell shares in London on the principal's behalf. A question arose whether the agent had validly sold some of the principal's shares to third parties. It was held that this was a matter for English, not Brazilian, law.

The rule of law which these cases illustrate is succinctly expressed in these words of Lord Esher:[18]

'If a contract is made in one country to be carried out between the parties in another country ... unless there appears to be something to the contrary, it is to be concluded that the parties must have intended that it shall be carried out according to the law of that other country.'

Despite this, however, it has been suggested[19] that, if the issue as between principal and third party relates to the agent's actual, as contrasted with ostensible or apparent authority, the law governing that issue should be not the law applicable to the contract between the agent and the third party but the law governing the relationship between the principal and agent, ie the law contained in the Rome Convention. Whether this suggestion is acceptable depends on the effect of the decision in *Ruby SS Corpn Ltd v Commercial Union Assurance Co*.[20] There the Court of Appeal held that New York law, the law which governed the contract of agency, also governed the agent's right to cancel the contract between the agent and the third party, which was an English contract of insurance. By English law such cancellation was not permissible. But it was held that since New York law allowed it, the cancellation, with the third party's consent, was valid. This case has been criticised as incorrect, since it conflicts with the principles expressed in the earlier cases cited above.[1] But it has been suggested[2] that the case is reconcilable with the earlier decisions in that it

---

16 (1882) 9 QBD 530; affd (1883) 8 App Cas 874.
17 [1891] 1 QB 79.
18 Ibid at 83.
19 *Dicey and Morris* at p 1461.
20 (1933) 150 LT 30.
1 Cheshire and North's *Private International Law* (11th edn 1987) at p 494, note 11.
2 *Dicey and Morris* at p 1462; and see the remarks of Ackner LJ in *Britannia SS Insurance Association Ltd v Ausonia Assicurazioni SpA* [1984] 2 Lloyd's Rep 98 at 101.

decides that the agent's authority is governed by the proper law of his own contract with the principal, but that he has such additional authority to bind the principal as is conferred upon him by the law governing his contract with the third party.[3]

CHAPTER 20

Agency in constitutional law

Relevance in public law. The preceding chapters have been concerned with the legal effects of an agency relationship created between private persons. They have, therefore, considered that relationship in private law. However, agency is of great importance in public life, that is, in the context of public, ie constitutional law.[1] The Crown, which is a corporation sole, and Government departments, which also may be corporations sole,[2] like other corporations, can only act through agents (or servants). Hence the law of agency is relevant to the legal position of the Crown and Government departments, most of all in respect of contract and torts. So far as those Government departments which are corporations sole are concerned, the general rules of the law of agency can apply since the fact that such corporations act for the Crown would not appear to affect the legal position.[3] But the Crown itself, and such Government departments as do not have separate legal existence because they lack incorporation, were in a special position at common law and still merit separate treatment, even after the passing of the Crown Proceedings Act 1947. The agents of the Crown and these departments must therefore be distinguished from agents appointed by private persons: hence the former use by Bowstead[4] of the expression 'public agents', which will be adopted here.

Contractual liability. As regards contractual liability, the position of the Crown and unincorporated Government departments before 1948 was that a third party who contracted with the Crown or such a department through a public agent could not make the principal liable. His only remedy was by petition of right, which was available for the recovery of unliquidated damages for breach of contract.[5] Such a remedy was strictly a matter of grace, not of right: although it would appear that in modern times it was regarded as a true remedy, in appropriate circumstances, available just as if it were right. Nor was it available

---

1 See generally Keir and Lawson *Cases on Constitutional Law* (5th edn 1967) pp 328–348.
2 Or may be agencies of the Crown without having been incorporated. Certain of these were incorporated by the Crown Agents Act 1979, which has been changed by the Crown Agents Act 1995.
3 But note what is said below on the subject of 'authority'.
4 *Bowstead on Agency* (12th edn) p 1. This terminology has been dropped by the editors of later editions.
5 *Thomas v R* (1874) LR 10 QB 44.

where the contract was one of *service*⁶ or was one by which the Crown appeared to fetter its own future executive acts.⁷ These limitations would appear to be still operative. By the Crown Proceedings Act 1947, the Crown (ie the authorised Government Department or the Attorney-General) may be sued on any contract made by a public agent on the Crown's behalf in any circumstances in which, before the Act, a petition of right would have been available.⁸ All the Act does, therefore, is to give statutory effect to the pre-existing practice, while changing the procedure to be employed by a plaintiff in the pursuance of his claim.

This still leaves for determination whether the Crown will be bound in any given situation by a contract purported to be made by its agent. The answer to that question depends upon the authority of the agent.⁹ If a public agent has actual authority under some statute or otherwise to make a contract, the Crown will be bound.¹⁰ But, from what was said by the Privy Council in *A-G for Ceylon v AD Silva*,¹¹ a public officer, merely as such, does not have actual authority to act on behalf of the Crown in all matters which concern the Crown. Nor is there any holding out of such an officer by the Crown, giving rise to apparent or ostensible authority, from employment in such capacity.¹² There must be a representation by the Crown.¹³ A representation by the public agent alone will not suffice. Nor will a representation by one public officer be sufficient to hold out another as having the requisite authority, unless there is some special power conferred on the public officer making the representation. But this is disputed.¹⁴

---

6 *Dunn v R* [1896] 1 QB 116, ie an agent or servant of the Crown had no legal claim against the Crown in respect of the agency or service. This would appear to be the law still after the Crown Proceedings Act 1947; see also now the Trade Union Reform and Employment Rights Act 1993, ss 31(1), 49(1), 51, Sch 7, para 3, Sch 10; Trade Union and Labour Relations (Consolidation) Act 1992, s 300(1), Sch 1.

7 *Rederiaktiebolaget Amphitrite v R* [1921] 3 KB 500, a case which has been much criticised by writers on constitutional law, and on which no subsequent decision has been based: Hood Phillips *Constitutional and Administrative Law* (6th edn 1978) pp 641–642, and cases cited; ibid, note 23. Note the comments on this case by Denning J in *Robertson v Minister of Pensions* [1949] 1 KB 227, [1948] 2 All ER 767, which were themselves criticised in the House of Lords in *Howell v Falmouth Boat Construction Co Ltd* [1951] AC 837, [1951] 2 All ER 278.

8 See s 1; on which see *Hood Phillips* pp 639–643.

9 And, possibly, upon the validity of a sub-delegation to the agent in question: *Hood Phillips* pp 607–608. See also Wade and Bradley *Constitutional and Administrative Law* (11th edn 1993) pp 745–748.

10 *A-G for Ceylon v A D Silva* [1953] AC 461 at 479. See also a Canadian case, *Verreault & Fils Ltée v A-G for Quebec* (1975) 57 DLR (3d) 403.

11 See previous note. Cf *Western Fish Products Ltd v Penwith District Council* [1981] 2 All ER 204, a case concerned with the conduct of officers of a local authority.

12 For discussion of the problems of apparent authority of public agents in relation to the doctrine of ultra vires, see Craig 'Representations by Public Bodies' (1977) 93 LQR 398, at pp 398–404. He attacks the present law as based on what has been called 'the jurisdictional principle', which requires that the agent have authority to act and is acting intra vires. See also Craig, *Administrative Law*, 1983, ch 16.

13 Cf *Miles v McIlwraith* (1883) 8 App Cas 120: though this was a criminal case and the 'agent' was not a Crown agent but was contracting *with* the crown.

14 On the ground that the *Silva* case turned on certain delegated legislation: *Bowstead and Reynolds on Agency* (16th edn) p 387: and conflicts with other authority, based upon something like the notion of usual authority: ibid, and see Treitel 'Crown Proceedings: Some Recent Developments' [1957] Public Law 321 at pp 335–339; Craig 'Representations by Public Bodies' (1977) 93 LQR 398.

Indeed in an earlier case,[15] Denning J held that a representation by one government department or official to which had been delegated a particular task or duty, was sufficient to bind the Crown with respect to the activities of other departments. However, the problem with permitting such estoppels is that, by their use, the ultra vires doctrine may be destroyed, since public bodies could than extend their powers by making representations which would bind them by estoppel. Hence, although some courts have applied estoppel to provide a remedy for what would otherwise be an injustice, viz, denial by a public body of the validity of the acts of their officials, the general applicability of estoppel has been negated.

The Act does not alter the legal position of the public agent. At common law such an agent (like any other agent making a contract on behalf of his principal) was not personally liable on such a contract, unless he had contracted in such a way as to show that he was contracting personally.[16] Moreover, it was decided in *Dunn v Macdonald*[17] (following the plaintiff's failure in a petition of right brought against the Crown for breach of a contract of service)[18] that the public agent who made the contract with the plaintiff was not liable to him for breach of any implied warranty of authority. The exact ground of the decision is a matter of some doubt, since it could be argued that the agent in that case in fact had no authority to make such a contract of service for a definite period. The answer suggested by Professor Hanbury[19] is that the plaintiff (who must be taken to know the law)[20] must be considered to have known that the agent had no authority to make the contract in question.

Liability in tort. The Crown's liability in tort for the acts of its agents is created by the Crown Proceedings Act 1947.[1] By the Act the Crown is liable where any other principal would be liable in respect of injury to agents or to others resulting from the ownership, occupation, possession or control of property[2] or from breach of any binding statutory duty[3] or from the performance of any functions imposed on an officer of the Crown by common law or statute.[4] But the Crown is *not* liable in tort for acts by an agent committed while discharging responsibilities of a judicial nature,[5] but will now be liable for torts by members of the armed forces of the Crown in the execution of their duties causing death or

---

15 *Robertson v Minister of Pensions* [1949] 1 KB 227, [1948] 2 All ER 767: cf note 7, above.
16 *Macbeath v Haldimand* (1786) 1 Term Rep 172: contrast *Clutterbuck v Coffin* (1842) 3 Man & G 842; *Graham v Public Works Comrs* [1901] 2 KB 781.
17 [1897] 1 QB 401, 555; cf *The Prometheus* (1949) 82 Ll L Rep 859. Note that these decisions were called in question, without deciding the issue, by Gray J of the High Court of Ontario in *Peaker v Canada Post Corpn* (1989) 68 OR (2d) 8 at 20–21.
18 *Dunn v R* [1896] 1 QB 116.
19 *Principles of Agency* (2nd edn) pp 149–150.
20 But was the law clear at that time? Cf above note 17.
1 See Atiyah *Vicarious Liability in the Law of Torts* pp 391–397.
2 Crown Proceedings Act 1947, s 2(1); on which see *Hood Phillips* pp 643–645; *Wade and Bradley* pp 733–736.
3 Section 2(2); on which see *Hood Phillips* pp 645–646.
4 Section 2(3). Note the definition of 'officer' in s 38: and see *Moukataff v British Overseas Airways Corpn* [1967] 1 Lloyd's Rep 396.
5 Section 2(5).

permanent injury to other members of the armed forces of the Crown who are on duty and will be entitled to a pension because of such death or injury.[6] The Crown will not be liable, however, for torts committed by certain officers not appointed, or paid out of the Consolidated Fund, by the Crown[7] nor for torts committed in the course of war or for the defence of the realm, etc.[8]

Moreover, there are two important restrictions on the tortious liability of the Crown (or a Government department). In the first place, the act of the agent must have been one which gave rise to a cause of action against the agent himself or his estate. Secondly, the Crown will not be liable if the defence of 'act of state' can be raised against the plaintiff's claim.[9] This defence is only available where an agent of the Crown, by command or subsequent ratification by the Crown, has injured an alien resident abroad.[10] It is not available where the injured plaintiff is a British subject (no matter wherever he is resident, or wherever the injury is suffered):[11] nor is it available against a friendly alien resident on British territory.[12]

The tortious liability of a public agent is similar. Generally speaking, unless otherwise personally immune from suit, such an agent can be sued in respect of torts committed by him, as can a private agent. However, the defence of 'act of state' is open to a public agent in the same circumstances as it is available to the Crown (and where an originally tortious act is made susceptible of the defence of 'act of state' by subsequent ratification on the part of the Crown).[13] Moreover, a public agent, as such, is not tortiously and vicariously liable for the wrongs of his subordinates, who are also agents or servants of the Crown,[14] but such an agent will be directly liable in tort for any wrong committed in obedience to his express orders.[15]

The general immunity of a public agent from suit is further illustrated by the rule that such an agent is not liable to account to a third person for any money which, as a public agent, he was obliged to give such third person. For example, the Secretary for War, in *Gidley v Palmerston*[16] was not liable to give a War Office clerk his retired allowance even if the Secretary had received the money

---

6 Crown Proceedings (Armed Forces) Act 1987, repealing s 10 of the 1947 Act. Note, however, the possibility of the resurrection of s 10 in certain circumstances: s 2 of the 1987 Act.

7 Section 2(6).

8 Section 11(1). Note also the immunity from suit in relation to postal packets: ibid, s 9, on which see *Triefus & Co v Post Office* [1957] 2 QB 352, [1957] 2 All ER 387: *Moukataff v British Overseas Airways Corpn* [1967] 1 Lloyd's Rep 396.

9 On this, see *Hood Phillips* pp 281–287, *Wade and Bradley* pp 329–331. It is not clear what this expression means: *A-G v Nissan* [1969] 1 All ER 629 at 645 per Lord Morris. It appears to be a principle of judicial restraint: *Buttes Gas and Oil Co v Hammer (No 3)* [1981] 3 All ER 616 at 628 per Lord Wilberforce.

10 *Buron v Denman* (1848) 2 Exch 167.

11 *Entick v Carrington* (1765) 19 State Tr 1029; *Sinclair v Broughton and Government of India* (1882) 47 LT 170.

12 *Johnstone v Pedlar* [1921] 2 AC 262. For the contrast, where the acts occur on non-British territory, see *A-G v Nissan* [1970] AC 179, [1969] 1 All ER 629.

13 *Buron v Denman* (1848) 2 Exch 167.

14 *Bainbridge v Postmaster-General* [1906] 1 KB 178. Cf in respect of contract, *A-G for Ceylon v A D Silva* [1953] AC 461, [1953] 2 WLR 1185: above.

15 *Raleigh v Goschen* [1898] 1 Ch 73.

16 (1822) 3 Brod & Bing 275.

for that purpose. Nor was the Secretary of State for India liable to account as trustee to people entitled to booty given by the Queen to the Secretary in trust for distribution.[17] The only liability on the agent is a liability to answer to the Crown.[18]

17 *Kinloch v Secretary of State for India in Council* (1882) 7 App Cas 619.
18 *R v Secretary of State for War* [1891] 2 QB 326. For discussion of the responsibility of agents of the Crown only to the Crown or to Parliament, see the judgment of the House of Lords in *Gouriet v Union of Post Office Workers* [1978] AC 435, [1977] 3 All ER 70, reversing the decision of the Court of Appeal, especially Lord Denning MR, [1977] QB 729, [1977] 1 All ER 696.

PART V

The termination of agency

SUMMARY

CHAPTER 21

Termination

A. Agency created by act of parties

A. BY ACT OF PARTIES

Agreement, revocation and renunciation. Since the relationship of principal and agent has been created by agreement between them, it follows that the relationship may be determined by both parties agreeing to the discharge of that relationship. It will also be determined if either party withdraws his original agreement. This will occur where the principal gives the agent notice of revocation of the agency or the agent gives the principal notice of renunciation.[1] Any such notice may be given in any form: a deed or document in writing is unnecessary, even if the original authority was contained in a deed.[2] To these general principles there are qualifications.

Irrevocable agencies

In the first place revocation is not allowed without the agent's consent where the agent has been granted authority to act on the principal's behalf but in respect or for the protection of any interest of the agent.[3] In such cases the authority is given either by deed or for valuable consideration as a security in respect of a liability of the principal to the agent. For example, in *Smart v Sandars*:[4]

> A factor was sent goods to sell on behalf of the principal. He made advances to the principal on the security of these goods. It was held that the authority was irrevocable.

The case was explained by Lord Atkinson in *Frith v Frith*[5] as one in which it was decided that:

---

1 *Lowe v Rutherford, Thompson McRae Ltd* (1971) 14 DLR (3d) 772.
2 *The Margaret Mitchell* (1858) Sw 382. But there *may* be a question as to the *amount* of notice to be given, ie, the duration of such notice: see, eg, *Dart & Oliphant Holdings Ltd v Yamaha Motor Canada Ltd* (1977) 10 AR 366; *Pratt Representatives (Newfoundland) Ltd v Hostess Food Products Ltd* (1978) 18 Nfld & PEIR 412, *Metz v Con-Stan Canada Inc* (1982) 16 Sask R 270, reversed on other grounds (1984) 33 Sask R 3; *Western Equipment Ltd v AW Chesterton Co* (1983) 46 BCLR 64; *Yamaha Canada Music Ltd v MacDonald & Oryall Ltd* (1990) 46 BCLR (2d) 363.
3 Cf Powers of Attorney Act 1971, s 4(1).
4 (1848) 5 CB 895. See also *Raleigh v Atkinson* (1840) 6 M & W 670.
5 [1906] AC 254 at 261.

'... the general authority of a factor in whose hands goods were placed for sale, to sell at the best price which could reasonably be obtained, could not be revoked after the factor had made advances on the security of the goods to the owner of them and while these advances remained unpaid.'

But this principle only applies where the purpose of the agency was to secure the agent, for example, in respect of a debt owed by the principal to the agent (as in the case just cited) or where the purpose of the agency was to create a beneficial interest in favour of the agent.[6] It does not apply where the sole purpose of the agency, as far as the agent is concerned, is to enable the agent to earn his commission by action on the principal's behalf.[7] Furthermore, where the agency is irrevocable for this reason, it will not be terminated, as other agencies would be,[8] by the death,[9] lunacy, or bankruptcy[10] of the principal.

Secondly, where the agent has incurred personal liability by acting in pursuance of his authority, such that the principal would be liable to indemnify the agent in respect of such liability, then the principal cannot revoke his authority so as to avoid the obligation of indemnifying the agent, while leaving the agent personally liable.[11] Thus in *Read v Anderson*:[12]

> The agent was employed to make bets on behalf of his principal: he was authorised to pay if he lost. The agent placed the bets and lost. It was held that the principal could not revoke after this had happened, but was still liable to indemnify the agent, since the agent, for the sake of his character and business, was bound to pay the amount that had been lost.

Thirdly, where the agent has made a contract on behalf of the principal, and, if he sued on that contract, would be able, as against the principal, to exercise a lien over any money or goods recovered as a result of such action, then the agent's authority is irrevocable.[13]

Lastly, in respect of certain powers of attorney, there are the provisions of the Powers of Attorney Act 1971, s 5 (applying s 205(1)(xxi) of the Law of Property Act 1925), which safeguard the donee of the power and the purchaser from such

---

6 *Kiddill v Farnell* (1857) 26 LJ Ch 818. Or to enable an underwriting agent to sue in the USA: *Daly v Lime Street Underwriting Agencies* [1987] 2 FTLR 277. Or to allow a landlord to take control of leased premises in the name of and as agent of the tenant so as to secure the landlord's interest in having his tenant carry out his obligations under the lease: *Re Hartt Group Ltd and Land Securities Ltd* (1984) 7 DLR (4th) 89.

7 *Frith v Frith* [1906] AC 254.

8 See below, pp 396–399.

9 *Kiddill v Farnell* (1857) 26 LJ Ch 818. Cf *McCallum v Trans North Turbo Air (1971) Ltd* (1978) 8 CPC 1 a decision of Tallis J of the Northwest Territories Supreme Court, relying on remarks of Addy J of the Ontario High Court in *Wilkinson v Young* (1972) 25 DLR (3d) 275 at 276.

10 *Yates v Hoppe* (1850) 9 CB 541.

11 *Warlow v Harrison* (1859) 1 E & E 309 at 317 per Martin B. See *Crowfoot v Gurney* (1832) 9 Bing 372.

12 (1884) 13 QBD 779. Note, however, the Gaming Act 1892, which affects the principal's obligation to indemnify his agent in the case of agreements or contracts affected by the Gaming Act 1845. This would mean a different result on these facts: but the principle still remains the same.

13 *Drinkwater v Goodwin* (1775) 1 Cowp 251.

donee in the event of what would otherwise be revocation by the donor of the power, or some other occurrence, such as the death of the donor.[14]

Other limitations on revocation

Apart from the instances given above, and any restrictions imposed by an express or implied term of the contract of agency, if there is a contract between the parties, the principal has complete freedom of revocation,[15] provided he revokes before the agent has completely exercised his authority, or the agent has been guilty of some wrongful conduct that justifies his immediate dismissal without notice.[16] Thus in *Campanari v Woodburn*:[17]

> The agent was employed to sell a picture, it being agreed that he should be remunerated only if he succeeded in making a sale. After he had tried, without success, to sell the picture, it was held that his authority could be revoked by the principal.

Again in *Hampden v Walsh*:[18]

> The principal deposited a sum with the agent in respect of a wager as to whether or not the earth was curved. Before the agent paid over the wager (which was lost) to the third party, the principal demanded it back. Despite the fact that the agent subsequently paid the wager to the winner, it was held that the principal had revoked in time, and could recover the sum from the agent.

If the principal does revoke, his revocation will not affect the principal's existing claims against the agent for failure to perform or for negligence. Nor will such revocation affect the agent's claim against the principal for an indemnity in respect of liabilities incurred on behalf of the principal before revocation, nor (possibly) his claim for commission or damages in respect of the prevention by the principal, as a result of revocation, of the agent's earning of commission.

---

14 The protection of this provision extends to situations where the donor of an 'enduring power of attorney' (below, p 408) is effected by subsequent mental incapacity: Enduring Powers of Attorney Act 1985, s 1. See also ibid, s 9, where the instrument registered under the Act does not create a valid power of attorney. Mental disorder of the donor when the power was executed will not render a power made under the 1985 Act invalid: *Re K, Re F* [1988] Ch 310, [1988] 1 All ER 358.

Similar protection of both 'attorneys', ie donees of the power, and those dealing with such attorneys can be found in British Columbia (RSBC 1979, c 334, as amended by SBC 1987, c 42, s 90, in consequence of the recommendations of the British Columbia Law Reform Commission, *Report on the Law of Agency, Part I: The Termination of Agencies*, 1975, pp 18–27). Cp also in Alberta, S Alta 1991, c P-17.5, s 14; cp RSPEI 1988 c P-16, s 3 (Prince Edward Island), RSM 1987 c P-97, s 2 (Manitoba). In Ontario the law was fundamentally altered, and the previous Powers of Attorney Act amended by the Substitute Decisions Act, SO 1992, c 30 and the Consent and Capacity Statute Law Amendment Act, SO 1992, c 32.

15 *Lowe v Rutherford, Thompson McRae Ltd* (1971) 14 DLR (3d) 772. Unless a statute governs the relationship, in which event termination can only be effected under its provisions, eg, proof of 'just cause'; *Adams-North Shore Insurance Services Ltd v Insurance Corpn of British Columbia* (1982) 42 BCLR 218.

16 As in *Boston Deep Sea Fishing and Ice Co v Ansell* (1888) 39 Ch D 339; above, p 204.

17 (1854) 15 CB 400.

18 (1876) 1 QBD 189: see also *Burge v Ashley and Smith Ltd* [1900] 1 QB 744.

Thus, notwithstanding revocation, the principal can sue for the agent's breach of contract or other wrongful conduct.[19] The agent can sue for indemnity.[20] Furthermore, and perhaps most important of all, the agent in some circumstances will be able to sue, not only for commission already earned, but also for commission which the principal's revocation has prevented him from earning. This is another aspect of a problem which has earlier been discussed.[1] In that context the point at issue was whether commission was payable without any benefit having occurred to the principal; and it was there stated that everything depended upon the way in which the contract was worded, or upon whether the principal had wrongfully revoked the agent's authority. Much of the previous discussion was concerned with the terms of the contract, and the effect of the language in which it was phrased. Here the point for consideration is, what amounts to wrongful revocation, such that the principal will be liable for the prevention of the earning of commission.

Closure of business. This has arisen in a number of cases in which the principal has ceased to carry on the business in respect of which the agent was employed.[2] Is the principal liable to pay compensation to the agent for his removal of the opportunity for the latter to earn commission? For example, in *Rhodes v Forwood*:[3]

> The agent was employed under a contract to sell the principal's coal. After four years the principal sold his colliery and went out of business. It was held that the principal was not liable to the agent for breach of contract.

This was because there was nothing in the contract by which the principal had bound himself to maintain the colliery. Nor was there any express term as to the length of the agent's service. But a different result was reached in *Turner v Goldsmith*:[4]

19 As to which see above, p 204.
20 *Warlow v Harrison* (1859) 1 E & E 309 at 317 per Martin B. It seems to be immaterial whether in such circumstances the agency is described as 'irrevocable' or it is said that the principal who revokes does so 'at his peril' as Martin B said. For all that the expression 'irrevocable' means (at least in these circumstances) seems to be that what the principal does, or what happens to the principal, cannot amount to unilateral termination of the agency so as to free the principal from the obligations which have already arisen under the agency.
1 Above, pp 194–200.
2 See *Luxor (Eastbourne) Ltd v Cooper* [1941] AC 108 at 142–144, [1941] 1 All ER 33 at 56–57, per Lord Wright. The 'estate agent' cases are only one example of this problem.
  Cf the issue that arose in *Alpha Trading Ltd v Dunnshaw-Patten Ltd* [1981] QB 290, [1981] 1 All ER 482, discussed above, p 198, in which the agents claimed that they had lost commission because the principals refused to complete the contemplated sale of the cement, from which the agents' commission was to have been paid. For this the agents were held entitled to sue for damages, on the basis of an implied term that the principals would not break their contract with the third party, the intended buyer of the cement. Contrast *Marcan Shipping (London) Ltd v Polish SS Co* [1988] 2 Lloyd's Rep 171; affd [1989] 2 Lloyds Rep 138, discussed above, p 198, where the agent's right to commission was excluded by an *express* term that commission would only be paid in accordance with market practice, which meant that if no sale occurred no commission was payable.
3 (1876) 1 App Cas 256; cf *Northey v Trevellion* (1902) 7 Com Cas 201; *Collier v Sunday Referee Publishing Co* [1940] 2 KB 647, [1940] 4 All ER 234.
4 [1891] 1 QB 544; cf *Devonald v Rosser & Sons* [1906] 2 KB 728. These were said to be cases where there was a 'contract of employment' into which a term had to be implied to give 'business efficacy' to the express terms: *Bauman v Hulton Press Ltd* [1952] 2 All ER 1121 at

The agent was employed on a commission basis by the principal to sell shirts. The principal's factory, at which the shirts were manufactured, accidentally burnt down. It was held that the principal was still liable to pay the agent a reasonable sum representing what he would have been likely to earn by way of commission.

Here, however, there was an express term in the contract by which the agent was employed for a period of five years, which had not expired when the factory burnt down. The contrast therefore seems to be between contracts which contain an express term about length of service and duration of the liability to pay commission and contracts which have no such express terms.

However, it may be that a term can be implied into the contract, by which the principal is bound to pay commission, notwithstanding that the business or enterprise from which the agent was to earn commission has come to an end.[5] This, *perhaps*, is the explanation of *Inchbald v Western Neilgherry Coffee, Tea and Cinchona Plantation Co Ltd*.[6] But it may be very difficult to imply such a term. In *French Ltd v Leeston Shipping Co Ltd*:[7]

The agent arranged a time charterparty by X of the principal's ship. The terms of the agent's contract were that he was to be paid commission during the continuance of the charterparty, on the basis of the hire earned for the principal. Before the time for the charterparty's duration had elapsed the principal sold the ship to X. It was held that no term could be implied into the agent's contract to the effect that the principal would not sell the ship but would continue to allow the agent to earn his commission. Hence the agent could not recover for loss of commission.

One test that was formulated by Phillimore J in *Northey v Trevillion*[8] and applied by Streatfield J in *Bauman v Hulton Press Ltd*[9] was as follows. Where there is a contract to employ another merely as agent, but with no service or subordination, there is no implied undertaking that the agent is to be supplied with the means of earning his commission. But, if the contract is one of service, the commission is

---

1123 per Streatfield J. But see the New Brunswick case of *Woodpulp Inc (Canada) v Jannock Industries Ltd* (1979) 26 NBR (2d) 358, the same result, ie liability of the principal for the agent's lost commission when the principal sold the business, was achieved by a construction of the *express* language of the contract, not by any implication of a term; cf the similar result in *Creditel of Canada Ltd v Gravure Graphics Ltd* (1987) 51 Man R (2d) 122.

5 As it was in *Alpha Trading Ltd v Dunnshaw-Patten Ltd*, above, note 2. Cf *George Moundreas & Co SA v Navimpex Centrala Navala* [1985] 2 Lloyd's Rep 515. But see the remarks of Bingham LJ in *Marcan Shipping (London) Ltd v Polish SS Co* [1989] 2 Lloyd's Rep 138 at 143, above, p 198.

6 (1864) 17 CBNS 733. See also above, p 200.

7 [1922] 1 AC 451. See the summary of this and other cases by Paull J in *Shackleton Aviation Ltd v Maitland Drewery Aviation Ltd* [1964] 1 Lloyd's Rep 293 at 317. In that case, too, no term could be implied to prevent a principal from disposing of the subject-matter of the contract of agency. Cf *Marcan Shipping (London) Ltd v Polish SS Co*, above, p 392, note 2. Contrast *Alpha Trading Ltd v Dunnshaw-Patten Ltd*, above, p 392, note 2, where the case of *French Ltd v Leeston Shipping Co Ltd* was distinguished. See also *George Moundreas & Co SA v Navimpex Centrala Navala*.

8 (1902) 7 Com Cas 201 at 203.

9 [1952] 2 All ER 1121.

merely intended to be in the place of salary, and the contract cannot be determined without compensation to the servant.

However, once the agent has acquired a vested right to commission, for example by fulfilling the terms of his contract, even if the principal does not benefit thereby,[10] then revocation by the principal, though otherwise valid, will be inoperative to deprive the agent of his rights to such commission. The problem is to determine whether the contract contains an express term which can be interpreted in such a way as to justify the agent's claim to commission as to work done, eg orders received, *after* the termination of his employment.[11] This right to 'continuing commission' was illustrated by the decision in *Sellers v London Counties Newspapers*.[12] There the agent was employed to obtain advertisements, and was paid commission on such advertisements as he obtained. It was held that, as soon as he got an *order* for an advertisement, he was entitled to commission thereon. Therefore, by dismissing the agent, the principal could not deprive him of the commission he had actually earned, nor of the commission from advertisements the order for which he had obtained, even if they were published after the date of his dismissal.[13]

Repudiation. Another aspect of the termination of the relationship of principal and agent (where that relationship stems from a contract between the parties) merits special attention. This is the possibility of termination of the relationship by unilateral repudiation.[14]

Generally an act which amounts to a repudiation of the contract prior to performance of the obligations under such contract will not determine the contract unless and until it is 'accepted' by the innocent, injured party.[15] What are

---

10 Eg the introduction of an 'able, ready, and willing purchaser': see *EP Nelson & Co v Rolfe* [1950] 1 KB 139, [1949] 2 All ER 584. See further above, pp 194–200, below, pp 411–421.

11 *Naylor v Yearsley* (1860) 2 F & F 41. For examples, see *Bilbee v Hasse & Co* (1889) 5 TLR 677; *Wilson v Harper, Son & Co* [1908] 2 Ch 370; *British Bank for Foreign Trade v Novinex Ltd* [1949] 1 KB 623, [1949] 1 All ER 155 (commission payable); *Barrett v Gilmour & Co* (1901) 17 TLR 292; *Crocker Horlock Ltd v Lang & Co Ltd* [1949] 1 All ER 526 (commission not payable); *Roberts v Elwells Engineers Ltd* [1972] 2 QB 586, [1972] 2 All ER 890 (commission payable).

See also, *G H Nolan (1956) Ltd v Watson & Co Ltd* (1965) 109 Sol Jo 288 (right to continuing benefit of commission or expectancy of such benefit). Contrast *Bronester Ltd v Priddle* [1961] 3 All ER 471, [1961] 1 WLR 1294 (advance commission repayable, as agent had no right to commission on orders for goods undelivered at termination of employment).

12 [1951] 1 KB 784, [1951] 1 All ER 544: followed in *Gold v Life Assurance Co of Pennsylvania* [1971] 2 Lloyd's Rep 164.

13 The Supreme Court of Canada also adopted the 'express term' approach in *Grover v Stirling Bonding Co* [1935] 3 DLR 481 (applied in *Rowles v Al-Wood Manufacturing Ltd* (1979) 9 Alta LR (2d) 61). But in *Graycombe Associates Ltd v Northern Stag Industries Ltd* (1976) 73 DLR (3d) 241, it was held that such commission could be paid *either* when there was an express term *or* where a similar term was to be implied of necessity, on the analogy of cases where the relationship of principal and agent could only be terminated by giving reasonable notice (cf p 389, note 2, above). See also *Lilley v Corynthian Restaurants Ltd* (1980) 7 Sask LR 110; *Royal LePage Real Estate Services Ltd v Church* (1991) 80 Alta LR (2d) 122. Is there, then, a difference between the law in England and in Canada?

14 For an illustration of this see an Australian case: *Imagic Inc v Futuretronics (Australia) Pty Ltd* (1983) 51 ALR 122.

15 Cheshire, Fifoot and Furmston's *Law of Contract* (12th edn 1991) pp 534–539, 541–546; Fridman *Law of Contract in Canada* (3rd edn 1994) pp 600–620.

acts of repudiation, and what constitutes an 'acceptance' of such repudiation are matters for the general law of contract, rather than the law of agency.[16] However, it was suggested in some earlier cases that the general principles of repudiation did not apply to the case of master and servant: and that a repudiatory act, whether by master or servant, immediately ended the contract, as well as the relationship between the parties.[17] The reason for this was the confidential, personal nature of that relationship, by virtue of which once there was an act inimical to the continuance of such relationship it would be unreasonable to permit the party not responsible for such act to hold the other party bound to him. This was confirmed, or emphasised by the fact that a decree of specific performance to order the master or servant to perform the contract (or an injunction to restrain the master or servant from committing or continuing to commit a breach) would not be available.

In more recent cases, there were dicta the opposite way.[18] Such dicta, and a decision which did in fact allow an injunction to issue in a master-servant contract,[19] were to the effect that the normal contract principles applied, and 'acceptance' of the repudiation was necessary. To this view, Megarry V-C adhered, after a lengthy review of the case-law, in *Thomas Marshall (Exports) Ltd v Guinle*,[20] a case of master and servant. This approach was applied by Lloyd J to a case of principal and agent, in *Atlantic Underwriting Agencies Ltd and David Gale (underwriting) Ltd v Compangia di Assicurazione di Milano SpA*.[1] In that case, therefore, the alleged act by the principals in repudiating the contract of agency, did not automatically terminate the contract of agency between them. Hence it was necessary to establish an act of acceptance of such repudiation, on the part of the agents, before the latter could sue for damages for breach of the contract of agency. This could not be done, therefore, apart from other reasons,[2] there was no basis for permitting the agents to sue the principals.

The approach favoured by Megarry V-C, and adopted by Lloyd J in this

---

16 Ibid.
17 *Vine v National Dock Labour Board* [1956] 1 QB 658 at 674, [1956] 1 All ER 1 at 8: per Jenkins LJ (approved by Viscount Kilmuir LC in the House of Lords: [1957] AC 488 at 500, [1956] 3 All ER 939 at 944); *Francis v Municipal Councillors of Kuala Lumpur* [1962] 3 All ER 633, [1962] 1 WLR 1411; *Denmark Productions Ltd v Boscobel Productions Ltd* [1969] 1 QB 699, [1968] 3 All ER 513. See also *Sanders v Ernest A Neal Ltd* [1974] 3 All ER 327. Cf a Canadian case, *Campbell v MacMillan Bloedel Ltd* [1978] 2 WWR 686.
18 *Decro-Wall International SA v Practitioners in Marketing Ltd* [1971] 2 All ER 216 at 223 per Salmon LJ, 228–229 per Sachs LJ; *Hill v C A Parsons & Co Ltd* [1972] Ch 305 at 319, [1971] 3 All ER 1345 at 1354 per Sachs LJ.
19 *Hill v C A Parsons & Co Ltd*, above, where despite the wrongful dismissal of the servant by the master the mutual confidence of the parties continued, ie, the contract was determined but not the relationship: see Donaldson J, delivering the judgment of the National Industrial Relations Court in *Sanders v Ernest A Neal Ltd*, above.
20 [1979] Ch 227, [1978] 3 All ER 193: criticised by Thomson 'Unacceptable Acceptance?' (1979) 42 MLR 91.
1 [1979] 2 Lloyd's Rep 240 (which was cited to the Court of Appeal in *Gunton v Richmond-upon-Thames London Borough Council*, above, but not referred to in the judgments). In the *Imagic* case, above, note 14, the effect of the principal's response to the repudiating act of the agent, viz, wrongful assertion of title to the principal's trade mark, appears to have been 'acceptance' of the discharge of the prior distributorship contract between the parties: (1983) 51 ALR 122 at 135 per McLelland J.
2 Arising under the pre-1990 conflict of laws.

agency case, was also approved by the majority of the Court of Appeal (over the dissent of Shaw LJ) in *Gunton v Richmond-upon-Thames London Borough Council*.[3] This, again, was a case involving master and servant, not principal and agent. However, it would seem that, if the doctrine that the ordinary principles of contract apply to a case of master and servant is the correct one—which may ultimately be approved by the House of Lords—there would seem to be no reason why it should not also apply to contracts between principals and agents, as was held in the *Atlantic Underwriting* case. Much the same considerations, viz, confidentiality and personal service, apply to the one relationship as to the other. Although the distinction has been drawn between the relationship of principal and agent and that of master and servant for most purposes,[4] there is less, if any reason to maintain such a sharp division where the rationale that underlies the attitude of the law with respect to one relationship can be said to apply equally to the other. Consequently, where either principal or agent performs an act, or makes a statement that purports to be, or may be interpreted as being, an act of repudiation of the contract, and there is no justification for such repudiation, such as breach of contract by the other party, then the contract of agency should not automatically end: the innocent party should have an option whether to insist upon the continuation of the contract or to accept the repudiation and seek the appropriate remedy, eg an action for damages for breach.[5]

B. BY OPERATION OF LAW

Normal termination. Aside from any agreement between principal and agent, or any unilateral act by either of them, the relationship between principal and agent will terminate when the transaction which has been undertaken has been performed. The execution of his authority by the agent brings that authority to an end. For example, a broker who has sold the goods, for the sale of which he was employed, is functus officio.[6]

Two points call for notice. In the first place, there is sometimes difficulty about ascertaining when the agent's authority has been executed.[7] Secondly, although the agent's express or implied authority may have been executed, it is possible that the agent may continue to act in a way that suggests to third parties that he has authority, ie he may assert an apparent authority. In such circumstances, the agency relationship that is then involved is one created by estoppel.[8] Such apparent authority will only cease when, either (a) it has been turned into a real authority by ratification and then terminated by performance of the undertaking or (b) notice of the agent's lack of authority has reached third parties dealing with the agent.

---

3 [1981] Ch 448, [1980] 3 All ER 577.
4 Above, pp 31–37, 303–312.
5 See, generally, McMullen 'A Synthesis of the Mode of Termination of Contracts of Employment' [1982] CLJ 110.
6 *Blackburn v Scholes* (1810) 2 Camp 341 per Lord Ellenborough.
7 Above, pp 194–200.
8 Above, ch 6.

The relationship will also terminate when the period for which it was created to endure has come to an end, provided that any limit upon the duration of the agency was fixed expressly by the parties, or can be implied into the relationship by trade or other usage or custom. A good illustration of this is provided by *Dickinson v Lilwal*:[9]

> A general authority to sell certain goods was given to a broker. It was a custom of the particular trade in which the broker was employed that such an authority, if not limited by express agreement, was to expire at the end of the day on which it was given. The broker made a contract on behalf of his principal two days after the day he was given his authority and it was held that this contract was therefore not binding on the principal.

Subsequent physical events. If the property which is the subject-matter of the agency is destroyed, or otherwise ceases to exist, for example where the principal sells the business with which the agent was connected,[10] the agency will end. As already seen, however, in some circumstances this will not mean that the agent's right to commission in respect of potential future business also lapses. On the contrary, the cases indicate that where the contract of agency is so expressed, or can be so construed, as to take into account the conclusion of the business, then the agent will still be entitled to commission, even though the agency has otherwise terminated.

Secondly, if the principal or the agent dies, the agency will be determined.[11] This is because the agency relationship is confidential and personal: hence the individual identity and existence of either of the parties are very material. The effect of the death of either the principal or agent is to fix the rights of the parties as they existed at the time of the death. Thus, if it is the principal who has died, the agent cannot recover expenses incurred after the date of the death, even if he had no knowledge of the death of his principal.[12] In *Campanari v Woodburn*:[13]

> An agent was appointed to sell a picture for the principal. He made several attempts but failed to sell it. Then the principal died. Unaware of the principal's death the agent continued with his efforts to sell the picture, and did so. It was held that the principal's personal representatives were not liable to pay the agent commission on the sale.

9 (1815) 4 Camp 279; cf *Lawford & Co v Harris* (1896) 12 TLR 275.
10 *Rhodes v Forwood* (1876) 1 App Cas 256: discussed above, p 392.
11 *Blades v Free* (1829) 9 B & C 167; *Pool v Pool* (1889) 58 LJP 67.
12 *Pool v Pool* above; see also *Re Overweg, Haas v Durant* [1900] 1 Ch 209. Curiously enough, none of the remedial legislation in, eg, England or British Columbia, which protects third parties dealing in good faith with the donee of a power of attorney after the termination of the power by, eg, death of the principal, has sought fit to give the agent an express right to recover such expenses as mentioned in the text. Perhaps a right to claim such expenses is implicit in the British Columbia provision that the agent is deemed to have authority to act when his authority has been terminated without his knowledge and his act was within the scope of his former authority: RSBC 1979, c 334, s 3, as included by SBC 1987, c 42, s 90. 'Agent' includes, but is not limited to, an attorney acting under a power of attorney: ibid, s 1 (but not partners: ibid, s 2(1)). 'Knowledge' includes knowledge of the occurrence that terminates the agent's authority: ibid, s 2(2).
13 (1854) 15 CB 400.

But the personal representatives were liable to pay the agent a reasonable sum for the services he had performed. However, they would have been liable to pay the agreed commission if they had ratified the agent's contract of sale.[14] If it is the agent who has died then the agent's personal representatives will not be bound to execute the agent's authority. Nor, if the agent is a firm, will the other parties be bound to perform the undertaking if one of the partners died.[15] Where the principal is a corporation then the dissolution of the corporation under the provisions of the Companies Act will terminate the authority of the company's agents, such as solicitors acting for it.[16]

Thirdly, the relationship may be affected by the subsequent insanity of either principal or agent. Such insanity will determine the relationship on the ground that an insane person cannot validly contract, so as to appoint or act as an agent.[17] But the termination of the agency may not affect the liability of the principal or the agent to third parties.[18]

In all these instances it must be remembered that these principles will not apply where the agency is 'irrevocable'.

Subsequent legal events. Here there may be two causes of the termination of the agency relationship.

The first is bankruptcy. When a principal or agent is adjudicated bankrupt his 'estate' vests in the trustee in bankruptcy.[19] 'Estate' includes the bankrupt's property (with certain exceptions not relevant here).[20] 'Property' includes money, goods, things in action, land, every description of property, and also obligations.[1] It would seem therefore that this would include the rights and liabilities arising out of the relationship of principal and agent.[2] Since agency is a personal relationship, that relationship was affected, under the old law, by the bankruptcy of either principal or agent.[3] Nevertheless, the provisions of the Bankruptcy Act 1914[4] gave protection to the agent and the third party who acted in ignorance of what was then a crucial event, namely an 'act of bankruptcy'.[5] Bankruptcy is

---

14 *Foster v Bates* (1843) 12 M & W 226.
15 *Tasker v Shepherd* (1861) 6 H & N 575.
16 *Salton v New Beeston Cycle Co* [1900] 1 Ch 43. For the continued personal liability of the agent, see below, pp 402–403.
17 *Drew v Nunn* (1879) 4 QBD 661, esp at 666 per Brett LJ; *Yonge v Toynbee* [1910] 1 KB 215; *Wilkinson v Young* (1972) 25 DLR (3d) 275. But see above, p 57 note 17. A change in the law, subject to certain conditions, was recommended by the Law Reform Commission of British Columbia's *Report on the Law of Agency, Part 2: Powers of Attorney and Mental Incapacity*, 1975, pp 19–28. This has taken the form of creating an 'enduring power of attorney': Power of Attorney Act, RSBC 1979, c 334, s 7. The same concept is now found in England: Enduring Powers of Attorney Act 1985: below, p 408.
18 Below, ch 22.
19 Insolvency Act 1986, s 306(1).
20 Ibid, ss 283, 385(1).
1 Ibid, s 436.
2 Cf the revocation of an enduring power of attorney (below, p 408) by the bankruptcy of the attorney: Enduring Powers of Attorney Act 1985, s 2(10).
3 Except where the agent's authority protected the agent's interest: also cf *Elliot v Turquand* (1881) 7 App Cas 79.
4 Section 45: see the 4th edition of this work at p 358.
5 These were abolished by the Insolvency Act 1985 which repealed the Bankruptcy Act 1914, and was itself replaced by the Insolvency Act 1986.

now regulated by Part IX of the Insolvency Act 1986. However, the consequences of adjudication appear to be the same as under the prior law, since some provisions of the 1986 Act[6] give similar protection from liability to that granted by the Act of 1914 where transactions are made in good faith before the making of a bankruptcy order under the statute.

Secondly, the relationship of principal and agent (if created by contract) will be terminated by the operation of the doctrine of 'frustration'—just as with any other contract. This means that if for any reason it becomes illegal, impossible, or useless to continue to execute the authority, or otherwise fulfil the obligations inherent in the agency relationship, then the parties are discharged from all further obligations. Thus if the principal becomes an alien enemy[7] or the agent is conscripted for military service,[8] or the property which the agent is to sell is expropriated,[9] the agency will be determined.

B. Agency created by operation of law

Agency of necessity. Since the agent's authority does not arise from any agreement between himself and the principal, but as a result of circumstances which justify his acting as agent, without any express authorisation, it is clear that this form of agency is not terminated either by agreement between the parties or by unilateral act. It would seem that this relationship terminates only when the 'necessity' which brought it into being has disappeared.[10]

Agency from cohabitation. This form of agency (described earlier as presumed agency) arises from the fact of cohabitation between husband and wife, or a man and woman who are not married. Hence, by way of a general rule, it can be said that the woman's authority ceases to exist when the parties cease cohabiting, unless the man continues to 'hold out' the woman as having apparent authority to act on his behalf: in which event the relationship of principal and agent will continue to exist, on the basis of estoppel. It may be, therefore, that the woman's authority will only terminate when notice is received by tradesmen that the parties have ceased to cohabit.[11] The above general rule must be considered in the light of the following remarks.

End of cohabitation. The wife's authority will certainly be terminated by cessation of cohabitation in the following circumstances: (1) if the marriage is terminated by decree or divorce, or declared void by decree of nullity; (2) if the parties no longer cohabit as a result of a decree of judicial separation, or an order

6 Viz s 284: cf Halsbury's Statutes (4th edn 1987) Vol 4, p 927.
7 *M'Connell v Hector* (1802) 3 Bos & P 113; *Stevenson & Sons Ltd v Aktiengesellschaft für Cartonnagen-Industrie* [1918] AC 239; (contrast *Tingley v Müller* [1917] 2 Ch 144) *Sovfracht (V/O) v Van Udens Scheepvaart en Agentuur Maatschapij* [1943] AC 203, [1943] 1 All ER 76. On this subject see Fridman 'Enemy Status' (1955) 4 ICLQ 614.
8 *Marshall v Glanvill* [1917] 2 KB 87; *Morgan v Manser* [1948] 1 KB 184, [1947] 2 All ER 666.
9 *Oxford Realty Ltd v Annette* (1961) 29 DLR (2d) 299.
10 On what is meant by 'necessity' in this context, see above, pp 134–144.
11 *Munro v De Chemant* (1815) 4 Camp 215; *Ryan v Sams* (1848) 12 QB 460 (discussed above, p 150).

from a magistrate's court containing a 'non-cohabitation' clause; (3) if the spouses have separated by mutual consent, with an agreement about the payment of maintenance by the husband provided such agreement is kept by him; (4) if the spouses have separated by mutual consent without any agreement as to maintenance and the wife has means of support;[12] (5) if the wife has deserted her husband, ie left him without his consent and without any justification for her going; (6) if the husband dies. However, the liability of the husband as principal, incurred before his death, will continue to exist.[13] Moreover, it may be that the wife's authority to act as agent will continue until knowledge of the husband's death has been received by her. In *Smout v Ilbery*:[14]

> A husband dealt with the plaintiff who supplied meat. He went abroad leaving his wife in England. Later he died abroad. Before either the plaintiff or the wife received news of his death, goods were supplied by the plaintiff to the wife. It was held that the wife was not personally liable for the goods, since she contracted as agent. Nor was she liable for breach of any warranty of authority, since she originally had authority to contract as agent, and such authority continued until revoked by knowledge of the death of her husband.

The ratio decidendi of this case has caused some difficulty; and the case has been criticised by some judges, and accepted by others.[15] Other cases[16] would seem to indicate that the death of the principal automatically terminates the relationship without any need for knowledge of the principal's death. The question of knowledge may be relevant, however, to the position of the agent vis-à-vis third parties, and the personal representatives of the principal.[17]

Other grounds. In earlier law, a wife's authority terminated, whether she was living with her husband or not, when she committed adultery,[18] unless the husband connived at or condoned the adultery,[19] or continued to hold her out as his agent.[20] All this would now seem to be irrelevant, in view of modern legal and social views about divorce.

It would appear however that the insanity of the husband will terminate the wife's authority:[1] but the wife may be personally liable for breach of the implied warranty of authority, and it may be that the husband, upon recovering his sanity, will be liable for goods supplied in the interim period, if the third party with whom the wife dealt did not know of the husband's insanity and the

12 *Eastland v Burchell* (1878) 3 QBD 432 (see above, pp 146–147).
13 *Re Wood's Estate, Davidson v Wood* (1863) 1 De G J & Sm 465.
14 (1842) 10 M & W 1.
15 See *Yonge v Toynbee* [1910] 1 KB 215 at 225 per Buckley LJ, 232 per Swinfen Eady J 235 per Vaughan Williams LJ; *Halbot v Lens* [1901] 1 Ch 344. On the personal liability of agents and warranty of authority, see above, pp 231–249.
16 *Blades v Free* (1829) 9 B & C 167 (a case which concerned an unmarried woman, but the position of a wife is the same) at 171, per Littledale J; *Pool v Pool* (1889) 58 LJP 67; *Re Overweg, Haas v Durant* [1900] 1 Ch 209; *Campanari v Woodburn* (1854) 15 CB 400.
17 Below, pp 406–407.
18 *Atkyns v Pearce* (1857) 2 CBNS 763.
19 *Wilson v Glossop* (1886) 20 QBD 354.
20 *Norton v Fazan* (1798) 1 Bos & P 226.
 1 According to *Yonge v Toynbee* [1910] 1 KB 215.

circumstances were such that it appeared that the wife had authority to act on behalf of the husband.[2]

If the husband provided his wife with a sufficient allowance, then her authority to pledge his credit will no longer continue,[3] just as if he had expressly prohibited her from doing so,[4] though the effect of such prohibition, as regards third parties, may depend upon whether the third party with whom the wife dealt, had notice of such prohibition.[5] If the wife is sufficiently supplied with necessaries, or exclusive credit is given by tradespeople to the wife, then her presumed agency will cease.[6]

Agency of unmarried women. The position of a woman cohabiting with a man not her husband, as already seen, is similar to that of a wife. The differences in the main, result from the fact that legal proceedings are not required to terminate such a relationship, or to bring about a legal separation between the parties. However, it may be that one important difference between the two situations lies in the fact that notice by third parties of the fact that the parties have separated may be required only in the case of a wife before the agency is terminated.[7]

2 On these points see *Yonge v Toynbee* [1910] 1 KB 215 and *Drew v Nunn* (1879) 4 QBD 661; cf the cases cited in note 11 above.
3 *Morel Bros & Co v Earl of Westmoreland* [1904] AC 11; cf *Debenham v Mellon* (1880) 6 App Cas 24.
4 *Lane v Ironmonger* (1844) 13 M & W 368; *Jolly v Rees* (1864) 15 CBNS 628.
5 See cases cited in previous note and *Jetley v Hill* (1884) Cab & El 239, cf above, pp 148–149 below, pp 404–406.
6 Above, pp 148–149.
7 See the cases cited in note 11 above. Cf above, p 149.

CHAPTER 22

Effects of termination

A. Position of agent

A. WHERE NOTICE OF REVOCATION WAS GIVEN

As between principal and agent. The difference between 'irrevocable' and other agencies has already been explained and discussed.[1] It was seen that any attempt by the principal to revoke an 'irrevocable' agency would be of no effect. In all other instances, where the principal can, and does, revoke the agency, the agent ceases to have any authority to act for the principal, and cannot make the principal liable for anything which he does after the notice of revocation has been received.

However, such revocation cannot affect the rights and liabilities of either principal or agent which have already vested at the time of revocation. Thus the principal can sue for breaches of contract or negligence, committed by the agent before the agency was terminated; and the agent can sue for remuneration earned before the revocation, and possibly, for remuneration which would have been earned had the agency not been terminated.[2]

As between agent and third party. Since, by revocation, the agent ceases to have authority to act on behalf of the principal, the agent can no longer bind the principal by any transaction which he enters into with third parties after notice of revocation has been received.[3] Hence the agent will be personally liable in respect of any such transactions, either because he must be taken to have contracted or otherwise dealt, on his own behalf, or because he contracted as

---

1 Above, pp 389–391.
2 Above, pp 391–392. Note, also, the question of 'acceptance' of repudiation, and the option that is available to the party who has not repudiated: see pp 394–396.
3 Unless the principal has not sufficiently notified third parties when the agency previously resulting from agreement may become an agency by estoppel, and the principal may still be bound: below, p 405. The protective provisions of the British Columbia Power of Attorney Act, RSBC 1979, c 334, as amended by SBC 1987, c 42, s 90, do not apply to this situation: ibid, s 4(2). Contrast the situation in Alberta and Manitoba where the attorney is protected against the donor of a power of attorney and third parties by SA 1991, c P-13.5, s 14; RSM 1987, c P97, s 2 (whether the power is terminated or becomes void by reason of the donor's mental incapacity or infirmity).

agent, in which event he will be liable for breach of the implied warranty of authority.[4]

B. WHERE NOTICE OF REVOCATION IS NOT REQUIRED OR GIVEN

Common law. The position as between principal and agent is clear, for the agent's authority is determined irrespective of notice of the fact which has terminated the relationship, whether that be performance of the undertaking, the death of the principal, or anything else. But this will not affect the rights and liabilities of the parties as they stood at the moment of termination; nor, presumably, will it affect the rights of the agent and principal inter se in respect of acts performed by the agent before the agent has notice of the terminating event.[5]

As between the agent and the third parties the position is more debatable. The agent's liability to the third party will depend upon whether the principal (or the principal's estate) can be regarded as being bound to the third party. If this is so, then the agent will not be personally liable to the third party, either on the contract made, or for breach of the implied warranty of authority. But if the principal is not liable, then the agent may well be personally liable to the third party.

Where the agency was determined by the death of the principal, it was held in *Blades v Free*[6] that the principal's executors were not liable for goods supplied after the principal's death—which presumably involves the personal liability of the agent.[7] But in *Drew v Nunn*,[8] where the principal became insane, it was held that this did not preclude the principal's liability to someone who supplied goods after the principal's insanity. This would appear to exclude the agent's liability to the supplier. However, in *Yonge v Toynbee*[9] it was held that an agent in such a position would be liable to the third party for breach of the implied warranty of authority. The whole question of the agent's liability to third parties seems to be connected with the question: when is notice that the agency relationship is terminated required to be given to third parties who deal, or may deal, with the agent?[10]

By statute.[11] The Powers of Attorney Act 1971, s 5(1) provides that a person acting in good faith in pursuance of a power of attorney will not be liable in

---

4 Above, pp 243–249. Cf *Sanford v Milburn* (1983) 51 NBR (2d) 137, where the sister of the owner of real estate was liable on this basis when she signed a listing agreement for the sale of the property on her brother's behalf without his authority to do so. But in some Canadian provinces the situation is different: see previous note. Cf on this, in Ontario, the Substituted Decisions Act, SO 1992, c 30 s 13.

5 Cf also, the agent's right to commission: above, p 392.

6 (1829) 9 B & C 167.

7 But contrast *Smout v Ilbery* (1842) 10 M & W 1 discussed above, p 400.

8 (1879) 4 QBD 661.

9 [1910] 1 KB 215.

10 Below, pp 405–408.

11 Note, in this respect, the provisions of the Insolvency Act 1986, s 284(4) (5) giving protection to good faith transactions, along similar lines to the protection given originally by the Bankruptcy Act 1914, s 45: cf above, p 398.

respect of such act, by reason of the fact that before the act the power had been revoked, if the fact of revocation were not known by the agent at the time he acted.[12]

B. Position of third party

Statutory protection. To some extent the third party is protected by statutory provisions.[13] In the event of the exercise of a power of attorney after the power has been revoked, s 5(2) of the Powers of Attorney Act 1971 protects a third party transacting with the agent, if there is no knowledge of the revocation.[14] By s 5(3) of the same Act, the person dealing with the donee of a power of attorney expressed to be irrevocable and given by way of security,[15] is also protected, unless he knows that the power was not given by way of security.

Effect of revocation at common law. The statutes referred to above only apply to agency relationships created by a power of attorney. Other agencies are still regulated by the common law. Unilateral revocation by the principal will not affect the third party as long as the agent is acting in an authorised or apparently authorised manner, unless and until the third party has notice of the fact that the agent's authority has been terminated. In other words, as long as the principal continues to 'hold out' the agent as having authority to act on his behalf, he will be bound by transactions between the agent and third parties and the principal will continue to 'hold out' the agent in this way, until the third party has notice that the agency has ended.[16] Thus, in *Trueman v Loder*[17] a third party who dealt

---

12 Knowledge of revocation includes knowledge of the occurrence of any event which has the effect of revoking the power: Powers of Attorney Act 1971, s 5(5). Note the application of this provision to the case of the invalid revocation of an 'enduring power of attorney' (as described in the Act) see the Enduring Powers of Attorney Act 1985, s 9(5): such a power is delineated in s 2. Revocation of such a power is dealt with in ss 7(1)(a), 8(3). See also below, p 409. Similar provisions are to be found in British Columbia (RSBC 1979, c 334, ss 3, 4(1), as inserted by SBC 1987, c 42, s 90. This applies to agency generally not only to agency created by a power of attorney: ibid, s 1.
13 Note also the Insolvency Act 1986, s 284(4) (5): above, note 11.
14 Where the interest of a 'purchaser' (as defined in the Law of Property Act 1925, s 205(1)(xxi)) is concerned, note the statutory presumption in favour of such purchaser contained in the Powers of Attorney Act 1971, s 5(4). Note also the provisions of the Enduring Powers of Attorney Act 1985, s 9(5): above, note 11. See also below, p 408. For similar protection in Ontario and British Columbia, see SO 1992, c 30, s 13 (dealing with enduring powers of attorney). See also SA 1991, c P-13.5, s 14(2), RSM 1987, c P97, s 2(2): above, note 3; RSBC 1979, c 334, s 4(2), as amended by SBC 1987, c 42, s 90.
15 Cf Powers of Attorney Act 1971, s 4(1): above, p 389.
16 Cf above, pp 122–132. Professor Seavey criticises the use of estoppel in relation to the principal and the third party, and substitutes the following reasoning. '[Agency] created by a statement to A . . . continues until A has been notified: if by communication to T it will not be revoked until T is notified. If the power was created by communication to both A and T, and A alone is notified of the revocation, he still possesses and can exercise the power, becoming a wrongdoer towards P. If T alone is notified, A may exercise the power rightfully, but what T may acquire by such exercise he will hold subject to the equitable right of P.' (29 Yale LJ 859 at p 892).
17 (1840) 11 Ad & El 589. This decision was followed by the Appellate Division of the Supreme Court of Alberta in *Morgan v Lifetime Building Supplies Ltd* (1967) 61 DLR (2d) 178, where an agent, after the termination of his authority, unknown to the third party, purported to cancel an

with the agent after his authority had been revoked, but without notice of such revocation, was able to sue the principal for the price of goods supplied. In *Curlewis v Birkbeck*:[18]

> The principal gave the agent horses to sell for him. This was done, and the third party who bought the horses paid the agent. Unknown to the third party, the agent's authority has been revoked before the sale. It was held that the payment was valid as against the principal.

Two questions are raised. First, in what circumstances has the principal held out the agent, so as to require notice on the part of the third party? On the basis of the earlier discussion of the term 'authority',[19] it can be said that wherever the agent is acting with an *implied* authority, or an *apparent* authority, notice of the termination (or restriction) of that authority will be necessary. Where the agent is acting with a *presumed* authority[20] (ie in the case of a woman, whether wife or unmarried, cohabiting with a man), it has already been seen that, unless the man has *actually*, not *implicitly*, held the woman out as having authority to pledge his credit, notice is not required: the man will not be liable where he has in fact revoked the woman's presumed authority.[1] This seems reasonable, in view of the fact that where the woman has no such presumed authority, because for example, she has a sufficient allowance, or the goods are not needed (even though normally they would be necessary),[2] the man will not be liable to the third party, irrespective of the third party's knowledge of such facts.[3]

Secondly, what amounts to notice? Must the third party be notified by the principal or can any knowledge from any source be regarded as satisfying this particular requirement? It would appear that it is immaterial whether the principal himself has supplied the requisite notice, as long as the third party is aware of the true facts. Thus in *Munro v De Chemant*[4] the liability of the man depended upon whether goods were supplied to the woman *after* the supplier knew that they had separated and, there, as Patteson J said in *Ryan v Sams*,[5] it was 'notorious that the parties had separated'. This seems to indicate that express notice by the man was unnecessary and, on principle, both in this case and in other instances, it would seem reasonable to state that the knowledge of termination may come from any source as long as it is reliable.[6] It would seem also that, if the third party himself is transacting through an agent, then, in certain

instalment contract previously negotiated for the principal, substituting a cash contract, and received the cash in his capacity as agent, thereupon fraudulently converting it to his own use. The principal was held liable to reimburse the third party.

18 (1863) 3 F & F 894; cf *Marsden v City and County Assurance Co* (1865) LR 1 CP 232; *Stavely v Uzielli* (1860) 2 F & F 30.
19 See pp 61, 68, 122.
20 Above, pp 133–134.
 1 See the discussion of *Jolly v Rees* (1864) 15 CBNS 628; *Lane v Ironmonger* (1844) 13 M & W 368; *Jetley v Hill* (1884) 1 Cab & El 239; and *Debenham v Mellon* (1880) 6 App Cas 24, above, pp 148–149.
 2 Above, pp 148–149.
 3 Cf Powell, *Law of Agency* (2nd edn) pp 401–402.
 4 (1815) 4 Camp 215 (see above, p 150).
 5 (1848) 12 QB 460 at 402.
 6 See also below, p 407 on the question of notice of principal's insanity.

circumstances notice to, or knowledge on the part of his agent that the other agency has been terminated, will be sufficient, at any rate where it is within the scope of the agent's authority to receive such notice, and part of his duty to communicate it to his principal.[7] In such circumstances the notice of the agent will be imputed to the principal.[8]

Involuntary termination. The preceding paragraphs have dealt with the case of unilateral voluntary revocation of the agency by the principal.[9] The agency relationship may be determined involuntarily, as already seen, for example as a result of the death or disability of the principal or agent, or it may be determined by effluxion of time, execution of the authority, frustration or impossibility.

In some of these instances, the third party will be aware that the agent's authority has been determined. Thus if the agent dies or becomes insane, or the circumstances are such that the purpose of the agency becomes impossible to fulfil, the third party will usually have notice of the fact that the relationship of principal and agent has come to an end. Where the agent incurs an incapacity or disability which is not patent to the outside world, or the time limit fixed by the parties for the continuance of their relationship expires, in circumstances which do not indicate to third parties that there was any such limit, it would seem that notice to the third party is necessary, if the principal is to avoid being made liable to such party by the operation of the doctrine of agency by estoppel.

That leaves cases where the principal dies or becomes incapacitated from acting as principal. What is the effect of the principal's death or insanity upon the position of the third party?

Death of principal. A good starting-point for any discussion is the case of *Blades v Free*.[10] There:

> X cohabited with a man who went abroad and later died. She had the same presumed authority as a wife,[11] but it was held that the man's executors were not liable to pay for goods supplied to X after the man's death, even though news of the death had not been received.

This case would seem to show that where the principal dies notice is not required to be given to the third party, in order for the principal's estate to escape liability. So that the third party is unprotected should the agency be determined by death of the principal.

But in *Smout v Ilbery*[12] the effect of the decision may well have been that a wife's authority (and possibly also the authority of *any* agent) will continue to

---

7 This subject is discussed in greater detail above, pp 348–352.
8 Cf cases dealing with the effect of an agent's notice of his principal's act of bankruptcy under the older law: *Brewin v Briscoe* (1859) 28 LJQB 329; *Re Ashton, ex p McGowan* (1891) 64 LT 28.
9 In the event of voluntary revocation by the *agent* it is not certain whether notice to the third party is required in order to terminate the principal's liability. There is no authority on this point, but it would seem on principle that, once the principal knows of the agent's renunciation then he must notify the third party, in order to prevent liability arising by way of estoppel (unless, of course, the third party has notice from some other source, eg the agent himself).
10 (1829) 9 B & C 167.
11 Ibid at 171 per Littledale J. See above, p 149.
12 (1842) 10 M & W 1 (see above, p 400).

exist after the death of her husband (or principal) until notice of that death has been received.[13] Admittedly, that case was primarily concerned with the personal liability of the *wife* for breach of the implied warranty of authority. But it would seem that such liability depends upon the question whether (and for how long) the original authority can be considered to continue: and that question, in turn, depends upon the issue of knowledge of the determining fact, ie the death of the principal. Moreover, in *Drew v Nunn*[14] Brett LJ considered, obiter, that on the death of the principal his estate would be liable to third parties who had dealt with the agent in ignorance of the principal's death. In the light of these contradictory opinions and the criticisms of *Smout v Ilbery* that have been voiced,[15] it is suggested that this question is far from settled.

Insanity of principal. The position at common law[16] where the agency is determined by the insanity of the principal, has been the subject of some debate. The decided cases appear to be based upon conflicting ideas. In *Drew v Nunn:*[17]

> A husband gave his wife authority to act on his behalf and held her out as his agent. Then he became insane. While he was insane, the wife ordered goods from the plaintiff, who knew nothing of the husband's insanity. Later the husband recovered his sanity. It was held that he was liable to the plaintiff for the price of the goods.

The basis of this decision appears to be that although the agency is terminated by the principal's insanity, his liability continues in respect of acts performed on his behalf by the agent, at least as long as the third party has no notice of the facts which terminate the agency.[18] Presumably, therefore, the agent still has authority, though this is no longer an *express* authority, but an *apparent* one.[19]

However, in *Yonge v Toynbee*[20] the Court of Appeal held that, where a principal became insane, the solicitors who were acting for him in certain litigation would be personally liable to the other party for the costs incurred in the proceedings which were continued in ignorance of the fact that the principal was insane, and before they were stopped once that insanity was known by the solicitors. The basis of this decision was that the solicitors (albeit ignorantly) had impliedly warranted that they had authority to act when, it would appear, they had no such authority since it had ended when the principal became insane. This clearly seems to contradict the idea in *Drew v Nunn* that the agent, in such circumstances, continues to have authority, though it is now *apparent* instead of *real*.

These cases have been criticised as being irreconcilable and as giving rise to the result that *both* principal *and* agent can be made liable to the third party who

13 Quaere by the *wife* (agent) or the third party.
14 (1879) 4 QBD 661 at 618.
15 Above, p 400.
16 In relation to agency created by a power of attorney the law is now contained in the Enduring Powers of Attorney Act 1985: below.
17 (1879) 4 QBD 661.
18 Ibid at 666 per Brett LJ.
19 Contrast the position where the principal dies, according to *Blades v Free*, above.
20 [1910] 1 KB 215.

transacts business with the agent in ignorance of the principal's insanity.[1] But in a Canadian decision, *Re Parks, Canada Permanent Trust Co v Parks*,[2] it was held by the New Brunswick Supreme Court, Appeal Division, that

> 'Unsoundness of mind . . . is . . . sufficient to determine a contract of agency between principal and agent, though the authority of an agent is not revoked with regard to a third person who has been dealing with the agent unless such third person has knowledge of the mental incompetency of the principal.'[3]

This would seem to support the view that the agent should not be liable personally to the third party, at least where the agent has acted in ignorance of the disability.[4]

It was further said that in such cases the third party does not need to have actual knowledge. Constructive knowledge or a knowledge of such circumstances as would put a reasonable man on his inquiry are sufficient notice to the third party that the contract of agency has been determined and that any authority which the agent had has been revoked.[5] In *Re Parks*, therefore, a power of attorney given by a doctor for the purpose of making certain payments in respect of her maintenance, was held to have been revoked by the doctor's insanity. But it was also held that, since the payees knew of that insanity, or knew sufficient facts from which that insanity would and should have been inferred or at least investigated, the payments were improperly made, and had to be reimbursed by the payee to the estate of the deceased doctor.

C. The Enduring Powers of Attorney Act 1985

The foregoing discussion reveals the unsatisfactory, unsettled character of the common law in respect of the effects of a principal's insanity. In consequence of recommendations made by the Law Commission, in 1983,[6] the Enduring Powers of Attorney Act was enacted in 1985. This provides for the creation of what is termed in the statute 'an enduring power of attorney'[7] which will continue to be effective despite the mental incapacity of the donor provided that the requirements of the Act are satisfied. In effect this statute alters the common law with respect to the termination of an agency relationship by the subsequent mental incapacity of the principal: and provides protection for the agent and third

---

1 See the criticism of Powell *Law of Agency* (2nd edn) pp 403–406; cf Seavey 'The Rationale of Agency' (1920) 29 Yale LJ 859 at 893; Wright 15 Can BR 196 at 198. For the position in some Canadian provinces see the statutes of Alberta, British Columbia and Manitoba, cited above, p 402 note 3. See also SO 1992, c 30, s 13.

2 (1956) 8 DLR (2d) 155. Discussed by Hudson (1959) 37 Can BR 497–503. Note the reference to these cases as *protecting third parties*, not aiding the donee of a power in *Wilkinson v Young* (1972) 25 DLR (3d) 275 at 276.

3 (1956) 8 DLR (2d) 155 at 162 per Bridges J.

4 This would seem to have been Powell's view: *Law of Agency* p 406.

5 (1956) 8 DLR (2d) 155 at 162; cf Turgeon JA in *Watson v Powell* (1921) 58 DLR 615 at 620.

6 Law Com No 122, 'The Incapacitated Principal', Cmnd 8977, 1983.

7 Cf Power of Attorney Act RSBC 1979, c 334, s 7.

parties in the event of the invalid creation of later revocation of the power. This alteration of the common law, however, has a restricted application.[8]

To come within the scope of the statute a power of attorney must be an enduring power of attorney. This means it was created by an instrument in the prescribed form, that was executed by the donor and the attorney in the prescribed manner, and incorporated in its provisions at the time of execution by the donor the prescribed explanatory information.[9] To be an attorney under such a power the attorney must be 18 and not bankrupt, or may be a trust corporation.[10] Certain powers of attorney cannot be enduring powers, viz, those made under the Trustee Act 1925, s 25 and those which give the attorney a right to appoint a substitute or successor.[11] Enduring powers of attorney are revoked by the bankruptcy of the attorney[12] and may be revoked by a court under the Mental Health Act 1983, Part VII.[13]

If an attorney under such a power has reason to believe that the donor is or is becoming mentally incapable, he must register the instrument creating the power.[14] But it was held in *Re K, Re F*[15] that an enduring power of attorney would be valid even though at the time the power was executed the donor was incapable by reason of mental disorder from managing his or her property or affairs. To be valid when executed the power must be executed by a donor who understood the nature and effect of the power, not whether the donor would have been able to perform all the acts which the power authorised. Hence, in that case, the powers were valid and could be registered under the Act.

If a power is an enduring power within the Act it will not be revoked by any subsequent mental incapacity on the part of the donor.[16] However, unless or until the power has been registered as set out in the Act, the donee, ie the agent, will not be able to do anything, without the authority of the court, except (a) maintain the donor or prevent loss to the donor's estate or maintain himself or other persons to the extent to which the donor might be expected to provide for the needs of the agent or some other person and then only to the extent the donor might be expected to have done; (b) make certain gifts of a seasonal nature, such as birthday or anniversary presents or gifts to charities to which the donor gave or might have been expected to give, as long as such gifts are not unreasonable in relation to the estate.[17] Section 5 of the Powers of Attorney Act 1971 applies, if and to the extent applicable, until the power is registered, as if the power had been revoked by the donor's mental incapacity.[18] Where the agent acts under the powers set out above, in favour of a third party lacking knowledge of any

8 Contrast the wider provisions of the British Columbia statute, as amended in 1987. See also SA 1991, c P-13.5, s 14, RSM 1987, c P-97, s 2.
9 1985 Act, ss 1(1), 2(1)(2): see SI 1990 No 1376.
10 1985 Act, s 2(7).
11 Ibid, s 2(8)(9).
12 Ibid, s 2(10).
13 Ibid, s 2(11): see also s 10, SI 1994 No 3047.
14 1985 Act, s 4: see also ibid, s 5 (functions of court prior to registration), s 6 (functions of court on application for registration), s 7 (effect and proof of registration). Once the instance has been registered the court has certain functions: ibid, s 8 (on which see *Re R* [1990] 2 All ER 893).
15 [1988] 1 All ER 358.
16 1985 Act, s 1(1)(a).
17 1985 Act, ss 1(1)(b)(2), 3(4) (5).
18 1985 Act, s 1(1)(c): for s 5 of the 1971 Act see above, pp 403–404.

impropriety on the part of the agent, the transaction will be validated as if the agent were acting under the statutory provisions.[19]

Such powers may confer general or specific authority upon the donee or agent. This includes the power to execute and exercise any trusts, powers or discretions vested in the donor.[20]

Where an instrument creating an enduring power of attorney failed to create a valid power but has been registered under the Act (whether or not such registration has been cancelled at the time of an act or transaction that is being called into question) certain consequences follow.[1] They are:

(a) freedom from liability of an agent acting in pursuance of the power by reason of the non-existence of the power unless at the time of acting the agent knows the instrument did not create a valid enduring power: or that an event has occurred which would have revoked the power if the power had been validly created, or the power would have expired even if it had been validly created;

(b) validity of the transaction vis-à-vis a third person, unless such third person had the knowledge referred to above;

(c) the application of a statutory presumption in favour of the validity of a transaction where the transaction involves the purchase[2] of an interest (subject to certain stipulated conditions[3]);

(d) the application of other protections for the agent and third parties as set out in Sch 2 to the Act, where the instrument failed to create a valid enduring power of attorney and the power has been revoked by the donor's mental incapacity.[4]

In relation to the provisions of s 5 of the Powers of Attorney Act 1971,[5] where the donor's revocation of the power is invalid because it has not complied with the provisions of s 7(1) of the 1985 Act (and such revocation has not been confirmed by the court under s 8(3) of the 1985 Act), it may be important to determine whether the attorney or the third party has knowledge of the revocation of the power. Hence the 1985 Act stipulates that 'knowledge of the confirmation of the revocation is, but knowledge of the unconfirmed revocation is not, knowledge of the revocation of the power.'[6]

19 1985 Act, s 1(3).
20 1985 Act, s 3(1)(2)(3).
 1 1985 Act, s 9.
 2 On which see Law of Property Act 1925, s 205(1): 1985 Act, s 9(7).
 3 1985 Act, s 9(4).
 4 1985 Act, s 9(6).
 5 Above, pp 403–404.
 6 1985 Act, s 9(5).

APPENDIX

Estate agent's commission

In the course of the discussion of the principal's duty to pay remuneration to the agent reference was made to cases concerning the right of estate agents to commission.[1] It was pointed out that the result of the decision in *Luxor (Eastbourne) Ltd v Cooper*[2] was to emphasise the importance of the exact wording of the contract between the principal selling property and the estate agent employed by him for the purpose of such sale. In the absence of clear, express binding terms in that contract, the courts are unwilling to make the principal pay commission to the agent when the sale of the principal's property has been effected by the principal himself and not the agent, even if the agent has purported to perform the agency, but has been prevented from achieving the completed performance of it by the intervention of the principal. This insistence upon a strict, literal interpretation of the contract between the principal and the estate agent is fully illustrated in cases concerning this matter which have come before the court since 1941. It is the purpose of this Appendix[3] to consider such cases, and to show how they exemplify the principles laid down by the House of Lords, which apply equally whether the agent is acting for the vendor or the purchaser.[4]

The first case is *Jones v Lowe*.[5] There the agent was paid commission in the event of his 'introducing a purchaser'. It was held by Hilbery J applying the *Luxor* case, that these words meant that the agent was only entitled to commission if he introduced someone who was not only ready and willing to purchase but 'goes so far as to sign a legal contract binding him to go through

---

1 Above, pp 194–200. Note also the possibility that certain commissions by such, or similar, agents may be illegal: see the Accommodation Agencies Act 1953: on which see *McInnes v Clarke* [1955] 1 All ER 346, [1955] 1 WLR 102. *Crouch and Lees v Haridas* [1972] 1 QB 158. [1971] 3 All ER 172. Note also, in relation to the making of false or misleading statements, the Property Misdescriptions Act 1991, ss 1, 2, 4.

2 [1941] AC 108, [1941] 1 All ER 33. On dicta in this decision, see *Alpha Trading Ltd v Dunnshaw-Patten Ltd* [1981] QB 290, [1981] 1 All ER 482, discussed above, p 197.

3 For further discussion see Gower (1950) 13 MLR 491: Ivamy 'Estate Agents and the Law' (1951) 4 Current Legal Problems 305 at pp 314–323. A different aspect of these problems is considered by Murdoch 'The Nature of Estate Agency' (1975) 91 LQR 357.

It is strange, in view of the difficulties evidenced by the discussion in the text, and the developments and experience in some Commonwealth countries, that the opportunity to legislate in this area was not taken when the Estate Agents Act 1979, which regulates 'estate agency work' (as defined in s 1(1)), was before Parliament.

4 *Garrard Smith & Co v Villiers* (1970) 114 Sol Jo 685.

5 [1945] KB 73, [1945] 1 All ER 194.

with the purchase'.[6] This had not happened: therefore the agent was not entitled to his commission. To allow the agent commission in such a case required an agreement to that effect worded in what Lord Russell of Killowen had called[7] 'clear and unequivocal language', which was absent in the case before Hilbery J.

This requirement was also stressed and was equally absent in *Murdoch Lownie Ltd v Newman*.[8] There the agents were to be paid commission 'in the event of business resulting'. What happened was that the agents introduced a prospective purchaser, with whom an agreement was made subject to his being able to arrange a mortgage. That agreement was subsequently rescinded. Were the agents entitled to commission? Various constructions of the phrase used in the agents' contract were suggested. But Slade J came to the conclusion that it was ambiguous and since it had been used by the agents it could be construed if necessary contra proferentem.[9] But that was held to be unnecessary in the light of the learned judge's conclusion that the words required a binding contract of purchase before commission was payable. Such a contract had not resulted from the agent's acts, therefore the house owner was not liable for any commission.

A very different phrase was used in *E P Nelson & Co v Rolfe*[10] for the agents earned their commission if they introduced 'a person, able, ready and willing to purchase' the principal's property. This they did, but before they had done so the principal had granted an option to purchase to X, who had been introduced to him by *other* agents. He therefore refused to deal with the other potential purchaser and the property was subsequently sold to X. The agents sued for their commission on the introduction of *their* purchaser and the principal argued that their contract was subject to two implied terms. The first was that commission was only payable in respect of the first introduction by *any* agent. The second was that if the vendor had 'justifiably' withdrawn the property from sale, commission would not be payable. By 'justifiably' was meant in the sense that the vendor felt morally, if not legally bound to some other person (X in this instance). The Court of Appeal rejected these suggested implied terms, on the ground that they were not necessary or inevitable for business efficacy.[11]

---

6 Ibid at 76, 197. Cf *Doyle v Mount Kidsbrom Mining & Exploration Pty Ltd* [1984] 2 Qd R 386, 'introducing a buyer': as long as the subsequent sale resulted from the introduction, commission was payable: *Max Christmas Real Estate v Schumann Marine Pty Ltd* [1987] 1 Qd R 325. Contrast *Tapley v Giles* (1986) 40 SASR 474 where the agent's introduction was not for the purposes of sale; *Trotter v McSpadden* [1986] VR 329, where the resulting sales contract was conditional not binding: no commission payable: so, too, in *Preston & Partners v Markheath Securities* [1988] 31 EG 57.

7 *Luxor (Eastbourne) Ltd v Cooper* [1941] AC 108 at 129, [1941] 1 All ER 33 at 47.

8 [1949] 2 All ER 783.

9 [1949] 2 All ER 783 at 787–788.

10 [1950] 1 KB 139, [1949] 2 All ER 584; Bucknill LJ followed three earlier cases which made mere *introduction* of someone sufficient; *Giddys v Horsfall* [1947] 1 All ER 460; *Dennis Reed Ltd v Nichols* [1948] 2 All ER 914; *Bennett & Partners v Millett* [1949] 1 KB 362, [1948] 2 All ER 929. On the situation where the contract specified the introduction of someone ready, willing and able to purchase, compare *Walters v John Crisp Pty Ltd* (1982) 64 FLR 299.

11 Cohen LJ also said that the implication of the first term could not have affected the matter, because the other agents were not entitled to commission from a mere introduction [1950] 1 KB 139 at 147, [1949] 2 All ER 584 at 588.

Hence the agents had fulfilled the contract and were entitled to their commission.[12]

The principles set out in these decisions were raised and discussed in some detail in a series of cases in the Court of Appeal in 1950. First in *Fowler v Bratt*[13] the decision in *Jones v Lowe*[14] as to the effect of instructing the agent to find 'a purchaser' was approved and affirmed. Then in *Graham and Scott (Southgate) Ltd v Oxlade*,[15] where the contract was to pay commission to the agents in the event of the agents' 'introducing a person . . . willing and able to purchase', the agents were held not entitled to commission where they introduced someone who offered to buy the principal's property 'subject to contract'. The principal in the end did not sell the property to that prospective purchaser, but sold it to someone else. Cohen LJ held that the mere introduction of a prospective purchaser was sufficient but the purchaser at least had to make a *firm* offer, one which did not leave him free to avoid completion without legal liability. Hence a prospective purchaser who offered to buy 'subject to contract' was not a purchaser for the purpose. In arriving at this conclusion the learned Lord Justice overruled *Giddys v Horsfall*[16] and distinguished *E P Nelson & Co v Rolfe*[17] on the ground that there a firm offer had been made. This was the ground upon which Singleton LJ based his decision: that where the person introduced makes his offer or acceptance 'subject to contract' the acceptance is a conditional acceptance and no more than that: hence the agent was not entitled to commission.[18]

In the next case, *McCallum v Hicks*[19] the principal instructed the agents to 'find someone to buy' his house. What the agents did was to introduce someone who made an offer 'subject to formal contract' but subsequently withdrew. It was held that the expression 'find someone to buy' was only another and a more colloquial way of saying 'find a purchaser'.[20] Hence the principle of the earlier cases (eg *Jones v Lowe*, and the *Oxlade* case) were clearly applicable, and no commission was payable. Denning LJ stated that whether the contract with the agent said find 'a purchaser' or someone 'willing' to purchase, the meaning was the same: the agent had to find someone who was 'irrevocably willing', that is, someone who had given 'irrevocable proof of his willingness by entering into a binding contract to purchase.[1]

---

12 In *A A Dickson & Co v O'Leary* (1979) 254 Estates Gazette 731, Lord Denning MR said that this case stood for the proposition that, where, as in the *O'Leary* case, a principal has used two agents, there is an implied term in the contract with each that commission is not payable if, before the introduction of the contractually stipulated client ready, willing, and able to purchase, the principal has entered into a binding contract to sell to another.

13 [1950] 2 KB 96, [1950] 1 All ER 662.

14 [1945] KB 73, [1945] 1 All ER 194.

15 [1950] 2 KB 257, [1950] 1 All ER 856. Contrast *Christie, Owen and Davies Ltd v Rapacioli* [1974] QB 781, [1974] 2 All ER 311, discussed below, p 416.

16 [1947] 1 All ER 460 and the other cases relied on by Bucknill LJ in *E P Nelson & Co v Rolfe* [1950] 1 KB 139 at 145, [1949] 2 All ER 584 at 587, see note 10 above.

17 [1950] 1 KB 139, [1949] 2 All ER 584.

18 [1950] 2 KB 257 at 269, [1950] 1 All ER 856 at 863.

19 [1950] 2 KB 271, [1950] 1 All ER 864.

20 Ibid at 274, 865, per Bucknill LJ.

1 Ibid at 276, 866. Cf the interpretation of 'sale' to mean 'completed sale' in *Alex Duff Realty Ltd v Eaglecrest Holdings Ltd* [1983] 5 WWR 61. The language of Denning LJ was criticised in *Christie, Owen and Davies Ltd v Rapacioli* [1974] QB 781, [1974] 2 All ER 311.

The same result followed in *Dennis Reed Ltd v Goody*,[2] where the agents were instructed to find 'a person ready, able, and willing to purchase' the principal's property. The agents introduced X, who agreed to buy the principal's property subject to the principal's agreeing to indemnify him against future road charges. As a result of delays caused by this question X withdrew from the agreement, so that there was no sale. When the agents claimed their commission their claim was rejected by the Court of Appeal. The case itself is another example of the application of the principles laid down in the decision referred to above. Its importance lies in the formulation by Denning LJ of the general law on estate agents' commission, which provides the background for the interpretation of an estate agent's contract with his principal.[3]

These may be summarised thus:[4]

1. The agent is only to receive commission if he succeeds in effecting a sale.[5]
2. Any language that is used in the contract will have this effect, as long as it shows that the agent is to introduce a *purchaser*.
3. If the agent is to be given a commission on *offers* only, he must use 'clear and unequivocal language'.[6]
4. The normal arrangement, the 'common understanding of men', is that the agent's commission is payable out of the purchase price.[7]
5. If a binding contract of purchase is signed by the principal and the third party then, if the principal repudiates the contract, he is still liable to pay commission, not because it has been earned and is payable, but because it is his own fault that the sale has not been completed.[8]

---

2 [1950] 2 KB 277, [1950] 1 All ER 919.
3 Ibid at 284–285, 923. See the language of the same judge in *Jaques v Lloyd D George & Partners Ltd* [1968] 2 All ER 187 at 190. Cf the formulation of the governing principles by Nield J in *Blake & Son v Sohn* [1969] 3 All ER 123 at 128–129. Note the criticism of some of Denning LJ's language in this case in the *Rapacioli* case, above note 1.
4 *Note*: that these principles of interpretation only apply where there are no express terms which conclude the matter. If such terms exist it is not possible to imply a term that the agent must be the 'effective cause' of the sale (or lease) in question: *Cooper & Co v Fairview Estates (Investments)* (1986) 278 Estates Gazette 1094; affd (1987) 282 Estates Gazette 1131.
5 Hence the need to show that the agent was the 'effective cause' of the sale: *Brodie Marshall & Co v Carpenter* (1984) 274 Estates Gazette 1149; *Bentleys Estate Agents v Granix Ltd* [1989] 27 EG 93. Even through a sub-agent: *Bruce & Partners v Winyard Development* (1987) 282 Estates Gazette 1255. Commission might be payable to two agents if both were instrumental as effective causes of the sale: *Lordsgate Properties v Balcombe* (1985) 274 Estates Gazette 493: with which contrast *John D Wood & Co v Dantata* (1985) 275 Estates Gazette 1278; affd (1987) 283 Estates Gazette 314. See also *Chesterfield & Co Ltd v Zahid* [1989] 29 EG 75. See also above, pp 191–194. For a more recent case in which no sale meant no commission, or damages, see *Property Choice Ltd v Fronda* [1991] 2 EGLR 249.
6 [1950] 2 KB 277 at 288, [1950] 1 All ER 919 at 925, per Denning LJ.
7 Cf Denning LJ [1950] 2 KB 271 at 274, [1950] 1 All ER 864 at 865; Bucknill LJ in [1950] 2 KB 271 at 274, [1950] 1 All ER 864 at 865. But in *(WA) Ellis Services v Wood* [1993] 31 EG 78 no term could be implied that commission was payable directly from the purchase money.
8 [1950] 2 KB 277 at 285, [1950] 1 All ER 919 at 923, correcting [1950] 2 KB 271 at 275, [1950] 1 All ER 864 at 866. This 'rule' and the ensuing one were cited with approval by the Manitoba Court of Appeal in *Carsted v Gass* (1980) 116 DLR (3d) 550 at 553.
    In *Alpha Trading Ltd v Dunnshaw-Patten Ltd* [1981] 1 All ER 482 at 489, Brandon LJ referred to this passage from the judgment of Denning LJ in the *Dennis Reed* case, and said that

6. But no commission is payable if it is the *third party*, not the principal, who has defaulted on a *binding* contract, unless the principal sues for specific performance and gets damages, in which event he will 'probably' be liable to pay the commission out of such damages.[9]

Everything, therefore, depends upon there being an enforceable contract between principal and third party. Or at any rate, in the opinion of Bucknill LJ and Hodson J[10] upon the *willingness* of the third party to enter into an enforceable contract, when it is the *principal* who refuses to complete the sale, even though as yet no enforceable contract has been made.[11]

The last of the Court of Appeal decisions in 1950 was *Bennett, Walden & Co v Wood.*[12] There the agents' commission was payable on their 'securing an offer' for the principal. It was held that obtaining an offer 'subject to contract' was not sufficient for this purpose. Although the phrase in question had not been mentioned among those dealt with by Denning LJ in *Dennis Reed Ltd v Goody* Evershed MR agreed with the earlier remarks of Denning LJ[13] that in contracts of this sort fine distinctions between one formula and another were undesirable.[14]

The question of the 'willingness' of the third party to purchase in so far as it is relevant to the agents' commission, was further clarified in *Boots v E Christopher & Co.*[15] In that case the agents were to be paid a percentage of the purchase price if they introduced a person able and willing to purchase on the principal's terms. Such an agreement was made and a deposit was given by the third party to the agents. But the third party failed to complete and directed the agents to hand the deposit to the principal. They did so after deducting what they claimed was their commission. This the principal sued to recover. In holding that he was entitled to succeed, the Court of Appeal stressed the importance of the fact that the

---

it indicated that Denning LJ considered that there could be a liability to the agent if the agent's employer failed to perform or defaulted on his contract with the third party: which was consistent with the language of Lord Wright in *Luxor (Eastbourne) Ltd v Cooper* [1941] AC 108, [1941] 1 All ER 33, referred to by Brandon LJ in [1981] 1 All ER 482 at 486–487.

9 For a Canadian example of this, see *Carsted v Gass*, above. See also *H W Liebig & Co Ltd v Leading Investments Ltd* (1986) 25 DLR (4th) 161; *Century 21 Suburban Real Estate Ltd v Duff* (1987) 62 Nfld & PEIR 190; *Royal LePage Real Estate Services Ltd v Harper* (1991) 85 Alta LR (2d) 31.

10 [1950] 2 KB 277 at 283, 291, [1950] 1 All ER 919 at 922, 927. Must it be binding and enforceable? See *Murdoch Lownie Ltd v Newman* [1949] 2 All ER 783 at 789 per Slade J; *Fowler v Bratt* [1950] 2 KB 96, [1950] 1 All ER 662; *McCallum v Hicks* [1950] 2 KB 271, [1950] 1 All ER 864. That it must would seem to be the inference from the language used by the Court of Appeal in *Wilkinson Ltd v Brown* [1966] 1 All ER 509, [1966] 1 WLR 194 at least unless there is some term in the agent's contract which permits a different interpretation. Cf also what is said in *Christie, Owen and Davies Ltd v Rapacioli* [1974] QB 781, [1974] 2 All ER 311.

11 Yet in the *Alpha Trading* case, above, the principal was liable to the agent for unearned commission when the principal's refusal to complete the contract that had been agreed upon, and was enforceable, was compromised by the parties thereto, and their obligations jointly and mutually released. This was not an 'estate agents' case: but the principles of law applicable were said to be the same whatever the nature of the agency involved.

12 [1950] 2 All ER 134.

13 [1950] 2 KB 277 at 288, [1950] 1 All ER 919 at 925.

14 [1950] 2 All ER 134 at 136–137.

15 [1952] 1 KB 89, [1951] 2 All ER 1045.

commission was payable out of the purchase price—which made expressly clear that a sale had to be effected before the agents were entitled to anything.[16] Furthermore, since the principal had not been guilty of default in respect of the sale, he could not be held liable for commission. It was the third party's unwillingness, not the principal's that had prevented the sale, nor was the principal obliged to sue for specific performance.[17]

On the other hand, the wording of the contract between owner and estate agent led to a very different conclusion in *Midgley Estates Ltd v Hand*.[18] There the commission was payable as soon as the agents' purchaser 'shall have signed a legally binding contract', effected within a stated period. The agents introduced someone who signed such a contract within such time. But that person subsequently was unable to complete the purchase and forfeited his deposit. It was held that, in view of the express terms of their contract, the agents were entitled to their commission, because they had done what was demanded of them by that contract. Jenkins LJ in more or less the same language, reiterated the general principles laid down by Denning LJ, referred to above.[19] However, they were really inapplicable here, because the language of the contract was 'reasonably plain'.[20]

The problem of interpreting words which were not 'reasonably plain' returned in *Christie, Owen and Davies Ltd v Stockton*.[1] There the contract inter alia provided that: 'should the owner withdraw after having accepted an offer to purchase by a person able and willing to enter into a formal contract then [the agents] shall be paid their commission'. Clearly this was an attempt to cover the gap in the principal's liability to pay commission by the 'subject to contract' cases of 1950.[2] What happened was that although the owner and the third party had entered into an agreement for the sale of the property, subject to contract, no formal contract was ever entered into between them. Despite the attempt by the agents to secure a contract which would protect him from being deprived of the remuneration which he might reasonably expect to have received for his services by what was lawful conduct on the part of the principal (with which attempt Slade J sympathised),[3] it was held, on the basis of the 1950 cases, that 'a person able and willing to enter a formal contract' meant 'a person able and willing to enter into a formal contract of which the terms have already been agreed, albeit orally'.[4] Here no such valid, if unenforceable, contract had been made: everything was still in 'the realm of negotiation'.[5] To cover the agents in such circumstances required 'clear and unequivocal language'.[6] This had not been

16 [1952] 1 KB 89, [1951] 2 All ER 1045, at 97–98, 1049 per Denning LJ.
17 Ibid at 98, 1049 per Denning LJ; at 100–101, 1050, per Hodson LJ.
18 [1952] 2 QB 432, [1952] 1 All ER 1394.
19 [1952] 2 QB 432 at 435–456, [1952] 1 All ER 1394 at p 1396–1397.
20 Ibid at 436, 1397 Jenkins LJ. Hence the distinction between this case and *Jaques v Lloyd D George & Partners Ltd* [1968] 2 All ER 187, [1968] 1 WLR 625: below, p 419.
1 [1953] 2 All ER 1149, [1953] 1 WLR 1353.
2 See above, pp 413–415.
3 [1953] 2 All ER 1149 at 1153.
4 Ibid at 1151.
5 Ibid at 1153.
6 Ibid at 1153.

used although the conduct of the agents was irreproachable. Hence commission was not payable.

The necessity for a 'binding contract' between principal and third party before commission was payable where the agent was to introduce a ready, willing and able purchaser was emphasised and exemplified in *Peter Long & Partners v Burns*,[7] where the contract of sale made with the third party was made as the result of an innocent misrepresentation on the part of the agents, and hence was rescinded by the third party. It was held that, although at first sight the contract made with the third party was a binding contract, it eventually became an invalid contract, not binding on the parties.[8] Therefore, the agents had not become entitled to their commission. It should be noted that in this case, unlike the one previously discussed, the conduct of the agents was subjected to criticism in that they had apparently hurried the third party into the contract in the interests of earning their own commission.[9]

Since the 1950s the courts have considered this part of the law on many other occasions.[10] The first is the case of *Ackroyd & Sons v Hasan*.[11] At first instance[12] Winn J applied 'the philosophy implied in the judgments in cases decided in 1950 and 1952' (ie the cases cited and discussed earlier) and held that no commission was payable where the contract called for 'the introduction of a party prepared to enter into a contract to purchase' and no sale eventuated. The Court of Appeal, however, considered that the language of the agency contract was not ambiguous and was to be construed as meaning that commission would be earned when a party fulfilling the necessary conditions was introduced, and not only when a binding contract was entered into with a third party.[13] The court, however, came to the same conclusion as Winn J, on the ground that the kind of offer that was required of a prospective purchaser for commission to be payable had not been procured by the agents. This was because the assent of the owner was necessary for the contract of purchase to be within the terms of the contract of agency: and the owner had not assented to the offer, because of a fundamental difference about the subject-matter of a sub-lease that was intended to be incorporated in the contract of purchase.

In contrast the agents succeeded in their claim for commission in *Drewery v Ware-Lane*.[14] There the obligation on the agents was to find a prospective purchaser to sign a purchaser's agreement. Such an agreement was signed by a

---

7 [1956] 3 All ER 207, [1956] 1 WLR 1083. See also *A A Dickson & Co v O'Leary* (1979) 254 Estates Gazette 731, where no such binding contract could materialise because the principal had exchanged contracts with a purchaser found by *another* agent prior to the introduction of a prospective purchaser by the agent not claiming commission. The latter's claim was unsuccessful. Cf *Preston & Partners v Markheath Securities* (1988) 31 Estates Gazette 57, sale was subject to contract: no commission payable.

8 Contrast *Midgley Estates Ltd v Hand* [1952] 2 QB 432, [1952] 1 All ER 1394; where the contract was binding although it was not completed.

9 [1956] 3 All ER 207 at 210 per Singleton LJ, 213 per Morris LJ, 215 per Romer LJ.

10 Some of these are discussed in Fridman 'Estate Agents' Commission' (1960) 110 LJ 375; (1964) 114 LJ 35; Bicknell 'Estate Agent's Right to Commission' (1966) 116 NLJ 603.

11 [1960] 2 QB 144, [1960] 2 All ER 254.

12 [1959] 2 All ER 370, [1959] 1 WLR 706.

13 [1960] 2 All ER 254 at 264 per Ormerod LJ.

14 [1960] 3 All ER 529, [1960] 1 WLR 1204.

person introduced by the agents: but that agreement was made subject to contract. Before the agreement could be implemented, the principal sold the property to another person. In this case, the agents did not have to find a 'purchaser', ie someone 'irrevocably willing' to purchase the property.[15] They had to find a *prospective* purchaser'. Though he never became a purchaser, the person introduced by the agents was none the less the person they had agreed to find, because there was a bona fide prospect of his buying the property in question. Therefore, the agents had fulfilled their undertaking. As long as the 'prospective purchaser' was bona fide, and the agents who introduced him were bona fide, the commission was payable. A principal could only escape liability to pay such commission if he could show that there was fraud or similarly unconscionable conduct on the part of his agents.[16]

That was where the agency contract specified a 'prospective purchaser'. In *Dellafiora v Lester*[17] the obligation on the agents was to introduce a person 'willing and able' to purchase a business. It was held here that commission was not payable to agents who introduced someone who wanted to purchase the property and was willing and able to put down the stipulated deposit, but was not suitable and acceptable to the principal on other grounds, because of which he refused to assent to the sale. From this case it is to be deduced that the personal as well as the financial character of the prospective purchaser may be material to the question whether the agents have earned their commission, at least where the obligation on the agents is to find a willing and able purchaser.

To return to situations in which the obligation on the agents was to bring about a legally binding contract, in respect of which different considerations have been held to apply, there is the case of *Sheggia v Gradwell*.[18] There the agents did obtain someone to sign such a contract, which the owner subsequently rescinded (as he was entitled to do because his landlords refused to give their assent to the assignment of the lease in question to the prospective purchaser). It was held that commission was payable. The case of *Peter Long & Partners v Burns*[19] was distinguished on the ground that in that case the principal rescinded because of the agents' innocent misrepresentation. It was the agents' fault that no legally binding contract eventuated. In the *Sheggia* case, however, the agents had done all possible to produce a legally binding contract, and had brought such a contract about. Their purchaser was not a man of straw, not someone introduced knowing that he would be unacceptable and that the contract would fail to materialise. As long as the agents acted in good faith (as the *Drewery* case emphasised), and a contract ensued, then even though it failed to end in a sale the

---

15 *McCallum v Hicks* [1950] 1 All ER 864 at 866; cf *Ackroyd & Sons v Hasan* above, at 258 per Upjohn LJ.
16 [1960] 3 All ER 529 at 532 per Ormerod LJ.
17 [1962] 3 All ER 393, [1962] 1 WLR 1208: cf *Dennis Reed Ltd v Goody* [1950] 1 All ER 919: above, pp 414–415.
18 [1963] 3 All ER 114, [1963] 1 WLR 1049; Lord Denning MR dissented, apparently willing to assimilate the 'ready, willing and able to purchase' cases, with the 'legally binding contract' cases.
19 [1956] 3 All ER 207, [1956] 1 WLR 1083: see above.

agents were entitled to their commission: they had done what was necessary to earn it.[20]

Subsequently it was said by Salmon LJ in *A L Wilkinson Ltd v Brown*[1] that the scope of the decision in *Sheggia v Gradwell* ought not to be extended. In the *Wilkinson* case commission was payable to an estate agent if he introduced 'a person prepared to enter into a contract to purchase' at an acceptable price. The third party eventually said he would sign a contract if he could sell his own property. By the time this had been done, however, the principal had sold his property to someone else not introduced by the estate agent. In these circumstances it was held that no commission was payable by the principal to the estate agent. As Harman LJ said,[2] before it is found that the commission is payable, the court must be satisfied that the conditions on which it is payable has been fulfilled. In this case the contract required a person 'prepared' to enter into a contract to purchase, which meant someone who was more than willing, someone who was ready and willing, though it might not also involve the qualification 'able'.[3] This explanation of the phrase 'prepared to purchase' was assented to by Diplock LJ.[4] Salmon LJ suggested that it meant someone who was ready, willing and able to enter into a contract, by which he meant not that the person necessarily must have the cash at the bank but that he must be in a position to make the necessary financial arrangements which would enable him to complete the purchase. A willing purchaser involved someone who sent forward an unqualified offer or acceptance.[5] Hence in this case there was never such a purchaser and no commission was payable.

The *Sheggia* case was also criticised, and what is more distinguished, in the subsequent decision of the Court of Appeal in *Jaques v Lloyd D George & Partners Ltd*.[6] Here the plaintiff, who was the owner of a cafe with a lease that had seven years to run, instructed the estate agents to obtain a suitable purchaser for the lease, and signed a contract which stated that should the agents be 'instrumental in introducing a person willing to sign a document capable of becoming a contract to purchase at a price, which at any stage in negotiations has been agreed by me' he would pay the agents a commission of £250. That clause was not explained to the principal, nor was a copy of it left with him. The agents introduced someone who signed a contract of sale: but this was subject to the landlord granting a licence to assign and the prospective purchaser supplying satisfactory references to that end. The prospective purchaser paid the deposit under the contract of sale to the agents but, his references being unsatisfactory,

20 Contrast the Ontario case of *Youngblut v Herzog* (1967) 66 DLR (2d) 200 where the Court of Appeal held that commission was not payable under a contract of agency which referred to 'completion of the sale', when the terms of the purchaser's offer were never fulfilled, so that his deposit on the purchase was returned. Throughout, the principal had acted in good faith. The same result followed in the Manitoba case of *Carsted v Gass* (1980) 116 DLR (3d) 550, where the purchaser's deposit was forfeited to, and retained by, the principal, the vendor of the property.
1 [1966] 1 All ER 509 at 515.
2 Ibid at 510.
3 Ibid at 511.
4 Ibid at 514.
5 Ibid at 515.
6 [1968] 2 All ER 187.

the landlord refused the licence. In those circumstances the principal told the agents to release the deposit to the prospective purchaser. The agents claimed they were entitled to the agreed commission. The prospective purchaser thereupon recovered his deposit from the principal, who now sought to recover it from the agents who were counterclaiming for their commission. The Court of Appeal held that the agents were not entitled to the commission for which they were counterclaiming. One reason for this was because the agent's representative had misrepresented to the principal the effect of the clause referred to above, so that they were not entitled to enforce it in order to recover the commission set out in that contract of agency. In this respect the *Sheggia* case was distinguished, on the ground that the principal there had a remedy against the prospective purchaser for damages for breach of contract.[7] Moreover the language used in this case was so uncertain that it was not capable of being enforced. Whereas in the *Sheggia* case the agent had gone to great pains to put in clear and unequivocal terms the precise circumstances under which he was to get commission even though the principal obtained no benefit, in the case before the Court of Appeal the language was too imprecise to permit the court to come to such a conclusion, particularly having regard to the strict way in which such contracts have been construed by the courts.[8]

This is also brought out in *Blake & Co v Sohn*.[9] Here again the prospective contract for the sale of some land failed to materialise, in this instance because, the principal, the vendor, failed to make a good possessory title to some of the land in question, whereupon the prospective purchaser rescinded the contract, as he was entitled to do. In those circumstances the agents claimed their commission on the ground that it was payable to them either when the purchaser introduced by them entered into a contract with the principal or when they, the agents, introduced a purchaser ready, willing and able to complete the purchase. In the alternative they argued that it was an implied term of the contract that the principal had and would make out a good title to the land to the purchaser introduced to them by the agents. Once again the agent failed to obtain his commission. Nield J held that there was no express term which governed the relations between the parties in this set of circumstances, nor was there any indication that a term to the effect argued by the agents could be implied into the contract.[10] Nor was there such default on the part of the principal as would entitle the agent to his commission. Default in this context meant 'wilful refusal or deceit'. In reaching this conclusion the learned Judge canvassed at great length many of the leading decisions already considered above in particular the decision in the *Luxor* case.[11] While this decision adds nothing new to the previous law, it affirms and consolidates the principles which have been enunciated in the decisions since 1941. So, too, in *Christie, Owen and Davies Ltd v Rapacioli*,[12] in

7 Ibid at 190–191 per Lord Denning MR, 192–193 per Edmund Davies LJ.
8 Ibid at 190 per Lord Denning MR, 193–194 per Cairns J.
9 [1969] 3 All ER 123, [1969] 1 WLR 1412 (cf *Oldfield, Kirby and Graham Real Estate Co v Kliewer* (1971) 18 DLR (3d) 762).
10 Ibid at 133.
11 Ibid at 129–133.
12 [1974] QB 781, [1974] 2 All ER 311, in which the Court of Appeal criticised and refused to follow dicta of Lord Denning in some earlier cases: cf above, p 413.

which, the agents' obligation being to effect the introduction of a person ready, able, and willing to purchase, they were entitled to commission even though the transaction was abortive because the vendor withdrew after the purchaser's offer, which was otherwise acceptable, because the vendor had received a better offer elsewhere. However, in *A A Dickinson & Co v O'Leary*,[13] commission was not payable to the agent when the principal had already sold the property through another agent by the time that the agent claiming commission had produced his 'ready, willing, and able' purchaser. A term to produce such effect was implied into the contract of agency by the Court of Appeal.

It is evident that there are many anomalies in this part of the law. As long as the courts treat different expressions in contracts with estate agents as involving different degrees of stringency in the duty of such agents, without actually altering the basic, fundamental duty of such agents to act bona fide, honestly, and with reasonable care and skill there will continue to be apparently irreconcilable decisions, and fine, subtle distinctions between cases.[14] The suggestion has been made that justice may best be done if an estate agent is appointed 'sole agent' for the property owner.[15] This would protect him against sale through another agent,[16] and, if properly worded (eg, 'the sole and exclusive right to sell'), the contract would protect the agent against a sale by the owner himself.[17]

13 (1979) 254 Estates Gazette 731: on which see also above, p 413, note 12, p 417 note 7.
14 Note that in Canada provincial legislation provides for the regulation of commission payable to estate agents: above, p 195, note 12. The same is also true of Australia and New Zealand, above, p 195, note 12.

    Nevertheless, problems arise, eg whether the agent was the effective cause of the sale, or whether the sale was within the duration of the 'listing' agreement: see, eg *NRS Realty Centre Ltd v Ikalcic* (1988) 59 Alta LR (2d) 308; *Quest Real Estate Ltd v R & W Holdings Ltd* (1987) 44 Man R (2d) 308; *First Group Real Estate Ltd v City of Edmonton* (1987) 76 AR 10; *Century 21 CG Realty Ltd v Trickett* (1986) 47 Alta LR (2d) 137; *Riverside Realty & Construction Co v Amanda Homes Ltd* (1987) 43 Man R (2d) 581; *Ain Realty Ltd v Riverbank Holdings Ltd* (1986) 46 Alta LR (2d) 161; *Style v Rogers Realty Ltd* (1987) 55 Alta LR (2d) 229; *United Real Estate Inc v Headrick* (1988) 65 Sask R 118, *Creditel of Canada Ltd v Gravure Graphics Ltd* (1987) 51 Man R (2d) 122; *Pleckham v Loofer* (1990) 85 Sask R 308; *Royal Le Page Real Estate Services Ltd v Church* (1991) 80 Alta LR (2d) 122.

    For an English case in which the sale was not effected within a time limit and no commission was payable, see *Fairvale Ltd v Sabharwal* [1992] 32 EG 51.
15 Gower, 13 MLR 491, 497.
16 *Hampton & Sons Ltd v George* [1939] 3 All ER 627; *E Christopher & Co v Essig* [1948] WN 461. This is just what happened in *H M Rendall v Lammas* [1967] CLY 36, where the commission was recoverable as damages for breach of contract when the principal sold through *another* agent, not the one appointed as 'sole agent' for three months.
17 See *Brodie Marshall & Co (Hotel Division) v Sharer* [1988] 19 EG 129: with which contrast a Canadian case *Empala H Ltd v Reidy Surety Ltd* (1988) 48 Man R (2d) 305; and with *Bentall, Horsley and Baldry v Vicary* [1931] 1 KB 253, where the agent was *not* protected.

Index

Agent – *continued*
  performance of duties, 155–6
    non-personal performance. *See*
      DELEGATION
  property disposition by. *See* DISPOSITION OF
    PROPERTY BY AGENT; PROPERTY
  remedies. *See* REMEDIES
    special, 39–40
  special responsibility, with, 49–50
  sub-. *See* SUB-AGENT
  suing, effect on principal's liability, 225–7
  tort committed by, 325. *See also* TORT
  trustee, also as, 24n, *see also* TRUSTS
  use of term in book, 37
Alter ego doctrine, 342
Armed forces
  tortious act of member of, Crown liability,
    384
Assignment
  unassignable rights, 263
Auction
  commission, sale not made at, 192
Auctioneer, 45, 157–8
  implied authority, 81
  suing in own name, right, 250
Authority, 19–21, 38, 61–2
  act outside, 61, 112–13
    undisclosed principal, where is, 264–6
  actual, 62–4
    categories of, 62–4
    meaning, 62
  apparent, 68, 70, 112, 289. *See also*
    ESTOPPEL
    company, of agent for, 358–60
  contractual agent, of, 61–8, 217–18
  customary, 62, 63–4, 76–9
    brokers, of, 77–9, 80–1
    examples, 79–83
    exclusion of, 79
    meaning, 76–7
    unreasonable custom, 77–8, 80–1
  deed, created by, 57, 64–6. *See also* POWER
    OF ATTORNEY
  duty to act within, 157–8
  exceeding. *See* 'acts outside' *above*
  express, 62–3, 64–8
    deed, contained in, 64–6
    document, contained in, 66–7
    undisclosed principal, where is, 265–6
    written/oral authorisation, 66–8
  general and special, 38–40
  implied, 62, 63, 68–9, 79–83
    company, of agent for, 357–8
    customary authority. *See* 'customary'
      above
    scope, 68–9
    usual authority. *See* 'usual' *below*
  inquiry into, third party duty, 218–19
  notice of lack of authority, effect, 118–19,
    124–7, 218–19

Authority – *continued*
  ostensible, 68, 112. *See also* ESTOPPEL
  payment, to accept, 224–5
  power of attorney gives, 57
  presumed, 133–4. *See also* OPERATION OF
    LAW
  real, 62
  usual, 62, 63–4, 69–76
    apparent authority distinguished, 70–3,
      122–4
    cases on nature of, 71–4
    disclosed and undisclosed agency, and,
      74–5
    examples, 69–70
    limitations on, 70–5
  vital feature of agency, 19
  warranty, breach of implied, 61, 233, 243–4
    cases on implied warranty, 244
    strict liability, 244

Bailment
  agency compared, 27
    agency of necessity, and, 139, 142
  agent as bailee, 27
  sub-bailment, 169–71
  undisclosed principal, and, 254–5
Bank manager, 362
Banker
  lien of, 207, 208
Bankruptcy, 278
  effect of, 398
  partner, of, 370
Barrister, 46–8
Betting, 156, 173
Bill of exchange, 372–76
  agent signing, 372–3, 375–6
    forged signature, 373
    personal liability, 375–6
    'presumption most favourable to
      validity', and, 374
    unauthorised signature, 373, 376
  company, for, 373–4
  necessity, agency by, and, 135
  partnership, in name of, 373
  principal's liability on, 372–5
    negligence of, 375
  signature of procuration, 372
  third party in good faith without notice
    taking, 374
Bribe, 181, 186–8
  conspiracy at common law, 188
  remedies for principal, 205
Broker, 42–4, 158. *See also* CREDIT BROKER;
  INSURANCE BROKER; SHIPBROKER;
  STOCKBROKER
  customary authority, 77–9
  implied authority, 77–9, 80–1
Buyer of goods
  agent, whether is, 28–9
  disposal by, 299–300